Deploying and Administering Windows Vista® Bible

Deploying and Administering Windows Vista® Bible

Bob Kelly
Danielle Ruest
Nelson Ruest

Wiley Publishing, Inc.

Deploying and Administering Windows Vista® Bible

Published by
Wiley Publishing, Inc.
10475 Crosspoint Boulevard
Indianapolis, IN 46256
www.wiley.com

Copyright © 2008 by Wiley Publishing, Inc., Indianapolis, Indiana

Published by Wiley Publishing, Inc., Indianapolis, Indiana

Published simultaneously in Canada

ISBN: 978-0-470-18021-1

Manufactured in the United States of America

10 9 8 7 6 5 4 3 2 1

For general information on our other products and services or to obtain technical support, please contact our Customer Care Department within the U.S. at (800) 762-2974, outside the U.S. at (317) 572-3993 or fax (317) 572-4002.

Library of Congress Control Number: 2008934806

Trademarks: Wiley and related trade dress are registered trademarks of Wiley Publishing, Inc., in the United States and other countries, and may not be used without written permission. Windows Vista is a trademark of Microsoft Corporation in the U.S. and/or other countries. All other trademarks are the property of their respective owners. Wiley Publishing, Inc. is not associated with any product or vendor mentioned in this book.

Wiley also publishes its books in a variety of electronic formats. Some content that appears in print may not be available in electronic books.

This work is dedicated to my family and friends. Thank you all for your support and patience.

—BK

We dedicate this book to you, the reader, who has to work with computers every day and want to get it right. We hope you find it useful and that it saves you time and effort every day.

—DR and NR

About the Authors

Bob Kelly has been working in the IT field for 18 years with a focus on application deployment, scripting, and the automated distribution of Windows systems and is a Microsoft MVP for Setup and Deployment. Bob served in the U.S. Navy for eight years, ending his service as Systems Administrator for the White House Communications Agency. He spent the next several years as a consultant supporting various commercial and government agencies in the Washington DC area as a systems architect. Bob currently works as Senior Product manager for KACE (www.kace.com) where his primary focus is support of the AppDeploy.com online community and its integration with the KBOX Systems Management Appliance.

Bob founded AppDeploy.com (www.appdeploy.com) in September of 1999 as the premier destination for administrators seeking application and systems deployment expertise and has been writing for the website ever since. He has produced several hours of free videos on deployment related topics as well as several product reviews. Bob is author of *The Definitive Guide to Desktop Administration* as well as *Start to Finish Guide to Scripting with KiXtart*. He has gone on to speak at events like the Microsoft Management Summit and has written several articles, white papers, and books on the topics of scripting and desktop management. For more on Bob, visit www.bkelly.com.

Danielle Ruest and Nelson Ruest are both enterprise IT architects with over 20 years of experience in migration planning and network, PC, change management projects, and server infrastructure design. Danielle is a Microsoft MVP for Virtual Machines. Nelson is an MCSE, Microsoft Certified Trainer, and Microsoft MVP in Failover Clustering. Both are very familiar with all versions of Microsoft Windows as well as security, Active Directory, systems management, intra- and extranet configurations, collaboration technologies, office automation, and virtualization solutions. Together they have co-authored *The Complete Reference for Windows Server 2008* (http://www.amazon.com/Microsoft-Windows-Server-2008-Reference/dp/0072263652), *The Definitive Guide to Vista Migration* (http://www.realtime-nexus.com/dgvm.htm) which is referenced on the companion CD, *Deploying Messaging Solutions with Microsoft Exchange Server 2007* (http://www.microsoft.com/MSPress/books/10938.aspx), as well as *Configuring Windows Server 2008 Active Directory* (http://www.microsoft.com/MSPress/books/11754.aspx), and that was just last year. This year they are working on two books on virtualization in the datacenter.

Danielle and Nelson work for Resolutions Enterprises Ltd. (www.reso-net.com), a consulting firm focused on IT Infrastructure and dynamic datacenter design. Resolutions has been offering OS migration solutions for every version of Windows since Windows 2.0. It now has offered virtualization solutions for the past ten years. These solutions range from testing and development support environments to the virtualization of enterprise production systems. Danielle and Nelson have been instrumental in the development of these offerings to meet customer requirements as well as their promotion through multiple articles, presentations, and conferences.

Bob Kelly, Danielle Ruest and Nelson Ruest have also participated in the production of the documentation for the Microsoft Deployment Toolkit, which was called Business Desktop Deployment (BDD) when Microsoft first prepared it for release in support of Windows Vista deployments. Together, they bring this expertise to this Bible.

About the Technical Editors

This book was written in two portions. Bob Kelly was responsible for the deployment section and Danielle Ruest and Nelson Ruest were responsible for the administration section. Each author then performed the technical review for the other's work: Danielle and Nelson were technical reviewers for Bob's work, and Bob was technical reviewer for Danielle and Nelson's work. The authors felt this would create the best possible result since all authors would have input in all sections of the book. You be the judge.

Credits

Senior Acquisitions Editor
Jody Lefevere

Project Editor
Jade L. Williams

Technical Editors
Bob Kelly
Danielle Ruest
Nelson Ruest

Copy Editor
Beth Taylor

Editorial Manager
Robyn Siesky

Business Manager
Amy Knies

Sr. Marketing Manager
Sandy Smith

Vice President and Executive Group Publisher
Richard Swadley

Vice President and Executive Publisher
Bob Ipsen

Vice President and Publisher
Barry Pruett

Project Coordinator
Kristie Rees

Graphics and Production Specialist
Stacie Brooks

Illustration
Resolutions Enterprises Ltd.
Bob Kelly
Danielle Ruest

Quality Control Technician
Caitie Kelly

Media Development Project Supervisor
Laura Moss-Hollister

Media Development Specialist
Joshua Frank

Media Development Coordinator
Jenny Swisher

Proofreading and Indexing
Christine Sabooni
Ty Koontz

Contents at a Glance

Contents

Part I: Developing the Deployment Strategy   1

Contents

Contents

Part III: Administering Windows Vista 293

Contents

Foreword

Deployment and Administration of new Operating Systems on new or reused hardware for most organizations of size is a continuous effort. Training is required for new technologies, new staff and the end users of the hardware as well. Change is everywhere and in the business of software, change comes fast. In the operating system deployment space, change has been slower than most other technology areas. Until the introduction of the Windows Vista® operating system, the deployment process had been essentially the same since at least the release of Microsoft® Windows NT®. With the release of Windows Vista and the Windows Server® 2008 operating system, many changes were made deep in the core yielding several benefits requiring we re-examine our old processes and tools and be willing to unlearn some of them. Many of the old tools will not work anymore. Some of our reasons why we deployed the way we did until now will have been forgotten, or just no longer applicable. Letting go of old habits and familiar tools is often difficult. Hardware standardization should be a goal for most organizations, but is still too often not achieved and like software it also changes fast so we must learn to deal with it efficiently. Our job is to manage all this change and look for more efficient ways to do what we do. Fortunately, the majority of the change we will manage will be recognized as a definite improvement.

The changes to Windows Vista in the administration and deployment areas are mostly invisible to the end user. That is a good thing. The end user should focus on leveraging productivity improvements and not the nuances of how to install or administer an OS. After all the OS is only there to serve the applications that run on it.

All OS images require periodic updates. We now have methods available to incorporate those updates in the core image, or apply them just-in-time to an offline OS so that it can always boot up the first time secure and with the right drivers or language. The different techniques available allow us to choose how much network bandwidth or media capacity is best for us.

The Windows Vista OS core is now language neutral, allowing us to install and uninstall the languages of our choice. Drivers, languages and updates can be applied to OS files (images) that have not yet been deployed to end users. These driver, update, and language configuration capabilities allow us to design a true single image that can be distributed and updated worldwide if need be, and customize it at the final destination, with very high levels of automation. We no longer need to maintain multiple images for different HAL types, language types, and rebuild, capture, test and redistribute our images for each change in hardware or security. We can now safely choose to update our core images just a few times over the image lifecycle. Fewer changes in the core image help reduce changes impacting the administration cost of those OS configurations.

Microsoft has released tools such as the Windows® Automated Installation Kit and solution accelerators such as the Microsoft Deployment Toolkit 2008, Microsoft Assessment and Planning Toolkit, 2007 Office System Security Guide, Data Encryption Toolkit, Security Compliance Management, and Windows Vista Security Guide to help both do-it-yourself shops and services partners. Additional resources like this book summarize and bring to light the various tools and steps to learn how to deploy and administer Windows Vista along with the real world experience of the authors. Armed with these resources your organization can better approach deployment and administration as the continuous process that is.

Mike Lewis
Architect Client/Server Deployment
Microsoft Corporation

Acknowledgments

This book would not have been possible without the dedication and talent of many people. Thanks to Shane Cribbs who began this project with Wiley. Without you, we would not have been part of it. Also thanks to Bob from Danielle and Nelson for his diligent job on the technical edits. The reverse is also true from Bob to Danielle and Nelson. We've wanted to put our combined experience together in a book for quite some time. This is the result. We hope you enjoy it and find it a useful guide.

We would like to thank everyone at Wiley Publishing who supported us as we researched and wrote, week after week. Beth Taylor, our project editor and copy editor, was very helpful throughout the project. Jody Lefevere, our acquisitions editor, proved understanding and resourceful as authors changed and the schedule lengthened. Thank you both.

Of course, this book would not have been possible without the dedicated work of the Microsoft developers that helped produce Vista. Thank you all as well. Finally, thank you to the Microsoft team who put together the Microsoft Deployment Toolkit. Though it has undergone many changes since the days of the BDD, they have all been for the better.

How to Get the Most out of This Book

Here are some things to know so you can get the most out of this book:

First, to indicate that you need to select a command from a menu, the menu and command are separated by an arrow symbol. For example, if we tell you to select a tool from the Start menu, the instructions will say to choose Start ➪ Tool.

Parts I and II are entirely dedicated to operating system deployment and getting your Windows Vista infrastructure ready. Parts III and IV explain how to manage, administer, secure, and protect the computer systems that run Vista once the deployment is complete. For information on deployment project management, look to *The Definitive Guide to Vista Migration*, a free eBook written by Danielle and Nelson for which you'll find a link to on the companion CD-ROM.

This is a real-world deployment and administration book: We've worked hard to ensure that our lessons, examples, and explanations are based on professional conventions. We've also culled these practices from the myriad deployment projects we've all worked on as well as drawn administration techniques from the many support projects of which we have been a part.

The CD-ROM that accompanies this book contains many of the third-party tools discussed in each chapter as well as documentation templates that can be used in support of your own deployment project.

Icons: What Do They Mean?

Although the icons are pretty standard and self-explanatory (they have their names written on them!), here's a brief explanation of what they are and what they mean.

 Tips offer you extra information that further explains a given topic or technique, often suggesting alternatives or workarounds to a listed procedure.

 Notes provide supplementary information to the text, shedding light on background processes or miscellaneous options that aren't crucial to the basic understanding of the material.

 When you see the Caution icon, make sure you're following along closely to the tips and techniques being discussed.

CROSS-REF If you want to find related information to a given topic in another chapter, look for the cross-reference icons.

WEB RESOURCE For related information, resources, or software available online, look for the Web resource icons.

ON the CD-ROM This icon indicates that the CD-ROM contains a related file and points you to the folder location.

How This Book Is Organized

This book has been written in a format that gives you access to need-to-know information very easily in every section (or Part) of the book. These parts make up two major sections of the book. The first section includes Parts I and II, which are aimed at deployment and therefore focus on the tools you use
to implement this powerful new operating system (OS) into your environment. The second section includes Parts III and IV, which focus on administration tasks and systems management once the new operating system has been deployed.

The second section takes an in-depth look at how you manage Windows Vista systems once they are deployed. It is built on the CASPR system, which is made up of five aspects:

- Controlling change in your environment
- Administering your systems
- Securing your infrastructure
- Protecting information your users generate
- Recovering systems or information when issues occur

Each of the chapters in this section covers one aspect of the CASPR system.

Relying on the CASPR system will ensure that each aspect of system management will be completely covered and will vastly reduce the efforts required to create a stable and solid Vista PC infrastructure.

Part I: Developing the Deployment Strategy

The first part of this book explores deployment in depth through a look at deployment planning (Chapter 1), working on your first Vista images (Chapter 2), and learning about Vista licensing as well as how to manage it in small or large organizations (Chapter 3). Use this part to learn more about the changes Microsoft has brought to both Vista deployment and licensing.

Part II: Customizing the Deployment Process

The second part of the book goes in depth covering the deployment process: working with application installations through an examination of the Windows Installer service (Chapter 4), working with user data, protecting this most valuable asset to users as you migrate systems (Chapter 5), performing advanced modifications to Windows deployment images (Chapter 6), relying on the Microsoft Deployment Toolkit to improve the results of your deployment project (Chapter 7), and finally, working with Windows Deployment Services in support of this and future deployments (Chapter 8).

Part III: Administering Windows Vista

Part III begins the administration portion of this book by addressing the first two aspects of CASPR: change management (Chapter 9) and administration (Chapter 10). Change management focuses on two core Vista technologies: group policy that lets you manage one or a multitude of computers, and event management — a technology that was completely rewritten for this edition of Windows — as well as task scheduling, another technology that is completely new in Vista.

Part IV: Protecting and Maintaining the System

Finish off with the last three aspects of CASPR: security (Chapter 11), protection (Chapter 12), recovery (Chapter 13), and the What's on the CD-ROM appendix. Microsoft has invested very heavily in Vista security and this section takes you through the paces required to protect all of your systems whether they be in-house or on the road. Microsoft has also revamped and updated the components that let you protect intellectual property both inside and outside your firewall. The first portion of this book has shown you how to build images and implement deployment strategies that can re-image a computer in less than half an hour. However, there will be situations where you will need to recover a particular system from a total failure or recover a single lost document. Whether you want to make sure your users can recover their own information on Vista or you need to recover a computer from a total loss, rely on this section to discover the ins and outs of Vista's backup and recovery capabilities.

Getting in Touch with Us

You can find additional information, resources, and feedback from Bob Kelly at www.bkelly.com.

You can find additional information, resources, and feedback from Danielle Ruest and Nelson Ruest at www.reso-net.com. You can also contact them at infos@reso-net.com for any feedback or additional questions.

For quality concerns or issues with the CD-ROM, you can call the Wiley Customer Care phone number: (800) 762-2974. Outside the United States, call 1 (317) 572-3994, or contact Wiley Customer Service by e-mail at techsupdum@wiley.com. Wiley Publishing, Inc. will provide technical support only for CD-ROM installation and other general-quality control items; for technical support on the applications themselves, consult the program's vendor.

Part I

Developing the Deployment Strategy

With such a significant task as deploying a new operating system, it can be difficult to know where to begin. This first portion of the book begins by summarizing some of the new technologies and tools provided to get the job done. Understanding the tools and technologies is important to making deployment decisions and is critical to a smooth deployment. There are several key questions answered in this section, including:

- What tools are available?
- How will you determine the contents of your deployment image?
- How will you automate the installation of Windows Vista?
- How will you handle license and activation requirements?

Each of the chapters in this portion of the book help arm you with the information you need to begin your deployment project with key information necessary to do so.

Chapter 1

Planning the Deployment

Maintaining computers can be an expensive venture. In recent years, however, the cost of computer hardware has dropped to a drastically low level. Organizations have been able to leverage the cost drops and other volume purchasing programs to lower the initial expense of purchasing computers and Windows licenses. However, these initial purchase costs can pale in comparison to the cost of deploying the new computer systems.

Microsoft has provided many tools and capabilities with Windows Vista to help you reduce those deployment costs. Microsoft has redesigned its deployment process to provide faster and more consistent deployments. In addition, it has provided tools to customize and streamline the deployment process for your organization.

The focus of this chapter is to help you properly plan your deployment. There are many new technologies to master and many choices that must be made. If care is taken when making these choices, deploying Windows Vista can be an efficient process. Diving in without understanding some of these choices can ultimately lead to slow deployments, inconsistent desktops, project restarts, and time-consuming manual steps. This chapter aims to offer a starting point by providing an overview of key details and tools you should be aware of in order to get things off to a solid start including:

- Choosing the right edition of Windows Vista for your organization
- Determining the right method of installation
- Getting familiar with the Windows imaging format
- Choosing what should be included in your deployment image
- Automating the installation of additional applications following installation
- Addressing application compatibility issues

IN THIS CHAPTER

Choosing the correct edition

Selecting a deployment type

Introducing Windows Vista Installation

Automating installations

Maintaining application compatibility

3

Selecting Windows Vista Editions

The most logical first choice in planning a Windows Vista deployment is to decide which edition or editions of Vista are to be used. With Windows 2000 and XP there was not much of a decision to be made — if you wanted to simply operate in a domain environment, Professional was the only choice. Vista makes this choice more complicated by offering several editions, but for most environments the choice will still be very clear. The key to making this decision is having a basic understanding of the differences.

For most organizations, only the Enterprise and Business editions will be a logical choice. That said, it is always good to be familiar with the real differences so you can make meaningful recommendations and defend any decisions made as to the edition to be deployed.

All editions support a maximum of 4GB of RAM on 32-bit systems. On 64-bit systems, Basic offers support for 8GB, Home Premium lets you work with 16GB, and the remaining Business, Enterprise, and Ultimate editions boast support for 128GB or more. With such a larger number of features available in the various editions of Windows Vista, it paints a clearer picture to state what you do not get with each edition. The list provides a quick summary of the features not included in each edition of Windows Vista:

- **Features not included with Windows Vista Ultimate:** None—that's why it's the ultimate.
- **Features not included with Windows Vista Enterprise:**
  - Parental controls
  - Windows Ultimate Extras
  - Themed slide shows
  - Windows Media Center (recording television, Xbox extensions, HD movie maker, and DVD Maker)
  - Small Business Resources
- **Features not included with Windows Vista Business:**
  - Parental controls
  - Windows Ultimate Extras
  - Themed slide shows
  - Windows Media Center (recording television, Xbox extensions, HD movie maker, and DVD Maker)
- **Features not included with the Windows Vista Home Basic and Windows Vista Home Premium editions:**
  - Support for two processors
  - Backup limitations including support for ShadowCopy or image-based system backup/ recovery

- File system encryption
- Desktop deployment tools
- Policy based QoS networking
- Rights Management Services (RMS) Client
- Control over installation of device drivers
- Network Access Protection Client agent
- Pluggable logon authentication architecture
- Integrated smart card management
- BitLocker drive encryption support
- Support for worldwide interface languages or simultaneous installations of multiple user interface languages
- Subsystem for UNIX-based applications
- Virtual PC Express
- Windows Ultimate Extras
- Small Business Resources
- Windows fax and scan
- Wireless network provisioning
- Full support for Windows Mobility Center (thought it does provide partial support)
- Ability to join a network domain
- Remote desktop client support (though it cannot serve as host)
- Group policy support
- Offline files and folders support
- Client-side caching
- Support for roaming user profiles
- Support for folder redirection
- Ability to install IIS

- **In addition to the preceding items, the following additional features are also missing from Windows Vista Home Basic:**
  - Support for scheduled backups or for the backup of files to a network device
  - Aero user interface (glass, live thumbnails, dynamic windows, and so on)
  - Themed slide shows
  - Windows Media Center (recording television, Xbox extensions, HD Movie Maker, and DVD maker) Note: Home Basic does provide Windows Movie Maker (just not the HD version)

- Premium games
- It is limited to 5 SMB peer network connections (vice the 10 supported by the other editions)
- Tablet PC support
- Windows Slideshow feature
- Windows Meeting space support is limited to "view only"
- PC-to-PC synchronization
- Network projection
- Presentation settings

Vista Home Basic

Windows Vista Home Basic is the base code from which all other editions are built. It includes the new Windows Vista kernel and most security enhancements. Home Basic does not include the ability to join a domain. It also lacks most other features that would be useful mostly in business environments. Although this may make a suitable operating system for average home users, it has no place in a business environment.

Vista Home Premium

Windows Vista Home Premium includes all of the features of Home Basic and includes some additional features. One additional feature is the Aero interface, which gives us the glass-like interface and Flip 3D. On the more useful side, Home Premium includes support for tablet PCs, Windows Meeting Space, Scheduled Backup, DVD Maker, Windows Media Center, and additional games. Although these features make the operating system more fun and a little more useful, Windows Premium still lacks the ability to join a domain and other useful business features. In short, the Home editions should be used at home.

Vista Business

When using Windows Vista for business use, Windows Vista Business should be the first edition considered. Business Edition includes most all of the features of Home Basic but includes many additional features targeted at business customers. The following partial list of features that Vista Business contains makes it a more suitable choice in most organizations:

- Ability to join a domain
- Ability to apply Group Policies
- Remote Desktop
- Offline Files and Folders
- Tablet PC support
- Encrypting File System

- Complete and Scheduled Backup
- Windows Meeting Space
- Windows Fax and Scan
- Multiple physical processor support
- Volume, OEM, and Fully Packaged Product licensing options

Windows Vista Business also includes some more *nonbusiness* features, such as the Aero interface and additional games. In addition a very small number of home features, such as Parental Controls, are not available in Vista Business. This edition is targeted at general business use and is the edition of choice unless additional features of Vista Enterprise or Vista Ultimate are required. Though there are some features missing, such as BitLocker Drive Encryption, the features that are included make the Business Edition a good choice for fixed desktops and workstations (particularly since it is not likely that you will need full drive encryption for these systems).

NOTE The features listed in this section simply document what is included in the editions of Windows Vista. This does not mean that you must install such features. The Windows Vista installation is customizable at a very granular level so that you may eliminate those elements of the setup you do not wish to include (games, for example).

Vista Enterprise

Windows Vista Enterprise Edition is based on Vista Business, but includes features that some organizations may require or find useful. This edition is available exclusively to Microsoft Software Assurance customers, which may eliminate it as an option for some smaller companies. The features included in Enterprise Edition include all of those listed for Business Edition plus the following:

- BitLocker Drive Encryption
- Subsystem for UNIX-based Applications
- License includes the host and up to four virtual machines
- Ability to support multiple languages
- Volume licensing only

Depending upon your needs, any of these features may require you to move to the more expensive Enterprise Edition. Probably the most compelling feature of Enterprise Edition is the BitLocker Drive Encryption (also available in Vista Ultimate Edition) which makes this edition more suitable for portable systems. For test lab environments, the license to run four virtual machines without having to purchase additional licenses can actually lower the licensing costs of Enterprise to below those of Business. Before excluding Vista Enterprise from your options, be sure to consider the advantages and potential cost savings associated with the virtual machine licensing.

Software Assurance

If you are a Software Assurance customer, you may be entitled to some free licenses. For each Windows Client License covered under Software Assurance, you are entitled to one Windows Vista Enterprise upgrade license. The following Volume Licensing programs are eligible for this benefit:

- Open License
- Open Value
- Open Value Company-wide
- Open Value Subscription
- Select License
- Select License Software Assurance Membership
- Enterprise Agreement
- Enterprise Subscription Agreement

For more on the Microsoft Software Assurance program see `www.microsoft.com/licensing/sa/default.mspx`

Vista Ultimate

Windows Vista Ultimate is pretty much what it says. The Ultimate edition includes all the features from all of the other versions. It includes all of the features from the Home editions as well as the features from Business and Enterprise editions. Although this may sound like the best option for the organization desiring the best of the best, it has one characteristic that will exclude most organizations from using it. Like the Home editions of Vista, it is not available with volume licensing. The result will be that each computer must have a unique product key entered after installation, which somewhat offsets the advantages of automating deployment. Also consider that some of the features included in Vista Ultimate are simply unnecessary or undesirable in a business environment, such as Windows Media Center or Parental Controls. You could, of course, remove the features you don't want from the installation of Windows Vista Ultimate, but for the most part this would mean stripping the most expensive edition down to appear as Business or Enterprise. One feature that could be desirable for some organizations is Windows DVD Maker, but it is hard to argue this feature is worth the price and trouble. Consider third-party tools, such as offerings from Roxio or Ulead for such features, if desired.

Other options

In addition to the major editions above, Microsoft has also provided a few additional options. For example, Microsoft has provided a Windows Vista Starter edition for markets that are not classified as high income (high-income markets include the United States, Canada, the European Union, Australia, Japan, and New Zealand). It is a low-cost version of Vista which can only run a limited number of processes. This edition is not appropriate in a business environment and won't be available to most markets.

The other variant you may encounter are the N editions of Windows Vista. Due to legal issues in Europe, Microsoft also offers editions without Media Player included. These editions are identical to the standard editions above except the missing Media Player application and the addition of an N after the edition name. Unless your corporate policy requires an N edition of Windows, it is a simple process to remove Media Player from the installation or even block its use by using Group Policy.

Choosing a Deployment Type

The deployment of Windows Vista could be a great opportunity to establish a new and improved desktop. Others may feel they have their computers just as they should be. Your assessment of your current environment will likely be a key factor in deciding if an upgrade or a replacement is best for your organization. Other factors including the receipt of new computer hardware can also have an impact on how you plan your deployment of Windows Vista. Key deployment types covered here include:

- Replace
- Upgrade
- Refresh
- New computer

CROSS-REF Key to a migration is the migration of user data and settings, which is detailed in Chapter 5

Replacing computers

If you are replacing a computer, user data will need to be collected and stored in a temporary location. The new computer can be imaged with your customized image of Windows Vista beforehand in a staging area, but data restoral is typically performed on location (when the computer has been physically placed on a user's desk). It is a common scenario to replace only a fraction of the computers on a network on a rolling schedule. As such, a network often has new, old, and older systems which benefit from a cascading deployment. Power users get the newer (more powerful) computers, and their computers are reimaged and used to replace computers in the next tier of users. Finally, the oldest computers are expired or allocated to dedicated uses such as Internet kiosk stations.

Upgrading computers

As an alternative to migrating to Windows Vista, computers running Windows XP SP2 (or Windows Vista) may be upgraded to Windows Vista in-place. An upgrade retains your applications, files, and settings as they were in Windows XP SP2. Business and Ultimate editions of Windows Vista may only be applied as an update to Windows XP Professional or Windows XP Tablet PC. When moving from home editions, Windows 2000 and even Windows XP Professional x64 require a clean installation and cannot be upgraded in place.

Upgrades are typically discouraged as the introduction of a new operating system is an ideal chance to perform clean-up, employ lessons learned, and get a clean start. Regardless, applications need to be tested for compatibility. Performing an upgrade does not make incompatible software any less likely to exhibit issues.

CAUTION   The upgrade process will fail on target computers that have users logged on by using Remote Desktop sessions so be sure no such connections are active before initiating an upgrade.

Refreshing computers

A refresh entails backing up user data and settings, installing a fresh Windows Vista image and then restoring user data and settings. Of course, this is a simple definition as there is much to be done including customizing the Vista image and addressing licensing and application needs.

Deploying new computers

Not so much a type of deployment, this scenario is in fact identical to that of a computer replacement. However, it is important to mention that new computers are often being shipped with OEM installations of Windows. So Windows Vista may well arrive installed and ready to go. However, unless you are a large organization with an arrangement with the manufacturer to provide a custom configured image, few corporate networks will accept the OEM installation as is. Often extra applications and promotional shortcuts are delivered with such systems. Therefore it is recommended that new computers arriving with Vista already installed be well scrutinized before accepting the provided image for use in your production environment.

Understanding Windows Vista Installation

When it comes to designing a deployment plan for Windows Vista, it is a good idea to first establish a basic understanding of its new deployment technologies and tools. If you are familiar with the deployment processes from previous Microsoft operating systems, you may be surprised by how many fundamental changes have been introduced with Windows Vista. Specifically, Vista now employs an image-based installation and leverages a detailed XML file for automation of the installation (as opposed to the simple INI file format used by previous versions).

Investigating the Windows Imaging format

Microsoft has significantly changed the installation process. Previously, numerous configuration screens were presented during installation, prompting for which components to install and other information to customize the installation. Using this information, extensive installation scripts were run to set up the initial environment. Installation times frequently ranged from 45 minutes to an hour for a standard installation. Microsoft has now moved to an image-based setup (IBS). This new image-based setup is based on Microsoft's new imaging format, the Windows Imaging format

(WIM). Depending upon the computer and the customizations made to the installation, applying the image may take as little as 15 minutes.

Imaging is the process of making a copy of an ideal configuration and then replicating that copy to other computers. As shown in Figure 1.1, making an image involves installing an operating system on a reference computer, adding software and utilities, making customizations, and then making a copy of the reference computer. This image can then be applied to other computers to both speed deployment and ensure consistency throughout an organization.

For quite some time, Microsoft has been under pressure to better support imaging technology. Although Microsoft has not offered its own imaging solution until now, there have been several third-party vendors offering such solutions but with some inherent problems. In particular, there has been a need to provide better support of a single image on multiple hardware platforms and a unified imaging toolset. Providing better support of a single image allows organizations to support a much smaller number of images, ideally only one, that lowers support costs and increases consistency among deployed systems. Providing a unified toolset helps IT departments standardize imaging tools and reduce costs associated with third-party imaging tools. With the release of Windows Vista, Microsoft has attempted to address both of those needs.

FIGURE 1.1

Reviewing the imaging process

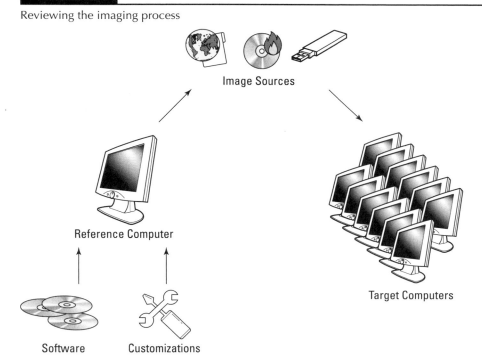

One limitation with imaging Windows has been the Hardware Abstraction Layer (HAL). Computers that use different HALs have typically required separate images. An example of computers that require different HALs is a single processor computer and a multiple processor computer, including hyper-threading and multi-core architectures. Another example of where HAL incompatibilities were often encountered was if one computer supported power management features and the other did not. Windows Vista now detects and installs the proper HAL, allowing you to use a single image.

Another factor that has forced many to use multiple images is supporting multiple mass storage controllers. Whether using SCSI, Parallel ATA, or Serial ATA, there are a large number of supported mass storage controllers available and most use a unique driver. For the most part, that still holds true. However, updating images to support new mass storage controllers has become much easier. Previously, extensive and often tedious answer file editing was required to update an image for new controllers. Now with only a few commands at the command prompt, your image can support the latest Windows Vista–capable mass storage controllers.

To address the problem of a unified imaging toolset, Microsoft has created the new Windows Imaging (WIM) format and several tools to manage and deploy WIM format images. The new format is file-based imaging rather than sector-based. Sector-based images are applied to the hard drive as raw data. The use of a file-based image format has several advantages.

One such advantage is that file-based images can be applied non-destructively. Microsoft is famous for their backwards compatibility and straightforward migration paths. An important migration path that must be supported for Windows Vista is an *in-place upgrade*. Although sector-based imaging is destructive and destroys all data on the partition to which it is applied, file-based imaging allows images to be applied leaving existing files in place.

Another advantage of file-based images is that they leverage the *single instance store concept*. Microsoft designed WIM files so that multiple images can be stored in a single WIM file. For example, a production image and a kiosk image can both be stored in the same file. Independently, this fact may seem rather esoteric. However, when combined with the fact that WIM files use single instance storage, this becomes a rather important advantage. If you were to compare two of your current desktop images, you would most likely find that a large majority of the files are the same, most likely over 90 percent. With single instance storage, only a single copy of each file is saved. This can drastically reduce image storage space. Microsoft has internally taken advantage of this technology by shipping one DVD with five separate editions of Windows Vista. This is possible because each of the editions shares a common code base, and only files not found in existing images are added to the WIM file for each additional image. Figure 1.2 illustrates the structure of a WIM.

WIM file structure

WIM files begin with a header. The header of the file contains information, such as the compression type used and the signature and GUID of the image file. There are three types of supported compression. The first type, *no compression,* stores all files in their original state without attempting any compression. The image capture and apply operations tend to perform marginally better with no compression because the CPU is not required to compress or decompress each file during the process. The second type of compression is referred to as *fast compression* and uses XPress compression. Finally, *LZX* compression, made famous by WinZip and PKZip, can be used to obtain high compression. Fast compression is the default method; it provides a good balance of CPU performance and space savings.

FIGURE 1.2

A Simplified diagram of Windows Imaging format file contents

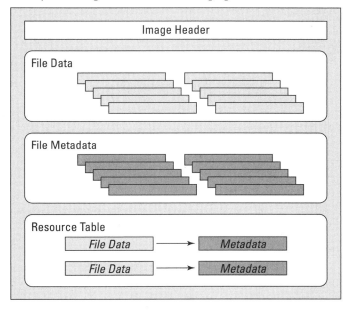

When applying images from a network location or slow optical drive, using no compression can provide worse performance than fast compression in many situations. This is true because the performance improvement of pulling a smaller image across the network often outweighs the extra work that must be performed by the CPU to decompress the data.

The next section of a WIM file is the file data portion. In this section, the data from each file is first compressed and then stored. The other attributes, such as permissions and directory structure, are not saved here. As a matter of fact, the filename is not used here. Instead a hash is generated for each file. When the data hashes of two files are identical, only one copy of the data is stored, even if the filenames and permissions are different. This is known as a Single Instance Store (SIS) and is the largest section of most WIM files by far.

Immediately following the file data is the file metadata. Each entry in the file metadata section includes information, such as a filename, an access control list, and other file system attributes. Each entry maps directly to a file, except there is no actual data stored here.

All of the magic happens in the next section, the *resource table*, which is a table that maps file data to file metadata. The resource table also includes resource locations that are used to rebuild the directory structure. If you are familiar with databases, you may recognize this as a mapping table. If you are not familiar with databases, you can think of it as a large spreadsheet that connects the file data to its metadata.

WIM file distribution

After you understand how a WIM file works, you can address the issue of image application. Third-party imaging formats require third-party tools to apply those images to a hard drive. Applying a WIM file can be performed by using either Microsoft tools or a WIM-compatible third-party utility. A standard installation of Windows is performed with `setup.exe`, which replaces `winnt.exe` and `winnt32.exe`. Microsoft has also provided another tool, called ImageX, which can both create and apply WIM files.

CROSS-REF   ImageX is discussed in more detail in Chapter 6.

Keep in mind, however, that WIM format images are file-based. File-based images do not store any partition or drive information. This offers the advantage of being very portable and being able to be used with varying-sized drives, assuming they can support the expanded data from the WIM file. File-based images do require, however, that the drive be prepared ahead of time. Disk partitioning and formatting must be performed before attempting to apply a WIM file image to a hard drive. This can be performed with any partitioning and formatting tool, but Microsoft provides the DiskPart utility to perform disk administration.

Third-party formats

Although this book focuses primarily on Microsoft's imaging format and tools, there are alternatives to consider (see Chapter 6). Microsoft has introduced its imaging format as the default distribution method, but that does not mean you are required to use it other than to initially install Windows Vista. Many organizations have significant time and money invested in other distribution solutions, such as Symantec Ghost and Acronis True Image. These alternative solutions often provide more than simple imaging features, so it is worth considering how you use them when deciding if such tools are truly replaced by the imaging tools now native to Windows. For some, combining Microsoft's tools with third-party tools may provide an efficient solution.

Leveraging Windows PE

Another major change to the deployment process is the manner in which installations are started. Before Windows Vista, Windows installation was typically started from DOS. DOS was used as the startup environment because of its small size and speed. Using such a small operating system allowed the installation to be launched from smaller media, such as floppy disks. DOS was also very familiar to systems administrators and fairly easy to customize and automate. Microsoft has now moved to a Windows-based installation environment, Windows PE. This section provides a simple overview of Windows PE; for more details see Chapter 6.

Windows Preinstallation Environment (PE) 2.0 is a scaled-down version of Windows Vista which uses a command prompt for the user interface, as shown in Figure 1.3. It does, however, have support for some very powerful features that make it very useful for both deployment and troubleshooting. Some of the included features are network support, Windows device driver support, Windows Scripting Host, and many other standard Windows tools and utilities. Utilities that aren't included can often be added or run from a network share. Due to the scaled-down features, Windows PE can be placed on a CD, DVD, or USB flash drive. A basic Windows PE implementation is less than 200MB in size.

FIGURE 1.3

Windows PE 2.0 user interface

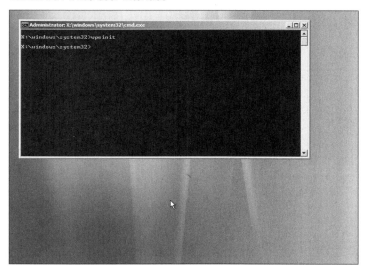

From a more technical standpoint, Windows PE is a Windows environment running entirely from memory. Successfully starting Windows PE requires two parts — boot files and a WIM image — to apply to a RAMDISK, as shown in Figure 1.4. During boot up, Windows PE boot media looks in a directory named sources for a file named boot.wim. Once found, boot.wim is imaged into a RAM Disk and given a drive designation of X. The portion of RAM designated as a RAM Disk is treated as a hard drive and is unavailable to the system for standard memory operations.

Boot.wim contains the entire Windows PE operating system. By default, the only other files present on the boot media are used to boot the system and image the boot.wim file into RAM Disk. By putting the operating system in RAM Disk, several things are accomplished. First, the boot media may be removed after boot because all necessary files are in RAM. Second, Windows PE requires read-write access to many of the system files, and RAM Disk is read-writable. This allows you to use read-only boot media. Using read-only media can be desirable, especially when dealing with virus outbreaks as the virus cannot infect read-only media.

FIGURE 1.4

An illustration of the Windows PE Architecture

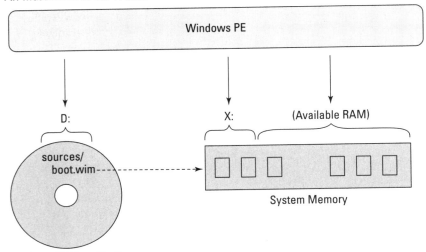

Notice in Figure 1.4 that a hard drive is not required. However, if a hard drive is not present or partitioned, the boot media will be assigned drive letter C:. If hard drives are present and partitioned, the boot media will begin its lettering after all local disk drive letters have been assigned. The implication is that the boot media drive letter is unpredictable while the RAM Disk drive assignment is statically set to X:. If you plan to write custom scripts, keep this in mind.

Obtaining Windows PE has become much easier with Windows Vista. The distribution media uses Windows PE to perform Windows Vista installation. Microsoft has also made Windows PE, along with customization tools, available as a free download called the Windows Automated Installation Kit (WAIK).

As you begin to plan your deployment process, one of the first decisions you must make is what type of images to use. No matter what technology you choose, you'll need to be somewhat familiar with the native imaging technology as discussed in Chapter 6.

Although it may be tempting to base an image on a system already up and running with your corporate applications, doing so can cause trouble down the road. It is always advisable to create images based off of a clean operating system installation in order to attain a more stable and predictable baseline image. Document what you install and how you install it for accurate reproducibility. In fact, it is best to automate the creation of this image entirely by using answer files and automated application installations as discussed later in this chapter and throughout the book.

Default images

Windows installation times have been drastically reduced since the native installation method now utilizes an imaging process. For many smaller organizations, this increased efficiency in the installation process may be sufficient. If your organization only requires a couple of applications and doesn't typically re-image more than one or two computers a week, standard installations may work fine.

When using the generic installation image from the Windows Vista DVD, you may wish to automate the few remaining steps of setup. Customizations may include providing answers to the setup process and/or running post-installation scripts to install software. A couple of good examples of automated software installation are antivirus software and Microsoft Office suites, because it's quite likely that everyone in your organization will require these applications.

Custom images

Most likely, you will want to deploy your own customized images. Although Microsoft provides a generic image, it may require significant post-imaging processing to modify it to meet your organization's requirements. If you support over 500 workstations, imaging is probably a daily task and saving even a few minutes each time can be a huge advantage.

The real power of imaging is that it allows you to create a customized image unique to the needs of your company, not just what Microsoft thinks you might need. WIM files were designed with customizations in mind. In addition, free tools are available so that you can create, apply, and update WIM files. However, there are three basic types of images from which you must choose. These distinctions are less technical, and more philosophical. Before creating any custom images you must decide which philosophy your organization should follow.

Thin images

The philosophy of using thin images is one of flexibility. The idea is to create a plain image with very little, if any, additional software and customizations. All organizational software and customizations would then be added by scripts or a management solution, such as System Center Configuration Manager or Group Policy.

The advantage of a thin image is that it would require less maintenance because there is less software included to have to update and maintain. When software updates are required, the installation sources can simply be updated.

Thin images have also been used to reduce the number of supported deployment images. Because there is no software included on the image, a single image can generally be used to support many different workgroups, for example, Sales, Marketing, Production, and IT.

Although using a thin image eases administration, it slows down deployments. After applying the image, it may take a considerable amount of time for post-setup scripts to run and complete.

NOTE   For more information on working with thin system images see *Deploy Vista with a Thin System Image*, by Ruest and Ruest at: `http://itmanagement.earthweb.com/entdev/article.php/11070_3675806_1`.

Streaming applications

An increasingly popular trend is the delivery of software as *virtual applications*. A virtual application is a way administrators may deliver software to users which isolates itself from the actual file and registry systems of the local computer. Chapter 4 discusses this in more detail, but virtual applications are often associated with another technology: *application streaming*. Application streaming allows for the delivery of software (typically virtual application packages) to computers over the network as they are requested by the user. Upon launching such an application, the required bits to start the application are downloaded to the client. As the application is running, additional bits are downloaded as necessary. Such data may also be cached so that it is only necessary to pull data from the network the first time the application is requested. While thin images may not seem practical, use of streaming technologies like this can make a thin image very compelling.

Thick images

Thick images are just the opposite. They are designed to include every possible piece of necessary software along with all desired customizations. The goal is speed and simplicity. After deploying a thick image, there is very little configuration to perform and no reliance on any external management software. Typically, naming the computer is all that is required.

The drawback of thick images is that the extensive customizations often make an image practical for only a small group of people. For example, including a Sales application in a thick image may preclude it from being used for the Human Resources department. The result is a larger number of supported images. Another drawback is keeping each application within each image up to date. The more applications you include in the image, the more updates and security patches you will have to apply.

Hybrid images

Most often, the ideal solution falls somewhere between thick and thin. These images are referred to as hybrid images. The goal is to support a minimum number of images while providing a relatively efficient deployment process.

A typical hybrid image would include customizations, such as:

- Microsoft Office suite
- Adobe Acrobat Reader
- Preconfigured Internet favorites
- Necessary desktop management agents
- Drivers for all supported hardware

Specialized or departmental applications are omitted to keep the image generic enough to be used throughout the organization. These applications would normally be installed by using a software distribution solution or post-imaging script, much like a thin image. However, by including software packages everyone will need in the image, the post-imaging processing times should be minimal.

Hybrid images are not without their problems. Because software packages are included in the image, it will require updating as each package is updated in your organization. However, hybrid images do strike a nice balance between performance and simplicity. This is the recommended image philosophy for most organizations.

When deciding just how "thick" or "thin" to make your images, ask yourself these questions:

- **Which applications are common to all workstations?** The more applications that all of your workstations have in common the more time can be saved by including them in the image. In addition, lengthy post-image scripts tend to be more error prone.

- **How long will it take to install each of the common applications?** It may make sense to include only the larger packages, such as Office suites. Often smaller packages, such as Acrobat Reader, can be installed quickly and more easily updated if excluded from the image. Keep in mind that you should only update the image if you update all of the existing machines in production.

- **Can the installation of the applications be automated?** If an application doesn't lend itself to automatic installation, it's certainly a good candidate to be included in the image.

- **What type of network connection will be available after imaging?** If you plan to image your machines with removable media in a remote location, thick images will require less network bandwidth. Properly designed, thick images will only require network access to join the domain, if applicable.

Automating the installation of Windows Vista

Building a corporate image is only the first step in planning your deployment. Although this image may contain the drivers and applications you want, its installation still requires the completion of a simple installation wizard. In previous versions of Windows, you could automate this process by dictating certain choices in your `Sysprep.inf` file or the `unattend.txt` file. While many administrators would edit this file directly, the key GUI tool for establishing these installation answer files was Setup Manager (`Setupmgr.exe`). The tool did not expose many of the customizations possible when editing directly, and with no error reporting or validation many administrators spent many hours fighting simple typos and confusing entries.

Like the installation format itself, the capability of automating the installation of Windows has also been drastically changed for the better. Today, System Image Manager (SIM) is the tool for not only creating these tools but also validating them to identify any problems that may exist prior to use. See Figure 1.5.

FIGURE 1.5

Reviewing the new System Image Manager tool

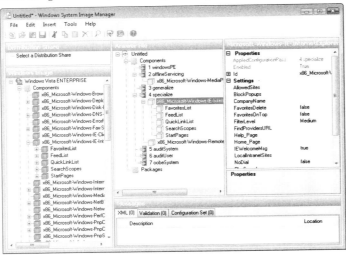

SIM is discussed in more detail in Chapter 2. The key thing to understand in the planning phase is the amount of power such a feature provides you and your deployment. Not only can you automate the installation options you see during an interactive installation, but there are also a great number of customizations you would otherwise never see.

A quick example of some things you can do by customizing an installation with SIM:

- Specify the owner and company names as well as the product key for the installation.
- Indicate whether to extend the partition to fill the remaining space on the disk.
- Customize IE home pages, control pop-up blocker, and dictate default favorites.
- Specify if users can use Remote Assistance to request help from a friend or support staff.
- Enable or disable the Windows Firewall.
- Dictate the name of the primary DNS domain to be searched for the name resolution.
- Specify the size and path of the page file.

TIP Within SIM, you can right-click on any value and choose help to be provided with more details about each setting and value you may specify.

CROSS-REF You can use a freeware tool that goes by the name of vLite, which provides the ability to remove the things you do not want from the WIM image entirely. This tool is discussed in more detail in Chapter 6.

Automating Application Installations

By using custom images, you can greatly reduce operating system deployment times. As discussed earlier, thick images can reduce deployment times but may very well require maintaining several images for your organization. For this reason, most organizations use a hybrid image. If using a hybrid or thin image, some or all applications must be installed after the imaging process. To create a more efficient and consistent deployment, the installation of these applications should be automated to the extent possible. This is not likely to be a new topic to you as it is common practice to automate installation. Further, this topic is covered in more detail in Chapter 4. This section provides a quick overview of some key software distribution techniques in use today to get you thinking about applications as part of your planned deployment.

Customizing application installation commands

The easiest option is often to use any automation or quiet installation support provided by the software vendor. Although it can sometimes be difficult to uncover them, many applications do provide command line arguments that can be passed to the installation program to force a silent installation. Depending upon the vendor you may be able to specify which options are installed and how much of the user interface is presented during installation. It is often this varying support for customized silent installations that can make automating application installations challenging.

Luckily, the Windows Admin community is a sharing one and many have shared details on the deployment of thousands of applications online at AppDeploy.com (`www.appdeploy.com`). This resource is a good starting point when working to identify which options exist. Although vendor Web sites often provide little to no information regarding deployment, what has been discovered or uncovered is organized here by application and version number.

The most ideal installation format to work with today is Windows Installer (MSI). As discussed in Chapter 4, Windows Installer offers a host of benefits including rollback, uninstall, logging, control of UI display, self-healing, nearly endless support for customization, and more. For applications to be certified as Windows Vista compatible, their installation package must be in the format of an MSI file. MSI files are small databases that instruct a service on your computer, the Windows Installer Service, what actions to perform to install, repair, or remove an application.

If the default installation options are acceptable, an application can often be installed using the /q option with Msiexec. An example of a quiet installation of Adobe Acrobat Reader with a progress bar during installation is

```
msiexec /i acroread.msi /qb
```

In most cases the MSI package and all supporting files can simply be copied off of the installation media. In some cases you must perform an administrative installation to a network share for silent installs to work properly. Two examples are Microsoft Office and VMware Workstation. As is the case for many applications distributed via the Internet, Adobe Acrobat Reader is actually a self-extracting archive that decompresses and then runs a Windows Installer setup. To get at these source installation files, start the setup, and when the Welcome screen appears, look in the `%TEMP%` folder for a new subdirectory (often with a random name), which contains the installation source. Copy these files to your network share and run such setups directly.

InstallShield (the most common ISV setup type) supports the ability to pass MSI command line parameters from the `setup.exe` so that it need not be extracted (or pulled from `%TEMP%`) if you do not wish. However many InstallShield setups are actually programmed to check if they are being run from the provided `setup.exe`. The reason is that some InstallShield setups rely upon an installed setup scripting component that must be installed prior to running the intended setup. Such setups require that you not call the MSI setup directly, which can be frustrating to administrators. Fortunately, you can use a couple of workarounds, including passing the property ISSETUPDRIVEN to the command line installation and assign it a value of 1. For example:

```
msiexec /i mysetup.msi ISSETUPDRIVEN=1 /qb
```

 A video presentation on working around such setups may be found online at www.
appdeploy.com/video/installscript.asp.

Creating transform files

When simply instructing an application to install silently is not sufficient, transform files provide you the ability to inject customizations. Microsoft Transform (MST) files can act as answer files that can be passed to the Windows Installer Service to select components to install and set preferences. Aside from choosing options, you can make any change you want to the provided setup including adding and removing files and registry entries. Some vendors even provide tools to help you create an MST file. For example, Microsoft Office MST files can be created with the Custom Installation Wizard.

However, most applications do not offer their own tool for generating an MST file. For such applications, you can rely on a third-party tool to customize the installation this way. If you are looking to make simple changes, such as adding or changing property values, it may suffice to make use of the free ORCA Windows Installer table editor from the Windows Installer SDK.

NOTE The Windows Installer SDK is available free from Microsoft at www.microsoft.
com/downloads/details.aspx?FamilyId=A55B6B43-E24F-4EA3-A93E-
40C0EC4F68E5&displaylang=en. Once installed, you can find the installation at
<InstallationDirecotry>\Microsoft SDK\bin\Orca.msi.

After an MST file has been created, it is passed as an option to the `msiexec` command to perform a silent installation. For example

```
msiexec /i mysetup.msi TRANSFORMS=mytransform.mst /qb
```

NOTE If deploying a Windows Installer setup via Group Policy, you can specify one or
more transforms as options in the GPO. If you desire to pass a property to an MSI
setup being deployed by Group Policy, you may use a tool such as ORCA to specify the value, as
command lines may not be specified in Group Policy.

Repackaging applications

If your application does not support a silent installation or the necessary level of customization can't be performed through silent installation, you need to repackage your application. Repackaging requires the use of third-party software (ORCA does not offer a repackaging feature). The two most widely used repackaging tools are AdminStudio from Acresso Software and Wise Package Studio from Symantec.

Repackaging tools typically work either by monitoring the changes made by a setup or by means of a *snapshot* that detects the differences made to a system by a setup. A snapshot has the user begin with a clean workstation that contains a minimal amount of additional software. The repackaging tool then takes a snapshot of the workstation before and after the installation of an application and determines those detected differences to be the needed contents for the newly created MSI setup.

Although MSI is the most common target for a repackaged application, application virtualization is developing as a popular alternative. Virtual applications run in memory and do not update the local computer's file system. While the act of creating a virtual application is often similar (or identical) to that of repackaging a setup to MSI format, the resulting package is instead managed by a client agent (or even its own internal mechanism) as opposed to being managed by Windows Installer. Repackaging a setup into a virtual application format is sometimes referred to as *sequencing* (a term coined by SoftGrid).

 A detailed list of applications that offer repackaging functions may be found online at www.appdeploy.com/techhomes/windowsinstaller.asp.

Selecting a Distribution Media

After you have determined if a thick or thin image will be used, the required distribution media may be chosen. Options include network, DVD, or USB drive distribution. Although variances and combinations may be used, these are your basic choices.

DVD

DVD distribution has several advantages if all of your computers have DVD-ROM drives. DVD media is relatively cheap, and there is little upfront cost because most modern computers do have DVD drives. DVDs are also large enough to handle modestly sized images. The generic image from Microsoft is about 1.8GB. Therefore, you will be able to add several applications and still stay within the size constraints of the DVD. When you take into consideration including Windows PE on the DVD, you have about 4GB available on a DVD with which to consider adding applications. Keep in mind that even if you have to use multiple images in your environment, WIM files allow multiple images to store a single instance of each file. Therefore it is very practical to store two or three images on the same DVD.

Like everything else, DVDs do have drawbacks. Three items that most often exclude DVD as a distribution choice are size, reliability, and maintenance. If your images turn out to be larger than 4GB, DVDs become very inconvenient. You may span an image across several DVDs, but that means an additional manual intervention. Reliability also comes into play, because DVDs are easily scratched, particularly those burned rather than pressed at the factory. Reaching the end of the last DVD of a three-DVD set and having the installation fail due to a damaged DVD can be very frustrating. Most problematic is the issue of version control. When your deployment image is updated, you must create new DVDs and distribute them to every technician responsible for imaging. If a single technician continues to use an older image, the network can be put into an inconsistent and potentially unstable state. This is particularly easy to see if you are moving to a new Windows service pack or Office Suite version.

USB drives

The newest edition to the list of distribution media is USB drives. With the inclusion of bootable and high-speed USB support on nearly every new computer, USB drives become a very attractive distribution media for some environments.

USB drives have several advantages over DVDs for distribution of your deployment images. One reason is that USB drives are typically much faster than DVD drives. A fast USB drive can boot and apply an image in less than half the time it might take to apply the same image from DVD. Secondly, they require no network connectivity and can be useful in remote locations or on overworked networks where bandwidth is a concern. Also, USB drives tend to be more reliable and are not susceptible to scratching in the way DVDs are. Lastly, the typical USB drive is much larger than the capacity of a DVD, allowing for more and larger images on a single drive.

USB drives suffer some of the same downfalls that DVDs do, namely not having a reliable means of version control. When new versions of the deployment image or images are created, every USB drive must be updated with the new image or images. Although the reliability of USB drives is higher than DVDs, they are still vulnerable to being dropped or broken.

NOTE If you are using DVDs or USB drives in a networked environment, consider including a simple script that checks a network share for a simple file containing the latest build number. This way the convenience of removable media may be enjoyed while minimizing the concern of version control.

Network

In environments that enjoy high-capacity and efficient networks, network distribution is recommended when possible. Using the network to distribute your image offers the advantages of centralized version control and, hopefully, reliability. Centralized version control is realized because all imaging is performed from the same distribution point. When new images are released, a simple update to the distribution point ensures that all new imaging will use the new image. Reliability is also increased as networks cannot be scratched or dropped as can DVDs or USB drives.

On the downside, your network must be able to handle the additional load of pulling deployment images across them. An unreliable or slow network can become even more so once gigabytes of information are being transferred for each image. If your network supports the ability to multicast, network impact can be minimized greatly by sending the data over the network only once with several target computers listening to receive it as a single stream. Another potential solution to minimize the impact of network-based imaging is to perform all of your imaging on an isolated or segregated network. In larger environments, a dedicated imaging server and network switch are often employed on a separate subnet from the production environment, which may also be used as a staging area for the introduction of new computer hardware, as shown in Figure 1.6.

FIGURE 1.6

Sample network configuration for imaging

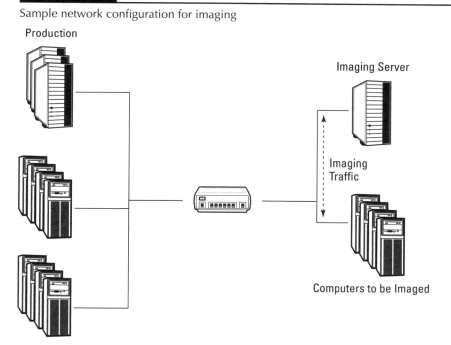

Evaluating Hardware Requirements

If you will be migrating existing machines to Windows Vista, you will first need to get an idea of what hardware you have deployed and how well it will handle Windows Vista. With its introduction, much hype and media attention was given to how much more hardware intensive Windows Vista is. In reality, Windows Vista is quite an adaptive operating system and will adjust its features to accommodate the hardware on which it is installed. However, there are some minimums that must be abided by and some recommendations to keep your users from becoming unduly frustrated at sluggish performance.

If you have an inventory system in place, you can do some quick checking against the requirements to identify those in need of updates. But even with a third-party inventory tool in place, it is advisable to check each machine representative of your environment for hardware compatibility using the Windows Vista Upgrade Advisor. More than a simple requirements check, this tool interrogates the local computer hardware and checks for compatibility using the latest information from Microsoft's Web site. If there are just a handful of different hardware types in your environment, running this on each of them can provide some valuable data.

Another option is the new Microsoft Assessment and Planning Solution Accelerator (MAP). This inventory, assessment, and reporting tool be used without requiring the installation of agent software on any computers or devices. While similar solutions often require installation of a client agent to collect local details, MAP users Windows Management Instrumentation (WMI), the Remote Registry Service, SNMP, Active Directory Domain Services, and the Computer Browser service to collect this information without a need to deploy remote agents. It provides identification of currently installed Windows Client operating systems, their hardware, and recommendations for migration to Windows Vista. In a medium to large environment this offering replaces the need for the Windows Vista Upgrade Advisor.

> **NOTE**   The Windows Vista Upgrade Advisor is available online at `www.microsoft.com/windows/products/windowsvista/buyorupgrade/upgradeadvisor.mspx` and the Microsoft Assessment and Planning Solution Accelerator is available online at `www.microsoft.com/downloads/details.aspx?FamilyID=67240b76-3148-4e49-943d-4d9ea7f77730&DisplayLang=en`.

As far as minimum requirements go, Microsoft has published charts outlining the bare minimums for use of Windows Vista as well as the recommended minimums to ensure support for full functionality (particularly to support the Aero interface). Table 1.1 outlines the recommended hardware requirements from Microsoft as they apply to the Business, Ultimate, and Home Premium editions of Vista.

TABLE 1.1

Recommended Hardware Requirements

Processor	1 GHz 32-bit or 64-bit processor
Memory	1GB of system memory
Hard drive	40GB (15GB free)
Video	WDDM driver 128MB Video Memory Pixel Shader 2.0 in Hardware 32 bits per pixel
Media	DVD-ROM drive
Sound	Audio Output

With these specifications, your computer may be able to perform basic tasks, such as working with e-mail and surfing the Internet, but the performance of more demanding applications will certainly suffer. In general, consider the following items when evaluating whether your current hardware should be reused, upgraded, or replaced:

- **Does my hardware meet the minimum requirements**? If your hardware doesn't even meet the manufacturer's recommended minimums, don't even try it!

- **What type of applications and processing will be performed on this computer?** Quite often computers are used for little more than e-mail and Internet access. Relatively humble hardware may do the job just fine. For other applications, always check with the application vendor for their recommended minimums.

- **How reliable is the existing hardware?** Typically, after four or five years, hardware tends to become less reliable, especially laptops. If hardware is unreliable it will cost the organization much more in IT support costs, repair costs, and end user downtime.

- **Will it be more economical to upgrade or replace?** If you decide that your hardware will not be sufficient for the tasks at hand, you must evaluate whether an upgrade or replacement will be more economical. Be sure to include factors such as warranties and time involved in performing upgrades versus fresh installs.

Also keep in mind the option of thin clients. If your existing hardware meets all of your needs with the exception of having an application or two, then using the old hardware as a thin client may extend the life of the hardware by several years. It may also help reduce management costs and have other advantages.

The most common hurdle during this part of deployment is to obtain an inventory of existing hardware. If your organization has an inventory system already in place, a simple report should give you the information you need to begin your planning. If not, there are several free options to get an inventory of your existing hardware.

The most flexible solution is to use some type of scripting to obtain the necessary information. Windows Vista supports scripting through the command line (batch or shell), Windows Scripting Host, and PowerShell. The great thing about creating your own script is that you can customize it to provide the data you need in the format you want.

If you don't already have an inventory system, there are several free tools, such as Open-AudIT (`winventory.sourceforge.net`) and Lansweeper (`www.lansweeper.com`) to help you get an inventory of your deployed systems. A search at `www.sourceforge.net` for hardware inventory returns numerous results of projects and applications to help inventory your network. Likewise, a search on Google for free hardware inventory returns several products to aid with the task. Ultimately, you will need to find a product that meets your corporate standards and provides you with the information you need.

 Lansweeper is included on the CD accompanying this book.

Ensuring Application Compatibility

Microsoft has introduced many new features with Windows Vista, and many of those focus on security. One of the problems with increasing security is that it typically implies a decrease in ease of use. One very visible example of this is application compatibility. If you've been in IT long enough to have been through an operating system migration, you know the potential for pains associated with application compatibility. When planning your deployment, you must take into account the compatibility of existing applications and the possibility of replacing or upgrading incompatible applications.

Understanding broken applications

Applications that have previously functioned correctly may now cease to function in Vista for many reasons. Microsoft has encouraged developers to write applications that run properly for standard users for some time, but now more implicitly enforces this as a requirement. When users must have Administrative rights to execute an application, it makes the system more vulnerable to accidental damage, virus attacks, and malware. With the strengthened file system and registry permissions, standard users are not generally able to damage a system to the point where it won't boot, nor are they generally allowed to perform actions required for most virus activity. Although it can initially seem easier to simply grant users administrative rights, doing so can cause a host of new problems by the unknowing (or even intentional) damage that may be done by users. With Windows Vista, simply giving users admin rights is much less of an option in that even when logged on as an administrator processes are not run with those elevated privileges without being prompted.

The prompting of the system for confirmation to perform administrative tasks (or changes that affect more than just the local user of the computer) is known as User Account Control (UAC). When an administrator logs into Vista, the shell is started without the administrative token. The result is that any applications are run as a standard user. When performing a task that requires elevated privileges, the system prompts to alert the administrator as to the seriousness of their actions. It will also prompt standard users, except they must enter account credentials for an administrative user, because they themselves don't have permissions to perform the action.

Of course, as with any prompt that pops up very often, users will begin approving them without reading the warning. Although effective, it is a rather unpopular feature and many have taken to disabling it rather than work around any issues. Obviously, the recommendation is to keep it in place and work around any issues encountered.

In some cases, the problem is not security related but is truly an application compatibility problem. One possible issue may be if an application requests direct hardware access. Because making a direct hardware request has not been allowed since Windows ME, this situation not very common. More common is that the operating system answers requests from applications in a slightly different fashion than in previous versions. This is due to changes in system files and the way in which API calls must be made. The good news is that these problems are probably the easiest to solve.

NOTE Application developers must be aware of new requirements and best practices when it comes to application security on Windows Vista. Particularly if you have an in-house development team, some useful reading to recommend would be:

Developer Best Practices and Guidelines for Applications in a Least Privileged Environment

`msdn.microsoft.com/library/default.asp?url=/library/en-us/dnlong/html/`
`AccProtVista.asp`

The Windows Vista Developer Story: Application Compatibility Cookbook

`msdn.microsoft.com/library/default.asp?url=/library/en-us/dnlong/html/`
`AppComp.asp`

Microsoft Standard User Analyzer included in Microsoft Application Compatibility Toolkit Version 5.0

`technet2.microsoft.com/WindowsVista/en/library/1082691c-8f61-44a8-a55f-`
`000c0b80e10f1033.mspx?mfr=true`

Identifying application incompatibilities

If your application is not functioning correctly under Windows Vista, check with the vendor or look for information on their Web site. Often application incompatibilities are known and patches or updates are released. If the vendor is unwilling or unable to correct the application, then you may need to proceed with correcting the problem yourself.

Identifying permission issues

You should begin by identifying whether the problem is permissions based. The easiest way to test this is to launch the application by right-clicking its shortcut and selecting Run as administrator. If the application functions correctly, you are most likely dealing with a permissions issue. These can usually be addressed by loosening security on a folder or registry key. Although this does slightly decrease the security of the system, it is far better than giving users administrative rights.

There are a few ways to identify permission issues with an application. One way is to use the Process Monitor utility; another is to enable auditing of object access failures, and yet another is to try Application Rights Auditor from BeyondTrust.

NOTE There are a couple of commercial tools available to detect permission issues on the fly such as BeyondTrust Privilege Manager (`www.beyondtrust.com/products/PrivilegeManager.aspx`) and Symantec (Altiris) Application Control Solution (`www.altiris.com/Products/AppControlSol.aspx`).

Using Process Monitor

Process Monitor has been around for some time as a freeware tool from SysInternals. The well-known File Monitor (FileMon) and Registry Monitor (RegMon) tools have been superseded by Process Monitor, which is now the tool to use for monitoring both the file and registry systems. The following steps illustrate how to use Process Monitor to identify where permission problems may be causing an application to fail.

1. **Start by downloading Process Monitor from Microsoft's Web site:** `http://technet.microsoft.com/en-us/sysinternals/bb896645.aspx`

2. **Extract the `Procmon.exe` utility from the downloaded archive and execute it (you will receive a UAC security prompt).** Process Monitor will immediately start recording everything the computer is doing.

   - To stop it, choose File ➪ Capture Events (or click Ctrl+E).
   - To clear the display choose Edit ➪ Clear Display (or hit Ctrl+X).

3. **Prepare to reproduce your problem; when ready, repeat the previous step to restart the monitoring process.**

4. **After you have reproduced your error, stop the capturing of events and review the information recorded.** Any file or registry permissions that may need to be modified should be recorded with a result of ACCESS DENIED. Double-click each such listing for full details.

Using audit policies

If permission issues are the cause of application compatibility problems, you may enable auditing to help locate the resources that are attempting to be accessed. Configure auditing to locate the problem by following these steps:

1. Open the Group Policy Object Editor by running gpedit.msc from a command prompt or Start Search box.

2. Navigate to Local Computer Policy ➪ Computer Configuration ➪ Windows Settings ➪ Security Settings ➪ Local Policies ➪ Audit Policy and double-click Audit object access.

3. Select the failure box to enable failure auditing. Click OK and close the Group Policy Object Editor.

4. Open the Properties window of the system drive, typically C:, and select the Security tab.

5. Click the Advanced button, change to the Auditing tab, and click the Continue button.

6. When presented with the Auditing interface, click Add and type Everyone as the account to audit. Click OK to continue.

7. Select the Failed box beside Full control to enable failure auditing for all events. Click OK until you exit the security window. You will get several errors that auditing can't be enabled for some folders and files. In general, these files and folders are not problematic and can be ignored.

8. Open the registry editor, `regedit.exe`. Right-click on `HKEY_LOCAL_MACHINE` and select permissions.

9. Use the previous steps used on the file system to enable failure auditing for everyone and close the registry editor.

10. Run the application once again, and once it fails, review the Security log with Event Viewer. You should see failure audits for folders or registry keys that the application failed to access or change.

After the file, folder, or registry key causing the problem has been located, it can be adjusted. Typically the files and registry keys causing the problem are beneath a vendor or application directory or key. Don't forget to reverse the procedures above to disable auditing after the process is complete. Otherwise, unnecessary auditing may slow down your system substantially.

Using BeyondTrust Application Rights Auditor

One (free) tool available is an Application Rights Auditor — a free product that automatically identifies and reports which Windows applications require users to have administrative rights. Application Rights Auditor uses a Microsoft Management Console (MMC) snap-in interface in conjunction with a desktop agent. The desktop agent is installed on computers to examine applications during execution. All application executions are automatically monitored silently in the background, and it sends pertinent data to a server where centralized reports may be configured and viewed within the MMC.

NOTE   Application Rights Auditor is available from www.beyondtrust.com/products/ ApplicationRightsAuditor.aspx

Addressing application incompatibilities

Depending on the compatibility issue you have identified, there may be one or more different approaches to realizing a solution. This section provides some basic guidance on addressing both application security issues as well as programmatic incompatibilities.

Modifying application security

After you have identified areas of the system that require permission changes in order to support needed applications, you will have several options for deciding how to implement those changes. Particularly if you determine the need before rolling out Vista, you have the option of including the permission changes in your custom image. Some choose to include such permission changes along with the automated installation package using Windows Installer or scripts. There is no correct answer; it really depends upon your environment and with what you are comfortable. The two most common methods for changing security are Group Policy and the XCacls command line utility.

Using Group Policy

Particularly if you are using Group Policy to deploy a Windows Installer setup already, enforcing required permission changes in the same Group Policy Object is ideal. You can create separate GPOs for permission changes like these, but consider the future when planning your strategy. If you later remove or upgrade an application from your environment, will you be able to easily remove those security changes along with it? Some choose to keep all file and registry permission changes in a single GPO for performance reasons. This is not a bad idea, but be sure to carefully document each change so you can easily associate it with the appropriate application in the future.

To apply or modify permission entries for objects using Group Policy:

1. **Open Microsoft Management Console (`mmc.exe`) and choose File ⇨ Add/Remove Snap-in and then select Add.**

2. **Select Group Policy Object Editor and click the Add button.**

3. **In the Group Policy Wizard, on the Select Group Policy Object page, click Browse and either select an existing Group Policy object in the appropriate domain, site, or organizational unit, click OK, and then click the Finish button.** (If you want to create a new GPO, right-click and choose new in the desired location.)

4. **Click the Close button and then click OK to complete the adding of the snap-in.**

5. **To edit the security of a file or folder navigate to Computer Configuration Windows Settings ⇨ Security Settings ⇨ File System. To edit the security of a registry key navigate to Computer Configuration ⇨ Windows Settings ⇨ Security Settings ⇨ Registry and click Add for the appropriate item.**

6. **To set permission for a group or user either select (it if it is already listed) or click the Add button (to specify an unlisted one). To allow permission, in the Permissions for User or Group box, select the Allow check box. To deny permission, in the Permissions for User or Group box, select the Deny check box.**

Using XCacls

XCacls is an updated version of the included cacls command line tool and offers much better command line support. XCacls is available online at `http://support.microsoft.com/kb/318754`. It offers several command line arguments to dictate its action (as shown in Table 1.2). Its syntax is as follows:

```
xcacls FileName [/T] [/E] [/C] [/G user:perm;spec] [/R user] [/P
    user:perm;spec [...]] [/D user [...]] [/Y]
```

TABLE 1.2

XCacls Command Line Arguments

Parameter	Description / Options
Filename	The file or folder to which permission should be applied (wildcards are supported)
/T	Recurse through the current folder and subfolders
/E	Edit the permissions instead of replacing them
/C	Continue if an Access Denied error message is encountered
/G	Grants the specified user the specified permissions in the following format:
	User: perm;spec
	User: The user or group name to be granted permissions
	Perm: The permissions to be granted
	C: Change (write)
	F: Full Control
	P: Change Permissions (special access)
	O: Take Ownership (special access)
	X: Execute (special access)
	E: Read (special access)
	W: Write (special access)
	D: Delete (special access)
	Spec: Applies only to folders and accepts the same values as perm, with the addition of the following:
	T: Not Specified. Sets the permissions on the directory without specifying permissions that are to be applied to new files created i n that directory. At least one access right has to follow.
/R	Revokes all access rights for the specified user

continued

TABLE 1.2	*(continued)*
Parameter	**Description / Options**
/P	Replaces access rights for the specified user in the following format:
	User: perm;spec
	User: The user or group name to be granted permissions
	Perm: The permissions to be granted
	C: Change (write)
	F: Full Control
	P: Change Permissions (special access)
	O: Take Ownership (special access)
	X: Execute (special access)
	E: Read (special access)
	W: Write (special access)
	D: Delete (special access)
	Spec: Applies only to folders and accepts the same values as perm, with the addition of the following:
	T: Not Specified. Sets the permissions on the directory without specifying permissions that are to be applied to new files created in that directory. At least one access right has to follow.
/D	Denies the user access to the specified file or folder
/Y	Disables confirmation prompt when replacing user access rights

An example of using the XCacls command line utility is provided here:

```
xcacls.exe "%ProgramFiles%\Application\settings.xml" /E /G
    "Authenticated Users":C
```

This example uses the /E switch to instruct the tool to edit and not replace the security settings for the specified file. The /G switch says to grant rights to the specified group Authenticated Users and the C specifies that it is to grant them Change permission.

Investigating compatibility modes

Some applications do not fail for lack of permissions. These applications often fail because of an unexpected response from an API call to Windows. One such situation is version checking during installation. Some older installation programs check to ensure that a particular version of Windows is present, for example Windows 98. When the system reports that it is running Windows Vista, the installer fails, stating that it requires Windows 98 or newer. Obviously Vista falls under *or newer*, but the install application simply doesn't recognize the new name.

A multitude of other examples and situations exist, but it all comes down to what to do to fix the problem. If running your application as an administrator doesn't indicate a permissions problem, next try setting a compatibility mode for the application.

Technically speaking, compatibility modes tell the operating system to respond to application calls as if it were a previous version of Windows. In addition, when the operating system is asked to identify itself to the application, it lies depending upon which compatibility mode has been configured. An example is shown in Figure 1.7 of setting a legacy application to run in Windows XP compatibility mode. You may also choose from Windows 95, 98, ME, NT 4, 2000, and Server 2003.

FIGURE 1.7

Viewing application compatibility options

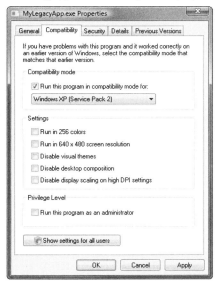

Depending upon the application, you may also need to adjust the visual settings. If a visual setting must be adjusted it is usually easy to recognize. Symptoms may include windows that don't resize properly, display improperly, or give an error stating they must be run with 256 colors. Do not use this setting unless necessary; as when launching an application with visual compatibility mode settings, the system has to make visual settings changes that sometimes cause problems with other running applications that need to be run with regular Vista display settings.

When selecting a compatibility mode, always start with the least intrusive. That is to say start with XP or Server 2003 compatibility modes first because Vista must only change a few responses to emulate those relatively new operating systems. Windows 95 compatibility mode requires that the system change a lot about the way it deals with the application, and changing too much can both slow down the application and possibly cause new problems due to unnecessary legacy emulations.

Aside from right-clicking on an executable and setting these options from the compatibility tab of the properties dialog, there is also a Program Compatibility Wizard which may be used. To access the Program Compatibility Wizard click the Start button, then Control Panel, then Programs, and then click Use an older program with this version of Windows.

Finally, there is the Program Compatibility Assistant (PCA) which is an automated feature that attempts to detect and apply solutions to known compatibility issues in an automated manner. A common scenario where you may see the PCA feature present itself is in a setup scenario. Some cases where PCA may assume a setup may have had issues include:

- No Add/Remove Programs (ARP) entry is created by the installation
- An Access Denied error level is returned by the setup executable when exiting
- UAC does not detect the executable as a setup so that the opportunity to execute as administrator is presented
- The executable uses the GetVersion function or the GetVersionEx APIs to get information on the Windows OS version and fails when hard-coded to look for version 5 (Windows XP)

When PCA detects these scenarios it will prompt the user to run the setup again with recommended settings. Then, based on the scenario PCA will run the setup and attempt to mitigate the detected issue by automatically applying the correct solution (running as Administrator, applying version compatibility settings, and so forth).

NOTE This is an automated feature and not a wizard or tool that can be executed manually. For details about the types of issues PCA addresses, and how it mitigates the problem when re-running the installation, see `msdn.microsoft.com/en-us/library/bb756937.aspx`.

Application Compatibility Toolkit

If your organization has been using Vista for some time, then only a small set of applications may need to be tested as the rest may have already been field tested. However, if you are migrating to Windows Vista, testing all of your critical organizational applications can be quite time consuming and costly. Because of time and cost, secondary applications are often left to be tested by the end users. This can lead to downtime and a general dislike for the IT department. Microsoft has introduced a free toolkit to help aid with inventorying and testing application compatibility, the Application Compatibility Toolkit.

NOTE Download the Application Compatibility Toolkit online at `www.microsoft.com/downloads/details.aspx?FamilyID=24da89e9-b581-47b0-b45e-492dd6da2971`

The Application Compatibility Toolkit (ACT) has been designed as a four-stage solution for addressing compatibility problems. First, it helps you gather information about your existing applications. Second, it can analyze existing applications to recognize potential compatibility problems. Third, it has the ability to create fixes for the problems, which you can then distribute to the appropriate computers. Finally, it provides the ability to share information with others via the Microsoft Compatibility Exchange.

To begin the process, you need to identify a computer to host the data collection process. Ideally, you would use a server and that server would be dedicated to the deployment process. The collection computer must have ACT installed as well as an available SQL server. If you have a production SQL server, ACT will create a new database for collection. If you prefer, you can install Microsoft SQL Server or even Microsoft SQL Server Express (free) on the collection computer to reduce the impact on production.

After installation, a collection plan is designed and ACT builds an executable that can be executed on target computers. This will collect application data and log it to the collection computer. It may take several days or weeks to get a complete list because some users may be out of the office temporarily. The ACT collection package is an MSI setup that requires administrative rights so you can deploy it via Group Policy, manually on a computer (as Administrator), or, if you have a systems management solution in place, you can also deploy the package as you would any application installation.

After a list of applications is compiled, an analysis can be performed. ACT identifies the logged applications and checks them against Microsoft, vendor, and community databases. Checking against an ACT community database allows different organizations to rate the compatibility of applications and give other organizations useful compatibility information that is vendor and OS independent.

Lastly, ACT can create fixes for applications. Many of the fixes are similar to setting compatibility modes except they only implement the exact needed legacy emulation. This eliminates the situation in which a compatibility mode fixes the original problem but causes another to do unnecessary legacy emulation. Other fixes are permissions fixes that can be overcome in various ways. One permission fix ACT can apply is to redirect sections of the registry that are not writable by a standard user to sections, which are writable by the user. Vista has a dynamic ability to virtualize changes the user does not have permission to make. The changes are stored in a virtual overlay that is maintained in the user profile and is transparent to the user.

The Application Compatibility Toolkit is a very useful and powerful tool when used correctly. Although it's useful during a migration, it can continue to be used for service pack updates and Internet Explorer upgrades. When planning your deployment, be sure to consider ACT as a part of your data collection stage as it can help reduce problems and downtimes after deployment.

Installing and configuring the Application Compatibility Toolkit

The steps are provided as a quick start to installing, deploying, and reviewing results using the Application Compatibility Toolkit. If you do not have a good inventory of what software is in your environment, doing this can prove a valuable tool even outside mitigating compatibility issues. Follow these steps:

1. Download the Application Compatibility Toolkit from the Microsoft Web site at `http://go.microsoft.com/fwlink/?LinkID=82101`

   It is recommended that a server be used to host ACT as the limited number of inbound network connections on a workstation (ten) may be insufficient if many computers are attempting to report results simultaneously.

2. **Run through the simple installation wizard and launch the Application Compatibility Manager tool using the generated shortcut.** A configuration wizard appears on first launch with a Welcome screen that describes its purpose as to help you establish a database, create a share where client systems will place generated log files, and to establish a log processing service account to process collected logs.

3. **Click Next to begin.**

4. **Choose to configure the local computer to process logs and view reports (Enterprise Configuration) or to simply view and manage reports from an existing database (View and manage reports only). In this case, choose Enterprise Configuration and click Next.**

5. **Configure the ACT database. If you do not have a SQL server available, SQL Server Express** (www.microsoft.com/sql/editions/express/default.mspx) **may be used. Choose a SQL server from the list and click the Connect button.**

6. **After a successful connection has been established, you may enter the name of the ACT database that is to be created (for example ACTdata) and click the Create button.** Once the database has been successfully created, the Next button will be enabled.

7. **Click the Next button to continue.**

8. **Specify a path to an existing folder be used to hold the data generated by clients reporting inventory information.** You can use the Browse button to locate or create a folder, but it must exist before proceeding beyond this screen.

9. **Specify a local path and then enter the name that you would like to share.** By default, a share name will be generated based on the physical path specified in the Path field.

10. **Edit as desired (for example, ACTlogs) and click Next to continue.** The configuration wizard completes its tasks by requesting credentials to be used to run as a service which will process the log files. The account requires read/write access to the database and the log file share.

11. **You may specify a specific service account or accept the default Local System option. Click Next to continue.** A Congratulations screen appears to advise you of the successful completion of ACT configuration.

12. **Leave the Automatically check for updates when launching check box selected and click the Finish button to close the ACT configuration wizard.**

Creating a data collection package for ACT

Once installed, it is necessary to create a collection package which is an MSI setup that may be run on clients to have them report data to the Application Compatibility Manager for processing and reporting. The following steps cover the creation of the collection package.

The home screen for the Application Compatibility Manager (shown in Figure 1.8) presents a simple menu for completing each of the steps necessary to utilize ACT. This screen may also be accessed by clicking the overview toolbar button at the top left that is represented by an icon image of a house.

FIGURE 1.8

Initial launch of the Application Compatibility Manager

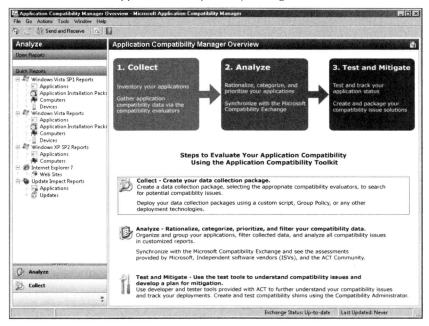

1. **Click the top item titled Collect – Create your data collection package to begin**. The new package screen appears which provides the following fields and options:
   - **Package Name**: Enter a friendly **name** for the package (for example ACTpackage).
   - **Evaluate compatibility when:** Three options are presented including Deploying a new OS or Service Pack (default), updating IE, or applying updates. Choose Deploying a new Operating System or Service Pack.

- **When to monitor application usage:** You can choose the starting time (default is "As soon as possible after installation"), the duration (default is three days), and frequency (the default period is eight hours).

- **Where to put collected data:** The default output location specified should already be that of the share specified during the previous configuration steps, but modify if necessary.

2. **When complete, click the save icon on the toolbar at the top left of the window.** A file location and filename prompt will allow you to choose the location and filename of the MSI setup which represents the data collection package for ACT.

Execute the collection package on client systems

There are a number of ways the collection package may be deployed from manual execution to deployment via an in-place systems management solution. As an MSI setup, Group Policy presents an attractive method of deployment for many organizations. The following steps take you through deploying the ACT package via Group Policy.

1. **Begin by running the Group Policy Management console (from the Administrative Tools program group on Windows Server).** The GPO object you choose will dictate what clients will install the package and report to ACT.

2. **Choose an existing GPO and choose Edit, or select a desired container, such as an OU and choose Create and Link a GPO Here.**

3. **If you create a new GPO, provide a descriptive Name such as ACT Client, click OK, right-click the newly created GPO, and choose Edit.**

4. **Choose ACT Client ⇨ Computer Configuration > Software Settings, right-click Software installation, and then choose New ⇨ Package.** A browse dialog will appear for you to specify the location of the MSI created in the previous steps.

5. **Select the MSI package and click OK.**

6. **In the resulting window, accept the default option of Assigned and click OK to continue.**

 The installation will take place without prompting for input, even if executed manually by double-clicking or running the installation from the command line.

Reviewing ACT reports

After data has been collected, several reports can be viewed from the Application Compatibility Manager interface (see Figure 1.9).

Several reports are provided, and you can identify and even address compatibility issues from within this console. Click the Send and Receive toolbar button to begin the process of obtaining compatibility information on the applications detected in your environment. You can create remediation packages and even share application compatibility ratings with the community. For more details on ACT, visit `http://technet.microsoft.com/en-us/windowsvista/aa905102.aspx`.

FIGURE 1.9

Reviewing results collected by the deployed ACT collection packages

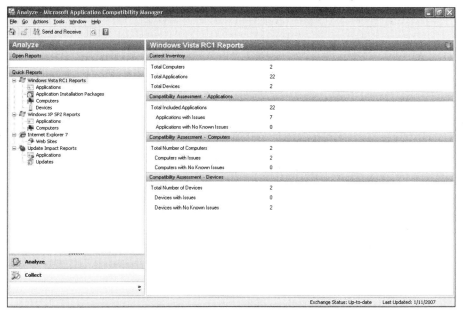

Documenting the Deployment Plan

When documenting your deployment plan, consider the following questions:

- What Edition(s) of Windows Vista should be used? Justify each.
- How many images will be supported? Justify each.
- Which applications will be included in the deployment images?
- Which applications will not be included and how will they be distributed?
- What type of distribution media will be used and why?
- Which hardware will be reused? Upgraded? Replaced?
- What critical applications are not Vista compatible by default and how can they be corrected?

Summary

Microsoft has significantly changed the installation process. Understanding the changes and taking advantage of them can greatly improve your organizational deployment of Windows Vista. The most drastic change implemented is the introduction of the WIM file images. However, WIM files only handle the problem of image storage and modification. Planning should be a very important part of your deployment process. Be sure to consider hardware requirements and upgrades as well as application compatibility. When proper planning has been done, the technologies in the rest of this book can used to simplify deployment and management as a well as increase the stability of your workstations.

Chapter 2

Creating Basic Windows Images

The benefit of using image-based installations has become apparent to even Microsoft; they have adopted it as their primary installation technique. However, the generic image that Microsoft supplies on its deployment media most likely will not meet the needs of your organization. Most organizations require additional applications, such as Microsoft Office suites and antivirus protection, and additional configuration changes, such as firewall and Windows Update configuration. Although many of these added applications can be configured after deployment, including these changes as part of the deployment process can save time and increase system security.

Your first step is to create customized Windows deployment images. Later chapters go into more detail about customizing (Chapter 6) and deploying images (Chapters 7 and 8). This chapter focuses on the direct steps you may perform in order to create stable, automated systems that you can use across a multitude of hardware models.

The process of creating and deploying customized images includes:

- Building a deployment server
- Creating an answer file
- Installing and configuring a reference computer
- Creating Windows PE boot media
- Capturing an image of the reference computer
- Applying the customized image

The following sections will walk you through the process.

Building a Deployment Server

Establishing a *deployment server* is the first step to building and deploying images. The term deployment server is used to refer to the computer you will be using to build, customize, and deploy your deployment images. Some technicians use their personal workstation or lab computers for this process. However, this is not always best because workstations and lab computers tend to be used for several purposes and may need to be reloaded on a regular basis. Consider the fact that you will probably deploy images after your migration as a weekly (or even daily) management task to correct problem workstations. If you have established a Windows Deployment Services (WDS) server, or are using the Microsoft Deployment Toolkit (a.k.a. BDD), a distribution share is established as part of their configuration and makes the most logical location for a deployment server. Consider this when selecting a system for this purpose; you can save a considerable amount of time if you don't have to reinstall the deployment tools and utilities on a regular basis.

When selecting a deployment server, you must keep a few things in mind. First, you want to make sure that the server has sufficient RAM. You will be loading several tools and Windows components on the server, and running low on RAM can slow down the process. Because this server will most likely also be used to distribute your images, larger amounts of RAM will provide for more file caching and thus faster imaging to multiple clients. It is recommended that you select a system with at least 1GB of RAM for testing and smaller deployments, while medium to large deployments are better suited for computers with at least 2GB of RAM. It is also important to plan for sufficient disk space. We recommend that the system have at least 60GB of free disk space dedicated to image testing and deployment. Again, larger deployments or those organizations supporting a large number of thick images may definitely require more space — so plan accordingly.

The deployment server may not be a server at all. It may be a workstation, especially during the testing phases or if your organization already has a deployment server and you are not allowed local access. In fact, the tools outlined in this book have been tested and work on Windows XP, Windows Server 2003, Windows Server 2008, and Windows Vista on both x86 and x64 platforms. You have flexibility in choosing and planning your deployment server.

Keep in mind that if you use a client operating system, such as Windows XP or Vista, you may run into issues when you deploy multiple machines at one time. Systems without a Windows server operating system installed are limited to ten inbound network connections.

Another recommendation is to use a *virtual machine* as a deployment server. A benefit is that the virtual machine can be configured with the proper tools and utilities and not interfere with the normal operations of your existing software. Equally important, your existing software won't interfere with your deployment tools. By storing the created image on a network share, you have the added benefit of shutting down the virtual machine until you need to update the image. In addition, when the machine is reloaded (which we all must do from time to time), you can save or move your deployment server without having to completely rebuild it.

Virtual machines are suitable for many consulting tasks, including image building and testing. If you haven't used them before, you've certainly heard of popular tools such as VMware and Microsoft's Virtual PC, both of which offer free products. If your company has a standard virtual machine application, follow that standard. Otherwise, you should consider the free VMware Server product as a feature-rich and capable solution. Many of the step-by-step tasks performed in this book were done by using a VMware-based virtual machine as the deployment server. One of the key strengths of virtual machines is their portability. To move the virtual machine from one host computer to another, you typically need to move only a single file or folder. You can use this to your advantage and begin building your deployment server now, on your workstation. As the deployment process proceeds you can then move the deployment server to a more powerful and secure host server.

If you do not already have a virtualization product installed, download and install VMware Server from the VMware Web site at `www.vmware.com/products/server/`.

The recommendation is to install on a Windows Server operating system, but most functions will run on XP/Vista as well. The reason is that it has a dependency on IIS, which is included in workstation editions of Windows, so as long as you have it installed, there should be no problems. While the software is free, it is necessary to register in order to receive a serial number via e-mail.

To build and prepare a virtual machine–based deployment server with VMWare Server, perform the following steps:

1. **Launch the VMware Server Console.**

> **NOTE** You can only have one default Web site running at a time, so if you have a default Web site running already, it may be necessary to stop it in order to start the VMware Management Interface Web or configure support for multiple Web sites.

2. **Click New Virtual Machine to launch the New Virtual Machine Wizard.**
3. **Click Next when the Welcome screen is displayed to begin.**
4. **Accept the default configuration as "Typical" and click Next to continue.**
5. **Next choose the operating system you will be installing on this Virtual Machine, such as Windows Server 2008, and click Next to continue.** Depending on how current the version of Virtual Server is, you may not see your operating system of choice listed. If this is the case, just choose something close, and you can always update the default settings such as allocated RAM after the virtual machine is created.
6. **Update the default name to Deployment Server and specify the location where you want the virtual machine files to be stored (see Figure 2.1).** By default, this path is in the current user profile. In an environment with roaming profiles in use, you must change this to a folder outside the user profile, such as a fixed local folder or a shared network location. When complete, click Next to continue.

FIGURE 2.1

Creating a deployment server in VMware Server

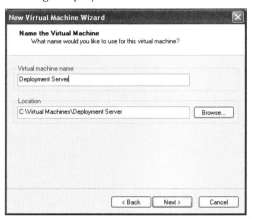

7. **Select the desired network connection option and click Next to continue.** In most cases the default option to Use bridged networking is desirable, which causes the virtual machine to establish its own IP on the external network of the host computer.

8. **Specify the disk size.**

    A. Start with a 30GB drive and select the option to allocate all disk space now (this will greatly improve performance of the drive).

    B. Click Finish to complete the wizard. It is recommended that you create two drives, one for your images and one for the operating system.

9. **To add the second hard drive, click Edit virtual machine settings from the Command pane. When the Virtual Machine Settings window appears, click the Add button.**

10. **On the Welcome screen for the Add Hardware Wizard, click Next to continue.**

11. **Select Hard Disk as the hardware type and click Next to continue.**

12. **Accept the default option Create a new virtual disk and click Next to continue.**

13. **Accept SCSI as the default virtual disk type and click Next to continue.**

14. **For the disk size, enter 100GB and check the option to have the drive split into 2GB files (Windows does not support a single 100GB file) and click Next to continue.**

15. **For the disk filename, accept the default or enter something more descriptive, such as** DeploymentServerDataDrive.vmdk. **Click Finish to complete the Add Hardware Wizard.**

16. **If you have a Windows Server 2008 DVD, you can insert it; if you have an ISO file, you can specify it as source for the virtual CD-ROM drive. To do so, click Edit virtual machine again from the Commands pane and select the CD-ROM device from**

the list. In the Connection area, select Use ISO image and browse to the path of your image file. Click OK to close the dialog when complete.

17. **Start the virtual machine, and the bootable installation media should automatically begin the installation of Windows Server 2008.** Complete the installation of Windows Server 2008 as you normally would, specifying the target drive as the 30GB disk created in Step 9 (as shown in Figure 2.2).

FIGURE 2.2

Selecting the Target Installation Drive for Windows Server 2008

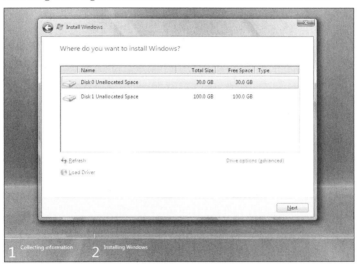

18. **When installation is complete, ensure the latest service packs and security patches have been applied via Windows Update.**

19. **Install your corporate antivirus solution and ensure the latest virus definitions are applied.**

20. **Join the domain.** Although not required, joining the domain can make the deployment process go much more smoothly.

21. **In Server Manager, choose to Storage ⇨ Disk Management. Right-click on the 100GB drive marked Unallocated and then choose New Simple Volume.** Allow for the maximum amount of space and assign it drive letter W. Have the wizard format the drive as NTFS with a default allocation unit size. A summary screen is provided at the end of the wizard.

22. **Click Finish to begin configuring this drive.**

After you have a functioning virtual machine and operating system, deployment tools may be installed and configured. The first toolset to use is the Windows Automated Installation Kit (WAIK).

Introducing the Windows Automated Installation Kit

In the past, building custom deployment images often involved writing complex custom scripts and using third-party tools. These third-party tools were needed to create and modify images, to create bootable media to capture, and to apply the images for creating automation tasks. Although many free tools and utilities were available, the most powerful and useful ones often cost more than many companies cared to spend. With Microsoft's embracing of imaging as its key deployment technology, you are now provided with a helpful set of free tools in the form of the Windows Automated Installation Kit (WAIK).

The Windows Automated Installation Kit is exactly what it sounds like — a toolkit with the sole purpose of helping administrators automate the installation of Windows. Although it is not the focus of this book, it is worth pointing out that it is not restricted to the automation of Windows Vista. Although the WAIK provides the most integration with Windows Vista, it may also be used to deploy images for other Windows operating systems, such as Server and XP. The computer used to run the WAIK tools need not be Windows Vista either. In fact, it is recommended that you install the WAIK on your deployment server. Regardless of platform, the Windows Automated Installation Kit is a full-featured and flexible toolkit.

1. **Download the WAIK (approximately 1GB) from the Microsoft Web site (validation may be required).**

   ```
   www.microsoft.com/downloads/details.aspx?FamilyID=C7D4BC6D-
       15F3-4284-9123-679830D629F2
   ```

   After you have the download, you will notice that it has an IMG file extension. This is a DVD image file that you may burn by using your preferred software.

2. **Rename the file extension from IMG to ISO and assign it as the ISO image for the virtual CD-ROM device.**

3. `STARTCD.EXE` **may auto run, but if it does not, browse to** `STARTCD.EXE` **on the drive and execute it. For an installation menu, choose "Windows AIK Setup" and follow the simple wizard through the installation.** The WAIK does require MSXML version 6 and .NET Framework version 2. While Windows Vista and Windows Server 2008 were shipped with the necessary versions, they must be installed on Windows Server 2003 and XP before installing the WAIK. On Windows Server 2008, you must add the .NET Framework feature first. Fortunately, these prerequisites are included on the WAIK DVD, as shown in Figure 2.3.

FIGURE 2.3

Windows Automated Installation Kit installation window

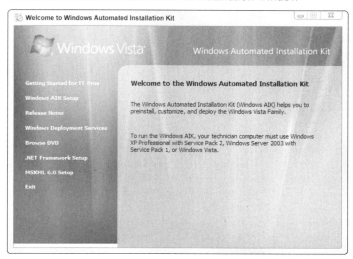

Creating Unattended Answer Files

Even with Vista's much improved image-based installation, installation naturally requires input from the user. Partitions must be created and formatted, product keys must be entered, network settings must be configured, and regular post-installation changes must be made. These steps hold true if you are using the default image on the Windows DVD or if you plan to use customized images.

You may be familiar with Setup Manager and INI formatted answer files from previous versions of Windows that allow you to automate these tasks and settings. Windows Vista has grown up, so to speak. It has outgrown the simplistic INI file format used with previous Windows versions and now uses XML formatted files to provide answers for setup. Figure 2.4 shows an example of an XML-based answer file.

NOTE Although the Setup Image Manager (SIM) is the tool to use when it comes to creating and editing these particular XML files, a handy tool for viewing (and also editing) XML files in general is the free XML Notepad 2007 utility from Microsoft: www.microsoft.com/downloads/details.aspx?familyid=72d6aa49-787d-4118-ba5f-4f30fe913628&displaylang=en.

FIGURE 2.4

Sample Windows Vista unattended answer file

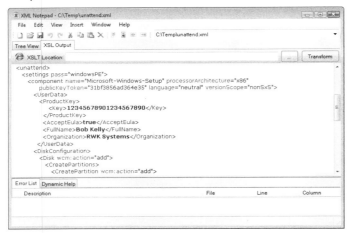

Although setup progresses normally without an answer file, it requires that the same settings and answers be provided for every individual installation. That's fine at home but clearly impractical when it comes to installing hundreds or thousands of computers at work.

Getting familiar with configuration passes

Windows installation is broken into various *configuration passes*. Configuration passes are generally separated by a restart. Specific actions may be performed during each configuration pass. Unattended answer files are broken into sections with corresponding names. For example, notice that on Figure 2.4, near the top, a line that specifies a settings pass of windowsPE. This means that all automation settings made in this section will be applied during the windowsPE configuration pass. The settings you specify here should match those you set during the Windows PE section of a manual Windows installation up to the first reboot after applying the Windows image. Those settings might include creating and formatting a partition, accepting the End User License Agreement, and specifying an installation product key. For the most part, settings have a specific configuration pass to which they must always be applied.

To effectively design and implement an unattended answer file, you must understand what happens during each configuration pass. Also, you need to understand which configuration passes are used for specific scenarios. The available configuration passes include:

- windowsPE
- offlineServicing
- generalize
- specialize

- auditSystem
- auditUser
- oobeSystem

windowsPE

The windowsPE configuration pass is used to automate the initial image installation. This includes configuring a setup language, partitioning and formatting the hard drive, configuring the upgrade type, and providing a product key. These actions take place while the system is booted to Windows PE, thus the name.

offlineServicing

The offlineServicing configuration pass is only used to edit an existing WIM file. In Chapter 6 the topic is covered in much more detail, but one feature of WIM files for image storage is the ability to edit the images in the WIM file offline. The Package Manager utility (pkgmgr) from the WAIK uses the offlineServicing configuration pass to add language packs, security updates, drivers, and packages to an image in a WIM file offline. When used, this is typically the only configuration pass defined in the answer file.

generalize

The generalize configuration pass is used to automate the Sysprep utility when generalizing the system for imaging. Typical settings for this section include power scheme configuration, owner information, and Plug and Play detection of devices after running Sysprep. The Sysprep utility is discussed in more detail later in this chapter.

specialize

The specialize configuration pass is typically run immediately following the windowsPE configuration pass, but before starting the Microsoft Windows Vista Out of Box Experience (OOBE). During this pass, machine specific settings are made. Settings may include assigning a computer name, configuring an IP address, and joining a domain.

auditSystem

The auditSystem configuration pass is used when starting in audit mode. Settings made in this configuration pass are run in the context of the local system. This section is used to typically add device drivers and configure a computer name for the audit pass.

auditUser

The auditUser configuration pass is used when starting in audit mode. Settings in this pass are applied immediately after the auditSystem pass. These settings are applied in the context of the locally logged-on user and would typically include scripts to install software or customize the system.

oobeSystem

The oobeSystem configuration pass is used to automate the Out of Box Experience, also called Windows Welcome. The settings typically made during this past would include creating user accounts, setting the time zone, and running post-installation scripts.

As you might have guessed, you will not use all configuration passes for any particular scenario. In Figure 2.5 you can see the configuration passes used in a generic installation of Windows Vista. If you are editing an existing image or preparing a reference image, you may use other configuration passes.

Confused? No need to worry. Although it is good to know what is done where, you need not edit your answer files by hand. The Windows System Image Manager (SIM) tool used to author your XML answer files will not let you place a component (action) in the wrong configuration pass. If you spent any time editing Sysprep and unattended files by hand in Notepad in the past, you are going to appreciate SIM.

FIGURE 2.5

Diagram of configuration passes used In standard Vista installation

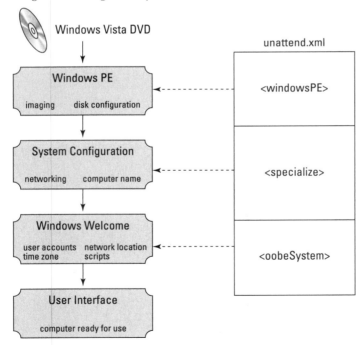

Navigating the Windows System Image Manager

You saw from the example in Figure 2.4 that the format and number of options can be daunting at first. The good news is that the Windows System Image Manager (SIM) offers a graphical tool to build these complex answer files. The interface is not as simple as a wizard, but neither is the setup. At first glance (see Figure 2.6), the tool can seem intimidating, but after you've worked with it for a little while, the logic of its operation becomes clear.

FIGURE 2.6

Getting familiar with Windows System Image Manager (SIM)

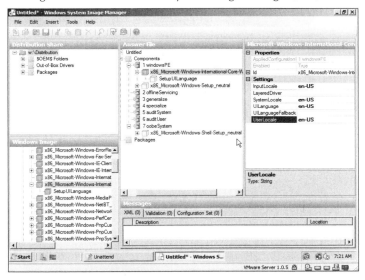

One of the first things to understand before you can become productive in SIM is to understand the various panes and their purposes. The panes provided are marked as follows:

- Distribution Share
- Windows Image
- Answer File
- Properties
- Messages

Understanding the Distribution Share pane

The first pane is used to manage the distribution share. Building customized images may require additional files, drivers, and applications to be included. A *distribution share* is a network share used to host these additional files. SIM can be used to both manage and create distribution shares. The primary benefit of using SIM to manage this share is that any answer files you create with the Windows SIM will automatically include the proper full path to the distribution share.

NOTE   If using unattended answer files is as far as you plan to take automation, then using this tool to create the distribution share can be helpful. However, if you plan to take advantage of the Microsoft Deployment Toolkit, its Deployment Workbench utility should be used to handle this task. The Microsoft Deployment Toolkit (MDT) is discussed in detail in Chapter 7.

Use of a distribution share is optional. It is possible to include all necessary files and applications directly in the customized image. However, some applications, such as those that employ a client agent (antivirus, systems management, and so on) will not function properly when included as part of the image without taking specific steps documented by the vendor. Including only necessary drivers is another advantage that can increase stability, and reduce the size of, the final deployment image.

To build a distribution share using Windows SIM, follow these steps:

1. **Start Windows System Image Manager.**

2. **In the Distribution Share pane, right-click in the Distribution Share pane and select Create a Distribution Share.**

3. **Browse to a drive and folder in which you want to store your distribution files.** You may select an existing folder or type in the name of a new folder (for example, W:\ Distribution).

4. **Click Open.**

NOTE   Answer files may contain sensitive information, but the NTFS and share permissions are created with access open to all users by default. You may choose to restrict access to the distribution share and files by modifying these permissions so that access is limited to only those accounts which require access. For details see `technet2.microsoft.com/ WindowsVista/en/library/31779ce6-cd71-4210-bd01-c679bd68a10e1033. mspx?mfr=true`.

Understanding the Windows Image pane

The bottom pane on the left is used to display components and packages that may be configured and referenced in your unattended answer file. This list is generated by creating a catalog of options read from the selected Windows Image (WIM) file.

 The Windows Image file that you want to catalog must be in a writable directory, which means it cannot be selected directly from DVD.

When an image file is selected, this pane contains a tree view of sections that make up its available contents including:

- Components
- Packages

Exploring the components section

The components section is a list of built-in Windows components and settings that may be customized or automated as part of Windows installation. Typical settings include disk configuration, network settings, and post-install configuration and scripts. The component names tend to be quite long and very descriptive. Each component begins with its architecture type and ends with a version number. While these have importance, they can initially be ignored as they tend to add more complexity while trying to learn the layout and location of the components.

 A full list of components that can be added to an unattended answer file can be found in the Unattended Windows Setup Reference, included as part of the WAIK. It comes in the form of a help file that can be most easily accessed by selecting the component of interest and pressing the F1 key.

After a specific component to be automated has been located, it may be added to the answer file by right-clicking on the component and selecting the appropriate configuration pass to add the setting. In most cases only one configuration pass is available. In the case where multiple configuration passes are available, you will have to make the decision as to which pass the component setting should be applied. A general rule in making such a decision would be to ask, "During a normal installation, when would this setting be configured?"

When adding components to your answer file, it is only necessary to add the root component to the answer file, and all parent components will be automatically added. For example, in Figure 2.7 the Administrator password can be added to the answer file by right-clicking the Administrator Password component and selecting Add Setting to Pass 7 oobeSystem (it is not necessary to first add the UserAccounts component specifically).

Exploring the packages section

The packages section of the Windows Image pane contains a list of packages that can be optionally included and configured with the installation. An easy example is the Microsoft Windows Foundation Package. It allows you to include and configure optional packages, such as fax services, games, IIS, and corporate help customizations.

FIGURE 2.7

Selecting components for an answer file in System Image Manager

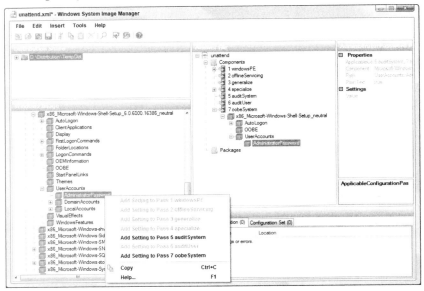

Understanding the Answer File pane

As each component and package is added to the answer file, it is displayed in the Answer File pane under the selected configuration pass. Essentially, this pane displays all of the sections that are included in the answer file. It serves as a browser for the answer file, where when selecting a component or package, its settings may be viewed and adjusted. Items may also be removed from the answer file by right-clicking on an item and selecting Delete.

TIP When a component is selected and configured, the building block icon for that component becomes dark blue. This differentiation provides a quick visual indicator of any settings that have been overlooked and left in an unconfigured state.

NOTE The numbers beside each pass are simply numerical identifiers that roughly indicate the order in which the configuration passes will be applied. The numbers are a bit esoteric but do occasionally show up in documentation and scripts, so it may be worth noting that configuration passes have not only friendly names but numerical identifiers as well.

Understanding the Properties pane

After an answer file has been created and various components and packages have been added, the Properties pane offers the place to dictate the values for any of the added components. Each specific setting is configured by first highlighting the component in the Answer File pane and then using the Properties pane to enter any desired values. Figure 2.7 shows how to add a section to the answer file for defining an Administrator password. Now by highlighting the AdministratorPassword component in the Answer File pane, the desired password may be entered, as shown in Figure 2.8.

FIGURE 2.8

Defining the Administrator's password in an answer file

Some properties offer free-form text boxes to enter a value while others provide pull-down menus. Some text boxes are limited to what can be entered. The very bottom part of the Properties pane often helps by listing the type of data that can be entered into each setting. Notice in Figure 2.9 that the ProtectYourPC setting must be an integer (Int32) ranging from 1 to 3.

FIGURE 2.9

Obtaining valid values for settings

Messages

The messages section of the Windows SIM is used to inform the user of detected configuration errors that may be present in the answer file. This feature does not prevent errors, but it does detect XML errors as well as mismatched or deprecated settings. XML errors should only exist if the answer file has been edited outside SIM. To display any detected errors, select Validate Answer File from the Tools menu to scan the answer file.

In general, messages are classified as messages with a small yellow icon or an error with a small red icon. As a general rule you should understand any warnings and eliminate them whenever possible. In some cases, the warnings are from situations that cannot be avoided. So long as the repercussions are understood, such warnings may be disregarded. Errors, on the other hand, should always be corrected when encountered.

You can use the following steps to create a generic answer file that will automate Windows Vista setup. It will most likely not meet the exact needs of your organization but can be used as a starting point for creating your own customized answer file.

CAUTION The following steps assume that you are deploying Windows Vista Enterprise Edition using a Volume Activation Key (VAK). If using a retail or OEM license to deploy an image, a prompt for the product key will be displayed during installation (or you may include it in the answer file). For more information on licensing and activation, see Chapter 3.

To create a new answer file using SIM, perform the following steps:

1. **Create a directory for working with your new answer file to keep it separate from your existing files, for example, W:\Unattend.**

2. **Copy the install WIM from the sources directory (\sources\install.wim) on the Windows Vista DVD to your new unattend directory.** Ensure that the read-only attribute has been removed from this file (right-click ➪ Properties).

3. **Launch the Windows System Image Manager (located in the Microsoft Windows AIK program group).**

4. **From the File menu, choose Select Windows Image and select the install.wim file you copied in Step 2 (W:\Unattend\install.wim).**

5. **Because the WIM file contains more than one image, a prompt is displayed so the desired image within the WIM may be specified. Choose Windows Vista Enterprise edition.** Because this is the first time the WIM has been opened, a prompt to build a catalog file will be presented.

6. **Select Yes to allow the system to build a catalog of the image.**

7. **From the File menu, choose New Answer File.**

8. **Use Table 2.1 to add the specified components to the answer file. Expand the components node of the Windows Image panel and either right-click and add, or drag and drop, the following components to the designated configuration pass in the Answer File pane.**

9. **Use Table 2.2 to make the settings on the components you have added to the answer file.**

10. **From the Tools menu, select Validate Answer File.** A warning appears about the SkipMachineOOBE setting; you may safely ignore it for now.

11. **Save your answer file in your unattend folder as** `basic_unattend.xml`.

TABLE 2.1

Step 8 Component Selections

Component	Configuration Pass
<arch>_Microsoft-Windows-International-Core-WinPE_<version>	1 - windowsPE
(Used to configure Windows PE for the correct locale)	
<arch>_Microsoft-Windows-Setup_<version>	1 - windowsPE
• DiskConfiguration	
• Disk	
• CreatePartitions	
• CreatePartition	
(Used to automatically create a single partition)	

continued

TABLE 2.1   *(continued)*

Component	Configuration Pass
<arch>_Microsoft-Windows-Setup_<version> • ImageInstall • OSImage • InstallTo *(Used to specify the partition to be used for installation)*	1 - windowsPE
<arch>_Microsoft-Windows-Setup_<version> • UserData *(Allows you to skip the EULA)*	1 - windowsPE
<arch>_Microsoft-Windows-Shell-Setup_<version> • AutoLogon *(Lets you enable AutoLogon as Administrator to enable the account)*	7 - oobeSystem
<arch>_Microsoft-Windows-Shell-Setup_<version> • OOBE8 *(Used to automate the Out of Box Experience (OOBE))*	7 - oobeSystem
<arch>_Microsoft-Windows-Shell-Setup_<version> • UserAccounts • AdministratorPassword *(Used to set the local Administrator's password)*	7 - oobeSystem

TABLE 2.2

Step 9 Component Settings

1 windowsPE

Microsoft-Windows-International-Core-WinPE

InputLocale	**en-US (or other valid locale)**
SystemLocale	**en-US (or other valid locale)**
UILanguage	**en-US (or other valid language)**
UserLocale	**en-US (or other valid locale)**

1 windowsPE

Microsoft-Windows-International-Core-WinPE ⇨ SetupUILanguage

UILanguage	**en-US (or other valid language)**

1 windowsPE	
Microsoft-Windows-Setup ⇨ DiskConfiguration	
WillShowUI	**OnError**

1 windowsPE	
Microsoft-Windows-Setup ⇨ DiskConfiguration ⇨ Disk	
DiskID	**0**
WillWipeDisk	**true**

1 windowsPE	
Microsoft-Windows-Setup ⇨ DiskConfiguration ⇨ Disk ⇨ CreatePartitions ⇨ CreatePartition	
Extend	**true**
Order	**1**
Type	**Primary**

1 windowsPE	
Microsoft-Windows-Setup ⇨ ImageInstall ⇨ OSImage	
WillShowUI	**OnError**

1 windowsPE	
Microsoft-Windows-Setup ⇨ ImageInstall ⇨ OSImage ⇨ InstallTo	
DiskID	**0**
Partition	**1**

1 windowsPE	
Microsoft-Windows-Setup ⇨ UserData	
AcceptEula	**true**
FullName	**<Owner Name>**
Organization	**<Company Name>**

continued

61

TABLE 2.2 *(continued)*

1 windowsPE	
Microsoft-Windows-Setup ➪ UserData ➪ ProductKey	
Key	**\<Database Master Key for Vista Enterprise\>**
WillShowUI	**OnError**

7 oobeSystem	
Microsoft-Windows-Shell-Setup ➪ AutoLogon	
Enabled	**True**
LogonCount	**1**
UserName	**Administrator**

7 oobeSystem	
Microsoft-Windows-Shell-Setup ➪ AutoLogon ➪ Password	
Value	**\<Password\>**

7 oobeSystem	
Microsoft-Windows-Shell-Setup ➪ OOBE	
HideEULAPage	**True**
NetworkLocation	**Work**
ProtectYourPC	**3**
SkipMachineOOBE	**True**
SkipUserOOBE	**True**

7 oobeSystem	
Microsoft-Windows-Shell-Setup ➪ UserAccounts ➪ AdministratorPassword	
Value	**Password1**

CAUTION Be careful when using the SkipMachineOOBE setting. By specifying a value of TRUE, you will not be prompted to create any user accounts. Because the local Administrator account is disabled by default, this may leave your installation in an unusable state. If specifying SkipMachineOOBE as true, be sure to enable the local Administrator account, create an alternate local Administrative account, or join the computer to a domain.

TIP You may have looked and noticed that there is no answer file setting to enable the local Administrator account. Microsoft has omitted this setting as part of Vista's increased security and it's recommended that you create a new local account for administration. If you are required to enable the Administrator account as part of your answer file, it can be done by assigning the Administrator account a password and configuring it to auto logon during setup.

Building a Reference Computer

With the deployment server in place and the unattended answer file created, we are now ready to move on to building a reference computer. This is the computer that will serve as the baseline image to be deployed across your organization. To review, so far you should have:

- Selected an appropriate edition of Windows Vista
- Decided how many images will be created and maintained and how thick to make each image
- Built a deployment server
- Installed the Windows Automated Installation Kit (WAIK) on the deployment server
- Created an unattended answer file for installation

CROSS-REF Chapter 6 describes the types of images (thin, thick, and hybrid).

The next step in creating a successful deployment is to leverage the unattended answer file to begin creating a *reference computer*. A reference computer is the computer used to create your customized image for deployment. Although this can be a virtual machine, you will need to test your image on all organizational hardware platforms before mass deployment.

The reference computer is an ideal computer of sorts. It includes not only Windows Vista with any customizations for your organization but also the latest service packs and updates for Windows. If you are implementing hybrid or thick images, you will also include applications.

The reference computer must be stable. One step to increase the stability of a reference computer is to start with a clean and automated installation. A clean installation ensures that you do not have any computer vendor software, malware, or trial software and also ensures that you know exactly what has been included and configured on the reference computer. Automating the installation of the reference computer ensures that rebuilding the image later can be done in a consistent fashion. If done correctly, the file used to automate the installation of the reference computer can also be used later in the process to automate the deployment of imaged computers.

Implementing an answer file

You now have a functioning Windows Vista answer file, but how do you actually use it to build a reference computer? Answer files are typically implemented in one of three ways. In the first, a generic Windows Vista installation will scan all removable media for a file named `autounattend.xml`. If the file is found, it will be copied to the local disk and read during the various configuration passes. By copying the file to the local hard drive, it is ensured that the file will be available during each configuration pass even if the removable media is disconnected. In this scenario, the windowsPE, specialize, and oobeSystem sections would be read and used.

In the second, if starting Windows Vista installation with the setup command, the answer file can be specified as part of the setup command using the /unattend command line option. In this case the file can be named any valid windows filename. Just like when using `autounattend.xml`, the file will be copied to the local hard drive and cached for future configuration passes. This allows you to store your answer file on network drives or other locations that may not be available during early setup stages. In this scenario, the windowsPE, specialize, and oobeSystem sections would be read and used.

The last way you can implement an answer file is to embed it into a customized image. This is done with the Sysprep tool, which will be discussed later in this chapter. Again, the file is cached to the local drive so that it is always available when needed. In this scenario, the generalize section would be used when running Sysprep, and the specialize and oobeSystem sections would typically be read and used unless the system was set to start in audit mode. The windowsPE section would not be read because by the time the custom image has been applied to a system, the Windows PE portion of setup is already complete.

> **TIP** When autounattend.xml is copied to the local drive, it is copied to C:\windows\system32\panther and renamed unattend.xml. For security reasons, passwords and other secure information will be removed from the file after use.

To start the process of creating a custom image, you should use the first method to automate a generic Windows Vista installation. This allows you to test your answer file and provides a method to easily rebuild the custom image later, if necessary. At this point in the deployment process, you should have at least two computers, a deployment server and a reference computer, as shown in Figure 2.10.

FIGURE 2.10

Deployment server and reference computer ready for Vista installation

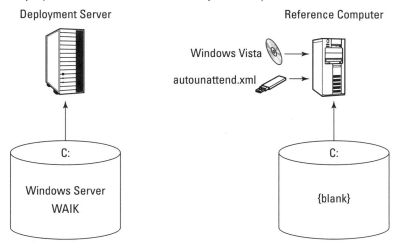

Walkthrough: Automating Windows Vista installation

In this walkthrough, the steps necessary to perform an automated Windows Vista installation will be covered. The computer having Vista installed will be referred to as the reference computer since it will eventually become the computer used to build your custom image. If you plan to use a virtual machine for this, create a new virtual machine for this purpose before proceeding.

To automate Windows Vista installation with your new answer file, follow these steps:

1. **Copy your answer file to a blank floppy disk or USB flash drive.** Although it is not critical that the floppy disk or flash drive be blank, using one avoids possible conflicts and boot issues.

   NOTE If you are using an answer file on a virtual machine, it is best to make use of a floppy disk image, as working with USB flash drives in this way can be problematic. To create a virtual floppy image in VMware Server, just go to the Virtual Machine Settings and select the Floppy device. Select Use floppy image and click the Create button. You will be prompted to browse to a path and filename where the file should be created. Then within your virtual machine you can make use of it as you would a floppy disk (format it and place the file on the disk). When you are done, disconnect and specify this floppy image as the image for another virtual machine to "insert the virtual floppy" elsewhere.

2. **Rename your answer file to** `autounattend.xml`. Note that the proper spelling of this file name is critical.

3. Place the removable media with the answer file into the reference computer.

4. Configure the BIOS of the reference computer to boot from DVD first.

5. Boot the reference computer from the Vista DVD.

Installation should proceed without any further interaction. If the setup stops and prompts for information, review the related section of your answer file. Although the steps listed here have been tested several times prior to printing, it may be that your setup requires additional settings not provided in the example. You can use the Unattended Windows Setup Reference from the WAIK to help identify the necessary components which may need to be included in your answer file.

Customizing the reference computer

After the reference computer has Windows installed, you are ready to begin making customizations. The customizations will involve the inclusion of drivers, updates, applications, and configuration changes.

Providing device drivers

When building your master image, you will need to take into account all hardware in your environment. The most common reason that organizations choose to support multiple images is that they must support varying hardware. This can be easily overcome and is a poor excuse for supporting multiple images when you consider the time and expense of maintaining many images. The concern for supporting multiple hardware platforms from a single image revolves around two areas: successfully applying the image and allowing users to access approved hardware.

In the past, successfully applying and starting an image on different hardware was quite a challenge. Mass storage controller drivers and Hardware Abstraction Layer (HAL) limitations drove many organizations into supporting multiple images. Although these challenges could be overcome, it was sometimes too difficult to implement or not documented well enough. The most common problem was applying an image to a different hardware platform and getting Stop Error 7B (Blue Screen of Death), which meant inaccessible boot device. Windows Vista handles different hardware platforms much more gracefully, including different drive controllers and HALs with no additional effort on your part.

Providing drivers to users can also be handled in a well-managed fashion. You may preload the drivers in your image, provide a DevicePath in the registry to search for drivers, or you may update the driver store to include drivers approved by the computer support department. Each method has advantages and drawbacks, depending upon the size of your organization and management tools that you have in place.

Preloading drivers

Perhaps the most simple and time consuming method of providing drivers for your users is to preload them. To preload drivers you simply apply an image to a hardware platform for which you want to include drivers. After the image application is complete, you can manually add any drivers for devices that require them. It's a bit laborious, but it works.

Preloading drivers has the advantage of not requiring any special configuration file changes. However, it does not allow for dynamic updating of drivers. If additional drivers must be added later, you must apply the image to new hardware, update the drivers, and then prepare and capture the image again. This method also leaves many unused drivers loaded and could lead to conflicts or instabilities if not carefully managed.

Updating the driver store

The cleaner method of adding device drivers to the reference system is to update the local driver store. When unrecognized devices are attached to a computer, the Plug and Play service will first check the local driver store to see if a driver can be found. To protect the integrity of the system, only Administrators are allowed to update the local driver store. However, once drivers are loaded into the local driver store, standard users can leverage the drivers to support hardware if the computer policy has been set to allow it.

You may add a driver to the driver store using the PNPUtil command line tool which is provided as part of Windows Vista and Server 2008. The –a argument is used to add a driver:

```
PNPUtil.exe -a mydriver.inf
```

Complicating things a bit more, signing the driver with a public key infrastructure (PKI) certificate trusted by your client systems is a common requirement. Signing drivers also requires that you obtain a certificate and configure your clients to trust it. For details on how to accomplish this see Signing Device Driver Packages at `http://technet2.microsoft.com/ windowsserver2008/en/library/fabaef98-fa7a-4535-90a1-3961adef009e1033. mspx`.

Although this method does provide a cleaner answer than simply preloading the drivers, it requires significant effort for each additional driver. In addition, updating the driver store on the image requires applying the image to a workstation, updating the driver store, and then again preparing and capturing the image. This method also does not provide the flexibility of being able to provide additional drivers to workstations that have been previously deployed.

Providing a driver directory

The most flexible method of providing drivers to users is by modifying a registry key that instructs the computer which directories to search for drivers. Providing a driver directory offers the advantage of being easy to update without loading unnecessary drivers associated with preloading drivers.

When building the image you may set the registry key manually or by using the appropriate component in the answer file. The driver directory may be a local directory, but would typically be a network path where drivers can be kept up to date more easily. When new devices are attached, the Plug and Play service will search the local driver store and then any paths listed in the following registry key:

```
HKEY_LOCAL_MACHINE\Software\Microsoft\Windows\CurrentVersion\DevicePath
```

If a driver is found in the DevicePath directory, then it is staged into the local driver store.

NOTE Multiple DevicePath directories should be separated by a semicolon. Also there is no recursive search of these directories, which means that you must specify each directory and not just the root. For example, specifying `\\server\files\drivers` includes only the drivers in that folder and not those in subfolders like `\\server\files\drivers\network`. Be careful to not remove the existing entry for `%SystemRoot%\inf`!

For drivers to be successfully staged into the driver store they must either be installed by an Administrator or signed by a trusted party. To have users install the drivers you provide, you must make sure that the drivers are signed by a trusted authority. All drivers included with Windows in the local driver store have been signed and may be installed by standard users. However, drivers obtained from third parties are sometimes not signed by Microsoft or other trusted parties and may require you digitally signing them yourself (as discussed in the previous section).

NOTE It is increasingly common for vendors to provide digitally singed drivers. One driving force for this movement is the fact that 64-bit editions of Windows Vista and Server 2008 will not install kernel mode drivers unless they are digitally signed.

Customizing the image

Install any Windows service packs or updates to the reference computer. Even if you have an enterprise patch management solution, keeping your image up to date on the latest security updates will lessen your exposure to security threats. It is very possible for your computer to become compromised before a freshly imaged system has time to update itself.

After getting Windows up to date, you may begin to install any applications. The applications you install here will be dependent upon what image type you have chosen to implement. If using a thin image, then no applications will need to be installed. If using hybrid or thick images, remember that each computer in your organization will need to be licensed for each application in the image. After installing the applications, ensure that they also have the latest patches and updates as necessary.

After installing Windows and verifying the successful execution of any necessary applications, you may proceed to make any special configuration changes. However, it is recommended that you do not make too many configuration changes at this stage of deployment — they can't be managed over time. Although scripting such changes will go a long way to ensuring reproducibility, it is a better solution to manage the settings and configuration through a persistent management solution (such as with Group Policy or using a desktop management solution, such as System Center Configuration Manager).

NOTE Although most every aspect of the user profile can be dictated by Group Policy, Group Policy enforces changes. To establish custom defaults, it is necessary to configure the Default User Profile as desired. This is typically done by logging on as a user, making the desired changes, and logging off. With this user profile configured as desired, it can simply be copied over that of the Default User Profile so that any new user profiles created by the system will use this as a starting point.

Preparing the reference computer for imaging

After the reference computer is customized for your environment, you must prepare it for the imaging process. When imaging computers, a copy is made of one computer and applied to others. This is both helpful and problematic. The advantages have been discussed and primarily deal with reduced deployment times and extremely consistent workstations.

The disadvantage of an exact copy is that it is an exact copy. More specifically, items such as the computer name, IP address, and Security Identifier (SID) are copied to each and every computer. This problem is overcome by *generalizing* the system before creating an image from it. This generalization process is carried out using the System Preparation Tool (`sysprep.exe`). You can see the System Preparation Tool, which is located on Windows Vista systems in the `c:\windows\ system32\sysprep` folder, in Figure 2.11.

FIGURE 2.11

System Preparation Tool user interface

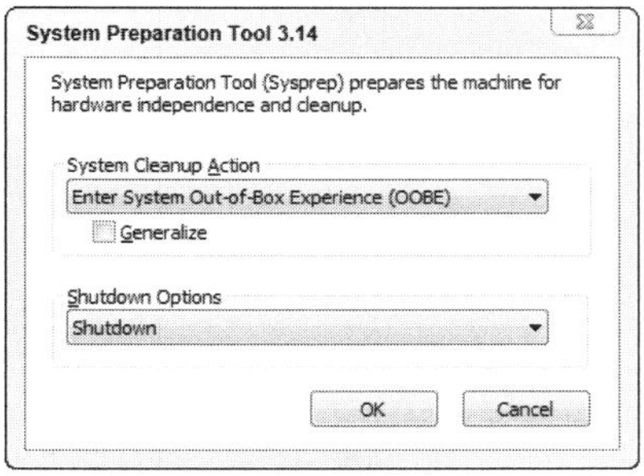

Cleanup action

The System Preparation Tool allows you to adjust three settings in the user interface. The first setting is the type of cleanup action. The choices are OOBE or audit modes. When the cleanup action is set to OOBE mode, the computer will begin Windows Welcome, also known as Out of Box Experience, on the next reboot. This setting allows the user to name the computer, configure network settings, join the computer to a domain, and create user accounts and other setup items. You see this interface when you turn on a new computer for the first time. In general, this is the cleanup mode you should use for creating your images.

You may also select System Audit Mode, which will bypass Windows Welcome on next reboot. By circumventing Windows Welcome, you are given access to the desktop without having to run through any wizards. On the other hand the computer has not been properly configured for use. Audit mode is used for either post-imaging configuration or multi-tiered image building, where an organizational image is built and remote locations will customize the image and then configure the cleanup action for OOBE, as shown in Figure 2.12.

FIGURE 2.12

Example of multi-tiered image building

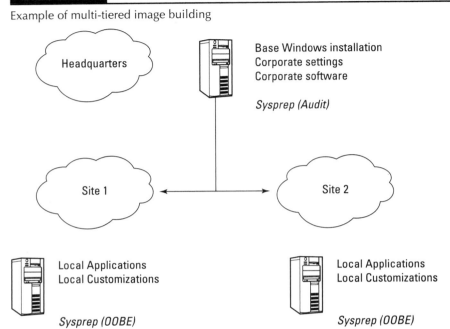

Headquarters

Base Windows installation
Corporate settings
Corporate software

Sysprep (Audit)

Site 1

Site 2

Local Applications
Local Customizations

Local Applications
Local Customizations

Sysprep (OOBE)

Sysprep (OOBE)

Generalize

The generalize option is the main focus of the tool. When this option is selected, all unique information is stripped from the computer. In particular, the computer name, network settings, End User License Agreement acceptance, Product Key, Security Identifier (SID), user name, and computer name are removed. In addition, other system cleanup is performed and the Windows activation grace period is reset. Typically, the machine would then shut down. On the next startup, the computer would then presumably start Windows Welcome to prompt the user for the missing information. However, before starting Windows again an image will be captured while the computer is in the generalized state.

Shutdown options

After the System Preparation tool has completed its work, it can exit the program, reboot the computer, or shut down the computer. When creating images, the most common desire is to have the computer shut down so that you may then proceed to capture an image. However, you may already have a bootable CD or USB flash drive (UFD) attached and wish to immediately reboot.

Understanding the limitations of Sysprep

Although an image can be generalized as many times as you like, the Windows activation grace period will only be reset a maximum of three times (five times for Vista Enterprise). When the grace period expires, the computer will enter a notification-based experience where the user is constantly prompted to activate and becomes virtually useless to your end users. This limitation is significant because it essentially limits the number of times you can apply, modify, and recapture an image. It should now be apparent why being able to modify an image offline is so useful.

Another approach to managing images offline is to use a virtual machine as a Reference Computer. Since a VM is nothing but a set of files, you just copy these files before running Sysprep and then you run Sysprep on the copy. Doing this means that the reference computer is not changed, so you can run Sysprep as many times as desired. Keeping a running copy of the reference computer also makes it a lot easier to update and patch without having to perform these actions in an offline mode.

Answer file

The System Preparation tool may also be run completely from the command line. You can see the available command line parameters in Figure 2.13. From the command line, Sysprep has the additional capability of specifying an answer file, which cannot be done from the graphical user interface. For this reason it is most likely you will desire to use Sysprep from the command line and not from its graphical user interface.

FIGURE 2.13

System Preparation Tool command line parameters

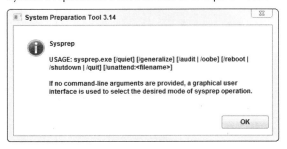

When the /unattend option is used with Sysprep, it specifies the answer file that should be used on next reboot. The assumption is that the system has been generalized and on next reboot will need information to be provided before being ready for use by the end user. Normally, this information would be provided as part of Windows Welcome. If you do not wish to manually enter a product key, accept the license agreement, create user accounts, or configure localization settings you may provide an answer file to be used. The process here is very similar to the answer file you provided to automate the setup of your reference computer, as the image shipped on the Vista DVD is in a generalized state.

The answer file may be given any valid Windows filename and may be stored in any currently accessible location. The Sysprep utility will copy the file to C:\Windows\panther and rename it to unattend.xml. Assuming there are no changes, you may reuse the answer file created to automate the reference computer installation created in a previous walkthrough.

Walkthrough: Preparing the computer for imaging

To generalize the system, specify an answer file, and shut down the reference computer, use the following command changing the path to the answer file to match your needs. The entire command should be entered on a single line, although it has been wrapped below due to length.

```
C:\windows\system32\sysprep\sysprep.exe /generalize /oobe /
    shutdown /unattend:w:\unattend\basic_unattend.xml
```

Capturing Custom Images

Now that your reference computer has been customized and generalized, it is ready to be captured to an image. There are numerous third-party utilities for capturing images and most use a proprietary imaging format that each vendor claims is superior. However, everyone can leverage ImageX, which is used here to capture a WIM file.

Windows PE

When powered on normally, your reference computer proceeds to run Windows Welcome and prompt for any needed information, so you must be careful to not start the locally installed copy of Windows on the reference computer. To capture the image, you will need to start the computer from an alternate operating system with access to imaging tools, and most likely it will need network access.

Windows PE is the Microsoft-supplied answer to this need (alternatives are discussed in Chapter 6). You will need bootable Windows PE media and an imaging utility. Microsoft supplies the tools necessary to build a customized Windows PE environment. They are shipped as part of the Windows Automated Installation Kit. If you have been following along, you should already have installed the WAIK on your deployment server, which can now be used to create a Windows PE boot image, and in turn, boot media.

 **Although provided here as part of the quick steps necessary to establish a custom Windows Vista image, this topic is covered in much more detail in Chapter 6.**

Walkthrough: Creating Windows PE boot media

Before completing the following walkthrough, ensure that you have successfully installed the Windows Automated Installation Kit. To create a basic Windows PE boot image, follow these steps:

1. **Right-click on the Windows PE Tools Command Prompt shortcut from its program folder on the start menu and choose Run as administrator.**

2. **To establish the file structure needed to customize a Windows PE image, run the CopyPE script with two arguments: the first is the target architecture (x86, ia64 or amd64), and the second is the target directory where you will manage your image.** If you are working with multiple architectures, it is a good idea to include it in your target folder name. However, this is a path that needs to be typed for most commands so keep the path short to save some typing. For the tasks documented in this section the following arguments are used:

   ```
   copype.cmd x86 c:\winpe_x86
   ```

If you are working with a VMware virtual machine as a client system, you must add its network driver to the image. Additionally, the same process (Steps 2 and 3) may be used to add any network driver if your physical machine is not natively supported by Windows PE. To add the VMware network driver to a Windows PE image, follow the steps below:

1. **Mount the Windows PE image for read/write updates:**

   ```
   imagex /mountrw c:\winpe_x86\winpe.wim 1 c:\winpe_x86\mount
   ```

2. **One way to obtain any of the VMware drivers is to start up a VMware session and choose the Install VMware Tools option.** Don't worry if you already have them installed — all this does is mount a VMware Tools installation CD (which may automatically start the installation wizard). In the virtual CD that appears in your session, go to `E:\Program Files\VMware\VMware Tools\Drivers\vmxnet\win2k\` and copy these files to your host system.

   ```
   Copy D:\program files\VMware\VMware Tools\Drivers\vmxnet\
       win2k\*.* \\server\drivers\network\vmware\
   ```

3. **Install the driver using its INF file with the PeImg INF command:**

   ```
   peimg /inf=\\server\drivers\network\vmware\vmware-nic.inf c:\
       winpe_x86\mount\windows
   ```

4. **When done editing your image, be sure to commit the changes back to the mounted image by using the ImageX Unmount command:**

   ```
   Imagex /Unmount /Commit c:\winpe_x86\mount
   ```

With your WIM file ready to go, the final step is to make a bootable disk image in the form of an ISO file. Using a virtual machine, you may easily attach the virtual machine to the ISO file, and it will be treated as a CD-ROM. If you are using physical machines, you may either burn the ISO file to CD/DVD or make a bootable USB flash drive (UFD). If you make a bootable CD or DVD, make sure to burn the contents of the ISO file to CD or DVD and not the actual file itself. Successfully booting to a UFD can depend highly upon the UFD and the BIOS of the computer you are booting. (The steps to create a bootable UFD for Windows PE are covered in Chapter 6.) To create the ISO, simply run the following two commands:

1. **Copy the updated Windows PE image over the existing boot.wim in the ISO sources directory (answer yes if asked to confirm the overwriting of the file):**

   ```
   copy c:\winpe_x86\winpe.wim c:\winpe_x86\iso\sources\boot.wim
   ```

2. **Use the OSCDImg command line tool discussed in Chapter 6 to generate the ISO:**

   ```
   oscdimg -n -bc:\winpe_x86\etfsboot.com c:\winpe_x86\ISO c:\
       winpe_x86\winpe_x86.iso
   ```

ImageX

After booting to Windows PE, you will need an imaging utility to capture the local hard drive to a file. Microsoft provides a utility for working with WIM files, which includes capturing them. The utility is named ImageX and is completely command line driven. You can customize the Windows PE disk to include ImageX, but in most situations it is more flexible to place the imaging utility on a network share. If new versions of ImageX are released, you will be able to update the network share without having to update all of your boot media. If you are using an imaging utility other than ImageX, it will most likely function from a network share as well. Windows PE also supports USB external drives if you prefer.

ImageX is provided as part of the WAIK and may be copied from the deployment server to a network share. In addition to capturing images, ImageX may also append an image to an existing WIM file, export images to new WIM files, mount images for viewing or editing, or split large WIM files into smaller, manageable files.

Standard options

If you are saving to a network location, the first thing you need to do is establish a network connection by supplying the necessary credentials. The easiest way to do this is with a simple NET USE command:

```
net use N: \\server\files /USER:mydomain\myname
```

The above will prompt for a password. Once established, you may make use of the N drive or use a UNC path. As long as you have taken this action and established credentials for accessing the share you need not actually use the mapped drive letter.

If you only plan to use ImageX for capturing and applying images, the only options you need to specify are /capture, a destination WIM filename, and a friendly name for the captured image within the file (remember that WIM files may contain multiple images!). If you plan to use Setup, which can also apply images, you need to specify the edition of Vista you are capturing with the / flags option. This is a relatively undocumented and annoying feature. Be aware that the Microsoft Deployment Toolkit (MDT) and Windows Deployment Services (WDS) both use Setup to apply your images, so if you plan to use either of these tools as part of your deployment process, be sure to specify a Windows edition. Because it doesn't hurt to specify an edition when it's not needed, always specify an edition with the /flags option when capturing an image. A common capture command looks something like the following:

```
N:\imagex.exe /flags "Enterprise" /capture c: N:\images\vista_
    custom.wim "Standard"
```

The preceding command would capture the local C drive to a new file named vista_custom.wim. This image would have the friendly name of Standard. If you wished to capture the local C drive and add it to an existing WIM file, simply use the /append option instead of /capture.

CROSS-REF Syntax, command line options, and the use of the /flags option for ImageX can be found in Chapter 6.

Compression

Another useful option of ImageX is its compression settings. The WIM file format supports three different compression types, all of which may be performed with ImageX. The first compression type is actually no compression at all. If space is of no concern, you may capture your image using no compression, in which case each file of the image is stored in its original format. This is configured by using the /compress none option with ImageX.

If space is the primary concern, the compression can be set to maximum, which uses LZX, with the /compress maximum option. This type of compression is very effective and can significantly reduce the size of the image. LZX compression, however, is very resource intensive, requiring significant CPU time to ensure that each file is compressed as much as possible.

The default behavior is to use fast compression, which uses XPress compression. This option provides a significant space savings over using no compression at all and is faster than maximum compression. When comparing the space saving of maximum compression to fast compress there is typically little to no difference in file sizes. However, when trying to squeeze the last 100MB of an image on a single DVD, fast compression may not be suitable. For most scenarios, however, it is the compression type of choice. If no compression type is specified or a /compress fast option is used, then fast compression will be used.

TIP Be careful when planning which images to store in a single WIM file and also when appending an image to a file for testing. ImageX has a /delete option which will remove an image from an image file, but it only removes the file metadata. File data and contents will not be removed from the WIM file. If several images are sharing the same files, then there is little need for concern because most of the files will still be used by other images. If images for different operating systems are stored in the same WIM file, there may be considerable wasted space after deleting an image from a WIM file. To optimize the WIM file after deleting an image, you may use the /export option to export the valid images into a new WIM file, where only the necessary file data is stored.

Walkthrough: Capturing a WIM file with ImageX

To use Windows PE and ImageX to capture the reference computer to a WIM file on a network share, perform the following steps:

1. Create two new groups on the deployment server or in the Active Directory Domain Services (ADDS). Name the first group Image Readers and name the second group Image Writers. Put any accounts that will be used to apply images into the Image Readers group. Put any accounts that will be used to capture or modify images into the Image Writers group.

2. **Create a network imaging share if you don't have one already prepared to store images.** For the following examples, a share named Images has been created for a new folder named w:\images.

3. Configure the share to allow the Image Readers group read permissions and the Image Writers group modify permissions.

4. Boot the reference computer to Windows PE.

5. Once Windows PE successfully starts, map a drive to imaging share using the following command as a guide. When prompted, provide credentials for an account in the Image Writers group.

   ```
   net use n: \\deploysvr\images
   ```

6. Capture an image of the reference computer C drive with the following command. **If you are not using Enterprise Edition, change Enterprise to Business or Ultimate.** The following command should be entered on a single line, although it is wrapped here due to length:

   ```
   n:\imagex.exe /flags "Enterprise" /capture c: n:\images\vista_
       custom.wim "Base Image"
   ```

7. **Wait.** It usually takes between 15 and 45 minutes to capture an image based on the speed of the computer, network speed, and the size of the image to be captured.

Deploying Custom Images

Deploying WIM files is different than deploying binary-based images used by some other vendors. Binary images contain drive and partition information, which is needed to successfully start an operating system. WIM files are file-based images and do not include partition information. The file-based nature of the WIM files allows it to be applied in a nondestructive manner. For example, you may re-image a problematic machine without deleting the locally stored data. However, it is not a very practical solution because with the registry as part of the image, it will be necessary to reinstall any applications. That said, the lack of partition information in the image does mean that it is necessary to properly prepare the hard drive before applying the image.

Preparing the hard disk

Although any drive partitioning and formatting software may be used, DiskPart is included with Windows and is included with Windows PE by default. DiskPart is an interactive command line utility which can perform even more tasks than the graphical Disk Administrator. For the purposes of imaging, it can be used to create partitions, make partitions active, and format partitions.

DiskPart is a very powerful utility. Its most significant power comes from its ability to run its commands from an input file and thus be run from a script. The process of automating DiskPart begins with first creating a text file with all necessary DiskPart commands and secondly running DiskPart with the /s option to specify the text file (referred to as a DiskPart script file). In the following walkthrough, you will create and store the script file on the network share, along with the customized WIM file. The advantage is that any necessary modifications can be made in a single location, which makes this a much more manageable solution.

To properly prepare a disk to receive an image, you must perform the following tasks within DiskPart:

Select disk 0

The first step is to select the disk you wish to operate against. Disks begin numbering with 0, which would be the most common option. If necessary, you may use list disk to show the available drives for selection (if your system has a hidden OEM image partition you may find it listed as disk 0) .

Clean

An optional step is to clear any existing partitions from the drive. This is a destructive option and should be used with care.

Create partition primary [size=XXXX]

If the drive has been cleaned or is new, a partition must be created. This command will create a primary partition which will extend to the full size of the drive. The size in megabytes of the partition may be specified by using the size option.

Active

This will simply mark the newly created partition as active. This is required if you wish to boot an operating system from this partition.

Format fs=ntfs

The format command in DiskPart will format the partition with the specified file system. This task may also be performed with the standalone format command.

Exit

Exit the user interface and close the DiskPart utility.

Walkthrough: Preparing a hard disk for an image

To use DiskPart to prepare a target computer's disk for imaging, follow these steps:

1. From your deployment server, open Notepad and enter the following text in a new document:

```
select disk 0
clean
create partition primary
active
format fs=ntfs
exit
```

2. Save the document on your images share (i.e. w:\images) as single_partition.txt.

3. Boot the target computer to Windows PE.

4. Once Windows PE successfully starts, map a network drive using the following command as a guide. When prompted for credentials, supply a user name and password with read permissions to the share.

```
net use y: \\deploysvr\images
```

5. Execute the following command on the target computer to prepare the local disk.

```
diskpart /s y:\single_partition.txt
```

Applying the image

Once the disk of your target computer has been properly prepared, there are two methods to apply the image. One is to use the ImageX command line utility with the /apply option. The other is to use `setup.exe` from the Vista DVD. Both methods imply that the computer has been booted to an operating system which supports them, typically Windows PE.

Deploying with ImageX

ImageX provides a very efficient and simple method to apply images to a prepared disk. As a command line utility, ImageX may be scripted to perform a customized installation and provides the most flexibility and efficiency. The most significant downside to using ImageX is that it does not provide a method to perform in-place upgrades. However, when combined with other tools, such as Windows Easy Transfer or User State Migration Tool, user data and accounts can be maintained during the imaging process.

To apply an image with ImageX, simply specify the `/apply` option. The first parameter after the `/apply` option is the name of the WIM file which contains the image you want to apply. The second parameter is the image number or name. Keep in mind that a single WIM file may contain multiple images, so it's necessary to specify the image to be applied. If you chose to use image numbers, the image numbers begin with 1. Lastly, specify the location to apply the image. Typically, this would simply be a drive letter, but in some circumstances you may want to apply an image to a subfolder. For an example, see the section "Walkthrough: Applying an image with ImageX."

NOTE If you don't know (or just can't remember!) which images are stored within a WIM file, the /info option of ImageX will list the images in a WIM file. Not only does it list the image names, but also their indexed numbers within the WIM file along with other information about the WIM file.

Deploying with Setup

Setup, the replacement for `winnt.exe` and `winnt32.exe`, may also be used to deploy images. Setup only accepts a few options as parameters. The one needed for the automated deployment process is the /unattend option, which allows an unattended answer file be specified. The unattend answer file specifies the image to use and the target drive to prepare. Setup may be used to perform a clean installation or an upgrade.

Walkthrough: Applying an image with ImageX

To apply a customized WIM file to a prepared hard drive with ImageX, complete the following step. Be sure that you have booted to Windows PE, prepared the hard drive, and mapped a network drive, as per the previous Walkthrough.

From the target computer, use ImageX with the /apply option, using the following command as a guide:

```
y:\imagex.exe /apply n:\images\vista_custom.wim 1 c:\
```

Automating the deployment

At this point you may be concerned about the amount of effort required to successfully deploy a captured image. You must:

1. Boot to Windows PE.
2. Map a network drive, if applicable.
3. Partition and format the local drive if necessary.
4. Run ImageX with appropriate parameters.

If you only plan to deploy one or two images per week, this may not seem like a significant amount of work. If you plan to deploy hundreds or even thousands of workstations, the process will need to be more automated. A simple technique to automate the process is to use a batch file. Chapter 6 discusses customizing Windows PE to automate the process. Chapter 7 discusses use of the Microsoft Deployment Toolkit, and Chapter 8 covers Windows Deployment Services, all of which can be used to significantly increase the efficiency of the deployment process.

Summary

To create an effective deployment solution, automation is very important. Using unattended answer files to automate the installation of Windows is a simple method to speed deployment and increase consistency. However, answer files alone will not satisfy the needs of most organizations. Because of this, Microsoft has provided additional tools to fully customize your installation images. By leveraging customized images and the tools of the Windows Automated Installation Kit, you can create a deployment solution well suited to meet the needs of your organization.

Chapter 3

Managing Windows Licensing and Activation

IN THIS CHAPTER

Understanding Windows licensing

Centralizing activation using KMS

Leveraging multiple activation keys

Resolving activation notifications and reduced functionality mode

Microsoft has a large group of people and a relatively large amount of resources dedicated to licensing. Some are responsible for ensuring that their customers are abiding by the license agreements, while others are simply there to advise customers on proper licensing options. Although fully understanding Microsoft's licensing model is probably outside the scope of all but a full-time specialist, it is important that you understand the technical differences between the available licensing options.

A major concern for Microsoft is the number of people who choose to avoid licensing issues altogether by pirating the software. Due in part to its popularity, Windows has become one of the most pirated pieces of software ever. To help curb the piracy and ensure customers understand the dangers of pirated software, Microsoft has implemented the Windows Genuine Advantage program.

Although the Windows Genuine Advantage program attempts to educate and appeal to the morals and ethics of customers, Microsoft has also begun to enforce measures to verify licensing by using the process of activation. An effective deployment solution must deal with the activation requirements of the operating system.

Licensing Windows

Understanding and managing Windows licenses can be a full-time job. Just as you think you understand it, it changes. The aim of this section is to provide you with the information necessary to build a successful deployment. You will need to ensure that proper licenses are purchased and obtained (better yet, have your purchasing department take care of it for you).

Although much of the purchasing process has to do with price, licenses also have technical restrictions about their deployment and activation.

In general, Microsoft offers three different Windows licensing types. Although all three types provide identical functionality inside the operating system, pricing and management should be concerns when deciding which licensing type to use.

To verify proper licensing, Microsoft began implementing activation with the release of Windows XP. Although obtaining a license gives you the legal right to use Windows, activation verifies your license is valid. As shown in Figure 3.1, the activation state for Windows Vista can be one of three states:

- Grace period
- Notification
- Activated

When Windows is initially installed, it is typically operating in its grace period. The grace period is a 30-day period in which Windows is fully functional and will attempt to activate itself until activation can be achieved. Ideally, Windows would then enter the activated state. It is important to note that Windows may also return to the grace period state, depending upon the license being used. However, if activation cannot be accomplished after remaining in the grace period for 30 days, then Windows enters Reduced Functionality Mode (RFM) in which the user interface is very restrictive and time limited. Thankfully, RFM has been eliminated with the release of Windows Vista SP1. Now the system enters a *Notification Experience,* where the user is repeatedly notified that they must activate (discussed in more detail later in this chapter).

FIGURE 3.1

Understanding the Activation process for Window Vista

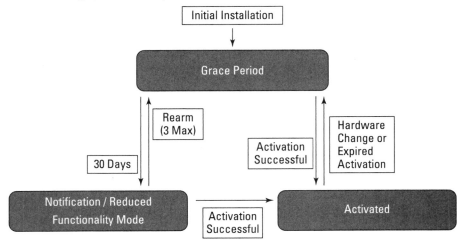

Managing Windows activation in your environment is highly dependent upon the licensing type you select. Choices include:

- Retail licensing
- OEM licensing
- Volume licensing

Understanding retail licensing

Retail products, or Fully Packaged Products (FPP), are versions purchased off the shelf of your local software store or from an online retailer. They come boxed with media and paperwork and are the most expensive of all licensing types. In addition to being the easiest to obtain, the primary advantage of a retail version of Windows is that its license may be transferred one time to another computer, which Microsoft defines as a motherboard. If your computer running Vista crashes or just becomes too old for your needs, you can retire it and reuse the existing retail Windows Vista license on a new computer. Because Microsoft defines the computer as a motherboard, you will also be able to upgrade your motherboard without having to purchase a new copy of Windows Vista. Although the Windows XP license did not explicitly specify the number of times, it was permissible to move a license, the Windows Vista license may be moved one time.

Retail licenses must be activated by the user through either the Internet or a phone call to Microsoft. Additionally each product key may only be activated against one machine. However, you may activate that product key against the one machine as many times as you like, for example, after reloading Windows. The exception is if you are transferring the license to another computer. In that case, you need to call Microsoft and explain the situation. The Microsoft licensing agent can provide you with a manual activation code. Once activated, retail versions of Vista remain activated unless multiple hardware changes are detected within a short period of time. Due to activation issues and expensive licensing, retail licensed media is seldom used to build deployment images.

Understanding OEM licensing

OEM is an acronym for original equipment manufacturer, which indicates OEM licensing is intended to be used by vendors who sell Windows Vista as part of a hardware purchase. Typically, vendors get very good pricing from Microsoft for OEM licenses in return for bundling the software with the hardware and purchasing large quantities. This price advantage is passed, at least in part, to the customer, which is this licensing technique's primary advantage. The easiest way to identify OEM licensing is by locating the product key sticker (usually found attached to the top of the computer).

OEM licensing has one major disadvantage, in that it is a nontransferable license. OEM licenses are tied to the hardware that they are bundled with and may not be reused on or transferred to other hardware. In its truest sense, the OEM license is tied to the motherboard of the computer. This means that if you decide to upgrade your motherboard or simply custom build a new computer for yourself, you will need to obtain a new Windows Vista license. Technically, Microsoft also may require you to purchase a new license if replacing a failed motherboard, although it is their current policy to allow reactivation for motherboard failures. Typically, you can call the activation number shown on the activation screen and explain the situation, at which time you would be given an activation code to enter manually.

Activation of OEM licenses is normally handled by the vendor before shipping out the computer and is referred to as OA, or OEM Activation. With OA, the vendor places a special marker in a BIOS table of the motherboard indicating that the computer was sold with a Windows Vista license. During installation, Windows Vista retrieves information from the licensing table (SLIC) and the OEM ID from the BIOS. This information is validated with a native digital certificate and, therefore, bypasses normal activation procedures.

The activation remains valid so long as the OEM ID and SLIC tables in the BIOS remain consistent. When using imaging to deploy to various hardware platforms, this may cause a problem as an OEM licensed image will not activate if moved to a hardware platform with a different OEM ID marker in the BIOS. Due to the large price discounts, OEM is a very popular licensing option among businesses and organizations. However, using OEM licenses to build images can generate a management nightmare. For this reason, most organizations do not use OEM media to build deployment images.

Understanding volume licensing

Volume licensing was designed for organizations with a large number of computers. Volume licenses are less expensive than their retail counterparts are, but are only sold as upgrades. This misunderstanding is common with Microsoft licensing. For a volume license of Windows Vista to be considered valid and legal, the computer must have a pre-existing full Windows license that satisfies the upgrade requirements for the version of Windows Vista you will be installing. Microsoft clearly states in its licensing documents and on its Web site that *all* Windows Volume licenses are upgrades.

Microsoft is beginning to use a new volume activation technology called Volume Activation 2.0. With Volume Activation 1.0, volume licensed products simply bypass activation altogether. Due to the piracy and key leakage in corporations, Microsoft now uses Volume Activation 2.0 for Vista and Server 2008.

NOTE Windows XP, Windows Server 2003, and Office 2007 and earlier continue to use Volume Activation 1.0.

Volume licenses offer better activation management for image-based deployments than retail or OEM activation. A large number of Windows Vista computers can be activated with a single product key, by using either a Multiple Activation Key (MAK) or the Volume Activation Key (VAK). Because of this, Microsoft provides what they call *re-imaging rights* with volume licenses. The main point of re-imaging rights is that a computer with a valid OEM or retail license may be imaged from a volume license-based image. To support the image building process, volume license media includes a full Windows installation rather than an upgrade installation. So although a volume license is only legal as an upgrade, the media can be used to perform a full install without having to perform an upgrade or check for a previous version of Windows.

When building customized images, you will almost certainly want to use Volume License media and product keys. For optimum activation management, it is sometimes considered best to purchase OEM licenses for the bulk of your computers (at the reduced price) and purchase a small quantity of volume licenses to build your deployment images. You may also purchase Enterprise Edition volume licenses to upgrade your Business OEM licenses, because Enterprise Edition is not available as an OEM license.

Understanding virtual machine licensing

It has long been established that for physical machines or virtual machines, licensing is the same. You cannot install Vista on a virtual machine without licensing and activating it just as you would a physical machine. However, there have been some changes as virtual machines become more commonplace.

The first good news for those working with virtual machines was the inclusion of four free desktop licenses with the Enterprise edition of Windows Vista. With a single license for Vista Enterprise, four installs in a virtual machine are provided in addition to the installation on the device. Enterprise customers can exercise their downgrade rights to run several different operating systems within virtual machines with Windows Vista Enterprise as the host.

Another licensing offering that has been recently unveiled is Windows Vista Enterprise Centralized Desktop (VECD). VECD provides unique licensing to run Windows in virtual machines (VMs) on servers for allowing remote access from users from their workstations or thin clients. VECD supports hosted desktop architectures, also known as centralized desktop or virtualized desktop infrastructures (VDI), and provides customers the flexibility to explore this particular model of desktop deployment. Windows VECD can be used with the Microsoft virtualization technologies or third-party partner solutions.

The new VECD licensing option provides for unlimited installs of Windows Vista Enterprise (or downgraded Windows operating system) on the server. It allows four concurrent accesses of virtual instances at a time and is licensed by access device (PC or thin client).

 **For details on the Windows Vista Enterprise Centralized Desktop, visit www. microsoft.com/virtualization/solution-product-vecd.mspx**

Managing Volume License Activation

When managing volume license activation of Windows Vista, you must choose to use Multiple Activation Key (MAK) activation, Key Management Services (KMS) –based activation, or a combination of both, whichever best meets your needs. To select an activation method, you first need to understand how each works.

Centralizing activation with KMS

The default activation method for volume license editions of Windows Vista is to use KMS. KMS is an organizational, centralized activation solution. The focus of KMS activation is to have a local server at your organization to activate the Windows Vista clients, as shown in Figure 3.2. The major advantage is that you only need to activate the KMS server itself with Microsoft, and after you activate your KMS server, no further communication with Microsoft is necessary to activate your Vista clients. In fact, you won't have to keep up activation counts either, because a KMS server will activate as many computers as many times as you want. Of course, proper licensing needs to be observed to remain legal, but activation should be much more manageable.

KMS volume activation works in two stages. In the first stage, you manually configure and activate a centralized server running the software licensing service. The software licensing service is included with Windows Vista and Server 2008 and is available as a download for Server 2003. You begin by changing the product key for the KMS server to the KMS key provided by Microsoft when purchasing volume licenses. Each key may activate up to six servers ten times each without having to call Microsoft for a manual exception. After the product key has been changed, the server must be activated either through the Internet or manually by calling Microsoft and entering the activation code by hand. For more details, see the KMS Walkthrough later in this chapter.

FIGURE 3.2

Example KMS activation infrastructure

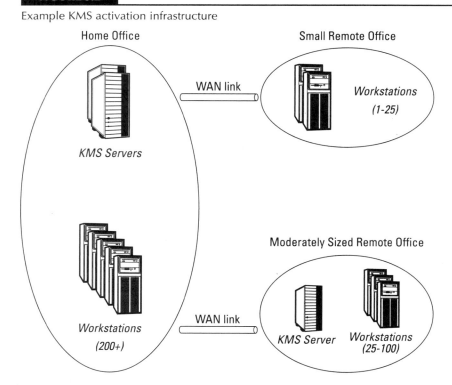

NOTE   Although Vista can host a KMS server, it can only activate other Windows Vista systems. If you need to activate Windows Server 2008 systems, you will need to host the KMS server on a Windows Server system. Further, a KMS key can be used to install up to six KMS host systems (if more are needed, requests can be made to Microsoft's Volume Activation Support Center).

Just as the new KMS key installed on the server dictates it will operate as a KMS server, there are KMS client keys that indicate a workstation or server should activate with a KMS server rather than against Microsoft activation servers. This key is referred to as the generic key and is included on the installation media in a file named pid.txt. To use this key, simply omit a product key when installing Windows and it will use the generic key and in turn attempt to activate with a KMS server. However, on which KMS server?

KMS server location

KMS servers are located by clients in one of two methods. The default and preferred method is to use DNS. When installing a KMS server key, the software licensing service will automatically attempt to register itself with its DNS server. If you are not using dynamic DNS, then you must manually create a DNS entry for the KMS service. When a KMS client requires activation, it performs a DNS query to locate a valid KMS server, as shown in Figure 3.3. Multiple KMS servers may be used and specified in DNS to provide fault tolerance.

FIGURE 3.3

A Windows Vista client activating against a KMS server

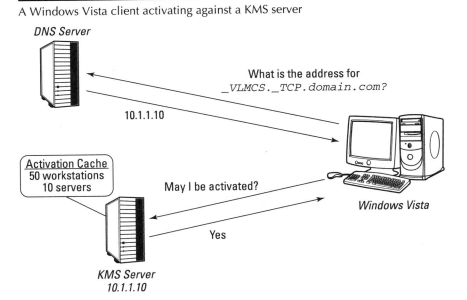

> **CAUTION** Although a KMS server will automatically register itself in DNS, it will not remove itself from DNS when retired. If you retire a KMS server or simply plan to move the KMS functionality to another server, be sure to remove the DNS entries manually for the KMS service referencing the server to be retired.

Second, clients can locate a KMS server by manual configuration. If DNS location of KMS servers is not feasible, then each client may be manually configured to access a KMS server. When manually specifying a KMS server, there is no fault tolerance. Therefore, we strongly recommend that you do not employ this manual configuration unless no other options are available. If manual configuration is necessary, you can use the `slmgr.vbs` script and its *skms* argument (discussed later in this chapter). This command line can be deployed as a simple task using a desktop management solution (such as Microsoft System Center Configuration Manager, Altiris Deployment Solution, or the KBOX Systems Management Appliance), or you can run this command as a startup script assigned through Group Policy.

Reviewing the limitations of KMS

Although KMS offers a relatively maintenance-free activation solution, it does have some shortcomings and limitations. Specifically, you must have a minimum number of systems requesting activations in order for it to succeed (activation threshold). You must also configure DNS manually if you have multiple domains or multiple KMS servers. Clients need to reactivate on a regular basis. Some OEM systems can have issues with upgrade verification functions. In this section, each of these issues will be discussed.

- Activation threshold
- DNS configuration
- Reactivation
- Upgrade verification

Understanding activation threshold requirements

The most notable is the *activation threshold*. The activation threshold is the minimum number of physical computers on a network that must request activation before activation will occur. The threshold for Server 2008 is five activation requests; for Windows Vista it is 25 activation requests. The intent is to ensure that KMS activation is only used in medium to large businesses, where proper licensing is more likely to be observed.

When the first computer requests activation from the KMS server, it responds with a count of one. The second is provided a count of two. When the fifth computer makes its request, it will succeed if that computer is Windows Server 2008; if that fifth computer is Windows Vista, it would not because its activation threshold is 25.

>  **NOTE** KMS can activate both physical and virtual computers, once the threshold of physical computers is met.

Understanding DNS requirements

Another thing you may need to watch out for in the current KMS implementation is the location of the required DNS entry. The entry in DNS for a KMS activation server is an SRV record in _VLMCS._TCP.yourdomain.com. Using this particular location in DNS poses two problems. One problem is that KMS entries are not site specific and may result in activations being performed across WAN links, even when a local KMS server is available. One possible solution is to use separate DNS domains for each physical location, each with its own list of available KMS servers.

Another problem is that the DNS entry is only automatically registered in the domain to which the KMS server is a member. If you are working in a multiple domain environment, you will need to create an SRV record underneath _VLMCS._TCP manually for each domain you would like the KMS server to service.

Understanding reactivation requirements

Another limitation, or feature, of KMS is the need for client reactivation. When activated using KMS servers, clients are only activated for 180 days and require reactivation to continue to be used. Under normal circumstances, the clients should manage the reactivations in the background without any administrative overhead. Until activated, clients will attempt to activate every two hours. After activated, clients attempt to reactivate every 7 days, which means that on a properly operating network with healthy clients and servers, workstations should always have at least 173 days of activation remaining.

This works well for environments where workstations are typically connected to the network. It even works well with portable computers as long as they connect to the network every few months. Remote locations that connect to the central office through VPN even work well with KMS activation and can help meet the activation threshold. What do not work well with KMS activation are portable computers that connect to the organizational network infrequently. For those, you might prefer to use MAKs as described in the next section.

Understanding upgrade verification functionality

Another less common issue associated with KMS activation is its upgrade verification functionality. As all volume licenses are upgrades, KMS activation will minimally attempt to verify that OEM computers were sold with Windows licenses. If the BIOS of a workstation contains a software licensing (SLIC) table, it must also contain a Windows marker in that table. This presumably means that the computer was sold with a valid Windows OEM license and that the volume license, which is an upgrade, is valid and should be activated. If your BIOS has an SLIC table but no Windows marker, activation against a KMS server will fail. The solution would be to use another activation technique or have your vendor correct the issue.

Leveraging MAK activation

When KMS activation doesn't meet your needs, Multiple Activation Key (MAK) activation can be used. MAK activation is similar to retail product activation in that each workstation must be activated against the Microsoft activation server. This process may be performed over the Internet or the phone.

The primary advantage to MAK activation is that it is relatively permanent. After a computer is activated using a MAK, clients are not required to reactivate at regular intervals. In fact, the only time reactivation should be necessary is after significant hardware or driver updates or after reinstallation of Windows.

With permanent activations, users can create images of the workstations after activating Windows, which bypasses any activation or validation procedures. To prevent this, Windows keeps track of the hardware on which it is installed. If a significant number of components change, then reactivation is required. Although the intent is to identify when the hardware has been changed, updating drivers can also cause a change to be detected. Each hardware component is assigned a weight. If the total weight of changed components reaches 25, then the computer must be reactivated. Table 3.1 shows the indexed hardware components along with their corresponding weights.

TABLE 3.1

Understanding Weight Values for Triggering Reactivation

Hardware Component	Weight
Physical System Hard Disk Drive Serial Number	11
BIOS Identifier	9
Processor	3
IDE Adapter	3
SCSI Adapter	2
MAC Address	2
Audio Adapter	2
RAM Amount (i.e. 0-512 MB, 512 MB-1 GB, etc.)	1
Display Adapter	1
CD/DVD Drive	1

Reviewing the limitations of MAK

Using MAK activation has its disadvantages as well. The primary disadvantage of MAK activation is that it uses an activation pool for each MAK issued.

When you purchase volume licenses and receive a MAK, Microsoft creates a pool of activations associated with your MAK. Although this number is loosely based on the number of volume licenses you purchase, it also is related to the licensing agreement you purchase them under. After the pool has been created on Microsoft's activation servers, you may activate computers with the corresponding MAK. Each activation decreases the pool count by one. The most notable implication here is that even reactivations will decrease the count by one. Therefore, if you frequently reload your computers, which will in turn require them to be reactivated, your activation pool may quickly become depleted.

However, there is not a one-to-one relationship between your activation pool and the number of licenses you purchased. In addition, the activation pool may be increased at any time by simply contacting Microsoft Activation. MAK activation is not intended to ensure that each activation represents a legal copy of Windows. Instead, it ensures that businesses and organizations are aware of the number of activations they are performing. In turn, it would be much more apparent if a key were to be leaked to the outside world or if it were being used inappropriately by unscrupulous staff members. If you legitimately reactivate computers very frequently, this can become quite a hassle, however. In this case, it is usually best to implement KMS activation.

The actual activation process for MAK activation can be performed by two methods, depending upon your network design. Figure 3.4 shows an example of independent MAK activation. Independent activation will be performed automatically if a MAK is used for installation and an Internet connection can be established. Otherwise, independent activation may be performed over the telephone. As the size of the network grows, phone activation becomes increasingly unpopular and ineffective.

FIGURE 3.4

Independent activation of MAK

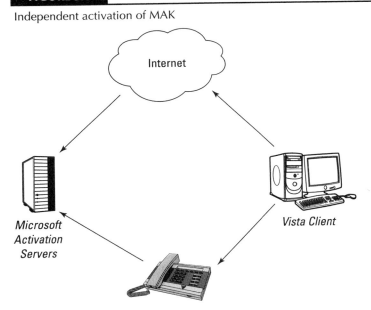

In some environments, Internet access may not be directly available and phone activation may not be practical. If the environment contains at least 25 workstations, KMS activation is typically preferred. If, however, there are not at least 25 workstations or MAK must be used for other reasons, proxy activation may be performed for MAK clients, as shown in Figure 3.5.

FIGURE 3.5

Proxy activation of MAK

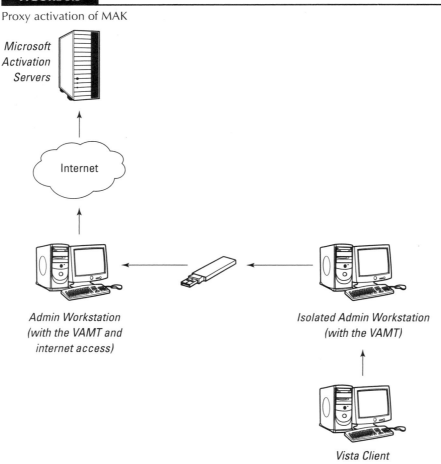

Microsoft
Activation
Servers

Internet

Admin Workstation
(with the VAMT and
internet access)

Isolated Admin Workstation
(with the VAMT)

Vista Client

To perform MAK proxy activation, the Volume Activation Management Tool (VAMT) is used. In proxy activation, the computer requiring activation generates a request that can then be passed on to Microsoft as a completely separate process. This feature eliminates the need for direct Internet access by the clients and eliminates the need to place a phone call for each workstation to be activated.

Comparing KMS and MAK activation

Licensing can be confusing, and there are several pros and cons to both the KMS and MAK approaches to activation. To help you make a decision, we've included Table 3.2, which highlights the differences between MAK activation and KMS activation.

TABLE 3.2

Comparing KMS and MAK Activation Methods

KMS Activation	MAK Activation
Clients use the default installation key	Clients must use a MAK installation key
Only the KMS server is activated with Microsoft	Each client is activated directly with Microsoft unless the VAMT is used
25 physical client minimum to implement for Vista, and 5 for Windows Server 2008	No minimum number required
No activation pool to manage allowing unlimited reactivations	Activation pool managed by Microsoft
Each activation is valid for 180 days	Activations are not time limited
DNS or manual client configuration is used to locate the KMS server	Internet access, a phone call or the VAMT is used for activation

Managing licensing and activation

As you can well expect, Microsoft provides various tools, technologies, and scripts with which you may manage licenses. This section introduces some tools, including the following:

- The Windows Software License Management Tool (`slmgr.vbs`)
- The Volume Activation Management Tool (VAMT)

Windows Software License Management Tool

All of the current license information for each workstation can be accessed using Windows Management Instrumentation, or WMI. In addition to querying information, you may also make changes and perform activations using WMI objects. Using WMI allows you to write scripts and applications tailored to the needs of your organization. However, Microsoft has also included with Vista a VBScript for basic management tasks. The script is referred to as the Windows Software License Management Tool and named `slmgr.vbs`.

When run without options, `slmgr.vbs` will provide you with a list of its available options (as shown in Figure 3.6). As you can see, the tool can both query the existing license and activation status as well as make changes, such as changing the product key. Although this script is very useful for individual machines and automation, it lacks the ability to report or act on multiple machines without further customizations of the script.

FIGURE 3.6

Windows Software License Management Tool options

```
Windows Script Host

Unrecognized option: -?
Windows Software Licensing Management Tool
Usage: slmgr.vbs [MachineName [User Password]] [<Option>]
         MachineName: Name of remote machine (default is local machine)
         User:     Account with required privilege on remote machine
         Password:   password for the previous account

Global Options:
-ipk <Product Key>
    Install product key (replaces existing key)
-ato
    Activate Windows
-dli [Activation ID | All]
    Display license information (default: current license)
-dlv [Activation ID | All]
    Display detailed license information (default: current license)
-xpr
    Expiration date for current license state

Advanced Options:
-cpky
    Clear product key from the registry (prevents disclosure attacks)
-ilc <License file>
    Install license
-rilc
    Re-install system license files
-rearm
    Reset the licensing status of the machine
-upk
    Uninstall product key
-dti
    Display Installation ID for offline activation
-atp <Confirmation ID>
    Activate product with user-provided Confirmation ID

                                              OK
```

Volume Activation Management Tool

For managing activations of multiple machines, use the Volume Activation Management Tool (VAMT). Although the tool is not included with Windows, it is a free download from Microsoft at www.microsoft.com/downloads/details.aspx?FamilyID=12044DD8-1B2C-4DA4-A530-80F26F0F9A99&displaylang=en. As shown in Figure 3.7, the VAMT allows you to see the activation status of many computers at once. It can also be used to initiate online activation or perform MAK proxy activation. Not only does the VAMT allow you to view volume license status, it also shows you the license and activation information for retail and OEM licensed computers.

To use the VAMT, you begin by adding computers. As you may have a large number of computers to manage, the VAMT requires that at least one group be created to organize these computers. This group is not related or associated with any security groups and is only used inside VAMT. With an initial group created, computers can be discovered by searching the Active Directory Domain Services or a Workgroup. You may also add individual computers by name or IP address, although in larger organizations it would not be practical to add all computers manually.

FIGURE 3.7

Volume Activation Management Tool user interface

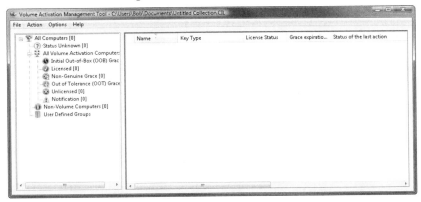

As computers are found and added to the tool, their licensing and activation status is queried and displayed. The list of computers and all of their information are stored locally as an XML file called the Computer Information List. Therefore, if you want to see this information from another computer, you can either re-create the groups and rediscover all of the workstations, or you may export the Computer Information List using VAMT, which can be imported on the other workstation.

After the Computer Information List is built or imported, the VAMT can be used to view licensing information, perform MAK proxy activation, initiate MAK independent activation, or manage MAKs. Importantly, the VAMT can query the MAK activation pool and report on the number of activations remaining on your MAK, a good thing to know before you actually run out!

> **NOTE** If the Windows Firewall is used, no configuration is required on the client computer because bidirectional TCP sessions that originate from the client computer are automatically allowed. You can configure the TCP port on the client computer or KMS host by using the `slmgr.vbs` script or setting registry values. An exception has been added to the Windows Firewall to facilitate opening the default port 1688.

Implementing KMS activation

Before attempting to deploy KMS activation, be sure to plan your layout ahead of time. One item to consider is the number of KMS servers to deploy. The load placed on a KMS server is very light when you consider that computers only communicate with the KMS servers every seven days during normal operating conditions. Additionally, the amount of information stored about activations is minimal. Lastly, the two network packets required for activation are very small, around 250 bytes, which should not overburden even the most modest of networks. In practice, a single KMS server should be able to handle well over 100,000 clients. In reality, you may want more than one server for redundancy reasons.

Fault tolerance is a strong reason to have multiple KMS servers. In most environments, we recommend that you implement at least two KMS servers. The only time this is not recommended is if your client count is not sufficient to keep both KMS servers at their 25-client minimum. In an environment with over 200 clients, for example, keeping both servers above their minimums should not pose a problem.

> **NOTE** For additional guidance, see the Microsoft home page for Volume Activation at `technet.microsoft.com/en-us/windowsvista/bb892849.aspx`. You can also find a video demonstration of how to set up KMS on Windows Server 2008 at `www.microsoft.com/downloads/details.aspx?FamilyID=bbf2eb61-2b30-4f2d-bccd-df53e220b8e9&displaylang=en`.

After you have properly planned your environment, implementing KMS activation is relatively straightforward process consisting of two primary steps. The first step is to deploy your KMS server or servers. If you plan to use Windows Server 2003 as a KMS server, you will first need to download and install the KMS Server component, the Software Licensing service. Windows Server 2008 and Vista include the necessary services, but for Windows Server 2003, an update for KMS 1.1 is online at `support.microsoft.com/kb/948003`.

> **NOTE** KMS for Windows Server 2003 v1.0 will activate only Vista RTM and Vista SP1 KMS clients. If hosting KMS on Windows Server 2003, make sure to install v1.1 of KMS to support activation of Windows Server 2008 KMS clients. You'll then need to install a new KMS key and then activate the KMS host before use.

As mentioned earlier, KMS hosted on a Windows Vista machine can activate only Windows Vista KMS clients; it cannot activate any editions of Windows Server 2008 as KMS clients. The Windows Server 2008 editions that can be activated by the KMS host depend on the KMS key that you install on the KMS host. It is also important to note that you will need to activate this KMS host before the host can begin accepting activation requests from KMS clients. The first step to configuring a KMS server is to install the KMS server activation key, which is obtained from Microsoft after purchasing Windows Server 2008 or Vista volume licenses. Although the Software Licensing service has WMI interfaces and an API you can leverage, the recommended method of configuring the activation key is by using the built-in VBScript, `slmgr.vbs`.

The following steps provide command line guidance for installing a VAK via VBScript:

1. **Launch a command prompt as administrator.**
2. **Use the following command to install your VAK key with the built-in VBScript:**
   ```
   slmgr.vbs -ipk <Product Key>
   ```
3. **Once the VAK key has been installed, the server must be activated either via the Internet or over the phone. If the server has Internet access, activate it with the following command:**
   ```
   slmgr.vbs -ato
   ```
   If Internet access is not available, run the following command and follow the prompts to activate by phone:
   ```
   slui.exe 4
   ```

After the VAK key has been installed and the server has been successfully activated, the KMS server should be ready to begin accepting incoming client requests. If you are using dynamic DNS, clients in the same domain as the KMS server may begin activating immediately. For other domains, you need to configure the server to register in additional domains, manually add DNS entries for the KMS server in other domains, or manually configure the clients to use the KMS server.

To configure the KMS server to register in additional domains, add and configure the following registry value using regedit:

Value: HKLM\Software\Microsoft\Windows NT\CurrentVersion \SL\
DnsDomainPublishList
Type: REG_MULTI_SZ
Value Data: <List of DNS domains to publish, each on a
separate line>

Instead of using DNS auto-discovery, the clients may also be manually configured for a specific KMS server and port. Static KMS server configuration is generally performed with the `slmgr.vbs` script. The most efficient way of implementing this would be though a startup script or similar mechanism. To configure a client for a specific KMS server manually, use the following command:

```
slmgr.vbs -skms <KMS Server>:<port>
```

Although using a fully qualified domain name for the KMS server, IP addresses and NetBIOS names also work. The port number is only required if using a nonstandard port number.

Implementing MAK independent activation

Implementing MAK independent activation is a very simple process for most scenarios. The key step in deploying MAK independent activation is configuring each client with the MAK. This is generally performed through one of the following ways:

- Manually during installation
- Using an unattended answer file
- With the System Control Panel applet
- Using a script
- Using the VAMT

If providing the MAK during installation manually, the computer will activate automatically and no additional administration is necessary. When using the System applet of the Control Panel, a simple process of clicking a link and typing in the MAK is required after installation. Although this requires minimal effort, performing this action on hundreds or thousands of computers is very inefficient. By providing the key in an unattended answer file or by using the `slmgr.vbs` script to configure the MAK, deployment can be automated so that no administrative effort is required during the deployment process to configure MAK activation. Finally, the VAMT also has the capability to install a MAK on any recognized workstations.

NOTE   **Regardless of the method chosen to install the MAK, the VAMT can both verify that the activation is successful and monitor the number of activations remaining in the activation pool.**

Implementing MAK proxy activation

When using MAK activation where a direct Internet connection is not available to clients, MAK proxy activation can be used. To activate a computer using MAK proxy activation, use of the VAMT is required. The process begins by configuring clients to use a MAK. The options for installing a MAK are the same as for independent activation. The difference is that the workstations will not be able to activate themselves after being configured for MAK activation.

Begin activation by first using the VAMT to discover the necessary clients requiring proxy activation. If necessary, this tool may be used to install a MAK as well. After the necessary clients appear in the VAMT, you may use the tool to obtain the Installation ID (IID) from the computer, send it to Microsoft, and obtain a Confirmation ID (CID). After the Confirmation ID has been obtained, the VAMT can be used to activate the client using the Confirmation ID.

Notification Experience and Reduced Functionality Mode (RFM)

The focus so far has been on ensuring that your computers are properly activated. However, what happens when activation can't be obtained or maintained? The general result is that the computer enters a grace period and then eventually into Reduced Functionality Mode.

Computers can enter the grace period for several reasons. Initially, the computer will be in a grace period immediately following installation until activation can be performed. After initial activation, MAK activated computers may enter their grace period if substantial hardware changes are noticed. In this case, Windows assumes it has been moved to new hardware and must reactivate to validate it is a legal copy. KMS clients may enter a grace period if they fail to reactivate 180 days following the last successful reactivation. While in the grace period, the computer functions normally except for occasional reminders that the computer needs to be activated.

Volume license editions of Windows will remain in a grace period for up to 30 days. If hardware is significantly modified on Retail or OEM licenses, the grace period is only three days. If activation is not performed during the grace period, the computer will see the Notification Experience (if Windows Vista Service Pack 1 or later is installed) or Reduced Functionality Mode (if the computer does not have Service Pack 1 or later installed).

Introducing the notifications-based experience

If a Windows Vista SP1 and Windows Server 2008 system are not activated within the grace period, persistent notifications will alert users of the need to activate. While in the notifications-based experience, the system will function normally, with the following exceptions:

- The desktop background will be black.
- A KMS host cannot activate or renew KMS clients.
- Windows Update installs only critical updates (optional updates and those marked as "Genuine Only" will not be made available).

Experiencing Reduced Functionality Mode

Prior to Windows Vista SP1, if activation was not performed during the grace period, the computer enters Reduced Functionality Mode (RFM), shown in Figure 3.8.

FIGURE 3.8

User interface in Reduced Functionality Mode

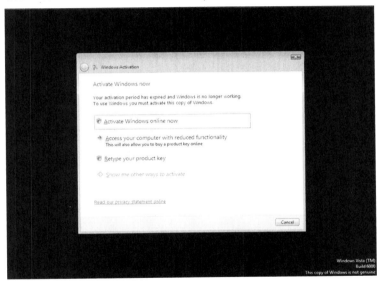

There are two flavors of Reduced Functionality Mode, depending upon the reason for entering RFM. If activation is not performed after the initial grace period, reactivation isn't performed at least 210 days after a KMS activation, or reactivation isn't performed after significant hardware change, the computer will enter out-of-grace RFM. In out-of-grace RFM the following limitations apply:

- One hour logon time limit
- No access to built-in games
- No access to premium features (such as Aero, ReadyBoost, and BitLocker)

If the Windows Genuine Advantage program detects a blocked key code or modified activation files, the computer will enter non-genuine RFM. Non-genuine RFM includes the following restrictions:

- Aero and ReadyBoost are not available
- Some content from the Microsoft Download center is not available

Resolving the notification experience and Reduced Functionality Mode

The first option is to activate Windows over the Internet immediately. If the computer needs to be reloaded or was only a test computer, you may reload the computer and format the hard drive to gain another 30 days of initial grace period. If in RFM, and there is a need to recover data from the workstation, it can be booted into Safe Mode or the `explorer.exe` process can be launched manually to provide a standard desktop with which any necessary data may be moved.

It does occasionally happen where immediate activation or reload are not options. The workaround in this situation is to use the `slmgr.vbs` script to re-arm the computer. Similar to how Sysprep will reset the grace period back to 30 days, the `slmgr.vbs` re-arm command performs the same function much quicker and without resetting the network and licensing information. Keep in mind that a computer may only be re-armed three times. Assuming that the computer was imaged from a Syspreped image file, two more re-arms would be allowed. For this reason, it is always recommended that image files be Syspreped no more than twice before re-creating the image from scratch. With a properly designed unattended answer file, that should be a relatively simple process.

 An exception to the rule, Windows Vista Enterprise SP1 can be re-armed up to five times.

Summary

While in the end it goes relatively unnoticed, a properly designed activation plan can prevent a lot of administration later. KMS activation is the recommended activation method for medium to large deployments as well as testing environments due to the unlimited client reactivations where the MAK activation pool can add significant management overhead. For more disconnected environments, MAK activation does provide a semi-permanent activation mechanism. If activation is not properly implemented and maintained, computers will begin to enter notification or reduced functionality modes and cause both a loss of productivity and additional work for technical staff. As usual, a little work upfront can save time in the end. This is sometimes referred to as *the 80/20 rule*. Meaning, spend 80 percent of your time to prepare and you'll only have to spend 20 percent of the time to administer once the service is in place.

Part II

Customizing the Deployment Process

Time to get to work! This portion of the book focuses on the specific use of the tools provided to develop and deploy Windows Vista. While the very capable tools offered by Microsoft are explained in detail, several third-party utilities and alternatives are also brought to light.

Windows Installer is covered in detail to prepare you for managing the custom installation of applications in your environment. Tools and methods available for handling user data and settings are detailed in Chapter 5, while Chapter 6 offers an explicit look at the tools for managing images. With your image created and customized, the remaining chapters focus on deployment covering the Microsoft Deployment Toolkit and Windows Deployment Services.

Chapter 4

Working with Windows Installer

The Windows Installer Service (WIS) is an engine for the installation, maintenance, and removal of software for Microsoft Windows systems. Much more than a new setup file format, WIS introduces a number of new features and challenges for administrators that warrant special attention.

Although not new to Windows Vista, it will be important to understand WIS in order to prepare applications for deployment effectively. There is a lot to know about Windows Installer, and it has become a specialty area that many administrators now focus on as a core area of expertise. It has also been regularly updated to provide improvements and new features. This chapter will introduce WIS and its architecture, management, and some best practices to keep in mind along the way.

Introducing Windows Installer

Most everyone who is involved in software management, be it software distribution or packaging, has heard of the Microsoft Windows Installer service (WIS). This powerful service has been created by Microsoft to help manage the software lifecycle on Windows systems. With the release of Windows Vista, Windows Installer is in its fourth edition. Version 4.0 was been specifically designed to run on Windows Vista and Windows Server 2008. Windows Installer version 3.1 runs on earlier operating systems back to Windows 2000. Therefore, version 3.1 will work with Windows 2000 Service Pack 3 and above, Windows XP Service Pack 2 and Windows Server 2003. If you're running an earlier version of Windows, you can obtain older versions of Windows Installer from Microsoft's Web site. The latest version 4.5 supports Windows Server 2003 and later, so for most environments, this one version will provide a consistent standard that may be applied across all client and server systems.

 For a full list of Windows Installer versions and its corresponding operating system, go to `http://msdn2.microsoft.com/en-us/library/Aa371185`.

The Windows Installer redistributable download can be found at `http://msdn2.microsoft.com/en-us/library/aa372856(VS.85).aspx`.

If you're aware of Windows Installer, you're most likely aware of some of its features. First and foremost, Windows Installer provides a consistent, single point of interaction for commercial software or in-house application installations. This is a major change from the pre–Windows Installer days when system administrators and packagers had to deal with a multitude of installation tools, each with its own particular commands and its own particular idiosyncrasies. Using Windows Installer for installations is one way to reduce administrative overhead for software management because you only have to learn one single installation method. Of course, not all software or all in-house applications are integrated to the Windows Installer service and this despite the fact that it has been around for a few years since it was introduced. This is one reason why you may want to use a packaging tool to prepare and customize your own Windows Installer installations.

Second, Windows Installer provides a set of features that tie in very closely with the software lifecycle. As you know, software has its own lifecycle, and managing this lifecycle after a piece of software has entered into your network is important. This lifecycle and the relationship the Windows Installer service has with it are illustrated in Figure 4.1.

The third and most important aspect of the Windows Installer service is that it provides a series of features that were heretofore unavailable through conventional installation systems. Much of this functionality is due to the fact that Windows Installer actually stores an installation database on the target computer system each time it installs a piece of software. This database contains information about the installation, the components that were installed by the installation, and the way those components were configured during installation. This gives WIS the ability to provide a comprehensive set of features in support of this installation.

For example, because WIS includes the computer's preinstallation state in its database, it can support complete installation rollbacks in the case of a problem during installation, returning the target system to the same state it was in before the installation began. In addition, because it stores the software configuration in its database, it can automatically repair an installation should a problem occur with the program. This repair mode can be run through a maintenance mode, but it is also automatically run each time a user launches a program through its shortcuts or through opening an associated file type (such as a document generated by the program). For managed environments, it can automatically elevate a user's privileges during installation to ensure that the installation will occur properly in locked-down environments. That's because Windows Installer is a service that runs in the background and, therefore, always is available. Finally, it can completely remove an application from a system when it is time to retire or upgrade a software program from a network.

These are only some of the features that make Windows Installer a powerful installation system. These features are part of the reason why many strive to integrate all of the installations to this service. Most, but not all, new software products on the market are now provided as MSI packages for these reasons.

FIGURE 4.1

Understanding the interaction of MSI In the software lifecycle

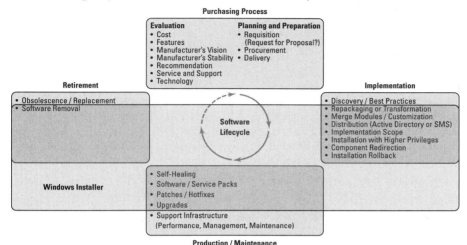

Integrating installations with the Windows Installer service

Taking advantage of WIS does not mean that you need to go out and buy a new version of all of the software products in your network. An average-sized network, say between 500 and 5,000 users, will most likely have between 100 to 300 different software programs and applications in use. Some organizations of this size may have over 1,000 such programs in use. This is before the organization performs a software rationalization — a formal exercise that reviews and justifies the existence of each software product or application within the network. If you haven't done so yet, it is highly recommended that you perform such a rationalization in your network. To do this, you must get rid of any programs that duplicate features or multiple versions of the same program. This greatly reduces your software administration burden and potentially reduces licensing costs. Rationalization is an important aspect of any Vista migration project because it helps significantly reduce the application preparation workload.

It is unrealistic to expect any organization to be able to simply go out and purchase new versions of each software product in their network to have versions that are integrated with the Windows Installer service. That's because of several reasons:

- The cost would be too prohibitive.

- New versions of your in-house applications aren't available on the market; you have to build them and doing so may also be cost-prohibitive.

- Some manufacturers simply don't offer new versions of their products.

- Though they are becoming fewer and fewer, some manufacturers still haven't integrated their software products to Windows Installer.

For these reasons, you have to consider your options for moving to Windows Installer–integrated installations. The first thing you should do is categorize your software into the following three program types:

- **Native Windows Installer software:** This software includes any product that bears the Designed for Windows Vista, Server 2008, Server 2003, Windows XP, or Windows 2000 logos or any software that does not include this logo but has been set up to be installed through Windows Installer. Obviously, software that supports the logo may be more reliable than software that does not include it. That's because the logo specifications include much more than Windows Installer integration.

- **MSI-Integrated Corporate applications:** These new versions of your corporate applications should be integrated to the Windows Installer service in all cases.

- **Repackaged Legacy software:** This software encompasses all products that are not upgraded and use an installation system other than Windows Installer. They should be repackaged to be integrated to this service. This also includes corporate applications that do not require recoding or cannot be recoded as well as legacy commercial software.

Examining the Windows Installer service

Like all system services, Windows Installer is a service listed in the Services section of the Computer Management console. This service is set to a manual startup and is activated only when you launch an installation that is integrated to it. This automatically starts the service and runs Windows Installer to perform the installation. You should not change the settings of this service because they are controlled by the operating system.

In addition, you need to know which version of the Windows Installer service you are running. Obviously, the newest version includes the most comprehensive feature set. To find out which version you are running, search for MSI.DLL in the Windows folder. After you locate it, you can verify its properties to view which version you are running. Figure 4.2 shows the version number for this file.

Another and even easier way to find out which version you have installed is to simply type one of the following commands at the command prompt:

```
msiexec /?
msiexec /help
```

This will display a dialog box that lists all of the switches supported by the command as well as display the installed version of the service (see Figure 4.3).

FIGURE 4.2

Identifying the Windows Installer service version in Windows XP and Vista

FIGURE 4.3

Getting help from `msiexec`

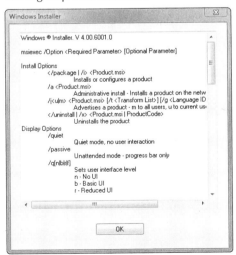

 A complete list of the switches supported by the `msiexec` command on Windows can be found at `http://support.microsoft.com/kb/314881`.

Windows security and software installations

Like Windows NT and Windows 2000, Windows XP, Windows Vista, Windows Server 2003, and Windows Server 2008 use the NTFS file system. The advantage of this system over its predecessors is that every object stored in the system includes *attributes*. These attributes can contain security features — security features that are different for users, power users, and administrators. The greatest limitations are applied to users. Because a user's main responsibility is to operate the system, they only need to read and execute permissions for system components. By nature, NTFS protects system and application files by restricting access to these files.

However, in Windows NT, users were given too much leeway. This is because software integration was not controlled effectively. Many software products would install into (and require constant read and write usage of) the system directories. Giving users these rights would open the system to potential damage and therefore higher support costs.

Realizing this, Microsoft released the Zero Administration Kit for Windows NT. This kit provided corporations with the tools to increase system "lock down" to limit user access further. But this system was complex to use, and organizations often had to invest heavily into its management.

With Windows 2000, Microsoft changed the nature of the NTFS system lock down. It added further restrictions to users and changed the way applications work with the operating system. As a comparison, users in Windows NT have the same rights that power users do in Windows 2000. Today, actual users have significant restrictions within the operating system directories and within application directories.

In Windows XP/2003, Microsoft added more complete support for protected software operation within the operating system itself, such as support for side-by-side dynamic link library (DLLs) in memory. Now with Windows Vista, Microsoft has updated the system to provide further protection for registry components along with the file components that belong to applications running on the system.

Software that follows the most recent guidelines for the Designed for Windows Logo program (see above) should not install any component in the system directories. That's because all software components now reside in the application's own directory in Program Files. In addition, every component that is modifiable by a user (including configuration settings and user preferences) is stored within the directories containing the user profile. Here users can read and write to their hearts' content. This is a good strategy because critical system and application files are protected for all users. If users damage something related to an application within their own profile, you can usually repair it by erasing the profile and re-creating it. Of course, care must be taken during this operation because the profile doesn't only store application preferences but also user preferences and sometimes user documents. It is a good idea to make sure that you back up and restore documents and preferences once the profile is recreated.

Windows resource protection

Since Windows 2000, Windows has included Windows File Protection (WFP). This feature stores a backup copy of many critical system files (within the `%SystemRoot%\System32\DLLCache` folder). A special agent is constantly watching the system directories. If a Windows system file such as a DLL is deleted or replaced, this agent will automatically correct the situation by restoring the original and proper file. Many files are contained within the cache folder and are restored quickly without notification. However, due to space considerations, Windows may attempt to pull an original file from the installation media (for which you may be prompted if it is not available at the time).

Files protected by WFP may be updated only by OS upgrades, service packs, and hot fixes released by Microsoft. To protect the operating system further, WFP allows only operating system operations to update files within the DLLCache folder.

> **NOTE**   **Windows Installer cannot update protected files. If a Windows Installer package attempts to update such files, it will return error 1933. For this reason, setups that are tightly integrated with the operating system, such as Windows Media Player and Internet Explorer, are not provided as MSI setups from Microsoft.**

In Windows Vista, Microsoft updated Windows File Protection and renamed it Windows Resource Protection (WRP). Along with the protection of system files, WRP now offers protection for key registry entries. If Windows Installer encounters any files or registry keys that attempt to modify protected areas of the system, it will log a warning and simply skip over the offending component. This is different from the behavior of Windows Installer with WFP. With WFP, Windows Installer would request that WFP install the offending file, but with WRP, the component is simply not installed and the installation proceeds without error. This may cause products to work erratically once the installation is complete. This is one more reason why applications should be updated to Windows Installer version 4 before they are deployed to Windows Vista systems.

Managing software in a locked-down environment

The new file structure for application location, application preference location, and the Windows File Protection make it even more difficult to update and install software on Windows systems, especially remotely. Of course, users who have local administration rights can install anything on a system. Standard users, who are on the lowest end of the totem pole in terms of installation rights, cannot install anything on the system because they are granted generic user access only.

Although this makes for more stable PCs, it does present a challenge for administrators: they need a proper vehicle to install software in locked-down environments, or grant all users administrative rights. Running a network where all users have administrative rights is like running a Windows 95 network, because you don't gain any of the advantages of a locked-down environment.

Although many desktop management solutions provide a client agent to address this issue, native support is also provided in Windows by Windows Installer because it can provide elevated rights to install software packages within the security context of the user. This makes it possible to have a locked-down environment and still allow installations in secure contexts. Of course, this does not solve all of the problems related to user installation rights, especially for those related to workstations or servers that are not connected to the network, but it does go a long way toward solving problems related to network-based software installations in a locked-down environment.

Understanding the Capabilities of Windows Installer

By now, you're starting to realize how many features and functionalities the Windows Installer service can offer you. Here's a more complete list of these features:

- **Restore the target system to its preinstallation state or rollback:** This is one of the nicest aspects of Windows Installer because it tracks the state of a computer system before it begins a software installation. If for some reason an installation fails, WIS returns the system to the previous state, making sure that failed installations do not destabilize systems. This is done through the creation of temporary files during the installation. These files are only available during the installation; once complete, you must use the uninstall command to remove the application (/x).

- **Provide application resiliency:** This gives WIS the ability to check the health of an application and repair or reinstall damaged pieces of the application. This requires access to the original installation source (or a copy available at a specified location) because the repair requires access to the original installation files.

- **Clean uninstallations:** Because WIS tracks all of the components making up an application during its installation, it can safely remove the application from a system, even if the application shares components with other applications on the same system. WIS also tracks which applications share the components and keeps them if there are still applications that require them on the system.

- **Control reboots during installation:** WIS gives you the ability to either call for or suppress reboots during the installation of your software. For example, this feature lets you install a required component, such as the Microsoft SQL Server Desktop Engine (MSDE), reboot the computer if required, and continue with the installation of your product.

- **Componentization or separation of the components of an installation into discreet units that are treated as whole components by the Windows Installer service.**

- **Source list control:** Windows Installer lets you control the source locations for the installation. Each time a package is updated, WIS updates the folder from which it is updated and adds it to the source list if it isn't already there. The next time it needs to repair an installation, it will look to this folder for an installation source. For increased resiliency, several source locations may be specified for any one MSI package. Source list control is a very important part of WIS package management.

- **Merge module inclusion:** You can include mini-packages into your own software installation. For example, this is how you would include MSDE into your own package.

- **Command line options for installations:** Because WIS uses a single command line tool for installations — the `msiexec.exe` command — it allows you to use standard command line structures to install products. In addition, the command line supports the modification of MSI packages through transforms and/or patches, letting you use one single interface for installation, patching, and customization. The `msiexec` command also includes several levels of logging, which make it quite practical to use when you are having problems with an installation. Because WIS installations are performed through the `msiexec` command, `setup.exe` commands are no longer really needed, though they are often included in applications to make the install more transparent to users. A WIS installation that uses a `setup.exe` normally installs any required prerequisites in support of the installation and then simply calls `msiexec` with the proper switches.

- **Taking the extensive command line support provided by Windows Installer even further, you may also specify the value of any public properties right at the command line:** Public properties act as variables that dictate the behavior of a Windows Installer Setup. There are several common public properties that control everything from how an application appears in the Add/Remove Programs applet to how a required reboot should be handled. Further, authors may dictate their own public properties to allow custom command line option support for their Windows Installer setups.

- **Group Policy control:** Windows includes a series of Group Policy settings both at the user and at the system level for the control and operation of the Windows Installer service.

- **Installation on demand:** Because this function lets you choose whether a software component is installed during the software installation, it speeds up installations. With Installation on Demand, the feature or function that was not installed originally can be installed when it is first used by the user. This is another reason why original installation sources must be maintained on the network. Be careful with this feature because many users find it extremely annoying to see the Windows Installer service launch when they are in the middle of using a product simply because the feature wasn't installed originally.

- **Application advertisements:** This function is much like the Installation on Demand function, but performs even faster because all it does is place the shortcut to the application on the user's desktop. The application isn't actually installed until either the user clicks the shortcut to use it the first time or the user tries to open a document associated with the application.

- **Administrative installations:** This allows you to perform a single network installation, which would then let users install the software without access to the original CD version. WIS provides one single standard format for these administrative installations.

Understanding the Windows Installer architecture

The Windows Installer package is everything that is required to perform the installation of a software product. The first part of the package is the .MSI file. This file includes all of the instructions for the installation. Along with the instruction file, you also have CAB files, which are compressed files that contain the software parts to be installed. These software parts do not necessarily need to be compressed into CAB files; they can simply be stored in a folder structure that is distributed with the .MSI file. In addition, the software parts could also be contained in CAB files that are stored within the .MSI file. It all depends on your preference based on the size of the bits that make up the software product. For example, a small program, such as WinZip Computing's WinZip compression tool, could be stored within a single .MSI file. On the other hand, a very large program such as Microsoft Office 2007 will contain an .MSI file, several .CAB files, and separate components as well, because the bits making up this installation take up several hundred megabytes.

Within the .MSI file is the installation database — a relational database that the Windows Installer service uses to perform the installation. The information in this database is hierarchical in nature and includes the following:

- **Product**: This is the highest layer of the hierarchy. It usually identifies what needs to be installed, for example Microsoft Office 2007. The product is identified by WIS through its product code, which is a globally unique identifier (GUID).

- **Features:** A product is composed of features. Features are units of installation that can be discretely selected during installation. For example, in Microsoft Office 2007, Microsoft Word, Microsoft Excel, Microsoft PowerPoint, and so on are all features, and users can select or deselect them when installing Office. Features can also include subfeatures. For example, in Microsoft Excel, the Help files are a subfeature. The same applies to Excel Add-ins, Sample Files, and so on. Each item that can be selected or deselected for installation is a feature or subfeature. Features can be shared across applications. One good example is the Spell Checker in Microsoft Office. It is shared between all Office applications, but it is not automatically removed when a feature that uses the shared feature is uninstalled. For example, if you want to remove Excel from a system, but keep Word, Windows Installer would not automatically remove the Spell Checker. In fact, WIS will not remove a shared component until it knows that no other installed product requires it. That's because it tracks which product uses which shared features.

- **Components:** Features are made up of components. A component is a collection of files, registry keys, shortcuts, and other types of resources (for example, an icon image) that make a feature work on a computer. As far as Windows Installer is concerned, components are single units that are identified with special GUIDs called the *component code* within the installation database. Because they are considered as single, cohesive units, components do not share files or any other object. If two components on the same computer include the same file, both will maintain a copy of that file on the system. Treating application objects as components helps speed up the operation of Windows Installer because it limits the number of items WIS needs to keep track of. Components can be shared between applications, but if two applications need to rely on the same component, both must include it in its installation. When the second product is installed, Windows Installer realizes that the component is already on the system and does not re-install it.

Instead, it adds a special counter called a refcount to the database to identify how many products use the component. The refcount ensures that the component is not removed until all the products that need it are removed from the system. Of course, because the identification of a component is based on its GUID, two applications sharing the same component must be sure to make use of the same GUID to have the component properly managed. A good example of how a component should be structured is related to all elements that a product will want to store in the HKEY_CURRENT_USER registry key. All of these elements should be contained within the same component because this way, when a new user tries to access the product, the resiliency features of WIS will automatically identify that these elements are missing from the user's profile and add them as a single group.

■ **Key paths**: Key paths are associated with components. Each component has a key path that the Windows Installer service associates with the component. Key paths identify whether or not a component is fully installed. This is through a special file or setting included in the key path. Windows Installer uses the key path to determine the health of each component within a product. If a key path is missing or incomplete, WIS can trace it back to the feature it belongs to and reinstall the entire feature or subfeature. This engine provides self-healing for WIS installations. The time it takes to repair an application depends on the number and size of the components within a given feature.

While some people who author Windows Installer setups choose to create one feature per component, it is not necessary to do so since a feature can be made up of multiple components. In addition, the same component can be used by multiple features. To ensure that self-repairs are not overly lengthy in time, authors have to balance the number of components they include in each feature with the number of features or subfeatures they include in their products. For example, if all components were stored in one feature, any self-repair operation would result in a reinstallation of the entire application.

Figure 4.4 illustrates the installation dialog box for Microsoft Office 2007. As you can see, Office 2007 is made up of multiple features and subfeatures. Users can discretely select each feature and subfeature during an interactive installation. In addition, they can determine how the feature or subfeature will be installed.

As shown in Figure 4.5, four choices are available for how you may choose to install each feature or subfeature:

■ **Run from My Computer:** This option installs the feature, but not all of its subfeatures.

■ **Run All from My Computer:** This option installs the feature and all of its subfeatures.

■ **Installed on First Use:** This option installs the feature only if you choose to use it while working with the product.

■ **Not Available:** This option does not install the feature.

FIGURE 4.4

Reviewing the makeup of the Microsoft Office 2007 Windows Installer package

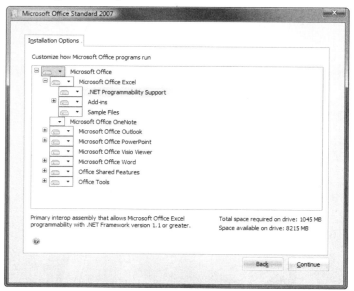

Run all from My Computer is often the best option to select because you are guaranteed that whatever you may need from this feature and its subfeatures is available to you whenever you need it. Installed on First Use is sometimes used in networks, but does result in annoying pop-ups of the Windows Installer dialog box while users are attempting to work with the software. When local drive space is an issue, this capability may make sense but is generally not a good idea. In addition, this option requires constant access to the installation source files. This is not very useful for mobile users who may not be connected to the network when they need the feature. For this feature to work for them, you would need to store the setup files locally (which defeats the purpose of saving drive space). While choosing Run All from My Computer may install unnecessary features and components, by far the option gives the most pleasant experience to the user. For this reason, it is often the best feature to use. If you decide you prefer not to use this option, make sure that whatever is not installed is set to Not Available. This ensures that no installations need to take place while users are working with a product.

FIGURE 4.5

Viewing feature installation options

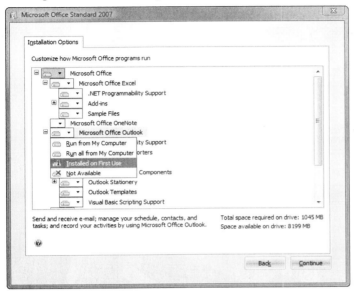

Reviewing the Windows Installer database structure

As mentioned previously, Windows Installer installations are based on the .MSI file that is included with the product setup. This file is nothing more than a set of installation instructions that are organized in tables within a relational database. Each table is defined by the Windows Installer Software Development Kit (SDK). This SDK includes Orca, an MSI database editor that has limited functionality. In an organization that invests in an Enterprise Software Packaging strategy, you will require much more comprehensive tools to view, edit, and create MSI installation databases.

The tables found in the MSI database contain a series of information types within rows and columns. For example, one commonly used table is the Launch Conditions table. This table sets out the conditions under which an installation may or may not be executed. A good example of this is when you create a package for a product that is designed to run on workstations and not on servers. In this case, you would put in a launch condition that verifies the operating system onto which the package is being installed, and if the OS query returned Windows Server 2008, 2003, or 2000, you would display a message stating that this is an unsupported OS and abort the installation process.

The tables that make up the body of an MSI database are the sequence tables. Sequence tables tell Windows Installer what to do during an installation and in which order it should be done. A common sequence of events is the verification of the Launch Conditions, and then if they are met, the copying of installation files, the modification of the registry, and the removal of temporary files, such as those used for rollback.

There are three types of sequence tables, each tied to a specific Windows Installer service feature. The first is the Admin table type. Admin tables are used for administrative installations or installation of a product into a network share to create a remote installation point for the product. The second type of sequence table is the Advertisement. This table type is used to advertise products and features. Advertised features and products are not actually installed until the user activates it by trying to use it. The final type is Installation and is the most commonly used sequence table because it controls how a product is installed. The Installation type can be used for either interactive or silent, background installations.

Along with each sequence table type, you have two associated subtables: InstallUISequence and InstallExecuteSequence. The first, InstallUISequence, is used for interactive installations and includes all of the dialog boxes that are displayed to the user during the interactive installation. The second, InstallExecuteSequence, lists the actual steps to perform during the installation. The InstallExecuteSequence table includes a column called Actions, which includes a set of predefined actions that the Windows Installer service can perform. Some of these actions include:

- Check for execution requirements (Launch Conditions)
- Search for previous versions of the product in order to upgrade it
- Create folders
- Create shortcuts
- Install or delete files
- Install or remove registry keys
- Move or copy existing files to new locations
- Install, remove, start, or stop Windows services
- Install or uninstall Common Language Runtime (CLR) assemblies within the .NET Framework
- Install or remove ODBC drivers and data sources
- Register COM classes or COM+ applications
- Modify environment variables

NOTE   When running a Windows Installer package silently, the InstallUISequence is not used. Therefore, if you are customizing an MSI setup that you intend to deploy in a silent, automated manner it is important to place such customizations in the InstallExecuteSequence table.

Windows Installer supports *custom actions*, or actions you define yourself. In support of custom actions, Windows Installer can execute VBScript or JScript code, run commands from the command line, or call functions that may have been defined in a special dynamic link library (DLL) that you programmed. Custom actions are very powerful and add almost any installation action to the Windows Installer service.

Finally, another table that is commonly edited by administrators within MSI packages is the Property table. Properties can be used to define installation variables. They work much like environment variables do in Windows itself. For example, the Property table helps you ensure that an installed product is available to only a single user or to all users of a computer. This is done through the ALLUSERS property which will tell WIS to either install product settings on a per user per machine basis. Note that property names are case sensitive so allusers does not mean the same thing to WIS as ALLUSERS (public properties are always named in uppercase letters). Properties can be applied during installation in one of two ways. The first is through the `msiexec.exe` command, but this command only works with *public* properties. The second is through another special WIS file type called a transform. Transforms can be used to manipulate any property; in fact, transforms can be used to manipulate any of the tables in an MSI package.

Another useful property is ROOTDRIVE. By default, WIS installs products into the drive with the freest space. If your workstation drives are split into more than one disk partition, for example, C: for system files and D: for data, and the D: drive has more free space than the C: drive does, WIS will automatically install programs on the D: drive. Specifying this public property with an explicit value (for example, ROOTDRIVE=C:\) will ensure that your packages are always installed on the C: drive.

The few tables mentioned here are not comprehensive lists of all the tables available within a Windows Installer database. There are quite a few tables within this database structure. For example, other tables include:

- Application design
- Feature
- Component
- Feature components
- Directory
- File copy
- File
- Media
- Registry entry
- Installation procedure
- User interface
- Desktop integration
- Installation validation

You will not need to understand all tables unless you choose to author an MSI setup without the aid of an authoring or repackaging tool.

Getting familiar with Windows Installer file types

All of the installation options are available programmatically as well. This is where the different file formats for the Windows Installer service come into play. You're already familiar with the MSI file extension. This is the file that contains the installation database and can also contain compressed CAB files, application settings, and other resources that make up the package required to install the product. Windows Installer also uses other file formats to perform special operations during installation.

The second most prevalent Windows Installer file type is the MST or *transform* file. The transform is a secondary file that is tied to the MSI database during execution to modify the behavior of the installation. One strong reason to make use of transform files is to adhere to the highly recommended practice of never modifying an MSI file received from a manufacturer. These files follow a specific structure and include specific content that will be required when it is time to upgrade or even simply remove a file from the system. If you modify the internal contents of an original MSI, you may break its upgrade or removal capability.

Therefore, when you want to customize the installation behavior of any given MSI, you need to transform it by adding all of your custom changes into an MST. When you run the `msiexec.exe` command to install the product, you use the TRANSFORM public property to apply the transform during installation. This maintains the integrity of the original MSI file while allowing you to customize the installation to your own needs.

Transforms can include most any type of customization but the most common are these:

- Identify which features of a product should be installed.
- Determine if and how users interact with the installation. Most often, there is little or no user interaction.
- Identify which answers need to be provided to the setup during installation. This includes items such as installation location and product activation keys.
- Identify which shortcuts should be created and where they should be placed. Get rid of special Internet offerings and other annoying bits from manufacturers' products.
- Include additional files, such as corporate document templates.
- Identify which registry settings are to be modified and how.

As you can see, transforms are a useful way to modify the original MSI.

The next most common Windows Installer file type is the MSP or *patch* file. Patches are updates to the product that do not affect the ProductCode attribute within the MSI database. It may increment the ProductVersion for the MSI. When the ProductVersion is modified, the patch is usually large enough to be considered a service pack or, in WIS terms, a major update. When it does not affect the ProductVersion, the patch is considered a minor update.

NOTE   If you modify the source code for a deployed product, you will need to update or refresh the deployed installation. The reason is that the source files for a deployed installation may reside on a network share in support of self-healing. If you modify these source files without updating the deployed installations, self-healing will no longer work, especially if the ProductVersion attribute has been modified by the patch. To reinstall the product on all deployed systems you should run the following command:

```
msiexec /fvomus name_of_the_package.msi REINSTALL=ALL
```

The switches used in the above command include the following functions:

```
f — fix or repair an application
v — run from the source and re-cache the local package
o — if file is missing or an older version is installed
m — rewrite all computer specific registry entries
u — rewrite all user specific registry entries
s — overwrite all existing shortcuts
```

As of version 3.1, you could actually use only /fv since all other switches are now the default repair behavior.

When you run an installation through the Windows Installer service, you actually create an installation database on the target computer. This installation database is then used to support long-term program viability features. Applying patches for software products that are integrated to the Windows Installer service means updating this installation database and modifying key components, often-dynamic link libraries (DLLs) of the program.

Although original MSI files are often transformed through MST files to customize their installation within corporate networks and adapt them to corporate standards, the MST does not modify the original MSI. Patches, on the other hand, modify the original installation database as well as key program components (see Figure 4.6). Therefore, when patches are made available, you need to apply them to installed copies of the product to update the deployed installation database as well as apply them to any administrative installation of the software you may have performed. This will ensure that anyone performing future installations or repair operations from this administrative install point will install an updated version of the product.

Yet another Windows Installer file type is the MSM or *merge module*. The merge module is designed to allow you to include subproducts into your installation. For example, several products require a database to operate. To ensure that such a database is available, they will include a copy of the freely distributable SQL Server 2005 Express Edition or the Microsoft SQL Server Desktop Engine (MSDE).

These are the major file types used with the Windows Installer service. For example, when you just export the installer database out of an MSI file, you create an IDT file (Installer Database Tables). During the preparation of installer patches, manufacturers will work with PCP files. During the creation and/or preparation of an MSI package, you may work with CUB or package validation files.

FIGURE 4.6

Reviewing the MSP patching process

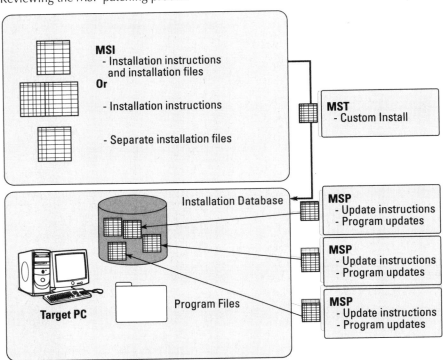

Finally, when you integrate a Windows Installer package with Group Policy to deploy it to a user instead of a computer, Group Policy will create an AAS file that is an advertisement script. This script is deployed to the user instead of the actual MSI. The script supports the automatic installation of the package after the user clicks on the product shortcut the script creates or on a document that requires the product to open. The full list of file extensions used with Windows Installer is in Table 4.1.

TABLE 4.1

File Types Associated with Windows Installer X

File Extension	Purpose
MSI	Installation database and possible installation resources
MST	Installation transformation instructions
MSP	Patch information to be applied to original MSI
MSM	Merge module to be integrated into MSI
IDT	Exported Installer database file
PCP	Patch creation file used during patch preparation
CUB	MSI package validation file
AAS	Group Policy advertisement script
CAB	Compressed file containing installation resources for a product

Managing the Windows Installer service

As you can see, there's a lot to the basic Windows Installer architecture. Now that you understand that Windows Installer is a transactional service that is based on the MSI database, you're starting to see the value of such a service in a managed network. Because Windows Installer is a service, it needs to be managed like all the other components in your network. Microsoft has made it easy to work with and manage this service. As mentioned previously, much of the service administration is performed through the `msiexec.exe` command. However, Microsoft has also given you the ability to centrally manage the behavior of the service through Group Policy Objects (GPO) and Active Directory.

Working with Windows Installer installations

Because it is a service, Windows Installer runs under the Local System account privilege. This means that it has the right to perform almost any installation operation even if users are in a locked-down environment. Note that you may control if and how the ability to run installations with elevated privileges should be handled via Group Policy (refer to the AlwaysInstallElevated policy). There are several ways to start this service, but they are all related to a Windows Installer or MSI installation. Without the MSI, you cannot access the service. This means you can launch a Windows Installer operation using any of the following actions:

- Double-click `setup.exe` for an MSI-based installation
- Double-click an MSI file
- Use the `msiexec.exe` command
- Use Add/Remove Programs
- Deploy an MSI product through Group Policy or through a software deployment tool that understands MSIs

When an interactive installation is initiated, it calls upon the Windows Installer application-programming interface (API) to start the service and present the appropriate dialog boxes to the user. To do this, the service runs several processes, one in your user context with your user rights and permissions and others in the Local System account context. This is why it is best to deploy MSIs centrally: even if WIS has access to the Local System account, if your credentials do not allow you to perform installations, you won't be able to install a product interactively. On the other hand, if you deploy the installation with the appropriate settings the service will be able to perform the installation even if the logged-on user does not have installation rights. In this case, the processes that run in the user context are only run to configure actual user settings and not to install the application. Remember that the user has complete control over the user profile so running in the user context allows WIS to complete installations properly.

One key element of an MSI installation is context. You can work with Windows Installer to deploy applications on either a per user or per machine basis. Using the ALLUSERS=1 property during installation will tell Windows Installer to perform a machine-based installation or an installation that will configure settings within the All Users profile, letting any user who has access to the machine have access to the installation. In most if not all cases, you'll want to use per machine installations. That's because if you install an application on a per user basis, only the user who installed the application can remove it from the system because only that user has access to the user profile in which the application hooks reside. If multiple users installed the same application on a per user basis, then it cannot be removed until each user has uninstalled it. In managed environments, this can be quite a headache.

NOTE The default installation that Windows Installer performs is a per user installation. That's because by default, the ALLUSERS property is not set and a user installation is the default behavior. Make sure that you change this value. As mentioned above, the value can be set directly within your own packages, can be modified through a transform, or can be added to the command line while installing a product.

There are a couple of possible values that may be assigned to the ALLUSERS property, and they can mean different things based on the rights of the individual performing the installation:

```
ALLUSERS = 1 (All Users)
```

If the user performing the installation is a standard user, the above will return an error as an unprivileged user does not have sufficient permission to install an application for all users. If the user has admin privileges, the installation will be performed for all users (to the "All Users" profile directory):

```
ALLUSERS = 2 (Current User)
```

While you would expect setting ALLUSERS to 2 would always install just for the current user, if the user has administrative privileges it will be installed for all users even if this setting is specified. If you really do want to install just for the current user and have administrative privileges, this property should not be set at all so the default behavior of installing just for the current user may be realized.

During the installation, Windows Installer will back up any file it replaces in order to support installation rollback. These files are copied to a temporary folder, often the c:\config.msi folder. Of course, once the installation is complete, it removes the files.

In addition, when it finishes an installation, WIS will copy the installation's MSI file and any associated MST file to a special folder called %windir%\installer and rename it with a cryptic name. This allows it to manage the installed product directly from the local machine without necessarily requiring access to the original installation source (see Figure 4.7).

NOTE   The %windir%\installer folder is a hidden folder by default. To view it, type the address in Windows File Explorer. In addition, you'll notice that all of the filenames are very cryptic. To view which product the file matches to, right-click the Explorer sort bar at the top of the Details pane and add both Title and Author to the detailed view. This will show you which manufacturer and to which product the file relates.

Alternatively, you can simply hover over the file in Windows File Explorer to see its properties in a tooltip.

FIGURE 4.7

Understanding how the components work together during a product installation

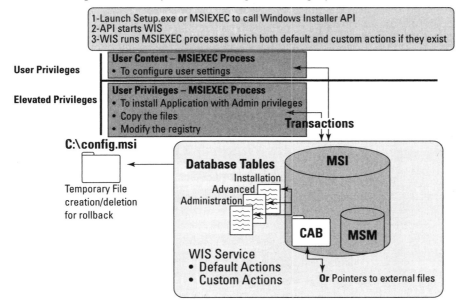

Leveraging GPO settings and policies

Corporate networks that run Active Directory can centrally control the Windows Installer service through Group Policy. If you don't have Active Directory, then you'll have to use another centralized management tool to control these settings or you'll have to do it through local policies.

There are quite a few policy settings for the Windows Installer service, especially after Server 2003 Service Pack 2. Table 4.2 outlines all of these settings and indicates some recommended settings for them as provided with Server 2008. All specific settings for Windows Installer are found by choosing Computer Configuration ➪ Policies ➪ Administrative Templates ➪ Windows Components ➪ Windows Installer or User Configuration ➪ Policies ➪ Administrative Templates ➪ Windows Components ➪ Windows Installer. Software deployment settings are located in either Computer Configuration ➪ Policies ➪ Software Settings ➪ Software Installation or User Configuration ➪ Policies ➪ Software Settings ➪ Software Installation. In most cases, you'll want to work with the Computer Configuration portion of a Group Policy because you want to avoid user-based software deployments as much as possible.

> **NOTE** Networks running Windows XP Service Pack 2 and Windows Server 2003 but without Service Pack 1 for Windows Server 2003 need to add a special hotfix for Windows Server. This hotfix allows you to open policies either from Windows Server or from Windows XP with no error. This is described in article number 842933 on the Microsoft Knowledge Base. It can be downloaded from here: `http://support.microsoft.com/default.aspx?kbid=842933`.
>
> In addition, to update your domain controllers with the admin template files that are contained in Windows XP Service Pack 2, you need to run the Group Policy Management Console (GPMC) from a machine running XP SP2 and open each of the policies you want updated. This automatically adds the appropriate admin template files to the policies. More on Group Policy is covered in Chapter 9.

TABLE 4.2

Group Policy Settings for Windows Installer

Group Policy Setting	Purpose	Recommended Setting	Notes
Computer Configuration ➪ Policies ➪ Administrative Templates ➪ Windows Components ➪ Windows Installer			
Disable Windows Installer	Controls the use of Windows Installer	Not configured in Windows Server 2003 and later. In Windows 2000 Server networks, change to For non-managed apps only.	This setting ensures only deployed software can be installed by normal users. This is the default in Windows Server 2003 and later.

Group Policy Setting	Purpose	Recommended Setting	Notes
Computer Configuration ⇨ Policies ⇨ Administrative Templates ⇨ Windows Components ⇨ Windows Installer			
Always install with elevated privileges	Tells WIS to use system credentials to install software	Not configured	When you have a systems management solution in place there is no need for this setting (the solution's own agent is used instead).
Prohibit Use of Restart Manager	Controls if Restart Manager should detect files and use and mitigate a system restart when possible	Not configured	Enabled by default, this feature is new to Vista and later systems and can reduce the need for system restarts due to in-use files.
Prohibit rollback	Stops WIS from creating temporary files for rollback	Not configured	The only reason to enable this setting is to save temporary disk space. Do not use this setting in either Computer or User Configuration because setting it in one automatically turns it on for the other.
Remove browse dialog box for new source	Stops users from browsing the file system when installing features in WIS	Not configured	The default behavior is sufficient in this case.
Prohibit patching	Stops users from patching WIS products	Not configured	By default, only administrators can patch products.
Prohibit Flyweight Patching	Controls the ability to turn off all patch optimizations	Not configured	By default, installations will be automatically analyzed to determine if optimization is possible.
Prohibit removal of updates	Protects updates from being removed	Not configured	By default, only administrators can remove updates.
Disable IE security prompts for Windows Installer scripts	Lets Web-based programs install without user knowledge	Not configured	Applying this can be a very high security risk.
Enable user control over installs	Gives users elevated privileges during installations	Not configured	Users should not have the right to install software except under special situations. In this case, there are better ways to give them these rights than this policy.

continued

TABLE 4.2   *(continued)*

Group Policy Setting	Purpose	Recommended Setting	Notes
Computer Configuration ⇨ Policies ⇨ Administrative Templates ⇨ Windows Components ⇨ Windows Installer			
Enable user to browse for source while elevated	Gives users access to restricted files and folders	Not configured	This would let users use the Local System account to access restricted files and folders during an installation. It is turned off by default.
Enable user to use media source while elevated	Gives users access to removable media during installations with high privileges	Not configured	Users can access removable media during installations in their own security context. Since you want only per machine installs, do not enable this setting.
Enable user to patch elevated products	Gives users the ability to patch software, even when running with elevated privileges	Not configured	Patches should be delivered centrally to end users.
Allow admin to install from Terminal Services session	Lets administrators install applications when in a TS session	Enabled	This affects only system administrators and lets them install software through Terminal Services sessions.
Cache transforms in secure location on workstation	Saves transforms in secure location on the desktop	Not configured on Windows Server 2003 and later Enabled on Windows 2000 Server	Caching transforms into secure locations protects them from malicious tampering. This is the default behavior in Windows Server 2003 and later. This is also key to per machine installs because transforms can only be used on the same machine when this setting is enabled.
Logging	Sets the logging level for WIS	Not configured	Use this only when required. Logs are saved to the Temp folder of the system volume. While logging is available at the command line, for deployments via Group Policy this can prove a valuable feature. When enabled, default logging is set to include status messages, warnings, error messages, start up of actions, and terminal properties.

Group Policy Setting	Purpose	Recommended Setting	Notes
Computer Configuration ⇨ Policies ⇨ Administrative Templates ⇨ Windows Components ⇨ Windows Installer			
Disable logging via package settings	Controls if MSI packages may be authored to dictate their own logging settings	Enabled Set to Disable logging via package settings on	Normally, you specify logging at the command line or for all installations via the Logging policy (above). This keeps setup authors from being able to dictate logging behavior via the MsiLogging property
Prohibit user installs	Controls how user installs are configured	Enabled Set to Hide User Installs	This setting will prevent per user installations and allow only per machine installations. Note: On Windows 2000, this setting disables all installs.
Turn off creation of System Restore Checkpoints	Protects user systems by creating restore points on Windows XP and later systems	Not configured	This setting is enabled by default.
Enforce upgrade component rules	Controls how upgrades occur	Not configured	If this setting is enabled, some upgrades may fail because you will have to follow strict upgrade rules. It is not always possible to control how upgrades are performed because you do not always control the source code for the upgrades.
Prohibit non-administrators from applying vendor-signed updates	Controls the ability of non-administrators to install updates that have been digitally signed by the application vendor	Not configured	By default, updates that are properly signed by vendors can be installed by users.
Baseline file cache maximum size	Controls the percentage of disk space available for the baseline cache	Not configured	By default, Windows Installer uses 10 percent of available free space for this cache. Change it only if you feel 10 percent is not sufficient for your needs.

continued

TABLE 4.2   *(continued)*

Group Policy Setting	Purpose	Recommended Setting	Notes
User Configuration ⇨ Policies ⇨ Administrative Templates ⇨ Windows Components ⇨ Windows Installer			
Always install with elevated privileges	Tells WIS to use system credentials to install software	Not configured	When you have a proper MSI deployment tool in place, there is no need for this setting.
Search order	Tells WIS where to search for installation files	Not configured	By default, WIS searches the network first, then removable media, then the Internet.
Prohibit rollback	Stops WIS from creating temporary files for rollback	Not configured	The only reason to enable this setting is to save temporary disk space. Do not use this setting in either Computer or User Configuration because setting it in one automatically turns it on for the other.
Prevent removable media source for any install	Controls if users can install software from removable media	Enabled	This setting stops users from being able to install software from removable media. Ideally, software should be installed from the network only. Even if it is enabled, administrators can install from any location.
User Configuration ⇨ Policies ⇨ Administrative Templates ⇨ Control Panel ⇨ Add or Remove Programs			
Hide the Add a program from CD-ROM or floppy disk option	Lets users add programs from removable media through the Control Panel	Enabled	This setting is used in conjunction with the "Prevent removable media source for any install" setting. Note: You might want to enable the Hide Add new Programs page as this will stop users from adding programs through the Control Panel.

Make sure that you apply the settings from Table 4.2 to your production network and that you include testing computers with these settings in your packaging lab. Doing this lets you test as a user under full user conditions when preparing packages. As for software delivery through Group Policy, it is recommended that you only use the Computer Configuration portion of the GPO because you want to ensure all installs be on a per machine basis.

Implementing software restriction policies

To protect your systems further from unwanted software installations, you should make use of Windows' Software Restriction Policies (SRP). SRPs are designed to help control the execution of code within your network. SRPs rely on four different rules to determine if software can execute in the network. These rules include:

- **Hash rule**: A hash is a special identifier that is generated by performing calculations on the binary elements of a file. Because of the way the hash is calculated, no two-hash rules are the same. It is also impossible to reverse the process to find the originating data. To use hash rules, you need a hash-generating program.

- **Certificate rule:** A public key certificate that is included in both the SRP rule and in the MSI packages. This is often the easiest way to use SRP because it is easier for you to control certificates, especially because Windows Server 2003 includes the ability to manage an internal public key infrastructure (PKI).

- **Path rule**: One of the simplest SRP rules because it simply states which paths are acceptable to host application setup packages. Be careful if you use this method because if you allow `*\softwaresource\*` for example, anyone can create a program that makes the C:\softwaresource folder and run program installations from there. The best way to use this rule type is to implement a distribution structure based on the Distributed File System (DFS) that can present the same installation source to all sites through DFS Namespaces.

- **Internet zone rule**: This rule is based on the zones perceived by Internet Explorer. This method is slightly more risky because after a zone is allowed, any installations from this zone will work.

Rules are applied in the order they are listed here. Often the easiest way to implement SRPs is to combine both a certificate rule with a path rule based on DFS Namespaces. Because DFS Namespaces use the domain name in the universal naming convention (UNC) rather than the server name, the same path can be used anywhere in the network.

If you decide to use certificate rules, you'll want to pre-deploy the certificates you will use in your packages. That's because when you deploy a package with an untrusted certificate, the user will have to accept the certificate before the installation can proceed. If on the other hand you have pre-deployed the certificate, then the installation can proceed uninhibited. Fortunately, Windows Server 2003 and later support certificate auto-enrollment. Therefore, users will not even be aware of the need for or the issue of certificates for software deployment and installation.

You might also consider the following:

- Administrative installations of MSI packages may change the nature of the package so it is always best to install a certificate in the package *after* it has been installed to the administrative location.

- Commercial MSI packages may also already include digital signatures. In this case, you can add the vendor's certificate to your SRP rules. If you modify the package once deployed, it needs to be re-signed.

- Make sure that your certificates are managed properly and accessible to anyone who needs to sign packages that are ready for deployment.

When you set up SRP, you'll need to first generate the SRP objects in the Group Policy you will use to manage them. These objects are not generated by default within GPOs. Next, determine how it will be enforced. It is best to enforce to all software except libraries (for example DLLs) and to all users. This way, administrators are not affected. You'll also want to configure how trusted publishers will be evaluated. It is a good idea to re-verify certificates before allowing the publisher to be trusted. This way, you won't allow publishers with outdated certificates to be trusted.

Managing source lists

Another aspect of MSI package deployment that you need to take into consideration is the installation source list. When you deploy an MSI package, Windows Installer needs to maintain the ability to access the original deployed package source for several reasons. One of the main reasons is package self-healing. During the self-healing process, Windows Installer has to connect to the original installation source to reinstall each feature that has a missing or damaged key path. If the original source is no longer available, WIS will ask the user to provide it with an appropriate location. This is definitely not something you want users to face because they have no idea where these files should be. As you know, many of them will still attempt to resolve this situation themselves before they think to call the Help Desk.

Another example is the product upgrade. In some cases, you may upgrade a product that requires access to the original source installation of the previous version in order to remove it properly. A third example is the installation of companion products. For example, if you install a third-party grammar checker in Microsoft Office, it might require access to the original Office installation files to add features that were not originally selected during install.

All of these situations can cause an installation to fail if source lists are not properly managed. Some good news came with the arrival of Windows Installer version 3.1, which mitigates the impact of these situations because it leverages the locally stored MSI file (in the `%windir%\installer` folder) to patch and upgrade products. Despite this, it is still very important to maintain constant source lists. The SOURCELIST public property can be used to specify more than one source, and Windows Installer will try all locations listed before prompting the user with a request for a valid location. In addition, the way WIS searches for valid locations is controlled through the search order GPO setting in user configurations. By default, WIS searches the network first, then removable media, then the Internet. The key to source list management is to make sure sources are available before WIS needs to verify their location. From the command line, the SOURCELIST public property can specify one or more paths separated by a semicolon as shown in the following example:

```
msiexec.exe /i \\server\share\folder\package.msi SOURCELIST="\\dfspath\
    folder\;c:\localsource;http://installationpoint.com/acnt"
```

There are a couple of ways to deal with source list management. One is to design a proper package delivery infrastructure in your network. As mentioned above, the best way to do this is to use DFS Namespaces. The DFS service lets you create a UNC, which is in the form of \\domainname\ share instead of \\servername\share. The advantage is that with a DFS Namespace, there should be no reason why the share name should ever change because Namespaces are stored within Active Directory and are linked to target shares hosted on servers throughout your infrastructure. This lets you modify the share targets to your heart's content without ever affecting users or installations. That's because the DFS Namespace can point to multiple targets that can be in different locations. In addition, DFS Replication (DFSR) can replicate data from target to target to make sure the contents of all targets are identical.

Although the first version of DFS relied on the File Replication Service (FRS) which only replicated entire objects — copying a whole file even if only 1 byte has changed — DFSR supports delta compression replications, replicating only changes to existing files. This makes the DFSR engine even more powerful and useful for this scenario.

The second prong of this approach is to make sure that the source lists you include inside your packages include all possible locations for a package. For example, DFS Namespaces are wonderful for any system that is connected to the network, but what happens when the package is on a portable that is no longer connected to the network? Once again, users would be prompted to specify a location for source files, and this situation would even be worse since there would be no way a user could fix this problem short of having the installation CD with them. One way to solve this issue is to create a hidden partition on the hard drive of portable systems and copy all packages to this location prior to their installation. That way the location is available in the event of a problem with a product while the user is traveling.

Of course, this means that you need to maintain these special locations, but that is part of your software deployment infrastructure design and operation. Also, the vastly expanding default disk size on portables makes an approach such as this quite viable today.

> **NOTE** If you have already deployed packages and you have not managed source lists properly, you have probably run into some issues with these installations. There are several ways to repair source lists in deployed products. One is by using features that are potentially provided with your deployment tool. For example, if you are using Microsoft Systems Center Configuration Manager 2007 (SCCM), you can modify source lists after the fact for per machine product deployments. It is also possible to use scripts to modify source lists. Finally, you can simply redeploy a properly managed package. This also gives you the opportunity to rectify other potential problems you may have introduced before you standardized your application installation approaches (such as per user installs instead of per machine installs).
>
> For more on managing source lists, see the Product Source Update Manager Whitepaper from Microsoft at www.microsoft.com/downloads/details.aspx?FamilyID=32F40DB4-6706-4E62-B867-AA1D332B6403&displaylang=en

Changes to Windows Installer 4.0

Windows Installer received a significant facelift to run with Windows Vista. Vista heralds a whole series of changes and modifications in terms of both user access and system protection. These changes affect application installations. Because of this, the most significant changes in WIS 4.0 are related to the following:

- Compatibility with Restart Manager
- Compatibility with User Account Control
- Compatibility with User Account Control Patching
- Support for Windows Resource Protection

Most existing MSI packages will run on Windows Vista, but it is always best to update your own packages to run with this version of WIS to make sure you have the latest built-in capabilities and compatibility.

Compatibility with Restart Manager

In order to avoid user disruptions as much as possible, Vista includes a new feature, the Restart Manager. By default, Vista relies on Restart Manager to stop and restart applications rather than stopping and restarting the system. It actually saves the state of applications and temporarily closes them to prevent the need to restart. The system is restored after the installation is complete without a restart.

Applications that are compatible with WIS 4.0 will include a new MsiRMFilesInUse dialog that will automatically link them with the Restart Manager's capabilities. For applications to run properly with Restart Manager once installed, they must include the new RegisterApplicationRestart function. Both can be added as a transform to packages that are not designed for WIS 4.0.

 More information on Windows Installer 4.0 and Restart Manager can be found at `http://msdn2.microsoft.com/en-us/library/Aa372466.`

Compatibility with User Account Control

User Account Control (UAC) is a new security feature of Windows Vista that is designed to let all users run with standard user privileges, even if you are logged in with an administrative account. Each time an action requires administrative privileges, UAC requests authorization from the user. The difference lies in how it does this. When logged in as an administrator, UAC simply requests you to allow or deny an action. When logged in as a standard user, UAC requests the name of an account with administrative privileges and its password to proceed.

Because of its integration with UAC, administrators can rely on WIS 4.0 to install all applications as managed applications. Managed applications are automatically installed with elevated privileges and are stored in the HKEY_LOCAL_MACHINE registry hive, which is the same as using the ALLUSERS=1 property. After an application is registered as a managed application, it will no longer prompt users or administrators during installation.

If applications are not registered as managed, then standard users will require over-the-shoulder credential assignment or asking someone else to fill in the user name and password for the installation to complete.

 More information on WIS 4.0 and UAC can be found at `http://msdn2.microsoft.com/en-us/library/Aa372468`.

Compatibility with User Account Control patching

Vista's UAC supports the ability to patch applications without requiring elevated privileges, but to do so, applications must be digitally signed. Several other conditions are required:

- The application must have been installed by WIS 3.0 or higher.
- If the application was installed on Windows XP, it must have been done with removable media — CD or DVD — otherwise it will not work. Note that this restriction does not apply to applications installed on Vista.
- The application must have been installed for all users or per machine.
- The patch or the original package must include the MsiPatchCertificate table, which in turn includes the digital certificate for the patch.

More conditions must be met, but when patches are properly prepared for Vista, they will install under standard user privileges. This is something you should always aim for in your patches.

 More information on patching with UAC can be found at `http://msdn2.microsoft.com/en-us/library/Aa372388`.

Support for Windows Resource Protection

Microsoft has renamed Windows System File Protection to Windows Resource Protection (WRP) in Windows Vista. WIS 4.0 may later integrate with WRP in the following manner:

- If system files are contained within a package, WIS skips its installation and logs an entry into the log file and continues the installation. This is different from Windows 2000 and XP as WIS would call on SFP to install the file for it.
- WRP protects both files and registry keys. As with files, if WIS encounters a protected registry key in the installation, it skips it, logs a warning in the log file, and moves on.

There is more to the integration, but for administrators preparing software packages, it is important to know that WRP does not allow WIS to update any protected resource.

More information on WIS and WRP can be found at `http://msdn2.microsoft.com/en-us/library/Aa372868`.

 Any internally created packages should include a digital signature in order to support User Account Control (UAC) patching. UAC patching enables the authors of Windows Installer installations to identify digitally signed patches that can be applied and removed in the future by non-administrator users. This functionality is available beginning with Windows Installer version 3.0. User Account Control (UAC) patching was called least-privilege user account (LUA) patching in Windows XP. LUA patching is not available on Windows 2000 and Windows Server 2003.

Changes to Windows Installer 4.5

Windows Installer is available as a redistributable for Windows Vista SP1, Windows Server 2008, Windows XP SP2, and Windows Server 2003 SP1. It offers some new functions and features including two worth mentioning specifically:

- **Transaction support:** As of this release, Windows Installer can now perform multiple-package installations using transaction processing.

- **Custom user interface support**: A custom user interface can now be embedded within a Windows Installer package.

It is a good idea to deploy Windows Installer 4.5 as part of your Windows Vista corporate image. Because it is not included, you will need to download and install it manually.

NOTE For more on what's new in Windows Installer 4.5, visit msdn.microsoft.com/en-us/library/bb736325(VS.85).aspx.

The MSI Package Lifecycle

In a way, this lifecycle is very similar to the software lifecycle, or the history of the software products you choose to use in your network. That's because they both begin with a request; someone somewhere decides they need to have or use a specific product, a product that will provide the particular features they need. In the packaging lifecycle (see Figure 4.8), this request can stem from a variety of sources, but most often it stems from the user community.

In many cases, these requests are informal — a manager decides a product is required to better the productivity of their team; some user tells a manager they can't do without a given product; IT decides it is time to upgrade or change one of the core products in the network. Ideally, you should be using a tracking system that automatically ferries this request through the proper channels, locating the budget required for the acquisition or the development project if no commercial product responds to your needs, providing approval for the purchase or project launch, and delivering the product to be packaged to your doorstep. At the same time, this tracking system can let users, or rather requesters, know of the status of their request and the expected delivery date for the product on their desktop.

FIGURE 4.8

Understanding the MSI package lifecycle

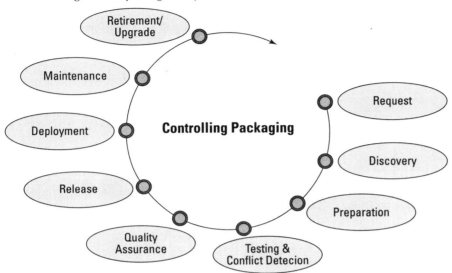

Next, you begin the actual packaging process by examining the product to be packaged. How does it behave when installed? Are there prerequisites for its operation? Will it run properly on your operating system of choice? Does it conform to given Windows standards? These are the types of questions you need to answer and document before you can move on to further stages. One of the most important questions at this stage will be, is the product designed to work with the Windows Installer service or not? The answer to this question will greatly influence how you proceed in the next stages of your packaging lifecycle.

A key step in the discovery process is research and review of existing documentation sources for the application installation. Help may be found in locations, such as a README.TXT file, included documentation, or the vendor's Web site (FAQs or knowledge bases). Unfortunately, this information can often be difficult to uncover. One place where such information can be found for most applications is the AppDeploy Package Knowledge Base. This knowledge base is a community-contributed resource of information on the automated installation of applications on a product-by-product basis with a separate living document available for each version of a product installation. Details include:

■ **Command Lines**: Command line syntax for installation and removal of the software, which may include available command line arguments and/or public properties.

■ **Notes**: Shared information on how to handle the automated installation of the software.

- **Virtualization**: Shared information regarding how to work with the software in sequencing or creating a virtual deployment package for products like Altiris Software Virtualization Solution (SVS), Microsoft's SoftGrid Application Virtualization, VMware's Thinstall, and Citrix XenApp.

- **Terminal Services**: Details on how to address problems working with this software in a Terminal Services session as with Citrix shared environments.

- **Related Links**: Links to official and unofficial information regarding the deployment of the software.

- **Security Lockdown:** Information regarding which files, directories, and/or registry entries must be opened to standard users for operation in a locked-down environment.

It should be noted that `AppDeploy.com` offers forums for questions and discussions on this subject, but its Package Knowledge Base is designed for the sharing of facts. The most commonly reported method of package development (repackaged, transformed, and scripted) as well as a simple difficulty rating is voted on by members, which can provide you with a quick starting point to judge how difficult packaging will be for the application with which you are working.

 The Package Knowledge Base may be found at `www.appdeploy.com/packages`.

The next step is what most people consider the packaging process itself. This is where you prepare the automation of the installation and configuration of the product you intend to deploy. If the product is compatible with Windows Installer, you can customize it by creating a transform manually or by capturing the installation and configuration settings in a file that may be applied to the original product installation to modify its behavior according to your needs and requirements. If the package is not compatible with Windows Installer, you'll want to convert its legacy installation into one that will work with this service. In this case, you can capture the installation and configuration settings into a special file that will serve as a new installation executable.

After you've created the initial package, you need to test it to ensure that it behaves exactly as you expect it to. There are a number of different tests you can perform at this stage for example: automated or silent installation test, pull installation (manually launched on the workstation or server from a network location), push installation (automatically deployed with your systems management software), uninstallation, and so on. But system tests are not the only tests you require. More often than not, software packagers find themselves preparing a product for deployment that they've never heard of nor have very little experience with. Therefore, it is difficult for you to understand if the configuration you devised for this product is properly designed or if the eventual user will approve of this configuration. To validate the configuration, you need to involve an experienced user in the testing process. His role will be to ensure that the product behaves as it should after it is deployed. This is normally referred to as *acceptance* or *integration* testing and is often formalized to identify the expert users who perform it as software owners, people who will be responsible for more than just testing, but also for recommendations on product evolution after it is in formal use in the network.

Another form of testing is conflict detection. It was only a few years ago that we began to realize the impact of "DLL Hell" or the impact of trying to make a multitude of products from different vendors, developed at different times behave properly on a single system. In fact, DLL Hell became so prevalent that Microsoft finally decided to implement a single installation standard for software products in Windows: the Windows Installer service.

Although this service has been rightly hailed as a savior by many systems administrators because of its many features for the support of the coexistence of misbehaved products on a single system, it is not the be all and end all of conflict resolution. Take, for example, the integration of two products on a system: product A and product B. Product B includes components that are not compatible with product A, yet both must be installed on the same system.

The solution is to convert both to an MSI installation to integrate them to the Windows Installer service if they don't already support it. Thanks to this service, incompatible programs can coexist and operate on the same system. Should product B's components damage product A's, Windows Installer's self-healing capabilities will automatically repair the damaged product the next time it is launched, so long as Windows Installer has access to the source installation files. However, you could find yourself in a DLL Hell Loop: When product B is launched, it breaks product A, but fixes itself; when product A is launched, it breaks product B, but fixes itself, and so on. This may be because each program uses a different version of the same DLL or requires the same registry keys with different settings. Nevertheless, you certainly don't want your users to see Windows Installer launch each time they start a program on their system.

That's why conflict detection and resolution are still required. Despite the fact that Windows Installer can handle conflicting situations on the fly, you want to control the behavior of packages in your network. This means ensuring that products are well behaved when delivered. Detection is handled by comparing the package you are working on with the others you have deployed (or a subset of those deployed) and conflict detection can even handle a snapshot of your baseline system image to ensure conflicts with Windows itself are accounted for.

After all testing and conflict detection is done, you need to perform a final quality assurance on the package. Ideally, the person performing this final QA activity will be different from the person who originally packaged the product. This will provide you with a better and more thorough verification. Don't forget to complete all documentation about this package at this stage. Too many organizations try to save time by leaving documentation until after the product is deployed only to find out some critical component was missed and they have no means to find out how to repair it.

So now, your package is ready for release. At this stage, users begin to hearten because your package tracking system has announced to them that they will soon see the package on their own desktop. All they have to wait for now is deployment. Your release process should fit smoothly with your deployment system, automatically integrating the package into the source package store that your software deployment team will use as the source for deployment.

Now that the package is out, you feel that your job is done. Unfortunately that is not so. *The packaging lifecycle does not end with deployment.* That's because today, it seems that released software must constantly be patched to maintain its operational consistency and protect those who have chosen to use it. Patches, hotfixes, and service packs are a fact and will have varying impacts on your packaging process depending on when in its own lifecycle you decide to deploy a product. If you deploy the product after it has been out for some time, you will need to integrate its patches and possibly service packs to the package before you deploy it. If you have decided to use a new product in its infancy, you will have to deploy patches for the product once it is in use in your network. In both cases, you must continue deploying hotfixes and other patch types throughout the lifetime of the package in your network.

To package or not to package?

Although Windows Installer offers strength and resiliency for product installations, unfortunately, there are some key products, which should not and cannot be packaged through the Windows Installer service. They include these:

- Service packs, hotfixes, and some system extensions cannot be repackaged with WIS. Good examples of this are core Windows system component updates, such as Windows Media Player or even the Direct X system. Along with the service packs, these components make low-level changes to the Windows system and therefore cannot be supported by Windows Installer.

- Windows File Protection (WFP) components excluded from WIS. As you know, components that are included in the SFP are automatically protected by the operating system; only the system can update files under this protection. Currently, only Microsoft has the ability to modify files at this level.

- Special packages that are already included in deployment kits. For example, Internet Explorer comes with its own Administration Kit (IEAK) that lets you package and deploy IE within your network. This type of product is best left to its original state because packaging it in WIS might break something that is automatically taken care of in the IEAK.

- Device drivers and network protocols. These special components must verify a system's configuration extensively before installation. It's not that WIS can't do that, it is mostly that the changes brought about by these installations are at such a low level that it is very difficult to package them into a WIS package. A good example is Adobe Acrobat. Because this product installed actual printer drivers, it took Adobe several years to modify its installation to the MSI format. Before this, many organizations invested heavily into the repackaging of Acrobat sometimes with little or no success. Now that it is an MSI, it is much simpler to work with.

- Commercial MSI products. Vendor provided MSI packages should never be repackaged. Remember that to modify these packages, you need to use a transform (MST) and apply it at the time of installation.

If, however, your only mode of deployment is through Active Directory and Group Policy, you can still use Windows Installer to help deploy these types of components. Windows Installer may be used as a wrapper that may use custom actions to turn the installation into an MSI. Windows Installer doesn't actually perform the installation, but it does perform the delivery of the package and launches the `setup.exe` that is required to perform the installation.

In addition, you must be constantly deploying new applications and updates on target systems that already include installed programs. Therefore, you always need to consider the installed applications whenever you test either the new program or the new update.

Then, after the package has reached the end of its usefulness to users or once the package has become obsolete, you need to retire it from the network. Retirement may also mean replacement if the business function the package fulfills is still required. If you plan to replace the package with a newer version of the same product, then you face an upgrade, which is a native feature of Windows Installer.

 To be fair, it is important to mention that using existing command line arguments to install a product that is not in MSI format preserves the vendors' provided installation logic and is supported by the vendor. Repackaging has many benefits, but it also adds complexity. If a problem with a repackaged installation cannot be reproduced in an interactive installation, the vendor is very unlikely to provide support.

NOTE For more on this subject, a video presentation entitled *To Repackage or Not to Repackage* is available online at `www.appdeploy.com/video/repackage-not.asp`

Best Practices for Using Windows Installer

Use the following best practices when customizing your packaging environment:

- Take the time to review the Windows Installer concepts covered in this chapter carefully. They will prove to be your guideline for package preparation from now on.
- Categorize all of your software packages into one of three categories: Native WIS Software, MSI-integrated Corporate Applications, and Repackaged Legacy Software.
- Make sure that you use the latest version of the Windows Installer service.
- Learn the ins and outs of the `msiexec` command so you can access Windows Installer features through the command line.
- Maintain your workstation lock-down status at all times. Use Windows Installer features to help maintain this environment.
- Work with the Windows Installer service as much as possible, but learn when to make exceptions. Keep your exceptions to a minimum at all times.
- Try to limit your feature installation to Run All from My Computer or Not Available. Avoid using Installed on First Use to provide a better experience to your users.
- Use per machine installations everywhere. This means using the ALLUSERS=1 property either inside the package or on the command line when installing packages. This will always create managed applications.
- Always use the ROOTDRIVE=C:\ property or better yet, design your workstations with a single disk partition, the C: drive.
- Always create and apply MST files to customize commercial MSI packages.
- If you create your own MSI files, make sure you store all user data into a single component.
- Make sure that all of your MSI files use unique product codes. Taking this step ensures that MSI products can coexist on the same machine.
- Make sure that you update all deployed packages when you modify the package by applying a patch.

- Make sure that you apply the proper GPOs to control the Windows Installer service in your network.

- Use Software Restriction Policies to control which MSI packages are installable in your network. The two best methods are Certificate and Path rules, often used together.

- If you use certificate rules for SRP, make sure you set up an auto-enrollment PKI before you deploy packages that are digitally signed. This will avoid placing this burden on users.

- Make sure you manage source lists properly. In fact, you should be using a domain-based DFS share strategy for package installation sources.

- Cache packages locally on portable systems.

- Adapt the MSI Packaging Lifecycle to your own environment and integrate it into your corporate packaging policy.

- When using WIS 4 and later, make sure your packages are integrated to the Restart Manager.

- When using WIS 4 and later, make sure packages are installed as managed applications. Doing this avoids upgrade issues in the end.

- When using WIS 4 and later, make sure that patches are digitally signed and that the certificate is in the MsiPatchCertificate table. The best way to do this is to add it to your custom MSI template so that it is automatically added to any new MSI that you create.

- Verify your packages to make sure they do not include any resources protected by WRP.

Now you're ready to use Windows Installer to its best abilities.

 **A video on the subject of Repackaging Best Practices may be found at www. appdeploy.com/video.**

Summary

This chapter provided some good background on the Windows Installer Service and what it offers the administrator by way of both benefits and challenges. Windows Installer is an important aspect of application delivery and management today. An emerging technology that may well replace Windows Installer in the future is application virtualization. Resource conflicts and dealing with protected files are all eliminated as obstacles as the application is not really installed but instead runs in memory with a virtual file and registry system that sit on top of the physical file and registry system. To uninstall a virtual machine, simply delete it. To update a virtual machine, simply replace it. Repackaging an application into a virtual application can a very similar challenge to doing the same for MSI setups, but there is no arguing the benefits of application virtualization.

For more on application virtualization, look at Chapter 6 of the eBook on Vista Migration at www. realtime-nexus.com/dgvm.htm.

Chapter 5

Migrating User Data

O dds are you have replaced one or two home computers over the last several years. Although you may have been happy to start fresh, you still spent the first hours customizing your desktop, shortcuts, favorites, and even configuring options in your favorite programs to get everything just so. In a corporate environment, you may have some users happy with a fresh start and many more that are not happy for the inconvenience. Regardless of how they feel about it, it is important to consider your experience and the time it took and then think about this on a scale of hundreds, thousands, even tens of thousands of systems. The disruption in service, the hours spent getting things back to how they should be can cost a company millions. Even something as trivial as a background wallpaper image can impact an organization if you consider that there could be thousands of people searching for that lost image and then trying to figure out how to set their background in Windows Vista. Extrapolate this example to application settings, shortcuts, Internet settings, and "favorites," and the importance of user data and settings migration becomes clear. In this chapter, we go over user data migration and some tools available to see you through the task.

Understanding User Data

A growing number of organizations are doing what they can to keep data off local workstations. The most obvious benefit is that server shares are routinely backed up. If something happens to the user's computer, data is safely waiting on the server. Data can also be replicated between sites so that it is not only available for users moving from computer to computer, but from site to site.

Often simply establishing a policy that instructs users to save data to a network share is not enough. Typically, a combination of policy, folder redirection, roaming profiles, and security restrictions are used to keep data off local workstations. However, in an environment where several dozen applications are deployed, it is common to have applications that don't behave as you would like. Some store data locally, even in the application directory. Further, because it is still often necessary to allow users access to some local folders, data could be stored here and would fall outside your server backup plan.

> **NOTE** If implemented, a combination of redirected folders and roaming profiles may actually serve as a method of natural and automatic migration. In fact, it may well be worth considering the implementation of folder redirection and roaming profiles as a precursor to your Windows Vista migration.

Even if you have worked hard and succeeded in ensuring all user data is maintained on network shares instead of the local system, there are often settings and configuration information for the system and for specific applications stored locally on the system. While arguably less important than data, loss of system and application settings can be very frustrating to users and significantly slow their first days with Windows Vista (which has plenty of changes for the user to deal with on its own).

Identifying the migration scenario

There are two basic scenarios for migrating data from one system to another:

- Wipe and load (targeting the same computer)
- Side-by-side migration (targeting a new computer)

Understanding the wipe and load scenario

In a wipe and load scenario, the user state is migrated from a source computer (computer A) to an intermediate store because the system drive is wiped in the process (so the data cannot be stored on this same drive). After Windows Vista is installed, the user state is migrated back to the source computer (computer A, see Figure 5.1). This is a common scenario when simply replacing the operating system on the same hardware.

Understanding the side-by-side scenario

In a side-by-side scenario, the user state is migrated from a source computer (computer A) to an intermediate store. After Windows Vista is installed, the user state is migrated to the destination computer (computer B, see Figure 5.2). This is a common scenario when new systems are being introduced as part of the Vista migration.

FIGURE 5.1

Wipe and load scenario diagram

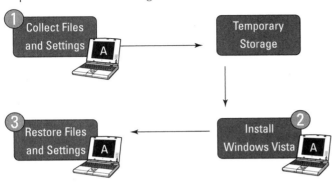

FIGURE 5.2

Side-by-side scenario diagram

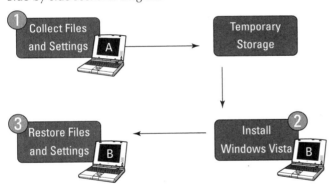

A side-by-side migration scenario is often used to take advantage of the introduction of new computers to a network during a Windows Vista migration. Computer cascades or rotations may be used to move systems from one user to the other. These new systems include improved capabilities over existing systems and, therefore, are delivered to the organizations' most demanding users. To make use of the replaced systems, the PCs recovered from the first delivery may be re-imaged and delivered to a second community of users whose systems are recovered and cascaded down to other users, and so on.

Determining the data and settings to be managed

One often overlooked step in planning a migration is to first identify what to migrate, including personal user settings, applications and application settings, personal data files, and folders. Identifying the applications to be migrated is especially important because there is no point in capturing data about applications that are not going to exist after the migration to Windows Vista. It is important that the information restored to the new system consist of only the information that is required. Restoring unnecessary data or settings for applications that are not present on the target system can introduce instability in newly deployed machines.

Additionally, it can be a waste of time and space to back up all profiles blindly. Consider the type of profiles that may exist on your systems:

- **Domain User Profiles**: These are likely to be needed most in a domain environment.

- **Local User Profiles**: If users log on to a domain, local profiles may be unnecessary, if users do logon locally it would be important to include them. Some migration software can even support migrating a local profile to a domain profile on the target system.

- **Roaming User Profiles**: If roaming profiles are in use, then the profile is downloaded from the server when logging on and copied back up when logging off. In this case the migration of user profiles may be completely unnecessary in your environment.

- **Unused User Profiles**: You may encounter profiles that have not been used in a very long time, or belong to users that have left your organization. These can be cleaned up ahead of time, or you can utilize features that limit migration to profiles that have been used within a specified period of time (for example, the ScanState tool discussed later in this chapter offers a /uel option which allows you to specify a number of days within which a user must have logged on for the profile to be included in the migration).

In fact, it will likely become clear during the migration-planning phase that some applications are simply not needed following the migration. Obviously, such application files and settings should be excluded from the migration.

Consider the following list as key things you may consider when identifying what it is you want to migrate:

- **Folders**: This can be specific folders you determine necessary for migration, including standard user profile folders, such as My Documents, My Video, My Music, My Pictures, Desktop files, Start Menu, Quick launch settings, and Favorites. It may also include All Users folders, such as Shared Documents, Shared Video, Shared Music, Shared Desktop files, Shared Pictures, Shared Start Menu, and Shared Favorites.

- **Files**: You can specify individual files, but most commonly *file types* are specified. File types are determined by their file extensions. Standard file types to back up might include .qdf, .qsd, .qel, .qph, .doc, .dot, .rtf, .mcw, .wps, .scd, .wri, .wpd, .xl*, .csv, .iqy, .dqy, .oqy, .rqy, .wk*, .wq1, .slk, .dif, .ppt*, .pps*, .pot*, .sh3, .ch3, .pre, .ppa, .txt, .pst, .one*, .mpp, .vsd, .vl*, .or6, .accdb, .mdb, .pub.

NOTE Wildcards are used to cover more file types without having to specify similar file extensions. For example, for Excel documents you can use .xl* to cover all the Excel file types (.xlsx, .xlsm, .xlsb, .xltx, .xltm, .xls, .xlt, .xls, .xml, .xml, .xlam, .xla, and .xlw).

- **Access Control Lists**: Migrate access control lists (ACLs) for files and folders to maintain file and folder level security. For example, if a file is marked as read-only for Users and Full Control for administrators, these settings will still apply after the file or folder is restored to the destination computer.

- **System Settings**: A number of valuable system settings may be migrated, though many such items may be better managed by using Group Policy. Such system settings may include Accessibility settings, custom wallpaper and wallpaper settings, dial-up connections, Internet Explorer settings, Outlook express mail files, regional options, remote access, and screen saver settings.

- Application Settings: Depending upon the tool being used, a limited set of application settings may also be available for migration. The options and settings stored by these supported applications can be migrated so long as the application is first installed on the destination computer prior to restoral of user data and settings information.

Depending upon the tool used, more or less such settings may be available to you. Microsoft's User State Migration Tool (USMT) handles all those items specified above. A third-party application or use of the optional Windows Easy Transfer Companion (beta) may provide alternate migration options.

Determining where to store data during the migration process

Data may be stored locally or remotely during the migration process. Locally stored migration data can mean a faster migration process overall. To store such data locally, you will need a separate partition or attached storage (such as a USB device).

No matter if you are going to store locally or on a network location, the major consideration to be made is just how much space will be required. Generally speaking, it is best to base calculations on the volume of e-mail, personal documents, and system settings for each user. The best way to estimate these is to survey several average desktops to estimate the size the data store that you will need.

One big differentiator when determining how much space will be needed is your organizations' e-mail storage location. If e-mail is stored centrally, such as by an Exchange Email server, data sets will naturally be smaller as compared to when e-mail is stored locally (as in offline storage files). When it comes to locally stored mail, automatically generated OST files will be regenerated when connecting to Exchange; it is Personal Storage files (PST) which require special attention as they cannot be recovered from Exchange. Mobile users typically have larger data sets than workstation users. When performing tests to estimate these sizes, we recommend that you separate the results of mobile and workstation users and average them separately. With local or remote e-mail also a major factor, these tips can be helpful in determining the size needed to store migration data (refer to Table 5.1 for typical requirements based on the type of user).

TABLE 5.1

User Storage Requirements to Support Migration

Type of User	Estimated Storage
Desktop user with centralized e-mail storage	50mb – 75mb plus size of collected files
Desktop user with local email storage	150mb – 200mb plus size of collected files
Laptop user	150mb – 300mb plus size of collected files

Considering user documents

As a rule, it is estimated that a typical user's documents will fit into 50MB of disk space. Naturally this depends upon the types of files with which the user works. The 50MB estimate assumes typical office work such as word processing documents and spreadsheets. Types of documents used in your organization can also have a significant impact on the size needed per user. A user that works with high-resolution images, audio, or video for example can quickly eat up a substantial amount of drive space.

Considering user system settings

For registry settings, 5MB is considered sufficient for a typical user. Naturally, the more applications on a system the more space may be required, but for the user-specific portion of the registry, it is rare that this would exceed 5MB.

Considering e-mail

As discussed, keeping mail locally on a computer as opposed to centrally stored on a mail server can take up a very large amount of disk space. Some users will deal with a larger volume of e-mail than others, but when it comes to estimating space, e-mail could be the biggest variable to consider. Regardless, it is a good idea to have users that keep some mail local though they have a central mail server synchronize any offline folders with their mail server prior to migration.

Estimating space requirements with the User State Migration Tool (USMT)

With so many variables, the estimates in Table 5.1 may or may not be applicable in your environment. The best way to know for sure how much space will be required is to investigate a subset of systems and get actual numbers for your organization. Using USMT is covered in more detail later in this chapter, but it is worth pointing out here that it offers a helpful command line option to assist in the size estimation process.

The /p option of the Scanstate tool generates a space-estimate file called Usmtsize.txt that is saved to the specified storage path. Running this command does not actually collect the user state but simply reports on the space requirements of *what would have been* collected.

NOTE   Consider this a bit of a bug, but except when migrating from x86-based computers running Windows XP, this estimate is often twice as large as the actual disk space needed on the destination computer. Consider this when calculating your size requirements.

You can choose to have the migration store compressed when using USMT to collect data; however, the estimates generated by the /p option are applicable for both compressed and uncompressed stores because the compressed store will always be smaller.

The following example turns off compression and creates a space-estimate file at \\server\ share\store\usmtsize.txt:

```
scanstate /i:miguser.xml /i:migapp.xml \\server\share\store /nocompress /p
```

As shown in Figure 5.3, the usmtsize.txt file produces a list of byte values broken down by cluster size. The first column of numbers is the cluster size, and the second column is what the store size will be for that cluster size. The first line is the cluster used for the drive where usmtsize.txt was created. The estimate to focus on is the line with the cluster size matching the storage drive (the cluster size of your file server or local storage destination). These estimates do use some assumed values that may not always provide a high degree of accuracy in the estimation process.

FIGURE 5.3

Reviewing the output of usmtsize.txt

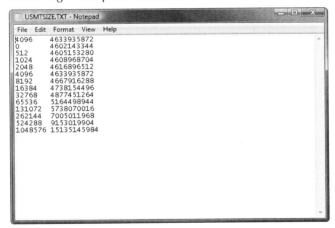

So how big are the clusters on your target storage drive? You can use Defrag.exe to determine cluster size by using the −a option to assess the need to defragment (without performing the actual defragmentation operation) and the −v option to produce a verbose output. Specify the target drive, and the report will provide the cluster size in the Analysis Report section at the top of the output, as shown in Figure 5.4.

FIGURE 5.4

Determining cluster size with `Defrag.exe`

```
C:\WINDOWS\system32\cmd.exe                              _□×

C:\>defrag e: -a -v
Windows Disk Defragmenter
Copyright (c) 2001 Microsoft Corp. and Executive Software International, Inc.

Analysis Report

        Volume size                     = 233 GB
        Cluster size                    = 32 KB
        Used space                      = 143 GB
        Free space                      = 90.24 GB
        Percent free space              = 38 %

Volume fragmentation
        Total fragmentation             = 13 %
        File fragmentation              = 26 %
        Free space fragmentation        = 0 %

File fragmentation
        Total files                     = 75,285
        Average file size               = 2 MB
        Total fragmented files          = 1,579
        Total excess fragments          = 8,732
        Average fragments per file      = 1.11

Pagefile fragmentation
        Pagefile size                   = 0 bytes
        Total fragments                 = 0

Folder fragmentation
        Total folders                   = 5,360
        Fragmented folders              = 30
        Excess folder fragments         = 113

You should defragment this volume.

C:\>
```

If you want to adjust the cluster size, the `convert.exe` tool may be used to convert the cluster size. In Windows 2000, `convert.exe` can be used to convert the partition to a 512-byte cluster size. In Windows XP, `convert.exe` will determine the best cluster size and will then (typically) convert the partition to a 4096-byte cluster size.

Given the relatively high complexity in determining space requirements for migration, it can be best to simply perform an actual collection of user data for migration on a sampling of systems and use the resulting file sizes in your calculations.

NOTE No matter what estimation you determine to be the best for your environment, it is naturally a good idea to ensure that you have more than enough space available. The recommendation is to allow a minimum buffer of an additional 20 percent more than your estimate.

Choosing migration tools

Microsoft provides two free tools to handle the migration of user files and settings:

- **Windows Easy Transfer:** Intended to be end-user tool
- **User State Migration Tools (USMT):** Provides a more automated and comprehensive method to migrate user data and settings

For most, choosing between these tools is a very simple decision: If you are migrating more than a handful of computers, USMT is going to be your choice when weighing these two tools.

However, it is important to keep in mind that there are more than just these two choices. Although the fact that they are free is a definite selling point for the Microsoft tools, other players in this market have established themselves over the years as reliable alternatives with their own enhancements and features that may mean a great deal to you. These tools are discussed at the end of this chapter, and naturally just how to use these tools is something covered in each tool's respective documentation. The Walkthroughs in this chapter focus on Windows Easy Transfer and USMT.

Windows Easy Transfer

Windows Easy Transfer is designed for interactive use and does not provide the automation features for mass usage as offered by the User State Migration Tool (USMT), which is discussed later in this chapter. However, if you are working with an individual system in a support role or if you are dealing with a small number of systems, the Windows Easy Transfer utility can be a welcome feature.

The Windows Easy Transfer tool comes with Windows Vista, so if you are moving a user from one computer to another, what you need is ready to launch. If you are moving a user from an earlier version of Windows, you'll need to obtain it in one of two ways:

- Run from installation DVD
- Download from Microsoft

Running Easy Transfer from DVD

In the support subfolder of the Windows Installation DVD, you will find a folder named migwiz, and this contains the Windows Easy Transfer application (for example. `D:\support\migwiz\migsetup.exe`). Simply run the `migsetup.exe` file to begin. (A standard installation wizard is not displayed; it simply prepares itself and executes the migration wizard directly.)

This does require that you run as Administrator. Under Windows Vista you are prompted by User Account Control (UAC) to allow execution as administrator. However, most commonly this tool will be run on a Windows XP system, so you need to consciously ensure execution as an administrator. As per usual, this can be done either by logging on as an administrator or using the "Run As" feature. Administrator privileges are required in order to successfully scan and collect data and settings from other profiles on the local computer.

Downloading Easy Transfer from Microsoft

You can download Windows Easy Transfer for Windows XP from Microsoft at `www.microsoft.com/downloads/details.aspx?FamilyId=2B6F1631-973A-45C7-A4EC-4928FA173266&displaylang=en`

The download does require validation, but the download is free and anyone running a valid installation of Windows is authorized to access the download. Running from Windows Vista? The Windows Easy Transfer utility is actually installed as part of the operating system so no download or install is necessary. You can find it in the Welcome Center application (also accessible by choosing Control Panel ➪ System and Maintenance and from its program group in Start Menu ➪ All Programs ➪ Accessories ➪).

Understanding the capabilities of Easy Transfer

Windows Easy Transfer lets you move files and settings from one computer to another. It does not remove any files or settings from the source computer in the process. It allows for the transfer of the following items:

- User accounts
- Folders and files
- Program settings
- Internet related items
- E-mail related items

NOTE During use of the Windows Easy Transfer tool, the computer cannot be used. Any running applications must be closed, and the desktop is completely taken over by the application during the process.

Although Windows Easy Transfer does not handle migration of applications, as of the printing of this book, a new tool is available as a beta download entitled *Windows Easy Transfer Companion*. It is based on a popular third-party migration tool named Alohabob PC Relocator, as part of Microsoft's acquisition of Apptimum, Inc. It provides for the migration of applications (beyond settings, the applications themselves). It works for a limited set of over 100 applications. It is not likely to address even most of your needs, but it certainly could be a help. At least for now, this technology is tied to Windows Easy Transfer and not USMT, so it is again more likely for use in migrations of very few computers.

The Windows Easy Transfer Companion beta is available for download at www.microsoft.com/downloads/details.aspx?FamilyID=39f724eb-4e37-4be0-adfc-786786e73e50&displaylang=en. An article discussing its use and a list of supported applications may be found at http://support.microsoft.com/kb/931696.

Using Windows Easy Transfer

After the Windows Easy Transfer application is launched, the desktop is taken over by the application. The application collects information on what it is you want to transfer, where you want to store it, and then does the work of collecting and storing the selected data.

Naturally, there are two distinct operations in using Windows Easy Transfer:

- Collecting files and settings
- Restoring files and settings

Collecting files and settings

The computer from which files and settings are to be migrated is referred to as the *old computer* by the Windows Easy Transfer tool. To make use of Windows Easy Transfer, sit down at the old computer and follow these steps:

1. **Launch Windows Easy Transfer.** The tool must be run as administrator in order to access all areas necessary. Therefore if launching Windows Easy Transfer from a Windows Vista system, a User Account Control (UAC) prompt must be acknowledged.

   A Welcome screen appears as the first screen of the wizard (see Figure 5.5). It contains a summary of the tool's capabilities and links to help.

FIGURE 5.5

Starting Windows Easy Transfer

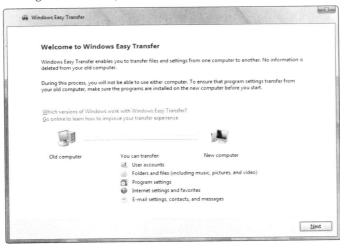

2. **Click the Next button to begin.** The resulting screen lets you continue a transfer in progress (if files and settings have been previously selected) or to start a new transfer.

3. **Choose Start a new transfer to continue.** The wizard prompts to identify what task it is you want to perform by asking which computer the tool it is on, which the application is being executed: My new computer (to restore files and settings) or My old computer (to collect files and settings).

4. **Choose My old computer to continue.** The next screen asks how you want to go about performing the transfer. Choices include using an Easy Transfer Cable, using a network connection, or using removable media (such as a writable CD, DVD, or USB drive). The first two options include using a network connection to perform a live migration directly from the old computer to the new one. If you are migrating operating systems, the target may actually be the same computer. Further, choosing the removable media option also provides the option to specify a network location (to store the payload as opposed to performing the transfer directly). Therefore, for the purpose of this walkthrough, choose Use a CD, DVD or other removable media to continue the process.

> **NOTE**   Unfortunately, an Easy Transfer Cable is not simply a standard USB cable, but a proprietary one with a chip that allows for the connection of two systems. You cannot use a simple USB cable for this task. This option is intended for home users who do not have a network to support the migration. A handful of partners manufacture the cable for Microsoft (including Belkin) and are available online for around $20 to $40.

Windows Easy Transfer next prompts for what removable media you want to utilize for the transfer. Options include CD or DVD, USB flash drive, or External hard disk or to a network location. Naturally, the right choice is dependent upon your environment.

5. **For purposes of this walkthrough, choose External hard disk or to a network location.**

6. **On the next screen, specify the path to where the payload should be stored in the Network location field.** We also recommend that this data be protected by entering an optional password (as is typical, the password must be typed twice to confirm it was entered as intended).

7. Press the **Next** button to continue. You are prompted to choose what is to be transferred.

8. **You can choose All user accounts, files and settings; My user account, files and settings; or Advanced options.** The recommended choice is All user accounts, files, and settings, but in order to see just what can be migrated, choose Advanced options.

   A progress bar appears briefly as Windows Easy Transfer determines what it will be able to migrate. When complete, a list of accounts, files and settings are presented with check boxes alongside each. All are checked by default, and any items you do not wish to migrate can be unchecked. There are also buttons to add specific files or folders or to specify other drives. At the bottom right, the size of the data to be transferred is displayed. Keep an eye on this if the space you have for the transfer is limited.

9. **After all desired items have been specified, click the Next button to begin collecting user files and settings.** When complete, a message that you are ready to transfer files and settings to your new computer is displayed.

Restoring files and settings

The computer to where files and settings are to be restored is referred to as the *new computer* by the Windows Easy Transfer tool. To restore the data collected from the old computer using the previous steps, sit down at the new computer and follow these steps:

1. **Launch Windows Easy Transfer.** If you have any running programs, you are prompted to close them before proceeding.

   A Welcome screen appears as the first screen of the wizard (see Figure 5.5). It contains a summary of the tool's capabilities and links to help.

2. **Click the Next button to begin.**

3. **On the next screen, choose Continue a new transfer in progress to continue.** You are prompted to identify how the data is to be retrieved: over the network or using removable media.

4. **Choose No, I've copied files and settings to a CD, DVD, or other removable media to continue.**

   The wizard then asks where the files were saved: On a CD or DVD, on a USB flash drive, or on an external hard disk or network location.

5. **Choose On an external hard disk or network location to continue.**

6. **On the next page, you can type or browse to the location of your settings file and optionally include a password in the field provided if you choose to enter one during the capture process. When you have specified the path (and if necessary the password) needed to access the data, press the Next button to continue.**

   The Windows Easy Transfer wizard next asks that you "Type a new user name or click a name in the list" in order to specify the target account. You can use the same name or a new one. If you create a new account the password is not transferred to the new computer; instead the user will be prompted to create a password the first time they log on to the new computer.

7. **After you have specified a target user account for those to be restored, click the Next button to continue.**

   A summary page is offered so you may review the selected files and settings. A tree-view is provided so you may browse what is to be restored, and at the bottom right, the transfer size is identified.

8. **Click the Transfer button to begin the restoral process.**

   During the restoral process, you are warned not to use the computer or you may need to restart the restoral process. After the transfer is completed, a transfer summary is displayed with the option to see a detailed list of what was transferred.

9. **Click the Close button to exit Windows Easy Transfer.**

Working with the User State Migration Tool (USMT)

As you know by now, the User State Migration Tool (USMT) is used to migrate user accounts during large deployments of Windows Vista operating systems (and Microsoft Windows XP). USMT captures user accounts, including desktop and application settings as well as user files, and then migrates them to a new Windows installation. Similar to Windows Easy Transfer, you can use USMT for both side-by-side and wipe-and-load migrations.

USMT is intended for administrators who are performing automated deployments. If you are only migrating the user states of a few computers, you can use the Files and Settings Transfer Wizard for computers running Windows XP, or Windows Easy Transfer for computers running Windows Vista. USMT enables you to do the following:

- **Configure the migration for your needs**. Using the migration rule files, you can control exactly which user accounts, files, and settings are migrated and how they are migrated.

- **Automate the migration**. Use the two USMT command line tools, which control collecting and restoring the user files and settings. These two tools provide the core functions of USMT:

  - **ScanState.exe** collects files and settings from a computer.

  - **LoadState.exe** restores files and settings to a computer.

In this section, we will discuss the requirements and limitations of USMT before going into customizing and using the tools provided.

Requirements

USMT supports Windows 2000, XP, and Vista. However, LoadState (the tool used on the destination computer) does not support Windows 2000. Therefore, you can migrate from Windows 2000, but your destination must be Windows XP SP2,Vista, or later. Windows Server is not supported.

> **NOTE** Both 32 and 64 bit editions of Windows XP and Vista are supported. When migrating between 32 and 64 bit editions, you can migrate from 32 to 64 bit, but you cannot migrate from 64 to 32 bit.

Earlier in this chapter we covered determining how much drive space would be required to perform a migration. Naturally, the target system also requires space to accept the restoral. In fact, it requires at least two times the space required by the largest backed up file plus the size of the uncompressed store. The reason is that when LoadState runs on the destination computer it migrates each file one at a time from the store to a temporary location on the destination computer. It then transfers the file to the target location and deletes the temporary copy before moving onto the next file.

Understanding USMT limitations

We have discussed things that can be migrated, but every tool has a number of things for which various reasons cannot be migrated by USMT. Such items include:

- Mapped network drives
- Local printers
- Network printers (if the destination computer is running Window XP)
- Microsoft Project settings (when migrating from Office 2003 to Office 2007)

- Taskbar settings (when migrating from Windows XP to Vista)
- Customized icons for shortcuts
- Permissions for shared folders (shares are normally maintained on servers)
- Files and settings between installations with different languages (both source and destination computer must have matching languages of Windows)
- Settings from older versions of applications (with the exception of Microsoft office, the version of the application being migrated must be the same on the source and destination computer)
- Hardware settings and drivers
- Passwords
- Application installations (some settings may be migrated, but the applications must first be installed on the target system through a separate mechanism)

Customizing migration with USMT

Although the command line options discussed later in this section dictate what actions are performed by the ScanState and LoadState tools, the XML-based configuration files dictate what is backed up.

Some default migration files are provided that suffice for many environments, including:

- **MigUser.xml**: Specifies user files and settings
- **MigSys.xml**: Specifies system settings to be migrated
- **MigApp.xml**: Specifies application settings to be migrated

Creating your own configuration files for USMT

It is best to use the included default migration files as models for your own custom migration files. To migrate user data files, model your custom .xml file on MigUser.xml. To migrate operating system settings to a computer running Windows XP, model your .xml on MigSys.xml. And to migrate application settings, start with MigApp.xml. However, these files are very large, and simply adding your own code to them can make changes difficult to read and edit. Therefore, it is recommended that you create your own separate XML files instead of adding to the existing ones. Plus, if you were to reinstall USMT, the default files would be overwritten and your changes would be lost.

We also recommended that you do not alter the operating system settings (MigSys.xml) file. These settings are migrated by manifests that should not be modified. If you have a need to exclude certain operating systems settings from migration, you should create and modify a Config.xml file.

> **NOTE** You can use the asterisk (*) wildcard character in migration XML files, but you cannot use the question mark (?) wildcard character — it is unsupported.

Modifying user files and settings is straightforward and will be discussed later in this section. A more challenging task is to create a custom configuration file that handles the migration of an application not supported by the default MigApp.xml. Creating a configuration file for USMT to migrate application settings may be realized by executing the following steps:

1. **Verify the correct version of the application is installed.**
2. **Identify what settings should be migrated.**
3. **Identify how to apply the migrated settings.**
4. **Author a migration component for the application.**
5. **Test the application settings migration.**

Each of these steps is covered in the following section.

Verifying that the correct version is installed

Although we have established that it is not advisable to migrate application settings for an application that will not be installed on the target system, it is also important to make sure that the version of the application is the same on both the source and target systems. A newer version of the application may not store settings in the same place, which could result in problems on the destination computer.

Although you can normally look to the About box under the Help menu of an application for version information, not all applications easily provide version information. Minor version changes in particular can be hard to determine within the application. A couple of ways to identify the version of the application are to check the registry's uninstall key and to check the version information on the application's executable file.

To check the uninstall key, launch RegEdit and browse to the following:

```
HKEY_LOCAL_MACHINE\Software\Microsoft\Windows\CurrentVersion\Uninstall
```

Here you find a subkey for each installed application which may be identified by a friendly name or GUID. In this subkey is normally a value specifying the version number of the application that may be used to ascertain the exact version number of the installed application in question.

You can also look to the application's executable file and view its properties to see the version number of the application, as shown in Figure 5.6.

To view the file version properties, follow these steps:

1. **Locate the executable for the program in File Explorer.** The file is typically named close to that of the application's title and stored under the Program Files folder in an easily identifiable subfolder.
2. **Right-click the file and choose Properties.**
3. **Click the Details tab (in Windows XP, the tab to choose is titled Version).**
4. **Record the full version number for comparison.**

FIGURE 5.6

Reviewing file properties to determine application version

Of course, if you are migrating to a new system you will be installing the applications on the system after Windows Vista has been applied (or the application may be part of your custom image). In either case, simply ensure that the version you plan to install as part of your migration matches that of the existing application from which you will be migrating.

If you are upgrading an application as part of your migration to Windows Vista, you need to determine how to best proceed. You can upgrade the existing operating system to the latest version of the application to be sure there will not be an issue in application setting migration, or you can consciously migrate from one version to the next and then perform testing to ensure everything functions as desired.

Identifying settings that should be migrated

The most tedious step is to identify what settings should be migrated. It is best to have a subject matter expert on the application with which you are working to help identify settings of importance. In order to identify where these settings are storing their values it is necessary to go through each setting in the application and modify it while running a file and registry monitor utility, such as Process Monitor.

The following steps take you through identifying where application settings may be stored:

1. **Download Process Monitor from** http://technet.microsoft.com/en-us/ sysinternals/bb896645.aspx.

2. **Shut down as many applications as possible to reduce the activity on the computer.** Process Monitor will record *all file and registry activity* so the less work the system is doing the less Process Monitor will be taxed to record.

3. **Launch the application for which you are working to identify migration settings.**

4. **Launch Process Monitor immediately to stop the capture process by choosing File ⇨ Capture Events (or press Ctrl+E).** Process Monitor begins automatically, and it is important to first filter what is captured so it is easier to determine the changes with which you are working to identify.

5. **Choose Filter ⇨ Filter from the menu at the top of the window to launch the Process Monitor Filter dialog.**

6. **To limit what is captured to the application with which you are working, choose Process Name, for an operator choose not a process name, choose that of your running application, and click the Add button (as shown in Figure 5.7).**

FIGURE 5.7

Applying a filter in Process Monitor

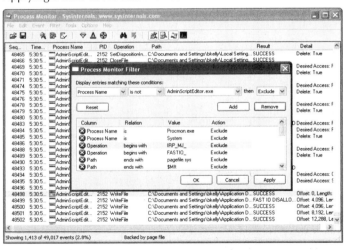

7. **Next, restart the monitoring process by again selecting File ⇨ Capture Events (or by pressing Ctrl+E).**

8. **In the application, change and apply any changes you wish to migrate and then view Process Monitor to see where the change is being applied to the system.** In this way, you should be able to identify any registry entries or files that require inclusion in your migration in order to support this application.

Some applications store information in the user profile that should not be migrated (for example, installation paths, computer name, and other computer-specific information). You should make sure to exclude such files and registry keys from the migration.

Identifying how to apply the migrated settings

In most cases, the target location is the same as that of the source computer. USMT automatically uses environment variables to determine destination paths. So for example, if you have a file collected from a Windows XP profile path (`C:\Documents and Settings\User1\My Documents`), the Vista destination folder will automatically be handled as its new location under the Users folder (`C:\Users\User1`). However, there may be cases when you need to modify the location of some settings, and USMT configuration files allow you to support these cases if they are encountered.

Authoring a migration component for the application

A migration file supports several XML elements that allow you to control the actions to be executed. It is beyond the scope of this book to go into detail regarding these elements, but an online reference is provided at `http://technet2.microsoft.com/WindowsVista/en/library/91f62fc4-621f-4537-b311-1307df0105611033.mspx`.

Testing the application settings migration

Perform the actual migration using test systems and verify the desired files and settings are transferred in the process. Launch the application on each system and compare settings to verify each was included as desired.

Excluding files and settings

To exclude files and settings, you can create a `custom .xml` file by using the `<include>` and `<exclude>` elements to exclude options with conditions. When specifying `<exclude>` you should always specify a corresponding `<include>`. The reason is that without an `<include>` there is no reason to exclude it (it would not be included to begin with).

For example, perhaps you know users have mp3 files in folders that you might otherwise be migrating. The solution would be to include all files from `C:\` *except* .mp3 files. For example, to get all files excluding mp3 files, you can use the following custom XML configuration file contents:

```xml
<migration urlid="http://www.microsoft.com/migration/1.0/migxmlext/mp3files">
    <component type="Documents" context="System">
        <displayName _locID="miguser.sharedvideo">MP3 Files</displayName>
        <role role="Data">
            <rules>
                <include filter='MigXmlHelper.IgnoreIrrelevantLinks()'>
                    <objectSet>
                        <pattern type="File">C:\* [*]</pattern>
                    </objectSet>
                </include>
                <exclude>
                    <objectSet>
```

```
                              <pattern type="File">C:\* [*.mp3]</pattern>
                        </objectSet>
                   </exclude>
              </rules>
         </role>
    </component>
</migration>
```

NOTE   The pattern elements you see here are written as regular expressions. Although regular expressions can be fairly intimidating to the uninitiated, they provide a powerful way to identify elements. The examples included here, online, and on user support forums will likely get you what you are looking for, but you may find a need to write your own. Should you need to write your own regular expressions, you could use some helpful tools, such as Expresso from Ultrapico, which is a free tool to help write and test regular expressions. Download Expresso from www.ultrapico.com/Expresso.htm.

Another, arguably easier, way you can exclude items is to use a Config.xml file (discussed later in this section).

Including files and settings

If you are aware of a specific area of the registry you would like to migrate, you can specify a subkey, value, or a subkey and its child subkey. To migrate a set of registry keys and its subkeys, the following XML file contents may be used:

```
<migration urlid="http://www.microsoft.com/migration/1.0/migxmlext/TestSubkey">
    <component type="Application" context="System">

    <displayName>Component to migrate all ApplicationName HKCU subkeys and values
    </displayName>
         <role role="Settings">
         <rules>
              <include>
                   <objectSet>

    <pattern type="Registry">HKCU\Software\Company\ApplicationName\* [*]</
    pattern>
                   </objectSet>
              </include>
         </rules>
         </role>
    </component>
</migration>
```

There may be a data folder or perhaps a folder specific to an application you are working to include in the migration. To specify the inclusion of a folder from a specific drive (and from any location) on a computer, the following XML file contents may be used:

```
<migration urlid="http://www.microsoft.com/migration/1.0/migxmlext/test">
<component type="Documents" context="System">
  <displayName>Component to migrate all ApplicationNameData folder contents on
  any drive on the computer </displayName>
  <role role="Data">
    <rules>
        <include>
          <objectSet>

  <script>MigXmlHelper.GenerateDrivePatterns ("\ApplicationNameData\* [*] ",
  "Fixed")</script>

  <script>MigXmlHelper.GenerateDrivePatterns ("*\ApplicationNameData \* [*] ",
  "Fixed")</script>
        </objectSet>
          </include>
    </rules>
  </role>
</component>
</migration>
```

Rerouting files and settings

There may also be files and settings you want to migrate, but you want to specify an alternate target location as part of the transfer process. For example, to migrate all .jpg files and have them restored to a folder named Images on the destination computer, the following XML file contents may be used:

```
<migration urlid="http://www.microsoft.com/migration/1.0/migxmlext/test">
<component type="Documents" context="System">
  <displayName>All .jpg files to Images</displayName>
  <role role="Data">
    <rules>
      <include>
        <objectSet>
          <script>MigXmlHelper.GenerateDrivePatterns ("* [*.jpg]", "Fixed")</
  script>
        </objectSet>
      </include>
      <locationModify script="MigXmlHelper.Move('C:\Images')">
        <objectSet>
          <script>MigXmlHelper.GenerateDrivePatterns ("* [*.jpg]", "Fixed")</
  script>
        </objectSet>
      </locationModify>
    </rules>
  </role>
</component>
</migration>
```

NOTE Sample XML configuration files for USMT may be found online at Microsoft's Web site at `http://technet2.microsoft.com/WindowsVista/en/library/38291110-5f95-4baa-a9f2-d4a30f32299b1033.mspx`

Working with Config.xml

Config.xml is an optional file you can create by using the /genconfig option of the ScanState tool. If you want to exclude certain elements of a migration, this is the preferred way to do so. This file does not contain any migration rules, just a list of system components, applications, and user documents that may be migrated.

Running the following command on a machine causes the config.xml file to be built containing every component that can be migrated. The components are organized into sections: <Applications>, <WindowsComponents>, and <Documents>. To choose not to migrate a component, simply change its entry to migrate="no" as shown in Figure 5.8.

FIGURE 5.8

Editing a Config.XML file to exclude items from migration

To create a Config.xml file in the current directory run the following command (note: this does not create a store, just the Config.xml file):

```
ScanState /i:migapp.xml /i:miguser.xml /genconfig:config.xml
```

To make use of this same Config.xml when creating a migration package, run the following command:

```
ScanState \\server\share\store /i:migapp.xml /i:miguser.xml /o /config:config.xml
```

> **NOTE** As specified in the documentation of the ScanState tool later in this chapter, the /o option will instruct the tool to overwrite any existing data in the store. If not specified, ScanState would fail if the store already contained data.

Collecting files and settings with ScanState

You must run ScanState as Administrator. On Windows 2000 and XP systems, you can simply log on and run the tool with an administrative account. On Windows Vista systems, you will be prompted by User Authentication Control (UAC) to allow the tool to run with this required access. Of course, if you have a systems management solution in place to distribute the command line, this is ideal. Using group policy, a startup script can do the job, but keep in mind that a logon script runs in the context of the user (which will fail unless all your users happen to be administrators).

ScanState is a command line tool with many options (Table 5.2 describes each of the options individually). Following this table are some typical examples of ScanState commands. The syntax for ScanState is:

```
scanstate [StorePath] [/i:[Path\]FileName] [/o] [/v:VerbosityLevel]
    [/nocompress] [/localonly] [/encrypt /key:KeyString|/keyfile:[Path\]FileName]
    [/l:[Path\]FileName] [/progress:[Path\]FileName] [/r:TimesToRetry]
    [/w:SecondsBeforeRetry] [/c] [/p] [/all] [/ui:[DomainName\]
    UserName]|LocalUserName] [/ue:[DomainName\]UserName]|LocalUserName] [/
    uel:NumberOfDays|YYYY/MM/DD|0] [/efs:abort|skip|decryptcopy|copyraw] [/
    genconfig:[Path\]FileName] [/targetxp] [/config:[Path\]FileName] [/?|help]
```

TABLE 5.2	

ScanState Command Line Parameters

Option	Description
StorePath	Specifies folder where the files and settings are to be stored.
/i	Specifies configuration xml file containing rules that define what state to migrate. This is typically used more than once to specify multiples of such files (such as MigUser.xml, MigApp.xml, MyCustom.xml).
/o	Overwrite any existing data in the store. If not specified ScanState will fail if the store already contains data.
/v	Specifies the verbosity of the output created in the ScanState log. The default is 0, but valid values range from 0 to 15.
/nocompress	Disables compression (enabled by default). This may be used for troubleshooting purposes so you can browse the contents or to use a virus scanning program to scan the contents.
/localonly	Limits migration to files stored on the local computer (regardless of the rules specified in included xml configuration files). If this option is not specified, data from external drives on the source computer will be included in the collection process.

continued

TABLE 5.2   *(continued)*

Option	Description
/encrypt	Encrypts the store with the specified key (password). The key is specified with the /key or /keyfile options.
/key:<KeyString>	Used with the /encrypt option to identify a KeyString between 8 and 256 characters long. If there is a space in the KeyString value, surround the string in double quotes.
/keyfile:<KeyFile>	Used with the /encrypt option to identify a text file that contains an encryption key (as opposed to providing the string on the command line with the /key option).
/l	Specifies the location of the ScanState log file. This can be specified as a relative path or a full path, but cannot be the same folder as StorePath.
/progress	Creates the optional progress log. This can be specified as a relative path or a full path, but cannot be the same folder as StorePath.
/r	Specifies the number of times to retry when an error occurs. The default is three times. This can be helpful in environments where network connectivity is an issue.
/w	Specifies the number of seconds to wait between retries (see /r option). The default is 1 second.
/c	Causes ScanState to continue to run even if there are nonfatal errors. Without this option, ScanState will exit on the first error encountered. Any such errors are ignored but will be logged in the progress log.
/p	Generates a space-estimate file called usmtsize.txt that is saved to StorePath. When this option is specified no user stat is collected. Note: You must also specify /nocompress with this option.
/all	This option explicitly migrates all of the users on the computer, which is the default behavior unless accounts are excluded with either the /ue or /uel options.
/ui:<UserID>	Migrates only specified users. You can specify the domain and user name or a local user name. All users are included by default, so this option is only helpful when using the /ue or /uel options to exclude users. The asterisk (*) wildcard is supported. For example, to migrate only the user named NCKELLY, you could use the following options: /ue:** /ui:domain\NCKELLY
/ue:<UserID>	Excludes specified users from migration. You can specify the domain and user name or a local user name.
/uel:<NumberOfDays>	Limits migration to only users that have logged onto the source computer within the specified number of days.

Option	Description
/efs:<Setting>	Specifies how the ScanState should handle EFS encrypted files. The following settings may be specified: /efs:abort: Fail with an error code if an EFS file is found on the source computer /efs:skip: Ignore all EFS files /efs:decryptcopy: Decrypt if possible before saving to store /efs:copyraw: Copy the file in its encrypted state EFS Certificates are migrated automatically. When migrating to Windows Vista it is recommended that you use the /efs:copyraw option
/genconfig	Generates a Config.xml file which identifies all items that would be collected. Instead of collecting the items, it generates a file identifying each component that would be migrated with the identifier **migrate="yes"** included with each item. By editing this file to reflect **migrate="no"** where items should be excluded, the /config option may be used to enforce these exclusions.
/targetxp	Optimizes the process for situations when the destination computer will be running Windows XP. This option is helpful when creating a store as it will limit the contents to those items that pertain to Windows XP. This may also be used with /genconfig to limit the contents of config.xml to those items that pertain to Windows XP.
/config	Specifies the optional Config.xml file that should be used when creating a store. This can be specified as a relative path or a full path (if you do not specify a path, Config.xml must be located in the current directory).

This example collects user data and settings (scanstate) by using the default MigUser.xml and MigApp.xml configuration files (/i:miguser.xml /i:migapp.xml) and saves the resulting store to \\ server\share\store. It creates a verbose log file with status messages that can be used with a debugger (/v:13) to a file named scan.log which is created in the current directory (/l:scan.log):

```
ScanState \\server\share\store /i:miguser.xml /i:migapp.xml /v:13 /l:scan.log
```

This next example generates an usmtsize.txt file (/p) that provides a space-estimate based on the collection of user data and settings (scanstate) using the default MigUser.xml and MigApp.xml configuration files (/i:miguser.xml /i:migapp.xml). The /nocompress option is required when generating a space estimate file with /p. Finally, because the destination for the store is a network location, a log file with the /l option must be specified. In this case, the log file would be created in the current directory and would record only default errors and warnings (as is dictated by the default logging level of zero).

```
ScanState /i:miguser.xml /i:migapp.xml \\server\share\store /nocompress /p
    /l:scan.log
```

This final example collects user data and settings (scanstate) by using the default MigUser.xml and MigApp.xml configuration files (/i:miguser.xml /i:migapp.xml) and saves the resulting store to E:\ localstore. However, only those users who have logged in within the last 45 days will have their data and settings migrated (/uel:45).

```
ScanState /i:migapp.xml /i:miguser.xml E:\localstore /uel:45
```

Restoring files and settings with LoadState

Although it is not always essential, installing all applications on the destination computer before restoring the user state is a good practice. Doing this ensures that migrated settings are preserved; otherwise some applications may overwrite or disregard existing settings restored by LoadState.

LoadState is a command line tool with many options (Table 5.3 describes each of the options individually). Following this table are some typical examples of LoadState commands. The syntax for LoadState is:

```
loadstate StorePath [/i:[Path\]FileName] [/v:VerbosityLevel] [/nocompress]
    [/decrypt /key:KeyString|/keyfile:[Path\]FileName] [/l:[Path\]FileName]
    [/progress:[Path\]FileName] [/r:TimesToRetry] [/w:SecondsToWait] [/c] [/all]
    [/ui:[[DomainName\]UserName]|LocalUserName] [/ue:[[DomainName\]
    UserName]|LocalUserName] [/uel:NumberOfDays|YYYY/MM/DD|0] [/
    md:OldDomain:NewDomain] [/mu:OldDomain\OldUserName:[NewDomain\]NewUserName]
    [/lac:[Password]] [/lae] [/q] [/config:[Path\]FileName] [/?|help]
```

TABLE 5.3

LoadState Command Line Parameters

Option	Description
StorePath	Specifies folder where the files and settings are stored.
/i	Specifies configuration xml file containing rules that define what state to migrate. This is typically used more than once to specify multiples of such files (such as MigUser.xml, MigApp.xml, MyCustom.xml, etc.).
/v	Specifies the verbosity of the output created in the ScanState log. The default is 0, but valid values range from 0 to 15: output
/nocompress	Specifies that the store is not compressed.
/decrypt	Decrypts the store with the specified key. The key is specified with the /key or /keyfile options.
/key	Used with the /decrypt option to identify a KeyString between 8 and 256 characters long. If there is a space in the KeyString value, surround the string in double quotes.

Option	Description
/keyfile	Used with the /decrypt option to identify a text file that contains an encryption key (as opposed to providing the string on the command line with the /key option).
/l	Specifies the location of the LoadState log file. This can be specified as a relative path or a full path, but cannot be the same folder as StorePath. running LoadState from a shared network resource.
/progress	Creates the optional progress log. This can be specified as a relative path or a full path, but cannot be the same folder as StorePath.
/r	Specifies the number of times to retry when an error occurs. The default is three times. This can be helpful in environments where network connectivity is an issue.
/w	Specifies the number of seconds to wait between retries (see /r option). The default is one second.
/c	Causes LoadState to continue to run even if there are nonfatal errors. Without this option, LoadState will exit on the first error encountered. Any such errors are ignored but will be logged in the progress log.
/all	This option explicitly migrates all of the users on the computer, which is the default behavior unless accounts are excluded with either the /ue or /uel options.
/ui	Migrates only specified users. You can specify the domain and user name or a local user name. All users are included by default, so this option is only helpful when using the /ue or /uel options to exclude users. The asterisk (*) wildcard is supported. For example, to migrate only the user named NCKELLY, you could use the following options: /ue:** /ui:domain\NCKELLY
/ue:<UserID>	Excludes specified users from migration. You can specify the domain and user name or a local user name.
/uel:<NumberOfDays>	Limits migration to only users that have logged onto the source computer within the specified number of days.
/md:<OldDomain>:<NewDomain> /md:<LocalComputerName>:<NewDomain>	Specifies a new domain for the user(s). This option may be used to change the domain for users on a computer or to migrate a local user to a domain account. *OldDomain* may contain the asterisk (*) wildcard character.
/mu:<OldDomain\OldUserName>:<[NewDomain\]NewUserName> /mu:<OldLocalUserName>:<NewDomain\NewUserName>	Specifies a new user name for the specified user. If the store contains more than one user, multiple /mu options may be specified. You cannot use wildcard characters with this option.

continued

TABLE 5.3	*(continued)*
Option	**Description**
/lac:<*Password*>	Specifies that if a user account is a local account, and it does not already exist on the destination computer, to create the account on the destination computer as a disabled account (to enable the account, the /lae option must be specified as well).
	If /lac is not specified, any local user accounts that do not already exist on the destination computer will not be migrated. Password is the password for the newly created account. By default, an empty password is used.
/lae	Enables the account that was created with /lac. You must specify /lac with this option.
/q	Allows LoadState to run without administrative credentials. This option only migrates the account for the user who is currently logged on.
/config	Specifies the optional Config.xml file that should be used during restore. This can be specified as a relative path or a full path (if you do not specify a path, Config.xml must be located in the current directory).

The following command restores all user data and settings (LoadState) by using the default MigUser.xml and MigApp.xml configuration files (/i:miguser.xml /i:migapp.xml) from the specified store at \\server\share\store. Finally, because the destination for the store is a network location, we must also specify a log file with the /l option. In this case, the log file would be created in the current directory and would record only default errors and warnings (as is dictated by the default logging level of zero).

```
LoadState /i:migapp.xml /i:miguser.xml \\server\share\store /c /l:load.log
```

This next command will restore all user data and settings (LoadState) using the MigUser.xml and custom.xml configuration files (/i:miguser.xml /i:custom.xml) from the specified store at E:\local-store. This store was encrypted using the /encrypted option, so to perform the restore, the /decrypt option is used and the password used as a Keystring during the ScanState phase is repeated here with LoadState (/key:NINRLS19).

```
LoadState /i:miguser.xml /i:custom.xml E:\Localstore /decrypt /key:NINRLS19
```

Reviewing best practices

The following are some best practices to keep in mind when working with USMT. Arguably the most important of these recommendations focus on security. Remember, when performing a migration you are taking personal information, potentially confidential information, and removing it from the environment where it was secured. Take care with user data by encrypting it, scanning it for viruses, and deleting the migration stores after the migration has succeeded.

- **Close all applications before running ScanState or LoadState:** While Windows Easy Transfer requires it, you could run the USMT tools with applications running, but doing so may result in a failure to migrate the settings of those applications.

- **Install applications before running LoadState:** To better ensure that migrated settings are preserved, it is best to install all applications on the destination computer before restoring user data and settings.

- **Log off after running LoadState:** Some system settings will not take effect until the next time a user logs in. To fully complete a restoral, log off of the system once LoadState has finished running.

- **Consolidate restored files:** To realize a more managed environment, you can redirect the restoral of documents to the smallest possible number of folders. For example, you can restore all office document types to the same profile folder (documents).

- **Encrypt the store:** Encrypting the store adds an element of security to the data. Use the / encrypt and /decrypt options to better protect user data and settings. At the same time, please keep in mind that the key (or password) is visible in plain text so anyone that has access to the command line (or your script that is running the command line) will also have access to this password.

- **Consider password migration:** USMT does not migrate passwords (including those for applications such as Outlook, Internet Explorer, Remote Access Service [RAS] connections, and mapped network drives). In order to ensure that all passwords are known, it is advisable to have end users change and record their passwords just prior to the migration.

- **Perform virus scans:** Scan both the source and destination computers for viruses before running USMT.

- **Maintain the security of the store while it is on your network:** Make certain that the file server where you save the store is secure. It is also important to secure the deployment server so that user data in the log files are not exposed.

- **Migrate in groups:** Particularly if performing the migration while users are using the network, it is best to migrate user accounts in groups. This both minimizes the impact on network performance and also allows you to make sure each phase is successful before moving on to the next. Finally, this also allows you to make any necessary modifications to your process between groups.

Investigating Third-Party Alternatives

While USMT could be an exception (it is a pretty comprehensive tool), going with the freely available tools offered by Microsoft is often not the ideal way to go. Third parties work hard to make themselves stand apart from these tools by focusing on a point solution as their specialty. While some systems management solutions offer user data and settings migration as one of their features, the following are a just a few of the tools which focus specifically on this task and are worth considering when choosing a solution:

- CA Desktop Migration Manager
- Tranxition Migration Studio
- PC Mover

CA Desktop Migration Manager

Formerly known as Desktop DNA, the product was acquired by Computer Associates and is now known as CA Desktop Migration Manager. It supports the full range of Windows platforms, including Windows 95, 98, NT, ME, 2000, XP, and Vista. It supports real-time migration over the network or using a simple crossover cable. It offers multiple ways to handle passwords: You can leave the current password, generate a password randomly using rules you define, or require the user to reset his or her password when logging on to the new PC after the migration is complete.

CA Desktop Migration Manager also provides the ability to perform Active Directory migrations (moving user profiles from Windows NT domains into AD). It supports redirecting users into AD, renaming them to a new naming convention, migrating file/folder and group security concurrently, and defining roaming users. This lets you migrate only those users who are active, effectively cleaning up your directory system.

Finally, some of the limitations discussed with USMT, such as the ability to map network drives and local printers, can be overcome with this solution.

Learn more about Desktop Migration Manager online at `http://ca.com/us/desktop-migration.aspx`.

Tranxition Migration Studio

Tranxition Migration Studio offers a drag and drop interface for creating predefined instructions to control the migration. This graphical tool helps you build your own custom migration scripts, and even the migration interface itself offers an interactive GUI to select the things you want to migrate. Naturally, the deployment tools offer command line support so they can be easily automated through your systems management software (or with a simple batch file).

Learn more about Tranxition Migration Studio online at `www.tranxition.com/tms.html`.

PC Mover

Laplink offers a solution named PC Mover which is geared toward end users or smaller interactive migrations for systems versions of Windows as far back as Windows 95. It supports the ability to move applications along with files and settings as part of the migration process. It does not provide a limited set of supported applications, but reports to move all applications, windows settings, and data files.

Other features of note include the ability to "undo" (reverse) a migration, and it offers several connection options including a parallel cable, Laplink cable, East Transfer Cable, network, or removable media.

Learn more about PC Mover online at `www.laplink.com/business_solutions/pcmover.html`.

Summary

A well-planned migration can save lots of user frustration and make your entire migration to Vista a much more successful project. After you assess just what it is you want to migrate, you need to choose a solution. No matter if you go with USMT, Windows Easy Transfer, or one of the third-party solutions covered here, it is important to understand the capabilities of the tool and how they support your needs. Keep security in mind throughout the process of moving this data and protect your user's data and settings. With proper planning, the migration of user data and settings can be a very simple and straightforward process. Of course, like anything, it can become a complex operation if you choose to include application settings for software that is not supported natively by your migration tool, so consider the payoff for this work before going too far down that path.

Chapter 6

Managing Windows Images

I n the early days of Windows deployment, Microsoft did not want to have anything to do with imaging. Imaging was just plain unsupported when it made its debut. Over time, they gave in a little and agreed it was okay to image prior to the GUI stage of a Windows NT installation.

The main concern was that the security IDs on the system needed to be globally unique and by cloning a system, the process of generating a unique security ID was bypassed. To address this issue, tools such as GhostWalker, SIDgen, and NewSID were introduced. Microsoft offered Sysprep, a tool designed to put the system in a state where at next boot it would run a Mini-Setup, which includes minimal steps required to ensure the system is unique.

Today, Windows Vista and Server 2008 use Microsoft's file-based imaging mechanism as its general installation technology right on the commercial DVD. Command line utilities to create and manipulate these image files are now provided free to all as part of the Windows Automated Installation Kit (WAIK). In fact, Sysprep is included as part of the installed operating system now at `c:\windows\system32\sysprep` (a hidden folder).

Chapter 2 covers the creation of a basic image; this chapter goes into more detail about customizing and maintaining your Windows PE and production deployment images by familiarizing you with the following:

- **WIM file format:** This new file format is the key technology leveraged by many of the provided tools for the creation, management, and use of Windows Images (and the format for the new Windows Vista setup routine).

IN THIS CHAPTER

Introducing WIM

Customizing images

Understanding Microsoft tools for image management

Getting familiar with third-party tools

- **ImageX:** This command line utility is used to create, apply, and service images offline (without the need to apply it to a computer).

- **PEImg:** This command line utility is provided for manipulating Windows PE images (such as installing drivers and optional components).

- **OSCDImg:** This command line tool is used to generate bootable ISO images (particularly for Windows PE).

- **vLite:** This third-party freeware tool can be used to customize a Windows Vista setup image. It supports slipstreaming service packs, removing unwanted installation components, and a host of other customization features.

Once a good overview of these tools has been provided, the chapter will cover some common tasks and how these tools may be used to accomplish them and finally, some third-party alternatives available for your review.

Introducing Windows Image File (WIM)

Before you dive into the benefits of how to work with WIM files, you need to look at the file format itself. One of the biggest things that set it apart from most other imaging formats you may have worked with previously is that it is not a sector-based image. WIM is a file-based image, and this implementation provides several benefits.

Exploring the benefits of WIM

Traditional images were essentially a single binary file representing all the contents of a hard drive or hard drive partition. While some solutions included an image-editing tool to manipulate these images, just what you could modify differed greatly between products and was often lacking. The approach taken with WIM offers several benefits worth exploring:

- **The image is hardware independent**: Now you can create one image and apply it to dissimilar hardware, so long as it uses the same processor architecture. For example, a 64-bit image will not work on a 32-bit system.

- **More than one image can be stored in a single WIM file, which stores only one copy of each unique file (functioning as a single instance store)**: Aside from lowering the number of potential image files you need to manage, this also reduces the storage space needed to hold your images.

- **Images may be serviced offline**: Many changes can be made to an image file directly without the need to reapply the image to a machine, make changes, and recapture the image.

- **Images may be applied to disk partitions of any size.**

- An API (WIMGAPI) is provided for developers to work with WIM files in their applications (see the section "Developing Custom Solutions," later in this chapter).

- A WIM image allows for nondestructive deployment by not affecting other files on a system when a reinstallation or upgrade takes place.

In summary, WIM offers a solution that lets you reduce the number of disk images to maintain, and maintaining those images is much easier and requires less time.

Exploring the limitations of WIM

Nothing is perfect, so some of the limitations of the WIM format are as follows:

- **You cannot install applications into a WIM.**

- **You cannot easily import registry changes to a WIM.**

- **The command line interface can be challenging for some:** To address this, you may check out some "unofficial" tools, such as GImageX, discussed later in this chapter.

Introducing Windows PE

Windows PE is a valuable tool, and many administrators are beginning to take full advantage of it as they begin to investigate the deployment of Windows Vista. It was actually introduced back with the release of Windows XP, but distribution has been very limited. If you were not an OEM or did not have an enterprise account with Microsoft, Windows PE was not available to you. During this time, an alternative Preinstallation environment came to be named BartPE (BartPE is discussed later in this chapter; see the section "Investigating Third-Party Alternatives"). First, you need to get a good look at just what Windows PE is and what it gets you before covering the tools you may use to customize it.

Understanding the benefits of Windows PE

Windows PE is a DOS replacement. Although it doesn't fit on a floppy disk, you can boot to Windows PE from CD, DVD, or USB flash drive. Windows PE offers a command line interface and a limited number of plug-ins to expand upon the default capabilities of this slimmed-down operating system. Windows PE 2.0 runs on a Windows Vista Kernel and therefore supports any network drivers that would be supported by Vista.

As compared to working with DOS, its ability to leverage the same drivers you would in Windows is a considerable step forward. If you have ever tried to make a network boot disk, you know it can be a frustrating process (depending largely upon the hardware with which you are working).

Windows PE supports both IPv4 and IPv6, but it does not support other protocols, such as Internetwork Packet Exchange/Sequenced Packet Exchange (IPX/SPX). Windows PE supports Distributed File System (DFS) name resolution only to standalone DFS roots.

Understanding the limitations of Windows PE

Part of the reason Windows PE was not so easy to get hold of (until the release of Windows Vista in fact) is that there was fear of its being used as an alternative operating system. As such, Microsoft has implemented a number of limitations designed to keep its use on target with what it was designed to do: provide a simple platform on which systems could be provisioned.

Windows PE provides no support for file sharing or inbound connections, which means that it cannot be used to run tools, such as Remote Desktop (the server service is missing). In fact, many applications will not run in Windows PE as it is built upon a limited subset of the files that make up a full Windows installation. This is both to reduce the size of Windows PE as well as to ensure it is not abused. Windows PE is designed strictly as a tool to help with the distribution of the Windows operating system. To a lesser extent, it may also be used as a recovery platform, but this functionality is not provided out of the box. To ensure the freely downloaded Windows PE is not abused:

- **It will reboot after 72 hours of use (up from 24 hours which was the limitation in the previous release).**

- **Windows on Windows (WoW) is not supported so 16-bit applications won't run in 32-bit versions of Windows PE, and 32-bit applications won't run in 64-bit versions of Windows PE.**

- **Windows PE doesn't support the .NET Framework:** It includes only a subset of the Windows Vista Win32 APIs, including I/O (disk and network) and the core Win32 APIs.

Meeting minimum requirements

The minimum requirements of Windows PE should not be a problem for any computers you support.

- The computer must have a minimum of 256MB of RAM.

- Windows PE requires a Video Electronics Standards Association (VESA)-compatible display device and will use the highest screen resolution it detects as supported.

 If Windows PE can't detect video settings, it uses a resolution of 640 × 480 pixels.

Using the provided Windows PE image

Mostly likely, you will want to modify a Windows PE image to somehow customize it for your own use. This may be to automate the mapping of a network drive, to add a command line tool, or to incorporate the automation of several desired actions into a script. However, the Windows PE image provided in the Windows Automated Installation Kit (WAIK) is capable of running on many computers with no customization required.

After it loads, you may use the provided command prompt to map network drives and run other commands by typing them out and pressing enter just as you would by using the command prompt window within Windows.

Doing this can be helpful to see the value of Windows PE, but in seeing its value it is likely to spark several ideas, from customizing the default wallpaper to match that of your corporate design to including tools and scripts to manually or automatically perform any number of actions.

Will the application you want to run function in Windows PE? The best way to find out is to try. With so much missing from Windows PE, you may find that many applications will not run. If you find yourself wanting to run something that cannot be run within Windows PE, it may be best to look to alternatives, such as BartPE or VistaPE that are discussed at the end of this chapter. These tools are designed for expansion. You either will find it is much easier than Windows PE to extend the capabilities of these alternatives through your own experimentation or by using any of the many plug-ins developed by other users of these tools.

Customizing Windows PE Boot Images

As discussed earlier in this book, there are several tools available within the WAIK to assist in the customization of WIM files. Beyond these, there are a handful of freeware applications that can also greatly assist in customizing Windows image files. This section discusses several such tools:

- ImageX
- ImageX GUI Tools
- PEImg
- OSCDImg
- vLite

Working with ImageX

ImageX is a command line tool provided with the WAIK for the creation, editing, and installation of WIM image files. As a command line tool, it is easy to script actions using a simple batch file. For a list of supported command line arguments, see Table 6.1.

TABLE 6.1

ImageX Command Line Options

Command	Purpose
/Capture	Captures a volume image to a new WIM file
/Append	Appends a new volume image to an existing WIM file
/Delete	Deletes an image from a WIM file that contains multiple images
/Split	Splits an existing WIM file into multiple WIM files
/Info	Returns XML descriptions for the specified WIM file
/Dir	Displays a list of files and folders within a volume image
/Mount	Mounts an image to a specified directory (read-only)
/MountRW	Mounts an image to a specified directory (read-write enabled)
/UnMount	Unmounts the image from the specified directory where it was mounted
/Export	Transfers an image from one WIM file to another
/Apply	Applies a volume image to a specified drive
/?	lList of command line help for any of the above specified commands

In the following section, each of the commands available and their options are covered along with an example of its use. This is meant as a reference or to quickly familiarize you with what is possible using ImageX. For more real-world scenarios, see the "Executing Common Tasks" section later in this chapter.

NOTE In the early days of Microsoft's foray into Windows Imaging, ImageX was sometimes referred to as *XImage*. Although you may still find older references online, don't be confused, the name was simply changed to ImageX for its final release. This was for legal reasons, as *Ximage* was already the name of a tool used by Dell for their own standard image process they perform for their customers.

NOTE Although many of the commands and flags are shown here in upper- and lowercase characters, this is only to help for readability — commands, flags, and arguments passed to ImageX are not case sensitive.

Using the Capture command

The Capture command does just what you would expect: it captures an image of the specified volume and produces a WIM file based on its contents. Less known is the fact that you may use the Capture command to specify a directory. One thing to keep in mind is that you can use the Capture command just once per WIM file. If you want to include another capture in a WIM file, you must use the *Append* command.

The syntax for the ImageX Capture command is as follows:

```
ImageX [Flags] /Capture ImagePath ImageFile "ImageName" ["Description"]
```

The flags and other parameters shown here are described as:

- **Flags:** Several optional flags may be specified to control the actions of the Capture command. (For a list and brief description of each, see Table 6.2.)
- **ImagePath:** The path to the volume image to be captured. This may also be a subfolder path to capture a directory instead of an entire volume (required).
- **ImageFile:** The path of the new WIM file (required).
- **ImageName:** The unique name for the image being captured (required).
- **Description:** Optional text used to provide additional reference information for the image.

TABLE 6.2

Flags Supported by the ImageX Capture Command

Flag	Purpose
/Boot	Marks a volume image as bootable. Available for Windows PE images only.
/Check	Enables WIM in egrity checking. Flag must be supplied during updates
/Compress	Specifies the type of compression used for the initial capture operation. Valid options are "maximum," "fast," or "none."
/Config	Enables use of a configuration file for exclusion and compression options. The Config flag is to be followed by the path and filename of a configuration file.
/NoRPFix	Disables reparse point tag fix up. If not provided, reparse points that resolve to paths outside of image_path will not be captured.
/Scroll	Scrolls output for redirection.
/Verify	Enables file resource verification.

For example:

```
imagex /capture c: c:\imaging\data.wim  "Drive C"
```

The above example captures the contents of the C volume of the drive and stores its contents in a WIM file named "data.wim" at the specified path. Finally, the optional description for this image in the WIM is specified as Drive C.

Using the Append command

After you have a WIM file with an image included, adding additional images to the WIM file is performed by using the Append command. As a single instance store, only files not already included in the image are actually appended to the WIM file. Those that already exist in the WIM file are simply added as pointers in the metadata in the existing WIM file.

The syntax for the ImageX Append command is as follows:

```
ImageX [Flags] /Append ImagePath ImageFile "ImageName" ["Description"]
```

The flags and other parameters shown here are described as:

- **Flags:** The optional flags that may be specified to control the actions of the Append command are similar to that of the Capture command. For a list and brief description of each, see Table 6.3.
- **ImagePath:** The path to the volume image to be captured (required).
- **ImageFile:** The path of the new WIM file (required).
- **ImageName:** The unique name for the image being captured (required).
- **Description:** Optional text used to provide additional reference information for the image.

TABLE 6.3

Flags Supported by the ImageX Append Command

Flag	Purpose
/Check	Enables WIM integrity checking before applying the additional image.
/Ref <wimfile.swm>	Enables the reference of split .wim files (SWMs). wimfile.swm represents the name and location of additional split files. Wildcards are accepted.
/Scroll	Scrolls output for redirection.
/Verify	Enables file resource verification.

For example:

```
imagex /append d: c:\imaging\data.wim "Drive D"
```

The above example would capture the contents of the D volume of the drive and add its contents as an additional image stored in the existing WIM file named "data.wim" at the specified path. Finally, the optional description for this image in the WIM is specified as Drive D.

Using the Delete command

The Delete command may be used to remove the reference to a specific volume image. However, it does not actually remove the data from the image. So if you are looking to reduce the size of a WIM file by removing the data from an image you may export it to create a new WIM file (see the section "Using the Export Command"), or if you are prepared to release the image, you may use the Prep command. There must always be at least one volume image in a .WIM file, so you can delete a volume image only if more than one image exists.

The syntax for the ImageX Delete command is as follows:

```
ImageX [Flags] /delete ImageFile ImageNumber | ImageName
```

The flags and other parameters shown here are described as:

- **Flags:** The only accepted flag for the Delete command is /Check which may be specified in order to enable WIM integrity checking.
- **ImageFile:** The path of the WIM file containing the image to be deleted (required).
- **ImageNumber or ImageName:** Either you may specify the number that identifies the image within the WIM file or the name of the image within the WIM file (required).

For example:

```
imagex /delete c:\imaging\data.wim 2
```

The above example would remove the reference to the second image in the WIM file named data.wim at the specified path.

Using the Split command

The Split command may be used to split an existing WIM file into multiple read-only split files (SWM files). This can be helpful when storing images on removable media, or when you need to move very large images across a network.

The syntax for the ImageX Split command is as follows:

```
ImageX [Flags] /split OriginalImageFile DestinationImageFile FileSize
```

The flags and other parameters shown here are described as:

- **Flags:** The only accepted flag for the Delete command is /Check which may be specified in order to enable WIM integrity checking.
- **OriginalImageFile:** The path and filename of the image file that is to be split (required).
- **DestinationImageFile:** The path and initial filename for the split files (required).
- **FileSize:** The maximum size (in megabytes) for each split file to be created. Note this is a maximum; the files created will not be larger than this but will often be of varying, slightly smaller size (required).

For example:

```
imagex /split c:\imaging\data.wim c:\imaging\datafiles.swm 750
```

This example splits the file data.wim into multiple read-only files of no more than 750MB; the files would be based on the name datafiles.swm (datafiles.swm, datafiles2.swm, datafiles3.swm, for example).

Using the Info command

The Info command will display the details of a specified WIM file. Among other details, it lists the GUID, number of images, and the compression algorithm used. It also identifies what part of a split image file you are dealing with (it will indicate "1/1" if the full image is included). There is a lot more information here too, including an XML formatted look at each image with details like size, name, description, language, version, number of files and directories, as well as the time it was created and last modified. For an example of the details provided for the default Windows PE image, see Figure 6.1.

FIGURE 6.1

Reviewing the output of the ImageX Info command

> **NOTE**   There are several commands that require an image number or name in order to specify which image within a file is to be addressed. The ImageX Info command is a quick and easy way to determine both.

The syntax for the ImageX Info command is as follows:

```
ImageX [Flags] /info ImageFile [ImageNumber | ImageName] [NewImageName]
    [NewImageDescription]
```

The flags and other parameters shown here are described as:

- **Flags:** One or more optional flags may be specified. For a list and brief description of each, see Table 6.4.

- **ImageFile:** The path and filename of the image for which you to review information (required).

- **ImageNumber or ImageName:** Particularly when there is more than one image in the WIM, you may specify either the number that identifies the image within the WIM file or the name of the image within the WIM file (optional).

- **NewImageName:** The new unique name for the specified image (optional).

- **NewImageDescription:** The new description for the specified image (optional).

TABLE 6.4

Flags Supported by the ImageX Info Command

Flag	Purpose
/Boot	Marks a volume image as bootable. Available for Windows PE images only.
/Check	Enables WIM integrity checking.
/XML	Returns the output as well-formed XML.

For example:

```
imagex /xml /info c:\imaging\data.wim 1 "My Image" "This is my image file"
    >data_wim_details.xml
```

This example generates information about the first image in the file data.wim as well-formed XML and pipes that information to create (or overwrite) a new file named `data_wim_details.xml`. It also updates the name of the image to "My Image" and changes the description of the image to "This is my image file."

Using the Dir command

As you might expect, the ImageX Dir command returns a list of files and folders within a specified volume image. Of course, you can always mount the image to view it as a browsing directory structure, but using this method can be more helpful for use when scripting. This command can also be helpful in quickly determining if a file you added to an image was successfully performed.

The syntax for the ImageX Dir command is as follows:

```
ImageX /dir ImageFile ImageNumber ⇨ ImageName
```

These parameters are described as (no flags are accepted by this command):

- **ImageFile:** The path and filename of the image for which you want to review information (required).

- **ImageNumber or ImageName:** Either you may specify the number that identifies the image within the WIM file or the name of the image within the WIM file (required).

For example:

```
imagex /dir c:\imaging\data.wim 1 >data_wim_contents.txt
```

This creates a text file named "data_wim_contents.txt" that lists the files and folders contained in the first (or only) image contained in the file data.wim file at the specified path.

Using the Mount and MountRW commands

The Mount command is used to load a WIM file as a directory structure. To view the contents of an image, you can use the Mount command to create a folder structure, which you may then browse. To make changes, you must mount the image using the MountRW command. Doing this establishes a directory structure ready for changes. Once loaded, you may modify the image just as you do for any file or folder on the file system. A mounted image may also be manipulated with the PEImg tool (discussed later). Changes made to an image do not take place right away but are cached until you use the ImageX UnMount command with the Commit option.

Like the Delete command, you'll need to export the image in order to completely clean the WIM of the older files or changes. This is because the changes made are appended to the end of the WIM file and the earlier reference to the change is replaced with the updated data.

You may mount more than one image at a time only in read only mode (using the Mount command). This is to ensure proper locking and safe updating of the file when it is unmounted. Mount images you wish to change in read-write mode and when you are done making any desired changes, you may simply unmount the image with the commit argument to commit the changes back to the WIM file (or without the commit argument to discard the changes). All changes are committed or they are not, there is no ability to commit changes to an image partially.

The syntax for the ImageX Mount and MountRW commands are as follows:

```
ImageX [Flags] /Mount ImageFile ImageNumber | ImageName ImagePath
ImageX [Flags] /MountRW ImageFile ImageNumber | ImageName ImagePath
```

These flags and other parameters are described in the following list:

- **Flags:** The only accepted flag for the Mount and MountRW commands is /Check which may be specified in order to enable WIM integrity checking.

- **ImageFile:** The path and filename of the image file to be mounted (required).

- ■ **ImageNumber or ImageName:** As with many of the other commands, you may identify the image within the file by number or by name.
- ■ **ImagePath:** Identifies the target directory where the image is to be mounted.

For example:

```
imagex /mountrw c:\imaging\data.wim 1 c:\imaging\mount
```

This example loads the contents of the first (or only) image in the file data.wim into a directory structure with a root of C:\Imaging\Mount. It would do so in a read-write state so that changes can be made and then optionally committed to the image with the UnMount command.

Using the UnMount command

When an image has been mounted, this command unmounts the image while optionally committing any changes that have been applied while it was mounted.

The syntax for the UnMount command is as follows:

```
ImageX /UnMount [/Commit] [ImagePath]
```

The parameters are described in the following list (no flags are accepted by this command).

- ■ **Commit:** Specify the optional commit argument in order to integrate any changes made to the image while it was mounted. If this argument is not specified, the image will be unmounted and any changes will be disregarded (optional).
- ■ **ImagePath:** Identifies the target directory where the image is currently mounted. To actually unmount an image, this value is required. If the image path is not specified, a list of mounted images will be returned detailing the location and name of the mounted image (optional).

For example:

```
imagex /unmount /commit c:\imaging\mount
```

This example moves the contents of the c:\imaging\mount folder back into the WIM file from which it was mounted. Because the commit argument is specified, any changes that were made to the mounted files and folders are written back into the WIM file as changes.

Using the Export command

The Export command exports the contents of a WIM file into another WIM file. It is often used to essentially defragment or clean up a WIM file. Edits to a WIM file, including the deletion of an entire volume image, only result in the removal of references to those files, so the files are not physically removed. When exporting the contents of a WIM file from one to another, only the files with active references are included in the process.

> **NOTE** When working with Windows PE images, you can make use of the Pelmg Prep command to optimize an image for file size. For details, see the "Using the Prep Command" section later in this chapter.

The syntax for the ImageX Export command is as follows:

```
ImageX [Flags] /Export SourceImageFile SourceImageNumber | SourceImageName
        DestinationFile DestinationName
```

The flags and other parameters shown here are described as:

- **Flags:** The optional flags that may be specified to control the actions of the Export command are similar to that of the Capture command. For a list and brief description of each, see Table 6.5.
- **SourceImageFile:** The path to the WIM file that contains the image to be exported (required).
- **SourceImageNumber or SourceImageName:** As with many of the other commands, you may identify the image within the file by number or by name (required).
- **DestinationFile:** The path of the WIM file that will receive the image copy (required).
- **DestinationName:** The unique name for the image in the destination WIM file (required).

TABLE 6.5

Flags Supported by the ImageX Export Command

Flag	Purpose
/Boot	Marks a volume image as bootable. Available for Windows PE images only.
/Check	Enables WIM integrity checking. Flag must be supplied during updates.
/Compress	Specifies the type of compression used for the initial capture operation. Valid options are "maximum," "fast," or "none."
/Ref <wimfile.swm>	Enables the reference of split .wim files (SWMs). wimfile.swm represents the name and location of additional split files. Wildcards are accepted.

For example:

```
imagex /export c:\imaging\data.wim 1 c:\imageing\newdata.wim "My Clean Image"
```

The above example would take the first image in the data.wim file and copy it to an image named "My Clean Image" in the specified newdata.wim file.

Using the Apply Command

Also very straightforward, the Apply command may be used to apply an image to a volume. You can also apply an image to a directory (even when a full volume has been included in the WIM file).

The syntax for the Apply command is as follows:

```
ImageX [Flags] /apply ImageFile ImageNumber | ImageName ImagePath
```

The flags and other parameters shown here are described in the following list:

- **Flags:** One or more optional flags may be specified. For a list and brief description of each, see Table 6.6.
- **ImageFile:** The path and filename of the WIM file that contains the image you wish to apply (required).
- **ImageNumber or ImageName:** To identify which image in the WIM file you wish to apply, you may specify either the number that identifies the image or the name of the image (required).
- **ImagePath:** Identifies the target drive (and optional directory) where the image is to be applied.

TABLE 6.6

Flags Supported by the ImageX Apply Command

Flag	Purpose
/Check	Enables WIM integrity checking. Flag must be supplied during updates.
/Ref <wimfile.swm>	Enables the reference of split .wim files (SWMs). wimfile.swm represents the name and location of additional split files. Wildcards are accepted.
/Scroll	Scrolls output for redirection.
/Verify	Enables file resource verification.

For example:

```
imagex /apply c:\imaging\data.wim 2 d:
```

This example applies the contents of the second image contained in data.wim to the D drive of the computer.

Working with an ImageX GUI

As a command line tool, ImageX can be very easy to automate using scripts (for more on this see, the section "Developing Custom Solutions" later in this chapter). However, if you are performing these tasks interactively and are not unaccustomed to command line tools and the many arguments they can require, a graphical user interface can be desirable. Microsoft provides no such solution, but other companies have taken it upon themselves to offer such an option:

- GImageX
- WIM Master
- OnDansWIM

Introducing GImageX

GImageX is probably the most popular solution of those listed here. It has evolved into a very helpful tool, which began its life as a tool that was written in the *AutoIt* scripting language as a learning tool for those interested in learning AutoIt. However, it was also offered in the form of a compiled executable, which made it a valuable tool for those with no interest in scripting at all.

Taking the fact that ImageX is a highly scriptable utility to a new level, this script utilized AutoIt's ability to produce simple Windows Forms to offer an intuitive interface, so you could avoid the command line entirely. It included tabs for each of the major functions and text boxes, combo boxes, and check boxes to specify simple details that were then translated to command line arguments when calling ImageX behind the scenes. Because GImageX was essentially a front end to generating ImageX command lines, it required the `imagex.exe` utility.

The current release of GImageX takes things forward even further. With the same look (see Figure 6.2), installation now requires only that the wimgapi.dll file (from the WAIK) be stored in the same directory as GImageX (which is provided as a single executable). This is because GImageX now handles actions programmatically by using Microsoft's provided API. In fact, the rather challenging API calls offered by Microsoft can be accessed through a COM version of GImageX using a well-documented COM interface that can be leveraged by programs and scripts (for more on this see the section "Developing Custom Solutions" later in this chapter).

Introducing WIM Master

WIM Master is another GUI solution for performing ImageX commands using a simple form. Its layout is almost identical to that of GImageX. This open source tool is written in Microsoft Visual C++.

Also distributed with the tool and its source code is a BartPE plug-in and a VistaPE script. (See the section "Investigating Third-Party Alternatives" for more on these alternative preinstallation environments.)

WIM Master is available from the discussion thread online at `www.boot-land.net/ forums/?showtopic=3001`

FIGURE 6.2

Taking a look at GImageX

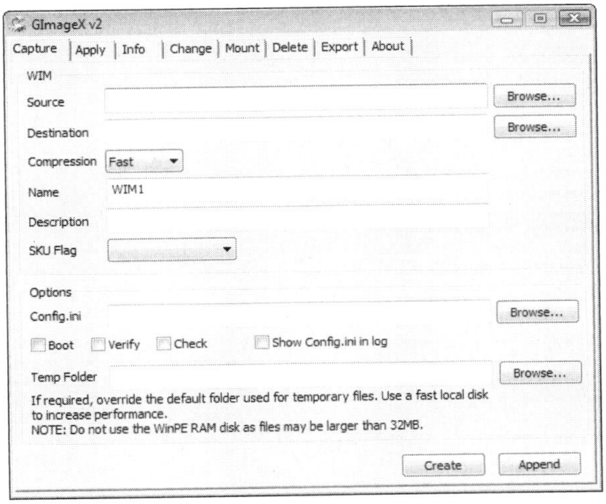

Introduc ing OnDansWIM

You can use another open source tool, OnDansWIM, which relies on several files distributed with the WAIK. Looking very similar to that of the tools previously discussed, it can be used to do everything that the command line ImageX offers. As you may expect, this is due to the fact that code simply calls ImageX behind the GUI. In fact, the command line being generated by the selected options is displayed at the bottom of the display for debug (and educational) purposes.

OnDansWIM is available at `www.msfn.org/board/Imagex-GUI-Open-Source-t99148.html`.

Working with PEImg

PEImg.exe is the Preinstallation Environment Image Setup tool. It is used to perform any of several actions upon a mounted Windows PE WIM file (see Table 6.7). Keep in mind that for each of these commands you must first mount the image using ImageX and then provide the path to the Windows directory of the mounted folder structure (specifically, <mounted location>\Windows).

In addition to the listed commands, the following flags may also be utilized along with the command:

- **/verbose:** Displays long names for packages (only short names are displayed by default)
- **/quiet:** Suppresses the progress bar
- **/f:** Suppresses prompts (provided for use in scripts, this flag is ignored for operations that would not normally prompt)

TABLE 6.7

PEIMG Command Line Options

Command	Purpose
/Import	Imports a package from a .CAB file or directory structure
/Install	Installs a specified package into a mounted image
/List	Displays a list of packages in the current image
/Uninstall	Uninstalls a previously installed package
/Inf	Installs an INF package (normally a driver) to a Windows PE image
/Prep	Optimizes the specified Windows PE image for size
/Lang	Sets the locale and the UI language of a Windows PE image
/TimeZone	Sets the default time zone of a Windows PE image
/TargetPath	Sets the location where the Windows PE image will reside on the disk
/?	List of command line help

Using the Import command

The Import command imports a package from a .CAB file or directory structure. The package is then available for installation, but must then be installed before it is available (see the section "Using the Install Command"). To confirm that an installation has successfully occurred, use the List command to see if the package is present in the image (and therefore available for installation).

The syntax for the PeImg Import command is as follo ws:

```
PeImg /import=<PackageSource> ImageWinDir [Flags]
```

The parameters shown here are described in the following list:

- **PackageSource:** The path and filename of a cab file or directory structure to be imported (wildcards are supported) (required).

- **ImageWinDir:** The path to the Windows directory of the mounted image (required).

- **Flags:** Optionally specify /verbose, /quiet or /f (see list at the start of this section for detail).

For example:

```
peimg /import=c:\updates\*.cab c:\imaging\mount\windows
```

This example imports all cab files located in the c:\updates directory and imports them into a mounted image located at `c:\imaging\mount`. Any such packages are then available for installation by using the Install command.

Using the Install command

The Install command is used to install a package into a mounted image. A list of available packages and their names can be obtained by using the List command. If wildcards are used when specifying a package name, any packages with matching names will be installed.

The syntax for the PeImg Import command is as follows:

```
PeImg /install=<PackageName> ImageWinDir [Flags]
```

The parameters shown here are described in the following list:

- **PackageName:** The name of the package to be installed (see the section "Using the List Command" for details on how to see what packages are available for installation)
- **ImageWinDir:** The path to the Windows directory of the mounted image (required)
- **Flags:** Optionally specify /verbose, /quiet or /f (see list at start of this section for detail)

For Example:

```
peimg /install=*Package* c:\imaging\mount\windows
```

This example installs all available packages that have a name containing the word "Package" to the mounted image located at `c:\imaging\mount`.

Using the List command

The List command is used to display a list of packages available for installation in the current image. This command can be used to verify that an Import command was successful or to determine the name of a package you want to install using the Install command.

The syntax for the PEImg list command is as follows:

```
PeImg /list ImageWinDir [Flags]
```

The parameters shown here are described as:

- **ImageWinDir:** The path to the Windows directory of the mounted image (required)
- **Flags:** Optionally specify /verbose, /quiet or /f (see list at start of this section for detail)

For Example:

```
peimg /list c:\imaging\mount\windows
```

This example lists all available packages in the mounted image located at c:\imaging\mount.

As shown in Figure 6.3, the output provides a table with four columns:

- **Lang:** Indicates the language of the package where applicable.
- **Version:** The version number of the listed package.
- **Ins:** Denotes installation state: a plus (+) indicates a package is installed, a minus (-) indicates a package is available, but not installed.
- **Name:** The name of the package (to be specified when using the Install command).

FIGURE 6.3

Reviewing the available packages in a mounted WIM image

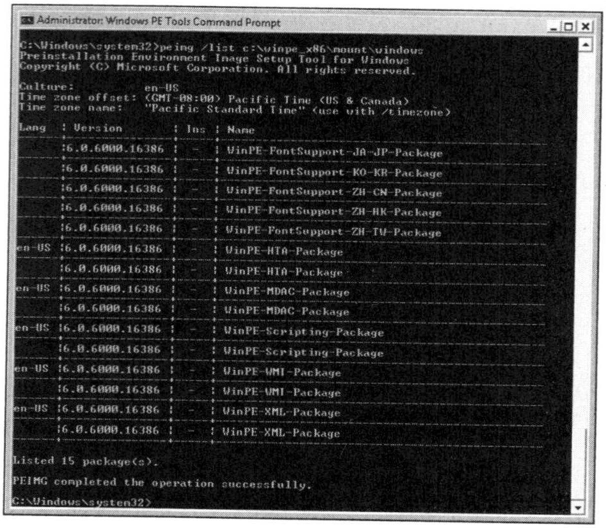

Using the Uninstall command

The Uninstall command is used to uninstall a previously installed package. A list of installed packages and their names can be obtained by using the /list command. In the INS column, (+) denotes installed packages. Wildcards can be used when specifying a package name. Any packages with matching long names will be uninstalled.

The syntax for the PeImg Uninstall command is as follows:

```
Peimg /Uninstall=PackageName ImageWinDir [Flags]
```

The parameters shown here are described in the following list:

- **PackageName:** The name of the package to be installed (see the section "Using the List Command" for details on how to see what packages are available for installation)
- **ImageWinDir:** The path to the Windows directory of the mounted image (required)
- **Flags:** Optionally specify /verbose, /quiet or /f (see list at start of this section for detail)

For Example:

```
peimg /uninstall=*Package* c:\imaging\mount\windows
```

The above example uninstalls all packages that have a name containing the word Package from the mounted image located at c:\imaging\mount.

Using the Inf command

The Inf command is used to install an INF package (which is normally used in the installation of drivers) to a Windows PE image.

The syntax for the PeImg Inf command is as follows:

```
Peimg /inf=<InfFile> ImageWinDir [Flags]
```

The parameters shown here are described in the following list:

- **InfFile:** The path and filename of the .INF file to be installed
- **ImageWinDir:** The path to the Windows directory of the mounted image (required)
- **Flags:** Optionally specify /verbose, /quiet or /f (see list at start of this section for detail)

> **NOTE** Like a few of the cases when a name may be specified as a PEImg value, you may make use of wildcards in the INF filename to install more than one driver in a single command.

For Example:

```
peimg /inf=c:\drivers\*.inf c:\imaging\mount\Windows
```

This example installs all .INF files from the c:\drivers folder in the mounted image located at c:\imaging\mount.

Using the Prep command

The PEImg Prep command optimizes the specified Windows PE image for size. If you use this command, do it last before the image is made available for production. The reason for this recommendation is that several other PEImg commands (including install, uninstall, import, and list) will no longer function after the Prep command is executed. However, the image is not completely locked; you can still execute the PEImg commands Lang, Inf, and TargetPath after Prep is executed. Due to the impact this command has on an image, a prompt is presented to confirm the command, which can be bypassed for scripting purposes using the /f flag.

The syntax for the PEImg Prep command is as follows:

```
PeImg /prep ImageWinDir [Flags]
```

The parameters shown here are described in the following list:

- **ImageWinDir:** The path to the Windows directory of the mounted image (required)
- **Flags:** Optionally specify /verbose, /quiet or /f (see list at start of this section for detail)

For Example:

```
peimg /prep c:\imaging\mount\windows /f
```

The above example optimizes the mounted Windows PE image for size with no prompts to confirm the action.

Using the Lang command

Prior to Windows Vista, Multilingual User Interface (MUI) packs were applied on top of an English version, and then language packs were installed to provide a localized user experience. Unfortunately, some languages had more complete support than others did, and the language packs had to be installed over an English version of Windows. In Windows Vista, the MUI architecture separates the language resources for the user interface from the binaries that make up the operating system. You can now change languages completely without changing the core binaries of Windows Vista, or to have multiple languages installed on the same computer. Languages are applied as language packs containing the resources required to localize part of, or the entire, user interface in Windows Vista.

The PEImg Lang command is used to set the locale and the UI language of a Windows PE image. A language pack for the specified language must already be installed. The language to be specified is identified as a *culture*. A culture is a two-letter identifier used to indicate a language.

NOTE If you are creating a Windows distribution (as opposed to Windows PE), you can use the Intlcfg.exe command line tool to recreate the Lang.ini file and select the default international values. When adding or removing language packs in a Windows image, the Lang.ini file must be recreated. The Lang.ini file is used during Windows Setup and contains a list of all available language packs, the locations of the language packs, and the default language to use during Windows Setup.

For example:

```
intlcfg -genlangini -dist:C:\WindowsFiles -image:C:\imaging\
    mount -defaultlang:fr-FR -all:fr-FR
```

The syntax for the PEImg Lang command is

```
PeImg /lang=<Culture> [/layerdriver=<ID>] ImageWinDir [Flags]
```

The parameters shown here are described in the following list:

- **Culture:** The culture name of the specified language (for example en-US, nl-NL, ja-JP or any of the available cultures provided).
- **ID:** For some cultures, this may be used to specify a numeric value that may be used to indicate which keyboard layer driver should be installed. Specifically, the ja-JP or ko-KR cultures support values between 1 and 6.
- **ImageWinDir:** The path to the Windows directory of the mounted image (required).
- **Flags:** Optionally specify /verbose, /quiet or /f (see list at start of this section for detail).

For example:

```
peimg /lang=en-us c:\imaging\mount\windows
```

In the above example, the English language is applied to the mounted image located at c:\imaging\ mount.

> **NOTE** For a list of available Language Packs and Language Interface Packs, see
> http://technet2.microsoft.com/WindowsVista/en/library/
> cfb72225-d7fd-46b0-9316-81769ec909791033.mspx

Using the TimeZone command

The PEImg TimeZone command is used to set the default time zone of a Windows PE image. This command can only be performed against an image that has previously been prepared by using the Prep command. The default English time zone is set to Pacific Standard Time. To view the current time zone of an image, use the PEImg List command.

The syntax for the PEImg TimeZone command is as follows:

```
PeImg /timezone=Culture ➪ TimeZoneName ImageWinDir [Flags]
```

The parameters shown here are described as:

- **Culture or TimeZoneName:** Either the culture or the time zone name reflecting the desired time zone (required)
- **ImageWinDir:** The path to the Windows directory of the mounted image (required)
- **Flags:** Optionally specify /verbose, /quiet or /f (see list at start of this section for detail)

For Example:

```
peimg /timezone="Eastern Standard Time" c:\imaging\mount\Windows
```

This example sets the image located at c:\imaging\mount to the Eastern (EST) time zone.

Using the TargetPath command

The TargetPath command sets the location where the Windows PE image will reside on the disk (for hard drive boot scenarios). This path must be specified as the root or a subdirectory of drive X. This command can only be executed against a Windows PE image that was previously prepared by using the Prep command.

The syntax for the PEImg TargetPath command is

```
PeImg /targetpath=<DriveX> ImageWinDir [Flags]
```

The parameters shown here are described in the following list:

- **DriveX:** Specifies the location where Windows PE should be applied on a hard drive. This value must be either X: or a subdirectory of drive X (required).

- **ImageWinDir:** The path to the Windows directory of the mounted image (required).

- **Flags:** Optionally specify /verbose, /quiet or /f (see list at start of this section for detail).

For example:

```
peimg /timezone="Eastern Standard Time" c:\imaging\mount\Windows
```

This example sets the image located at `c:\imaging\mount` to the Eastern (EST) time zone.

Working with OSCDImg

The Operating System CD Image (OSCDImg) utility is a CD-ROM and DVD-ROM Premastering Utility, which is actually not a new tool; however, it is getting some renewed life as a critical element of the WAIK in its ability to generate ISO files based on the content of your WIM file.

OSCDImg supports ISO 9660, Joliet, and Universal Disk Format (UDF) file systems. The syntax for the OSCDLmg command is:

```
OSCDIMG [options] SourceLocation TargetFile
```

The parameters shown here are described in the following list:

- **Options:** Choose from a long list of available options to control the behavior of OSCDImg, which are detailed in Table 6.8.

- **SourceLocation:** Specifies the location of the files that you intend to build into an .iso image (required).

- **TargetFile:** Specifies the name of the .iso image file (required).

TABLE 6.8

Reviewing OSCDIMG Command Line Options

Option	Purpose
-a	Causes the tool to display the allocation summary for files and directories.
-b <Location>	Specifies the location for the *El Torito boot sector* file. An El Torito boot sector file is a simple disk image like that of a boot floppy (including a boot sector and special CD-ROM structures). It is included in the Windows PE distribution at <WindowsPE>\etfsboot.com (where WindowsPE is the root installation directory for your Windows PE tools).
-c	Directs the tool to use ANSI filenames instead of OEM filenames.
-d	Causes the tool to not force lowercase filenames to uppercase.
-e	Instructs the tool to not use floppy disk emulation in the El Torito catalog. This option can only valid for single boot entry images and cannot be combined with any multi-boot entry switches.
-g	Directs the tool to use the Universal Coordinated Time (UCT) for all files instead of the local computer time.
-h	Causes the tool to include hidden files and directories.
-j1	Instructs the tool to encode Joliet Unicode filenames and generates DOS-compatible 8.3 filenames in the ISO 9660 namespace. Note: These filenames can be read by either Joliet systems or conventional ISO 9660 systems, but OSCDImg may change some of the filenames in the ISO 9660 name space to comply with DOS 8.3 and/or ISO 9660 naming restrictions.
-j2	Instructs the tool to encode Joliet Unicode filenames without standard ISO 9660 names. Note: A Joliet operating system is required to read files encoded this way.
-js<TextFile>	Directs the tool to override the default text file used with the j2 option (for example, -jsc:\Readme.txt).
-k	Causes the tool to continue creating an image even with it fails to open some of the source files.
-l<LableName>	Specifies a desired volume label. Note: No spaces should be inserted between the -l and <LabelName> (for example, -lMYLABEL).
-m	Instructs the tool to ignore the maximum size limit of an image.
-maxsize:<Limit>	Directs the tool to override the default maximum size of an image. The default value is configured to support a 74-minute CD-ROM (unless UDF is being used, in which case there is no maximum default size). The Limit value is specified in megabytes (for example, -maxsize:4096 limits the image to 4096MB).
-n	Causes the tool to utilize long filenames
-nt	Causes the tool to utilize long filenames compatible with Windows NT 3.51.
-o	Instructs the tool to optimize storage by encoding duplicate files only once using a MD5 hashing algorithm to compare files.

continued

TABLE 6.8	*(continued)*
Option	**Purpose**
-oc	Instructs the tool to optimize storage by encoding duplicate files only once using a binary comparison of each file (a method slower than the MD5 hash utilized by –o).
-oi	Instructs the tool to optimize storage by encoding duplicate files only once (when comparing files, this method ignores Diamond compression timestamps).
-os	Instructs the tool to optimize storage by encoding duplicate files only once (shows duplicate files when creating the image).
-ois	Instructs the tool to optimize storage by encoding duplicate files only once (when comparing files, it will ignore Diamond compression timestamps and will show duplicate files when creating the image).
-p	Allows you to specify the value to use for the Platform ID in the El Torito catalog (the default is 0x00, representing the x86 platform). This option can only be used for single boot entry images and cannot be combined with any multi-boot entry switches.
-t<Time>	Causes the tool to use the provided timestamp for all files and directories. The U.S.A. date format and 24-hour clock format should be used with no spaces when specifying this value. Any delimiter may be used between the items (for example: -t12/31/2008,23:59:59).
-u1	Directs the tool to produce an image that has both the UDF and ISO 9660 file systems. The ISO 9660 file system will be written with DOS-compatible 8.3 file names. The UDF file system will be written with Unicode filenames.
-u2	Directs the tool to produce an image that uses only the UDF file system. Any system not capable of reading UDF will only see a default text file alerting the user that this image is only available on computers that support UDF.
-ur	Directs the tool to override the default test file used with the -u2 option (for example, -urc:\Readme.txt).
-us	Causes the tool to create a sparse file when available (this can only be used with the -u2 option).
-ue	Instructs the tool to create embedded files (this can only be used with the -u2 option).
-uf	Directs the tool to embed UDF file identifier entries (this can only be used with the -u2 option).
-uv	Causes the tool to provide UDF Video Zone compatibility during DVD Video/Audio disk creation (meaning that UDF 1.02 and ISO 9660 are written to the disk). Additionally, the files in the VIDEO_TS, AUDIO_TS, and JACKET_P directories are written first (these directories take precedence over all other ordering rules used for this image).
-ut	Causes the tool to truncate the ISO 9660 portion of the image during DVD video/audio disk creation (when this option is used, only the VIDEO_TS, AUDIO_TS, and JACKET_P directories are visible from the ISO 9660 file system).

Option	Purpose
-w1	Directs the tool to report all filenames or depths that are not ISO-compliant or Joliet-compliant.
-w2	Directs the tool to report all filenames that are not DOS-compliant.
-w3	Directs the tool to report all zero-length files.
-w4	Directs the tool to report each filename that is copied to the image.
-x	Instructs the tool to compute and encode an AutoCRC value in the image.
-yd	Instructs the tool to silence warnings for nonidentical files with the same initial 64,000 bytes.
-yl	Causes the tool to produce long allocation descriptors instead of short allocation descriptors.
-y5	Dictates file layout on disk by writing all files in an i386 directory first and in reverse sort order.
-y6	Specifies that directory records be exactly aligned at the end of sectors.
-yo	Instructs the tool to control the file layout using a supplied text file that has a layout for the files to be placed in the image which follows these rules: The order file must be in ANSI format and the file must end in a new line. You must list only one file per line. The files listed must be specified relative to the root of the image and each file must be specified as a long filename (no short names are allowed). Finally, each file path cannot be longer than MAX_PATH, including volume name. It is also helpful to note that not all files must be listed in the order file — any that are not listed will simply be ordered as they would be if there was no ordering file.
-yw	Causes the tool to open source files with write sharing.

For example:

```
oscdimg -n -bc:\imaging\etfsboot.com c:\imaging\iso c:\imaging\
    winpe.iso
```

This example creates a bootable image named winpe.iso in the c:\imaging folder supporting long filenames and using the standard El Torito boot sector file supplied with Windows PE.

NOTE Simply copying an .iso file to a CD-ROM does not successfully apply the .iso file to a CD. To create a bootable CD-ROM, you must use CD-recording software that supports applying an .iso file as an image to a CD-ROM (a very common feature among such software).

Working with vLite

vLite (Vista Lite) is a freeware application written by Dino Nuhagic (AKA nuhi), which provides features that allow you to customize a Windows Vista setup prior to its use. Its features include:

- Support for the integration of hotfixes, language packs, and drivers
- Slipstreaming of Windows Vista service packs (not natively supported by Microsoft)
- The ability to remove undesired components of the installation
- Creation of an unattended setup
- Splitting and merging of Windows Vista installation CDs
- Creation of an ISO with the ability to burn it to a bootable CD or DVD
- A facility to perform other changes and tweaks

Although it is not a supported Microsoft tool, the features it offers are compelling and take advantage of Windows Vista's new setup architecture in a compelling way. The following section takes you through the following aspects of vLite while covering its key functions:

- Getting setup
- Slipstreaming service packs
- Integrating hotfixes, drivers, or language packs
- Selectively excluding components from setup
- Configuring defaults for certain options (tweaks)
- Generating an unattended setup
- Creating and/or burning an ISO image of the customized Windows Vista installation

Setting up vLite

The following steps take you through the download and installation of vLite:

1. **Download and install vLite from** `www.vlite.net`
2. **Select a folder where the Windows Vista installation media is stored.** This can be a local or network folder, a physical DVD, or a mounted virtual DVD ISO.
3. **Select a file where the installation will be stored locally on the computer for modification (this should be an empty folder).** After the paths are specified, the files are copied from the source media to the specified local folder. The files are about 2.5GB in total so, depending on your computer, this could take several minutes.
4. **Specify the editions of Windows Vista you want to work with.**
5. **Click the Tasks button on the left and select the boxes for each of the functions you want to exercise (see Figure 6.4).**

FIGURE 6.4

Specifying desired tasks in vLite

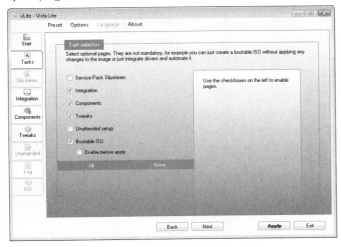

Slipstream ing with vLite

You can merge Vista service packs into your image such as with Windows Service Pack 1. Again, this feature was not provided by Microsoft so you should be warned that using this function might result in an implementation of Vista that is not supported by Microsoft. The following steps specify how to slipstream Windows Vista Service Pack 1 into a Windows Vista image.

1. **Download Windows Vista Service Pack 1 offline installation:** `www.microsoft.com/downloads/details.aspx?FamilyId=B0C7136D-5EBB-413B-89C9-CB3D06D12674`

2. **If you have not already, you must choose Service Pack Slipstream from the task list.** Any other tasks you choose along with this option will remain disabled until after the slipstream task has been completed.

3. **Choose the slipstream button from the list on the left and click the Select button at the bottom-right of the screen.**

4. **Choose your downloaded service pack. vLite will immediately begin extracting what it needs from the service pack binary.** This process can take up to an hour and a half to complete.

> **NOTE** To support the slipstreaming feature of vLite, you must be working with a fresh image of Vista RTM which has not been edited by vLite or any other application. You can remove components and make other desired changes *after* slipstreaming (not before).

Integrating with vLite

The Integration task allows you to integrate hotfixes, drivers, and language packs. Any currently installed items are also displayed for your information. The following steps take you through the integration options of vLite:

1. **If you have not already, you must choose Integration from the task list. If you chose Service Pack Slipstream, you will need to complete this task prior to any desired integration of hotfixes, drivers, and language packs.**

2. **To make use of the tabs for each of the elements, select the Enable box at the top left of the selected tab.**

3. **Click the Insert button and browse to the source for the item to be integrated.**

4. **Repeat the process for any other elements you wish to integrate.** You need not hit the Apply button until you have completed all of the desired changes across all tasks.

Excluding components with vLite

A core feature of vLite is to allow for the creation of a more lightweight installation of Vista. When choosing the Components task, you can specify any features of Windows Vista that you do not want to include in your Windows Vista installation. The following steps take you through how to exclude components from a Windows Vista installation with vLite:

1. **If you have not already, you must choose Components from the task list. If you chose Service Pack Slipstream, you need to complete this task prior to any desired changes to the components and files to be included in your Windows Vista installation.**

   The first time you utilize this task, the Compatibility dialog appears so that you may choose the features and applications you wish to utilize in your Vista installation. Based on these choices, certain components may be automatically included to support them.

2. **To bring this dialog up in the future, choose Compatibility from the bottom of the Components window display.**

3. **Select the items you want to exclude from your installation of Windows Vista.** This main Compatibility task window provides a tree view of accessories, drivers, games, hardware support, languages, multimedia, network, services, and system components. When hovering over any of the listed items, a simple description is provided to the right to help you in your decision.

4. **Choose the Protect files menu item from the bottom of the Compatibility tasks window for any files how wish to specifically include.**

5. **Repeat the process for any other components you wish to exclude.** You need not hit the Apply button until you have completed all of the desired changes across all tasks.

NOTE Service packs are designed to update the entire installation. If you have used vLite to remove any components, the installation of Windows Vista Service Pack 1 (and future service packs) may fail. The update issue applies only to service packs; you will still get Windows Updates for the components you did not remove.

Selecting Tweaks with vLite

There are a handful of changes you may specify to control the default behavior of supported options. These options are broken down into categories: security, system, explorer, and Internet Explorer. You may specify if listed options are to remain with their default setting or force them to be enabled or disabled automatically when the installation of Windows Vista is complete.

Follow these steps take you through how to make use of the Tweaks feature of vLite:

1. **If you have not already, you must choose Tweaks from the task list.** If you chose Service Pack Slipstream, you will need to complete this task prior to any desired changes to the setting default options for your Windows Vista installation.

2. **Select any of the groupings from the list on the left to see the available options for configuration.**

3. **Click the value for the option to select the desired setting or double-click the option name to toggle through the available settings.** Typically the options are default (don't change), enabled, or disabled. For example to disable User Account Control (UAC) in your setup, choose Disabled as the value for User Account Control (UAC) option listed under Security.

4. **Repeat the process for any other options you want to configure.** You need not click the Apply button until you have completed all of the desired changes across all tasks.

Creating an unattended setup with vLite

Another feature of vLite is a helpful interface to creating an unattended installation file, which may be used to automate your customized installation. This is typically done with Windows System Image Manager (Windows SIM). Although Windows SIM is a powerful tool with many more capabilities, vLite is handy because it is kept simple. Windows SIM can be a very confusing tool when compared to the simplicity of this feature. The following steps take you through how to create an unattended setup using vLite:

1. **If you have not already, you must select Unattended setup from the task list.** If you chose Service Pack Slipstream, you will need to complete this task prior to specifying the desired options for an unattend.xml file.

2. **Choose any desired User Data settings. You have a few choices including:**
   - Specify product key or skip the prompt to collect it
   - Skip automatic activation
   - Accept the end user license agreement (EULA)
   - Specify the name and organization for the installation
   - Enter the desired computer name for the unattended installation

3. Choose any desired Welcome Center settings from the list provided:

- Specify the network location (home or work, for example)
- Set default computer protection options (disabled, only install updates)
- Skip user creation
- Set an administrator password
- Specify the number of times an automatic admin logon should occur

A second tab is also offered so that you may have the installation prompt for such information (default). Alternatively, you can specify desired regional settings, such as UI language, time, and currency format, keyboard region, and time zone so that the installer will not be prompted.

Creating and burning an ISO image with vLite

Before generating an ISO image, you must apply your choices to the customized image. Click the Apply button after you have completed all desired tasks. When you click Apply you are prompted to choose a build method. You can simply save your changes, rebuild the entire installation (all editions), or you may build only the edition of Windows Vista that you are working with. When working with editions other than Ultimate, this reduces the size of the image by eliminating the need for them to be included in the image. It is this last option (Rebuild one) that is recommended.

After you have applied your changes, you may create an image and optionally burn it to writable media using the ISO task. The following steps take you through how to create and burn an ISO image using vLite:

1. **Choose a mode: Direct Burn, Burn Image, Create Image or Erase RW.** By default, the option is Create Image

2. **When creating an image (ISO) you need only specify a volume label (VistaLite by default) and then click the Make ISO button at the bottom right to be prompted for a filename.** After a name is specified the process will begin and should take no more than a few minutes.

3. **If you choose to burn an image, you may select the target device and burn speed.** Advanced settings are also provided to specify an alternate boot sector and to control if burned contents should be tested, verified, or erased.

4. **Finally, you may also split the image into manageable sizes if you want by pressing the Split button.**

Executing Common Tasks

The following sections are intended to walk you through some common tasks. As a command line tool with many options, even the most regular users will rely upon a reference and some simple step-by-step instructions.

To keep the examples meaningful, we will describe the setup of Windows PE and the file paths used. These paths are used in all of the common tasks documented in the remainder of this chapter, but you may naturally substitute any of these paths with your own source and target locations based on your own needs. To prepare your system to employ the tasks documented in this section, follow these steps:

1. **Download the WAIK (approximately 1GB) from the Microsoft Web site (validation may be required).**

   ```
   www.microsoft.com/downloads/details.aspx?FamilyID=C7D4BC6D-
       15F3-4284-9123-679830D629F2
   ```

   After you have the download, you will notice it has an IMG file extension. This is a DVD image file which you may burn using your preferred software. It may be necessary to rename the file extension from IMG to ISO in order for your software to properly recognize the file. Alternatively, you can use a drive emulator, such as Daemon Tools (`www.daemon-tools.cc`) to mount the file as a drive without burning. Yet another option is to make use of some tools like WinRar or 7zip, which support ISO files just as you would any other archive file (like ZIP).

2. **After you have downloaded and have access to the setup, run** `STARTCD.EXE` **for an installation menu, choose Windows AIK Setup, and follow the simple wizard through the installation.**

3. **Right-click the Windows PE Tools Command Prompt shortcut from its program folder on the Start menu and choose Run as administrator.** The many command line tools covered are typically executed from the Windows PE Tools Command Prompt and must be run as administrator so this is an important step.

4. **To establish the file structure needed to customize a Windows PE image, run the CopyPE script with two arguments; the first is the target architecture (x86, ia64 or amd64), and the second is the target directory where you will manage your image.** If you are working with multiple architectures, it is a good idea to include it in your target folder name. However, this is a path that needs to be typed for most all commands so keep the path short to save some typing. For the tasks documented in this section the following arguments are used:

   ```
   copype.cmd x86 c:\winpe_x86
   ```

5. **Mount the Windows PE image for read/write updates:**

   ```
   imagex /mountrw c:\winpe_x86\winpe.wim 1 c:\winpe_x86\mount
   ```

Adding packages to a Windows PE image

There are a number of packages available in the default Windows PE image which you may optionally choose to have installed (see Table 6.9.) If you are looking to install a package not included by default, see the section "Adding hotfixes to a Windows PE image" for how to first import the package into the image.

TABLE 6.9

Default Packages Provided with Windows PE

Name	Description
WinPE-FontSupport-JA-JP-Package	additional Japanese font support
WinPE-FontSupport-KO-KR-Package	additional Korean font support
WinPE-FontSupport-ZH-CN-Package	additional Chinese font support
WinPE-FontSupport-ZH-HK-Package	additional Hong Kong font support
WinPE-FontSupport-ZH-TW-Package	additional Taiwanese font support
WinPE-HTA-Package	HTML application (HTA) support
WinPE-MDAC-Package	Microsoft Data Access Component (MDAC) support
WinPE-Scripting-Package	Windows Script Host (WSH) support
WinPE-WMI-Package	Windows Management Instrumentation (WMI) support
WinPE-XML-Package	Microsoft SML (MSXML) parser support

NOTE There was a package for the Windows System Recovery Tools (WinPE-SRT-Package) available in earlier builds of Windows PE which was unfortunately dropped. This has led many to exercise alternatives, such as BartPE for this purpose, but workarounds are available online at www.vistaanswers.com/index.php/2008/03/31.

The following task covers how to install any of the packages provided in Windows PE by default:

1. **List the available packages to see what is available, what is currently installed, and to verify the proper names for the available packages using the PEImg List command:**

   ```
   PeImg /List c:\winpe_x86\mount
   ```

   Any currently installed packages will be denoted with a plus (+) sign in the "Ins" column of the listed packages table.

2. **Install the desired package by name, using wildcards if desired, with the WinPE Install command.** For example, to install the Windows Script Host, you could use the following command:

   ```
   PeImg /Install=WinPE-Scripting-Package c:\winpe_x86\mount
   ```

3. **When done editing your image, be sure to commit the changes back to the mounted image by using the ImageX Unmount command:**

   ```
   Imagex /Unmount /Commit c:\winpe_x86\mount
   ```

Adding hotfixes to a Windows PE image

You may want to apply service packs to your Windows PE image and this is something that is supported by PEImg. After you download and extract the CAB file from the update, you can use the import function to make it available as a package in the image. Then you can simply install the package as you would any of those included (detailed above).

1. **Create directories for downloads and to store your patches:**

   ```
   md c:\downloads
   md c:\updates
   ```
   Download any desired updates to the updates folder, for example www.microsoft.
   com/technet/security/bulletin/ms07-032.mspx

2. **Updates such as this are provided as MSU files. Extract the contents using the Expand command:**

   ```
   Expand c:\downloads\*.msu c:\updates -f:*
   ```

3. **Run the PEImg Import to make the updates available as packages:**

   ```
   PeImg /Import=c:\updates\*.cab c:\winpe_x86\mount
   ```

4. **List the packages to see the one you have added is now available as expected using the PEImg List command:**

   ```
   PeImg /List c:\winpe_x86\mount
   ```

5. **Install the new package by its name, or for updates you can specify the name using a wildcard, such as *KB* that can perform the installation for any packages with a name containing KB.** For example:

   ```
   PeImg /Install=Package_for_KB931213 c:\winpe_x86\mount
   ```

6. **When done editing your image, be sure to commit the changes back to the mounted image using the ImageX Unmount command:**

   ```
   Imagex /Unmount /Commit c:\winpe_x86\mount
   ```

Adding drivers to a Windows PE image

Many of the most common drivers are available in the default Windows PE image and will not require any work on your part. However, there are those times when devices, such as network devices will not function and getting the latest driver in your image is the logical course of action.

One such driver is the VMware network driver. VMware is used by many to test environments, such as Windows PE, particularly because it is easy to provide it a bootable image as an ISO file. To get network support from Windows PE from a VMware session it is necessary to add the VMware network driver to your image and use the PEImg INF command to perform the installation.

1. **Start up a VMware session and choose the Install VMware Tools option.** Don't worry — if you already have them installed — doing this simply mounts a VMware Tools installation CD (which may automatically start the installation wizard). In the virtual CD that appears in your session, go to E:\Program Files\VMware\VMware Tools\ Drivers\vmxnet\win2k\ and copy these files to your host system.

   ```
   Copy D:\program files\VMware\VMware Tools\Drivers\vmxnet\
   win2k\*.* \\server\drivers\network\vmware\
   ```

2. **Install the driver using its INF file with the PEImg INF command:**

   ```
   peimg /inf=\\server\drivers\network\vmware\vmware-nic.inf
   c:\winpe_x86\mount\windows
   ```

3. **When done editing your image, be sure to commit the changes back to the mounted image using the ImageX Unmount command:**

   ```
   Imagex /Unmount /Commit c:\winpe_x86\mount
   ```

Incorporating service packs

If you make use of Windows PE 2.1, this release of Windows PE is based upon Windows Vista SP1. Incorporating SP1 into a production Windows Vista image is not as simple as you may have hoped. In the past, a practice known as slipstreaming could be used to incorporate the service pack contents with the original installation source. Apparently, there were plans to provide such a deployment mechanism with SP1, but having run into problems it is now hoped that such a feature will be seen with the release of Windows Vista SP2.

Imaging is covered in more detail elsewhere in this book, but the basic steps to include Windows Vista SP1 to an existing Windows Vista production image are as follows:

1. Boot to Windows PE and use ImageX to Apply image to reference PC.

2. Reboot, log in to the computer, and Install Vista SP1.

3. Run Sysprep with the generalize switch to prepare the image for deployment.

4. Reboot to Windows PE and recapture the image with the ImageX Capture command.

NOTE   The freeware tool vLite supports slipstreaming of Windows Vista SP1 though Microsoft recommends against the unsupported practice (see the section "Slipstreaming with vLite" earlier in this chapter for details).

Editing the registry of a Windows PE image

Although you cannot work with the registry as easily as you might hope, you can make changes to the registry of your image. From within Windows, you need only mount the image and then import the registry hive file into a temporary path in RegEdit. After you have made any desired changes, you can export the image path back to a file and replace the original file to realize the changes with your image.

Depending upon which area of the registry you wish to edit, you will need to load the appropriate hive file (see Table 6.10).

TABLE 6.10

File Locations for Registry Hives

Registry Hive	Mounted File Location
HKLM\SOFTWARE	mount\windows\system32\config\SOFTWARE
HKLM\SYSTEM	mount\windows\system32\config\SYSTEM
HKEY_CLASSES_ROOT	mount\windows\system32\config\SOFTWARE (browse to classes)
HKEY_USERS and HKEY_CURRENT_USER	Comprised of ntuser.dat files of your local user profiles (i.e., mount\Users*\ntuser.dat)

The steps to modify the registry of a WIM image are provided for your reference:

1. **With the image mounted for read/write (/MountRW), run RegEdit and select the HKEY_LOCAL_MACHINE hive.**

2. **Choose File ⇨ Load Hive from the menu bar and browse to the location of the registry hive you want to modify (refer to Table 6.10) from within the Windows PE mounted file structure** (`c:\winpe_x86\mount\windows\system32\config\systemprofile\ntuser.dat`)

3. **Enter a temporary name for the hive, such as WINPE.**

4. **Browse to the WINPE node under HKLM and make any desired modifications.**

5. **When you are done making edits, click the WINPE folder under HKLM and choose File ⇨ Unload Hive.** You will be prompted to confirm this action.

6. **When done editing your image, be sure to commit the changes back to the mounted image using the ImageX Unmount command:**

   ```
   Imagex /Unmount /Commit c:\winpe_x86\mount
   ```

RegEdit is also available in Windows PE so you can run this to verify your results within Windows PE. However, changes made with RegEdit while running Windows PE won't take effect because the registry is temporarily loaded in memory.

Incorporating scripts in a Windows PE image

It is recommended that you keep your actual script on an accessible network share and not within the Windows PE image so that you may easily test and modify it without a need to rebuild and deploy the WIM.

There are a couple of ways to trigger the execution of scripts:

- Edit the StartNet script to perform actions or call your own script
- Change the default shell to that of your own script

Editing the StartNet script

Editing the StartNet script (STARTNET.CMD) is the easiest and most effective way to customize Windows PE startup actions. You may edit the script directly or you may have this script make a call to one of your own. If you are familiar with a batch file (.BAT), a CMD file is the very same thing.

The script is located at C:\winpe_x86\mount\Windows\System32\Startnet.cmd. By default, the script contains a comment and one command: wpeinit. Wpeinit is a command line tool that initializes Windows PE each time it boots. It installs PnP devices, processes Unattend.xml settings, and loads network resources.

Specifying an alternate shell

The default shell that is called by Windows PE is cmd.exe (the command prompt). You can, however, change this behavior to launch your own script or supported executable.

To specify an alternate shell, follow these steps:

1. **With the image mounted for read/write (/MountRW), run** notepad.exe **and enter the following text in a new file to be saved in the Windows\System32 folder of your mounted image as "myscript.cmd"** (C:\winpe_x86\mount\Windows\System32\ myscript.cmd)

   ```
   @echo off
   echo starting network...
   wpeinit
   echo mapping network drive...
   net use q: \\server\share\tools Password1 /USER:appdeploy\
      bkelly
   echo launching new cmd instance...
   cmd /k
   echo Ready to reboot.
   pause
   ```

2. **Create a second file in Notepad to be saved in the same location with a name of winpeshl.ini** (C:\winpe_x86\mount\Windows\System32\winpeshl.ini) **and enter the following text:**

   ```
   [LaunchApp]
   AppPath = %SYSTEMROOT%\System32\myscript.cmd
   ```

 The AppPath entry does not support command line options.

3. After you are done editing your image, commit the changes back to the mounted image using the ImageX Unmount command:

```
Imagex /Unmount /Commit c:\winpe_x86\mount
```

WARNING   When the shell closes, Windows PE reboots, so make sure to control the completion of your script.

After following the above steps, Windows PE will run the script that initializes the network, map drive Q to a network share, and then start a new command shell so that the user can perform actions without the script closing (see Figure 6.5). If the script were to close, the computer would be restarted. This method allows the user to enter commands, and when done, typing exit would return them to the script (where they would see the Ready to reboot message).

FIGURE 6.5

Testing automatic startup commands with a custom shell

NOTE   If you search for Windows Shell online, you'll find a number of alternative shells for Windows, many of which are compatible with Windows PE. For example: BS Explorer (www.kursknet.ru/~boa/en/index.html) and LiteStep (www.litestep.net/).

Create a bootable ISO from WIM image

Creating a bootable ISO image is a typical final step in customizing Windows PE. You can burn this to a CD or DVD to use in production. For testing, a virtual machine is the perfect tool due to a common feature that allows you to mount an ISO as a virtual disk from which you can easily boot.

With the details of each of these command lines already covered, here is an example of using these tools to get your edited image in the form of an ISO.

1. **Unmount the image and commit any changes:**

   ```
   imagex /unmount /commit c:\winpe_x86\mount
   ```

2. **Copy the updated Windows PE image over the existing boot.wim in the ISO sources directory (answer yes if asked to confirm the overwriting of the file):**

   ```
   copy c:\winpe_x86\winpe.wim c:\winpe_x86\iso\sources\boot.wim
   ```

3. **Use the OSCDImg command line tool discussed earlier to generate the ISO:**

   ```
   oscdimg -n -bc:\winpe_x86\etfsboot.com c:\winpe_x86\ISO c:\
       winpe_x86\winpe_x86.iso
   ```

Configure a UFD to boot to Windows PE

A USB flash drive (UFD) can be a handy deployment mechanism for Windows PE as compared to a CD or DVD in that it can hold more, it can be accessed more quickly, and it fits much better in your pocket. Not all computers will support booting from a USB device, but most new computer motherboards do offer such support. Enter your BIOS menu at startup to see what boot devices are available (you can typically reorder such devices to dictate priority).

1. **Unmount the image and commit any changes:**

   ```
   imagex /unmount /commit c:\winpe_x86\mount
   ```

2. **Copy the updated Windows PE image over the existing boot.wim in the ISO sources directory (answer yes if asked to confirm the overwriting of the file):**

   ```
   copy c:\winpe_x86\winpe.wim c:\winpe_x86\iso\sources\boot.wim
   ```

3. **Now launch a command prompt as administrator by right-clicking the command prompt icon and choosing Run as administrator.**

4. **To launch the DiskPart command line tool, type:**

   ```
   DISKPART
   ```

5. **List the available disks to determine which is that of your UFD.** *It is very important that you determine the proper disk number* because all data will be removed from the specified disk when following these steps. To list the disks, type the following command and, based on its capacity, note the number that corresponds with your UFD (see Figure 6.6):

   ```
   LIST DISK
   ```

FIGURE 6.6

Reviewing listed disks to determine which your UFD is

```
C:\winpe_x86>diskpart

Microsoft DiskPart version 6.0.6000
Copyright (C) 1999-2007 Microsoft Corporation.
On computer: BOBKELLY-PC

DISKPART> list disk

  Disk ###  Status        Size     Free     Dyn  Gpt
  --------  ------------  -------  -------  ---  ---
  Disk 0    Online        149 GB     9 MB
  Disk 1    No Media         0 B      0 B
  Disk 2    No Media         0 B      0 B
  Disk 3    No Media         0 B      0 B
  Disk 4    No Media         0 B      0 B
  Disk 5    Online        125 MB   125 MB

DISKPART>
```

6. **Select the disk by number based on what was determined to be the correct drive in the previous step** (be *certain* to select the correct disk!):

   `SELECT DISK 5`

7. **Now that the proper disk is selected, prepare it with the clean command**:

   `CLEAN`

8. **Now create a partition on the clean drive:**

   `CREATE PARTITION PRIMARY`

9. **Select the newly created partition:**

   `SELECT PARTITION 1`

10. **Set the partition as active with the Active command:**

    `ACTIVE`

11. **Format the partition with the Format command:**

    `FORMAT`

12. **Assign the new partition with the Assign command:**

    `ASSIGN`

13. **To quit DiskPart use the Exit command:**

    `EXIT`

14. **Now copy to the contents of the c:\winpe_x86\ISO folder to the USB disk.** In the following sample command, the USB disk is on the E drive (substitute as needed):

    `XCOPY C:\WINPE_X86\ISO\*.* E: /E`

> **NOTE** If you have trouble locating your drive, go back into DiskPart, select the disk and the volume and then run the Assign command again using the optional argument Letter to specify a specific drive letter:
>
> ```
> ASSIGN LETTER=E
> ```
>
> There are situations where this is necessary, for example, when a disconnected network drive was mistakenly assigned the same drive as the UFD. Specifying an explicit drive letter like this will alleviate any such problems.

Now you should be able to boot from the USB flash disk. Make sure to select the right boot device during the boot cycle or to change the boot order in your computer's BIOS.

Developing Custom Solutions

What constitutes development can vary greatly depending upon who you talk to. You could say you developed an image at this point, so how about developing an automated way to handle some of the more repetitive tasks of building a Windows PE image? We saw some solutions that aim to help you do this, but many are keen to do it themselves. You can do just about anything from a simple batch file to leveraging the Windows Imaging API (Wimgapi.dll) directly, both of which are briefly covered in the following sections.

Leveraging scripts for automation

A script can be a series of command lines in a batch file or something more. For example, to have a script mount an image, import any packages, and then unmount the image, you need only to create a batch file containing each of the required commands:

```
imagex /mountrw c:\winpe_x86\winpe.wim 1 c:\winpe_x86\mount
PeImg /Import=c:\updates\*.cab c:\winpe_x86\mount
PeImg /Install=*KB* c:\winpe_x86\mount
Imagex /Unmount /Commit c:\winpe_x86\mount
```

You can also write a script to act on input from the user. Typically user input is provided to a script by a simple text menu or via command line arguments. However, today there are tools to let you go far beyond this. One of the features of the Admin Script Editor provides a GUI editor (see Figure 6.7) for creating windows forms for PowerShell (natively using the .NET Framework) or for VBScript and KiXtart (using the freeware KiXforms COM component).

> **NOTE** Admin Script Editor is a suite of scripting tools designed to help create, manage, and distribute scripts. A trial of this application may be found on the included CD and online at www.adminscripteditor.com.

FIGURE 6.7

Creating a script with a graphical interface

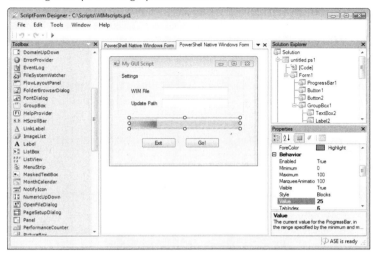

Developing solutions with SmartDeploy Imaging Component

The SmartDeploy Imaging Component (AKA SmartWIM) from SmartDeploy provides a documented ActiveX control to allow for the incorporation of WIM format support into your applications or scripts.

Capture and apply disk volumes directly from script, get information about images through a Web page, or provide a state-of-the-art user interface complete with progress bar. SmartWIM eliminates the need to wrap command line tools or learn Microsoft's provided APIs by offering a straightforward, fully documented ActiveX control (see Figure 6.8). Some of the functions and features include:

- Capture and apply images using VBScript, Visual Basic, VB.NET, C#
- Create delta files that contain only the differences between images
- Real-time imaging status with percent complete and estimated time remaining
- Single fully self-contained COM object and ActiveX control written with ATL 3.0
- Small footprint (~300KB)
- Requires no MFC DLLs or runtime libraries
- Works on Windows 2000, XP, 2003, Vista, and Windows PE 2.0

FIGURE 6.8

Understanding the architecture of SmartWIM

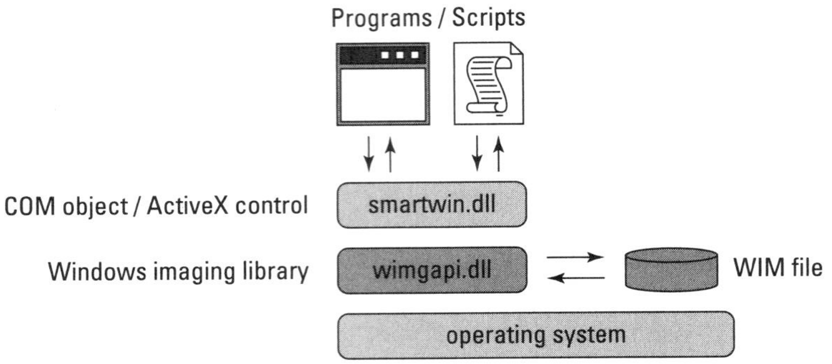

Programs / Scripts

COM object / ActiveX control   smartwin.dll

Windows imaging library   wimgapi.dll   WIM file

operating system

Which is the better tool is a matter of opinion, but keep in mind that the new (and free) GImageX v2 provides a COM interface for scripting as well (see Introducing GImageX earlier in this chapter).

NOTE   **It is possible to utilize the APIs provided by Microsoft directly, although it is more challenging. For an example project in C# to get you started, visit** `www.code` `project.com/KB/vista/wimgapi.aspx`

Investigating Third-Party Alternatives

This section discusses some third party alternatives. Two different technologies were covered earlier in this chapter: preinstallation environments and imaging tools. The two products listed in the following sections are preinstallation environment alternatives. This section takes a brief look at some other imaging solutions you may wish to investigate further.

BartPE

BartPE is a free tool for building your own PE image based on Windows XP or Server 2003. It does not support Vista as a source for building a preinstallation environment, but it can still be used in the deployment of Windows Vista just the same. BartPE is available online at `www.nu2.nu/` `pebuilder/`.

NOTE   **A couple of plug-ins are available to support imaging products, such as Drive Snapshot, Image for Windows, and Acronis True Image.. For details on Acronis True Image support for BartPE, visit** `www.acronis.com/homecomputing/support/bartpe/`

BartPE is a DOS replacement and alternative to Windows PE. Its focus is to provide a "next generation rescue platform" as opposed to a deployment tool, but it is fully capable of handling both tasks. Unlike Windows PE, BartPE is designed as a more interactive tool with menus and applications.

Perhaps most compelling is its plug-in facility for which hundreds of add-ins have been written to extend the capabilities of BartPE to serve a wide array of uses.

BartPE exists because Windows PE was unavailable to anyone without an OEM or Enterprise Assurance relationship with Microsoft. BartPE provided an alternative solution during this time. The initial release of BartPE was in violation of Microsoft Licensing and had to been taken down. This was remedied in the second release, which is now perfectly legal.

The BartPE Builder tool (see Figure 6.9) allows you to supply source files used to create the pre-installation environment, which can also build an ISO and even burn the resulting image to removable media all with one click.

FIGURE 6.9

Using BartPE Builder to create an alternative preinstallation environment

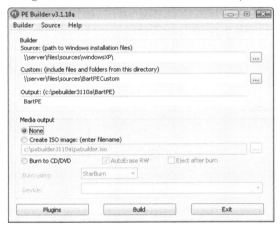

 For a video demonstrating the use of both Windows PE and BartPE (as well as the pros and cons of each solution), visit www.appdeploy.com/video/leveragingpe.asp.

VistaPE

VistaPE is very similar to BartPE, in that it features a graphical shell, an expanded set of supported devices and functions, and can run almost any Windows program. Although arguably more difficult to work with compared to BartPE, the key technological difference is that VistaPE is built on a Windows Vista kernel (BartPE is based on Windows XP or Server 2003). It is designed to be a universal tool with the flexibility to grow with your needs. VistaPE is available online at http://vistape.net/vistape.html.

The following list describes key VistaPE functionality:

- Possibility to fully or partially loading VistaPE at startup into memory (boot.wim)
- Support for a large number of SATA/RAID/SCSI/NIC drivers
- Capable of reading/writing to NTFS/FAT32/FAT/Ext2/Ext3 partitions
- Full networking support
- Automatic hardware detection (PnP)
- May be booted from CD/HDD/UFD/Network
- Fully compatible with Microsoft Windows Vista
- Support for a wide range of programs and shells
- No limits regarding the maximum number of open processes
- Automatic creation of shortcuts for programs
- Ability to remove VistaPE boot media while VistaPE is running (using boot.wim)
- Full multilingual support

Working with VistaPE

The following steps take you through basic use of VistaPE to get a feel for its capabilities:

1. **Download WinBuilder, which is distributed as a RAR file (an archive file similar to zip).** If you don't have a program that supports the RAR file type, do a quick search for tools, such as 7Zip or WinRar.

2. **Copy the two files contained in the archive to the folder from which you want to work.** It is recommended that you create a new folder for this purpose (this may be a network share if desired). When you run the winbuilder.exe application and download the VistaPE project, the files downloaded will be stored in a folder named Projects that is automatically created as a subdirectory of the folder containing WinBuilder.

3. **Select the Download tab and from the server tab in the download center, choose vistape.net/project, and click the Download button**. A progress bar will be presented as the VistaPE files are downloaded. After the download is complete, the VistaPE project will be loaded as shown in Figure 6.10.

4. **Click the Paths button and enter the path to your Windows Vista DVD or Windows Vista installation media as the source directory.**

5. **To add optional components, simply choose them from the tree view on the left.** For example, select DotNet 2.0 from VistaPE MultiBoot v.11 ⇨ Addons ⇨ DotNet 2.0 (3.0) for VistaPE.

6. **Click the Play button at the top right to begin the process of generating your bootable ISO.**

FIGURE 6.10

Loading VistaPE in WinBuilder

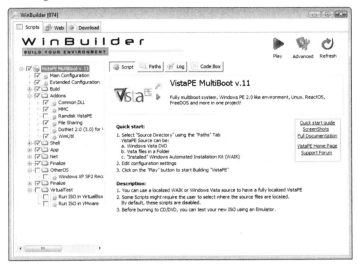

Symantec Ghost

Symantec Ghost is probably the most well known imaging solution. Few administrators have been in the field for more than a couple of years that have not been exposed to it at some point. The latest offering known as *Symantec Ghost Solution Suite 2.0* aims to provide a rapid and reliable Windows Vista migration tackling many phases. Key features include:

- Support for Microsoft Windows Vista and 64-bit operating systems
- A single centralized management console for management of migration tasks
- Built-in Vista inventory filters for identification and targeting of Vista ready machines
- Hardware and software inventory

To learn more about Ghost Solution Suite 2.0, visit `www.symantec.com/business/products/overview.jsp?pcid=2260&pvid=865_1`

KBOX Systems Deployment Appliance

The KBOX Systems Deployment Appliance from KACE is interesting in that it also utilizes a file-based imaging format. It stores all images on an appliance that manages all images as a single instance store (without having to keep all the images in an individual file).

It is provided as an appliance solution so setup is relatively fast and simple. It supports file-based imaging as well as scripted deployments and utilizes a custom Windows PE implementation (dubbed KPE) for its deployment console on target systems, as shown in Figure 6.11.

FIGURE 6.11

Viewing the KPE client interface (based on Windows PE)

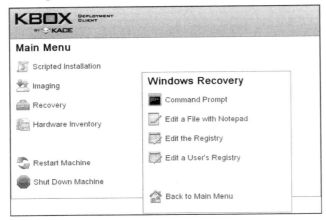

Key features of the KBOX Systems Deployment Appliance include:

- Agentless computer hardware inventory (no client deployment needed)
- Support for "bare-metal" system deployments
- Remote disk imaging or unattended network installations from a central, Web-based console
- Integrated library for centralized image archiving and management
- Windows and Linux support for imaging
- Image editing (such as the ability to inject a driver) from the Web-based console
- Ordered execution of pre- and post-deployment configuration tasks
- State management to re-provision or reconfigure machines back to a clean state (affecting only changed files)

To learn more about KBOX Systems Deployment Appliance, visit www.kace.com/products/kbox2000.php.

Summary

We discussed the many valuable tools: ImageX, some graphical tools for making ImageX easier to work with, PEImg, OSCDImg, and vLite. Hopefully you have been exposed to some new tools to help you along and may reference this material when leveraging the tools. We wrapped up the reference material with some real-world scenarios you may need to accomplish with step-by-step instructions covering how such tasks might be completed. Also, note that there is very good documentation on these tools not only at Microsoft's Web site but in a number of community Web sites as well. Some of these tools may seem challenging, but if you run into a roadblock, odds are you are not the first, and someone has discussed the situation out there!

Chapter 7

Using the Microsoft
Deployment Toolkit 2008

he Microsoft Deployment Toolkit 2008 (formerly known as the BDD)
provides guidance on the deployment of Windows systems. You can
use it to leverage a number of Microsoft tools and scripts to address
such tasks as establishing a lab environment for the development and testing
of imaging servers. You can create automated tasks for the installation of
Windows Vista and desired applications, create custom images, and even
automate the population of key values that dictate how an installation is to
take place on a computer by computer basis.

The Microsoft Deployment Toolkit (MDT) contains a substantial amount of
guidance and documentation on its own. To help illustrate the value of this documentation, this chapter provides a summary description of each of the included
documents before going into a step-by-step walkthrough covering how you can
configure and make use of MDT in your own environment. Finally, we cover
some third-party tools you can look to as alternatives to the MDT.

Introducing the Microsoft Deployment Toolkit

The Microsoft Deployment Toolkit (MDT) is made up of both documentation and tools designed to help tie together several different utilities and
scripts. These utilities and scripts are collected here in order to provide a
cohesive end to end solution for deploying Windows systems.

Microsoft Deployment Toolkit (MDT) 2008 is available from Microsoft's
Web site at www.microsoft.com/downloads/details.
aspx?familyid=3bd8561f-77ac-4400-a0c1-fe871c461a89.

Until recently Microsoft Deployment Toolkit 2008 was known as Business Desktop Deployment (BDD). The initial BDD 1.0 was released in November 2003. It focused on the deployment of Windows XP systems. Subsequent Versions 2.0 and 2.5 were released to provide increasingly enhanced guidance. Updated for Windows Vista and Office 2007, the BDD was renamed BDD 2007. When the BDD name was first abandoned it was often titled as Microsoft Deployment, but today, in yet another renaming, it is referred to as Microsoft Deployment Toolkit (or MDT) because it now supports the deployment of both desktop and server operating systems. Still, it is also some-times referred to as the Microsoft Deployment Solution Accelerator, and some earlier references may actually call it BDD 2008. Confusing as this all may be, the main idea to take away is that when you see references to BDD, the acronym is simply referring to the latest version of the BDD, now known as Microsoft Deployment Toolkit (MDT). Aside from yet another change in how it is identified, MDT contains a number of enhancements, including:

- Microsoft System Center Configuration Manager 2007 support
- Lite Touch Installation support for Windows Server 2008
- Several Lite Touch Installation enhancements including multicast support

Earlier releases of the BDD were broken up into two separate editions: Standard and Enterprise. This served to confuse things even more, so it was eventually abandoned. Now, it is one set of doc-umentation and tools with three different paths that can be taken to deploy systems:

- Zero Touch Installation (ZTI) uses Microsoft System Center Configuration Manager 2007 (SCCM) or alternatively, its former incarnation, Systems Management Server 2003 (SMS) with the Operating System Deployment (OSD) Feature Pack to completely automate the deployment of Windows XP SP2, Windows Vista, and Windows Server 2003 or 2008 as well as any needed applications.
- Lite Touch Installation (LTI) requires a more hands-on approach (though interaction can be minimized with some effort) for the deployment of Windows XP SP2, Windows Vista, as well as any needed applications.

 **The step-by-step instructions in this chapter focus on LTI because LTI does not require the acquisition of a Microsoft systems management tool.**

So what is the third path? LTI can be accomplished with or without using SMS (depending upon your environment). Essentially, zero touch aims to provide complete automation, whereas Lite Touch is mostly automated, but requires a few key configuration details to be collected before the automated installation begins.

Zero Touch Installation requires Microsoft System Center Configuration Manager 2007 (or the older Systems Management Server 2003), Windows Server 2003 with Windows Deployment Services (WDS), and Active Directory. In contrast, Lite Touch Installation requires only a local area network with one server. In both cases, it is MDT that pulls together the other tools required for a complete deployment solution.

Although many administrators will be using MDT to deploy the very latest operating systems such as Windows Vista (which is the focus here), it can be used to manage desktop migrations as far back as Windows 2000. Beyond new system deployment, MDT also provides functionality for migrating operating systems, such as moving from Windows 2000 to Windows XP with Service Pack 2.

Going over documentation

When you think of MDT, you probably think of the Deployment Workbench and tools, but the documentation and job aids provided can be a huge factor in your successful deployment of Windows Vista. MDT contains documentation for project management and technical guidance for administrators and project managers. Totaling over 1000 pages, the guides are broken down into several process segments (see Figure 7.1), and this section aims to highlight each of them. A thousand pages is a lot of reading, so you'll be happy to hear you need not read most of it. Some documents can be very helpful depending upon your situation, most others you will probably skip over. Determining which documents may be helpful can be enough of a challenge that you could be inclined to skip it completely. What we recommend is that you skim this list of resources and make note of those you feel would benefit you in your own environment. Taking advantage of these documents and job aids can mean both a more smooth and successful deployment *and* less work (writing) for you at the same time!

 **NOTE**   Several experts participated in the writing of these documents and job aids. In fact, the authors of this book were also authors of some of the MDT guides!

FIGURE 7.1

Browsing MDT Process documentation

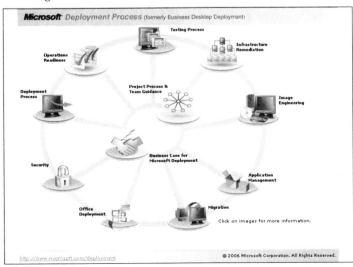

> **NOTE**   Another helpful set of free deployment guidance is available through the *Definitive Guide to Vista Migration* by Ruest and Ruest. This guide takes a more direct approach to the structuring of deployment projects at about 250 pages in length. It also includes business case templates and other documentation tools. Go to `www.realtime-nexus.com/dgvm.htm` to download it.

Business Case for Microsoft Deployment Toolkit

With the idea that IT projects are expected to yield positive and measureable returns, it is common for organizations to develop a business case for approval before any project may begin. MDT provides a sample business case for its fictitious organization (Woodgrove Bank) to assist in the development of your own business case.

This consists of two documents:

- **Woodgrove Business Case.doc:** This sample document follows many of the corporate and academic content standards often required. Although you may want to add or remove from the many elements of the sample document, having a full business case for MDT available as a starting point can be a timesaver. (38 pages)

- **Woodgrove Business Case.ppt**: A PowerPoint presentation is also provided for the business case that helps walk viewers through the problem statement, proposed solution, financial analysis, and next steps. (14 pages)

Microsoft Deployment Project, Process & Team Guidance

The MDT solution provides fully developed processes for computer imaging, software and hardware inventory, application compatibility evaluation and remediation, application packaging and scripting, network inventory and analysis, and desktop computer deployment, including data migration. The processes provided here in MDT are based on real-world experience in actual deployments from small offices to enterprises of over 50,000 desktops.

Several documents and job aids are provided here including:

- **Planning Guide.doc:** Taking up where the "Quick Start Guide" leaves off, this is a comprehensive document describing how to start, carry out, and complete an MDT project. It provides information on assembling the project team, and defines the vision, goals, scope, and project plans. (58 pages)

- **Preparing the Lab.doc:** This guide contains information about how to set up a lab environment for the building phase of an MDT project. (14 pages)

- **Release Management Guide.doc:** This guide provides procedures for achieving a managed secure rollout for a new operating system as well as the hardware, software, personnel, and processes that come along with such a deployment. (32 Pages)

- **Enterprise Learning Framework User Guide.doc:** This guide covers the Enterprise Learning Framework (ELF) which is an online guidance tool for the development of user training and communication as it pertains to the deployment of Windows Vista and Office 2007 applications. (17 pages)

- **Woodgrove Enterprise IT Archetype.doc:** This document provides a detailed description of a fictional enterprise organization intended to describe a representative IT organization. This sample describes the roles and responsibilities of each administrator in the organization and can be helpful in visualizing how your own project might be executed. (38 pages)

- **Functional Specification.doc:** This job aid is a template that may be used to create your own Functional Specification document. By referring to the above Woodgrove Enterprise IT Archetype document, it provides an example of how such a specification may be drafted. (43 pages)

- **Deployment Plan.doc:** The deployment plan is provided to serve as a high-level checklist of milestones and tasks with examples of deliverables. (39 pages)

- **Pilot Plan.doc:** The pilot plan job aid is a template you may use to document your own pilot including what aspect of the deployment project will be delivered as pilot and details needed to successfully conduct a pilot. (26 pages)

- **Request for Change.doc:** A request for change (RFC) collects change details as a critical step of a controlled change management process. This document provides a template from which you may base your own RFC form. (12 pages)

- **Risk Template Tool.xls:** This spreadsheet helps to work through identifying possible risks, as well as analyzing, planning and costing those risks. See Figure 7.2. (6 worksheets)

FIGURE 7.2

Reviewing the Microsoft Deployment Risk Template tool

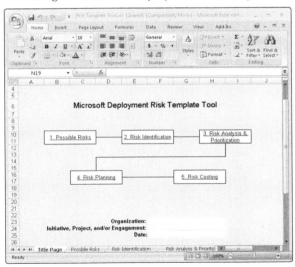

- **Test Plan.doc:** This job aid provides yet another template for your use. This one describes the strategy and approach used to plan, organize, and manage a project's testing activities. It identifies testing objectives, methodologies, tools, expected results, responsibilities, and resource requirements. (41 pages)

- **Test Specification.doc:** This technical outline is a template for conducting the testing process. It defines the input, output, environment, and procedural guidelines at the deployment project level and for each test case. (33 pages)

- **Test Cases Workbook.xls:** This spreadsheet provides actual test cases for LTI and ZTI covering type and scope complete with a description of each test, steps to conduct the tests, and the expected result for each. (More than 300 tests are included)

- **Training Plan.doc:** Another template, this job aid identifies the needs and processes for training the people who will participate in creating the deployment project. This can cover a particular software package or development environment. It focuses on the project teams and does not address the training needs of users or support staff for ongoing operations. (28 page)

- **Vision Scope.doc:** This last template helps you to create a document that represents the ideas and decisions developed during the Envisioning Phase, the goal of which is to achieve team and customer agreement on the desired solution and overall project direction. (30 pages)

Infrastructure Remediation

Understanding your network environment is important for a project such as the deployment of Windows Vista. To properly prepare for such a change, this step in the process helps you understand the status of your organization's environment, identify other sources of change that may affect the project, and perform risk mitigation approach to those changes.

With the idea that most organizations can avoid most networking problems by creating and maintaining adequate network documentation, the following documents and job aids are provided:

- **Infrastructure Remediation Feature Team Guide.doc:** This comprehensive guide aims to help establish or improve existing network documentation which may then be maintained after the project is complete. This process does require an inventory collection and reporting tool such as SMS/CCM or the Application Compatibility Toolkit (ACT). (33 pages)

- **Communications Plan.doc:** This document provides a template that may be used to describe how the project establishes a reliable means of ensuring visibility and cooperation by communication status and news about the project to its stakeholders. (8 pages)

- **Network and Workstation Hardware Upgrades List.xls:** This simple spreadsheet is provided to assist in collecting an installation requirements list. It is used to record the device, manufacturer, and model of the system as well as the component that requires upgrading and a description of that item. (1 page)

- **Inventory Template.xls:** Particularly if you do not have a robust inventory and reporting tool, this spreadsheet can help you to break down your collected data in an effort to more clearly standardize the client computer deployments. Inventory is broken up into unmanaged infrastructure, hardware, operating systems, applications, inventory, and audits. (7 worksheets)

- **Assessment Template.xls:** This spreadsheet may be used to document your assessment of the network, active directory, servers, desktops, applications, etc. (over 75 worksheets)

- **Current State Assessment Template.doc:** This template may be used to document a system in order to accelerate and standardize client computer deployments and upgrades. It divides the assessment into the areas of network environment, infrastructure, client environment, client computer deployment process, user state, and application compatibility. (21 pages)

Image Engineering

The Image Engineering process covers creating a build server, configuring supplementary applications, creating a computer installation boot CD, building initial reference computer images, and preparing the WDS server. There are four documents provided to support this process:

- **Image Engineering Feature Team Guide.doc:** The imaging process consists of several phases such as planning, developing, and deploying. Aside from project management, this document also discusses technical topics such as the concept of thin, thick and hybrid images, a development checklist, and the handling of updates. (27 pages)

- **System Center Configuration Manager Imaging Guide.doc:** This document extends the previous Feature Team Guide by covering the use of Systems Center Configuration Manager and its functions in the imaging project. (26 pages)

- **Workbench Imaging Guide.doc:** This document offers a step-by-step extension of the Image Engineering Feature Team Guide, specific to creating LTI images in the Deployment Workbench. (42 pages)

- **Image Customization Guide.doc:** This guide describes how to customize images by customizing the task sequence, writing scripts, customizing existing scripts, adding applications, and customizing actions. (33 pages)

Application Management

Inconsistency between client systems on your network can result in usability and support issues that may be mitigated by ensuring that applications are installed the same way on all systems. Aside from the obvious need to save time, automating installations is a key to ensuring systems are as similar as possible. The Application Management process offers guidance on how to mitigate application compatibility issues, automate installations, and manage requests for change in your environment. Once again, Feature Team Guides, reference materials, and job aids are provided to help smooth the process:

- **Application Management Feature Team Guide.doc:** This guide provides guidance on the automation of application installations in order to achieve a more managed environment. Among other related topics, the guide discusses the creation of a project plan, analysis of application inventory, package creation and testing. (39 pages)

- **Application Compatibility Guide.doc:** Particularly with Windows Vista, application compatibility is a key factor in the success of a deployment project. This document describes strategies for identifying potential problems, addressing those problems with a mitigation package, and then deploying those mitigation packages. (58 pages)

- **Application Packaging Guide.doc:** This guide provides coverage of how to go about establishing automated installation routines for the customization and deployment of applications in your environment. It provides step-by-step instructions on use of the Deployment Workbench to automate the installation of applications for both LTI and ZTI deployment methods (with and without SMS/SCCM). (21 pages)

- **The 20 Commandments of Software Packaging.pdf:** This document outlines 20 guidelines to follow when repackaging software. The paper is sponsored by Macrovision, but most all of the tips provided also translate well to competitive packaging solutions. (31 pages)

- **Macrovision Application Preparation Roadmap.pdf:** This document includes a poster which aims to summarize the application preparation and deployment process. (1 page)

- **MSI Repackaging and Customization Best Practices Guide.pdf:** This document provides best practices for the repackaging and customization of installations for those migrating legacy setups to MSI format. (12 pages)

- **Macrovision Brochure.pdf:** You can find some tips on the importance of application preparation and an overview of the products offered to address these needs from Macrovision. (11 pages)

- **Application Knowledge Sheet.doc:** This job aid provides a worksheet with several fields to help document an application and how it is to be managed in your environment. (1 page)

- **Client Build Requirements.doc:** Again using the Woodgrove Bank Company as an example, this document provides policies, procedures, methodologies, and approaches instituted to support the desktop computer lifecycle. (33 pages)

> **NOTE** The software division of Macrovision has been sold to a new company named Acresso, but the documents and titles had not yet been updated as of this writing. Find Acresso at www.acresso.com.

> **NOTE** Although AdminStudio gets some good coverage here, there are a number of other solutions for migrating and creating Windows Installer setups of which you should be aware. For a comprehensive list of such solutions, visit www.appdeploy.com/techhomes/windowsinstaller.asp.

Migration

Identifying data files and settings and saving and restoring them is what the migration process is all about. Handling user data and settings properly make the migration experience much easier on users. Save users from spending hours looking for files and trying to get things back they way they like by automating the migration of as many files and settings as possible. The process is documented here in two guides covering the migration as a project and the technical documentation on the use of provided tools:

- **Migration Feature Team Guide.doc:** This guide covers the decisions and concepts to be considered when migrating desktop configurations to a new Windows Vista. It addresses the issue of migration as a full project with step-by-step plans to smooth and successful execution. (22 pages)

- **User State Migration Guide.doc:** For Microsoft Management, the User State Migration Tool (USMT) provides key functionality in the migration process and this guide provides documentation for the use of this tool. (20 pages)

Office Deployment

For many businesses, Microsoft office among the most used software. Office is a very large suite of tools and is treated by the MDT process as a core application (normally included within the desktop computer image for Vista). A guide and a large number of job aids are provided to assist in establishing a lab, identifying key issues, creating the deployment package, integrating the package with the core image, testing, and running a successful pilot:

- **Office Deployment Guide.doc:** This guide covers each phase of an Office rollout. It is intended as a sub-guide to the Application Management Feature Team Guide which includes guidance on team structure and organization. (26 pages)

- **Office Assessment Template.xls:** This job aid provides a template for use with the Office Deployment Guide with worksheets for all of the information that pertains to this project. (86 worksheets)

- **Office Budget Plan.xls:** This job aid provides an Office System budget plan broken down into several line items with columns for projected budget and actual amount spent for each. (1 worksheet)

- **Office Communications Plan.doc:** This document provides a template for describing how the project will be established and a reliable means of ensuring visibility and corporation by communicating status about the project to stakeholders. (15 pages)

- **Office Configuration Plan.doc:** This configuration plan document is yet another template to help you document your project. It helps to document the features each user has access to, the default settings for your environment, and how to maintain Office throughout its lifecycle. (21 pages)

- **Office Current State Assessment Template.doc:** This document offers a template to assessing your environment including the client, deployment process, SMS infrastructure, user state, and application compatibility. (16 pages)

- **Office Distribution Plan.doc:** Yet another template, this document describes the strategy and approach used to plan, organize, and manage the project's distribution activities. (22 pages)

- **Office File Migration Plan.doc:** This template is used to document the planning required in order to use all Office documents and solutions and provides insight into the overall configuration strategy. (16 pages)

- **Office Functional Specification.doc:** This template is designed to document the exact and specific terms for what the team is building and deploying. (30 pages)

- **Office Hardware Upgrades List.xls:** This spreadsheet offers a simple list of hardware upgrade items for tracking purposes including what kind of device, manufacturer, model, part number, cost, etc. (1 worksheet)

- **Office Inventory Template.doc:** This template is provided in support of your deployment project to help standardize the corporate office automation suite across an organization by offering a place to record an inventory of unmanaged and managed computers, applications, and more. (15 pages)

- **Office Management Plan.doc:** This template offers a basis for documenting the changes to user settings for a custom configuration of Office 2007 and the creation and/or enforcement of those settings. (19 pages)

- **Office Pilot Plan.doc:** This template is provided to help document what aspect of the solution will be delivered in the pilot deployment and provides the details to successfully conduct the pilot. (20 pages)

- **Office Project Plan.mpp:** This project plan written in Microsoft Office Project breaks out each of the necessary tasks and milestones with their dependencies and estimated durations for each. See Figure 7.3. (191 tasks)

- **Office Risk Template Tool.xls:** This risk template tool breaks down possible risks, risk identification, risk analysis and prioritization, risk planning, and risk costing. (6 worksheets)

- **Office Test Plan.doc:** The test plan document describes the strategy and approach used to plan, organize, and manage the project's testing activities, and this template serves to help detail this information for your own test plan. (32 pages)

- **Office Training Plan.doc:** This template is for establishing a training plan which identifies the needs and processes for training the project team (it does not address training of end users or support staff). (22 pages)

- **Office Vision Scope.doc:** This last Office template is designed to represent the ideas and decisions developed during the Envisioning Phase, designed to achieve team and customer agreement on the desired solution and project direction. (23 pages)

FIGURE 7.3

Updating the provided Migration Plan for Office deployment

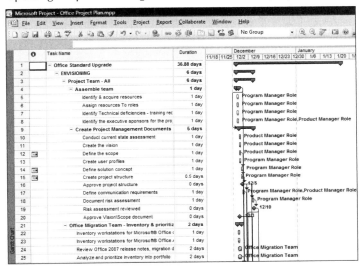

Securing the Desktop

It is the goal of the security team to secure an organization's data. To ensure adequate security measures are in place it is necessary to analyze and determine existing security, identify vulnerabilities, and ensure security measures are current. The following job aids are provided to help you in this task:

- **Security Feature Team Guide.doc:** This document provides information on the subject of security measures for client computers to be deployed with MDT and how to protect the deployment infrastructure from security threats. (35 pages)

- **Windows Vista Security Guide:** This guide provides instructions and recommendations to help strengthen desktop and laptop security for those systems running Windows Vista in a domain with Active Directory in place. Unlike the others, this document is actually an online link to the article, which is multiple chapters in length. (online)

Deployment Process

This section details the steps to streamline deployment and describes specific deployment steps to simplify the process. The process is broken up into four phases: Planning server placement, evaluating server and network capacity, installing the deployment tools, and deploying the desktops.

- **Deployment Feature Team Guide.doc:** This guide serves as the MDT documentation for guidance through deployment tasks and checkpoints. (39 pages)

- **Preparing for LTI Tools.doc:** This guide provides specific details on how to use MDT to deploy Windows and Office. It also covers how to run the automated deployment process to replace earlier versions of the operating system. (56 pages)

- **Preparing for Systems Management Server 2003.doc:** This guide details how to deploy Windows XP and later using MDT much as the previous *Preparing for LTI Tools* document does, but with a process leveraging a SMS infrastructure. (56 pages)

- **Preparing for System Center Configuration Manager.doc:** This guide offers detailed information on using Windows Deployment to deploy Windows and Office with MDT leveraging a Systems Center Configuration Manager (SCCM) infrastructure. (25 pages)

- **Deployment Customization Guide.doc:** This guide takes the Image Engineering feature team through the process of using SMS or SCCM during the imaging process. It goes on to describe how to customize images using the task sequence and scripting. (76 pages)

- **Deployment Customization Desktop Samples.doc:** This guide is designed to provide sample configuration settings for specific desktop deployment scenarios using MDT. (76 pages)

- **Toolkit Reference.doc:** This large reference guide documents configuration settings that may be leveraged in the deployment process. The many properties, scripts, and more are all documented in this valuable reference guide. (266 pages)

- **Troubleshooting Reference.doc:** This reference provides information on current known issues, possible workarounds, and brief troubleshooting guidance. (43 pages)

- **Volume Activation TechNet Center:** This is a link to the online document entitled "Volume Activation 2.0 for Windows Vista and Windows Server 2008" which describes the options and operations of working with Volume Activation. (Online)

- **Volume Activation Download Center:** This is a link to a downloadable document that documents the planning, deployment, and operations of Volume Activation 2.0 for Windows Vista and Windows Server 2008 with an overview, planning guide, deployment guide, operations guide, and other resources and answers to frequently asked questions. (Multiple documents totaling 152 pages)

Operations Readiness

The operations feature team is responsible for the rollout of the solution through its hand off to IT staff. Critical to deployment success, this aspect of the deployment includes such tasks as analyzing and evaluating the management tools currently in use, assessing the current maturity of the operations environment, and preparing the operation staff for pilot. This section includes:

- **Operations Readiness Feature Team Guide.doc:** This guide is intended to help you to prepare to hand off a completed deployment project to an in-place IT operations team. (32 pages)

- **Enterprise Learning Framework User Guide.doc:** The Enterprise Learning Framework (ELF) is an online guidance tool that helps Microsoft customers develop user training and communications plans for the deployment of Windows Vista and Office. ELF is not intended for use directly by users, but for training, communication, and deployment managers. This guide provides step-by-step guidance on how to use the ELF tool. (17 pages)

Testing Process

An element of the Envisioning Phase, it is the objective of the testing process to have the decisions that the test team makes align with that of the overall project goals. The materials created by the Testing feature team should also be well integrated into the overall migration project.

To help facilitate this, Microsoft includes Test Feature Team Guide.doc. This guide is intended to guide a team through test tasks and checkpoints for the process of deploying Windows. (37 pages)

Getting familiar with the tools of MDT

The documentation supports a process which leverages a number of free tools provided by Microsoft. In addition to some custom scripts, these individual solutions are brought together by MDT. Before delving into how to use these tools, a quick look at what tools are leveraged by MDT will be discussed in this section.

Knowing when to use Microsoft Management tools

It can be intimidating to see such a long list of tools, but there is no need to become an expert in any one of them to make good use of Microsoft Deployment. In Table 7.1, a quick breakdown of the tasks performed by MDT is provided to summarize how each of the tools fit in. Even if the end-to-end solution MDT aims to provide is too much for your environment, there is still plenty of value in picking out select documentation and tools as guidance in those areas of need.

TABLE 7.1

Tools Associated with Microsoft Management

Tasks	Tools
Hardware and Software Inventory	Application Compatibility Analyzer, Microsoft SQL Server/Microsoft SQL Server 2005 Express Edition, Microsoft Office Access
Application Compatibility Testing and Remediation	Application Compatibility Toolkit 5.0.2, Microsoft Virtual PC 2007
Core Application Packaging	Office Professional Edition 2007, the Microsoft Office Resource Kit
Imaging	ImageX, System Image Manager, Microsoft Windows Preinstallation Environment 2.0 (Windows PE 2.0), Sysprep, Deployment Workbench
Project Management	Microsoft Project 2007
Application Packaging	Third party solution (Acresso AdminStudio, Altiris Wise Package Studio, ScriptLogic MSI Studio, InstallAware Studio, and so forth).
New Methods of Activation	Volume Activation 2.0
User Data and Settings	User State Migration Tool 3.0.1
Deployment Process	Windows PE 2.0, Sysprep, Windows Deployment Services, Microsoft Deployment Windows Deployment Wizard
Encryption	BitLocker™ drive encryption support for Lite Touch Install scenarios

NOTE Office products are not included free, but are necessary to leverage all the provided documents. However, you can use the free Office Viewers to work with all of the documentation (with the exception of Microsoft Project) in read-only mode. Naturally, third-party repackaging tools are also not included, but are often necessary.

The Deployment Workbench

Figure 7.1 shows the Deployment Workbench, which is the glue that aims to tie the many tools used by MDT together into a more cohesive deployment solution. This Microsoft Management Console snap-in provides a familiar tree-view for navigation to the various MDT components:

- Information Center provides areas to access documentation, news, and updates for Microsoft Management.

- Distribution Share facilitates the execution of tasks that need to be performed, including installation of required components, source files, and drivers.

- Task Sequences allow the ordering of the tasks to be automated.

- Deploy is where action is taken to manage deployment points and the deployment database.

Microsoft Application Compatibility Toolkit 5.0

The Microsoft Application Compatibility Toolkit (ACT) provides a toolset for the identification and remediation of known compatibility issues. For those who do not have an asset management system in place, the reports generated by ACT can provide a very good start to establishing some much needed software inventory data. With the inventory data collected, you can then analyze the data and rectify the issues identified. See Figure 7.4.

The process of evaluating application compatibility challenges that may be faced in Windows Vista deployment should include the following steps:

1. Collect information about your current applications.
2. Prioritize the applications to test and support.
3. Test the applications against your baseline workstation configuration.
4. Mitigate issues (remediate, upgrade, migrate, remove).

NOTE For details on the configuration and use of ACT, see *Getting Started with Application Compatibility in a Windows Deployment* online at http://download. microsoft.com/download/5/a/a/5aa544b0-e938-48d3-a2ab-6a7540e6387d/ Getting%20Started%20with%20AppCompat%20FINAL.pdf.

FIGURE 7.4

Starting the Microsoft Application Compatibility Toolkit

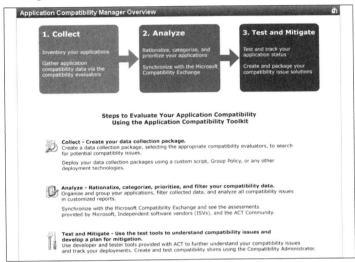

Microsoft User State Migration Tool 3.0.1

Version 3.0.1 of the Microsoft User State Migration Tool (USMT) is provided with MDT to support the migration of user accounts during deployments of Microsoft Windows XP and Microsoft Windows Vista operating systems. USMT captures user accounts (desktop settings, application settings, and user files) and then migrates them to a new Windows installation. USMT is intended exclusively for administrators who are performing automated deployments and want to handle user data migration. USMT enables you to do the following:

- **Configure the migration specifically for your environment.** Files and settings are migrated based on xml-based rule files that control exactly how user accounts are to be migrated.

- **Automate migration using USMT command line tools.** Two tools are provided, which control collecting and restoring the user files and settings.

Microsoft Windows Enterprise Learning Framework User Kit

The Enterprise Learning Framework (ELF) is a tool designed to help corporations develop a training and communication plan for employees during Windows Vista and the 2007 Microsoft Office system deployment. It identifies the most relevant learning topics on Windows Online Help and

Office Online for different stages of deployment and different types of users. ELF enables you to do the following:

- Prepare employees for deployment and raise awareness of the new versions' benefits
- Minimize disruption on deployment day by getting employees up to speed with a list of "must know" topics
- Select productivity topics to help employees get the most from Windows Vista and the 2007 Office release after deployment

Windows Automated Installation Kit (WAIK) User's Guide for Windows Vista

The Windows Automated Installation Kit (Windows AIK) is designed to help you deploy Windows onto new hardware in an automated fashion. The Windows AIK is a set of deployment tools provided to support the automated deployment of Windows including:

- **Microsoft Windows Preinstallation Environment 2.0**: The latest version of this MS-DOS replacement designed for the installation of Windows. Windows PE is a streamlined operating system designed to get a computer up and ready to begin installation as quickly as possible while supporting standard Windows Vista hardware drivers and security.
- **ImageX**: This command line tool supports the creation, maintenance, and application of file-based images (WIM files).
- **Windows System Image Manager (SIM)**: Previously, you could use Setup Manager to generated unattended setup files. Today, SIM provides this functionality and more by allowing you to complete several tasks with unattended setup files. You can create a new unattended setup file, edit existing ones, and even verify the settings in an existing file. SIM can also show you the potential configuration options given a specific image of Windows Vista.

Standalone task sequencer

Also included in MDT is a standalone task sequencer derived from System Center Configuration Manager (SCCM) 2007. Provided as a key element of the Deployment Workbench, his task sequencer is used to control which events should occur and when during the installation of Windows Vista. In fact, even those that already have SCCM 2007 can benefit from this delivery of the task sequencer in that it provides extensions to task sequencing capabilities, three additional task sequence templates, and enhanced post-operating system installation provisioning tasks. More on how to leverage this task sequencer is discussed later in this chapter in the section "Creating task sequences."

Installing and Configuring MDT

Installing MDT is quite simple as it is provided as a basic Windows Installer setup. However, it does rely upon a number of additional technologies and tools which must also be downloaded and installed separately. The good news is that there is an interface provided within the Deployment Workbench tool which facilitates the downloading and installation of these additional components.

Start by downloading MDT from the Microsoft Web site and run the simple setup. Like most any setup, you must be an administrator to perform the installation and go through a simple wizard interface for accepting the license agreement, choosing a target directory, and initiating the actual installation.

Getting MDT set up can take a little while, but is a fairly straightforward process:

1. **Install the required components and hotfixes.**
2. **Establish a distribution share including the WAIK and required OS source files.**

NOTE MDT is available from Microsoft's Web site at `www.microsoft.com/downloads/details.aspx?familyid=3bd8561f-77ac-4400-a0c1-fe871c461a89`. Microsoft does reorganize its Web site often, so if it does move, a search for "Microsoft Deployment" or "BDD" should quickly uncover its new location.

In order to use Deployment Workbench for anything other than simply reviewing the documentation, it is necessary to do so using an account that is a member of the local Administrators group. In Vista, this means using Run as Administrator to launch the program.

TIP Open only a single instance of Deployment Workbench. Opening two or more instances of Deployment Workbench can result in unpredictable behavior.

Installing components

Before you begin installing the additional components, ensure you have the latest list of available components by performing the following steps:

1. **Right-click the Deployment Workbench shortcut and choose Run As Administrator.**
2. **Choose Deployment Workbench ⇨ Information Center ⇨ Components**
3. **From Window's main menu bar, choose Action and then click Check for Updates.**
4. **Choose Check the Internet as the source for locating updates.** If you are installing in an offline environment, you can perform this step from a different Internet-attached computer and then copy the downloaded files to removable media. To then make use of this removable media as the source for locating updates, you can use the second option, Check a local path, and specify the path to your locally staged source files. Click the Check button to initiate the process.

Now that you have the latest manifest of available components, begin downloading and installing each of the components you require (see Figure 7.5). Choosing Download will change the selected components status to Queued and the Download button itself will be updated to function as a Cancel Download button. You can queue several components to download. How long it takes will naturally depend upon your Internet connection. When a download begins, you will see the percentage of completion reflected in the status for the downloading component (it will complete the download of one component before beginning the next queued download).

FIGURE 7.5

Installing the components of the Deployment Workbench

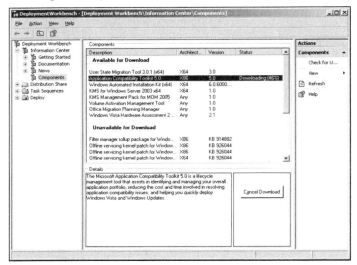

> **TIP** Within the Deployment Workbench, click the News node under Information Center to see if there are any new updates or changes for which you should be aware.

Once all the required components have been downloaded, you can select each to see either an Install or Browse button. The Browse button simply opens the folder where the installation resides (a subdirectory of the installation directory) using Windows Explorer where you may double-click the setup to perform the installation.

As each item is downloaded and installed, it will move between the labeled sections as appropriate — Available for Download, Unavailable for Download, Downloaded, and Installed.

> **TIP** Although some hotfixes may be listed under Unavailable for Download, what is provided is a button to view the knowledge base article online. Once online, you may or may not find the update in question is available to be downloaded (outside of the Deployment Workbench).

Establishing a distribution share

As shown in Figure 7.6, in order to establish a distribution share, you must install the Windows Automated Installation Kit (WAIK), create the share, and import the necessary files. The following section details each of these steps.

FIGURE 7.6

Establishing a distribution share

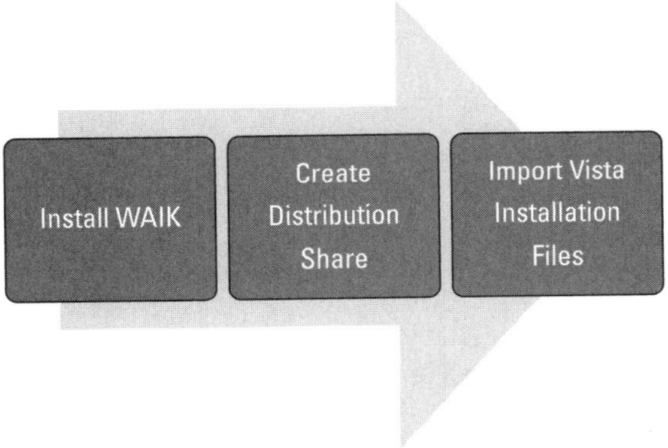

Clicking the Distribution Share node will provide checklist of steps you must perform before an operating system may be deployed. Use this checklist as a simple reference to track your progress:

- Install the WAIK
- Create a distribution share directory
- Add operating system files
- Add applications (optional)
- Add OS packages (optional)
- Add drivers (optional)

Installing the WAIK

The first step is to install the Windows Automated Installation Kit. This is something that should have been accomplished when downloading and installing the required components as discussed previously. If you did not perform the installations of listed components, this required component will prevent you from continuing any further.

1. Select Deployment Workbench ⇨ Information Center ⇨ Components, choose Windows Automated Installation Kit from the Available for Download list, and then click the Download button.

2. Click the Install button to initiate the installation of the WAIK.

3. When installed, you should see it listed in the Installed section of the Components view, and the first item in the Distribution Share checklist should reflect it has been completed.

Creating a distribution share directory

The next step is to create a distribution share directory. This step establishes the directory and share where MDT will store its configuration files and source binaries to be used in creating builds.

1. Choose Deployment Workbench ➪ Distribution Share and click the Create distribution share action from the pane on the right.

2. In the Create Distribution Share Wizard, you will see a Specify Directory page. Click Create a new distribution share and enter the location for the share on the local system.

3. Click Finish to complete the step and close the Create Distribution Share Wizard.

Adding operating system files

The last required step in establishing a distribution share is to add operating system files. You need only add those you wish to deploy, keeping in mind that with Vista, the WIM file you specify will contain each of the editions, as they are all present in the file-based image. The following steps walk you through adding a Vista image to the Deployment Workbench:

1. Choose Deployment Workbench ➪ Distribution Share ➪ Operating Systems and click the New action from the pane on the right.

2. From the OS Type page, select Full set of source files and then click Next to continue.

3. On the Source page, for Source Directory enter the root of the DVD drive where you have inserted your Windows Vista setup DVD, or the root of the folder where you have copied its contents and click Next to continue.

   In this process, the last page in the New OS Wizard is the Destination page. Here you are prompted to provide a Destination directory name.

4. Enter a unique and descriptive name (such as "Windows Vista") and click Finish to initiate the copying of the required files to the distribution share.

If you had already created one, this wizard also allows you to easily specify a custom captured image (a WIM file), or you can even choose to add a Windows Deployment Services image from a WDS server.

> **TIP** Although you cannot specify an ISO file for your image, you make use of an ISO image file by mounting it with a tool such as the free DAEMON Tools (www.daemon-tools.cc) utility. You can also rely on WinImage from Gilles Volant Software (www.winimage.com/).

Optionally, Applications, OS Packages (to include Windows), and Out of Box (OOB) drivers may also be added using a similar wizard interface in this section.

Adding applications

To automate your build as much as possible you need to include the installation of those applications that apply to all client systems in your environment. To add an application, follow these steps:

1. **Expand the Distribution Share node of the Workbench tree, right-click Applications, and click New from the Actions pane on the left.**

2. **For Application Type, choose either Application with source files or Application without source files or elsewhere on the network.** If you specify that an application with source files is being specified, the source files will be copied to the distribution share during deployment. If you already have a share that contains your prepared application installations, you may choose the latter option and simply provide a UNC or DFS location to access them from their current location. A third option, Application Bundle, is provided in the event that there is no application installation command associated with the application. This is for use in scenarios where you wish to install application dependencies such as when applications must be installed as a group.

3. **On the Details page, enter information such as Publisher, Application Name, Version, and Languages and then click Next to continue.**

4. **On the Source page, type the path of the application to be added.** This step is shown only if Application Type specified an Application with source files. If application source files are configured to be copied to the distribution share, all data in the specified folder will be copied. If the source files being specified are located on the local system and not a centrally available network share, an option to Move the files to the distribution share instead of copying them will be enabled so the files may be moved to the distribution share where they can be reliably accessible.

5. **On the Destination page, specify the name of the directory in your distribution share where the application files will be copied or moved.** Like the previous step, this too is shown only if Application Type specified an Application with source files.

6. **On the Command Details page, you may specify the quiet install command line and working directory needed to install the application.** The Command Line need not specify a path; the path is known to the application entry by the value provided to the Working Directory field. See Figure 7.7 for an example.

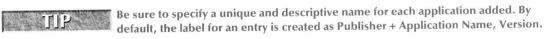 **Be sure to specify a unique and descriptive name for each application added. By default, the label for an entry is created as Publisher + Application Name, Version.**

You may also specify dependencies for an application by right-clicking it from the list, clicking Properties, and managing the list on the Dependencies tab.

FIGURE 7.7

Specifying the installation command for an application

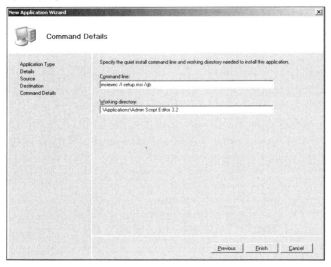

Adding OS packages

For the purpose of establishing a build in MDT, a package is defined as a security update, service pack, or language pack, and normally has a .cab or .msu file extension. You can add these to the Deployment Workbench by following these steps:

1. Choose Deployment Workbench ⇨ Distribution Share ⇨ OS Packages and then click the New option from the actions pane on the right.

2. On the Specify Directory page, type the Package source directory to be added to the distribution share. Then click Finish to complete the operation.

Adding out-of-box drivers

An out-of-box (OOB) driver refers to a driver that is not already included in the Windows Vista image. Adding one is as easy as the previous items and may be accomplished by performing the following operation:

1. Choose Deployment Workbench ⇨ Distribution Share ⇨ Out-of-box Drivers and click the New option from the actions pane on the right.

2. On the Specify Directory page, specify the Driver source directory path as the folder or share containing the device drivers to be added.

3. Select the driver group to assign the driver, or accept the default All Drivers. Then click Finish to complete the operation.

This operation adds all the device drivers found in the specified folder and subfolders to take care in how you establish this driver directory before adding it here.

Imaging with MDT

With everything installed and ready to go, it is time to put the workbench to work. Because the most common use of MDT is establishing and configuring LTI deployment, this section focuses on LTI development and deployment. Follow these steps:

1. **Create the task sequences that will automate the development of a baseline image.**
2. **Establish a distribution point from which to deploy the installation.**
3. **Take a time out to investigate the options provided by the task sequencer.**
4. **Create a deployment point for handling the deployment of our reference system.** At this stage, you will be ready to prepare a reference computer.
5. **With the reference computer established, you can then add the custom image to the distribution share.**
6. **After the custom image has been added, you can create a deployment build for it.**
7. **To realize the full power of MDT, you also need to create and configure a deployment database.** After it is ready, you will need to populate it with data.
8. **Take time to understand the deployment rules and how they may be leveraged.**
9. **Apply a level of customization to better automate an LTI image.**
10. **Deploy the custom image to test the deployment process.**

The key functionality of the Deployment Workbench is its Task Sequencer. Start by creating task sequences to automate the creation of the baseline image.

Creating task sequences

With a focus on the deployment of Vista, the first thing you need is to establish a build. A build is made up of several components including source files, configuration settings, and the installation process (task sequence) which defines how to create an image.

It should be the goal of any administrator to automate the build process as much as possible. Consistent reproducibility is crucial in controlling your baseline configuration as changes, updates, and new hardware are introduced to your network in the future.

Before you begin creating task sequences it is important to establish a naming scheme to use for task sequence IDs. While task sequence names can be modified later, these task sequence IDs cannot. An example would be to use the version of Windows, the edition, the service pack, and a descriptive label to identify the customizations. Before you are carried away, know that there is a 16-character limit to the task sequence ID value. This information pertains to a full build and not to an individual task so you may have only a limited number of such configurations. Table 7.2 provides some sample task settings to use as a guide, including one that specifies a "configuration set." The concept here would be that you may have multiple ways you wish to create a build of the same Vista edition and service pack level. In this case, you name the configuration in your build documentation and reflect it in the task sequence ID by letter or numeral.

TABLE 7.2

Descriptive Task Setting Properties

Task Sequence ID	Task Sequence Name	Task Sequence Comments
WinVistaBusSP0	Windows Vista Business	Windows Vista Business Edition with no service pack
WinVistaEntSP1	Windows Vista Enterprise SP1	Windows Vista Enterprise Edition with Service Pack 1
WinVistaUltSP1-a	Windows Vista Ultimate SP1 with Configuration Set A	Windows Vista Ultimate Edition with Service Pack 1 and a set of customizations documented and titled as configuration "Set A."

The Task Sequencer is the tool to create, manage, and execute this build automation. To create a task, follow this procedure:

1. Choose Deployment Workbench ➪ Task Sequences and click the New option from the actions pane on the right.

2. On the General Settings page, enter the Task Sequence ID, Task sequence name, and Task sequence comments as described previously. Click the Next button to continue.

3. On the Select Template page, you may choose to select one of the four default templates, including:

   - **Standard Client Task Sequence** may be used to specify a default task sequence for deploying operating system images to client computers.

   - **Standard Client Replace Task Sequence** may be used to back up an entire system, its user state, and then wipe the disk.

   - **Custom Task Sequence** may be used to establish a blank task sequence which you can customize from scratch.

   - **Standard Server Task Sequence** may be used to create a default task sequence for the deployment of system images to server computers.

For the purpose of establishing a Windows Vista build task, choose Standard Client Task Sequence. Press the Next button to continue.

4. **On the Select OS page, choose the operating system image to be installed with this task and press the Next button to proceed.**

5. **On the Specify Product Key page, you may choose to provide a product key (or not) and click the Next button to continue.** Normally, you would want to enter this to create an automated installation process, but with no volume license key available, you may not need to not use a product key when installing. This will prompt the user for the key (in a LTI scenario) or you can make use of a Key Management Service. There are actually a few ways to go about handling the distribution of product keys including using the BDD database capabilities to automate the process. For more details visit: `http://blogs.technet.com/mniehaus/archive/2007/08/10/can-i-deploy-windows-vista-ultimate-with-bdd-2007.aspx`.

6. **On the OS Settings page, you may enter the Full Name, Organization, and Internet Explorer Home Page; then click Next to continue.** Each of these values is required, but may be overridden during deployment using a wizard or rule.

7. **On the Admin Password page, you can specify an Administrative password for the build.** The local administrator password is also specified in a task sequence so you may choose: Do not specify an Administrator password at this time. Furthermore, while protected to some degree, any password specified is written into the `unattend.xml` file, which may not be secure against someone wishing to reverse the process used to obfuscate the password in this file.

8. **Click Finish to complete the process.**

Investigating Task Sequencer options

The Task Sequencer is a standalone task sequencer derived from System Center Configuration Manager 2007. To better understand the full capabilities offered by this powerful tool, we recommend that you browse the following options:

1. **Choose Deployment Workbench ⇨ Task Sequences, right-click the task sequences created previously, and choose Properties.**

2. **Next, click the Task Sequence tab.**

3. **Explore the options available by pressing on the Add button in the toolbar and reviewing the options in each of the task groups listed (see Figure 7.8).**

FIGURE 7.8

Exploring the actions available in the Task Sequencer

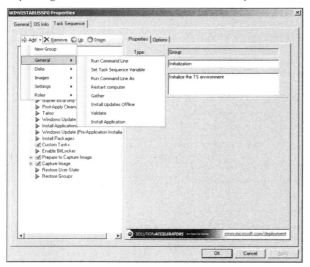

NOTE   **This example is based on an x86 deployment. For a deployment of an x64 operating system, replace all of the x86 entries with amd64.**

Creating a deployment point

With the deployment task established, the next step is to create a deployment point from which it may be distributed. In this case, you are not performing a live distribution, but are instead automating the installation of a reference system which will be used to create our deployment image. Do so by following these steps:

1. Choose Deployment Workbench ⇨ Deploy ⇨ Deployment Points and click the New option from the actions pane on the right.

2. On the Choose Type page, select the default Lab or single-server deployment option and then click Next.

3. On the Specify Deployment Point Name page, enter Image Creation for Deployment point name and click Next.

4. On the Application List page, you may choose to allow users to select additional applications when upgrading. In this case, you are provided with a menu of applications to include in your baseline image. Select the option and click the Next button to continue.

5. On the Allow Image Capture page, leave the Ask if an image should be captured option selected and click Next.

6. On the Allow Admin Password page, you may select the Ask user to set the local Administrator Password option, but because you will likely wish to specify this when deploying the image, the setting is inconsequential and should only be selected if needed. Click Next.

7. On the Allow Product Key page, you may select the option titled, Ask user for a product key. Click Next. As with the previous setting, you may leave this deselected because the image creation process will provide the ability to override what is specified here.

8. On the Network Share page, you can change the default share name; then click Next. In most cases, the default "Distribution$" share name will be fine, but you may specify an alternate name if you wish.

9. On the Configure User State, you can specify user data defaults. In this case, you are not going to migrate any user data so you may choose the Do not save data and settings option and click the Finish button to complete the creation of the deployment point. However, if you were to use this in a live deployment scenario the other options available are:

   ■ **Automatically determine the location on the network.** This instructs the deployment process to browse the local network to determine the location for storing the user-state data.

   ■ **Automatically determine the location on the Local System.** This instructs the deployment process to browse the local system to determine the location for storing the user-state data.

   ■ **Specify a location.** This option lets you dictate manually to specify the location to save user-state data.

10. If further customization is necessary, right-click the new listing titled Image Creation and choose Properties.

11. On the Windows PE tab ensure the Generate a Lite Touch bootable RAM disk ISO image option is selected in the Images to Generate section at the top left of the window and click OK to proceed.

12. In Deployment Workbench ➪ Deploy ➪ Deployment Points right-click the newly created Image Creation deployment point and choose Update to create the file structure that represents this newly created deployment point.

Preparing a reference computer

At this point, you are ready to automate the installation of the machine that will become your baseline image for deployment. Most labs today make extensive use of virtual machines for the money and time it saves. Because the image of Windows Vista you create is not hardware dependant, you may generate it on a virtual machine without fear of issues regarding Hardware Abstraction Layer (HAL) compatibility.

1. Copy the LiteTouchPE_x86.iso image from the directory structure created in the previous step to your local computer (for example, \\server\distribution$\ Boot\LiteTouchPE_x86.iso).

2. Configure your virtual machine to boot from this ISO file by mounting it as a CD image. Alternatively, you could burn the ISO image to a CD.

3. Boot the virtual machine from the mounted ISO image. Alternatively, if you burned the ISO to a CD, you may boot from it in order to load the Lite Touch image.

4. Accept the default **Run the Deployment Wizard to install a new operating system option**. The menu provided lets you choose if you want to run the Deployment Wizard or exit to the command prompt. After you have made your choice, click Next to continue.

5. On the **User Credentials page, enter the User Name, Password, and Domain of the account to be used for accessing the distribution share and click OK to proceed.**

6. On the **Select a task sequence to execute on this computer page, you can choose the deployment task you want to execute.** If following these directions, there will be one choice for the installation of Windows Vista Business. Accept this default choice and click Next to continue.

7. The next page of the Windows Deployment Wizard is **Configure the computer name**. The name will not remain once it is generalized for imaging with Sysprep, so leave the automatically generated default name in place and click **Next** to continue.

8. You can Join the computer to a domain or workgroup. You can choose a domain name and credentials, but as you are generating an image for deployment, you may simply accept the default **Join a workgroup** option and click **Next** to continue.

9. The next page prompts you to **Specify whether to restore user data**. Again, this is not a production deployment, so accept the default **Do not restore user data and settings** option and press the **Next** button to continue.

10. The next page prompts for **Locale Selection**. If you wish to specify an alternate locale and keyboard setting, you may do so here and press the **Next** button to continue.

11. The next parameter requested in the wizard is to **Set the Time Zone**. Here, you may select you local time zone and press the **Next** button to continue.

12. The next page allows you to **Select one or more applications to install**. Check the box by any of the applications you wish to have incorporated in this build and press the **Next** button to continue.

13. You are then prompted to **Specify whether to capture an image**. By default, it will be set to **Capture an image of this reference computer**, with two fields to specify the filename and path: **Location and File name**. By default, the path will be your Distribution$ share and the filename will be that of your Task ID. Press the **Next** button to review your settings.

14. Finally, the next window of the wizard states **Ready to begin**. You may optionally click **Details** to view the settings you have chosen, and then press the **Begin** button to start the process. Figure 7.9 shows the progress dialog shown to advise you of the current status.

FIGURE 7.9

Monitoring installation progress

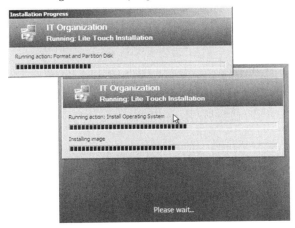

15. You may be prompted to **Type your product key for activation** if it was not specified earlier. The progress dialog will be on top, so you may need to drag the window out of the way to enter the product key (see Figure 7.10). If prompted, enter a valid product key and press **Next** to continue.

FIGURE 7.10

Entering your product key

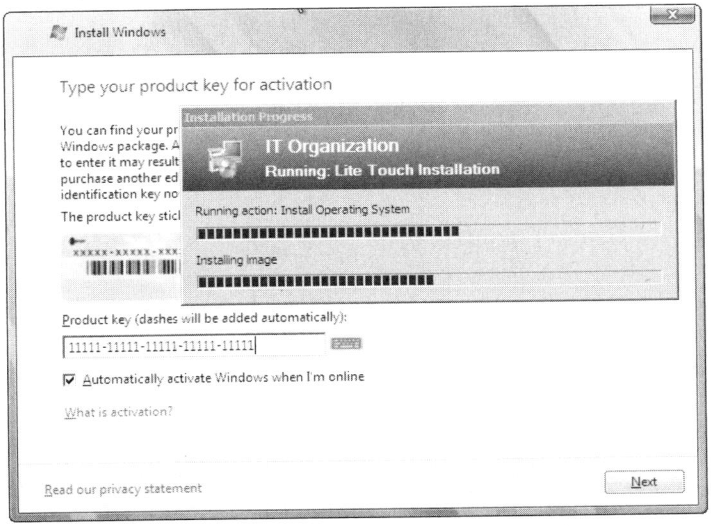

The automated process installs Vista, reboots, automatically logs on, and continues the installation process including the installation of applications and Windows PE. Sysprep is used to generalize the system, and it then reboots to Windows PE and creates the image (WIM) over the network on the server share.

Adding the custom image to the distribution share

When the image was created in the previous step, it was saved directly to the distribution share, but there are a couple more steps required to make it available as a custom image.

1. Choose Deployment Workbench ➪ Distribution Share ➪ Operating Systems and click the New option from the actions pane on the right.

2. On the OS Type page, choose Custom image file from the menu and click Next to continue.

3. On the Image page, fill in the Source file field with the path to your newly created image. By default this will be *servername*\distribution$\Captures\<task sequence id>.wim.

4. On the Setup page, you may accept the default Setup and Sysprep files are not needed option. This is due to the fact that Windows Vista contains Sysprep and the files needed to perform an automated installation. Click Next to continue.

5. On the Destination page, you can specify the target directory name for the operating system files. By default this will be filled in using the same name specified as your task sequence ID. If you have chosen meaningful names for task sequence IDs as suggested, take advantage of it by accepting this default and clicking Finish to complete the addition of the custom image to the Deployment Workbench.

Creating a deployment build for a custom image

As you had previously created a deployment build for establishing the reference computer, you now need to establish one for the deployment of your custom image.

1. Choose Deployment Workbench ➪ Deploy ➪ Deployment Points and click the New option from the actions pane on the right.

2. On the Choose Type page, select the default Lab or single-server deployment option and then click Next.

3. On the Specify Deployment Point Name page, enter Image Deployment for Deployment point name and click Next.

4. On the Application List page, deselect the option to Allow users to select additional applications on Upgrade as the applications you wish included in your image have already been installed within the image and click Next.

5. On the Allow Image Capture page, deselect the Ask if an image should be captured option and click Next.

6. **On the Allow Admin Password page, you may select the Ask user to set the local Administrator Password option if you wish installers to be prompted. Click Next to continue.**

7. **If you want the installer to prompt the user, you may select Allow Product Key presents an option to Ask user for a product key; then click Next.**

8. **The Network Share page lets you change the default share name if you want.** In most cases, the default "Distribution$" share name is fine, but you may specify an alternate name if you want. Click Next to continue.

9. **On the Configure User State page, you can specify user data defaults.** If you want to handle the migration of user data, you may choose one of the following options and then click the Finish button to complete the creation of the deployment point. Available options include:

   ■ **Automatically determine the location on the network.** This instructs the deployment process to browse the local network to determine the location for storing the user-state data.

   ■ **Automatically determine the location on the Local System.** This instructs the deployment process to browse the local system to determine the location for storing the user-state data.

   ■ **Specify a location.** Lets you dictate manually specify the location to save user-state data.

10. **Choose Deployment Workbench ⇨ Deploy ⇨ Deployment Points, right-click the newly created Image Deployment point, and choose Update to create the file structure that represents this newly created deployment point.**

Creating the MDT database

To better automate image deployments, you can take advantage of the MDT database. With it, you may query for settings, roles, software assignments, and more based on computer, location, or make/model. By leveraging this database, you can dynamically provide details during a deployment that would otherwise need to be manually input through the Lite Touch Installation wizards. Alternatively, there are other methods to handle the various properties that may be specified by the database (See the section "Understanding deployment rules" later in this chapter for details). To establish a deployment database, follow these steps:

> **NOTE** If you do not have a SQL server already, you may install SQL Server Express Edition, which is free and available online at www.microsoft.com/sql/editions/express/default.mspx. However, if you are serious about Windows deployment, and you should be, you will install a real version of SQL Server and make this database part of your ongoing systems management infrastructure. This lets you avoid the limitations inherent in Microsoft's free database tool. You can, however, virtualize this role. For information on doing so, see *Build a SQL Server Virtual Appliance* at itmanagement.earthweb.com/article.php/31771_3718566_2.

1. **Choose Deployment Workbench ⇨ Deploy ⇨ Database from the tree and click the New option from the actions pane on the right to start the New DB Wizard.**

2. **On the SQL Server Details page, enter the SQL Server Name and click Next.** You may also optionally provide values for **Instance** (the name of the instance of SQL Server to be used for querying property values) and Port (if needed in your environment for connectivity to the SQL server). You may also specify if Named Pipes or TCP/IP Sockets should be used for server communications. In most environments, the SQL Server Name will be the only field that requires attention here.

3. **On the next page, Database, you can specify the name of a new database to be created (or recreated) on the server and click Next to continue.** Optionally, if you have already established a database for this purpose, you may choose Use an existing database that already contains the required tables and views and choose from the list of databases retrieved by the wizard.

4. **On the SQL Share page, you can specify a SQL Share to be used by Windows PE to establish a secure connection to the server.** What share specified here is not important, only that a valid share is specified which is accessible by the deployment account. Only the share name should be specified, for example: admin$.

Configuring the MDT database

With the database created and ready to go, the next step is to configure how it is to be used by your deployment. There are a number of options here, and which of those you choose depends greatly on your environment. This section provides a walkthrough of the steps and options available for your consideration.

1. **Choose Deployment Workbench ⇨ Deploy ⇨ Deployment Points, right-click the Image Deployment point, and choose Configure DB from the context menu to start the Configure DB Wizard.**

2. **On the first page of the wizard, specify which of the computer-related queries you want to configure and click Next. Choose from the following options:**

   - Query for computer-specific settings
   - Query for roles assigned to this computer
   - Query for applications to be installed on this computer
   - Query for SMS packages to be installed on this computer
   - Query for administrators to be assigned to this computer

3. **Next on the Location Options page, specify which location-related queries should be configured and click Next. Choose from the following options:**

   - Query for location names based on default gateways
   - Query for location-specific settings
   - Query for roles assigned for this location

- Query for applications to be installed for this location
- Query for SMS packages to be installed for this location
- Query for administrators to be assigned for this location

4. **Next on the Make/Model Options page, specify which of the make/model-related queries you wish to configure and click next. Choose from the following options:**

- Query for model-specific settings
- Query for roles assigned to computers with this make and model
- Query for applications to be installed on computers with this make and model
- Query for SMS packages to be installed on computers with this make and model
- Query for administrators to be assigned to machines with this make and model

5. **On the Role Options page, specify which role-related queries you wish to add and click Finish to complete the database configuration. Choose from the following options:**

- Query for role-specific settings
- Query for applications to be installed for this role
- Query for SMS packages to be installed for this role
- Query for administrators to be assigned for this role

> **NOTE** For more detail on use of the MDT database, see *Simple, Scalable Deployment with BDD 2007* at `www.microsoft.com/technet/technetmag/issues/2007/11/ExtendingBDD/?loc=en`.

Populating the Microsoft Management database

For the queries specified in the previous steps to succeed, you must populate the database with information about your target environment. Depending upon your needs you may populate one or more sections of the database to support your deployment. These sections are Computers, Roles, Locations, and Make and Model. Following are the basic steps of adding a computer entry. Note all follow the same interface for entry creation.

1. **Choose Deployment Workbench ⇨ Deploy ⇨ Database ⇨ Computers from the tree and click the New option from the actions pane on the right to view the property form where you may specify the details of a new computer entry in the database.**

2. **For an Asset tag, enter one or more values to identify the computer.** This represents the default primary method of identifying a computer on this form, so (as in all form fields that require entry) a red circle with an explanation mark inside is displayed alongside the field until it contains required data. In this case, however, you may specify any one of these key values to identify a computer (Asset tag, UUID, Serial number, or MAC address). If an invalid value is specified, the field indicator will blink until it is cleared or the value is properly updated.

If using MAC address, you must use all capitals and separate each two digits with a colon to satisfy the field requirement

3. The Details tab contains a list of the properties available for customization. Because this is something to be done for each computer added to the database, it is often desirable to enter a minimal number of unique values. For example, **ComputerName** is very commonly specified in this way.

4. Click the Applications tab and then configure the applications to install and the order of the application installations.

5. Click the Packages tab, and then configure the packages to install and the order of the package installations.

6. Click the Roles tab and then configure the roles to associate with the computer.

7. Click the Administrators tab, configure the accounts to be made members of the local Administrator group on the target computers, and then click OK.

NOTE A script for the bulk importation of computer entries based on the contents of a CSV file is provided online at http://blogs.technet.com/benhunter/archive/2007/08/05/bdd2007-bulk-database-loads.aspx.

Understanding deployment rules

In addition to the database method above, you can use other options to leverage the ability to define properties such as the computer name or the local administrator password. To specify general deployment options there are other options that should be understood. Depending on your environment or on the item to be defined, one or more of these other methods may be desirable.

NOTE There are a number of standard properties available for customization, and each is documented in the Toolkit Reference.doc file included in the Deployment Process documentation. It should also be noted that you can define your own custom properties if a standard property is not found that meets your needs.

In addition to the database method described in the previous section, there are a few other ways you can assign values:

- Hard-coded values
- Variable substitution
- Script functions
- Dynamic keys

NOTE The values are collected by a script which gets standard properties from its definition file (ZTIGather.xml). It then uses the *CustomSettings.ini* file to determine what custom properties it should use as well as the actual values for all of the properties required by the deployment.

Each of these methods is discussed briefly in the following section.

Using hard-coded values

One of the simplest ways to specify values is to use hard-coded values in the CustomSettings.ini file. For example, you could statically define the time zone (TimeZone) to the desired time zone offset:

```
TimeZone=005
```

Using variable substitution

Similar to the method above, you can also include variables to make hard-coded values more dynamic. For example, you could statically define your logging share (SLShare) to point to the "LOGS" folder on a currently connected SCCM deployment point:

```
SLShare=\\%SMSDP%\Logs
```

Using script functions

Rules can call script functions as well. A script known as the user exit script serves as a function library. You may create your own script functions to return desired values and then place them in a user exit script. These custom scripts have full access to the global variables and can leverage them in the creation of dynamic values. By placing the script in the same directory as the custom-settings.ini file, you can then reference these functions with it by typing the function call along with any desired parameters within pound symbols. For example, you may want to assign the ComputerName based on information gathered from the Asset Tag. To do so you would first create your UserExit script, and then reference it in the CustomSettings.ini file as shown.

Example UserExit Script:

```
Function UserExit(sType, sWhen, sDetail, bSkip)
      UserExit = Successfs
End Function
Function MakeName(sAssetTag)

   Set wmiRoot = GetObject("WinMgmts:root/cimv2")
   Set wmiColl = wmiRoot.ExecQuery("Select * FROM Win32_ComputerSystem")
   For Each wmiObj In wmiColl
          sMan = wmiObj.Manufacturer
   Next
   Select Case sMan
          Case "Dell Inc."
                 sManCode = "D"
          Case "Compaq"
                 sManCode = "C"
          Case "HP"
                 sManCode = "H"
          Case Else
                 sManCode = "U" ' unknown
   End Select
   MakeName = sManCode & "-" & sAssetTag
End Function
```

257

The preceding MakeName function is intended to determine the computer's manufacturer and then use a single character identifier and the asset tag passed to the function to return a name meeting the organization's desired naming convention. In order to make use of this, the above would be saved as UserExit.vbs and then placed in the same folder as the CustomSettings.ini file. The CustomSettings.ini file would finally need to be updated to reference the script and function as shown in the following example:

Example CustomSettings.ini Segment:

```
ComputerName=#MakeName("%AssetTag%")#
UserExit=UserExit.vbs
```

Using dynamic keys

Rules can also be selected based on the value of dynamic keys. The following example will return the computer name "LabSystem01" if the MAC Address is "00:03:FF:39:CC:67".

```
[Settings]
Priority=MACAddress,…

[00:03:FF:39:CC:67]
ComputerName=" LabSystem01"
```

In the example above, the settings section leads with Priority which can list multiple methods for identifying a system in order of how they should be used. Many other values would also be listed in the setting section of CustomSettings.ini, but it is simplified here for clarity. The second section is actually that of a valid MAC address on the network. The values in this section are used when the computer's MAC address matches that of the section name (00:03:FF:39:CC:67).

Configuring LTI deployment for full automation

Even specifying many of these values for the setup, the wizard dialogs will still be displayed by default. The good news is that you have very granular control over what elements of the wizard are displayed by adding properties to the CustomSettings.ini file. In fact, the SkipWizard property results in suppression of the entire Windows Deployment Wizard. To skip individual pages, the following properties are available:

- SkipAdminPassword
- SkipApplications
- SkipAppsOnUpgrade
- SkipBDDWelcome
- SkipBitLocker
- SkipBitLockerDetails
- SkipBuild
- SkipCapture

- SkipComputerBackup
- SkipComputerName
- SkipDeploymentType
- SkipDomainMembership
- SkipFinalSummary
- SkipLocaleSelection
- SkipPackageDisplay
- SkipProductKey
- SkipSummary
- SkipTimeZone
- SkipUserData

Although the names of most properties are self-explanatory, just what is available requires a bit of searching the Toolkit Reference.doc file, which is included in the Deployment Process documentation. Here, each of the available properties is documented in some detail.

CAUTION   **When you update your deployment, such as making changes to the CustomSettings.ini file, it is necessary to right-click the update deployment point and choose Update to commit the changes. At this point you will also want to update your LTI media (ISO file, CD, USB device, and so on).**

Deploying the custom image

Now you can deploy your image. The steps are nearly identical to that of when you prepared your reference system for imaging, but this time you are dealing with a production deployment. For testing you can stick with a virtual machine, or you can apply the LiteTouchPE.iso image to a CD or portable USB memory drive in order to use this same procedure in the deployment of physical systems. Just be sure to update the deployment point and use the updated version of the LiteTouchPE.iso file moving forward.

1. **Choose Deployment Workbench ⇨ Deploy ⇨ Deployment Points, right-click the deployment you have been working with, and choose Update to re-create the file structure and support file.**

2. **Copy the LiteTouchPE_x86.iso image from the deployment point's distribution share to your local computer** (for example, `\\server\distribution$\Boot\ LiteTouchPE_x86.iso`).

3. **Configure your virtual machine to boot from this ISO file by mounting it as a CD image.** Alternatively, you could burn the ISO image to a CD.

4. **Boot the virtual machine from the mounted ISO image.** Alternatively, if you burned the ISO to a CD you may boot from it in order to load the Lite Touch image. Depending on how you have customized the deployment values and what wizard pages you have suppressed, the Windows Deployment Wizard will prompt for the values as specified.

Investigating MDT Alternatives

MDT was established to help provide guidance on the use of the tools provided by Microsoft and how to use them together to provide a complete solution. While some of the more advanced capabilities do rely on Microsoft's Systems Center Configuration Manager product, it is possible to get quite a lot done with the free tools discussed here. While MDT does not assume that any network management system or specific deployment servers already exist within an organization, much of the guidance is written in a generic enough fashion to support implementation of other tools.

Free is always an attractive selling point; however, it is Microsoft's common approach to its offerings such as MDT to get a grade of "a solid C" or to provide an "80% solution." Aside from Microsoft's obvious focus on Microsoft client systems, it relies on its third-party vendors to provide a complete solution and often avoids direct competition. While the free tools don't cost any money up front, they can be expensive in the time they take to implement and master, and then to discover those features you wanted were unavailable. As is the case in most any technology area, it is the goal of the third-party vendors to offer something that may be easier, more comprehensive, and to introduce innovations in the form of unique time-saving features or processes that can make them a more attractive solution.

There are a number of other tools on the market that aim to provide solutions to the task of desktop deployment and systems management, which span a wide range of capabilities, cost, and complexity. A few of the most popular solutions are covered in this section briefly as a starting point in your investigation in researching the following alternative deployment systems:

- Altiris Client Management Suite
- Novell ZenWorks Suite
- KBOX Systems Management Appliances
- LANDesk Management Suite

Client Management Suite

Altiris Client Management Suite is built on a Web-based framework known as Notification Server. Its many available add-ons provide support for desktop management with role-and-scope-based security features. It supports imaging and remote deployment of images for OS deployment including bare-metal provisioning. Hardware and software inventory with Web-based reporting, license management, through reporting and metering features are also available.

For more on Client Management Suite, visit `www.altiris.com/Products/ClientManagementSuite.aspx`.

ZENworks Suite

Novel offers ZENworks Suite. Windows support for their management product was added years ago, and it has become the preferred tool of many administrators. ZENworks Suite is a set of integrated tools designed to automate IT management and business processes across the lifecycle of desktops, laptops, servers, and handhelds. It uses policy-driven automation to reduce administrator effort in desktop management.

For more on ZENworks, visit `www.novell.com/products/zenworks/`.

KBOX Systems Management Appliances

KACE offers KBOX, which is an appliance-based approach to desktop management. With most of the features offered by its competitors, KBOX strives to be comparatively simple to operate. It is aimed at the mid-market (companies of less than 8500 seats) which, aside from its relatively simple installation and operation, is what most sets the KBOX apart from the other products listed here. Two appliances are offered, a KBOX Management Appliance for systems administration and the KBOX Deployment Appliance for system deployment. These appliances are available as physical rack-mount servers, or as virtual appliances leveraging VMware. A major advantage the KBOX has over its competitors is that no installation or deployment is required to set it up. This saves considerable time to administrators.

For more on KBOX management appliances, visit `www.kace.com/products/systems-management-appliance/desktop-management-software-alternative/systems-management-appliance.php`.

LANDesk Management Suite

LANDesk offers its LANDesk suite of tools, which is designed to handle the management of all your client systems. It provides a means to automate systems and security management tasks and see, manage, update, and protect all your desktops, servers, and mobile devices from a single console application. It offers several features out of the box as well as several add-ins to extend that functionality to features like antivirus, process management, patch management, asset management, and more.

For more on LANDesk, visit: `www.landesk.com`.

Most of these tools offer a similar set of features (see Table 7.3). However, each implements the features in their own way. For example some use Web-based consoles, some use locally installed management consoles. It is beyond the scope of this book to cover these tools in much detail, but it may be well worth considering a more tightly integrated set of commercial solutions as compared to Microsoft Deployment. Microsoft offers many management tools, and it is in fact Microsoft Deployment that provides the integration of these many tools to produce a "suite." For windows-only organizations with skilled staff in place, Microsoft Management can arguably be considered a competitive alternative to these and other commercial offerings.

TABLE 7.3

Key Features of Popular Third-Party Management Systems

	Altiris	ZENworks	KBOX	LANDesk
Inventory	X	X	X	X
Web-Based Management Console	X	X	X	
Web-Based Reporting	X	X	X	
Software Metering	X	X	X	X
Imaging	X	X	X	X
Unattended OS Installation	X	X	X	X
Remote Management	X	X	X	X
Handheld Management	X	X		X
Patch Management	X	X	X	X
Software Deployment	X	X	X	X
Linux Client Support	X	X	X	X
Mac Client Support	X	X	X	X

NOTE   AppDeploy.com provides a directory of systems management tools including official company and product links as well as general descriptions of most products available. It is updated by users and vendors and provides a good starting point for those looking for competitive deployment products. This resource is found in the "Tools" section of the site at www.appdeploy.com/tools.

Summary

MDT provides the tools and guidance for deployment of Windows systems. This chapter covers the many valuable documents included with this offering as well as the actual installation and configuration of these tools and how to use many elements of the solution. This was intended to familiarize you with its capabilities and use so you can best determine if MDT can help streamline your own deployment process. For detailed information on MDT, look to the included documentation as outlined earlier in this chapter.

Chapter 8

Windows Deployment Services

Microsoft Windows Deployment Services (WDS) provides a network-based installation of Windows Operating systems to reduce the complexity and potential differences in installation choices that may be encountered as compared to manual installations. Thanks to PXE and environments such as Windows PE, it is capable of deploying images to computers that have no operating system. Replacing the previous Remote Installation Services (RIS) feature of Windows Server 2003, this latest incarnation provides several features that take advantage of the new file-based imaging capabilities of Windows Vista while also adding more robust features, such as multicast and improved transfer speeds. This chapter discusses WDS, how you can go about replacing a current RIS implementation, installation, and configuration steps and basic operation in real-world, step-by-step guides to help you get the most out of WDS.

IN THIS CHAPTER

Introduction to Windows Deployment Services

Migrating from Remote Installation Services (RIS)

Installation and configuration

Basic operation

Introducing Windows Deployment Services

Windows Deployment Services (WDS) replaces the previously named Remote Installation Services (RIS). It is included by default in the upcoming Windows Server 2008, and the functionality can be added to Windows Server 2003 with the Windows Automated Installation Kit (WAIK).

Not just for Windows Vista deployment, WDS supports deployment of the following operating systems:

- Windows Vista
- Windows Server 2008
- Windows XP
- Windows Server 2003

Many administrators that have leveraged Microsoft's Operating System deployment features in the past will have invested to some degree in Remote Installation Services (RIS). WDS replaces RIS and offers a much improved set of features. Knowing that many environments cannot so easily abandon RIS, much work has gone into providing a migration route that can let you continue to leverage your investment in RIS.

> **NOTE**   WDS also replaces Automated Deployment Services (ADS), which was provided to focus on the deployment of server operating systems. Now, the installation of both clients and servers is handled the same way.

Replacing Remote Installation Services

WDS and RIS address the same task: the remote deployment of Windows operating systems over the network.

Improvements introduced with WDS include:

- Use of the new file-based imaging format (WIM)
- Use of Windows PE as boot OS
- The ability to deploy both client operating systems such as Windows Vista and server operating systems such as Windows Server 2008
- The ability to send a deployment as a multicast targeting multiple destinations at once instead of sending a separate data stream to each target

There are three functionality modes provided by WDS to better support those moving from a RIS environment. Depending on your selection, you will see different functionality, support for different image file formats, and even a different boot environment. The three available modes are:

- Legacy mode
- Mixed mode
- Native mode

More details on the installation of WDS in Native mode for both Windows Server 2003 and Windows Server 2008 are detailed later in this section, but a brief summary of how to establish each of these modes for WDS is covered in the following sections.

Running WDS in Legacy mode

In Legacy mode, WDS functions just as RIS does. The old OSChooser is the boot operating system, and only RISETUP and RIPPREP images are supported. If you are not going to be deploying Windows Vista, Legacy mode is a perfectly acceptable mode of operation. Key aspects of WDS Legacy mode include:

- Utilization of OSChooser as its boot environment
- Support for RISETUP and RIPREP image types
- The RIS toolset drives the administration experience

To set WDS for Legacy mode, start by installing the RIS component on Windows Server 2003 SP1, install WDS, and then run RISETUP to add an image.

Operating WDS in Mixed mode

In Mixed mode, both boot operating systems are supported (OSChooser and WDS tools). You can use OSChooser to deploy RISSETUP and RIPREP images, and you can deploy WIM files using the WDS management tools. You can choose to boot into RIS or an image containing Windows PE, which gives you excellent support for a RIS and WDS environment. Key aspects of WDS in Mixed mode include:

- Utilization of both OSChooser and Windows PE as their boot environments
- Support for .WIM as well as RISETUP and RIPREP image types
- The RIS toolset and WDS management tools drive the administration experience

To set WDS for Mixed mode, start by installing the RIS component on Windows Server 2003 SP1, then run RISETUP, and add an image. Then install WDS, and then run the following command:

```
WDSUTIL /initialize-server
```

Operating WDS in Native mode

In Native mode, WDS may be used to deploy only WIM images. OSChooser and the RIS toolset are not available as they are in the other modes. The WDS management console is used to handle all aspects of WDS management. Key aspects of WDS in Native mode include:

- Utilization Windows PE as its boot environment
- Support for .WIM image types only
- The WDS management tools drive the administration experience

To set WDS for Native mode, start by installing the RIS component on Windows Server 2003 SP1, then install WDS, and then run the following command:

```
WDSUTIL /initialize-server
```

 Native mode is the only option in Windows 2008.

Reviewing components of Windows Deployment Services

WDS is made up of several services and technologies, some of which are covered in this section to help you become familiar with these key components of WDS, including:

- Pre-Boot Execution Environment (PXE)
- Trivial File Transfer Protocol (TFTP)
- Multicast
- WDS Client
- WDS Management Tools

Understanding the role of the Pre-Boot Execution Environment (PXE)

To avoid the need for boot disks and to eliminate the need for an operating system on client computers, WDS leverages PXE. Most modern computers (network cards) support this technology that allows systems to "boot to the network."

When a PXE boot is initiated, the PXE ROM requests an IP from a DHCP server. As part of the initial DHCP discovery request, the client computer identifies itself as being PXE-enabled, which indicates to the PXE server that it should respond to the client. After the client has an IP address from the DHCP server, the client locates and establishes a connection with the DHCP server to download a network boot image. Based on the choice made, TFTP is used to download a Windows PE image that serves as the operating system for the WDS client.

Understanding the role of the Trivial File Transfer Protocol (TFTP)

TFTP is used to download files needed by the network boot process provided by PXE. The TFTP server downloads files, such as `Pxeboot.com`, `Wdsnbp.com`, `Bootmgr.exe` and `default.bcd` as well as the full boot image that contains Windows PE. With Windows Server 2008, TFTP download performance has been enhanced to provide faster uploads and downloads of WDS images.

Understanding the role of multicast

Windows 2008 introduces multicast support that is leveraged by WDS to handle the deployment of an image to many computers simultaneously without bogging down the network. When you send an image with a multicast transmission, the data is sent over the network only once for all the computers being targeted, as shown in Figure 8.1.

The multicast broadcast is a rotating broadcast of file streams that continues to broadcast until every client computer's needs have been met. What this means is that it doesn't matter when clients come online, they can join in on the multicast data at any time in the transfer. Each client listens to the WDS server, and when it has completed sending the image file, it starts over from the beginning. So, if a client misses a file, it can pick it up when the file is sent again the next time. Once all clients have received the entire image file, the multicast session is terminated.

FIGURE 8.1

Understanding multicast

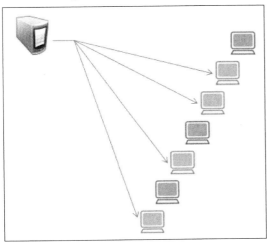

The WDS management tools enable you to monitor real-time transmission progress to clients, and even remove clients from the transmission, and also provide logging and reporting features. Use of multicast with WDS is discussed more later on in this chapter.

Understanding the role of the WDS Client

WDS Client is a graphical wizard that runs under Windows PE. It is used to capture and apply images from the WDS server. This can be interactive (by default) or it can be configured to run in a fully unattended fashion. The Windows Deployment Services client unattend file uses the Unattend.xml format, and it is stored on the WDS server in the \WDSClientUnattend folder. It automates the WDS client user-interface screens (such as entering credentials or specifying an Install image).

Understanding the role of the WDS Management tools

WDS Management tools are a set of tools that may be used to manage the server, operating system images, and client computer accounts. It consists of the WDS Console (an MMC Snap-In) and WDSUtil, which is the WDS Management command line utility. WDSUtil is just as capable (if not more so) than the WDS Console when it comes to managing WDS. For a list of commands supported by WDSUtil, see Table 8.1.

TABLE 8.1

Reviewing Supported WDSUtil.exe Command

Command	Description
/add	Adds images, image groups, or devices
/approve-AutoAddDevices	Approves pending Auto-Add devices
/convert-RiprepImage	Converts an existing RIPrep image to a Windows Image (.wim) file
/copy-Image	Copies an image within the image store
/delete-AutoAddDevices	Deletes devices in the auto-add device database
/disable	Disables all services for WDS
/disconnect-Client	Disconnects a client from a multicast transmission or namespace
/enable	Enables all services for WDS
/export-Image	Exports an image from the image store to a .wim file
/get	Retrieves properties and attributes from WDS servers, devices, images, image groups, or Transport Servers
/initialize-Server	Configures a WDS server for initial use
/new	Creates new capture and discover images as well as multicast transmissions and namespaces
/progress	Displays the progress status while a command is being executed
/reject-AutoAddDevices	Rejects pending auto-add devices
/remove	Removes images, image groups, multicast transmissions, and namespaces
/replace-Image	Replaces a boot or installation image with a new version of that image
/set	Sets properties and attributes on WDS servers, devices, images, image groups, or Transport Servers
/start	Starts all services on the WDS server, including multicast transmissions, namespaces, and Transport Server
/stop	Stops all services on the WDS server
/uninitialize-Server	Reverts changes made during server initialization
/update-ServerFiles	Updates server files on the RemoteInstall share
/verbose	Displays verbose output for the specified command

NOTE   If you want to manage WDS from a remote server running Windows Server 2008, you can install the Remote Server Administration Tools: From Server Manager, right-click Features and click Add Features. Select Remote Administration Tools (RSAT) to have the Windows Deployment Services MMC snap-in installed with the WDSUtil.exe command line utility to support remote administration. See Chapter 10 for information on installing the RSAT on Windows Vista with or without SP1.

Installing Windows Deployment Services

This section focuses on the installation of WDS. Starting with ensuring the prerequisite requirements are met, we cover installation on both Server 2003 (with SP1 or SP2) and then installing WDS as a role for Windows Server 2008.

Satisfying prerequisites

There are a handful of requirements to consider when installing WDS. Some require only that certain services be available on the network and not necessarily on the local server where WDS is being installed. WDS requirements include:

- **Active Directory Domain Services (AD DS):** The server to host WDS must either be a member of an AD DS domain or a domain controller for an AD DS domain. The forest version does not matter as all domain and forest configurations support WDS.

- **Dynamic Host Configuration Protocol (DHCP) Server:** While it does not need to be on the local server, you must have a working DHCP server on the network because PXE relies on this for IP addressing, which is used by WDS.

- **Domain Name System (DNS):** Again, it need not be installed locally, but a DNS server is required on the network before you can run WDS.

- **NT File System (NTFS) Volume:** The server must have at least one NTFS volume to the image store.

> **NOTE** When working with Windows Server 2003, RIS must be installed prior to installing WDS.

As you would expect, installation requires that you are a member of the Local Administrators group on the server (of which Domain Administrators will be a member when a member of a domain).

When adding Roles for Server 2008, the Add Roles Wizard may be accessed from Server Manager. Here you may choose the required services if needed. If setting up a new server for this purpose it is important to note that you must install the AD DS role first, then you can run the AD DS Installation Wizard (DCpromo.exe) to install AD DS and DNS Server together (shown in Figure 8.2). Once this process is complete you may then add DHCP.

> **NOTE** In a test lab, you may have all these services on one server, but in a production environment you are likely to have servers such as ADDS, DNS, and DHCP already established.

FIGURE 8.2

Installing DNS from the AD DS Installation Wizard

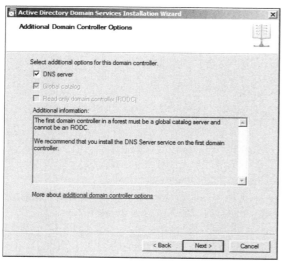

Setting up Windows Deployment Services for Server 2003

In addition to the prerequisites listed earlier, when installing on Windows Server 2003 it is also necessary to have RIS installed before you begin. It need not be configured, but it must be installed. The steps that you need to take depend upon the service pack level of your Windows Server 2003 system.

Installing WDS on Server 2003 with SP1

For systems with Service Pack 1, you must install RIS and then the WAIK before starting the installation of WDS.

1. Launch Add/Remove Programs from the control panel and click the Add/Remove Windows Components option on the left sidebar.

2. Select the option for Remote Installation Services and click the Next button to initiate the installation.

3. When the installation is complete, you may be prompted to reboot the server; do so and then continue to the next step.

4. Download the WAIK (approximately 1GB) from the Microsoft Web site (validation may be required).

   ```
   www.microsoft.com/downloads/details.aspx?FamilyID=C7D4BC6D-
   15F3-4284-9123-679830D629F2
   ```

After you have the download, you will notice it has an IMG file extension. This is a DVD image file that you may burn using your preferred software. It may be necessary to rename the file extension from IMG to ISO in order for your software to properly recognize the file. Alternatively, you can use a drive emulator, such as Daemon Tools (`www.daemon-tools.cc`) to mount the file as a drive without burning. Yet another option is to make use of some tools such as WinRar or 7zip which support ISO files just as you would any other archive file (like ZIP).

5. **Run the WDS installation from the WAIK DVD image titled Windows-Deployment-Servies-Update-x86.exe (or –amd64 depending on your system) located in the WDS folder** (`D:\WDS\Windows-Deployment-Servies-Update-x86.exe`).

6. **You see a welcome screen and then a license agreement to accept as the Software Update Installation Wizard begins. Simply click the Next button to begin (there are no configuration options).**

   When the update is complete, you will be prompted to restart the server.

7. **If you do not want to restart it now, be sure to select the Do not restart now check box before clicking the Finish button.**

Installing WDS on Server 2003 with SP2

For systems with Service Pack 2, WDS is already included. Steps here depend upon the status of RIS on the server at the time the service pack was applied. Service Pack 2 contains the same version of WDS that is available in the Windows AIK, so installation of the Windows AIK is not necessary for installation of WDS (though you may still want the tools for image management).

If you had RIS installed and configured at the time Service Pack 2 was applied, the computer was automatically upgraded to WDS (no further installations are needed).

If you had RIS installed but it was not configured at the time Service Pack 2 was applied (or if you had not previously had RIS installed on the server at all), you can install it from Add/Remove Windows Components as described below:

1. **Launch Add/Remove Programs from the control panel and click the Add/Remove Windows Components option on the left sidebar.**

2. **Select the check box for Windows Deployment Services (as shown in Figure 8.3) and press the Next button to initiate the installation.**

3. **Click the Finish button to close the installation wizard once the installation is complete.** You will then be prompted to restart you server. When possible, restart the server to finalize the installation.

FIGURE 8.3

Installing WDS from Add/Remove Windows Components

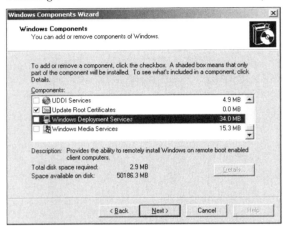

Setting up Windows Deployment Services for Server 2008

For Windows Server 2008 WDS is provided as a role you may add and is much more straight-forward than the steps previously discussed for handling a Windows Server 2003 installation. The steps to perform this installation on Server 2008 are provided below:

1. **Launch Server Manager, navigate to Server Manager ⇨ Roles, and choose Add Roles from under Roles Summary.**

2. **From the second screen in the Add Roles Wizard (the first may be optionally disabled from appearing), select Windows Deployment Services from the list of available roles and click Next.**

 **You can also initiate the installation from the command line:**
`ServerManagerCmd –install WDS`

The first window of the Add Roles Wizard dedicated to the installation of WDS starts with an introduction to Windows Deployment Services with links to more information. Click the Next button to continue.

3. **Select Role Services.** Both are selected by default. You can choose to install only Transport Server if you want to leverage multicasting without utilizing WDS, but choosing Deployment Server requires Transport Server as a dependency.

4. **Leave both services selected and click Next.** A confirmation page is provided to confirm your desire to install Windows Deployment Server with the Deployment Server and Transport Server services.

5. **Click the Install button to begin the installation.** A page showing the results of the installation is presented.

6. **Click the Close button to exit the Add Roles Wizard.**

After installation is complete, the next step is to configure Windows Deployment Services.

Configuring Windows Deployment Services

This section highlights some potential configuration issues and then covers the use of the Windows Deployment Services Configuration Wizard to establish a basic configuration and progresses through providing images and finally configuring the Boot Menu.

Understanding potential WDS configuration issues

There are a handful of issues you should be aware of when configuring WDS. The following list describes these known issues:

- Use Windows Server 2008 media for your boot image. You should use the Windows Server 2008 media without modification for best results. You can use the `Boot.wim` from Windows Vista media if it includes SP1. However, you need to obtain the media with SP1 already included because it cannot be slipstreamed. (See Chapter 6 for details.)

- IPv6 is not supported.

- If you are running WDS on a network with a non-Microsoft DHCP server, you will need to configure the server to not listen on port 67, and you'll need to configure DHCP to add *Option 60* to your DHCP scopes.

- If DHCP is installed on a server on a different subnet, you must configure IP Helper tables. DHCP traffic is not normally forwarded to other networks, but to support use of PXE across subnets you should configure UDP port 67 to be forwarded directly to both the DHCP server and the Windows Deployment Services PXE server. Additionally, all traffic on UDP port 4011 from the client computers to the PXE server should be properly routed.

 **Alternatively, you can add DHCP options 66 and 67. Option 66 must be set to the WDS server and option 67 should be set to** `boot\x86\wdsnbp.com`.

Running the Windows Deployment Services Configuration Wizard

Like so many setups and installations, a helpful wizard walks you through the configuration options available to configure WDS. To configure WDS, perform the following steps:

1. As a member of the Domain Administrators group, launch Windows Deployment Services from Administrative Tools.

2. Expand the list of servers on the left, and the unconfigured server will be listed with a yellow caution sign in its icon indicating it is in an unconfigured state (see Figure 8.4).

Preparing to configure your WDS server

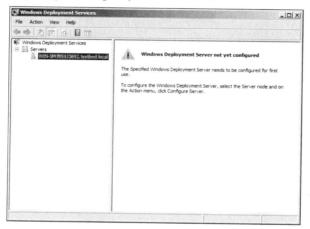

3. **Right-click the server and choose Configure Server.** The first page of the Windows Deployment Services Configuration Wizard warns of the prerequisites covered earlier in this chapter.

4. **Click Next.** The next page of the wizard prompts for the Remote Installation Folder Location where you may specify the path and folder name for the remote installation folder. This folder contains the OS images. Make sure you choose a location with plenty of space. Unlike RIS you do not need to specify a volume that acts as a single instance store, as the WIM files themselves actually provide this functionality. The default path is C:\RemoteInstall. However, the C drive is normally the Windows system volume, and it is recommended that you choose a different volume (or even a different disk if possible).

5. **Change the default if desired and then click the Next.** The next step in the wizard is for handling DHCP option 60. If DHCP is running on the WDS server, it must be configured not to listen on port 67, and DHCP option 60 must be added to all DHCP scopes on the server. If you are not running a Microsoft DHCP server, you will have to configure it manually, but with Microsoft DHCP server, the wizard will detect and offer the appropriate options to be checked (see Figure 8.5).

FIGURE 8.5

Configuring DHCP for WDS

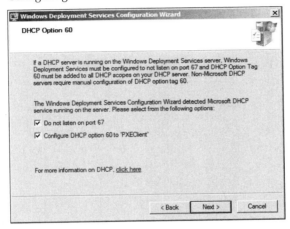

Next you are prompted to specify the PXE Server Initial Settings. PXE client computers can be pre-staged in Active Directory Domain Services, and doing so designates them as *known client computers*. Whereas not pre-staging clients designates them as *unknown client computers*. This page allows you to specify how PXE should respond to known and unknown clients based on your own preferences.

6. **Choose your desired setting and click the Finish button to commit your configuration choices.** A Configuration Complete screen is displayed with the option to Add images to the Windows Deployment Server now check box (checked by default).

7. **Deselect the Add images to the Windows Deployment Server now check box and click Finish to close the Wizard.**

Adding the default boot image

A boot image is an image containing Windows PE that the client boots into to select the image they want to install. When you have multiple images available, you may want to customize the boot image menu (this is covered later in this section). Aside from adding a default Install image (covered below), you cannot make use of WDS without first providing a default boot image. To provide the default boot image, perform the following steps:

1. **From within the Windows Deployment Services MMC, navigate to Windows Deployment Services ⇨ Servers ⇨ <your server>, right-click Boot Images, and choose Add Boot Image to launch the WDS Add Image Wizard.**

2. **Use the Browse button to select the location of the boot.wim file you want to provide.** Normally this will be the boot.wim from the sources folder on the Windows Server 2008 DVD (or DVD image). Remember, if you want to use a Windows Vista boot. wim you'll need to get it from a Windows Vista with Service Pack 1 DVD (where service pack one is included in the installation media on the DVD). When you have selected the boot.wim file, click **Next** to continue.

3. **Next, you may modify the name and description of the image (pulled from the installation media).** For example, it may read "Microsoft Windows Longhorn Setup (x86)" and you can change this to "Windows Server Setup (x86)". Particularly if you are working in an environment with multiple architectures it is a good idea to include the architecture in the title as shown here.

4. **Make any desired changes and click Next to continue.** A Summary page is provided to provide a quick review of your choices.

5. **Click Next to have the boot image added to WDS.** A progress bar and messages appears until the copy process is complete.

6. **Click the Finish button to close the WDS Add Image Wizard.**

Adding the default Install image

A boot image is one requirement for using WDS and the other is to add an Install image. To add an Install image, follow the below steps:

1. **From within the Windows Deployment Services MMC, navigate to Windows Deployment Services ⇨ Servers ⇨ <your server>, right-click Install Images and choose Add Install Image to launch the WDS Add Image Wizard.**

2. **Create a new image group option to specify a name such as "Test Images," "Vista Images," "Server Images," and so on and then press the Next button to continue.** This Image Group window lets you select an existing group or create a new group. Groups are used to collect similar images for purposes of organization. Because this is the first time you are adding an Install image, you will have to use the Create a new image group option and specify a name for the new group.

3. **Enter the path to Windows Image (WIM) file that contains the image (or images) you wish to add and click Next to continue.** You may click **Browse** to select an image such as the default Windows Server 2008 image, which may be found at D:\sources\ install.wim (assuming your DVD drive is D).

4. **On the List of Available Images page, leave the box selected to use the default names and press the Next button to continue.** By default, all are checked but select only those you wish to add to WDS. At the bottom of the display is a check box to Use default name and description for each of the selected images. If you deselect this box, the next pages of the wizard request a desired name and description for each selected image being added. This may be desirable in cases where a meaningful name was not provided, or in the case of Windows Server 2008, where the name and description may refer to Windows Server 2008 as Windows Longhorn.

5. **Review the Summary presented, and click Next.** This Summary page is provided to confirm the group name, image file path and filename, as well as a list of all the image names to be added from that file. You can use the Back button to make any desired changes. At this point, the Task Progress window is displayed during the process of adding the images where integrity of the source-install image file is performed before adding the image. A progress bar and status message are provided as this process can potentially take some time to complete.

6. **When the operation is complete, the Finish button will enable and you can use this to exit the wizard.**

Configuring the boot menu

When a system boots to a boot image it loads Windows PE and then presents a menu to the user so they may select which image they wish to install. When there is more than one boot image, clients will be presented a menu to choose the boot image to be used. Once the user selects a boot image, it will load and display the available Install images. When customizing boot images, it is often the case that you may have different boot images for different tasks (such as architecture type). You may configure a boot image for the following reasons:

- Start setup to install Windows Vista.
- Load a Windows PE image for use by administrators (such as yourself).
- Provide the Windows Recovery Environment (Windows RE).
- Reformat the hard drive to support BitLocker Drive Encryption.
- A second instance of any of the above to handle 64-bit systems.

You should also be aware of the following known issues and limitations:

- **You can use only 13 boot images per menu**: The number of characters that can be displayed within the Boot Menu necessitates this limitation. Thirteen boot images is quite a lot and you will likely not approach this limitation.

- **The name of the specified image file cannot contain any spaces:** Only numbers and letters are supported in WIM image names here.

- **Use the Boot.wim from the Windows Server 2008 media:** As mentioned earlier, you must use the boot.wim from the Windows Server 2008 media or from the media of a Windows Vista Service Pack 1 image (using the boot.wim from Windows Vista media prior to inclusion of Service Pack 1 will result in multicast issues).

To configure the boot menu, first you need to add an additional boot image. To do so, follow the steps below:

1. **From within the Windows Deployment Services MMC, navigate to Windows Deployment Services ⇨ Servers ⇨ <your server>, right-click Boot Images and choose Add Boot Image to launch the WDS Add Image Wizard.**

2. **Use the Browse button to select the location of another boot.wim file such as one for a different architecture. When you have selected the** `boot.wim` **file, click Next to continue.**

3. **Make any desired changes and click Next to continue..** Particularly if you are adding an image with a different architecture it is a good idea to include the architecture in the title which will appear in the boot image menu.

4. **Click Next on the Summary page to have the boot image added to WDS.** A progress bar and messages will appear until the copy process is complete.

5. **Click the Finish button to close the WDS Add Image Wizard.**

 It is also possible to add additional boot images from the command prompt by using the WDSUtil command line as follows:

```
WDSUTIL /Add-Image /ImageFile:c:\temp\MyBoot.wim /
    ImageType:boot
```

For ImageFile, you would naturally specify the path and filename of whatever boot image it was you were working to have added.

Customizing the Boot Menu with BCDEdit

Now that you have two images, the Boot Menu will automatically be updated to include both images based upon the information you provided in the steps above. None of the steps in this section need to be configured for many environments. However, to customize the Boot Menu further, you may use the `BCDEdit.exe` command line tool to edit the default.bcd file (located at `%REMINST%\boot\<architecture>\Default.BCD`). Some common commands are detailed here including:

- View the Contents of the BCD Store
- Configure the Default Selection Time-out Value
- Set the Desired Default Selection
- Configure the TFTP Block Size
- Configure the TFTP Window Size

 It is always a good idea to back up the BCD Store before modifying it.

The command below will create a backup to the specified path (W:\BCDRecover):

```
bcdedit /export "w:\bcdrecover\bcd"
```

The command below will restore the above backup:

```
bcdedit /import "w:\bcdrecover\bcd"
```

For more information on working with BCDEdit and its command line options, visit http://technet2.microsoft.com/WindowsVista/en/library/08d64d13-4f45-4a05-bd86-c99211a93dd91033.mspx?mfr=true.

An alternative to the BCDEdit utility is offered by a third party in the form of VistaBootPro. This tool aims to provide a more user-friendly GUI experience for customizing your boot configuration (see Figure 8.6).

FIGURE 8.6

Customizing advanced BCD settings with VistaBootPro

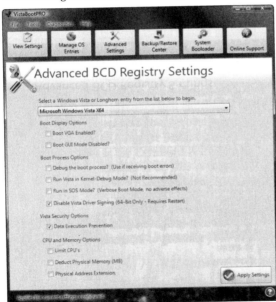

 For more on working with VistaBootPro or to download it, visit www.vistabootpro.org.

Viewing the contents of the BCD store

The BCD store dictates the behavior of the boot process. Key to making any changes is first knowing what is included and what the current settings are. This may be accomplished with the following BCDedit command line (the output of which is shown in Figure 8.7):

```
Bcdedit /enum all /store w:\remoteinstall\Tmp\x86.{9DADDE7B-4978-
    43D9-844E-B2AAAD0C27C1}.bcd
```

FIGURE 8.7

Viewing the contents of the BCD Store

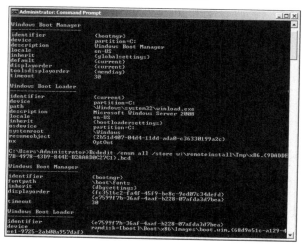

Configuring the default selection timeout value

The default timeout value for the Boot Menu is 30 seconds. In the older (more simple) days you might have made this change by editing the `boot.ini` file. Today, the BCD store replaces the `boot.ini` file even for the local system boot process so the steps are actually identical for each if you should want to adjust this for your Windows Vista or Server 2008 computers locally:

1. **View the existing configuration settings in the Default.bcd store by running the following command:**

   ```
   bcdedit /enum all /store w:\RemoteInstall\Boot\x86\default.bcd
   ```

   When you view this, you should see two Windows Boot Loader sections with descriptions matching that of the two boot images you added to WDS.

2. **Set the timeout for the default BCD store to ten seconds by running the following command:**

   ```
   bcdedit /store w:\RemoteInstall\Boot\x86\default.bcd /set
       {bootmgr} timeout 10
   ```

3. **Force regeneration of the BCD store in the \Tmp folder by sending a control signal to the WDSServer service.** You may do so by running the following command:

```
sc control wdsserver 129
```

Setting the desired default selection

After the default timeout value expires the default item will be chosen. If you have multiple items, you may specify the default item by following these steps:

1. **Determine the GUID of the boot loader you wish to specify as default by running the following using bcdedit with the /enum switch as shown below:**

```
bcdedit /enum all /store w:\RemoteInstall\Boot\x86\default.bcd
```

2. **Use the determined GUID value with the default switch to specify your desired default Boot Menu item:**

```
bcdedit /default {68d9e51c-a129-4ee1-9725-2ab00a957daf}
```

Configuring the TFTP block size

The default TFTP block size value is 1432 bytes. Some networking equipment, such as cryptographic devices, can add overhead that makes it necessary to reduce this default. Although larger packets run a higher risk of being fragmented at the IP level, increasing the block size improves the transfer performance while allowing larger files to be transferred.You can configure this value by setting the appropriate value in the default BCD store by performing the following actions:

1. **Determine the GUID identifier of the boot manager application by running the following using** `bcdedit` **with the** `/enum` **switch as shown.** The GUID you should be looking for is shown in Figure 8.8:

```
bcdedit /enum all /store w:\RemoteInstall\Boot\x86\default.bcd
```

FIGURE 8.8

Determining the Boot Manager Application GUID

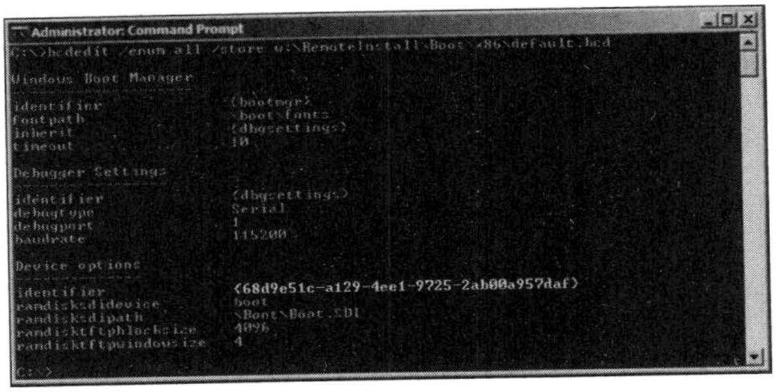

---

2. Set the appropriate TFTP block size value by running the following command:

```
bcdedit /store w:\RemoteInstall\boot\x86\default.bcd /set
    {68d9e51c-a129-4ee1-9725-2ab00a957daf} ramdisktftpblocksize
    4096
```

> **NOTE** It is recommend that you go up in multiples (4096, 8192, and so forth) and also that you not set a value higher than 16384. It is also important to consider that the configured block size applies to all clients. You should set this value only as high as the block size upper limit that all the clients on the network support.

3. Finally, it is necessary to force regeneration of the BCD store in the \Tmp folder by sending a control signal to the WDSServer service. You may do so by running the following command:

```
sc control wdsserver 129
```

Configuring the TFTP window size

TFTP is an inherently slow protocol because it requires an acknowledgment (ACK) packet for each block of data that is sent. Because the server will not send the next block in the sequence until the ACK packet for the previous block is received, the round-trip time can be very long on a slow network. You can optimize this by manipulating the TFTP size. TFTP windowing enables you to define how many data blocks it takes to fill a window. Data blocks are sent back to back with no ACK packets until the window is filled and then an ACK packet is sent. The result is fewer ACK packets and faster download times for the client. The default TFTP window size is 8. To change this value, perform the following actions:

1. Determine the GUID identifier of the boot manager application by running the following using bcdedit with the /enum switch as shown below. The GUID you should be looking for is highlighted above in Figure 8.9:

```
bcdedit /enum all /store w:\RemoteInstall\Boot\x86\default.bcd
```

2. Set the appropriate TFTP window size value by running the following command:

```
bcdedit /store w:\RemoteInstall\boot\x86\default.bcd {68d9e51c-
    a129-4ee1-9725-2ab00a957daf} ramdisktftpwindowsize 9
```

3. Finally, it is necessary to force regeneration of the BCD store in the \Tmp folder by sending a control signal to the WDSServer service. You may do so by running the following command:

```
sc control wdsserver 129
```

Working with Windows Deployment Services

With WDS installed and configured, you will find the actual use of WDS is very straight forward. See Chapter 2 for details on creating an unattended installation of Windows Vista. Here we will cover several tasks associated with the use of WDS including:

- Creating a Capture image
- Creating a Custom Install image
- Creating a Discover image
- Preparing Media for a Discover image
- Deploying an Install image
- Leveraging the Windows Deployment Services API

Creating a Capture image

To create your own Install image, it is first necessary to create a Capture image. A Capture image is one that you boot to in order to capture the operating system to a .WIM file. This is essentially an alternative to using ImageX as described in Chapter 6, but you can of course create a custom Capture image using the WAIK tools.

1. **Right-click one of the boot images you have added to WDS and click Create Capture Boot Image**. Choose one that matches the architecture for which you want to target with this Capture image.

2. **In the initial form presented by the Create Capture Image wizard, you can enter an Image Name and Image description to identify the capture image.** You must also specify a Location and filename where the new file should be generated. A progress bar is provided as the capture image is generated.

3. **When complete, click the Finish button to close this wizard.**

4. **Add this newly generated image to the Boot Images in WDS. Right-click Boot Images and choose Add Boot Image.**

5. **Browse to the File Location specified in Step 2 to select the new Capture image. When selected, click Next to continue.** You are presented the opportunity to update the name and description you entered in Step 2.

6. **Click Next.** The Add Image wizard provides a summary of the image to be added based on your selections.

7. **Click Next.** Progress is given as the image is added.

8. **When the image has been added to the server, click the Finish button to complete the process.**

With the Capture image created, the next steps are to establish a reference computer to capture an Install image as a WIM file for deployment.

Creating a Custom Install image

Prepare a reference computer and then create an Install image based on that system. The following steps take you through the creation of a Custom Install image for Windows Vista:

1. **Create a reference computer.** This includes Windows Vista, Service Pack 1, and any updates or applications you may want to deploy as part of your Custom Install image.

2. **You need to generalize the installation by using Sysprep so that it may be deployed to other systems. Run Sysprep from** \Windows\System32\Sysprep\sysprep. exe **(the folder is hidden by default). Leave the System Cleanup Action set to OOBE, select the Generalize check box, and leave Reboot as the Shutdown Option, as shown in Figure 8.9.**

Running Sysprep to generalize your Custom Install image

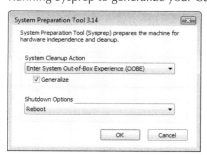

3. **When the computer restarts, boot to the network and press the F12 key when prompted.** Depending on your hardware, you may need to edit the boot order of the system or hit a key to be presented with a boot choice menu. Because there is more than one boot image active in WDS, you'll be presented with the option to choose a Capture image.

NOTE When working with Microsoft Virtual PC 2007, you must make sure the focus is set to the boot window for the virtual machine, then hold down the DEL key during the startup process to enter the BIOS Setup Utility. From here, you can go to the boot menu and change the Boot Priority to move PXE to the top of the list.

4. **Choose your Capture image from the list, as shown in Figure 8.10** After you have made your choice, the Windows PE image will be loaded over the network using PXE, as shown in Figure 8.11. When the image finishes loading, the Windows Deployment Services Image Capture Wizard will appear.

FIGURE 8.10

Choosing the Capture image from Windows Boot Manager

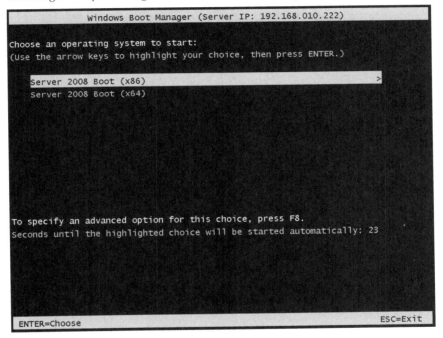

```
        Windows Boot Manager (Server IP: 192.168.010.222)

Choose an operating system to start:
(Use the arrow keys to highlight your choice, then press ENTER.)

   Server 2008 Boot (x86)                                          >
   Server 2008 Boot (x64)




To specify an advanced option for this choice, press F8.
Seconds until the highlighted choice will be started automatically: 23




ENTER=Choose                                              ESC=Exit
```

FIGURE 8.11

Loading a Windows PE image by using PXE

```
                Windows is loading files...

IP:192.168.10.222
```

5. Click Next on the Welcome screen to begin.

6. On the Image Capture Source screen, choose the appropriate volume to be captured from the Volume to Capture drop-down list. Enter an Image Name and Image Description in the fields provided and click Next to continue.

7. **Click the browse button and select the location and filename for where you want to store the image.** The location you specify here must be a local location on the computer (this is enforced to avoid image corruption in the event that there could be network issues during the capture process). Be sure to specify a filename with a .WIM extension.

8. **Select the Upload image to WDS server box and specify the Server Name in the provided field.** Once entered, click the **Connect** button (depending upon your environment, you may be prompted to provide credentials with sufficient privilege to connect to the WDS server).

9. **In the Image Group drop-down box, choose the image group in which you want to keep this image. Finally, click the Finish button to begin the process.**

> **NOTE** On Windows Server 2003 systems, two files are generated during the image creation process: an ImageName.WIM file and a Res.RWM file. The Res.RWM file contains the file streams that are associated with the images (each image group will have its own Res.rwm file).
>
> Because the actual files that make up the image are stored in this Res.RWM file, the ImageName. WIM file is much smaller and contains only metadata, which describes the files, folders, and permissions that make up the image.
>
> The reason for this separation is to differentiate the resource-only .WIM file from the metadata in order to speed up the image enumeration process. Image enumeration works only on .WIM files, and so the Res.rwm file is not used. The data in the Res.rwm file and in the Image_name. wim file is single-instanced and compressed.

Creating a Discover image

A *Discover image* is used to deploy to systems where PXE is not available. Discover images are saved and booted to physical media such as CDs, DVDs, or USB drives. The Discover image locates the WDS server and then the server installs the image to that computer. If you have more than one WDS server, you can create Discover images to target specific ones. To create a Discover image, follow these steps:

1. **Right-click one of the boot images you have added to WDS and click Create Discover Boot Image. Choose one that matches the architecture for which you want to target with this Capture image.**

2. **Enter the desired Image name and Image description in the fields provided on the Create Discover Image Wizard page.**

3. **Specify the location and filename for the Discover image.** You can choose any location, but ultimately this is to be placed on some kind of removable media that can be inserted into computers you want to image with WDS (normally those systems that do not support PXE).

4. **Click the Browse button to select the Windows Deployment Server to Respond.** This brings up the standard computer selection dialog where you may enter the name of the WDS server.

5. **Click the Check Names button to verify you have it correctly specified. When you have the server name properly selected, click OK to close the Select Computer dialog box. Then, click Next to continue.** A progress dialog appears while the discover image is generated and saved to the specified location.

6. **When complete, click the Finish button to close the wizard.**

Preparing media for a Discover image

With the WIM file generated, the next step is to place it on removable media so you may take it to those systems you want to image by using WDS. To prepare a bootable CD/DVD as a delivery mechanism for the Discover image, follow these steps:

1. **If you have not done so by now, you need to download and install the WAIK (approximately 1GB) from the Microsoft Web site (validation may be required).**

   ```
   www.microsoft.com/downloads/details.aspx?FamilyID=C7D4BC6D-
   15F3-4284-9123-679830D629F2
   ```

   After you have the download, you will notice it has an IMG file extension. This is a DVD image file that you may burn using your preferred software. It may be necessary to rename the file extension from IMG to ISO in order for your software to properly recognize the file. Alternatively, you can use a drive emulator, such as Daemon Tools (www. daemon-tools.cc) to mount the file as a drive without burning. Yet another option is to make use of such tools as WinRar or 7zip that support ISO files just as you would any other archive file (like ZIP).

2. **Run STARTCD.EXE for an installation menu, choose Windows AIK Setup, and follow the simple wizard through the installation.**

3. **Right-click the Windows PE Tools Command Prompt shortcut from its program folder on the start menu and choose Run as administrator.** The many command line tools covered are typically executed from the Windows PE Tools Command Prompt, but as they often require administrative rights, it is important to launch it in this way.

4. **To establish the file structure needed to customize a Windows PE image, run the CopyPE script with two arguments: the first is the target architecture (x86, ia64 or amd64), and the second is the target directory where you will manage your image.** If you are working with multiple architectures, it is a good idea to include it in your target folder name. However, this is a path that needs to be typed for most all commands so keep the path short to save some typing. For the tasks documented in this section the following arguments are used:

   ```
   copype.cmd x86 c:\winpe_x86
   ```

5. **Copy your Discover image created in the previous section over the existing boot. wim in the ISO sources directory (answer yes if asked to confirm the overwriting of the file):**

```
copy c:\winpe_x86\winpe.wim c:\winpe_x86\iso\sources\boot.wim
```

6. **Use the OSCDImg command line tool discussed earlier to generate the ISO:**

```
oscdimg -n -bc:\winpe_x86\etfsboot.com c:\winpe_x86\ISO c:\
    winpe_x86\discover.iso
```

7. **You may then use a utility to burn the discover.iso image to a CD or DVD.** For details on how to place this image on a USB flash drive, see Chapter 6.

Deploying an Install image

Interactively deploying an Install image from WDS is a very straightforward process after everything has been set up. With no automation provided, the process is as follows:

1. **Boot the computer using PXE or removable media (using a discovery image) and choose the desired boot image to start Windows PE.**

> **NOTE**   Although it should not be a problem for most computers today (certainly not one you are planning to deploy Windows Vista to), client computers must have at least 512MB of RAM — the required amount for using Windows PE.

2. **Accept the defaults for Locale and Keyboard or input method and click Next to continue.** You are initially presented with a wizard that begins by providing an option to specify a **Locale** and **Keyboard or input method**. Naturally, you should make the appropriate choice based on your own environment.

3. **If prompted, provide the credentials of an account with sufficient privileges to access the WDS server and click OK to continue.**

4. **Choose the desired image from the menu, as shown in Figure 8.12, and click Next to continue.** If you only have one image, you will not see this menu.

5. **The next screen prompts for where Windows is to be installed. Choose the desired drive and click Next to continue.** The WDS client then reports "Waiting for server" while it communicates your choices. Once ready, the installation of the image begins. After the image is applied it will restart into the newly installed operating system, and you will see a standard installation (if a generic Install image was provided) or a minimal installation wizard (if a custom Install image that has been generalized was provided.

Too much interaction for you? See the "Automating the installation of an Install image" section later in this chapter.

FIGURE 8.12

Choosing an Install image from within Windows PE

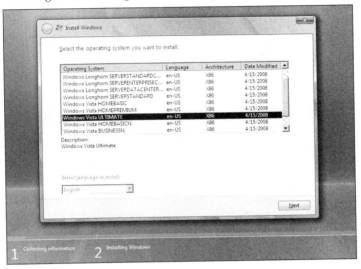

Deploying an Install image using multicast

For Windows Server 2008, you can make use of multicast to minimize network traffic when targeting many machines at once. To configure a multicast deployment, follow the steps below:

1. In the WDS Console, right-click the Multicast Transmissions node and choose Create Multicast Transmission.

2. Start by providing a name for the transmission that can help you to identify it and then press the Next button to continue.

3. Select the image that you want to deploy by choosing the image group name and then selecting the desired image from the list provided. Click Next to continue.

4. Specify the Multicast type and then click Next. Choose from the following:

   ■ Choose AutoCast to start immediately.

   ■ Choose Scheduled-Cast to have the multicast transmission begin when one or more of the following triggers are specified: Start automatically when the number of clients ready to receive this image meets the specified threshold or Start automatically later (where you may then provide a desired date and time).

   A Task Complete dialog box is shown to confirm the multicast transmission has been created.

5. Click the Finish button to close the Create Multicast Transmission wizard.

Automating the installation of an Install image

Use the Windows System Image Manager (SIM) from the WAIK to create an unattend.xml for use by WDS. This is covered in more detail in Chapter 2, so use the following steps to focus primarily on those elements unique to WDS:

1. **Launch the Windows System Image Manager (SIM) from the Windows AIK.** The SIM tool is shown in Figure 8.13.

FIGURE 8.13

Creating an Unattend.xml file for WDS

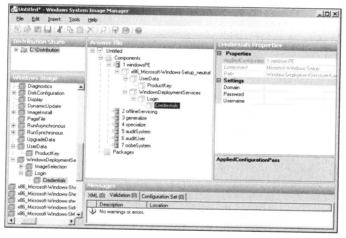

2. **In the lower-left panel titled Windows Image, choose Components ⇨ x86_ Microsoft-Windows-Setup_neutral ⇨ WindowsDeploymentServices ⇨ Login, right-click Credentials, and select Add Setting to Pass 1 windowsPE.** The selected component is added to the center pane titled Answer File.

3. **Click the Credentials node. Its properties appear in the left pane (Credentials Properties), where you can fill in values for Domain, Password, and Username.**

4. **You may also specify which image is to be installed by doing the same for the ImageSelection component. Drill down to Components ⇨ x86_Microsoft-Windows-Setup_neutral ⇨ WindowsDeploymentServices, right-click ImageSelection, and select Add Setting to Pass 1 windowsPE.** The selected component will then be added to the center pane titled Answer File.

5. **Click the InstallImage node and you will see its properties appear in the left pane (InstallImage Properties) where you can fill in values for Filename, ImageGroup, and ImageName. You can also click the InstallTo node to specify the desired DiskID and PartitionID numbers (typically 0 and 1, respectively, on systems with a single hard drive).**

6. You can, of course, modify any number of other parameters to control the installation in the same fashion. Other components of interest include:

   - x86_Microsoft-Windows-Setup_neutral ➪ UserData ➪ ProductKey (to specify a desired product key)

   - x86_Microsoft-Windows-Security-Licensing-SLC-UX__neutral_31bf3856ad364e35_ nonSxS (to skip automatic activation of Windows Vista)

7. When done, save the file to a safe place and close the Windows System Image Manager.

8. In the WDS console, right-click the desired Install Image, choose Properties, and select the check box at the bottom of the General tab labeled Allow image to install in unattended mode.

9. Click the Select File button and browse to the unattend.xml file saved in Step 7..
   The previous step associated the unattend file with the image installation. Now we need to tie it to the WDS client to automate its actions. Place a copy of it in the RemoteInstall\ WDSClientUnattend folder (with the file name *unattend.xml*).

> **NOTE** The reason there are two files is to provide support for Windows XP and Windows Server 2003 which do not support the unattend.xml format.

10. Click the OK button to apply the change.

> **NOTE** There is one more place you can specify a unattend.xml for WDS, and that is in the properties of the WDS server where you may specify a different file for any supported architectures. When configured, the unattend.xml will be used by WDS based on the computer's architecture if the client is found to have one specified this way. Begin in the WDS console by right-clicking the WDS server node and choosing Properties, selecting the Client tab and checking the box labeled Enable unattended installation. Then, by each architecture that you wish to support, click the Browse button to select the appropriate unattend.xml file, and then click OK to enforce the setting.

Leveraging the Windows Deployment Services API

You may also use the Windows Deployment Services (WDS) Application Programming Interface (API) to develop you own solutions based on WDS. The API is offered for Server and Client functions, but not for WDS management components.

- WDS Server Functions that are provided offer programmatic access to the WDS PXE server. WDS server components include a PXE server and TFTP server for booting to the network in order to load and install an operating system.

- WDS Client Functions provide programmatic access to the WDS client. The WDS client components include a GUI that runs within Windows PE and communicates with the server components to select and install an operating system image.

The WDS PXE Server consists of both a PXE server and a PXE provider. The PXE server contains the core networking capability and supports plug-in interfaces that are known as PXE providers. This provider model enables development of custom PXE solutions while continuing to use the core PXE server networking code base.

A sample custom PXE provider, filter provider, and WDS client application is available in the Microsoft Windows Software Development Kit (SDK).

> **NOTE** For more details on the WDS API visit http://msdn2.microsoft.com/en-us/library/bb530732(VS.85).aspx.

Summary

Windows Deployment Services (WDS) provides a powerful means of rolling out new systems. This chapter covered the excellent support for moving up from Remote Installation Services (RIS) as well as how to go about installing WDS on Server 2003 and Server 2008. The steps for proper configuration were also provided, and finally we covered some ways you can take advantage of WDS through step-by-step instructions for creating and deploying images. The topic of WDS is closely related with the tasks of creating images (Chapter 2) and managing Windows images (Chapter 6) so be sure to review those chapters as well.

For alternatives to WDS, see Chapter 6, which discusses Symantec Ghost and the KACE Desktop Deployment Appliance as alternative imaging solutions. Each of these solutions also provides its own deployment mechanisms with all the functionality of WDS (and more) which may well be worth investigating, depending upon your needs.

Part III

Administering Windows Vista

The administration portion of this book begins by taking an in-depth look at how you manage Windows Vista systems once they are deployed. It is built on the CASPR system, which is made up of five aspects:

- Controlling change in your environment
- Administering your systems
- Securing your infrastructure
- Protecting information your users generate
- Recovering systems or information when issues occur

Each of the chapters in this portion of the book covers one aspect of the CASPR system.

Relying on the CASPR system will ensure that each aspect of system management will be completely covered and will vastly reduce the efforts required to create a stable and solid Vista PC infrastructure.

Part III begins by addressing the first two aspects of CASPR: change management (Chapter 9) and administration (Chapter 10). Change management focuses on two core Vista technologies: Group Policy, which lets you manage one or a multitude of computers, and event management — a technology that was completely rewritten for this edition of Windows — as well as task scheduling, another technology that is completely new in Vista.

Chapter 9

Managing Change in Vista

Change management is one of the key aspects of system administration. Yet, change is at the heart of Information Technology (IT) because IT systems are constantly evolving and mutating as new hardware or software is released and new ways of doing things are implemented along with them.

The key to change management is structured control: planning and making sure that when change does occur, it occurs the way you want it to and does not adversely affect the systems you manage. In Windows Vista, this means dealing with two administrative activities:

- **First, you need to control change:** This is performed both locally and centrally through Group Policy.

- **Second, you need to track change:** Here, you can rely on the Vista Event Log, which along with the Task Scheduler, can help you know which events occur on a system and automatically trigger activities when expected events do occur.

These tools should form the core of your change management and change tracking strategies with Windows Vista.

Managing Change through Group Policy

System settings in Windows are controlled through changes in either the graphical interface or the command line. These changes are recorded in the System Registry, a central database that is located on each Windows system and is used to store configuration settings and otherwise control the behavior of a computer. As seen in Figure 9.1, the Vista registry is divided into hives or sections that either affect the computer or the users who rely on it to perform work. The registry can be controlled both locally and centrally, most often through a special control engine called Group Policy. Group Policy works through Group Policy Objects, special components of Windows that contain thousands of settings — about 2,450 settings in fact — each designed to control one single aspect of the operating system.

FIGURE 9.1

The Vista System Registry

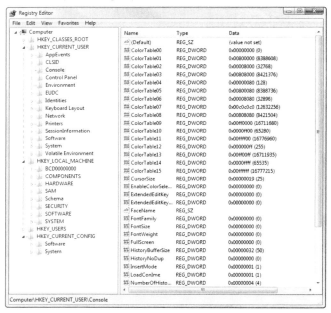

GPOs are designed to define the way a system — desktop or server — appears and behaves. This includes items such as the contents of the Start menu, icons on the desktop, ability to modify the desktop, ability to run various software products, and more. GPOs can be used to manage settings that affect PCs, servers, and users. This makes GPOs not only the most powerful management infrastructure for Windows systems, but also the engine of choice for object management. This is why you should endeavor to work with and understand GPOs as much as possible.

GPOs can control several aspects of a computer. They can

- Modify the contents of registry hives
- Assign logon, logoff, startup, and shutdown scripts

■ Be used to redirect data folders, moving precious user data to central locations so that it can be backed up and otherwise protected

■ Deploy software to PCs

■ Manage security settings

In addition, if you don't find the one setting you need to control, you can always add a custom administrative template to the mix and make your own modifications to the systems you administer.

As seen in Figure 9.2, GPOs contain thousands of settings. Each can be modified within the GPO and then saved into one object. This object can then be applied to hardware, affecting computer settings and therefore any user that interacts with them. Or the object can be applied to the users themselves, making sure that no matter which system they use, it will behave in exactly the same way each time they log on to Windows Vista.

FIGURE 9.2

A Group Policy Object

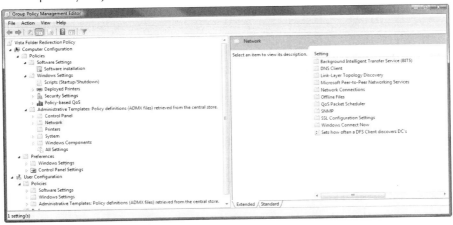

GPOs can be applied singly or in combination with other GPOs. GPO settings are assigned first for computers and then for users. GPO settings are cumulative and, depending on the order they are assigned, some settings may be overridden by others. Because of this, properly designing both the content of each GPO and the order in which the GPOs will be applied to the systems under your care is important. You should ensure that each GPO you design is targeted at a single object type, whether users or computers. Segregating GPOs in this manner will not only improve the speed with which each GPO is processed, but will also help in your delegation of administration structure.

Working with Local Policies

Each Windows computer system includes a local Group Policy, called the Local Security Policy (LSP). The local GPO is read each time the computer is started. However, if the computer is part of a domain — a network managed by Active Directory (AD) — this local GPO is often superseded by domain or central GPOs. Generally, the Local Security Policy contains fewer settings than do its central counterparts, partly because of its purpose and intent and partly because of the mechanism it uses to apply the settings.

Although central or directory GPOs include thousands of settings that control everything from the look of the desktop to the power settings of a computer, the LSP only includes items that are focused on security. As shown in Figure 9.3, this includes the following:

- Account Policies or the policies that control both password settings and account lockouts
- Local Policies or the policies that determine if you will audit activity on the computer, which user rights you will grant, and which security options you want to set
- Windows Firewall with Advanced Security or the settings that control which programs can talk to your computers and which programs can talk from your computer to others
- Public Key Policies or the policies that let you encrypt data on your computer
- Software Restriction Policies or the policies that control which software is allowed to run on your computer
- IP Security Policies or the policies that control how secure your communications with other computers will be

Organizations often elect to include content that is normally excluded from central GPOs into the local GPO. LSPs are often ideal to special settings that need only be applied locally or because their application is resource intensive. Because the LSP is applied as soon as the computer starts, it can provide a first line of defense, even and especially if your computer is no longer connected to the network. For this reason, you should include as many settings in the LSP as possible and then copy it to each system as it is installed.

Local policies are a boon for disconnected systems, but like the connected system, they presuppose that you have some form of control over the PC. To standardize systems, you must copy the policy you want to implement onto each one and then reboot them to make sure the policy is actually applied because it is only applied at system startup. Doing this is not very effective unless you need to rely on the local policy for specific purposes.

Every computer running Windows XP, Windows Vista, or Windows Server includes a local GPO by default. The settings in this default file are applied to each computer at every startup. Organizations that want to standardize certain elements of the desktop and other computer behavior should configure this policy object with default organizational settings and make sure this file is part of the installation set for each computer. Because these GPOs are local, they can also be different on each computer. To make the best of local GPOs, you should define a given set of parameters for each computer type (workstations, mobile systems, or kiosk computers) and change them as little as possible.

The local GPO is located in the %SYSTEMROOT%\SYSTEM32\GROUP POLICY folder. To view this folder, you must enable two settings in the Folder view options (Windows Explorer ⇨ Organize Menu ⇨ Folder and Search Options ⇨ View tab):

- Show hidden files and folders
- Hide protected operating system files (Recommended)

If you disable the later this generates a warning dialog box. The best practice in this regard is to enable the setting to capture a copy of the local GPO you want to deploy, then disable the setting afterward.

Local Security Policies are managed through a special console called Local Security Policy. This console is located in Administrative Tools.

1. **To launch the Console, go to Start Menu ⇨ Administrative Tools ⇨ Local Security Policy.**

2. **Accept the User Account Control (UAC) prompt, and the Console opens.** LSPs are saved in .INF format. After you've configured an LSP, you can export it by using the Action ⇨ Export policy command. Doing this is much easier than trying to use the default GPO in the Group Policy folder.

3. **Make sure that you click on the Security Settings node in the tree pane of the console to export all of the settings in the policy.** By default, policies are saved to the Documents ⇨ Security ⇨ Templates folder. Subsequently, you can import the LSP into another computer by once again using the Action ⇨ Import policy command. When imported, the LSP will automatically update each of the settings you previously configured. You should add a custom LSP to each computer system as you build it.

NOTE If Administrative Tools does not appear on the Start Menu, add it by right-clicking the Start button and then selecting Properties. Click the Customize button on the Start Menu tab, scroll down to the bottom, and select Display on the All Programs menu and the Start menu under System administrative tools. Click OK twice. Administrative Tools will now be displayed both on the Start Menu and under the All Programs banner.

FIGURE 9.3

The Local Security Policy

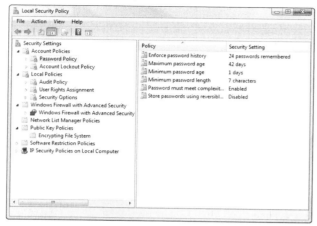

Local Security Policy contents

LSPs can contain several different security settings and, because they are your first line of defense, should be configured to provide a minimum level of security for each computer system connected or not in your network. Look to the recommendations of Table 9.1 to configure your LSP.

TABLE 9.1

Recommended Settings for Local Security Policies

Setting	Recommendation
Account Policies: Password Policy	By default, there is no password policy on Vista computers except for a request to change your password once every 42 days. Your password policy should be set as follows: ■ 24 passwords remembered in password history ■ 42 days as the minimum age ■ 1 day as the minimum age ■ 7 characters as the minimum length ■ Enable complexity requirements ■ Ignore any other settings.

Setting	Recommendation
Account Policies: Account Lockout Policy	By default, there are no account lockout restrictions. Set your account lockout to: ■ 30 minutes as the lockout duration ■ 3 invalid logon attempts ■ Reset lockout counter after 30 minutes
Local Policies: Audit Policy	Audit success of every item. Audit failure only if your systems contain sensitive information. Auditing fills up the Event Log very rapidly so apply failure audits with care.
Local Policies: User Rights Assignment	These settings are generally better left as is unless you have specific security requirements.
Local Policies: Security Options	These settings are generally better left as is unless you have specific security requirements.
Windows Firewall with Advanced Security	The firewall should be configured as on for all profiles (Domain, Private, and Public) and especially for the Public profile since it is the one that puts computers at most risk. Most applications that are designed for Vista will automatically configure firewall settings during installation so leaving the firewall on should not limit communications.
Public Key Policies	Turn on all recommended settings (settings with the word recommended beside them) for both Certificate Path Validation Settings and Auto-Enrollment.
Public Key Policies: Encrypting File System	Turn this on only for computers containing sensitive data.
Software Restriction Policies	Turn this on only for computers running sensitive roles in your network.
IP Security Policies (IPSec)	IPSec policies are linked with the Windows Firewall. Turn them on only for computers transferring sensitive data over the network.

NOTE Although some of the settings in the LSP are not configured, you must remember that it is because these settings are for local computers only. Most computers linked together in a network will rely on Active Directory. They receive the most important settings from a domain controller — the server that provides central authentication services — and these settings will override those in the LSP. In fact, when computers are part of a domain, settings that include a small lock on the folder icon are provided centrally by default and cannot be changed locally.

To make any changes in the Group Policy Editor — the engine that lets you modify the contents of the LSP — use the Tree pane to click on the item to change, then move to the Details pane to double-click on the setting to change. Modify the setting through its dialog box. Use the Explain tab to find more information about each one of the settings.

Using Multiple Local Security Policies

Windows Vista has the ability to include more than one single local GPO on each computer system. It applies these local GPOs in layers much as it applies central GPOs. As in previous versions of Windows, the first layer applies it to the computer system itself. The second applies to a local group, either the Administrators or a Users group. The third can apply a local policy to specific local user accounts. This gives you a lot more control over computers that may or may not be connected to an AD structure — computers in a workgroup, for example — but it still limits you to the content of the local policy only.

By default, you can only edit one single LSP with the Local Security Policy editor in Administrative Tools. The LSP lets you modify the behavior for the local computer system only. In order to modify and create more than one LSP on a system, you need to create a custom LSP console. To do so, follow these steps:

1. **Go to Start Menu, and type** mmc **in the Search box and press Enter. Accept the UAC prompt.** This launches a new, empty Microsoft Management Console.

2. **Go to the File menu and select Add/Remove Snap-in.** The Add or Remove Snap-ins dialog box appears.

3. **Select Group Policy Object and click Add.**

4. **In the Select Group Policy Object dialog box, verify that it states Local Computer and click Finish.** Your first LSP is added.

5. **Repeat the process by clicking Add again. This time, click Browse in the Select Group Policy Object dialog box. Go to the Users tab and select either the Administrators or Non-Administrators group. Click OK and Finish. Your second LSP now applies to a group.**

6. **Repeat Step 5 again to add the third LSP that applies to a single user, as shown in Figure 9.4.**

7. **Click OK to close the Add or Remove Snap-ins dialog box.**

8. **Choose File ⇨ Save and then name the console and click Save.** By default, this console will be placed in your own personal Administrative Tools folder.

9. **Modify the GPO settings according to your requirements.**

10. **Save when done and close the console.**

NOTE   Windows Vista and Windows Server 2008 (WS08) both support multiple local GPOs. This is done by assigning different security descriptors to each local GPO. Multiple LSPs contain much more information than a single LSP because they are actually complete Group Policy Objects.

Multiple LSPs can be useful when you have kiosk systems that require tight security when *users* are logged on, but that require less security when *administrators* are logged on. For more information on how to work with these local GPOs, go to `http://technet2.microsoft.com/WindowsVista/en/library/5ae8da2a-878e-48db-a3c1-4be6ac7cf7631033.mspx?mfr=true`.

FIGURE 9.4

Creating a Multiple Local Security Policy

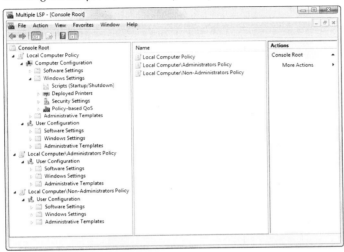

Working with central policies

In addition to local Group Policy Objects, networks that run Active Directory have centralized GPOs. Compared to local GPOs, centralized GPOs are management GPOs because you can modify them in a central location and have them affect any group of objects. By default, every AD network includes two default policies:

■ The Default Domain Policy

■ The Default Domain Controller (DC) Policy

A specific default domain policy is applied to every domain in a network. The same applies for the default DC policy, except that instead of being applied at the domain level, this policy is applied specifically to domain controllers. Although these two GPOs have little impact on PCs, they do provide central control elements that affect all users.

The Default Domain Policy is often called the Account Policy because it provides central control of account settings in the network. If your servers are running Windows Server 2003, then you will have only a single account policy. If your servers are running Windows Server 2008, then you can have multiple account policies, all contained within the same GPO. Most organizations use a single account policy and apply it to all users. In some rare cases, organizations use multiple account policies to provide more secure login restrictions for key groups of users, for example, the Administrators group. This lets them use a more open policy for normal users and a more restrictive one for administrative staff. Your base account policy should include the settings listed in Table 9.1 for both the Account Policies and Local Policies sections. Passwords are an important aspect of any security policy and should be enforced in every organization.

Working with PC-related Group Policy Objects

PC-related GPOs do not exist by default; they must be created and customized. As mentioned earlier, a GPO can manage thousands of settings on computers; in fact, in Vista, GPOs include 2,450 settings by default. These settings are divided into different categories as shown in Table 9.2.

TABLE 9.2

Group Policy Object Contents

Managed Object	Description
Computer and User Settings	Vista includes options that can control both computer (HKEY_LOCAL_MACHINE or HKLM) or user (HKEY_CURRENT_USER or HKCU) registry settings.
Scripts	Vista machines can run startup, shutdown, logon, or logoff scripts. Scripts are assigned through GPOs. Startup and shutdown scripts apply to PCs while logon and logoff scripts apply to users.
Folder Redirection	Vista machines can automatically protect user data through the use of folder redirection — the automatic move of local folders to remote servers. In addition, redirected data is available to users from any PC in the network. Finally, redirected data is automatically cached locally through offline folder settings so that users can work on the data even if the network connection is lost. In the event of a connection failure, data is re-synchronized as soon as the connection returns.
Software Delivery	Software installations that are packaged in Windows Installer format can automatically be assigned to either PCs or users through Group Policy Objects.
Security Features	All of Vista's security features can be controlled centrally through GPOs.

GPOs are divided into two major sections. The first includes computer settings and is designed to apply to a PC no matter who logs on or what their user rights are. The second is focused on user settings and is designed to apply to specific users no matter which computer they log on to. Both sections include many of the same settings, but because of their very nature, both also include settings that are not available in the other.

A good practice is to create GPOs for either users or computers and configure them as single-purpose GPOs; that is, as GPOs that are designed to affect only one single type of object. This makes it easier to control and otherwise manage GPOs. Another good practice is to create as few GPOs as possible. The more GPOs you create, the more confusing your system management practices will become.

Group Policy application concepts

Group Policy settings are applied in a specific order. Computer settings are applied first because these settings are applied when the computer starts up. User settings are applied second as users log onto the system. Computers have their own machine account that must be authenticated in the Active Directory domain when they boot up. During this authentication process the Group Policy is applied.

When multiple GPOs are applied to the same object, for example, if multiple GPOs are applied to a PC, they are applied in order of precedence, as shown in Figure 9.5.

1. The local GPO or LSP is applied at computer startup.

2. If available, GPOs that are assigned to a site are applied next.

3. Domain GPOs are applied after site GPOs.

4. Organizational unit GPOs are applied last.

5. If the object (either computer or user) is located within a child OU and the child OU contains an additional GPO, this GPO is applied last.

This process is often called the L-S-D-OU process for the Local-Site-Domain-OU application order. If conflicts arise between policies, the settings in the last policy override all of the others. For example, if you deny access to an item in the Start menu in the domain policy, but it is allowed in an OU policy, the resultant policy will allow access to the menu.

FIGURE 9.5

The Group Policy application process

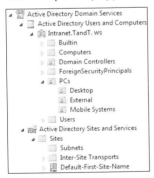

For this reason, understanding some basic Active Directory concepts before you can proceed with GPO assignment and management is important. AD structures are designed to control how objects are managed in a network. These structures include several basic components:

- **Active Directory Forest:** The base structure of a directory that contains all of the objects in the network.

- **AD Domain:** A container and an account policy boundary. A domain can contain several different object types: printers, user accounts, machine accounts, groups, shared folders, and much more. A forest can contain several domains. Organizations usually create a single production domain which is designed to contain all of their computer and user accounts. Each domain's objects are managed by domain controllers.

- **Site:** A local network that contains domain controllers but that is separated from the rest of the network by a wide area network (WAN) connection.

- **Organizational Unit (OU):** A container that is located within a domain. OUs are designed to help regroup objects for better management. Domains can contain millions of objects; therefore, using OUs to properly categorize these objects is important. OUs have four purposes:

  - To categorize objects; that is, to regroups objects of one particular type, for example computers

  - To manage objects by applying GPOs to them

  - To delegate object management, for example, taking all of the computers in an OU and assigning their management to a specific group of PC technicians

  - To hide objects by placing them in an OU and controlling its access rights

As mentioned before, there is at least one GPO that is assigned to each domain: the Default Domain Policy. Site GPOs are fairly rare because they apply to groups of objects within a specific remote office and not to others. Instead of using sites, many organizations will choose to apply a GPO for remote office management to a container that will include every remote office. This is why most organizations apply GPOs to Organizational Units because these can span multiple sites.

As you can see, the structure of your AD domain has such an impact on your PC management strategy.

> **NOTE** In Windows Server 2008, Active Directory is called Active Directory Domain Services (ADDS) because WS08 includes several different technologies which are all labeled with the Active Directory name. Along with Active Directory Domain Services, these include Active Directory Certificate Services, Active Directory Lightweight Directory Services, Active Directory Rights Management Services, and Active Directory Federation Services. However, because the previous two versions of Windows Server, 2000 and 2003, referred to Active Directory as Active Directory alone, most people still refer to ADDS as Active Directory.

Controlling GPO inheritance

In addition to the application order, you can control how GPOs will be inherited from one location to another. Remember that by default, GPOs are assigned through the LSDOU rule. However, if you assign a GPO at the domain level and you want to make sure that its settings are not overridden by GPOs that are assigned after it (GPOs that are assigned to an OU, for example), you can force the application of your settings. You do this by forcing GPO inheritance.

When GPOs are inherited through the LSDOU inheritance order, they automatically override each other if they contain conflicting settings. If settings are applied in a domain GPO, but are removed in an OU GPO, then the OU GPO contains the setting that will be applied. If a setting is applied in a parent OU and then removed in a child OU, then the setting in the child OU will be applied. But, in certain situations, you want to make sure that global policies are not overridden by more focused policies. To do this, you can assign the Enforced attribute to the GPO. Using the Enforced attribute ensures that the GPO will not be overridden by any other.

Conversely, you might want to ensure that certain more focused GPOs are not overridden by global GPOs. You can also do this by assigning a Block Inheritance attribute, but this time, not to the GPO itself, but rather to the Organizational Unit itself.

As you can see, you could assign the Enforced attribute to a GPO while someone else assigns the Block Inheritance attribute to his or her OU. Enforcing and Blocking at the same time could lead to quite a bit of confusion in the overall settings that would be applied, but fear not: Enforced always wins. Despite the fact that Enforced always wins, you should use the Enforced and Block Inheritance attributes sparingly and make sure your overall GPO strategy is coherent and does not require either setting.

Controlling GPO updates

By default, Group Policy Objects are updated on a regular schedule on all systems, PCs and servers. Domain controllers are updated every 5 minutes because they provide an essential service. PCs and member servers are updated at 90-minute intervals. If the contents of a policy have not changed since the last time it was applied, it is not applied again.

Each Group Policy Object includes a file named GPT.INI. This file contains the version number for the GPO. Each time a change is applied to the GPO, this version number is incremented. When the GPO refresh is applied, the system reads the GPT.INI to see if the version number has changed. If it hasn't changed, then there are no updates to the system. If it has, then the system reads the policy and applies any changes.

You can modify the default behavior, once again, through GPO settings.

You can also force the reapplication of GPOs to any system. Do this by using a command line tool:

```
gpupdate /force
```

Using this command on any system updates both computer and user GPOs and reapplies all settings even if the version number has not changed.

Structuring GPO application for PCs

Group policy is a very powerful management tool that can be applied to four different object categories:

- Domain controllers
- PCs

- Member servers
- User accounts

In terms of Vista, you should be concerned about the application of GPO settings to PCs and user accounts. Domain controllers and member servers are under the purview of other administrators in the network. These won't change until your servers are upgraded to Windows Server 2008. At that point, they will benefit from the many features Microsoft has enhanced in Vista. Until then, the only items that can profit from Vista's new GPO settings will be PCs running Vista and the users who have access to them.

> **NOTE** Group Policy is an excellent vehicle for system administration, but it is possible to overdo it. Begin your Vista GPO strategy by inventorying the GPOs you have in place and then look them over to see if there is room for rationalization. Because Vista brings so many new settings, you don't want to find yourself in a situation where you are proliferating GPOs.
>
> To assist this process, download the Microsoft tool to inventory Group Policy from www. microsoft.com/downloads/details.aspx?FamilyID=1d24563d-cac9-4017-af14-8dd686a96540&DisplayLang=en.
>
> To learn how to rationalize the number of GPOs in your network while providing complete management services, download Redesigning GPO Structure for Improved Manageability at www.reso-net.com/download.asp?Fichier=P73.

PCs should be further segregated into different categories. Because GPOs are inherited and are mostly applied to organizational units, you should create a hierarchical OU structure that will refine settings as your categories are developed. For example, you should create a main GPO that will affect all PCs whether they are workstations or mobile computers. Then, you should create sub-GPOs that would refine settings based on whether a system is a desktop or a mobile PC. For example, desktops will rarely rely on wireless networks whereas mobile systems will often do so. Desktops will rely on wired communications and may not require communication encryption whereas mobile systems will.

For this strategy to work, you need to create a corresponding OU structure as seen in Figure 9.6. This structure includes a main OU that will include two sub-OUs. The main OU is named PCs and includes a targeted GPO that contains settings for all PCs. Sub-OUs include desktops and mobile systems. Each sub-OU contains a corresponding GPO to further refine settings. Note that the Desktops GPO is optional since you may not need to further refine settings beyond those applied to all PCs. It is still important to create this OU though in order to categorize desktop systems and separate them from mobile systems.

FIGURE 9.6

Creating an OU structure for PC management

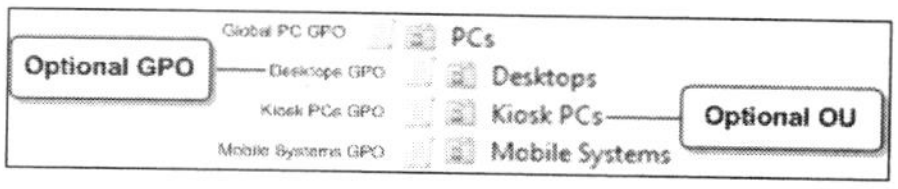

A third sub-OU can be used when you have Kiosk PCs or PCs that are exposed to the public and require advanced security settings. These PCs will rely on GPO Loopback settings. Loopback settings always ensure that computer settings are applied no matter who logs on. This is performed in one of two ways. Merged settings will append computer settings once user settings are applied. Replaced settings will completely replace user settings with computer settings. Policy loopback is controlled in the Computer Configuration under Administrative Templates ⇨ System ⇨ Group Policy.

NOTE By default, computer accounts created in Active Directory are stored in the Computers container. Similarly, user accounts are stored in the Users container. Both of these containers are special containers that do not behave as OUs and therefore cannot be the target of Group Policy Objects. Because of this, you must create new OUs that will contain PC and user accounts. To make sure that you do not confuse these new OUs with the default containers, call them PCs and People. Then, after these OUs are created, move the PC and user accounts to the appropriate levels in the OU structure to begin their management through GPOs.

In some cases, organizations decide to group PCs on a regional basis because doing this lets them delegate PC administration to regional technicians. In this case, you still need to create the PCs, Desktop and PCs, and Mobile OU structures to differentiate between desktops and mobile systems.

Structuring GPO application for users

Designing policy application for users is a bit more complicated because user GPOs can become quite granular if you're not careful. We recommended that you keep user GPOs to a minimum. In fact, you can often have one single user-oriented GPO and have it apply to all users through the People top-level OU.

You can refine the structure of the People OU by including sub-OUs, but unless you have the need to provide separate management settings for different types of users, there should be no need for other user-oriented GPOs as shown Figure 9.7.

Follow the keep it simple, stupid (KISS) rule and keep it as simple as possible. Doing this makes it much easier to manage GPO content and will make GPO troubleshooting much more straightforward when required.

FIGURE 9.7

The People OU structure and applicable GPOs

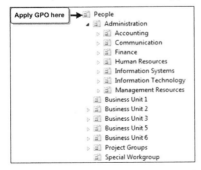

> **NOTE** For more information on the structure of a directory for management purposes and for information on the structure of a directory to manage server objects, see http://www.reso-net.com/livre.asp?p=main&b=WS08.

Working with GPO tools

GPOs are managed through a series of different tools. You've already had a look at the Local Security Policy console and you've created a custom console for the management of multiple LSPs. Each of these tools gave you a foretaste of central GPO management. Now, you can access the best GPO management tools.

> **NOTE** You must run the GPMC from a Vista computer if you want to control all of the settings that apply to Vista. You can also rely on the GPMC found in Windows Server 2008, but it is rare that organizations rely on servers to manage GPOs.

The first tool is the Group Policy Management Console (GPMC). Prior to Service Pack 1, the GPMC was located on every Vista system in your network. It did not however have an available shortcut, even in Administrative Tools. To start the GPMC, you needed to type **GPMC.MSC** in the Search box under the Start Menu and press Enter. Doing so launches a UAC prompt. Accept the prompt to open the console. Remember that you must use a domain account to do so.

In Vista SP1, you must download and install the GPMC separately because Service Pack 1 removes the GPMC from Vista PCs when it is applied. You must then install the Remote Server Administration Tools (RSAT) update to get access to this console once more. See Chapter 10 for the instructions on using RSAT with Vista SP1.

As shown in Figure 9.8, the GPMC is divided into several different sections. By default, the GPMC opens with the current AD forest selected. To view its contents, you must expand the forest in the Tree pane. After it is expanded, the GPMC Tree pane lists the following items:

- **Domains:** They contain normal domain contents.
- **OUs:** The main structure you use to apply GPOs.
- **Group Policy Objects:** The container for all GPOs.
- **WMI filters:** The container that includes filters you can assign to GPOs based on Windows Management Instrumentation queries or queries that let you identify systems based on specific selection criteria. Criteria can include available disk space, model type, manufacturer name, and any other object you can use to identify systems.
- **Sites:** The container that lists all of the sites in your AD structure.
- **Group Policy Modeling:** Allows you to perform "what if" scenarios with GPOs to help determine how systems or users would be affected by GPO changes.
- **Group Policy Results:** Lets you view Resultant Set of Policy (RSoP) results on a specific object. This tool is very valuable when you try to determine why systems are not behaving as you would expect.

In addition to the listed items, the GPMC includes GPO Links. Links are differentiated from actual GPOs by their icon. The link icon includes a small arrow to show that it is a shortcut to the actual GPO. All actual GPOs are stored in the GPO container and cannot be removed from this container. To apply a GPO to a given object, you need to link it to that object. Both links and GPOs will contain properties, but these properties will differ between the two. For example, the Enforced attribute is not actually applied to a GPO, it is applied to a GPO Link. You can however edit a GPO's content and properties by editing a link. The GPMC will alert you that you are working with a link instead of the actual GPO as shown in Figure 9.9. Do not check the Do not show this message again if you want to know each time you are working with a link instead of a GPO option.

FIGURE 9.8

Working with the Group Policy Management Console

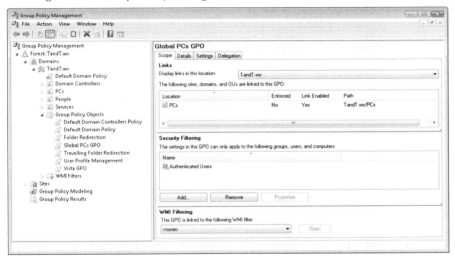

FIGURE 9.9

The GPMC Link warning

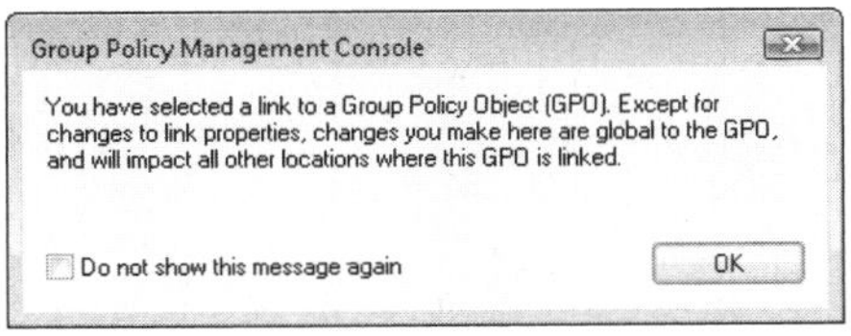

The items in the Details pane vary with the objects you select in the Tree pane, but when a GPO or a GPO Link is selected, the GPMC will list four tabs in the Details pane. These tabs outline various details for each GPO. Scope will outline how the GPO is applied. It lists where the GPO is linked, which Security Filter is applied and which WMI Filter is applied. By default, all GPOs are filtered to Authenticated Users, a special group that includes both user and computer accounts, and do not include any WMI Filter. You can control the application of a GPO by modifying the group to which it applies under Security Filtering. For example, if you wanted a GPO to apply only to the Finance Users group, you would modify its Security Filtering by removing Authenticated Users and adding a security group named Finance Users.

Security filtering is also useful when you do not want to create multiple links for a GPO. For example, in an organization with multiple regional sites, you might create an OU for each region and create the corresponding PCs and People structures inside each Regional OU. When it comes to linking GPOs to this OU structure you have two choices. First, you can choose to link the GPO to each appropriate OU, creating as many links as required and having to manage all of these links. Second, you can create a security group that regroups all objects of one type — PCs, Desktops, Mobile Systems, and People — and then link the appropriate GPO to the entire domain so that all objects are affected, but filter this GPO with the appropriate security group. Only the members in this group will have access to the contents of the GPO, all others will ignore it. The difference between both strategies is shown in Figure 9.10. Ideally, you will create a central OU structure and limit the use of Security Filtering or the creation of multiple GPO links.

FIGURE 9.10

Options for using a Regional OU Structure

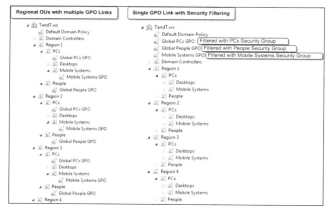

The second tab of the Details pane of the GPMC, Details, lists the name of the GPO, its owner, when it was created and modified, its version, unique ID, and status. The Settings tab lists the settings that have been enabled in the GPO. The Delegation tab lets you view who can control this GPO. For example, PC-related GPOs should be delegated to PC administrators.

The GPMC offers several GPO management features:

- You can create and link GPOs.
- You can backup, restore, and otherwise protect GPOs.
- You can create OUs to better manage GPO application, but you cannot control the contents of the OU.
- You can create WMI Filters and apply them to GPOs.
- You can view AD sites and assign GPOs to them, but you cannot create new sites.
- You can perform "what if" GPO modeling.
- You can troubleshoot GPO settings by performing Resultant Set of Policy analyses.
- You can generate reports on your GPOs.
- You can import settings from GPO templates into GPOs.
- You can migrate GPOs from one domain to another.
- You can link to other domains or forests in your network.
- You can delegate portions of the console to other groups so that they can manage GPO contents and/or application.

Overall, this tool provides powerful GPO management features.

NOTE To find more information on the GPMC see http://technet2.microsoft. com/windowsserver/en/library/af452421-4839-40f2-8892-ccf-670f5a27a1033.mspx?mfr=true

Creating a Group Policy Object

The creation process for GPOs is relatively simple:

1. Right-click the Group Policy Objects container and select New.
2. In the New dialog box, name the GPO with a clear name outlining its purpose and click OK. At this point, the GPO is created inside the GPO container, but it does not include any modified settings and it is not applied to any object.
3. Now that the GPO is created, right-click on it and select Edit. Doing this opens another GPO management tool, the Group Policy Editor (GPEdit). GPEdit lets you view all of the settings you can control in the policy as shown in Figure 9.11. As mentioned before, each policy is divided into two sections: computer settings and user settings. GPEdit is a live editing tool. There is no save feature. Each time you make a change, you've modified the GPO. This is one more reason why you need to be careful when working with GPOs.

a. To make modifications, navigate to the portion you want to modify through the Tree pane, move to the setting you want to control in the Details pane, and double-click on it. Choose the setting you want in the dialog box and click OK.

b. When a section includes multiple settings, you can simply move from one to the next by using the Next Setting button. This automatically makes your modification and moves to the next setting. Also note that each time you select a setting, its description will be displayed in the Details pane.

FIGURE 9.11

Working with the Group Policy Editor

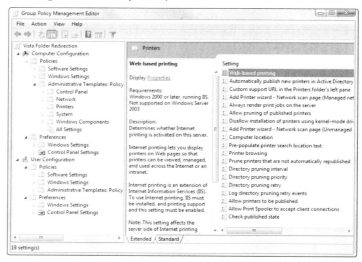

4. When you have completed your modifications, close GPEdit and return to the GPMC. Review the changed settings by clicking on the policy name in the GPO container, then moving to the Settings tab in the Details pane. Make sure that all of the settings you wanted to modify have been updated before proceeding. If something is amiss, then launch GPEdit again.

5. Now, you're ready to apply the GPO. To do this, you need to link it to a container. Drag and drop the GPO to a destination container, whether it is a site, a domain, or an OU. Make sure that the destination for the link exists before you try to link it. When you link the GPO, GPMC will ask if you are sure; click OK to continue and generate the link.

> **NOTE** GPOs are not "live," that is, they do not affect any objects until they are linked to a destination container. This means you can create GPOs in the Group Policy Objects container in the GPMC, edit them as much as you need, and when you feel you have them right, link them to their final destination. This provides a form of change control over the GPOs you create.

6. Now that the GPO is linked, you can modify the link properties. Possible changes include applying the Enforced attribute, disabling Computer or User sections of the GPO, and so on. For example, you should disable the User section if the GPO is targeted at PCs and vice versa when it is targeted at users.

7. Review the container's properties. Remember that containers such as OUs can also include attributes that affect GPOs. For example, you might need to apply the Block Inheritance attribute to the OU. Blocking inheritance is useful when you want to store objects in your container and you want to give them different settings than those that are set globally.

> **NOTE** Use the Enforced and Block Inheritance attributes sparingly because they can greatly complicate your GPO management efforts.

That's it. Simple, isn't it? Yet, GPOs provide one of the most powerful management capabilities in Windows. Take the time to explore the various settings that are available in each GPO. Make sure that you use a Vista PC to run the GPEdit tool, otherwise you will not have access to all of Vista's GPO settings.

> **NOTE** A spreadsheet listing all of the new GPO settings in Vista can be found at `www.microsoft.com/downloads/details.aspx?FamilyID=41dc179b-3328-4350-ade1-c0d9289f09ef&DisplayLang=en`. Rely on this spreadsheet to document your own GPO changes.

It is easily possible to apply any number of GPOs to objects. It is also easy to become confused with GPOs. The organizational unit structure has a direct impact on how GPOs are applied. Rely on it to keep your GPO application structure straight.

Also, backup each of the GPOs you create each time you create or modify a GPO. Store the backups in a safe place. You'll need to rely on them to restore your policies in the event of a system breakdown.

Working with Windows Server 2008 Group Policies

In Windows Server 2008, Microsoft has added even more functionality to Group Policy. In addition to the standard division between computers and users, each section of a Group Policy Object now includes two subsections as shown in Figure 9.12. The first, Policy, contains the actual policy contents. This changes the path to all policy settings. For example, in previous versions of Windows, the path to Software Settings was Computer Configuration\Software Settings. In Windows Server 2008, the path is now Computer Configuration\Policy\Software Settings.

FIGURE 9.12

A Windows Server 2008 GPO

The reason for the change is the new second section of GPOs: Preferences. This section now controls specific client-side settings and can be used to reduce post-installation configuration tasks. Preferences includes two subsections: Windows Settings and Control Panel Settings. You use each to remotely configure system settings on any Windows XP Service Pack 2, Windows Server 2003 Service Pack 1, Windows Vista, or Windows Server 2008 machine.

NOTE   In order for Windows XP SP2, Windows Server 2003, and Vista to process the new Preferences section, they must all have updated client-side extensions. You need a specific update for each OS. Updates are detailed in Microsoft Knowledge Base article number 943729, which can be found at http://support.microsoft.com/kb/943729.

The contents of the Preferences section and the components you can control through it are described in Table 9.3. The big difference between Preferences and Policies is that users are allowed to reset the changes made to their computers through the Preferences section. Changes made by the Policies section are permanent unless modified centrally. However, using the Preferences section can often greatly reduce the need for logon scripts. Using the Preferences section is, after all, much easier than writing a Visual Basic or even a PowerShell script.

TABLE 9.3

The Preferences Section of a WS08 GPO

Preferences Subsection	Setting	Application
Windows Settings	Applications	Lets you configure multiple application-specific settings through custom plug-ins. For example, plug-ins for Microsoft Office are available at (http://go.microsoft.com/fwlink/?LinkId=90745). A Group Policy development kit is available at (http://go.microsoft.com/fwlink/?LinkId=144).
	Drive Maps	Create, modify, delete or hide dynamic drive mappings using the user's credentials or alternate credentials.
	Environment	Create, modify, or delete user or system environment variables. Variables can also be used as conditions for other preference settings.
	Files	Copy, modify, or delete a file on a system. Also modifies the attributes of a file.
	Folders	Copy, modify, or delete a folder on a system. Can rely on conditions. For example, you can delete a folder only if it is empty.
	INI Files	Add, replace, or delete settings in existing .ini or .inf files or even delete an entire .ini or .inf file.
	Network Shares	Create, modify, or delete a file share on a system. Can also modify user limits, Access-based Enumeration settings, or comments on a share.
	Registry	Create, replace, or delete entries in the registry. Can also copy multiple settings from one system and add them to other systems. Relies on a wizard to create multiple entries.
	Shortcuts	Create, modify, or delete a shortcut.
Control Panel Settings	Data Sources	Create, modify, or delete data sources.
	Devices	Enable or disable different device classes or specific hardware types on target systems. For example, can be used to control USB device classes.
	Folder Options	Configures folder options and file associations.
	Internet Settings (IE)	Configure IE settings. Supports IE 5, 6, and 7.
	Local Users and Groups	Control the contents of the local users and groups contained in member servers and PCs belonging to the domain.
	Network Options	Configure virtual private network (VPN) or dial-up networking connections.

continued

TABLE 9.3	*(continued)*	
Preferences Subsection	**Setting**	**Application**
	Power Options	Configure power settings on Windows XP or Windows Server 2003. To configure Power Options for Vista and WS08, use the Administrative Templates | System | Power Management section of either Computer or User Policy settings.
	Printers	Configure multiple printer connections for a system.
	Regional Options	Control regional options.
	Scheduled Tasks	Create, modify, or delete scheduled tasks. Can be used to run commands as soon as GPOs refresh, automate recurring tasks, wake computers from sleep mode, or even launch processes when users log on without requiring a script.
	Services	Modify the configuration of existing services.
	Start Menu	Control the structure and the options of the Start menu. Can also be used to add read-only sections of the Start menu while letting users control the read-write sections. Supports Start menu standardization.

Working with ADMX/ADML files

Despite the fact that Vista GPOs include up to 2450 settings, there is always one setting that you cannot find but want to control. This is done by using administrative templates. Administrative templates are structured text files which allow you to modify components in the system registry. These templates are imported into the GPO of your choice through GPEdit. In GPEdit, go to the settings you want to control: either computer or user, right-click on Administrative Templates in the Tree pane and select Add/Remove Templates. In the Add/Remove Templates dialog box, click the Add button. Navigate to the appropriate template, select it, and click Open. Close the Add/Remove Template dialog box when done.

Prior to Windows Vista, all GPO definition templates used an ADM file format — pure text files that were organized in a structured manner. With Vista, Microsoft introduces the ADMX format — a format based on the Extended Markup Language (XML), which provides much richer content for GPO templates. Note that ADMX templates no longer need to be imported into GPOs; they are automatically referenced when GPEdit is opened.

ADMX templates are now language independent, globalizing Group Policy settings. Each ADMX file is accompanied by one or more ADML files which include language-specific content. Global organizations will want to include an ADML file for each language their administrators work in. In addition, ADMX files can be centrally stored as opposed to the distributed approach used by ADM files — one on each domain controller in a particular AD domain. And, because of the increased number of policy settings in Vista, 132 ADMX files are included in the release version of Vista by default.

Because of the changes to Group Policy in Vista, the ADMX format is incompatible with the ADM format. Environments who manage a mix of Windows 2000 and/or XP with Vista need to either translate their existing templates to ADMX format or create new ones. Organizations that want to make sure critical settings are applied to all of their Windows clients need to put in place a strategy that supports the translation of ADM to ADMX and vice versa, but of course, only for the settings that apply to specific Windows versions. ADM and ADMX files can coexist together. End users and end machines will have no awareness as to whether the policy settings were configured from Vista or Windows 2000 or XP. However, it is a good idea to think about migrating your existing ADM files to ADMX format.

The location of administrative templates has also changed with Vista. In the earlier Windows versions, ADM files were located in the directory %WINDIR%\INF. Note that text-based ADM templates are still located in this folder. Now ADMX files are located in %WINDIR%\ PolicyDefinitions and the corresponding ADML files are placed in %WINDIR\ PolicyDefinitions\<LanguageFolder>.

 **NOTE** Microsoft licensed an ADM to ADMX conversion tool from FullArmor Corporation. This free utility is available at www.fullarmor.com/ADMX-download-options.htm.

In previous versions of Windows, each time a new ADM template was created it would be copied from the local system to the SYSVOL share on a domain controller. It would then be copied to every DC in the domain. This method was cumbersome and could lead to errors. If a user had an outdated ADM template on their system, it could overwrite the proper one. It was difficult to have an authoritative store for ADM templates.

In Vista, ADMX template files are obtained by default from the PC they are generated from. If you have multiple technicians working on ADMX templates, then it is a good idea to create a central ADMX file store that will be referenced each time someone needs to edit a GPO no matter which machine they use. The central store is usually created by a server administrator because it involves changes in a domain controller, something PC technicians often don't have access to. Follow these steps to create the central store:

1. **Log on with domain administrative rights**.

2. **Locate the PDC Emulator domain controller in your network.** The easiest way to do this is to open the Active Directory Users and Computers console and right-click on the domain name to choose Operations Masters, click on the PDC tab to find the name of the DC. Then use Explorer to navigate to its SYSVOL shared folder. You use the PDC Emulator because it is the engine which drives GPO changes in the network.

3. **Navigate to the SYSVOL\domainname\Policies folder where domainname is the DNS name of your domain.**

4. **Create a new folder called PolicyDefinitions.**

5. **Copy the contents of the C:\Windows\PolicyDefinitions from any Windows Vista PC to the new folder created in Step 4.**

6. **Include the appropriate ADML folders.** For example, U.S. English systems would use the en-US folder.

7. **Launch the Group Policy Editor.** From now on, it will automatically reference the new central store as will all editors on any Vista PC in your domain.

Make sure that you create this central store as soon as possible to help mitigate any potential versioning issues with your templates.

> **TIP** There is no Group Policy interface for loading ADMX files into a GPO. If you want to add new settings based on an ADMX file, create the ADMX file and copy it to your central store. It will appear in the Group Policy Object as soon as you reopen GPEdit. To learn more about creating ADMX files, go to http://technet2.microsoft.com/windowsserver2008/en/library/22f34dbd-1d72-4ddd-9b14-4ba8097827771033.mspx?mfr=true.

Assigning PC-Related GPOs

To create your own GPOs, you need to think through each one of the changes you want to apply to your systems. There are lots of different settings you can apply, but the most common are listed in Table 9.4. Remember that if you are using Windows Server 2008 domain controllers, you must use Policy in the path after either Computer Configuration or User Configuration.

TABLE 9.4

Recommended Computer Configuration Group Policy Object Settings

Setting	Application
Software Settings	Use this setting to deploy software in your organization. Deploy software to PCs (Computer Configuration section) instead of users. This automatically makes the software available to all users on a PC and makes it easier to manage. Multiple packages can be deployed in the same GPO.
Windows Settings	This section lets you control scripts, deploy printers, security settings, and Quality of Service (QoS) communications. Scripts are normally applied to users (User Configuration section). Printers are deployed to groups of users or groups of computers. Security settings are most often assigned in the Default Domain Policy so that they apply to all systems and user accounts. This section is in Chapter 11. QoS policies are defined mostly in environments that stream audio and video to PC endpoints.
Administrative Templates	Administrative templates let you control most of the settings in a GPO. You can set regional and language options, control user account behavior, control network and printer behavior, and work with both system and Windows components.

Setting	Application
Administrative Templates ⇨ Network ⇨ Offline Files	Offline files allow users to work on local copies of files that are normally stored on a server. Configure these settings to control the synchronization behavior between PCs and servers.
Administrative Templates ⇨ Network ⇨ Windows Connect Now	This section is useful for mobile workers because it controls the behavior of their system when a wireless connection is available.
Administrative Templates ⇨ Printers	Controls how Vista PCs interact with printers.
Administrative Templates ⇨ System	Controls items such as logon or logoff messages, as well as the locations of service pack and Windows Installer installation files.
Administrative Templates ⇨ System ⇨ Device Installation	Controls whether or not users can plug in USB storage devices. This is quite useful when you do not want users to walk away with confidential data. More on this will be covered in Chapter 11.
Administrative Templates ⇨ System ⇨ Driver Installation	Controls whether non-administrators can install specified device drivers or not. This is useful for mobile workers who need to add devices while on the road.
Administrative Templates ⇨ System ⇨ Folder Redirection	Controls the location (local versus remote) of user data folders such as Documents, Pictures, Videos, and more. Helps protect user data by moving it to centralized storage areas. More on this will be covered in Chapter 12.
Administrative Templates ⇨ System ⇨ Group Policy	Controls the general behavior of Group Policy.
Administrative Templates ⇨ System ⇨ Internet Communication	Controls any Vista activity that requires either use of the HTTP protocol or an Internet connection to function.
Administrative Templates, System, Locale Services	Allows you to automatically switch the PC's language to match a user's when they log in to Vista.
Administrative Templates ⇨ System ⇨ Logon or Net Logon	Control the local or network logon behavior of the system.
Administrative Templates ⇨ System ⇨ Power Management	Helps reduce the power consumption of PCs in your organization by putting them on stand-by when not in use.
Administrative Templates ⇨ System ⇨ Remote Assistance	Controls the behavior of the Remote Assistance tool built into Vista. This section will be discussed in Chapter 10.
Administrative Templates ⇨ System ⇨ Removable Storage Access	Controls whether or not users can rely on removable storage to access data. Use in environments that need to protect sensitive data. This item is covered in Chapter 11.
Administrative Templates ⇨ System ⇨ Scripts	Controls general script behavior such as timeouts and display settings.
Administrative Templates ⇨ System ⇨ Trusted Platform Module Services	Controls the Trusted Platform Module (TPM) that can be used in conjunction with BitLocker Full drive Encryption. Used in environments that are sensitive to laptop theft. More information will be covered in Chapter 12.

continued

TABLE 9.4	*(continued)*
Setting	**Application**
Administrative Templates ⇨ System ⇨ User Profiles	Controls how user profiles are managed in Vista. Should be reviewed to set all defaults for your organization.
Administrative Templates ⇨ Windows Components	Includes controls for over 50 Vista components from Movie Maker — something you probably don't need in your network — to the Task Scheduler and the Event Viewer. You should take the time to review each of the settings in this section and assign those you think are best for your organization.

> **NOTE** Most settings have default configurations even if they are listed as Not configured. Make sure you read the details of the Explanation before you change behavior that might already be set by default.

As you can see, GPOs can be quite granular and can control almost any aspect of a PC's behavior. Take the time to review all of these settings and then determine which ones should be set to meet your organization's security and system usage policies.

> **TIP** For additional guidance on deploying Group Policy with Vista go to http://technet2.microsoft.com/WindowsVista/en/library/5ae8da2a-878e-48db-a3c1-4be6ac7cf7631033.mspx?mfr=true. For best practices guidance, go to http://technet2.microsoft.com/windowsserver/en/library/6ffcfdc1-d5de-49cd-a531-79ffea50e4431033.mspx?mfr=true.

Troubleshooting and monitoring Group Policy

GPO issues arise most often when too many technicians have access to the ability to create GPOs and they proliferate GPOs at all levels of the directory. It gets even worse when these technicians do not document the GPOs they create. The first step you should take to reduce GPO issues is to limit who has control of GPOs and make sure they always document their changes.

> **NOTE** For organizations that want tighter control over their policies, Microsoft offers Advanced Group Policy Management (AGPM), a tool that is designed to provide change management on all GPOs. The AGPM is available through the Microsoft Desktop Optimization Pack for Software Assurance. More information can be found at http://download.microsoft.com/download/6/4/f/64f5dc66-832a-4df3-baf4-3b4e7fb9e500/Datasheet%20-%20AGPM.pdf.

If you do run into issues anyway, you can rely on two tools to resolve them. Both are found in the GPMC. RSoP allows you to identify the resultant settings on an object that might have several GPOs applied to it. Modeling lets you perform "what if" scenarios to see how changes might affect objects.

Troubleshooting GPOS

If a computer or user account is behaving oddly, then perform an RSoP test on the object. Use the following procedure to do so:

1. Go to Start Menu, Search and then type GMPC.MSC and press Enter. Accept the UAC prompt.

2. After the GPMC is launched, expand the Forest to view all subitems in the Tree pane.

3. Right-click on Group Policy Results and select Group Policy Results Wizard. Click Next.

4. Select which computer you want to test the policy on. If you are troubleshooting a policy for a user, select the user's main computer. Click Another computer and click Browse. Type the computer name and click Check Names. Click OK.

5. If you are testing for a user account only, select the Do not display policy settings for the selected computer in the results. Otherwise, click Next.

6. Identify the user account for which you want to test settings. Click Next.

7. If you only want computer settings, then select Do not display user policy settings in the results, otherwise, click Next.

8. Review your selections. Click Back to change settings. Click Next when ready.

9. Click Finish once the results are generated.

10. Name the Report and review its contents. Repair any untoward setting assignment.

Reports include several items as shown in Figure 9.13. The Details pane includes three tabs. The first, Summary, provides a summary of all settings. The second, Settings, provides a list of the actual settings that are applied to the object. The third, Policy Events, lists all of the events that have occurred on the system in relation to Group Policy application. Each provides valuable information in the troubleshooting of GPO application.

FIGURE 9.13

Troubleshooting resultant set of policies

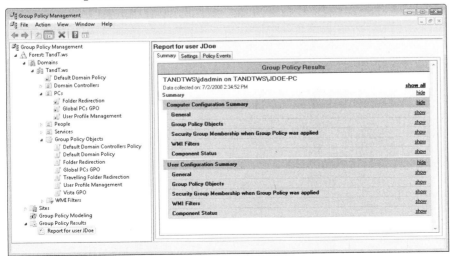

> **CAUTION** Be very careful when moving objects in the directory. Objects are located in specific containers because they are managed from that particular container. When you move an object, it will automatically change its management scope and will now receive the GPO settings that are applied to the new location. If a user or computer system is facing GPO issues, begin by identifying if the object was recently moved in the directory. Use the change tracking feature outlined later in this chapter to find out how.

Performing what-if scenarios

What-if scenarios are also quite useful when troubleshooting GPOs. They let you identify what would happen if an object were moved or if a new GPO setting were applied. They are similar to RSoP but instead of detailing the actual results, they detail potential results.

Follow these steps to perform a what-if scenario:

1. **Choose Start Menu, ⇨ Search,** type GMPC.MSC, **and press Enter. Accept the UAC prompt.**

2. **After the GPMC is launched, expand the Forest to view all subitems in the Tree pane.**

3. **Right-click on Group Policy Modeling and select Group Policy Modeling Wizard. Click Next.**

4. **Select the domain controller to perform the modeling and click Next.** Note that you should not perform this first thing in the morning as users log on to the network because it affects the domain controller's performance.

5. **Select either the container or the object.** To simulate for users in a container, select the OU by using the Browse button. Do the same for computers in a container. For individual simulations, select the actual object, computer, or user. Click Next.

6. **Identify that you want to test for Slow network connections or Loopback processing. Also identify the Site if you need to. Click Next when done.**

7. **Select the security user group used to filter the policy.** In most cases, this is the Authenticated Users group. Click Next when ready. Repeat for the security computer group.

8. **Select the applicable WMI filter for users if required. Click Next when ready. Repeat for computer WMI filters.**

9. **Review your selections. Click Back to change settings. Click Next when ready. Click Finish once the results are generated.**

10. **Name the Report and review its contents.**

Note that the resulting report is very similar to the RSoP report. One significant difference is the last tab in the Details pane. It includes the contents of the query you generated instead of the events related to GPO processing. Use these two tools to troubleshoot and repair policy settings in your network.

Tracking Change in Vista

Managing change in any network is a daunting task. You have to really know what is happening to be able to understand how your network evolves with use. In Windows, the best way to find out what is going on is to audit all system and user activity. The only way to do this is to use a two-part approach. First, you must create an audit policy. Second, you have to indicate which objects and which users you want to audit.

Turning on the audit policy

You need to turn on the audit policy. Do this by using either the Local Security Policy or through central Group Policy. Use the Local Security Policy if you want to audit a single computer or if it is part of a workgroup. If you have more than one system, then use Group Policy. That's because it provides centralized policy deployment to multiple systems — create the policy once and deploy it to any number of systems.

Despite the fact that Vista now brings 800 new settings to Group Policy management, the audit policies have not changed. Vista allows you to audit nine different types of events just as you could in Windows XP and Windows Server 2003, as shown in Figure 9.14. Whether you use Group Policy or the LSP, you need to turn on each of the events you want to monitor. Use the following process:

FIGURE 9.14

Modifying the Audit Policy

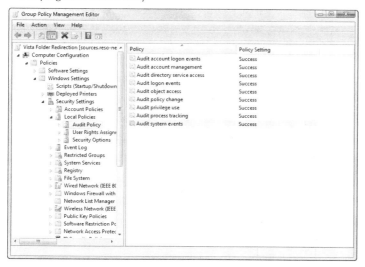

1. Click Start Menu, Search, type GMPC.MSC, and press Enter. Accept the UAC prompt.

2. After the GPMC is launched, expand the Forest to view all subitems in the Tree pane. Navigate to the Default Domain Policy, right-click on it, and select Edit. The Default Domain Policy is used because it applies to every system in the network.

3. In GPEdit, choose Computer Configuration ➪ Windows Settings ➪ Security Settings ➪ Local Policies ➪ Audit Policy.

4. Double-click each setting to modify it.

Modify the settings as appropriate. To learn more about each setting, click on the Explain tab in the setting's dialog box.

Preparing the policy, local or central, is only the first part of the auditing process. The second step is to change the security descriptor of the items you want to audit. For example, to audit file access on a given shared folder, you need to:

1. Right-click the shared folder and select Properties.

2. Select the Security tab, click the Advanced Security button, and move to the Audit tab.

3. Select whom you want to audit.

Fortunately, you can use groups to monitor the activities of all the users in your organization, which makes it simpler to assign. You must repeat this activity on each server or workstation you want to monitor and for each object you need to watch.

Audited events are recorded in the Security Event Log and can be seen through the Event Viewer. Because events are recorded locally on each system that is affected, you need to visit each and every system to obtain a global picture of events on your network. Doing this is a bit tedious if you don't have an event collection mechanism — or a system that automatically collects key events and forwards them to a central location. Fortunately, Vista can also collect events.

Vista's Event Log can now automatically act on events and send them to a central location, which can be another Vista system or a server running Windows Server 2008. In addition, you'll soon discover that the Event Log now records a host of events that were unheard of in previous versions of Windows.

In these previous versions, Microsoft used a number of different mechanisms to record events. Many products and subfeatures of Windows recorded information in their own logs as if they didn't even know the Event Log existed. It's no wonder that most administrators didn't even bother to verify any logs unless an untoward event occurred and they were spurred on by others: security officers, for example. It was just too much work. With Vista, most of these tools now record events properly and store them into the Event Log. This is bound to make your life easier, but of course, only when all your systems have been upgraded to Vista.

Exploring the Vista Event Log

For Windows Vista, Microsoft scrapped all of its previous Windows code and started from scratch to rewrite the whole thing. With all the security issues Windows had been facing in the past few years, rewriting the code with security in mind was a must. But this approach also provides added benefits. For example, when Microsoft programmers were working on the Vista Event Log, not only did they rewrite the code, but they also took advantage of the opportunity to give it a complete overhaul. The new Vista Event Log sports a new interface and a significant number of new event categories making it much more useful than ever before. It now includes the following new features:

- New Event Viewer Interface
- New Event Categories
- New Event Filters
- New Event Language: XML
- New Event command line tool

The Event Viewer interface

The first thing you'll notice when you launch the Event Viewer in Windows Vista is the new look and feel. When you first open it, the Event Viewer presents its summary view. The new Event Viewer lays out its contents into three panes, as shown in Figure 9.15, because it is based on the Microsoft Management Console version 3.0. The left pane is still the tree view which will be familiar to most Windows technicians. It includes several nodes: Custom Views, Windows Logs, Applications and Services Logs, and Subscriptions. The center pane is as it was before: the details pane. When the focus is on the Event Viewer node, you see a summary view which lists all events according to importance as well as audited events. Finally, the right pane lists actions you can perform. Like context menus, the contents of this action pane will change with the views you select.

When you change views, for example, when you focus on a specific log and view the events it contains, the details pane becomes your Event Viewer, showing the actual contents of events without having to open each event and having to juggle windows to try to see event listings at the same time as you see event details as shown in Figure 9.16. This makes it much easier to work with events.

FIGURE 9.15

Summary view of the Event Log

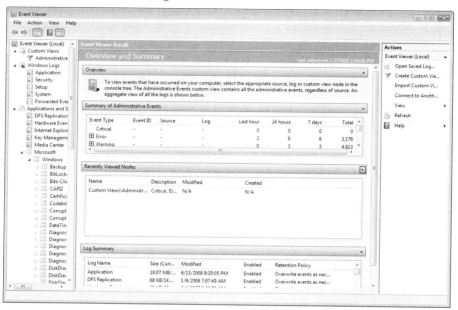

FIGURE 9.16

View the details of an event

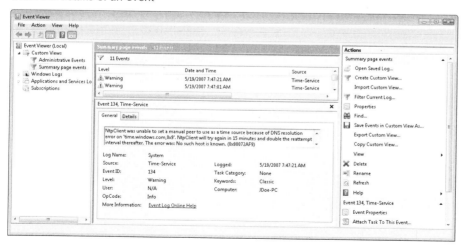

New event categories

Another major improvement of the Event Log is that it is now designed to collect every single event on the system. Although previous versions of Windows stored event information in different locations — databases, flat files, event logs — Vista now stores all events in the Event Log. Therefore, it now includes a whole series of new event categories. These are located under the Applications and Services Logs node in the tree pane. Perhaps the most important change is in the Microsoft sub-node. This sub-node now includes 53 different categories under the Windows sub-node. Each category is focused on a specific service within Windows — BitLocker, Event Collector, Group Policy, User Access Control, and much more. Subcategories are listed for each — administrative, operational, analytic and so on — making it very easy to drill down deep into any issue.

In addition, each application that is Vista-ready will store its events inside this event category. Windows includes its own — Distributed File System (DFS) Replication, Hardware Events, Internet Explorer, Key Management Service, and Media Center. Third-party applications also store their events here. This proves that the Event Log is now the one and only store for events in Vista.

New event filters

In addition, in the Custom Views node under the tree pane, you see that Vista already includes a custom view: the Administrative Events view. This view is based on a filter as shown in Figure 9.17 and is used to automatically collect events that are of interest to system administrators, saving you from having to generate your own filters. Because this is a default view, this filter is read-only, but you have full flexibility to create other filters based on any event attribute.

FIGURE 9.17

Details of the Administrative Events filter

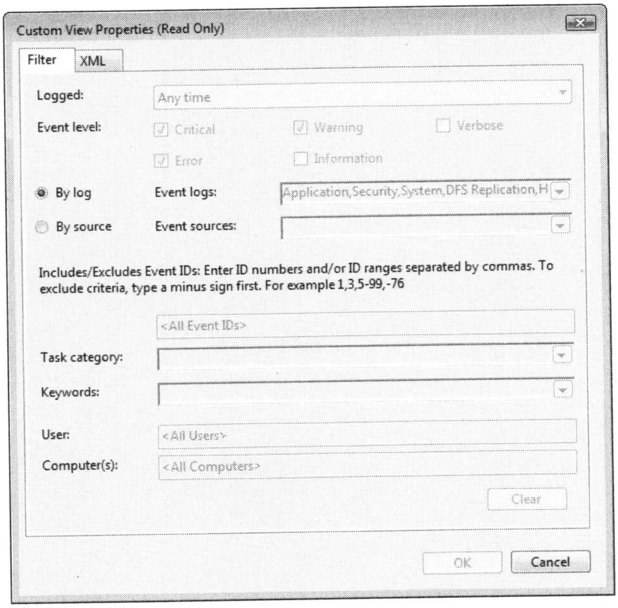

The filters can be based on a whole series of attributes. Logged time is one of the first attributes you can focus on with six predefined time periods and the ability to create your own custom time period. Event level is next, letting you select critical, errors, warning, verbose, or information events. Then, you can filter either by log or by source. By log gives you a tree pane that lets you check the logs you need. Source lets you select any potential event source. Finally, you can filter by event ID, tasks that may be associated with the event, keywords contained inside the event, user, and computer generating the event.

New event language: XML

Filtering is now so powerful because Vista events are now completely structured, using an Extended Markup Language (XML) structure. Previous versions of Windows provided some structure for event reporting, but it was mostly only evident to programmers using the Win32 application programming interface. With Vista, everything changes because they rely on XML with a published schema as shown in Figure 9.18. Each event now includes an XML description, which makes filtering out events (that might be considered garbage) much easier and lets you focus on the events that are of interest to you. This filtering strategy will go a long way toward making it easier to audit change and manage systems running Windows Vista.

FIGURE 9.18

The XML details of an event

New event command line

For those who love the command line, you won't be disappointed with the new Event Log. Vista includes a new command that is designed to let you manage and administer events in character mode:

```
wevtutil.exe
```

Wevtutil, for Windows Event Utility, includes a whole series of functions and switches, all aimed at event management. For example, you can find out all of the publishers who are registered on a system. That's because with the new Event Log, publishers must register themselves on the system. Wevtutil lists not only publishers but also their configuration on the system and all of the events they might log on a system. Nobody can hide from administrators anymore!

Wevtutil will also let you install or uninstall event manifests, run queries against events, export and archive logs as well as clear them, all from the command line. If you're into the command line, then take the time to explore this powerful new tool.

As you can see, the Event Viewer is considerably different from previous versions of Windows, even at just the interface level. But that's not all. With Vista, you can integrate events with tasks, you can automate tasks based on events, and you can forward key events to central locations.

Exploring the Vista Task Scheduler

Event management includes close ties to system automation because you often need to generate automatic actions when specific events occur. For example, one of the most common tasks that is related to events is the automatic deletion of temporary files when disk drives get too full. Or in another scenario, you may require an automatic notification when unauthorized users try to log on to workstations that contain access to highly sensitive or confidential information.

In order to automate either notifications or tasks, you need to rely on the Task Scheduler. In Vista, the Task Scheduler has become much more of a real job scheduler. Like the Event Viewer and the Event Log system, the Task Scheduler has been completely rewritten and now offers several enhancements over the Task Scheduler found in previous versions of Windows. For one thing, the Task Scheduler now maintains a complete library of all scheduled tasks, all categorized according to source. In addition, like the Event Viewer, the Task Scheduler profits from a new interface based on the Microsoft Management Console (MMC) version 3.0 as shown in Figure 9.19.

FIGURE 9.19

The new Task Scheduler interface

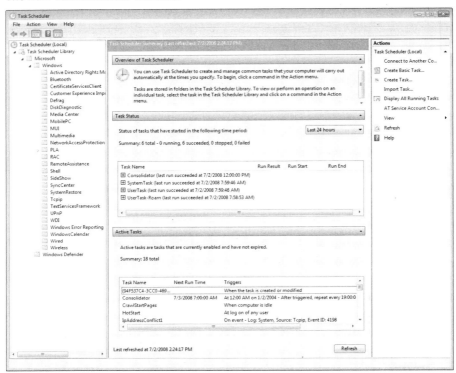

As with all MMC version 3 interfaces, this one sports three panes — moving from left to right, the first is the Tree pane, the second is the Details pane and the third is the Action pane. As you can see, the main Task Scheduler details pane displays task summaries, task status, and active tasks, giving you ready access to any task information.

Tasks in Vista are based on two main components:

■ Launch conditions which can include up to three components:
  ▪ Triggers which are the elements which actually start a task
  ▪ Conditions which outline when and how the task can run
  ▪ Settings which outline the options for a task
■ Actions which tell a task what to do

So far, this isn't very different than previous task automation features found in other versions of Windows, but Vista's Task Scheduler is a far cry from the Windows NT AT command. Previous versions of Windows had serious drawbacks when it came to system automation. In Vista, all of these situations have been corrected.

Vista now includes a whole series of new triggers — events; machine status such as idle, startup, logon, and so on; session state changes such as opening or closing of Terminal Services sessions, or lock or unlocking of sessions; or even the more conventional time-based task startups. Tasks can even use other tasks as triggers, letting you create new, conditional, or chained tasks and then, once the task has been initiated, have it repeat regularly or in other situations, add delays or other limits to a task. In addition, tasks can run on universal time so that global organizations can create tasks in one time zone and ensure they run properly in any time zone.

Each task can include more than one trigger ensuring the task will run if any of the launch elements occur. Along with triggers, tasks include conditions that determine how the task will behave as can be seen in Figure 9.20. Conditions control if the task should run while the system is idle, if the task should run while the system is on battery power, if the system should be booted up to run the task should it be turned off, or even if the system should be linked to a network for the task to run.

Settings control whether the task can be run manually, what should happen if the system was turned off when the task start time occurred, what to do if the task does not complete or fails or even runs too long. Settings can also apply rules to a task. These rules can include what to do if the start time occurs and an instance of the task is already running, or even delete the task once it has run.

FIGURE 9.20

Setting task conditions

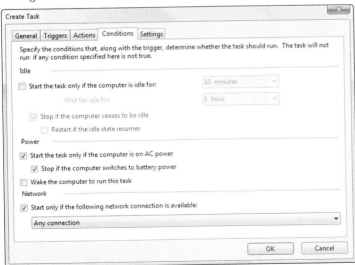

Actions can be any number of items including running a program, sending an e-mail, or simply displaying a message. This makes the Task Scheduler very powerful indeed since you could automatically display a warning message to users whenever they try to access protected areas of their system. This makes a strong case for running locked-down systems, and the Task Scheduler gives you the tools you need to make sure the systems stay locked down and users curb their habits.

Of course, actions can also be more traditional and actually run programs. This is after all what the Task Scheduler was originally designed to do. And sending messages is also quite useful because administrators can receive notifications when tasks occur. For example, if you want to make sure that a critical task was performed on a system, then create a conditional task that sends an e-mail after the other task completes. Doing this saves you from having to verify task logs after the task was scheduled to run.

Vista even hides tasks and otherwise controls which credentials should be used when a task is run. In most cases, credentials are not stored in the task so you can change account passwords centrally without having to worry about all tasks failing. In some scenarios, though, credentials are stored in the secure Credential Manager store. In these cases, you still need to modify passwords locally but not in the task.

You can also use the Task Scheduler to create tasks either for Vista systems or for down-level versions of Windows. Tasks can be exported in XML format and reimported to any other system. This makes it very easy to generate tasks on one system and ensure that they run on all the systems in organizations of all sizes.

Finally, each task includes a history of operation, listing all of the events that indicate when the task was run and for how long. This feature makes monitoring tasks and making sure they run when expected very easy.

Tasks can be created in one of three ways. The first lets you create a basic task and runs you through a wizard that takes you through each step required to build the task. Advanced tasks are created by using the Create Task command that can be found either in the Context menu or in the Action pane. Create Task opens the Task dialog box and gives you access to each of the elements that make up a task. Finally, you can create and manage tasks through the command line through an updated "schtasks.exe" command. This command lets you script operations, such as importing tasks on different systems.

Overall, the Task Scheduler is a much more powerful engine for task management and automation on Vista, and when it is linked to the Event Log, Task Scheduler becomes a very strong engine for proactive systems management.

Automating Vista Events

When you manage events, you often wish you could generate automatic actions when specific events occur. For example, it would be nice if you could automatically delete temporary files and send a notification to desktop technicians when PC disk drives get too full. Or, it would be nice if you could receive automatic notification when unauthorized users try to log on to workstations that contain access to highly sensitive or confidential information. Or even better, display a message telling users they are trying to access unauthorized systems and then send an e-mail to appropriate authorities. All of these things are now possible in Windows Vista.

Linking events to automated tasks is a very straightforward process. It can be done in one of three ways:

- Through the Task Scheduler
- Through the Event Viewer
- Through the command line

When you create either a basic or an advanced task in the Task Scheduler, you can select an event as the trigger for the task. Use the following procedure:

1. **Create a new task from the Action menu. Choose Action ⇨ Create Task.**

2. **Name the task and set the credentials under which the task will run.**

3. **Move to the Trigger tab and click** New. Select **On an event** as the task trigger from the drop-down list.

4. **Choose either Basic or Custom as the event setting.**
   - Basic settings let you select which Event Log will be the source of the event, then which event source and finally, which event ID to look for.
   - Custom settings let you create an Event Filter, letting you determine exactly how the task should be launched based on a series of filtered conditions.

5. **Then continue adding the task properties such as conditions, actions, and settings.**

It gets even better when you generate the task from the Event Viewer. Here you repeat much the same process, except that the task is generated from the event itself instead of the other way around.

When you create an automated task from the Event Viewer, use the following procedure:

1. **Locate the event to which you want to attach the task.** You can either drill down to the event or create a filter to locate the event.

2. **Right-click on the event to select Attach Task To This Event or use the Action pane to click on the same command.** This option automatically launches the Basic Task wizard.

3. **Run through the wizard's panes to generate the task.**

The advantage of using this method to create the task is that it automatically fills in all of the information required to generate the trigger from the event. The disadvantage is that you can only create a basic task using this method. Of course, after the task is created, you can go to the Task Scheduler to add features and properties to the task, but this requires more steps to do so.

The last method is to use the command line to link a task to an event. To do so, you need the following values:

- The Event Log from which the event is generated
- The source of the event
- The event ID

These values can be obtained either through the Event Viewer or through the wevtutil.exe command by using the proper switches. For example, you might use:

```
wevtutil qe Security /c:n /rd:true /f:text
```

This command would query the Security Event Log to obtain the latest events by reversing the list of events /rd:true and displaying then in text format /f:text as opposed to the default XML format. In this command line, the value for *n* should be a number indicating how many events you want returned by the command.

Then, after you have the values you need, you can use the Task Scheduler command to generate the task. For example, you might use:

```
schtasks /create /TN taskname /TR action /SC ONEVENT /EC System /
    MO *[System/EventID=IDnumber]
```

Where "taskname" is the name you want to assign to the task, "action" is the action to perform or command to execute, and "IDnumber" is the ID number of the event, which will act as a trigger for the task.

In this example, the source Event Log is the System log. The task schedule is based on the occurrence of the event and is modified to identify the event ID.

As you can see, the combination of the Event Log with the Task Scheduler opens the door for several system management activities. And, because Vista offers a much more detailed and rich event management structure, the possibilities are endless. Tasks can be generated on one machine and exported in XML format to be imported to any other system.

Collecting Vista Events

Windows Vista includes an updated implementation of Microsoft's remote management infrastructure: Windows Remote Management (WinRM). The Vista Event Log uses WinRM along with the Windows Event Collector service as the engines for collecting events from remote machines and sending them to a central event collector system. This feature makes it very easy to troubleshoot problems or otherwise be aware of the type of events that occur on multiple systems because you only need to look at the collector system to review all events.

WinRM relies on WS-Management or Web Services Management, which is a special protocol that integrates a series of operations within a Web services architecture. This architecture is an industry standard that allows organizations to perform management operations over commonly used TCP/IP protocols such as the HyperText Transfer Protocol (HTTP) or secure HTTP (HTTPS). The advantage of WS-Management is that the common protocols on which it relies are often open in firewalls for other purposes. Therefore, you can manage remote systems without turning your firewall into Swiss cheese. This Vista feature is very valuable.

Several tasks must be completed to prepare systems for event collection:

- Each system that will forward events must be running one service: WinRM.
- Each system that will receive events must be running two services: WinRM and the Windows Event Collector. These services are set to manual by default.
- WinRM must be configured on both the forwarding computers and the collector computer.
- The Windows Event Collector service must be configured on the collector system.
- Access rights must be granted to the collector system on each of the forwarding computers.
- Then, after each of the above steps is performed, you can move to the creation of an event subscription.

Of course, elevated rights are required to perform the operation. Remember that because of User Account Control (UAC), all users, even administrative users, run with a standard user token. Therefore, you must make sure you use elevated rights when running these commands.

If you are working with machines that are part of an Active Directory (AD), then use the following procedure:

1. **Log on to the source computer or the computer that will forward events.**
2. **Right-click on the Command Prompt and select Run as Administrator. Provide appropriate credentials, usually domain credentials that have local administrative privileges.**
3. **Using the newly elevated command prompt, type the following command:**
   ```
   winrm quickconfig
   ```
4. **Then, press the Y key followed with Enter to make the changes.**

This command sets up the source system to accept WS-Management requests from other computers. In fact, this will set the WinRM service to delayed autostart, start the service, create a WinRM listener on HTTP, and enable WinRM exceptions in the Windows Firewall as shown in Figure 9.21.

FIGURE 9.21

Using the WinRM Quick Configuration Command

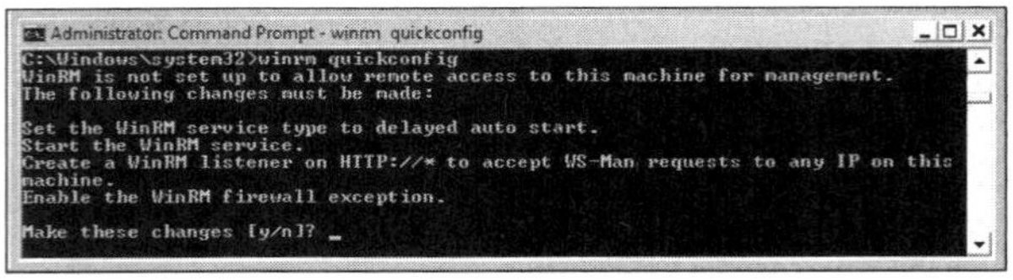

Next, you need to add the collector computer's account to the local Administrator's group. There are two ways to do this. Either add the collector computer account by itself to the Administrator's group or create a new group in AD, add the computer account to this group, and then add this group to the local Administrator's account. The second method is the preferred method since it will allow you to add more collector systems in the long run simply by adding them to the group in AD. Here's how:

1. **Open AD Users & Computers with a Run as Administrator command and apply the appropriate credentials for administrative rights in AD.**

2. **Locate the appropriate organizational unit (OU) and if one is not available, create one.** This OU should be designed to contain computer groups.

3. **Create a new security group. Name it Event Collection Systems.**

4. **Add the computer account of the collection system to this group.**

5. **Use Computer Management, under Local Users & Groups to add the Event Collection Systems group to the local Administrator's group.**

6. **Repeat Steps 1 to 4 on each source system.**

7. **Move to the collection system. Repeat the WinRM command used in Step 3.** Doing this allows you to control bandwidth usage or latency of the event forwarding process.

8. **Next, using the same elevated command prompt, run the following command:**
   `wecutil qc`

9. **Press** Y **followed with Enter to make the changes.** This configures the Windows Event Collector service to delayed autostart and start the service.

Now you're ready to prepare your first subscription.

1. **Open the Event Viewer by using Run as Administrator and provide the proper credentials.**

2. **Go to the Subscriptions item in the Tree pane.**

3. **Right-click on the Subscriptions item to choose Create Subscription You can also use the command in the Action pane.**

4. **Name your collection and provide a description.**

5. **Identify the destination log. By default, all collected events go to the ForwardedEvents log.**

6. **Click the Add button to select computers from AD. Add all the computers you want to collect events from. You can also use the Test button to verify that communication works between the forwarders and the collector.**

7. **Click Select Events to identify which events to collect.** This step launches the Query Filter dialog box. Set the options to collect the events you need or use an existing filter.

8. **Click the Advanced button.** This step opens the Advanced Subscriptions Settings dialog box. This dialog box allows you to control three settings:

   - **The account used for collection:** Leave this as is since the machine account is often best to use.

   - **Event Delivery Optimization lets you either control bandwidth used or increase the bandwidth used to ensure prompt delivery of the events:** The Normal mode is a pull mode — the collector pulls events from forwarders. The other two modes are push modes — the events are pushed from the forwarders or source systems to the collector. If latency is not an issue, then select Minimize Bandwidth.

   - **The protocol to use — HTTP or HTTPS:** If events are forwarded in your network, then HTTP is probably fine, but if events have to go over open connections or if they contain sensitive data, then use HTTPS. This will encrypt all data between forwarders and collectors, but additional configuration will be required.

9. **Click OK when done to finish the preparation of the collection.** If they exist on the source computers, selected events will begin accumulating almost immediately.

If you choose to configure HTTPS as the transport protocol, you will need to enable port 443 in the Windows Firewall. Pull or Normal subscriptions only need this setting on the source computers. Push subscriptions need this port enabled on both forwarders and collectors.

If you do not have an Active Directory and are working in a workgroup, you need to be aware of some limitations and special configuration requirements.

- Workgroup subscriptions only work in pull or normal mode.

- Windows Firewall exceptions for Remote Event Log Management must be enabled on each system.

- Because computer accounts do not trust each other in workgroups, you must create a special account on each system. Use the same account name and password on each system.

- You must also tell the collector system to trust each source computer. Once again, this is done through the WinRM command.

There you have it. Central event management through Windows Vista. You can now track the changes you manage through Group Policy.

Summary

Microsoft has significantly changed the change management process in Windows Vista. With the Local Security Policy, multiple LSPs, and centralized Group Policy, you can manage the behavior of any computer in your network or even that of any user. These tools provide a powerful engine for change management. In addition, you can determine exactly which changes will affect an object through the troubleshooting techniques provided by the best tool for Group Policy control: the Group Policy Management Console. But, because Group Policy is deployed through the structure of your Active Directory, you need to work with appropriate administrative authorities to make sure that this structure reflects what you need and what you want for your organization.

After your GPO strategy is set, you can begin to track changes in your network. You do this by relying on the Event Log along with the Task Scheduler to first discover which changes are occurring and then control what happens when certain events occur on a system. And, along with the new capabilities of these two tools, you can centrally collect events on one single system, making it much easier for an administrator to know what is going on in the network. For PC administrators, these changes are a boon. Make sure you take full advantage of these new features to help reduce your administrative workload.

Chapter 10

Administering Workstations

PCs are usually quite reliable. In fact, the best PC is the PC that just runs and runs without any major maintenance requirements. Many PC technicians dream of finally obtaining an operating system that will vastly reduce their workload by proving to be reliable and providing constant operation. Unfortunately, as most technicians know, this is rarely the case.

When issues arise, you need to have ready access to the tools of your trade so that you can mitigate the downtime that a broken PC can cause. With the arrival of Windows Vista, Microsoft once again endeavors to create an operating system that will provide a sound foundation for productivity workloads. It has achieved this goal to some degree, but despite it's best efforts, there will always be issues with PCs — be it a problem with the system's hardware, a problem caused by an application, a problem caused by misconfiguration, or even a problem caused by an inattentive end user.

Ideally, you can implement some form of proactive administration and then rely heavily on automation to ensure that the most common issues are dealt with even before you need to be alerted to a problem. But, in order to establish this proactive administration schedule, you need to be aware of the administration capabilities in Vista for both local and remote computers. You also need to build the appropriate toolkit. To do so, you need to investigate several different aspects of computer administration. These include:

- Identifying available workstation administration tools
- Identifying common administration tasks
- Learning to work on local PCs
- Learning to work on remote PCs

IN THIS CHAPTER

Performing local PC administration

Identifying common administration tasks

Performing remote PC administration

Automating recurrent tasks

Helping users with via remote assistance

Relying on the remote desktop

- Understanding tools that support remote PC administration

- Learning how to automate tasks either through the command line or through the downloadable Windows PowerShell interface

- Learning how to support users remotely in Windows Vista

Each of these elements helps you build your administrative toolkit and ensures that when issues do arise, you'll be ready to address them to the best of your ability. After all, even though you as a technician spend a lot of time tinkering with PCs running Windows Vista, it isn't and it shouldn't be the type of activity other personnel in your organization should perform. Their primary role is to perform work in support of the business your organization is in. And, to do that, they need functioning computers. That's where you come in.

Performing Local PC Administration

You've already seen how you can centrally manage change on Vista PCs and then, how you can track the changes that occur on each system. When configured properly, these tools reduce the administrative workload. But instances occur in which you need to interact directly with a PC to make sure it is working properly. When you do so, you need to know which tool is required when and how to get to it fast so that issues are resolved as soon as possible.

NOTE When issues arise on PCs, you need to determine the extent of the issue and then, determine whether you need to fix it or use another tactic to restore the PC to a functioning state. For example, if a system becomes corrupted and you estimate that it will take more than one hour to fix, then perhaps you should consider rebuilding the PC from scratch instead. Windows Vista offers significant improvements in deployment capabilities, and in some shops, it takes less than 30 minutes to rebuild a PC from the ground up. If this is the case in your shop, then keep this in mind when troubleshooting PC issues. If it takes less time to rebuild the system than it does to repair it, then rebuild it. Your users will be back to work a lot quicker and you won't be wasting your time.

The best place to start is with a list of the tools Windows Vista includes for administration purposes. Tools can be found in a series of different places on the system; therefore, it is important that you build your own desktop to facilitate systems management. Then, after you're aware of the various tools you have access to, you can begin to examine the most common administration tasks you'll need to deal with.

Working with workstation administration tools

Vista includes several enhanced tools for administration. You've already worked with several of them as you deployed your systems and created your change management and tracking strategy. Others will let you control each and every aspect of the Vista system. Table 10.1 lists the various tools you can use and where you can find them. Note that this table focuses on the tasks PC technicians need to perform.

Also, remember that for each of these tools, you must rely on the Run As Administrator command available from the context menu. This elevates the privilege of the tool and lets you perform all administrative tasks.

TABLE 10.1

Windows Vista Administration Tools

Tool	Purpose	Location	Obtain From
Active Directory Users and Computers	Use this console to create OU structures and pre-populate objects, such as computer and user accounts. Also useful to reset user passwords.	Start Menu ⇨ Administrative Tools ⇨ Active Directory Users and Computers Start Menu ⇨ Run ⇨ dsa.msc	Installed from Windows Server 2003 (WS03) Administration Kit
Backup and Restore Center	Use this console to protect both data and full system settings.	Start Menu ⇨ All Programs ⇨ Maintenance ⇨ Backup and Restore Center Control Panel ⇨ System and Maintenance ⇨ Backup and Restore Center Command Line ⇨ wbadmin.exe	Installed during Windows setup
Backup Status and Configuration	Use to determine backup status and configure backups.	Start Menu ⇨ All Programs ⇨ Accessories ⇨ System Tools ⇨ Backup Status and Configuration Start Menu ⇨ Run ⇨ sdclt.exe	Installed during Windows setup
BitLocker Full Drive Encryption	Use to protect a system's information by encrypting the system drive along with all other data drives.	Start Menu ⇨ Administrative Tools ⇨ BitLocker Full drive Encryption	Installed after Windows Setup but must be taken into consideration at installation because it requires a separate partition
Command Prompt	Use to perform operations without a graphical user interface. Useful for automating operations.	Start Menu ⇨ All Programs ⇨ Accessories ⇨ Command Prompt Start Menu ⇨ Run ⇨ cmd.exe	Installed during Windows setup

continued

TABLE 10.1	(continued)		
Tool	**Purpose**	**Location**	**Obtain From**
Computer	Use to view disk drives and other hardware attached to the computer through the Windows Explorer.	Start Menu ⇨ All Programs ⇨ Accessories ⇨ System Tools ⇨ Computer Start Menu ⇨ right-click on Computer ⇨ Explore	Installed during Windows setup
Computer Management	Use this console to access most system settings. Includes access to local users and groups, services, events, disk management, and more. Most useful console on the system.	Start Menu ⇨ Administrative Tools ⇨ Computer Management Start Menu ⇨ right-click on Computer ⇨ Manage Start Menu ⇨ Run ⇨ compmgmt.msc	Installed during Windows setup
Control Panel	Use this central panel to configure Windows Vista elements.	Start Menu ⇨ Control Panel Start Menu ⇨ All Programs ⇨ Accessories ⇨ System Tools ⇨ Control Panel	Installed during Windows setup
Data Sources (ODBC)	Use this console to manage data source connections for applications.	Start Menu ⇨ Administrative Tools ⇨ Data Sources (ODBC) Start Menu ⇨ Run ⇨ odbcad32.exe	Installed during Windows setup
Default Programs	Use to control which programs are launched at startup.	Control Panel ⇨ Programs ⇨ Default Programs	Installed during Windows setup
Device Manager	Use to control device drivers and general status of devices on a system.	Control Panel ⇨ System and Maintenance ⇨ System ⇨ Device Manager Also found in Computer Management	Installed during Windows setup
Disk Cleanup	Use to clean up temporary and other unnecessary files when disk drives are low in space.	Start Menu ⇨ All Programs ⇨ Accessories ⇨ System Tools ⇨ Disk Cleanup Start Menu ⇨ Run ⇨ cleanmgr.exe	Installed during Windows setup
Disk Defragmenter	Use to restructure disk data to improve file access and overall computer speed.	Start Menu ⇨ All Programs ⇨ Accessories ⇨ System Tools ⇨ Disk Defragmenter Start Menu ⇨ Run ⇨ dfrgui.exe	Installed during Windows setup

Tool	Purpose	Location	Obtain From
DNS Resolver	Use to troubleshoot Domain Name System (DNS) issues.	Start Menu ⇨ Run ⇨ dnsdiag.exe	Download from the Windows Server 2003 Resource Kit Tools
Event Viewer	Use this MMC snap-in to view logged events, such as errors and warnings.	Start Menu ⇨ Administrative Tools ⇨ Event Viewer Start Menu ⇨ Run ⇨ eventvwr.msc	Installed during Windows setup
Group Policy Management Console	Use this MMC to manage and apply Group Policy Objects to servers and workstations.	Start Menu ⇨ Administrative Tools ⇨ Group Policy Management Start Menu ⇨ Run ⇨ gpmc.msc	In Control Panel, install by clicking Programs, and then clicking Turn Windows Features on or off. With Service Pack 1, the Remote Server Administration Tools (RSAT) must be installed first.
Help and Support	Use to locate both local and online information about Vista components.	Start Menu ⇨ All Programs ⇨ Maintenance ⇨ Help and Support	Installed during Windows setup
Indexing Options	Use to configure Windows Search Indexing.	Control Panel ⇨ System and Maintenance ⇨ Indexing Options	Installed during Windows setup
Internet Explorer (No Add-ons)	Use to run a limited environment Internet Explorer without any ActiveX controls. Useful when issues arise with Web sites.	Start Menu ⇨ All Programs ⇨ Accessories ⇨ System Tools ⇨ Internet Explorer (No Add-ons) Start Menu ⇨ Run ⇨ iexplore.exe -extoff	Installed during Windows setup
Internet Information Services (IIS) 6.0 Manager	Use to configure Microsoft Internet Information Services 7 settings.	Start Menu ⇨ Administrative Tools ⇨ IIS Manager Start Menu ⇨ Run ⇨ iis.msc	Installed with Windows Server 2003 Administration Tools
iSCSI Initiator	Use to configure iSCSI connections from the desktop. Mostly useful for servers.	Start Menu ⇨ Administrative Tools ⇨ iSCSI Initiator Start Menu ⇨ Run ⇨ iscsicpl.exe	Installed during Windows setup

continued

TABLE 10.1   (continued)

Tool	Purpose	Location	Obtain From
Local Security Policy (LSP)	Use to configure security policies on the local system. Most useful for PCs in a workgroup or disconnected from a domain.	Start Menu ⇨ Administrative Tools ⇨ Local Security Policy Start Menu ⇨ Run ⇨ secpol.msc	Installed during Windows setup
Manage Network Connections	Use to control the settings assigned to network interfaces. Supports both IPv4 and IPv6.	Control Panel ⇨ Network and Internet ⇨ Network and Sharing Center ⇨ Manage Network Connections	Installed during Windows setup
Memory Diagnostics Tool	Use to analyze memory chips for potential problems.	Start Menu ⇨ Administrative Tools ⇨ Memory Diagnostics Tool Start Menu ⇨ Run ⇨ mdsched.exe	Installed during Windows setup Also available from the installation media DVD
Microsoft Baseline Security Analyzer (MBSA)	Use to scan local or remote systems for common configuration errors and to verify security best practices.	Start Menu ⇨ All Programs ⇨ Microsoft Baseline Security Analyzer Start Menu ⇨ Run ⇨ mbsa.exe Command Line ⇨ mbsacli.exe	Download from www.microsoft.com/ downloads
Network Monitor	Use to diagnose issues with server connectivity.	Start Menu ⇨ All Programs ⇨ Microsoft Network Monitor 3.1 ⇨ Microsoft Network Monitor 3.1 Start Menu ⇨ Run ⇨ netmon.exe	Download from www.microsoft.com/ downloads/details. aspx?FamilyID= 18b1d59d-f4d8-4213-8d17-2f6dde7d7aac& DisplayLang=en.
Notepad	Use to edit text files. Useful for creating command files to automate tasks.	Start Menu ⇨ All Programs ⇨ Accessories ⇨ Notepad Start Menu ⇨ Run ⇨ notepad.exe	Installed during Windows setup
Performance Information and Tools	Use these tools to review the performance of a system.	Control Panel ⇨ Performance Information and Tools ⇨ Advanced Tools	Installed during Windows setup
Print Management	Use to manage printing system on Vista PCs.	Start Menu ⇨ Administrative Tools ⇨ Print Management Start Menu ⇨ Run ⇨ printmanage-ment.msc	Installed during Windows setup

Tool	Purpose	Location	Obtain From
Problem Reports and Solutions (PRS)	Use to collect crash dumps and debug information. It enables administrators to track and address errors relating to the Windows operating system, Windows components, and applications.	Start Menu ⇨ All Programs ⇨ Maintenance ⇨ Problem Reports and Solutions Start Menu ⇨ Run ⇨ wercon.exe	To learn more about PRS, go to http://tech-net2.microsoft.com/WindowsVista/en/library/03a97dba-6b24-42c7-81f0-fb-751f6e839d1033.mspx?mfr=true
Registry Editor	Use to modify settings within the System Registry.	Start Menu ⇨ Search ⇨ regedit or regedt32 Command Line ⇨ regedit or regedt32	Installed during Windows setup
Reliability and Performance Monitor	Use to establish a baseline of performance and to troubleshoot performance issues.	Start Menu ⇨ Administrative Tools ⇨ Reliability and Performance Monitor Start Menu ⇨ Run ⇨ perfmon.msc Also found in Computer Management	Installed during Windows setup
Remote Desktop Connection	Use to establish a desktop connection on a remote computer in your own security context.	Start Menu ⇨ All Programs ⇨ Accessories ⇨ Remote Desktop Connection Start Menu ⇨ Run ⇨ mstsc.exe	Installed during Windows setup
Remote Desktops	Use this console to bring together multiple remote desktop connections into one single environment. Very useful when managing several remote systems.	Start Menu ⇨ Administrative Tools ⇨ Remote Desktops	Installed from Windows Server 2003 (WS03) Administration Kit or through RSAT For information on its use, go to http://searchwincomputing.techtarget.com/originalContent/0,289142,sid68_gci1243095,00.html
Security Configuration and Analysis	Use this console to configure security settings on a system and to compare existing security settings with those in a template.	Start Menu ⇨ Run ⇨ mmc then add the Security Configuration and Analysis snap-in	Installed during Windows setup

continued

	TABLE 10.1	*(continued)*		

Tool	Purpose	Location	Obtain From
Security Templates	Use this console to capture security settings into a template for application to other systems.	Start Menu ⇨ Run ⇨ mmc then add the Security Template snap-in	Installed during Windows setup
Services	Use to control startup state of various Windows services.	Start Menu ⇨ Administrative Tools ⇨ Services Start Menu ⇨ Run ⇨ services.msc Also found in Computer Management	Installed during Windows setup
Snipping Tool	Use to capture portions of screens and turn them into images. Very useful for creating supporting documentation or for documenting issues.	Start Menu ⇨ All Programs ⇨ Accessories ⇨ Snipping Tool Start Menu ⇨ Run ⇨ snipping tool.exe	Installed during Windows setup
Sync Center	Use to control synchronization settings for offline files as well as for portable digital assistants (PDA).	Start Menu ⇨ All Programs ⇨ Accessories ⇨ Sync Center Start Menu ⇨ Run ⇨ mobsync.exe	Installed during Windows setup
System Configuration	Use to display system configuration information.	Start Menu ⇨ Administrative Tools ⇨ Services Start Menu ⇨ Run ⇨ msconfig.exe	Installed during Windows setup
System Information	Use to display information about the system.	Start Menu ⇨ All Programs ⇨ Accessories ⇨ System Tools ⇨ System Information Start Menu ⇨ Run ⇨ msinfo32.exe	Installed during Windows setup
System Restore	Use to restore a system to a given point prior to configuration changes.	Start Menu ⇨ All Programs ⇨ Accessories ⇨ System Tools ⇨ System Restore Start Menu ⇨ Run ⇨ rstrui.exe	Installed during Windows setup
Task Manager	Use to control running processes on a system. Also provides a real-time view of performance.	CTRL-ALT-DEL ⇨ Task Manager Right-click Taskbar ⇨ Task Manager	Installed during Windows setup

Tool	Purpose	Location	Obtain From
Task Scheduler	Use to automate tasks on either a schedule or an event basis.	Start Menu ⇨ Administrative Tools ⇨ Task Scheduler Start Menu ⇨ Run ⇨ taskschd.msc Also found in Computer Management	Installed during Windows setup
Telnet	Use to perform remote administration.	Command Line ⇨ telnet.exe	In Control Panel, install by clicking Programs, and then clicking Turn Windows Features on or off
User Accounts	Use to control accounts on the local system.	Control Panel ⇨ User Accounts Also found in Computer Management	Installed during Windows setup
Windows Defender	Use to defend against general malware and to clean infected systems.	Control Panel ⇨ Programs ⇨ Windows Defender Start Menu ⇨ Run ⇨ msascui.exe	Installed during Windows setup
Windows Easy Transfer	Use to transfer settings from one Vista PC to another. Use only when dealing with single PCs.	Start Menu ⇨ All Programs ⇨ Accessories ⇨ System Tools ⇨ Windows Easy Transfer Start Menu ⇨ Run ⇨ migwiz.exe	Installed during Windows setup
Windows Explorer	Use to navigate through folder structures on local and remote PCs and servers.	Start Menu ⇨ All Programs ⇨ Accessories ⇨ Windows Explorer Start Menu ⇨ Run ⇨ explorer.exe Start Menu ⇨ right-click on Computer ⇨ Explore	Installed during Windows setup
Windows Firewall with Advanced Security	Use to control incoming and outgoing TCP/IP connections on Vista systems.	Start Menu ⇨ Administrative Tools ⇨ Windows Firewall with Advanced Security Start Menu ⇨ Run ⇨ wf.msc	Installed during Windows setup
Windows Recovery Environment (WinRE)	Use to restore damaged systems.	Boot from the Windows Vista Installation Media Boot from the Installed WinRE system	Installed after Windows Setup but must be taken into consideration at installation since it requires a separate partition

continued

TABLE 10.1	*(continued)*		
Tool	**Purpose**	**Location**	**Obtain From**
Windows Remote Management (WinRM)	Use this command shell to execute commands remotely on other Windows Vista systems.	Command Line ⇨ winrm.exe	Installed during Windows setup but must be activated to work
Windows Remote Assistance	Use to provide assistance to users when they have issues by sharing their desktop in their security context.	Start Menu ⇨ All Programs ⇨ Maintenance ⇨ Remote Assistance Start Menu ⇨ Run ⇨ msra.exe	Installed during Windows setup

NOTE   Some tools must be obtained from the Web while others must be activated. Administrative tools for example, are not displayed by default. Use the Start Menu Properties to enable them as well as the Run command. See Chapter 9 for more information on how to do this. Other tools such as the Windows Server 2003 Resource Kit tools or the Remote Server Administration Tools must be downloaded. Obtain the WS03 Resource Kit from http://go.microsoft.com/fwlink/?linkid=16721. Obtain RSAT from http://support.microsoft.com/kb/941314. The Windows Server 2003 Administration Pack is located in the %WINDIR%\System32 folder on a Windows Server 2003 system. See below for installation instructions on Vista.

As you can see, there are many administrative tools in Windows Vista. In fact, it is sometimes difficult to keep up. Obviously, some will be much more useful than others. The best way to deal with these tools is to first, rely on Table 10.1 to figure out the correct tool to use for a specific purpose. Then make the tools you use the most often readily available by placing them on your Quick Launch toolbar. You use the Quick Launch toolbar instead of the Desktop because Quick Launch is always available no matter which tool you are working with. If you rely on the Desktop to place your shortcuts, then you always need to get back to the Desktop to access your tools, an operation which takes more time and several more mouse clicks.

Use the following procedure to prepare your environment:

1. **Make sure your Quick Launch Area is displayed and then right-click on the Taskbar. Choose Toolbars ⇨ Quick Launch.** Do not uncheck it if it is already checked.

2. **Size your toolbar appropriately. Make sure that your Taskbar is unlocked by right-clicking it and deselecting the Lock the Taskbar.** Doing this lets you view each individual toolbar and its limits in the Taskbar.

3. **Double the size of the Taskbar by positioning your cursor at the very top of the Taskbar until your cursor changes to an up-down arrow; then click and drag the Taskbar until it takes up two lines.**

4. **Now take the Programs toolbar — the one where open programs are listed — by clicking its double-edged border at the left and dragging it to the bottom-left beside the Start button**. Programs should now be listed at the bottom and the Quick Launch toolbar should be at the top.

5. **Lock the Taskbar again by right-clicking it and checking Lock the Taskbar.** Your Taskbar should now look like the one in Figure 10.1.

FIGURE 10.1

A locked two-line Taskbar displaying the Quick Launch Toolbar

6. **Now you can begin to populate your Quick Launch Area; do it by locating the item you want to add in the Start Menu, right-clicking it, and selecting Add to Quick Launch. Add the following items:**
   - Command Prompt
   - Computer Management
   - Control Panel
   - Help and Support
   - Internet Explorer
   - MBSA
   - Network Monitor
   - Notepad
   - Reliability and Performance Monitor
   - Custom Security Configuration and Analysis and Security Templates
   - Snipping Tool
   - System Configuration
   - System Information
   - System Restore
   - Windows Explorer
   - Windows Firewall with Advanced Security
   - Windows Remote Assistance

   The resulting Taskbar is illustrated in Figure 10.2. Note that in addition to Quick Launch, this Taskbar also includes the Desktop toolbar. Add it by right-clicking on the Taskbar and selecting Toolbars ➪ Desktop. Just like the Quick Launch toolbar, the Desktop toolbar adds ready access to any items on your desktop.

A well-configured Administrative Taskbar

Now you're ready to get to work. In fact, the tools covered in this chapter include most of the tools you'll find on this Taskbar. Other tools are covered in their respective chapters as you run through the CASPR system for Vista management.

Obtaining additional administration tools

As you build your Vista management and administration toolkit, you'll notice that you can add a significant number of tools to the default set found in the operating system. For example, as mentioned in Chapter 9, when you run Windows Vista without Service Pack 1, the Group Policy Management Console (GPMC) is installed by default, but when you run Vista with SP1, it is no longer available. In order to run the GPMC on Vista SP1, you must install a special toolkit called the Remote Server Administration Tools. Another source of tools is the Windows Server 2003 Administration Pack.

RSAT can help you manage environments running with any version of Windows Server from 2008 down. However, the RSAT for Windows Vista does not include all of the tools included in the Windows Server 2003 Administration Pack. For this reason, you might still want to install and run tools from the Windows Server 2003 administration toolkit in order to have access to administration features unavailable with RSAT. Table 10.2 lists the different tools available with either RSAT or with the Windows Server 2003 Administration Pack.

TABLE 10.2

Tools Available in RSAT and the WS03 Administration Pack

RSAT	Windows Server 2003 Administration Pack	Comment
Active Directory Certificate Services Tools	Public Key Management, Certification Authority	
Active Directory Domain Services Tools	Active Directory Tools	
Active Directory Lightweight Directory Services Tools		Available separately through the Active Directory Application Mode (ADAM) download
BitLocker Drive Encryption Tools		BitLocker is only available for Vista and above

RSAT	Windows Server 2003 Administration Pack	Comment
DHCP Server Tools	DHCP	
Distributed File System Tools	Distributed File System	
DNS Server Tools	DNS	
Failover Clustering Tools	Cluster Administrator	
File Server Resource Manager Tools	File Server Resource Manager Tools	Only available from WS03 R2 and above
Group Policy Management Tools	Group Policy Management Tool	
Network Load Balancing Tools	Network Load Balancing Manager	
Online Responder Tools		Only available for WS08 and above
Server for NIS Tools		Only available from WS03 R2 and above
Share and Storage Management Tools		
SMTP Server Tools		
Storage Manager for SANs Tools		Only available from WS03 R2 and above
Terminal Services Tools	Terminal Services Tools	
UDDI Services Tools	UDDI Services	
Windows System Resource Manager Tools		Separate download for WS03 and lower
	WINS Server Tools	
	Connection Manager Administration Kit	
	Internet Information Services 6.0 Manager	
	IP Address Management	Integrates DNS, DHCP, and WINS management tools into one.
	Microsoft .NET Framework 1.1 Configuration and Wizards	
	Telephony	

Installing the Remote Server Administration Tools

Installing the Remote Server Administration Tools is performed in two steps. The first installs an update on the client system and the second installs the actual tools themselves.

NOTE If you are installing the RSAT on Windows Vista, you must have at least Service Pack 1 installed.

1. Begin by installing the update. The update for RSAT is available in Knowledge Base article number 941314 at `http://support.microsoft.com/kb/941314`. Download and install this update. Double-click on it to launch the installation process. This process requires elevated rights and is performed through the Windows Update Standalone Installer. Accept the license agreement to begin the installation. Once the installation is complete, the local Administration Tools will include a help topic for the Remote Server Administration Tools.

2. Next, once the update has been installed, you need to enable the new RSAT Windows tools you want to use. Move to Control Panel ⇨ Programs and select Turn Windows features on or off. Accept the UAC elevation prompt and scroll down to Remote Server Administration Tools. You'll note that the RSAT section is divided into two subsections: Feature Administration Tools and Role Administration Tools. Expand both and check the tools you need on this system, as shown in Figure 10.3.

3. Click OK to launch the addition of these tools.

FIGURE 10.3

The RSAT Toolkit in Windows Vista

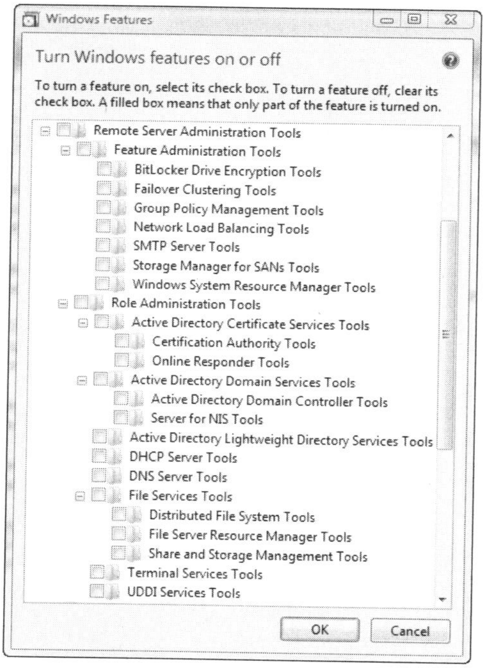

You can also use the Windows Package Manager (pkgmgr.exe) along with the Windows Update Stand-alone Installer (WUSA) to do this with two command lines. The first relies on WUSA to install the update using the update file itself. Using the /quiet switch will perform the operation without user interaction. If you want to see the results, then omit this switch. And the second installs the feature you require. Note that there is a reboot after WUSA runs (first command).

```
wusa path\Windows6.0-KB941314-x86.msu /quiet
start /w pkgmgr /iu:WindowsAdministrationTools
```

Where *path* is the location of the update. You use start /w with Package Manager because it causes the command to wait until the operation is finished before moving to the next command, letting you know when it has completed. Of course, if you are running an x64 version of Vista, you would use the x64 version of the update package. Table 10.3 lists the available Remote Server Administration Tools in the RSAT package.

NOTE The Update and feature names used in these commands are case sensitive and must be type exactly as they are displayed. For example, the update name must be Windows6.0-KB941314-x86.msu.

TABLE 10.3

Tools Available in RSAT

Tool Type	Full Tool Name
Remote Server Administration Tools	
Feature Administration Tools	BitLocker Drive Encryption Tools
	Failover Clustering Tools
	Group Policy Management Tools
	Network Load Balancing Tools
	SMTP Server Tools
	Storage Manager for SANs Tools
	Windows System Resource Manager Tools
Role Administration Tools	Active Directory Certificate Services Tools
	Certificate Authority Tools
	Online Responder Tools
	Active Directory Domain Services Tools
	Active Directory Domain Controller Tools
	Server for NIS Tools

continued

TABLE 10.3	_(continued)_
Tool Type	**Full Tool Name**
	Active Directory Lightweight Directory Services Tools
	DHCP Server Tools
	DNS Server Tools
	File Services Tools
	Distributed File System Tools
	File Server Resource Manager Tools
	Share and Storage Management Tools
	Terminal Services Tools
	UDDI Services Tools

If you want to add tools for the administration of Internet Information Server, then you must add additional tools on your workstation since they are not included in the RSAT. Once again, these tools are listed in the Windows Features dialog box. You can install tools for the management of the FTP service, IIS version 7.0 and IIS version 6.0, through this dialog box (see Figure 10.4). You can also install these tools using Package Manager with the following command line:

```
start /w pkgmgr /iu:IIS-WebServerRole;IIS6ManagementCompatibility
    ;IIS-LegacySnapIn;IIS-Metabase
```

FIGURE 10.4

Adding Web Management Tools to Vista SP1

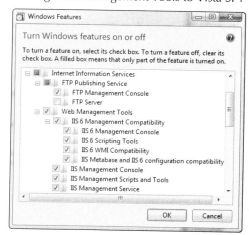

 The IIS 6 management tools are also required to manage the Simple Mail Transfer Protocol (SMTP) even if you do not run IIS 6 Web sites.

Installing the Windows Server 2003 Administration Kit

The Windows Server 2003 Administration Kit (AdminPak.msi) provides additional management consoles that are simply not available by default on Vista. But, unless you are using the version available on a server running Service Pack 2, this administration package will not install on Vista whether you have Service Pack 1 or not. In order to get it to run, you will need to first install it, then run a command to register its components on Vista. If you use a server running SP2, then you only need to install it. Use the following procedure to do so:

1. **Locate an updated copy of the Administration Kit on one of your servers.** Ideally, this server will be running at least Windows Server 2003 Service Pack 2 or even better, WS03 R2 SP2. The **adminpak.msi** file is located in the `%WINDIR%\System32` folder. The easiest way to access this file is to connect to the server's administrative share on the system disk; in most cases, this is `\\servername\C$`.

2. **Navigate to the** `%WINDIR%\System32` **folder, locate** `adminpak.msi`, **and copy it to your PC.**

3. **Double-click the** `adminpak.msi` **file once it is copied.**

4. **Accept the UAC prompt and follow the onscreen instructions.**

5. **If you used a version from WS03 SP2, then you're done. If for some unknown reason your servers are not at SP2, then copy the following commands into a text file and name it** `adminpack_vista.cmd`. **Run it when ready.**

```
@echo off
set filelist=adprop.dll azroles.dll azroleui.dll ccfg95.dll
set filelist=%filelist% certadm.dll certmmc.dll certpdef.dll
    certtmpl.dll
set filelist=%filelist% certxds.dll cladmwiz.dll clcfgsrv.dll
    clnetrex.dll
set filelist=%filelist% cluadmex.dll cluadmmc.dll cmproxy.dll
    cmroute.dll
set filelist=%filelist% cmutoa.dll cnet16.dll debugex.dll
    dfscore.dll
set filelist=%filelist% dfsgui.dll dhcpsnap.dll dnsmgr.dll
    domadmin.dll
set filelist=%filelist% dsadmin.dll dsuiwiz.dll imadmui.dll
    lrwizdll.dll
set filelist=%filelist% mprsnap.dll msclus.dll mstsmhst.dll
    mstsmmc.dll
set filelist=%filelist% nntpadm.dll nntpapi.dll nntpsnap.dll
    ntdsbsrv.dll
set filelist=%filelist% ntfrsapi.dll rasuser.dll rigpsnap.dll
    rsadmin.dll
```

```
set filelist=%filelist% rscommon.dll rsconn.dll rsengps.dll
   rsjob.dll
set filelist=%filelist% rsservps.dll rsshell.dll rssubps.dll
   rtrfiltr.dll
set filelist=%filelist% schmmgmt.dll tapisnap.dll tsuserex.dll
   vsstskex.dll
set filelist=%filelist% w95inf16.dll w95inf32.dll winsevnt.dll
   winsmon.dll
set filelist=%filelist% winsrpc.dll winssnap.dll ws03res.dll
for %%i in (%filelist%) do (
echo Registering %%i ...
regsvr32 /s %%i
)
echo.
Echo All done!
```

Not all tools are useful, but if you are part of a large network, you'll see that many of them are.

This installation is monolithic; it does not let you choose which tools to install. If you want to install only specific tools, for example, Active Directory tools, without any of the other tools, then use a command line to do so. The following command line installs the AD tools and only these tools. Make sure that you use an elevated Command Prompt.

```
msiexec /i adminpak.msi ADDLOCAL=FeADTools /qb
```
Doing this helps keep your system uncluttered with tools you do not need.

 More information on extracting specific tools from the Administration Kit can be found at http://support.microsoft.com/kb/314978.

Performing common workstation administration tasks

When you administer workstations, you quickly notice that systems administration focuses on three key tasks:

- Day-to-day administration of systems, often called proactive administration because it is performed before issues occur.

- Building a proper set of tools for administration, both local and remote.

- Troubleshooting when issues arise, often called reactive administration because it is performed after an issue has occurred.

The first task is easy because you can schedule its activities between daily, weekly, monthly, and ad hoc timelines. The second task is also easy because this is a one-time operation. The third task is more difficult because you never know when it will occur. However, if you create a proper administration schedule, you should have free time every day that allows you to deal with unexpected issues. And, if you set up your management and administration environment properly, you should be able to limit the occurrence of these unexpected issues.

> **TIP** One key element that greatly limits the number of unexpected issues is user education. Spend as much time as possible showing them how to do things right in Vista. It will save you a lot of time in the end because you won't have to deal with the simplest user issues.

> **NOTE** A great tool for sharing information is Windows SharePoint Services (WSS). WSS is a collaboration environment that provides a team site structure for groups of people working on the same subject. For example, one great site would be to have a central Vista PC administration site where information is shared among PC technicians and administrators and additional information is made available, especially reference information, such as Vista's online Help and the Microsoft Vista TechNet Center (`http://technet2.microsoft.com/WindowsVista/en/library/90a564b9-34af-4a6b-937f-324e1862244b1033.mspx?mfr=true`). Another good site would be an informational site full of tips and tricks for end users. Investigate this opportunity. WSS is free to organizations who own Windows Server 2003 so cost is no obstacle.

Building an administrative task schedule

Ideally, you will be using a schedule of operations to perform administrative tasks. You have to deal with daily, weekly, monthly, and ad hoc tasks. The best way to do this is to use the following approach:

- Daily tasks are performed first thing in the morning.
- Weekly tasks are performed on Monday and Wednesday afternoons.
- Monthly tasks are performed on Tuesday afternoons.
- This leaves Thursday and Friday afternoons for ad hoc tasks.

In addition, you can automate several tasks. For example, you can get the Event Log to forward notifications of low disk space. You can also set a scheduled task to automatically clean temporary files from systems when low disk space notifications occur. Although you still need to monitor this task, it will be performed automatically for you so, instead of performing the task, your responsibility will be to verify that the task has been performed.

Ideally, your schedule will stay firm and if you set everything up right, overtime will be kept to a minimum.

> **TIP** Use Outlook's Task Management features to build your administrative task schedule. It will remind you of all the tasks you need to perform and when you need to perform them.

Table 10.4 outlines the tasks to perform and their frequency.

TABLE 10.4

Windows Vista Administration Tasks

Task Number	Task Name	Frequency	Comment
VA-01	Run As Administrator	Daily	Although this is not really an administrative task, you should make a habit of using a standard user account to perform everyday work and then, use Run As Administrator to perform any administrative task.
VA-02	General System Status Verification	Daily	Review Event Logs on each PC to determine if there are any issues.
VA-03	Security Event Verification	Daily	In secure environments, you need to review auditing information on each sensitive system to identify if any untoward events occur.
VA-04	Anti-malware Update Management	Daily	You need to verify that anti-virus and anti-spyware definitions update work correctly in your environment.
VA-05	Backup Generation and Verification	Daily	User data should be backed up on a regular basis. Ideally, it will be redirected from local PCs to shared folders residing on servers. In addition, you need to provide overall systems protection. Finally, you need to test backups to make sure they work properly.
VA-06	Uptime Report Management	Weekly	Review uptime reports for each system. Identify reboots and find out why.
VA-07	Free Space Verification	Weekly	You need to verify that users are not running out of space on their systems.
VA-08	Network Traffic Monitoring	Weekly	You should regularly monitor network traffic from select points on your network to ensure everything is working properly.
VA-09	Volume Shadow Copy Operation Verification	Monthly	You need to make sure that Shadow Copies are operating properly on your user's PCs so that they can recover data as needed.
VA-10	Search Service Configuration	Monthly	Verify that the search configuration is set properly on each system.
VA-11	Disk Integrity Checking	Monthly	Run the disk checking tool on each system to correct any potential issues.
VA-12	Disk Defragmentation	Monthly	Verify the status of disk defragmentation on each system.
VA-13	Temporary File Cleanup	Monthly	Proactively clean up temporary and other file clutter on each system.
VA-14	Wireless Connection Status Verification	Monthly	Review wireless connectivity in your network and make sure users have full access to this service.

Task Number	Task Name	Frequency	Comment
VA-15	Wired Network Connection Setup/ Verification	Monthly	Review wired network connectivity and make sure user configurations are set properly.
VA-16	Remote Access Verification	Monthly	Review remote access settings and make sure users have secure access to internal systems.
VA-17	Security Patch Update Management	Monthly	Review security updates, test them and apply them to affected systems.
VA-18	Security Policy Review and Update	Monthly	Review the security policy and determine whether updates are required. Keep user communication on security issues current.
VA-19	Security Template Creation/Modification	Ad hoc	Security templates allow you to control overall security settings on your systems. They often need to be reviewed when untoward events occur.
VA-20	Inventory Management	Monthly	Review inventory details. Determine if components are missing and review changes to overall inventory.
VA-21	Script Generation and Maintenance	Ad hoc	Create scripts for operation automation and make sure they are working properly.
VA-22	Service Pack Deployment	Ad hoc	Review applicable service packs, test their installation and perform their deployment.
VA-23	System Documentation	Ad hoc	Much as you hate to do it, you need to document the state of your environment on an ongoing basis.
VA-24	System BIOS and Firmware Management	Ad hoc	When new firmware and BIOS software is delivered for your systems, you need to test and then apply it.
VA-25	Device Management	Ad hoc	You need to review and approve new devices as they become available for use in your network.
VA-26	PC Rebuilds	Ad hoc	Occasionally, you need to repair a PC that is damaged beyond recovery.
VA-27	User Support through Windows Remote Assistance	Ad hoc	Users will require assistance on an ad hoc basis. You need to be familiar with the procedure.
VA-28	User Password Reset	Ad hoc	Occasionally, you must reset a user password so that they will be able to access the network.
VA-29	PC RDC Management	Ad hoc	You need to properly manage the Remote Desktop Connections you create to access PCs in your network.
VA-30	Software Installation Management	Ad hoc	Occasionally, new software must be deployed to PCs.

continued

TABLE 10.4	*(continued)*		
Task Number	**Task Name**	**Frequency**	**Comment**
VA-31	GPO Management	Ad hoc	Occasionally, you need to create or modify existing GPOs to control more settings on your systems.
VA-32	Computer Object Provisioning	Ad hoc	As new systems are brought on board in your network, you need to pre-populate the Active Directory with their accounts so that when they join the network, they will immediately be subject to appropriate Group Policies.
VA-33	Internet Information Services Operation	Ad hoc	IIS should not be located on a PC except for development or testing purposes. Nevertheless, you need to verify its proper operation when it is installed.
VA-34	System Diagnostics	Ad hoc	When things go wrong on a system, you need to perform diagnostics to discover where the issue lies.
VA-35	Encrypted Folder Recovery	Ad hoc	When users lose access to their encrypted files, you need to use the recovery agent to restore them.
VA-36	BitLocker Drive Encryption	Ad hoc	When users lose access to their encrypted drives, you need to restore them through the recovery agent.
VA-37	Transfer User Settings	Ad hoc	Occasionally, you must change individual user's PCs. When this occurs, you must transfer their settings from one PC to the other.
VA-38	Set Up Accessibility Options	Ad hoc	Some users have disabilities which require different accessibility options. In this case, you must work with them to identify the appropriate settings.
VA-39	Set Up Multilingual Configurations	Ad hoc	If you work in an international organization, you may have to set up different languages for users to work in.
VA-40	Resolve Printing Issues	Ad hoc	In some cases, your users will have difficulty working with printers or print jobs. You will need to assist them in identifying and resolving the issue.

Table 10.4 lists administrative activities you need to perform on PCs. Networked environments normally host servers and it is these servers that normally provide centralized or shared services. Because of this, this table does not mention items such as Printer Management because printers should not be shared on PCs, but on servers. In addition, several activities such as those related to security or information protection and system restoration are not covered in this chapter, but are covered in future chapters as you run through the CASPR system for PC maintenance. And, of course, activities related to controlling change on PCs were discussed in Chapter 9.

 For a comparable list of activities on servers, look up *Windows Server 2008: The Complete Reference* by Ruest and Ruest from McGraw-Hill Osborne.

Building an administration toolkit

The key to proper systems administration is having the right toolkit. You've already begun to create a standard administration desktop. Now, you need additional tools. Vista offers unparalleled support for comprehensive management tools. For example, you can rely on the Microsoft Management Console version 3.0 to build your own administration console, one that will give you access to almost every tool you need to administer both your own local PC and remote PCs. In addition, you can use the Windows Sidebar to display custom gadgets — gadgets that report information on system performance and on system operation. This turns your desktop into an administrative control system, one that provides a central base of operations for the support of PC operations in your organization.

First, begin by creating a custom console that gives you access to most of the operations you need. As you've seen before, the most useful of existing console is the Computer Management console found in Administrative Tools. Although this is a good general purpose console, it is not an all-encompassing tool. As shown in Figure 10.5, Computer Management includes the following capabilities by default:

- You can use it to manage either local or remote systems. The console opens the local system by default. To change to a remote system, right-click on Computer Management (Local) and select Connect to another computer. Type in the name of the other computer or select Browse to locate it and click OK. Some minor functionality will not be available on remote systems, but this console still gives you access to almost everything you need.

- System Tools lists the Task Scheduler, the Event Viewer, Shared Folders, Local Users and Groups, Reliability and Performance tools and the Device Manager. The first two were described in Chapter 9. Shared Folders are seldom used on PCs. Local Users and Groups are used mostly to manage accounts stored in the local Security Accounts Manager (SAM) database. In networked environments, few accounts are local. Reliability and Performance is covered in Chapter 13 and Device Manager is used to troubleshoot device issues on systems.

- Storage gives you access to disk management features for both local and removable storage.

- Services and Applications gives you access to installed Services and WMI Control lets you configure the Windows Management Instrumentation settings on a system.

Several of the tasks you perform on an ongoing basis can be performed from here. For example, the Disk Management node gives you access to disk drives and especially their Properties (right-click on the drive). Here you can view free space, perform disk cleanup, check the disk volume, defragment it, and back it up as shown in Figure 10.6. You also have access to hardware information for the disk, previous versions to restore data, and security descriptors for the data. These capabilities make Computer Management quite powerful. In addition, Computer Management automatically includes additional console contents as you add Windows Components to the system.

FIGURE 10.5

The Details of the Computer Management console

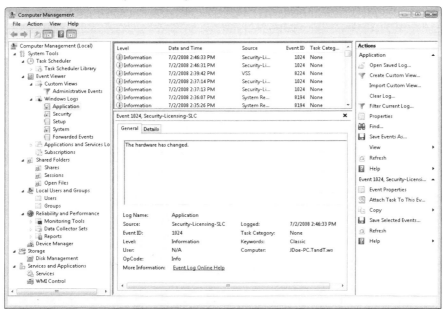

FIGURE 10.6

Performing Disk Management from the Computer Management console

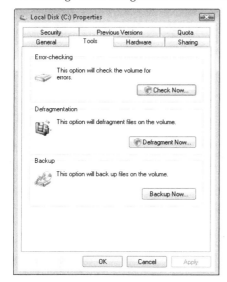

However, Computer Management does not provide default access to everything. For this reason, you may want to modify it to create a custom MMC, one which will build on Computer Management's features and add even more tools.

In addition to all the features of the Computer Management console, this custom console should include the following snap-ins:

- The Active Directory Users & Computers snap-in
- Group Policy Management
- NAP Client Configuration for the local system
- Print Management for the local system
- Security Configuration and Analysis
- Security Templates
- Windows Firewall with Advanced Security for the local system

You can add more snap-ins if you would like, or simply add them to discover their use. Note that many of the snap-ins listed in the snap-in dialog box are already part of Computer Management. To create this console:

1. **Use Start ⇨ Run to execute the following command:**

    `mmc /a %SystemRoot%\system32\compmgmt.msc`

    This launches the Computer Management console in editing mode.

2. **Choose File ⇨ Save As to save the console as Custom Management Console.msc under the Documents folder.** You save it in Documents to ensure it is protected and to make it easier to locate later.

3. **Choose File ⇨ Add/Remove Snap-in to open the dialog box.**

4. **Click the Advanced button and check the Allow changing the parent snap-in option. Click OK.**

5. **Use the drop-down list to select Computer Management (Local) under Parent Snap-in.** Doing this places additional snap-ins under Computer Management.

6. **Double-click each of the snap-ins listed earlier. Click OK when done.**

7. **Choose File ⇨ Options, name the console Custom Management Console, make sure it is set to User mode - full access, and deselect Do not save changes to this console. Click OK when done.**

8. **Choose File ⇨ Save to save your changes.**

9. **Close the console.**

10. **Open the Documents folder in Windows Explorer and use the right mouse button to drag the console to the Quick Launch area; select Create shortcut here.** Now, you can simply right-click on this shortcut and select Run As Administrator each time you need it.

There are several uses for this console as you will see, but it is basically the most common tool you will use to manage your network of PCs. The resultant console is displayed in Figure 10.7.

Second, get access to some cool gadgets you can add to yours and end users' Windows Sidebar to display system information. Gadgets can be found at the `www.gadgetsforvista.net/` site. Some cool gadgets that support system administration include the following:

- **Battery Gadget:** This feature displays battery status information for notebooks and tablet PCs.

- **Drive Information Gadget:** This gadget lists the status of your disk drives in Vista.

- **Network Utilization Gadget:** This gadget shows a graphical display of network throughput from your system.

- **Remote Desktop Gadget:** You can use this gadget to quickly link to any remote desktop.

- **Uptime Gadget:** You can find out how long a system has been running.

This list is not exhaustive, but it displays a selection of tools you can use to make your life as an administrator easier. The resultant desktop including the custom console is displayed in Figure 10.7.

> **NOTE** New gadgets come out almost every day. Make sure that you check the `www.gadgetsforvista.net/` site on a regular basis to discover what other cool tools you can rely on.

FIGURE 10.7

Working with a Custom Administration Desktop

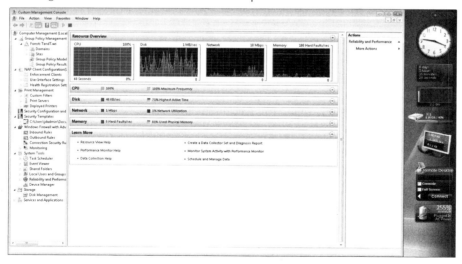

Using a standard troubleshooting strategy

Despite your best administrative efforts, your users will run into situations that will either be due to their inexperience or to their use of tools or components they shouldn't normally have access to. When this occurs, you need to troubleshoot the issue and discover how to fix it.

> **NOTE** Users should not run computers in administrative mode even if User Account Control is enabled. Users should be locked down and have only standard user access rights. Vista has made vast improvements in the ability a standard user has to control the computer environment and this should be sufficient. You'll soon find that if you lock down computer systems, you'll have a much more stable PC environment.

Troubleshooting is usually based on a series of questions you need to answer. Common questions should include:

- Who was using the PC when the problem first occurred?
- Who else has been using the PC, and have they experienced similar problems?
- Who has worked on this problem previously (if it has happened before)?
- Who has the same problem on another PC (that you know of)?
- When did this problem occur the first time, and has it occurred since?
- When was the last time you downloaded or installed application?
- When was the last time you installed new hardware?
- When did you last clean up the PC with Disk Cleanup or Disk Defragmenter, delete files or cookies, or perform similar deletions of data?
- What are your thoughts on what caused the problem?
- What have you tried to troubleshoot the problem yourself?
- What do you think can be done to solve the problem?
- Why do you think the problem occurred?
- How do you think the problem occurred?

> **NOTE** Windows Vista includes a new set of tools for event management. Many of the questions listed above can be answered by reviewing the information in the Vista Event Viewer.

Then, you need to use general troubleshooting procedures to resolve the issue. These procedures should include:

- Locate a solution by searching the PC's help and support center
- Locate a solution by searching the company's support files
- Search manufacturer's Web sites
- Search technical sites (MS Knowledge Base, TechNet)

Basically, you need to use a troubleshooting process, as shown in Figure 10.8, to resolve the issue. Relying on this process ensures that issues are resolved as quickly as possible, and documenting solutions will ensure you can build a list of solutions for future reference.

FIGURE 10.8

Using a standard troubleshooting process

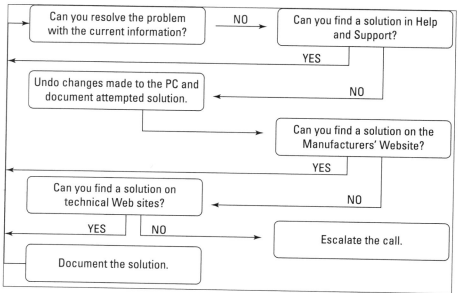

Performing Remote PC Administration

Even though you've created a custom console and you use it to administer remote systems, you sometimes need to rely on different means to resolve issues. Windows Vista includes several technologies in support of remote administration. Two of the most powerful remote administration tools are the Remote Shell and Telnet. The Remote Shell is a new feature built into Vista that relies on Microsoft's WS-Management Web Service. Telnet is an older technology that was adopted from UNIX environments to support remote command execution on Windows environments. Both offer support for remote command execution on Vista PCs.

Working with the Remote Shell

The Vista Remote Shell is built on WS-Management. The advantage of WS-Management is that it allows you to perform remote administration through common Internet ports, such as 80 (HyperText Transfer Protocol) or 443 (secure HTTP). Therefore, when you enable WS-Management on a Vista system, you will be able to administer it even if it is located outside your internal network, for example, when a mobile user is on the road. This is a great advantage. Of course, everything is secured through proper access controls, so your PC is still secure.

To use WS-Management, Vista relies on the Windows Remote Management (WinRM) engine to actually perform remote management. WinRM is enabled by default on Windows Server 2008, but it is not configured or enabled on Vista PCs, though it is installed.

> **NOTE** Enabling WinRM was discussed in Chapter 9 when you were working with the Event Viewer to collect remote Vista events. That's right, the Vista Event Log Collector service also relies on WinRM to operate.

As a reminder, you use the following command from an elevated Command Prompt to enable and configure WinRM:

```
winrm quickconfig
```

You need to confirm your operation. Doing this produces output that identifies what has been done to the system. This command needs to be applied to any system that wants to either issue or receive remote commands.

Most of the IP addresses inside your network will be trusted to perform operations on the system. You will require, of course, a proper administrative username and password on the system to perform these commands. This is one more reason why you must protect these credentials as much as possible and another reason for removing administrative credentials from end users.

If you know the IP addresses of your administrative workstations, you can add the to the trusted IP address list on each system:

```
Winrm set winrm/config/client @{TrustedHosts="workstationID"}
```

Where the *workstationID* is either its IP address or its fully qualified domain name (FQDN), for example, myPC.mydomain.com. To add more than one workstation, separate each workstationID with a comma or repeat the command several times. Then, when you have added these systems, you can enumerate listeners with the following command:

```
winrm enumerate winrm/config/listener
```

Perform these activities on each PC. You might consider putting this in the build of every PC so that they are configured by default.

Now you're ready to issue remote commands. These are performed through the winrs.exe command. Basically, you use the winrs.exe command to pass on normal commands to the remote system. For example, to view a list of files and folders on the remote system, you would use:

```
winrs -r:http://workstationID -u:Username -p:Password dir -s
```

Once again, the *workstationID* is the IP address or FQDN of the system, the *username* and *password* are your administrative credentials and the last part is the actual command you want to run. That's it. Simple, isn't it? Rely on the command list further in this chapter to discover which remote commands you can execute on the system.

NOTE More information on Windows Remote Management can be found at http://msdn2.microsoft.com/en-us/library/aa384426.aspx.

Relying on Telnet

Telnet uses an older technology to operate and relies on a different TCP/IP port (port 23), a port you probably don't want open in your Firewall configuration. Therefore, it is not recommended, especially for use outside your internal network. However, if you want to rely on Telnet anyway, follow these steps:

1. **Choose Start Menu ⇨ Control Panel ⇨ Programs.**
2. **Click Programs and Features.**
3. **In the left pane, click Turn Windows features on or off.**
4. **Enter your administrative credentials, and once the dialog box is displayed, scroll down to Telnet Client to select it and click OK.**
5. **Close all dialog boxes when done.**

Only the Telnet client is required to be able to work with Telnet. Telnet is a command interpreter. Therefore, if you type telnet at the Command Prompt, it puts you into the Telnet prompt. Here you must use Telnet commands to continue. Typical commands include:

- open \\PCname portnumber where *PCname* is the name of the machine you want to connect to and *portnumber* is the number of the TCP/IP port you want to connect to, will open a connection and determine if the target PC is listening on that port.
- close \\PCname will close an open connection.
- set \\PCname ntlm will turn on NTLM authentication on the remote PC.
- set \\PCname term vt100 sets the terminal emulation mode to VT100. You can also use ansi, vt52 or vtnt.
- send \\PCname ayt will send an "Are you there?" command.
- display will list the current parameters for the Telnet prompt.
- quit will close the Telnet prompt.
- You can also use the tlntadmn command if the Telnet Server is installed on the remote PC.

One very useful function of Telnet is the ability to connect to any TCP/IP port. This lets you find out if the remote system is listening on that port or not. It may be the best use of Telnet today because you can use it to troubleshoot any service that runs on a TCP/IP port. But, this function is more useful on servers than on PCs.

NOTE More information on Telnet commands can be found at www.microsoft.com/ resources/documentation/windows/xp/all/proddocs/en-us/telnet_ commands.mspx?mfr=true.

Automating Recurrent Tasks

As you can see, both WinRS and Telnet are character-based commands that do not rely on the graphical user interface to operate. The advantage of using character-based command interpreters is that they can be captured into batch or command files and can then be used to automate tasks. You can of course, automate tasks in the graphical interface through the Task Scheduler, but being able to trap commands into command files makes it easier to perform multiple tasks at once.

In Vista, you can automate operations by using three methods. Of course, there are more, but they often require third-party tools to execute. Two of the methods are available by default and the third must be downloaded and installed separately. They include:

- **The Command Prompt: A** built-in character-based command interpreter
- **Microsoft PowerShell: A** new downloadable command interpreter based on the .NET Framework
- **The Task Scheduler**: A powerful automation engine, which was already examined in-depth in Chapter 9

Ideally, you will create command files either in the Command Prompt or in PowerShell, and then you can use the Task Scheduler to schedule these tasks to run automatically whenever you need them.

Working with the Command Prompt

The Windows Vista Command Prompt has been greatly enhanced since Windows XP. It now boasts more than 120 commands with 40 new or updated commands. This gives the command line quite a bit of power. For example, if you want to see the network configuration of a system in one quick way, all you do is open a Command Prompt and type ipconfig/all. This will automatically list all of the network connections with each one of the settings for each connection.

Commands usually require switches to modify their operation and operators to indicate the object on which you want to run the command. The easiest way to discover information about each command is to simply open a Command Prompt and type:

```
commandname /?
```

Doing this automatically displays help information about the command you list. In some cases, commands include sub-items. For information on using these subitems, type the command, the subitem and then the help request (/?).

Table 10.5 lists the available commands in Windows Vista, updated or new commands, and where possible, the corresponding graphical interface tool. Use this table to identify which commands you need to work with.

TABLE 10.5

Windows Vista Commands

Command	New or Updated in Vista	Description	Corresponding GUI Tool
ASSOC		Displays or modifies file extension associations.	Windows Explorer
ATTRIB		Displays or changes file attributes.	Windows Explorer
	AUDITPOL	Modifies audit policies.	Security Templates
			Security and Configuration Analysis
	BCDEDIT	Sets properties in boot database to control boot loading.	Computer System Properties
BITSADMIN		Administers the Background Intelligent Transfer Service (BITS), the service which is used to download updates to PCs.	
BREAK		Sets or clears extended CTRL+C checking.	
CACLS		Displays or modifies access control lists (ACLs) of files.	Windows Explorer
CALL		Calls one batch program from another.	
CD		Displays the name of or changes the current directory.	Windows Explorer
	CHANGE	Sets special terminal server modes for logons, COM port mappings, and software installations.	Add or Remove Programs for Terminal Server
CHCP		Displays or sets the active code page number.	
CHDIR		Displays the name of or changes the current directory.	Windows Explorer
	CHGLOGON	Controls session logins.	
	CHGPORT	Control COM port mappings for DOS application compatibility.	
	CHGUSR	Change application installation mode.	Add or Remove Programs for Terminal Server
CHKDSK		Checks a disk and displays a status report.	Computer ➪ Disk Management

Command	New or Updated in Vista	Description	Corresponding GUI Tool
CHKNTFS		Displays or modifies the checking of disk at boot time.	
	CHOICE	Lets you select one item from a list of choices and returns the result..	
	CLIP	Redirects output from the command line to the clipboard.	Clipboard
CLS		Clears the screen.	Show Desktop Icon
CMD		Starts a new instance of the Windows command interpreter.	Command Prompt
	CMDKEY	Controls stored user names and passwords.	
COLOR		Sets the default console foreground and background colors.	
COMP		Compares the contents of two files or sets of files.	Windows Explorer
COMPACT		Displays or alters the compression of files on NTFS partitions.	Computer ⇨ Disk Management
CONVERT		Converts FAT volumes to NTFS. You cannot convert the current drive.	Computer ⇨ Disk Management
COPY		Copies one or more files to another location.	Windows Explorer
DATE		Displays or sets the date.	Control Panel ⇨ Date and Time
DEL		Deletes one or more files.	Windows Explorer
DIR		Displays a list of files and subdirectories in a directory.	Windows Explorer
DISKCOMP		Compares the contents of two floppy disks.	Windows Explorer
DISKCOPY		Copies the contents of one floppy disk to another.	Windows Explorer
DISKPART		Displays or configures Disk Partition properties.	Computer ⇨ Disk Management
	DISKRAID	Used to access the Diskraid command window.	Computer ⇨ Disk Management
	DISPDIAG	Displays diagnostics.	System Configuration

continued

TABLE 10.5 *(continued)*

Command	New or Updated in Vista	Description	Corresponding GUI Tool
DOSKEY		Edits command lines, recalls Windows commands, and creates macros.	
DRIVERQUERY		Displays current device driver status and properties.	Device Manager
ECHO		Displays messages, or turns command echoing on or off.	
ENDLOCAL		Ends localization of environment changes in a batch file.	
ERASE		Deletes one or more files.	Windows Explorer
	EXPAND	Allows the extraction of Microsoft Update files (.MSU) and launches the Microsoft Update Standalone Installer.	Windows Explorer
EXIT		Quits the CMD.EXE program (command interpreter).	
FC		Compares two files or sets of files, and displays the differences between them.	
FIND		Searches for strings in files.	Search
FINDSTR		Searches for a text string in a file or files.	Search
FOR		Runs a specified command for each file in a set of files.	
	FORFILES	Used to select a file or files to execute a command on it; used mostly in batch jobs	
FORMAT		Formats a disk for use with Windows.	Computer ⇨ Disk Management
FSUTIL		Displays or configures the file system properties.	Windows Explorer
FTYPE		Displays or modifies file types used in file extension associations.	Windows Explorer
GOTO		Directs the Windows command interpreter to a labeled line in a batch program.	

Command	New or Updated in Vista	Description	Corresponding GUI Tool
GPRESULT		Displays Group Policy information for machine or user.	Group Policy Management Console
GPUPDATE		Updates Group Policy Settings for machine or user.	Group Policy Management Console
GRAFTABL		Enables Windows to display an extended character set in graphics mode.	
HELP		Provides Help information for Windows commands.	Help and Support
	ICACLS	Display, modify, backup, or restore ACLs for files and directories.	Windows Explorer
IF		Performs conditional processing in batch programs.	
	ISCSICLI	Initiates iSCSI.	iSCSI Initiator
LABEL		Creates, changes, or deletes the volume label of a disk.	Computer ⇨ Disk Management
MD		Creates a directory.	Windows Explorer
MKDIR		Creates a directory.	Windows Explorer
	MKLINK	Creates Symbolic Links and Hard Links.	
MODE		Configures a system device.	Device Manager
MORE		Displays output one screen at a time.	
MOVE		Moves one or more files from one directory to another directory.	Windows Explorer
	MUIUNATTEND	Control Multiple User Interface (MUI) unattend actions.	
NET		Controls service status, adds users or groups, changes network configuration, shares folders, and more.	Control Panel ⇨ Network and Internet
	NETCFG	Network installer for Windows PE (WinPE).	Control Panel ⇨ Network and Internet
	OCSETUP	Windows optional component setup.	Control Panel ⇨ Programs ⇨ Turn Windows features on or off

continued

TABLE 10.5   *(continued)*

Command	New or Updated in Vista	Description	Corresponding GUI Tool
PATH		Displays or sets a search path for executable files.	
PAUSE		Suspends processing of a batch file and displays a message.	
	PKMGR	Windows package manager.	
	PNPUNATTEND	Unattended online driver installation.	
	PNPUTIL	Microsoft PnP utility	
POPD		Restores the previous value of the current directory saved by PUSHD.	
PRINT		Prints a text file.	
PROMPT		Changes the Windows Command Prompt.	
PUSHD		Saves the current directory then changes it.	
	QUERY	Used to query information about Terminal Services sessions. Can query users, processes, terminal servers or sessions.	Terminal Services Manager
	QUSER	Displays information about users logged on to the system through Terminal Services.	Terminal Services Manager
RD		Removes a directory.	Windows Explorer
RECOVER		Recovers readable information from a bad or defective disk.	Computer ⇨ Disk Management
REM		Records comments (remarks) in batch files or CONFIG.SYS.	
REN		Renames a file or files.	Windows Explorer
RENAME		Renames a file or files.	Windows Explorer
REPLACE		Replaces files.	Windows Explorer
RMDIR		Removes a directory.	Windows Explorer
	ROBOCOPY	Advanced utility to copy files and directory trees.	Windows Explorer
	RPCPING	Pings a server using remote procedure call (RPC).	

Command	New or Updated in Vista	Description	Corresponding GUI Tool
RUNAS		Changes the credentials used to execute a command. **Note**: This command cannot generate an elevated status like the Run As Administrator command can. In Vista, it can only be used to lower credentials, not elevate them.	Run As Administrator
SC		Displays or configures services (background processes).	Services
SCHTASKS		Schedules commands and programs to run on a computer.	Task Scheduler
SECEDIT		To work with security templates and update security configurations.	Security Templates Security and Configuration Analysis
SET		Displays, sets, or removes Windows environment variables.	
SETLOCAL		Begins localization of environment changes in a batch file.	
	SETX	Controls environment variables in the user or system environment.	
SHIFT		Shifts the position of replaceable parameters in batch files.	
SHUTDOWN		Allows proper local or remote shutdown of machine.	Start Menu ⇨ Shutdown
SORT		Sorts input.	
START		Starts a separate window to run a specified program or command.	Windows Explorer
SUBST		Associates a path with a drive letter.	Computer ⇨ Disk Management
SYSTEMINFO		Displays machine specific properties and configuration.	System Information
	SXSTRACE	Windows side-by-side (WinSxS) tracing tool.	
	TAKEOWN	Controls file ownership.	Windows Explorer

continued

TABLE 10.5 *(continued)*

Command	New or Updated in Vista	Description	Corresponding GUI Tool
TASKKILL		Kill or stop a running process or application.	Task Manager
TIME		Displays or sets the system time.	Control Panel ⇨ Date and Time
	TIMEOUT	Controls wait times in batch files.	
TITLE		Sets the window title for a CMD.EXE session.	
TRACERT		Determines the path taken to a destination by sending Internet Control Message Protocol (ICMP) Echo Request messages to the destination.	
	TRACERPT	Used to generate trace reports.	Event Viewer
TREE		Graphically displays the directory structure of a drive or path.	Windows Explorer
TYPE		Displays the contents of a text file.	Notepad
VER		Displays the Windows version.	System Information
VERIFY		Tells Windows whether to verify that your files are written correctly to a disk.	
VOL		Displays a disk volume label and serial number.	Computer ⇨ Disk Management
XCOPY		Copies files and directory trees.	Windows Explorer
	WAITFOR	Used to send, or wait for, a signal on a system.	
	WBADMIN	Controls backups and restores.	Backup and Restore Center
	WCEUTIL	Controls the Windows event collector.	Event Viewer
	WEVTUTIL	Control Windows events.	Event Viewer
	WHERE	Used to display the location of files matching a given search.	Search
	WHOAMI	Gets user name and group information along with security identifiers (SID), privileges, logon identifier (logon ID) for the current user (access token) on the local system.	System Information

Command	New or Updated in Vista	Description	Corresponding GUI Tool
	WINRS	Launches the Windows remote shell.	
	WINSAT	Launches the Windows system assessment tool.	
WMIC		Displays WMI information inside interactive command shell.	

There are several ways to work with the Command Prompt. Usually, you need to access an elevated Command Prompt to perform a given operation. Remember that to do this, you need to right-click on the shortcut in your Quick Launch area and select Run As Administrator. This way, everything you run from the Command Prompt will be elevated.

Creating command files

In addition, you'll want to run multiple commands in a series. For example, you can run uptime reports on a series of PCs. To do this, you use the uptime command. This tool is designed specifically to report on system uptime.

 **The uptime tool is available as a download only. Go to Knowledge Base article number 23243 to obtain it (http://support.microsoft.com/kb/232243/).**

Using this tool and a little ingenuity, you can produce your uptime reports automatically. Basically, you need to run the following command:

```
uptime \\PCname
```

To run a report on multiple computers, you would repeat the line one after another. To simplify the process, put these commands into a command file:

1. **Choose Start Menu ➪ Search ➪ Notepad to open the Notepad.**

2. **Type** uptime \\PCname **and repeat for each PC. Make sure each command is on its own line.**

3. **When you're done, choose File ➪ Save. In the Save dialog box, use the drop-down list under Save as type to choose All Files.** You can change the extension of the text file; otherwise all files are created with the TXT extension.

4. **Name the file** UptimeReport.cmd **and save it under your Documents folder.**

5. **To generate a report, open an elevated Command Prompt, change folders to your Documents folder, and type:**

```
UptimeReport
```

This will produce a report of uptime on each PC in the list.

Now, you'll find that this report isn't so useful because it produces output on the screen and you need to review the screen to see the results of each PC. This is why you should use the pipe (>) command. Using the pipe command will automatically output the results of your command into a text file so that you can review them through Notepad. This makes it a lot easier to verify report outputs. You can even schedule the task in Task Scheduler and review the resulting output at your leisure. Use the following structure to pipe output into a text file:

```
UptimeReport >UptimeReportDate.txt
```

You include the date into the title of the file so that you can differentiate output reports.

Creating an elevated Command Prompt Here hack

One of the most annoying things with the Command Prompt is the location it leaves you in when you launch it. If you need to get to another location in your folder structure, you often have to use the cd command several times to get to the appropriate location. This takes time, time you don't have when dealing with issues. Ideally, you should be able to navigate to the proper location through Windows Explorer and then, when you're there, generate a Command Prompt, even an elevated Command Prompt, in that location. For this, you need a registry hack.

1. Use Notepad to type the following text into a text file:

```
Windows Registry Editor Version 5.00
[HKEY_CLASSES_ROOT\Directory\shell\cmd]
@="Comm&and Prompt here"
"NoWorkingDirectory"=""
"Extended"=-
[HKEY_CLASSES_ROOT\Directory\shell\cmd\command]
@="cmd.exe /k \"pushd %L && title Command Prompt\""
[HKEY_CLASSES_ROOT\Directory\shell\runas]
@="Ele&vated Comm&and Prompt here"
"NoWorkingDirectory"=""
[HKEY_CLASSES_ROOT\Directory\shell\runas\command]
@="cmd.exe /k \"pushd %L && title Command Prompt\""
[HKEY_CLASSES_ROOT\Drive\shell\cmd]
@="Comm&and Prompt here"
"NoWorkingDirectory"=""
"Extended"=-
[HKEY_CLASSES_ROOT\Drive\shell\cmd\command]
@="cmd.exe /k \"pushd %L && title Command Prompt\""
[HKEY_CLASSES_ROOT\Drive\shell\runas]
@="Ele&vated Comm&and Prompt here"
"NoWorkingDirectory"=""
[HKEY_CLASSES_ROOT\Drive\shell\runas\command]
@="cmd.exe /k \"pushd %L && title Command Prompt\""
```

> **NOTE** Make sure you type in the text displayed here exactly as it appears. Double-check your text after you typed it. Making Registry changes is a tricky proposition at best so make sure you do it right.

2. **Save the text file as CommandPromptHere.reg.** Make sure you use the All Files option in the Save dialog box, otherwise your file will also have a .TXT extension. You use the .REG extension because it is the extension used to update Registry settings through text files.

3. **Close Notepad.**

4. **Now, double-click the CommandPromptHere.reg file through Windows Explorer. Accept the UAC prompt and then accept the Registry Editor warning. Click OK when the Registry has been updated.**

5. **Now, you can go to any folder in Windows Explorer, and right-click it to select either Command Prompt Here or Elevated Command Prompt Here from the context menu, as seen in Figure 10.9.**

FIGURE 10.9

Using a Registry Hack to create Command Prompt Here options

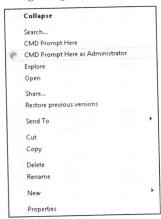

Now you can save time by being able to get the Command Prompt exactly where you need it.

NOTE There is a lot more to be said about the Command Prompt, but it would require its own book. Use a little ingenuity to figure out what you want to do with command files. You can become quite versed in batch file programming if you want to, but in most cases, all you really need is to use the right command once in a while.

TIP Rely on the information in the following link to find out more information on the Command Prompt and how to work with it in Windows Vista: `http://command windows.com/vista-commands.htm`.

Working with Windows PowerShell

Much as the Command Prompt has been used over the years and much as it offers powerful tools for both local and remote management, many people found that running character-based commands in Windows just wasn't powerful enough. That's because in UNIX or Linux environments, operating systems are built first in character mode, then a graphical user interface (GUI) is tacked on. In Windows, of course, it is the reverse. Windows is built with a GUI first, and the Command Prompt is tacked on later. That's why the character-based commands in UNIX or Linux are more powerful by default than in Windows.

Microsoft felt it needed to respond to this requirement. To do this, it created Microsoft Windows PowerShell, a new command interpreter built on top of the .NET Framework, which because of its access to .NET objects, can provide much more comprehensive programming capabilities than the Command Prompt ever will. PowerShell is not installed by default in Vista, at least not in the original release to manufacturing (RTM) version. Because of this, you must download it and run its installation before you can use it.

> **NOTE** Download Windows PowerShell for Vista here: `www.microsoft.com/downloads/details.aspx?familyid=c6ef4735-c7de-46a2-997a-ea58fdfcba63&displaylang=en`. This update is in MSU format and will call the Windows Update Standalone Installer to perform the update. PowerShell requires the .NET Framework to run, but this Framework is already installed by default on Vista.

PowerShell command reference

Table 10.6 lists the various commands you can find in Windows PowerShell. In addition to each command, PowerShell relies on *aliases*. Aliases let you create a shortcut to a command. For example, Microsoft has built a series of aliases in PowerShell by default. These aliases let you run most of the commands found in the Command Prompt through PowerShell; the alias calls the corresponding PowerShell command to execute the action you requested.

Just like the Command Prompt, you need to open a PowerShell interpreter to run the commands. After PowerShell is installed, choose Start Menu ⇨ All Programs ⇨ Windows PowerShell to open a PowerShell Prompt. Use the Documents folder within the Windows PowerShell Start Menu item to access PowerShell documentation and reference information.

TABLE 10.6

Windows PowerShell Commands

Command	Description
Add-Content	To add contents to a specified item.
Add-History	To add a list of commands used during a current session to the end of the session history.

Command	Description
Add-Member	To add a user-defined custom member to an instance of a Windows PowerShell object.
Add-PSSnapin	To add one or more Windows PowerShell snap-ins to a current console.
Clear-Content	To delete the contents of an item.
Clear-Item	To delete the contents of an item.
Clear-ItemProperty	To delete a value of a property.
Clear-Variable	To delete a value of a variable.
Compare-Object	To compare two sets of objects.
ConvertFrom-SecureString	To convert a secure string into an encrypted standard string.
Convert-Path	To convert a Windows PowerShell path to a Windows PowerShell provider path.
ConvertTo-Html	To create an HTML page that represents an object or a set of objects.
ConvertTo-SecureString	To convert encrypted standard strings to secure strings, to convert plain text to secure strings. Use with ConvertFrom-SecureString and Read-Host.
Copy-Item	To copy an item from one location to another within a namespace.
Copy-ItemProperty	To copy a property a value from a specified location to another.
Export-Alias	To export information about currently-defined aliases to a file.
Export-Clixml	To create an XML-based representation of an object(s) and stores it in a file.
Export-Console	To export the configuration of a current console to a file to be reuse or share.
Export-Csv	To create a comma-separated values (CSV) file that represents the input objects.
ForEach-Object	To perform an operation against each of a set of input objects.
Format-Custom	To use a customized view to format the output.
Format-List	To format the output as a list of properties in which each property appears on a new line.
Format-Table	To format the output as a table.
Format-Wide	To format objects as a wide table that displays only one property of each object.

continued

383

TABLE 10.6   *(continued)*

Command	Description
Get-Acl	To get the security descriptor for a resource, such as file or registry key.
Get-Alias	To get the aliases for a current session.
Get-AuthenticodeSignature	To get information about the Authenticode signature in a file.
Get-ChildItem	To get the items and child items in one or more specified locations.
Get-Command	To get basic information about cmdlets and other elements of Window PowerShell commands.
Get-Content	To get the content of an item at the specified location.
Get-Credential	To get a credential object based on a user name and password.
Get-Culture	To get information about the regional settings on a computer.
Get-Date	To get the current date and time.
Get-EventLog	To get information about local event logs or their entries.
Get-ExecutionPolicy	To get the current execution policy for the shell.
Get-Help	To display information on Windows PowerShell cmdlets and concepts.
Get-Host	To get a reference to a current console host object. Displays Windows PowerShell version and regional information by default.
Get-Item	To get an item at a specified location.
Get-ItemProperty	To retrieve the properties of a specified item.
Get-Location	To get information on a current working location.
Get-Member	To get information about objects or collections of objects.
Get-PfxCertificate	To get information on .pfx certificate files on a computer.
Get-Process	To get processes that are running on a local computer.
Get-PSDrive	To get information on Windows PowerShell drives.
Get-PSProvider	To get information on a specified Windows PowerShell provider.
Get-PSSnapin	To get the Windows PowerShell snap-ins on a computer.

Command	Description
Get-Service	To get a service on a local computer.
Get-TraceSource	To get Windows PowerShell components that are instrumented for tracing.
Get-UICulture	To get information on the current user interface culture for Windows PowerShell.
Get-Unique	To return a unique items from a sorted list.
Get-Variable	To get variables in a current console.
Get-WmiObject	To get instances of WMI classes or information about available classes.
Group-Object	To group objects that contain the same value for specified properties.
Import-Alias	To import an alias list from a file.
Import-Csv	To import comma-separated value (CSV) files in the format produced by the Export-CSV cmdlet and to return objects that correspond to the objects represented in that CSV file.
Invoke-Expression	To run a Windows PowerShell expression that is provided in the form of a string.
Invoke-History	To run commands from a session history.
Invoke-Item	To invoke a provider-specific default action on a specified item.
Join-Path	To combine a path and child-path into a single path. The provider supplies the path delimiters.
Measure-Command	To measure the time it takes to run script blocks and cmdlets.
Measure-Object	To measure characteristics of objects and their properties.
Move-Item	To move an item from one location to another.
Move-ItemProperty	To move a property from one location to another.
New-Alias	To create a new alias.
New-Item	To create a new item in a namespace.
New-ItemProperty	To set a new property of an item at a location.
New-Object	To create an instance of a .NET or COM object.
New-PSDrive	To install a new Windows PowerShell drive.
New-Service	To create a new entry for a Windows Service in the registry and the Service Database.
New-TimeSpan	To create a TimeSpan object.

continued

385

TABLE 10.6 *(continued)*

Command	Description
New-Variable	To create a new variable.
Out-Default	To send an output to the default formatter and the default output cmdlet.
Out-File	To send output to a file.
Out-Host	To send output to a command line.
Out-String	To send objects to a host as a series of strings.
Pop-Location	To change the current location to a location most recently pushed onto the lack.
Push-Location	To push a current location onto the stack.
Read-Host	To read a line of input from a console.
Remove-Item	To delete a specified items.
Remove-ItemProperty	To delete a property and its value from an item.
Remove-PSDrive	To delete a Windows PowerShell drive from its location.
Remove-PSSnapin	To remove Windows PowerShell snap-ins from its current location.
Remove-Variable	To delete a variable and its value.
Rename-Item	To rename an item in a Windows PowerShell provider namespace.
Rename-ItemProperty	To rename a property of an item.
Resolve-Path	To resolve a wildcard characters in a path and to display the path contents.
Restart-Service	To stop and then start one or more services.
Resume-Service	To resume one or more paused services.
Select-Object	To select specified properties of an object or set of objects.
Select-String	To identify patterns in strings.
Set-Acl	To change the security descriptor of a specified resource, such as a file or registry key.
Set-Alias	To create or change an alias for a cmdlet or other command element in a current Windows PowerShell session.
Set-AuthenticodeSignature	To use an Authenticode signature to sign a Windows PowerShell script or other file.
Set-Content	To write or replace the content in an item with new content.

Command	Description
Set-Item	To change the values of an item to the value specified in a command.
Set-ItemProperty	To set the values of a property at the specified location.
Set-Location	To set a current working location to a specified location.
Set-PSDebug	To turn script debugging features on and off, to set the trace level and toggles strict mode.
Set-Service	To change a display name, description, or to start the mode of a service.
Set-TraceSource	To configure, start and stop a trace of Windows PowerShell components.
Set-Variable	To set a value of a variable, and create a variable if one with the requested name does not exist.
Sort-Object	To sort objects by property values.
Split-Path	To return to a specified part of a path.
Start-Service	To start one or more stopped services.
Start-Sleep	To suspend shell, script, or run space activity for a specified period of time.
Start-Transcript	To create a record of all or part of a Windows PowerShell session in a text file.
Stop-Process	To stop one or more running processes.
Stop-Service	To stop one or more running services.
Stop-Transcript	To stop a transcript.
Suspend-Service	To pause one or more running services.
Tee-Object	To pipe object input to a file or variable, then to pass the input along the pipeline.
Test-Path	To determine whether all element of a path exist.
Trace-Command	To configure and to start a trace of a specified expression or command.
Where-Object	To create a filter that controls which objects will be passed along a command pipeline.
Write-Debug	To write a debug message to a host display.
Write-Error	To write an object to an error pipeline.
Write-Host	To display objects by using a host user interface.
Write-Output	To write objects to a success pipeline.

continued

TABLE 10.6	*(continued)*
Command	**Description**
Write-Progress	To display a progress bar within a Windows PowerShell command window.
Write-Verbose	To write a string to a verbose display of a host.
Write-Warning	To write a warning message.

 You can also access the PowerShell Owner's Manual online at `www.microsoft.com/technet/scriptcenter/topics/winpsh/manual/default.mspx`.

Running PowerShell scripts

Unlike command files, PowerShell script files use the .PS1 extension. Use the same process as you would normally use for creating a command file, but save the script with a .PS1 extension.

In addition, while you need to install Windows PowerShell on your computer to be able to create and run PowerShell scripts, you do not need to install it on remote systems to be able to execute PowerShell scripts against them. That is because the script actually executes on your own system and only executes commands on the remote system. This makes it easier to work with PowerShell scripts in a Windows Vista environment.

By default, PowerShell does not support the ability to run scripts. That is because its execution policy, the policy that runs scripts, is set to Restricted which means that no scripts are allowed to run. Make sure you've opened the PowerShell command and then use the following PowerShell commands to set your PowerShell policy.

```
Get-ExecutionPolicy
Set-ExecutionPolicy RemoteSigned
```

The first command lists the current policy. The second lets all of your own scripts run, but will run downloaded scripts only if they are digitally signed. This is the best policy. After all, you trust your own scripts but do you trust downloaded scripts?

Now, you can run scripts. Note that in order to run a PowerShell script, you need to type its full pathname along with the script file name. To run a script, type:

```
C:\foldername\scriptname.ps1
```

Where the script name and the folder name list the complete location of the script. If the folder name or the script name includes blank spaces, for example, the folder name is PowerShell Scripts, so you must add an ampersand before the script name and you must put the script name and path in double quotes:

```
& "C:\foldername\scriptname.ps1"
```

You do this because PowerShell is a bit particular about running scripts. These commands run scripts inside the PowerShell command shell. In order to run scripts outside PowerShell, you need to call the PowerShell command:

```
powershell.exe "c:\foldername\scriptname.ps1"
```

You can run this command either in the Run command in the Start Menu or simply in a Command Prompt, or even, through the Task Scheduler if you want to schedule the script to run. Use double quotes as a best practice to make sure your scripts always run.

> **NOTE** There is no elevation command in Windows Vista so that your scripts will run with administrative privileges. However, you can use a great little utility written by Michael Murgolo, a consultant with Microsoft Consulting Services that does just that. Download it at `/www.microsoft.com/technet/technetmag/issues/2007/06/UtilitySpotlight/default.aspx`.

Working with PowerShell

Now that you know how to run scripts, you need to learn how to build them. Learning a new scripting language is a significant task and teaching it is beyond the scope of this book, but there are ways you can take shortcuts.

- Use the Owner's Manual to learn some basics.

- Rely on prewritten or sample scripts. Microsoft hosts the TechNet Script Center that lists a whole series of PowerShell scripts all oriented toward administration tasks at `www.microsoft.com/technet/scriptcenter/topics/msh/cmdlets/index.mspx`.

- Learn to use the Get- command. Just type Get- at the PowerShell Prompt and then, press the **TAB** key. This will automatically scroll through the available commands associated with Get-. Use **SHIFT-TAB** to go backwards in the list.

- Get the PowerShell Help from Sapien Technologies. Sapien is the maker of PrimalScript, a powerful graphical scripting engine that supports several scripting languages. PowerShell Help offers help on all of the PowerShell commands in a nice graphical layout as can be seen in Figure 10.10. PowerShell Help is available for free at `www.primalscript.com/Free_Tools/index.asp`. While you're at it, get the free Logon Script Generator. It will also save you lots of time.

- Get the free PowerGUI. PowerGUI is a free graphical user interface for PowerShell script development. In addition, Quest, the makers of PowerGUI, has built a community of users that keep adding functionality to the PowerGUI. Find the community and download PowerGUI from `http://powergui.org`. As can be seen in Figure 10.11, PowerGUI can save you a lot of time.

These tips and free tools should get you going in PowerShell quite rapidly. Use it, you'll love it.

NOTE Third-party tools such as Admin Script Editor (ASE) from iTripoli Inc. (www. itripoli.com) can greatly help as well. ASE in particular can give you a significant jump start by offering wizards that generate code, syntax help as you type and keyword documentation right within the editing environment making it very simple to write complex scripts.

FIGURE 10.10

Working with PowerShell Help

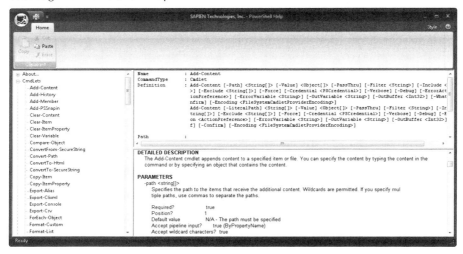

Finally, just like there is no default way to normally generate a Command Prompt at the location you are in, there is no default way to do this with PowerShell either. This means you need to use a hack to do so. Use the utilities mentioned earlier for elevation (by Michael Murgolo) to create similar entries in the context menu as those created for the Command Prompt earlier. Michael's files are not in REG format, but in INF format. This means that you must right-click on the appropriate file and select Install to get it to run. Once installed, you will have appropriate prompts in the context menu of any folder through Windows Explorer, as can be seen in Figure 10.12.

FIGURE 10.11

Working with PowerGUI

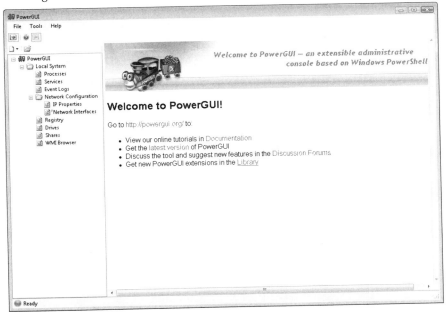

FIGURE 10.12

Accessing the Elevated PowerShell Prompt

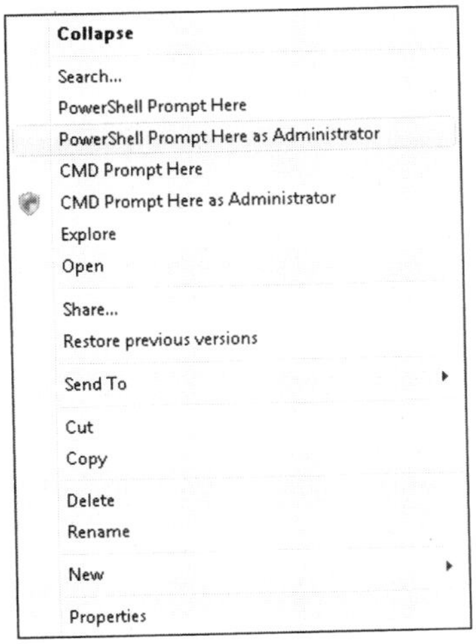

Collapse
Search...
PowerShell Prompt Here
PowerShell Prompt Here as Administrator
CMD Prompt Here
CMD Prompt Here as Administrator
Explore
Open
Share...
Restore previous versions
Send To ▶
Cut
Copy
Delete
Rename
New ▶
Properties

Scheduling automated tasks

Both PowerShell and Command Prompt items can be automated via the Task Scheduler. Rely on the information in Chapter 9 to create these automated tasks. But there are caveats when you use command files to create automated tasks:

- If your task is calling on a special command, for example, the uptime command, then you must make sure that the command will be available to the task when the task runs. Placing a command in your Documents folder will not work because the task may not have access rights to this folder. Ideally, you will create a C:\Toolkit folder and set its permissions so that the account you run the task under will have access to it.

- You must make sure that if your task will perform an action on a remote computer, that it will have appropriate access rights. To do this, run the task under the appropriate credentials. You might consider creating a special task management account that will have administrative rights on each PC and use it to run automated tasks.

- Make sure the command file or the PowerShell script you run will be available to the task. Once again, it is a good idea to place these scripts within the C:\Toolkit folder.

- You can use events to create tasks. For example, run a disk cleanup task as soon as a disk space warning is generated in the Event Log. You should also get the task to send you a notice of this event. Do this by creating conditional tasks.

- Use the Task Scheduler to help out in your administrative schedule. Create appropriate tasks for most of the monitoring activities you need to perform and output the result into a text file. Place the resultant text files in the C:\Toolkit folder and verify the output based on the schedule you set for each task. This will save you inordinate amounts of time since you will only need to verify the output instead of actually performing the task.

Using a combination of PowerShell, the Command Prompt, other utilities and a little ingenuity, you should be able to rely on the Task Scheduler to do most of your monitoring work for you. This is just one more way Vista helps reduce administration costs.

Supporting Users

The last activity you need to be familiar with is supporting users. There is really only one way to help users remotely in Windows Vista, even though several people use two different methods. The two tools people use are:

- Windows Remote Assistance (the right way)
- Remote Desktop (the wrong way)

Each provides access to an environment through a remote connection of some type.

Helping users with Remote Assistance

When you need to provide remote support to a user, especially while the user is still logged on and within the user's context, use Windows Remote Assistance (WRA). Remote Assistance works in one of two ways. It can let users request assistance from the Help Desk or it can let Help Desk operators offer assistance to users. Users must explicitly accept assistance before either can proceed.

Remote Assistance is controlled through two GPO settings: Solicited Remote Assistance and Offer Remote Assistance. Both are found in Computer Configuration ➪ Policies ➪ Administrative Templates ➪ System ➪ Remote Assistance. Each includes the ability to identify Helpers in your organization. Each lets you determine the type of assistance to offer, identifying whether support personnel can interact with the desktop of simply watch. Interaction provides the fullest support but can possibly represent a security risk. Both settings require a list of helpers. Helpers are user groups that are typed in the format domainname\groupname. Ideally, you want to create a special PC Technicians or Help Desk security group within Active Directory and rely on the members of this group to provide assistance.

CAUTION Before a Helper can assist a user or interact with their desktop, users must first accept the offer for remote assistance. Be sure to warn users never to leave their desktops unattended while someone else is interacting with it.

Again, ideally, you should not let users request assistance as it is fairly complex for them. You should instead offer assistance through WRA and get them to simply accept it. You can offer help in the following manner:

1. **Launch Windows Remote Assistance from Start Menu ➪ All Programs ➪ Maintenance.**
2. **Click Offer to help someone.**
3. **Type the DNS name or the IP address of the PC you want to connect to, and click Next.**
4. **Click Finish when the connection is established.**
5. **Wait for the user to accept the connection before beginning your support.**

You can also use a command line to offer assistance:

```
msra /expert
```

This command will automatically launch the Offer user interface. If you want to perform and offer from the command line, use:

```
msra /offerRA computername
```

A check box appears on the user's computer listing Allow «helper» to respond to User Account Control prompts when the helper asks to share control of the desktop. If the user selects this check box, you will be able to respond to requests from the computer for administrator consent or administrator credentials. Having this consent allows you to run programs at the administrator level without the end user's participation.

WRA in Windows Vista creates an encrypted connection between two computers over the Internet or the network. This connection is further secured through password protection. This method is the preferred method for supporting users because it does not require sharing the user's password.

CAUTION   **Never request a user's password to provide assistance. This is the worst of bad practices in systems administration. In fact, you should warn users that if someone requests their password, then they are not from your organization, and the user should never share the password. If this occurs, they should alert the Help Desk immediately.**

Relying on the Remote Desktop

Remote Desktop Connections are very useful to provide access to a computer remotely. But, they are useless when it comes to assisting users or resolving issues that occur in their security context for two reasons:

- Windows Vista does not allow two connections to a computer at the same time even though it allows multiple local connections at the same time through Fast User Switching. As shown in Figure 10.13, when you try to log on to a computer either locally or remotely and another user is currently using it, Vista offers to disconnect the other user. This makes it quite difficult to assist someone since all they can see is a logoff screen.

FIGURE 10.13

Using Remote Desktop to connect to a system with a user already logged on

> Logon Message
>
> Another user is currently logged on to this computer. If you continue, this user has to disconnect from this computer. Do you want to continue?

- To log on to a computer in a user's context, you must have access to their user name and password. Because you will never ask for a user's password, Remote Desktop cannot let you resolve issues within a user's context. To assist a user in their context, you must use Windows Remote Assistance.

However, there are still quite a few uses for Remote Desktops:

- They are great to perform administrative activities on servers because no single user is logged on locally to a server.
- With Windows Server 2008, you can rely on RemoteApps to publish just an application and not an entire desktop to a user. This feature makes sharing applications very easy.
- Users can access their own desktops with their own profile and application settings from anywhere in the organization through Remote Desktop. In many ways, this way is much easier than using Roaming Profiles because everything stays on the user's PC and does not need to be transferred from one PC to another.
- You can use Remote Desktop to troubleshoot issues on a remote PC when no user is logged on.

Make sure that the Remote Desktop connection is allowed on the target PC if you want to make use of RDC within these parameters. Once again, this is done through a Group Policy Object. You can accomplish this two ways:

- The setting is Allow users to connect remotely using Terminal Services and can be found by choosing Computer Configuration ⇨ Policies ⇨ Administrative Templates ⇨ Windows Components ⇨ Terminal Services ⇨ Terminal Server ⇨ Connections.

- You can also enable this interactively under the Control Panel ⇨ System and Maintenance ⇨ System section by using the Allow remote access command. Make sure you select Allow connections only from computers running Remote Desktop with Network Level Authentication (NLA) (more secure) as your settings since it is the most secure setting available.

After the remote connections are allowed, choose Start Menu ⇨ All Programs ⇨ Accessories ⇨ Remote Desktop Connection to create a connection to the remote computer. You can also use the Remote Desktop Connection gadget mentioned earlier to do this.

TIP Make sure you use the Remote Desktop after hours or when you know that the user is not logged on to their system because connecting to the system and saying Yes when there is a warning message of a user logged on will log them off with no warning. This is a good way to get irate users.

Summary

This chapter covers a series of different techniques for PC administration and user assistance. It identifies common administration tasks and begins the process of outlining how they are executed. The following chapters continue this explanation as different topics such as security and information protection are discussed.

In addition, this chapter covers how to perform local versus remote administration activities. It identifies the most common administration tools for use in Vista, many of which support both local and remote administration through the graphical user interface. It also outlines how you should create and configure your administrative workstation.

To relieve the administrative burden, it outlines how you can automate tasks either through the Command Prompt or through Windows PowerShell and then shows you how to link these automated commands with the Task Scheduler to perform them on a recurring basis. Then, because the task is already performed, you can spend time reviewing results instead of actually performing the task itself.

Finally, it outlines the difference between Windows Remote Assistance and the Remote Desktop when it comes to assisting users. WRA is the best tool to use in this context because it lets you view end users' desktops without compromising security at any level. Make sure that you rely on this tool when it comes to helping your users with the issues they deal with when working with Vista.

Part IV

Protecting and Maintaining the System

Part IV finishes off Vista administration with the last three aspects of CASPR: security (Chapter 11), protection (Chapter 12), and recovery (Chapter 13). Microsoft has invested very heavily into Vista security and this section takes you through the paces required to protect fully all of your systems whether they be in-house or on the road. Microsoft has also revamped and updated the components, which let you protect intellectual property both inside and outside your firewall. The first portion of this book has shown you how to build images and implement deployment strategies that can re-image a computer in less than half an hour. However, there will be situations where you will need to recover a particular system from a total failure or recovery one single lost document. Whether it be by making sure your users can recover their own information on Vista or because you need to recover a computer from a total loss, rely on this section to discover the ins and outs of Vista's backup and recovery capabilities.

Chapter 11

Securing the Workstation

This chapter continues to build on the CASPR system, this time focusing on the security aspects of system maintenance and administration. Whether you work with a computer running Windows Vista at home or whether you are part of a corporate network, you know you must secure the system at all times. Fortunately, Windows Vista includes a host of new features that are geared toward system protection. Service hardening, Security Center, User Access Control, Network Access Protection, Windows Defender, Windows Firewall are only a few of the integrated features this new version of Windows includes to make your systems more secure.

Somehow, knowing that there are more than one billion PCs running Windows in the world gives malicious attackers a hungering need to destroy them. Attacks range from viruses, Trojans, worms, root kits, phishing, password thefts, and much more. This is why your defense strategy must be wide-ranging and must include a very tight integration between your administrative security policy and the computerized methods you put in place to protect yourself.

To build secure systems, you need to make sure that you have all the components in place for a complete security strategy. This should include:

- A comprehensive security policy
- A defense in depth strategy
- A documented security plan
- A strategy for communicating this approach to security to your end users

These are the elements that are covered in this chapter. After you begin to put them in place, you will be able to completely harden your Vista environment, Although you can't expect that security issues will not occur, you can expect that you will be ready to deal with them and mitigate their impact.

Beginning with Basic Security

Microsoft, as the provider of Windows, offers several tools and guidelines to secure the information your systems host as well as securing the systems themselves. One excellent example is the Windows Vista Security Guide. It offers a structured way for you to further protect your systems beyond the base protections enabled when you install Windows. However, securing a computer system is more than just applying a set of configurations to the system; it also involves a comprehensive administrative outlook on how systems are used and how people are responsible for them.

> **NOTE** Look up the Windows Vista Security Guide at www.microsoft.com/technet/windowsvista/security/guide.mspx.

Microsoft has gone the extra mile to protect their systems just because they are so often under attack. In fact, one of the most important efforts Microsoft has made in terms of security with Windows Vista is to submit the operating system for evaluation against industry standards for security. One of these is the Common Criteria. Vista has been evaluated against the Common Criteria and has passed this security evaluation. Organizations that have very tight security requirements, for example, the Federal Government, can rely on Vista's built-in security features to create highly secure environments. Of course, this level of security is not for everyone, but it is comforting to know that should you require it, you can secure your systems thoroughly.

> **NOTE** More information is available on the Common Criteria at www.commoncriteriaportal.org.

Vista also supports Federal Information Processing Standard (FIPS) approved cryptographic algorithms to secure client/server communications. For even tighter security, Vista implements the Suite B cryptographic algorithms defined by the U.S. government. Because of this, it supports data encryption, digital signatures, key exchanges as well as hashing, which can let third-party vendors create more comprehensive security solutions.

> **NOTE** More information on Suite B can be found at www.nsa.gov/ia/industry/crypto_suite_b.cfm. In addition, a good resource site for security and vulnerability information is http://oval.mitre.org/.

Security deals with almost every single aspect of your network. The ultimate goal of your security strategy should always be to protect the information that is stored on your systems. Sometimes this information is the information that makes your organization run; other times, it is your own personal information you want to protect at all times.

Your security strategy should aim to cover the following aspects of computer activity:

- Each person that enters your network must be identified.

- Each person who has access to your organization's premises must be cleared and you must provide them with only appropriate levels of access once they are authorized.

- Your security strategy must implement non-repudiation principles, or otherwise make sure that when someone modifies something it is the person who is authorized to do so.

- Information in your network must be protected at the appropriate level. For example, confidential information must be kept confidential at all times.

- Information must also be available when it is needed.

- Information must have a high degree of integrity.

- Network activity must be monitored to some degree so that you know that traffic patterns are approved traffic patterns.

- Access to your systems must be audited so that you know who is doing what when.

- Your security strategy must be surrounded by the appropriate administrative activities to ensure it is maintained at all times.

Although this list is not comprehensive, it does identify the type of preoccupation you must have in mind when putting together your security strategy. In addition, you need to consider the scope of interaction users will have with your network:

- **Local:** When people log on to a system, they interact with it at the local level.

- **Intranet:** When people log on to your network, they can interact with all of the systems that are connected with each other. Most often, users will interact with servers offering services and may interact with each other. When the network is internal, it is called the Intranet.

- **Internet:** Users will interact with public systems that may or may not belong to you.

- **Extranet:** When users connect to your network from outside your premises or when partners interact with components of your network, they interact with your Extranet — a network that is under your control, but that is not part of the internal network.

Whatever its scope, security is an activity (like all IT activities) that relies on three key elements: people, PCs, and processes.

- **People** are both the executors and the users of the security process.

- **PCs** represent the technology people use to manage information.

- **Processes** make up the administrative aspects of the security strategy. They include workflow patterns, procedures, and standards used for the application of security.

Each of these three key elements must integrate with the other to create a strong security strategy.

Designing a security policy

Begin your security design for Vista with the design of your security policy. Your policy will encompass several aspects, but at the very least it should cover every aspect of computing, each of the different scopes of interaction, and it should be built upon sound principles and administrative practices. Don't wait until you are the victim of an attack. Act now so if you are attacked, you can mitigate the impact.

Look to your business model. Analyze the processes that make your organization run and identify those that are critical to its operation. This is much like business continuity. Many organizations who do not have a business continuity strategy in place will fail in the event of a major disaster to their datacenter. Although it won't be PC security that will cause a disaster of this magnitude, it is through the PC that most malicious attackers have access to your systems. Consider it as the first point of interaction or the Point of Access to Secure Services (PASS). This is why it must be secured.

Most organizations will already have some form of security policy in place, if so; use it as the starting point of the elaboration of your Vista security strategy. Then update it with new settings and features. Identify which standards you want to implement; include both technical and non-technical processes. For example, you might include technical security parameters when you pre-pare computers for delivery to end users. In another instance, you might make sure your end users never share their passwords with anyone from within or without your organization. Then, after you have the entire strategy defined, communicate it to your users and provide continuous security communications.

Using the Castle Defense System

One good way to make security simpler for everyone in your organization is to use a security model. For example, we have been using the Castle Defense System (CDS) security model for several years now. This model is easy to understand because everyone is more or less familiar with the concepts inherent in the protection of medieval castles. Using a descriptive illustration lets you show your end users, including management, that computer security is a multilayered activity that does not rest only on your shoulders.

In the days when the world was younger, it was also more dangerous. To protect themselves and their belongings, people built castles with multiple layers of protection. There are at least five different layers of protection in all castles. The first layer is the moat. It protects the castle by creating a physical barrier to entry. When the drawbridge is up, no one can enter and when it is down, only authorized people have access. The second level is the walls themselves. They are high and cannot be climbed except under duress. On top of the walls are crenellations that let archers defend from attackers. The third level is the courtyard; it is designed to let defenders fend off attackers because it does not offer cover from their arrows. The fourth level, the castle itself, offers a second massive layer of defense should the walls be breached. Finally, you have the vault that is designed to protect the crown jewels from attackers.

This rudimentary description gives a good impression of how you should defend your own "crown jewels" and ensure that they are protected at all times. It is a good analogy with which you can drive home the concept of multilayered security strategies.

When you transform it into a computer protection mechanism, the Castle Defense System also includes five layers of defense. In addition, like the castle, you begin the in-depth defense strategy from within and expand it to cover all aspects of computer security, as shown in Figure 11.1.

These five layers include:

- **Layer 1: Critical Information.** Identify what you want to protect.
- **Layer 2: Physical Protection.** Implement some physical level of protection for your offices.
- **Layer 3: Operating System Hardening.** Address the computer systems themselves.
- **Layer 4: Information Access.** Apply controls to the people whom you trust to interact with computers within your network.
- **Layer 5: External Access.** Control how people outside your own domain can interact with your network and the systems it contains.

And because you must work with people, PCs, and processes, two additional aspects — people and processes — must be included in the CDS to round out your illustration of a complete defense and security strategy.

Using this layered approach also makes it easier to identify what needs to be covered. Of course, before you can design or review your security strategy, you must have a thorough understanding of your own organization. You also need to have a good understanding of the technical components of your IT infrastructure to ensure that you cover them all.

As far as PC security is concerned, you need to address each of the five layers with respect to what does apply and what doesn't apply to these endpoint systems.

NOTE The Castle Defense System also applies to servers. For information on how to apply the CDS to server infrastructures, look up *Windows Server 2008: The Complete Reference* by Ruest and Ruest from McGraw-Hill Osborne.

FIGURE 11.1

The five layers of the Castle Defense System

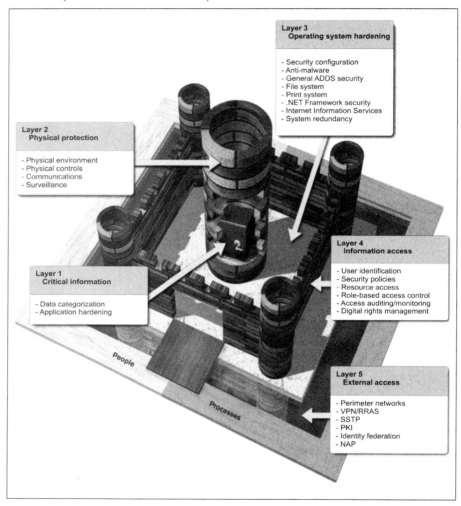

Layer 3
Operating system hardening

- Security configuration
- Anti-malware
- General ADDS security
- File system
- Print system
- .NET Framework security
- Internet Information Services
- System redundancy

Layer 2
Physical protection

- Physical environment
- Physical controls
- Communications
- Surveillance

Layer 1
Critical information

- Data categorization
- Application hardening

Layer 4
Information access

- User identification
- Security policies
- Resource access
- Role-based access control
- Access auditing/monitoring
- Digital rights management

Layer 5
External access

- Perimeter networks
- VPN/RRAS
- SSTP
- PKI
- Identity federation
- NAP

People

Processes

Building a security plan

Each security strategy includes a security plan. The plan must address more than the security policy itself. It must address how you will manage and update the security policy. In fact, the plan builds upon the first activity — security policy definition — to provide you with a complete approach to security. The next parts of the plan address every day approaches to ongoing security. They include:

- **Defense planning:** Mostly a budgeting and project management activity that ensures you will continue to update your defenses.

- **Security monitoring:** An activity focused on continuous monitoring of your network to ensure nothing untoward is occurring.

- **Security testing:** A final activity that ensures that the protection mechanisms you have in place are appropriate for your requirements.

The security plan and its interaction with the Castle Defense System are shown in Figure 11.2. As you can see, it is a continuous cycle that comes back to the policy definition when complete. If your testing determines that modifications are required, then you must update the policy, include the update in your planning, continue to monitor the update, and test it and so on. Security is never final and must always be an ongoing activity.

FIGURE 11.2

Security management activities

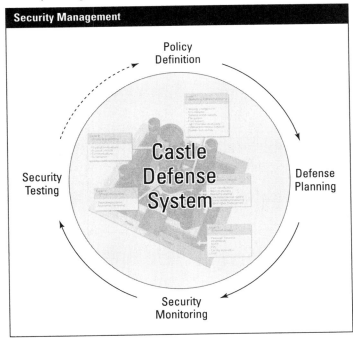

One key focus of the security plan is the understanding of the types of threats you face. Although you may not face all of the known threats, you will face some; therefore, it is better to understand as many as possible so that if they occur, you can to recognize them. Several types of threats exist, including:

- **Accidental security breach:** This type of threat often occurs because people are just not aware that they must protect your systems. For example, users from all over the world give out their passwords to people they trust. The next thing you know someone is impersonating the user because they have access to their account. You should make sure your users are aware that they should never give out their password to anyone.

- **Internal attack:** Often this attack stems from giving users too much access. This usually occurs because IT administrators believe that anyone having access to the internal network is a trusted person. Because of this, internal resources are not explicitly protected. Therefore, when contractors have access to your network, they also have access to all of your crown jewels.

- **Social engineering attack:** This attack derives from people impersonating someone users will trust. For example, sending someone a message from the "Internal Help Desk" and asking them for their credentials is a very common form of social engineering. Make sure that your users don't fall prey to this type of attack. Teach them to always call back if they are not sure they are actually talking to the help desk.

- **Organizational attack:** This attack is launched from a competitor — one who wants to have access to your confidential information to gain a competitive advantage over you and your organization.

- **Automated attacks:** These attacks are the most common attack type you and your end users will face. Automated programs scan computer ports at various addresses until one of them responds. Then, when they get a response, they begin to identify what type of opening the user has left on. Systems that do not run personal firewalls are excellent examples of the victims of this attack type.

- **Denial of Service (or Distributed Denial of Service) attack:** This threat relies on multiple systems to try to overwhelm a service you offer. For example, if someone can overwhelm your Domain Naming Service (DNS), then users may no longer be able to find your organization on the Web.

- **Viral attacks:** Viruses or other malicious code is inserted into the organization and begins to infect systems. This is often due to the fact that organizations do not run locked down computer environments. When a user runs with local administrative privileges, anything that can take control of their machine will automatically have the same privileges. Locking down systems prevents many of these attacks.

- **Malicious e-mails and phishing:** These attacks try to fool your users into doing something that will compromise your systems. The best defense for this type of attack is a strong offence: make sure your users are educated and won't fall prey to stupid gimmicks.

Although they do not all apply to the PC, each type of attack must be addressed by your security plan.

 More information on attack types and defense strategies can be found at Microsoft Security Central at www.microsoft.com/security/default.mspx. Microsoft

also publishes a Threats and Countermeasures document at www.microsoft.com/technet/ security/guidance/serversecurity/tcg/tcgch00.mspx#EDD. You should also consider accessing Microsoft's Threat Analysis and Modeling Tool (http://go.microsoft.com/ fwlink/?LinkId=86405). This tool lets you enter information about your organization to produce a rich list of the potential threats you may face. The results will let you better understand which aspects of the layers of the CDS you need to concentrate on for your systems.

Using the Windows Vista Security Guide

One of the best resources you can rely on to secure your PCs is the Windows Vista Security Guide. This guide includes both textual information as well as tools that help you implement security on PCs running Vista. It assumes that you are running a network in an Active Directory (AD) domain and that you have access to Group Policy to centrally control change on your PCs. It provides a GPO Accelerator — a tool that can generate either Local or Group Policies to further protect systems. When using Group Policy, the tool relies on a specific organizational unit (OU) structure, one where PCs are categorized according to type and are secured according to role.

 **This OU structure was used in Chapter 9 when discussing Group Policy.**

NOTE **Microsoft publishes a Group Policy Best Practices Analyzer which can be used to validate all of the GPOs in your network. Find the GPO BPA at** http://support. microsoft.com/?kbid=940122.

No security strategy for Windows Vista is complete without including contents from this guide. Make sure that you review it fully and incorporate its recommendations in the security strategy you prepare for your PCs.

Learning Windows Vista security features

Windows Vista includes a host of new features, many of which are focused on security. In fact, Microsoft's goal with Vista was to rewrite the Windows code to remove as many security flaws as possible. Although it is evident that Microsoft's new Trusted Computing Initiative has borne some fruit, it is almost impossible for an organization to go over millions of lines of code and remove every single flaw that it contains, especially when all too many experts are only happy to prove that they missed something. Despite this, Vista is much more secure than any other Windows operating system has ever been and, with the application of its security features in a judicious manner, you'll be able to make sure breaches of security won't happen in your network.

New security features in Vista include:

- **Service Hardening:** Microsoft has reduced the amount of privilege system services include by default. By creating new, restricted services, Vista will not allow attackers who take control of a service to perform tasks for which the service is not designed.

- **Data Execution Prevention** (DEP): A system which is built into most modern processors. DEP stops code from using certain memory areas to run malicious software. Vista integrates directly with DEP to ensure that the famous buffer overrun flaw is mitigated on the PCs it runs on.

- **x64 editions:** 64-bit editions of Vista also offer more protection than their x86 counterparts. Device drivers must be signed by their manufacturer before they can be installed. This ensures that it has not been tampered with from the time it was written to the time you install it. In addition, x64 systems include PatchGuard, a system that prevents code from modifying the Windows Kernel and ensures that your system runs as it was intended.

- **User Account Control** (UAC): With UAC, everyone runs with a standard user token when using Vista, even administrators. UAC makes it easier to run locked down systems because everyone is locked down by default.

- The **Vista Credential Manager**: This tool powers the logon architecture, removing the older graphical identification and authentication (GINA) architecture and making it easier for security providers to integrate to the logon process.

- **Smart Cards:** The new Credential Manager also makes it easier to integrate Smart Cards to the logon process and with the new cryptographic service provider (CSP), the deployment of smart cards is greatly simplified.

- **Network Access Protection (NAP):** This service is built into Vista from the start. You can use the Vista NAP client to integrate with either Cisco's Network Access Control or use a Windows Server 2008 backend to create a full NAP infrastructure. NAP protects your networks by quarantining systems that do not pass health status validations. Once quarantined, systems are updated, and when they have a clean bill of health are allowed access to full network resources.

- **Windows Security Center:** This Center provides you with a single integrated control panel for all things secure. If clearly outlines the status of updates, antivirus, anti-malware, and other security features on the Vista system.

- **Windows Defender:** A tool which provides built-in protection for malware including spyware and rootkits. Defender automatically obtains updates from Microsoft.com and provides one easy way to clean infected systems.

- **Windows Firewall with Advanced Security:** A tool which lets you completely control the inbound and outbound connections on any Vista PC. The Windows Firewall can be completely configured through Group Policy and can provide conditional behavior, letting you configure one behavior for systems connected to the internal network and another for systems that are traveling.

- The **Microsoft Malicious Software Removal Tool**: A tool that runs each month on your systems to ensure no malicious software is lurking in its depths.

- **Internet Explorer version 7**: This version of IE also includes a host of security advancements. Its Protected Mode automatically reduces its attack surface when surfing on the Internet. Its ActiveX Opt-In option lets you control the behavior of unauthorized ActiveX code. Other protections include URL handling and cross-domain scripting barriers. The new Fix My Settings command lets users rapidly return to a working IE environment. Also, its new security status bar lets users immediately know it the site is secure (green) or if the site is potentially unsafe (red). And the built-in Phishing Filter lets you know if a site is authentic or not.

■ **BitLocker Full Drive Encryption:** BitLocker lets you protect the entire system on portable computers so that no content can be stolen in the event of a computer loss.

■ **Rights Management Client:** The integrated client also helps protect user data by controlling how others can use the information you create.

■ **The Encrypting File System** (EFS): EFS can now integrate with smart cards and provide more complete protection for information stored on any PC.

■ **USB Device Controls:** These settings are managed through Group Policy and allow you to completely control which devices can be plugged into your Vista systems. This lets you control who can or cannot use removable disks to copy data from your network.

■ **Software Restriction Policies:** A tool that lets you control what software is allowed to run in your network. You should apply this to any software installations or scripts you want to allow to run in your network and block all other code from execution.

■ **Temporary and Offline Files:** These files can now be protected through EFS as well as protecting files while in transit through the Secure Sockets Tunneling Protocol (SSTP). This means that the contents of folders such as %tmp% and %temp% is protected at all times, even when the user logs off from the system.

This list includes a series of features that build on all of the security elements Microsoft put into Windows XP especially after the delivery of Service Pack 2. These features make it easier for you to deploy completely secure endpoints.

However, security does not only come from the client. It must be married with services that are rendered by servers. These services differ depending on whether your network is running Windows Server 2003 or 2008. The ideal and most secure combination is obviously Windows Server 2008 with Windows Vista. Nevertheless, running a Windows Server system with Vista should give you access to additional security components.

Applying the Castle Defense System

Armed with the list of new Vista security features and with the five layers of the Castle Defense System, you can now begin to view how you will protect your own Vista PCs. Table 11.1 outlines each of the five layers of the CDS and identifies how you can use the Vista feature set to secure each PC.

TABLE 11.1

Applying the CDS to Vista PCs

Layer	Contents	Contents
Layer 1 — Critical information	Data categorization	Categorize all data to determine the level of protection each type of data requires on your PCs.
	Application hardening	Make sure the applications your users have access to are well-designed and provide a protection layer of their own.
Layer 2 — Physical protection	Physical environment	Make sure entry to your offices is protected.
		Make sure your PCs are tagged and identified.
		Make sure the external systems you allow to connect to your network can provide a clean bill of health.
	Physical controls	Pay attention to the physical access to your PCs.
	Communications	Make sure all users, including administrators, understand their responsibilities in terms of security practices.
	Surveillance	Make sure everyone in the organization understands their responsibilities in terms of vigilance.
Layer 3 — OS hardening	Security configuration	Pay special attention to the following: service hardening, security configuration settings for the base PC installation, BitLocker Drive Encryption for portable systems whose configuration is sensitive, Encrypting File System data protection for others, User Account Control (UAC) for all users and administrators, Device Control to ensure that unauthorized USB disk drives cannot be connected to any PC, and wireless networking security.
	Anti-malware	Implement Windows Defender along with proper antivirus technologies.

Layer	Contents	Contents
	General Active Directory Security	Implement very tight permissions management.
		Implement Software Restriction Policies to ensure no malicious code is allowed to run in your domain.
	File System	Secure the file system to protect PC stability.
		Implement access-based enumeration to further protect information.
		Rely on digitally signed Windows Installer Packages for all third-party or custom product installations.
	Print System	Implement a full security strategy for all printers. Make sure standard users can install their own printers.
	.NET Framework Security	Any PC that includes this Framework needs special care. For example, PCs running Windows PowerShell will also include the Framework.
	Internet Information Services (IIS)	If you choose to install IIS on PCs, then make sure it is securely configured.
	System redundancy	Redundancy on PCs is provided through the application of sound principles, the protection of user data and the availability of additional systems for replacement.
Layer 4 — Information access	User identification	Rely on smart card or two-factor authentication for administrators in very secure environments.
		Highly secure environments will use two-factor authentication for all users.
	Security policies	Assign proper policies for the PC pool.
	Resource access	Tightly control all resource access.
		Implement EFS for mobile users.
	Role-based access control	Applicable only at the server or application level.
	Access auditing/monitoring·	Turn on auditing to track all changes on critical systems.

continued

TABLE 11.1 *(continued)*		
Layer	**Contents**	**Contents**
	Digital rights management (DRM)	Rely on Rights Management Services to apply DRM to all documentation that is copyrighted or sensitive in any other fashion.
Layer 5 — External access	Perimeter networks	Configure the Windows Firewall with Advanced Security to control access to Vista PCs and mobile workstations.
	Virtual Private Networks (VPN)	Rely on Virtual Private Network (VPN) connections for all remote access.
	Routing and Remote Access (RRAS)	Implement a remote access authentication service for users working remotely.
	Secure Sockets Tunneling Protocol (SSTP)	Ensure all remote communications as well as sensitive internal communications are encrypted.
	Public Key Infrastructures (PKI)	Implement PKI in support of smart card deployment and software restrictions.
	Identity Federation	Rely on Active Directory Federated Services for Extranet access if it is required.
	Network Access Protection (NAP)	Implement Network Access Protection (NAP) to ensure all machines that link to your network have approved health status.

Layer 1: Protecting information

Information is the basis of any effort that relies on the PC, but if organizations are properly structured at the IT level, then this information will most usually be stored on networked servers. That's because when it is stored centrally, information is easier to protect, back up, and secure. But, given the distributed nature of the client-server system, you'll often find that information, sometimes information that is critical to your organization, will be located on PCs. In those cases, you must protect the information as much as possible, especially if the PC is a mobile PC that is used outside of your offices.

Ideally, you will have performed some form of information categorization, one that will give you a better understanding of the information you need to protect if your organization is to run properly. There are usually four categories of information:

- Public information is information that may or may not be related to your organization, but that does not require protection. For example, information on products your organization sells through your Web site is deemed public information.

- Private information is information that you need to run your operations, but this information is not sensitive and may not require heavy protection. For example, information on how you run your Web site is usually private, but if it is leaked outside your organization, it will not be a major disaster.

- Confidential information is information that should only be divulged to authorized personnel. For example, the salaries you pay to your employees are usually deemed confidential.

- Secret information is information that is critical to the operation of your business. If secret information is leaked out, it may have a negative impact on your organization's ability to operate.

Each category of information can find itself on a PC at some point in time. For this reason, you need to make sure it is protected at all times.

CROSS-REF See Chapter 12 for more information on Information protection.

In addition to protecting the data on your PCs, you must make sure that your applications — the applications that generate and manipulate your organization's information — are hardened or otherwise configured in a fashion that makes it difficult for unauthorized personnel to obtain it. Stories about organizations that have leaked out information, such as credit card numbers of their clients because their applications are not hardened are too often on the news.

Layer 2: Working with protection

Physical protection is also more difficult with PCs because they are distributed by nature. There are four categories of PCs to protect.

The first category focuses on the workstations that are located in your office are easier to protect because they are on your physical premises; hopefully, you have system checks in place for anyone who wants to remove them from your premises.

However, physical protection becomes more difficult when you consider the second category: mobile or tablet PCs. According to researchers, more than 600,000 PCs are lost or stolen in the U.S. each year. That is a considerable number, so you want to make sure you've properly protected them.

In addition to mobile systems, you might also be faced with a third category: working with or preparing kiosk PCs. Kiosk PCs are still under your control, but they present a different problem because they are exposed to users over whom you have little or no control. Therefore, these PCs must have a very tight physical security mechanism put in place so that they are locked down and cannot be removed from your facilities.

The fourth category of PC that requires some form of physical security is the teleworker's PC. Although these are often mobile systems, they sometimes include actual workstations that you provide to your users so that they can perform work from home. In this case, you are faced with two issues:

- You must find a way to protect the system at a physical level in an environment — the user's home — where you have no control.

- The second is that this corporate PC will often be accessed by noncorporate users in the form of the user's family members. One feature of Vista that makes it easier to deal with this aspect is the ability to use Fast User Switching, assigning a personal account to each family member. But in some cases, families all use the same user account and this can cause a major risk since any family member will have access to the data on your network — at lease the same level of access as the user has.

With each of these different categories of systems, you have few choices for protection at the physical level. You can

- Tag each system and include them in an asset inventory. Bar code tags are the ideal method because they can be entered into a database.

- Use a loss tracking mechanism, one that will offer an online reward for the return of your lost items. Several exist. One that is well rated is www.trackit.com, but you can find many more if you search for them.

- Load your PCs with tracking software, software that will automatically identify the location of the system if it is lost or stolen and someone tries to use it. A good example of this software is AbsoluteTrack from Absolute software (www.absolute.com). Once again, you can search for others as there are several choices.

Make sure your kiosk PCs are bolted to the casings that hold them so that they are impossible to remove. It would be nice to do the same with mobile PCs, but that is unlikely. You can however protect your mobile systems with cable locks. You should include these with each mobile system you provide to your users and instruct them in their use. As for systems that you provide to your teleworkers, you can only recommend that they place them in secure rooms. The best way to do this is to provide your teleworkers with information and procedures they should follow when bringing a computer home.

Layer 3: Hardening the system

Layer 3 is where you can begin to rely on Vista's features to protect your systems. On this layer, you have access to several different methods for system protection. Vista does a great job of limiting attack surfaces, but you still need to apply additional protection configurations. At this layer, you need to work with the following Vista features:

- Local Security Policy and Security Configurations
- BitLocker Full Drive Encryption

- User Account Control
- USB Device Control
- Windows Defender
- Automatic Update Management
- Wireless and Wired Network Configurations

Each of these items is part of the configuration of this layer. Of course, you also need to keep in mind your staging practices for the PC itself, but this was covered in the first section of this book.

 **Of these items, only BitLocker is not covered in this chapter since it is part of the Protection aspect of the CASPR system. As such, BitLocker is covered in Chapter 12.**

Local Security Policy and security configurations

Chapter 9 outlines how you should work with the Local Security Policy (LSP) and identifies how you should link the LSP to Group Policy Objects (GPO) to centralize the management of security settings. In addition, Chapter 9 identified how you could create multiple LSPs to work with certain types of systems. One very good example of a system type where you would use multiple LSPs is the kiosk PC. This PC needs to be locked down when normal users work with it. Therefore, you apply the three LSPs in the following manner:

1. Apply the LSP at the computer level to completely lock down the system. This LSP will apply to the public when they work with the kiosk PC.

2. Apply the second LSP to users who are nonadministrators, but have an account in your network. These users may have a less restricted environment.

3. Apply the final LSP to administrators, letting them modify settings and update the configuration of the PC.

In addition, you should apply GPOs to the system by using the Loopback feature to ensure that no matter who logs on, the system's settings will always reset to a locked-down environment after it is put back to public usage.

You can of course export and import individual settings from an LSP to another. But when you create a comprehensive configuration for a system and you want to apply this configuration to every system of this type as soon as it is built, you must go beyond the LSP. For this reason, Vista includes the ability to create Security Templates and apply these templates to any system through the Security Configuration and Analysis tool. Both tools are snap-ins that are assigned to custom Microsoft Management Consoles. To work with these tools, you must create your own console because one does not exist by default. This operation is tied to task number VA-19: Security Template Creation/Modification as identified in Chapter 10.

To create your custom console, follow these steps:

1. **Choose Start Menu ⇨ Search to type** mmc **and press** Enter.

2. **Accept the UAC prompt**. Doing this opens a blank MMC console.

3. **Choose File ➪ Add/Remove Snap-in, scroll down the list to the left, select Security Configuration and Analysis (SCA), and click Add. Repeat for the Security Templates snap-in.** The two snap-ins should be listed in the selected snap-ins column as shown in Figure 11.3.

4. **Click OK.** You should now have a new console with two items contained within it. Save the console.

5. **Choose File ➪ Save and save it under your Documents folder (this will make it easier to find later on). Name it Security Console.**

FIGURE 11.3

Adding the security snap-ins

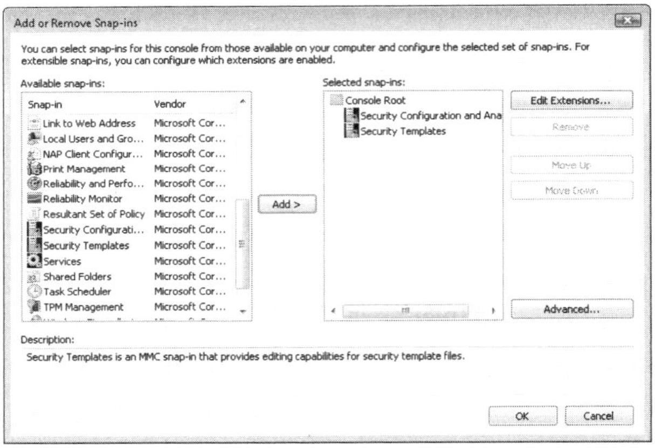

Now you're ready to begin working with your security console. Security templates can include several settings from the LSP:

- Account Policies
- Local Policies
- Event Log
- Restricted Groups
- System Services
- Registry
- File System

Each of these lets you configure how the elements it controls will be configured on the local system. Also, remember that when you apply an LSP, it will be overridden by the settings found in Group Policy because of the GPO application order. Therefore, you can use security templates in two different situations:

■ You can use templates to apply settings to standalone computers — computers that will not be part of a domain and will not receive GPO settings that may override the local settings.

■ You can use templates to apply settings that would not normally be applied by a GPO. This way, there are no conflicting settings, and the settings you apply locally will always remain the same.

The most common application of security templates, especially in a Vista environment, is the second one. And, as funny as it sounds, most often, administrators do not use the template to apply additional security, but rather to loosen security settings. That's because Vista has a very tight configuration by default. Windows Resource Protection (WRP), the system that protects core system files and registry keys, does a great job of locking down the system. But this great job often has a negative impact on *legacy applications,* applications that have not been designed for Vista and must write in some protected areas of the system.

Therefore, what you need to do is identify which files and registry keys an application needs access to and change its security settings. The best way to do this is to use two utilities FileMon and RegMon. FileMon scans the file system and captures any files that are accessed by the application during operation. RegMon does the same for registry keys. Basically, you run both tools, run the application, and perform as many operations with the application as possible. You capture the affected files and registry keys by outputting them from the two utilities. Once armed with the files and registry keys to change, you use your security console to generate a template that will modify the files and registry keys appropriately for the application to run with standard user rights. The resulting template you create can then be delivered and applied each time you install the application on a system, guaranteeing that the application will run on a locked-down Vista system.

NOTE   FileMon and RegMon are both from Microsoft and can be found at www. microsoft.com/technet/sysinternals/utilities/filemon.mspx and www.microsoft.com/technet/sysinternals/utilities/regmon.mspx. Microsoft has also released a new tool called Process Monitor which integrates the functionality of FileMon and RegMon. You can use Process Monitor if you prefer to perform the same task. Find Process Monitor at www.microsoft.com/technet/sysinternals/Utilities/processmonitor. mspx.

You can also rely on templates provided by other organizations to tighten security on your systems. For example, the Vista Security Guide includes templates and GPOs for additional security. But Microsoft is not the only source of templates. The National Security Agency (NSA) and the Center for Internet Security (CIS) also offer templates that help you secure systems. You can download and use these templates to secure your own systems. Finally, you can also obtain security templates from third-party vendors.

NOTE   Obtain NSA templates from www.nsa.gov/snac/ and CIS templates from www. cisecurity.org.

What's really nice is that the Security Configuration and Analysis snap-in lets you run these templates in analysis mode so that you can simply view what settings would be changed, letting you understand the content of the templates before adding them.

Whether you want to tighten or loosen security settings, the operations will be the same. Do the following:

1. **Return to your security console. Expand the Security Templates section until you see the search path.** Templates are automatically loaded into this console when they are found. By default this search path is `%UserProfile%\Documents\Security\ Templates.` If you obtain new templates from an external source, place them in this folder to automatically view their contents. You can change this folder location by selecting New Template Search Path from the context menu of the Security Templates item.

2. **If you don't have a third-party template, select New Template by right-clicking on the Search Path. Name the template and give it a description and click OK.**

3. **To ensure that your settings will not be modified by Group Policy, restrict your own changes to the Registry and the File System items. To modify either, first expand the template, then right-click on the item and select Add Key for registry settings or Add File for files.** After the file or setting is selected, a security dialog box appears.

4. **Apply appropriate settings and click OK.**

5. **As shown in Figure 11.4, you now need to decide if you want to Propagate inheritable permissions, Replace permissions or Block permission replacement on this object. Click OK when done.**

6. **Repeat for each of the files or registry settings you want to change.**

7. **Save the changes to the template by right-clicking the template name and selecting Save.**

There it is. Your first template is created. Now you use the Security Configuration and Analysis tool or its command line equivalent to apply it or you can apply it to a GPO and assign it appropriately.

FIGURE 11.4

Applying Propagation Settings to objects

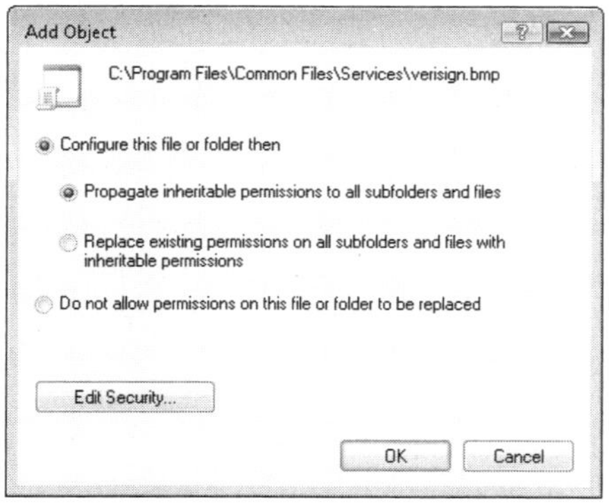

418

1. **Use the Security Configuration Analyzer (SCA) to analyze your computer and compare its settings to those in the template. Click on the SCA to change the focus of the console and then right-click SCA and select Open database.**

2. **Find a database if one exists or type in a new database name; then click OK.** Like the templates, the databases are stored in `%UserProfile%\Documents\Security\Databases`.

3. **Now select the template you want to test and click OK.** The Details pane now displays the next steps, as shown in Figure 11.5.

FIGURE 11.5

Preparing to analyze a computer

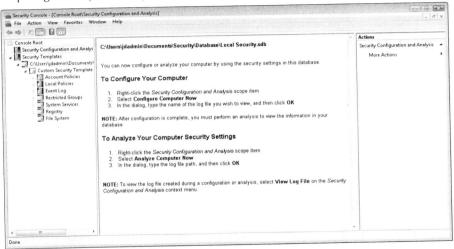

---

4. **To analyze your computer, right-click SCA and choose Analyze Computer Now.** Doing this opens a dialog box requesting the location of the log file for the analysis.

5. **Type in the name and click OK.**

6. **The analysis is performed. To view differences between the template and the system, move to the setting you wish to view in the Tree pane.** Differences will be displayed in the Details pane. Items that are changed include a small question mark on their icon.

7. **If you want to update the database setting by using a setting originating from the computer, double-click it and select Define this policy in the database; modify the setting and click OK.**

8. **Choose Save from the SCA context menu to save your changes.**

9. **Select Configure Computer Now from the SCA context menu. Identify the log file and click OK.** Doing this applies the changes and saves the database when done.

10. If you want to create a template from a preconfigured computer, then repeat the steps to generate the database, name a new template, analyze the computer, and then select Export Template from the SCA context menu.

Preconfiguring a system and then capturing the template from it may be easier than generating a template manually and doing the reverse. You can also analyze and configure computers from the command line. Use the following command to configure computers automatically:

```
secedit /configure /db filename.sdb /log filename.log
```

Make sure that you create these templates and then use the `secedit` command to apply them at computer setup. You can use the `Runonce` command to automatically apply your security templates after the system reboots the first time once Vista is installed.

User Account Control

User Account Control is a new feature in Vista. It lets you know each time an administrative task or a task that requires elevated privileges is performed on a computer. Part of the reason for UAC is that when people run with administrative privileges, it is possible for malicious code to execute with high privileges without your knowledge. When you run with UAC, you always know when any event requires elevated privileges because UAC always requests acceptance for the operation. In fact, UAC can display two different types of prompts, as shown in Figures 11.6 and 11.7. The prompt in Figure 11.6 appears when you are already logged on as an administrator. In this case, you only need to approve or decline the operation. The prompt in Figure 11.7 appears when you are logged on as a standard user. In this case, you must provide both an administrative user name and the corresponding password to allow the operation. A third prompt, shown in Figure 11.8, appears when a program wants to access administrative rights on your behalf. Here you decide to approve or decline the operation. This third prompt is similar to the one you would see when malicious code tries to infect your system.

As you can see, UAC has its uses and should be part of any Vista security strategy. In fact, your administrators should always run with a standard user account and access their administrative account only when they need to perform a task that requires elevation. To do this, they need to work with the Run As Administrator command, which is available through the context menu of any shortcut.

FIGURE 11.6

Working with UAC as an Administrator

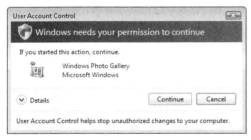

FIGURE 11.7

Working with UAC as a standard user

FIGURE 11.8

Accepting or Denying an Elevation Operation on behalf of a program

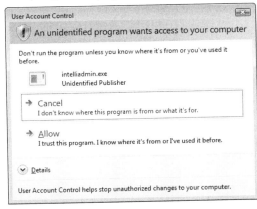

Because of its ability to protect your systems, you should not deactivate UAC. You should, however, configure it properly to avoid UAC prompts for your normal users. UAC is configured through Group Policy under Security Settings ⇨ Local Policies ⇨ Security Options as can be seen in Figure 11.9. The best way to configure this is to set the User Account Control: Behavior of the elevation prompt for standard users: Automatically deny elevation requests to on so that end users will not see any UAC prompts.

FIGURE 11.9

Working with the Group Policy Settings for UAC

User Account Control: Admin Approval Mode for the Built-in Administrator account	Disabled
User Account Control: Behavior of the elevation prompt for administrators in Admin Approval Mode	Prompt for consent
User Account Control: Behavior of the elevation prompt for standard users	Automatically deny elevation requests
User Account Control: Detect application installations and prompt for elevation	Enabled
User Account Control: Only elevate executables that are signed and validated	Disabled
User Account Control: Only elevate UIAccess applications that are installed in secure locations	Enabled
User Account Control: Run all administrators in Admin Approval Mode	Enabled
User Account Control: Switch to the secure desktop when prompting for elevation	Enabled
User Account Control: Virtualize file and registry write failures to per-user locations	Enabled

UAC also disables the default administrator account. Leave this account as is and provide different administrative accounts for your technicians. Taking this step gives you the best opportunity to lock down your computer systems and therefore reduce the number of support calls related to modifications to the base settings you configure for your Vista systems. In some cases, locked down environments have seen a 500 percent reduction in calls related to system configurations. This reduction rate makes a good case for keeping your systems locked as tight as you can. In addition, Vista now lets standard users perform many tasks they could not in previous versions of Windows. They can install signed software, signed software updates, printers, and change clock settings, to name a few. There is no reason to run an unlocked environment when you run Windows Vista.

USB Device Control

With Vista, you can now lock down USB devices, once again through Group Policy. With iPods and other portable music devices abounding, it is becoming more and more important for organizations to control which devices users can connect to their systems. For example, a user should not be able to connect their iPod to their office PC to download music. In addition, they should not be able to connect it to use as a hard drive to transport information they gather from your network. For these reasons, you must configure the USB Device Controls in Group Policy and control which devices are deemed acceptable — mice, keyboards, smart phones, and printers — and which are not — portable disk drives and flash memory devices, for example.

Although you can use these controls to prevent installation of all devices, it is best to allow the installation of authorized devices. To do this, you need to be able to identify devices. There are two ways to do this:

- You can use *device identification strings,* which are contained both within the device and within the .INF file that comes with the driver to block or authorize devices. There are two different types of device ID strings. The first is the hardware ID. These provide the most direct match between a device and its driver. The second are compatible IDs. These provide a list of compatible drivers that could give you at least basic functionality for the device. If you use these IDs to allow or deny devices, then you must include all of the possible IDs for the device. If not, multifunction devices especially, might be blocked at one level, but not at another.

 Find out more about device identification strings at http://go. microsoft.com/fwlink/?linkid=52665.

- You can use *device setup classes* to control devices. Classes divide devices into groups that use the same installation process. Classes are identified by globally unique identifiers (GUID) which are complex numbers that uniquely represent a class of devices. For example, if you want to block USB disk drives, then block the GUID for these devices and no USB disk drive will be able to be installed on your systems.

 Find out more about device setup classes at `http://go.microsoft.com/fwlink/?linkid=52662`.

Set up your authorizations through Group Policy.

1. **Launch the Group Policy Management Console (GPMC), choose Start Menu ⇨ Search ⇨ gpmc.msc, and press Enter.**

 If you are running Service Pack 1, you must download and install the GPMC onto your management PC before you can use it.

2. **Because this policy affects every computer, apply it to the PCs OU you created in Chapter 9. This can be applied through any GPO that would affect all PCs. If the GPO exists, right-click on and select Edit.** If it doesn't, then create it, name it, link it to the PCs OU, and then edit it.

3. **Go to the Device Installation settings (Computer Configuration ⇨ Policies ⇨ Administrative Templates ⇨ System ⇨ Device Installation). Also set up the policies for Removable Storage (Computer Configuration ⇨ Policies ⇨ Administrative Templates ⇨ System).**

4. **Set up the policies according to the recommendations in Table 11.2.** Examine the explanation for each setting to learn more about its intent and configuration possibilities. Each setting that is not configured relies on the default behavior for that setting.

5. **Test the settings with various devices of each type you authorized and de-authorized.**

TABLE 11.2

Assigning Device Installation Settings

Location	Setting	Recommendation
Device Installation	Treat all digitally signed drivers equally in the driver ranking and selection process	Not configured
	Turn off Found New Hardware balloons during device installation	Not configured
	Do not send a Windows Error Report when a generic driver is installed on a device	Not configured
	Configure device installation timeout	Not configured
	Do not create system restore point when new device driver installed	Not configured

continued

TABLE 11.2 (continued)

Location	Setting	Recommendation
	Allow remote access to the PnP interface	Not configured
Device Installation Restrictions	Allow administrators to override Device Installation Restriction policies	Configure only if you fully trust your administrators or anyone with administrative access rights.
	Allow installation of devices using drivers that match these device setup classes	Enable and add the appropriate GUID entries.
	Prevent installation of devices using drivers that match these device setup classes	Enable and add the appropriate GUID entries.
	Display a custom message when installation is prevented by policy (balloon text)	Enable and type in an appropriate violation of policy message.
	Display a custom message when installation is prevented by policy (balloon title)	Enable and type in an appropriate message title.
	Allow installation of devices that match any of these device IDs	Not configured
	Prevent installation of devices that match any of these device IDs	Not configured
	Prevent installation of removable devices	Not configured
	Prevent installation of devices not described by other policy settings	Enable.
Removable Storage Access	Time (in seconds) to force reboot	Not configured
	CD and DVD: Deny read access	Not configured
	CD and DVD: Deny write access	Enable only in very secure environments. Users often rely on this for backups.
	Custom Classes: Deny read access	Enable only if you have appropriate GUIDs.
	Custom Classes: Deny write access	Enable only if you have appropriate GUIDs.
	Floppy Drives: Deny read access	Not configured
	Floppy Drives: Deny write access	Enable only in very secure environments.
	Removable Disks: Deny read access	Not configured
	Removable Disks: Deny write access	Enable.
	All Removable Storage classes: Deny all access	Enable in very secure environments.

Location	Setting	Recommendation
	All Removable Storage: Allow direct access in remote sessions	Enable in very secure environments.
	Tape Drives: Deny read access	Enable.
	Tape Drives: Deny write access	Enable.
	WPD Devices: Deny read access	Enable only if your users do not use smart phones or Pocket PCs.
	WPD Devices: Deny write access	Enable only if your users do not use smart phones or Pocket PCs.

TIP Rely on classes instead of IDs because they are more comprehensive. To obtain the classes for a specific device group, look up the listings available on the Microsoft Web site at `http://msdn2.microsoft.com/en-us/library/ms791134.aspx`. Use these classes to set up your device restrictions.

NOTE Find out more about device restriction at `www.microsoft.com/technet/windowsvista/library/9fe5bf05-a4a9-44e2-a0c3-b4b4eaaa37f3.mspx`.

Windows Defender

Windows Defender is a spyware utility that automatically protects your computer from malicious content, such as spyware and rootkits, and automatically removes them if they are identified. Defender is built into Vista and does not require an additional installation. As shown in Figure 11.10, you access it through the Vista Security Center (Control Panel ⇨ Security ⇨ Security Center). This center gives you access to Windows Update settings, the Windows Firewall, Defender, and Internet Options, all of which are related to the health of your PC.

FIGURE 11.10

Accessing Windows Defender through the Security Center

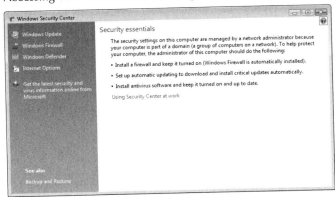

Defender is launched by clicking on its link in the left pane of the Security Center. As shown in Figure 11.11, Defender offers a very simple control panel. From here you can perform a quick or a full scan, look up your scanning history, and access Defender tools. Most often, you will not access Defender through this interface, but rather configure it through Group Policy.

FIGURE 11.11

Working with Windows Defender

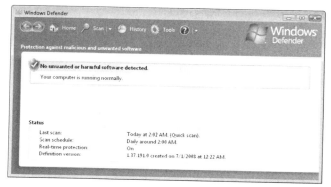

Use the recommendations in Table 11.3 to configure Defender settings in your network. Rely on the procedure outlined earlier for Device Control to modify the Group Policy that is applied to all PCs. You can find Windows Defender settings by choosing Computer Configuration ⇨ Policies ⇨ Administrative Templates ⇨ Windows Components.

CROSS-REF This configuration is related to task number VA-4: Anti-malware Update Management as outlined in Chapter 10 because you configure update settings through this GPO.

TABLE 11.3

Configuring Windows Defender GPO Settings

Location	Setting	Recommendation
Windows Defender	Turn on definition updates through both WSUS and Windows Update	Disable only if you have a custom Windows Server Update Services server in your network.
	Check for new signatures before scheduled scans	Not configured
	Turn off Windows Defender	Not configured

Location	Setting	Recommendation
	Turn off Real-Time Protection prompts for unknown detection	Not configured. Your users should be aware of untoward behavior on their systems.
	Enable logging known good detections	Enable only in troubleshooting situations.
	Enable logging unknown detection	Enable only in troubleshooting situations.
	Download entire signature set	Not configured
	Configure Microsoft SpyNet reporting	Configure only if you want to change your default participation in SpyNet. All organizations should participate to SpyNet as it relies on massive amounts of information to provide top-level protection.

Automatic Update Management

Windows Vista obtains Windows Defender updates from one of two sources: the Microsoft Update Web site or from an internal Windows Server Update Services (WSUS) server. The latter connects to Microsoft Update instead of the individual computers on your network. Organizations with more than a few computers will want to install their own WSUS server or servers so that they can better control the application of updates for Windows Defender as well as those for Windows itself. Because both updates originate from the same source, they are managed in the same way.

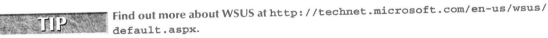 **Find out more about WSUS at** http://technet.microsoft.com/en-us/wsus/ default.aspx.

When originally configuring PCs during installation, one of the post-installation tasks you need to perform is to configure Vista to obtain updates for more products than only Windows. This lets you obtain updates for hardware components as well as Microsoft Office tools. This way, you only need to use one single tool for update configuration and management.

CROSS-REF **Applying updates addresses tasks number VA-17: Security Patch Update Management and VA-22: Service Pack Deployment as outlined in Chapter 10 since both use the same approach for their application. Once again, Updates are managed through Group Policy under Computer Configuration ⇨ Policies ⇨ Administrative Templates ⇨ Windows Components ⇨ Windows Update. Use the recommendations in Table 11.4 to configure your settings. Also rely on the procedure outlined previously for USB Device Control to perform these modifications.**

TABLE 11.4

Configuring Windows Update Settings through Group Policy

Setting	Recommendation
Do not display 'Install Updates and Shut Down' option in Shut Down Windows dialog box	Enabled. You want to control when updates are deployed.
Do not adjust default option to 'Install Updates and Shut Down' in Shut Down Windows dialog box	Not configured
Enabling Windows Update Power Management to automatically wake up the system to install scheduled updates	Enabled. This should be used in conjunction with the Power Management settings in the GPO to reduce the power costs of PCs in your network.
Configure Automatic Updates	Enabled. Ideally, configure to obtain updates from your server and install them on a regular schedule.
Specify intranet Microsoft update service location	Enabled and point to your WSUS server(s).
Automatic Updates detection frequency	Not configured. The default setting is appropriate.
Allow non-administrators to receive update notifications	Not configured. You should let administrators be the only ones to get these notices.
Allow Automatic Updates immediate installation	Enable only if you set a schedule in the Configure Automatic Updates item above.
Turn on recommended updates via Automatic Updates	Enable.
No auto-restart for scheduled Automatic Updates installations	Enable only if you intend to deliver updates during daytime hours.
Re-prompt for restart with scheduled installations	Enable only if you think you need emergency updates because this will disrupt users' work.
Delay Restart for scheduled installations	Not configured. Your schedule should apply updates at night.
Reschedule Automatic Updates scheduled installations	Not configured.
Enable client-side targeting	Enable to create test beds for update testing.
Allow signed content from intranet Microsoft update service location	Enable and configure in highly secure networks.

 Microsoft releases updates on the second Tuesday of each month. Be sure to test all patches and service packs fully before deploying them to your network.

Wireless and Wired Network configurations

When connected to a Windows Server 2008 network, Vista allows you to configure the operation of a wired or wireless network through Group Policy. In fact, these policy settings let you configure exactly who or what can connect to your own internal network through either wired or wireless networks. Settings in these policies are controlled through the Network Policy Server role which is part of Windows Server 2008's Network Access Protection. Basically, you configure a network policy for both wired and wireless connections and then set the policy controls in the Group Policy settings of each PC to allow them to connect to the network. Any device that does not receive this Group Policy setting cannot connect to the network. This provides very tight control over rogue network devices, especially wireless devices, which are a lot easier to spoof.

CROSS-REF This configuration addresses tasks number VA-14: Wireless Connection Status Verification and VA-15: Wired Network Connection from the task list provided in Chapter 10.

NOTE This configuration cannot exist without a Windows Server 2008 environment. Look up more information on this configuration at `http://technet2.microsoft.com/windowsserver2008/en/library/8d0a7ffc-a154-43ea-ba30-f51c678bccae1033.mspx?mfr=true`.

Layer 4: Managing information access

Layer 4 focuses on how users access information. Because of this, you need to concentrate on the following items:

- Smart Card Deployment
- Encrypting File System
- Auditing of User Access
- Rights Management Services
- Internet Explorer Configurations

Two of these items are covered in Chapter 12 because, like BitLocker, they deal with information protection. This includes both EFS and RMS. In addition, event auditing was covered in Chapter 9. Refer to this chapter for more information on working with security events.

The other items, Smart Card Deployments and IE Configurations, are covered here.

NOTE For more information on EFS and Vista, go to the Microsoft Data Encryption Toolkit for Mobile PCs which provides a Microsoft Encrypting File System Assistant at `http://www.microsoft.com/technet/security/guidance/clientsecurity/dataencryption/efsassistant/default.mspx`. For information on how to configure Active Directory Rights Management Services in Windows Server 2008, look up MCTS Self-Paced Training Kit (Exam 70-640): Configuring Windows Server 2008 Active Directory by Holme, Ruest, and Ruest.

Deploying smart cards

Smart cards come in all flavors and all types. The least expensive smart cards are USB smart cards because they come in the form of a small footprint USB device and do not require the implementation of additional hardware devices to read them. All you need to do is plug it in and away you go.

> **TIP** If you use USB smart cards, make sure that you enable them as removable devices in your Device Control settings.

In Vista, smart cards can be used for logon authentication as well as for use with the Encrypting File System. This makes them very valuable. When you select your smart card vendor, make sure that their products are compatible with Vista. Products compatible with XP do not work with Vista because Microsoft has modified the logon architecture in Vista. Use only certified products.

> **NOTE** For a list of compatible smart card readers, go to `http://winqual.microsoft.com/HCL/ProductList.aspx?m=v&cid=406&g=d`.

Then, when you're ready to perform your deployment, you can control smart card behavior through Group Policy. Smart Card settings by choosing Computer Configuration ⇨ Policies ⇨ Administrative Templates ⇨ Windows Components ⇨ Smart Cards. Use the procedure outlined under Device Controls to modify and apply the settings recommended in Table 11.5.

TABLE 11.5

Configuring Settings for Smart Cards in Group Policy

Setting	Recommendation
Allow certificates with no extended key usage certificate attribute	Not configured
Allow Integrated Unblock screen to be displayed at the time of logon	Verify with hardware manufacturer before using this setting.
Allow signature keys valid for Logon	Not configured
Allow time invalid certificates	Not configured
Turn on certificate propagation from smart card	Enable to provide multiuse certificates.
Configure root certificate clean up	Not configured
Turn on root certificate propagation from smart card	Not configured
Filter duplicate logon certificates	Not configured
Force the reading of all certificates from the smart card	Not configured
Display string when smart card is blocked	Not configured
Reverse the subject name stored in a certificate when displaying	Enable to properly display user names.
Allow user name hint	Not configured

Configuring Internet Explorer

Internet Explorer version 7 is much more comprehensive than any previous version of IE. In fact, Windows Vista lists 13 categories of settings under the Security Features of IE (Computer Configuration ➪ Policies ➪ Administrative Templates ➪ Windows Components ➪ Internet Explorer ➪ Security Features). These categories include:

- Add-on management
- Binary behavior security restriction
- Consistent mime handling
- Information bar
- Local machine zone lock-down security
- Mime sniffing safety feature
- MK protocol security restriction
- Network protocol lock down
- Object caching protection
- Protection from zone elevation
- Restrict file download
- Scripted Window security restrictions
- Enable native XMLHTTP support

As such there are too many settings to list here. The best recommendation is for you to take a close look at each of the various security features you can control in IE and apply them judiciously. This will let you create a secure IE environment.

NOTE   Perhaps the easiest way to do this is to look up the explanation of each feature online. If so, go to www.microsoft.com/windows/products/winfamily/ie/features.mspx for more information.

Layer 5: Working with external access

The final layer of defense involves external access. In PC terms, this means working with the way PCs access your resources when outside your network. As such, this means working with the following items:

- Windows Firewall with Advanced Security
- Virtual Private Network (VPN) Connections
- Public Key Infrastructures
- Network Access Protection

Each of these is discussed here as they apply to PCs.

Working with the Windows Firewall with Advanced Security

Vista includes a powerful firewall that helps protect each individual PC running it. In fact, it includes two different firewall products. The first is a basic firewall that focuses on whether or not protection is turned on. The second is a much more comprehensive tool that is once again managed through Group Policy.

Like Windows Defender, the Basic Firewall is accessed through the Security Center (Control Panel ⇨ Security ⇨ Security Center), just click the link in the left pane to launch the Firewall. You'll also remember that the firewall comes up immediately after you install Windows Vista as part of the initial security configuration of your PC. Of course, you need administrative credentials to view or modify its settings.

As shown in Figure 11.12, the basic firewall has two main settings: On or Off. You should keep it on at all times. There are also two additional tabs for basic firewall configuration. Exceptions list the type of exceptions you can set on the firewall. Firewalls basically control which of the 65,000 TCP/IP ports are open or not on your machine. You can of course manage the firewall at the port level if you want (just click the Add port button), but it is much easier to manage it at the application level. You want to be able to make Remote Assistance connections to a PC and then allow the application in the basic firewall settings.

FIGURE 11.12

Working with the Windows Firewall

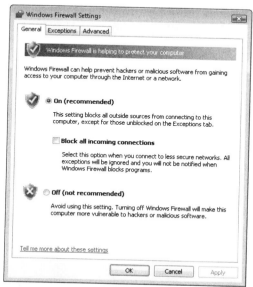

Many applications will be Windows Firewall aware — in fact, you should make sure that each application you choose is Firewall aware — and will automatically make the appropriate changes in the firewall when installed. Being Firewall aware is part of the Windows Logo compliance settings Microsoft publishes for independent software vendors so that they can make their applications as compatible to Vista as possible.

The last tab is the Advanced tab. This tab lets you configure different Firewall settings for different network connections if they exist. You need to make sure the Basic Firewall is turned on at all times.

The best way to ensure your firewall is turned on at all times is to use the Windows Firewall with Advanced Security (WFAS). This firewall control center is accessed through Group Policy (Computer Configuration ⇨ Policies ⇨ Windows Settings ⇨ Security Settings ⇨ Windows Firewall with Advanced Security). As shown in Figure 11.13, WFAS provides much more comprehensive control over firewall behavior.

FIGURE 11.13

Working with the Windows Firewall with Advanced Security

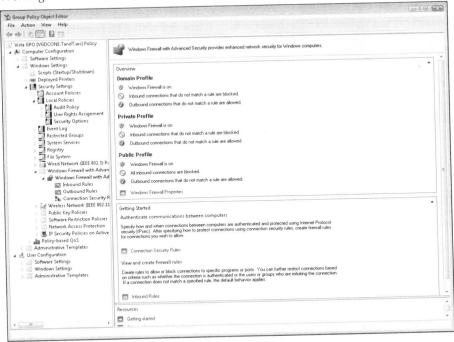

The first thing you will notice is the network profiles associated with the firewall. Each time Windows Vista connects to a network, it identifies what kind of network you are connecting to. Three choices are possible from the end user point of view: Private, Public, and Home.

Vista configures the firewall settings for the network depending on the choice made by the user. Private networks allow some connections as do Home networks. But Public networks are very restrictive and do not allow inbound connections. For this reason, you should instruct your users to always select Public network when they connect to an unknown network. When they do so, Vista will create the most restrictive con nection, protecting their PC from potential malicious content.

WFAS, however, includes one different network profile, the Domain profile. The Domain profile controls firewall behavior when the system is connected to your network. This feature is what makes WFAS so much more comprehensive than the Basic Firewall: being able to control the behavior of the Firewall based on the type of connection profile it is using.

As shown in Figure 11.13, the Firewall state is not configured by default. You should configure these settings for each of the three profiles even if they are not currently in use. By taking this step, you ensure that your PCs are protected no matter what happens. The three profiles include:

- **Domain:** This profile applies when the computer is connected to the network containing an Active Directory with the computer's account, normally your own network.

- **Private:** This profile applies when the computer connects to a network that does not contain its account, for example a home network that runs through a Workgroup.

- **Public:** This profile applies when the computer connects to an unknown network such as one in airports or coffee shops.

The configurations you should apply in WFAS should become more and more restrictive as you work through the profiles. To configure the settings for each profile, follow these steps:

1. Launch the Group Policy Management Console by choosing Start Menu ⇨ Search ⇨ gpmc.msc.

2. Locate a GPO that applies to all systems. This GPO should be assigned to the PCs OU, right-click it, and select Edit.

3. Navigate to the WFAS by choosing Computer Configuration ⇨ Policies ⇨ Windows Settings ⇨ Security Settings ⇨ Windows Firewall with Advanced Security), expand its contents, and click the Windows Firewall with Advanced Security subnode.

4. In the Details pane, click Windows Firewall Properties under the list of profiles.

5. Begin with the Domain Profile. At the very least, use the Recommended and Default settings, as shown in Figure 11.14. The Firewall should be turned **on**, Inbound connections should be Blocked unless explicitly allowed, and Outbound connections should be Allowed.

FIGURE 11.14

Working with the Firewall Profile Settings

6. **Click the Customize button under Settings to open a second dialog box that displays several settings. Once again, select the Defaults at the very least.**

   ■ It is a good idea to display notifications, so that users will know when a program is attempting a connection that is blocked.

   ■ Allow Unicast responses because this option will let the system wait up to three seconds for a response. After three seconds, all responses will be blocked. Note that this does not affect DHCP responses, which are always allowed.

   ■ Allow local firewall rules only if you want to allow non-GPO rules to apply to the PC as well. The default is to allow them.

   ■ Allow local connection security rules only if you want to allow non-GPO rules to apply to be defined on the PC as well. The default is to allow them.

   ■ In most cases, you should set only GPO rules. Although allowing local rules can be convenient when you configure a new application on a PC, it can become quite cumbersome when you are troubleshooting a non-functioning device. If you want to test new applications, do it in a test environment, not in your production network.

7. **Repeat the operation for the Private and Public tabs.**

   The last tab focuses on **IPsec Settings**. Click the Customize button to modify these settings. These settings deal with secure connections from the PC to other systems. Each of the settings in this dialog box is set to defaults. This means that some form of IPsec is turned on by default. To view the default values, click on the **What are the default values?** link at the bottom of the dialog box. You can change each setting by clicking on Advanced and then the Customize button. Click on **OK** when done.

NOTE Make sure you verify with your server administrators to coordinate these settings with them. IPsec will be configured on the server as well as on the PC and settings must match for the connection to occur properly.

If you do modify the IPsec settings, you can also allow exemptions for ICMP from IPsec. This means you could use the PING utility to identify if a computer is awake or not. While this might be useful inside your network, it is definitely not a good idea for portable systems that travel outside your network. The best bet is to leave it off.

8. Click OK to apply the changes to the profiles.

You can also create Inbound, Outbound and Connection Security Rules for your systems. Each node uses a wizard to generate the rule, as shown in Figure 11.15. Once again, it is easiest to base rules on programs rather than ports. You can also rely on the Predefined rules that come with the Firewall. Use custom rules only if you have a specific unknown program to install.

FIGURE 11.15

Creating Inbound, Outbound, or Connection Security Rules in WFAS

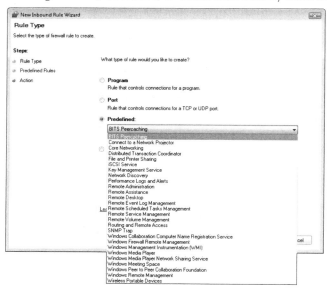

The best way to create Inbound, Outbound, or Connection Security Rules is to work with both Firewalls. Do this through the following steps:

1. Set up a PC using a typical configuration.

2. **Enable all of the applications you deem necessary for this PC.** This may include items such as Remote Assistance, Remote Desktop, and Windows Remote Management among others.

3. **Open the Windows Firewall through Control Panel and move to the Exemptions tab.**

4. **Go to your GPO and apply each of the rules found in the Exemptions tab of the Basic Firewall to your Group Policy.**

5. **Test the policy before deploying it.**

This approach will let you more easily configure the Group Policy and it will ensure your systems are working as they should while protecting them from malicious connections.

> **NOTE** Virtual Private Network connections rely on IPsec to connect to the system. WFAS allows you to configure both the Firewall and IPsec in the same integrated environment. If you are relying on Windows Server to create the VPN connections, then work with your server team to properly configure these settings. If you are using a third-party VPN tool, then look up the appropriate client from the list found at http://support.microsoft.com/kb/929490.

Working with Public Key Infrastructures

Public Key Infrastructures are quickly becoming a must in most computing environments today. PKI systems generate certificates that use a third party to prove who you are to others. This is because each time a PKI certificate is generated, it has had to undergo a validation process to identify who you are. For this reason, PKI certificates provide non-repudiation; that is, they absolutely prove who you are, no one can impersonate you because they need access to both the private and the public keys included with the certificate. Normally, you are the only one to have access to the private key.

> **TIP** For more information on PKI systems and how they can help build a world of trust, look up the Advanced PKI section on Resolutions' Web site at www.reso-net.com/articles.asp?m=8#c.

PKI systems in Vista can support several uses, including the following:

- Encrypting File System
- Smart Card Deployments
- Secure Sockets Tunneling Protocol (SSTP) VPN connections
- Secure Online Transactions
- Secure Web Site Connections
- Digital Rights Management
- Digital Signatures for e-mails and documents

Any document, even an e-mail, that includes a certificate will ensure that the document cannot be modified when delivered to others. In addition, certificates allow you to rapidly identify a computer or a user in a manner that a simple user name and password cannot. Windows Server makes it very easy to automate the entire certificate management and deployment process. You should integrate them to your infrastructure to enhance the security level of your network.

However, keep in mind that for certificates to work seamlessly, they have to be trusted by the recipient. Windows Vista includes an embedded series of trusted root certificate authorities that is updated regularly by Microsoft through Windows Update. If you purchase certificates from one of these authorities—for example, Thawte, VeriSign, GoDaddy, or others—then, your certificate will be trusted by any computer, both those you control and those you do not control. If you issue your own certificates, then they will not be trusted by any computer until you import the root certificate into the target PC. You can do this through Group Policy on computers you control. But when you are working with user's home computers or computers in public locations, you will not be able to rely on your own certificates. Ideally, each certificate you rely on will originate from a trusted authority so that it can be used either internally or externally with no worries.

> **NOTE** For information on how to configure Active Directory Certificate Services in Windows Server 2008, look up MCTS Self-Paced Training Kit (Exam 70-640): Configuring Windows Server 2008 Active Directory by Holme, Ruest, and Ruest.

Remember that internal certificate settings are managed through Group Policy (Computer Configuration ➪ Policies ➪ Windows Settings ➪ Security Settings ➪ Public Key Policies), as shown in Figure 11.16. Take the time to learn what each policy setting does before applying it. Also, work with your server team to coordinate certificate implementation and deployment strategies.

FIGURE 11.16

Working with Public Key Infrastructure Group Policy Settings

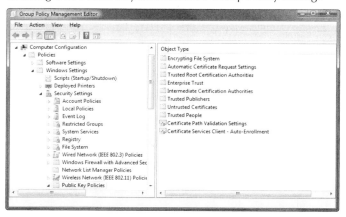

> **NOTE** As with everything, even Vista can have problems with certificates. Microsoft publishes a guide on how to troubleshoot these potential issues at www.microsoft. com/downloads/details.aspx?FamilyID=FE8EB7EA-68DA-4331-9D38-BDBF9FA2C266&displaylang=en.

Working with Virtual Private Network connections

Another aspect of working with external access is allowing remote users to access your internal network from the Internet. These remote connections can originate from users of mobile computers while they are on the road or users working from their home on either a corporate or a personal computer. While these connections relied on telephone lines in the past through modem connections, today, they rely on high-speed Internet connections. Because of this, the ideal way to support these connections is through a virtual private network (VPN) or a connection that creates an encrypted tunnel from the external computer to the internal network protecting all data that transfers between the two. Encryption is critical because you use a public network to connect from the remote point to your internal network and you want to ensure the content of the communications are protected at all times as shown in Figure 11.17.

FIGURE 11.17

Using a VPN creates a private tunnel through a public Internet connection

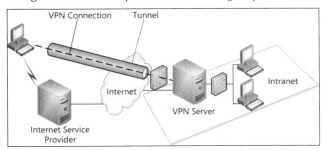

When the client makes a VPN connection, the following activities occur:

1. The user initiates an Internet connection. This connection can be a wired connection, a wireless connection or even a modem connection, though the latter are very rarely used today.

2. Once the Internet connection is active, the user launches the Connect to a network tool in Vista to make the connection (through Control Panel, Network and Internet, Connect to a network, or through a right-click on the network connection icon in the Tray area, then selecting Connect to a network). If this is the first time this connection is made, then the use must use the Connect to a workplace wizard which prompts for either a VPN or a direct dial connection as shown in Figure 11.18. The user then walks through the wizard pages to identify the address of the connection, its connection method and the credentials required for the connection. If the connection is already established, then the user only needs to select it and click the Connect button.

FIGURE 11.18

Creating a VPN connection in Vista

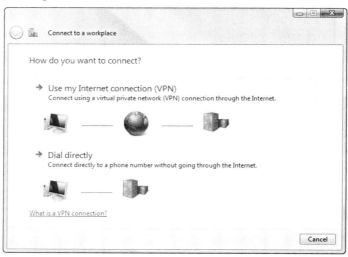

3. As the connection is launched, the client system contacts the hosting server and initiates the authentication process.

4. The hosting server authenticates the user and security information is exchanged between the client and the server.

5. The VPN server will then provide the client with a new IP address. The client system will then use this new address to communicate with the internal network through the VPN server. All communications are encrypted through a tunnel that only the server and the client are party to.

Virtual private networks can also be used for site to site connections, linking remote sites to central locations through inexpensive Internet connections rather than through expensive dial-up connections.

Windows Vista with Service Pack 1 and Windows Server 2008 support VPN connections using three different protocols:

■ Point-to-Point Tunneling Protocol (PPTP)

■ Layer Two Tunneling Protocol (L2TP) with Internet Protocol Security (IPSec)

■ Secure Socket Tunneling Protocol (SSTP)

These protocols are used to encapsulate communications from point to point to ensure they are fully encrypted. PPTP is the oldest protocol Microsoft supports for VPN connections; this protocol was introduced by Microsoft as early as with Windows 95. It supports user authentication, access controls, and the ability to apply a connection profile that may limit the access the end user will have to the internal network. By providing an IP address that is part of the internal IP address pool to the end point, PPTP lets the external computer behave as if it was directly connected to the network. In addition, PPTP can compress data through the VPN tunnel to improve communication speeds.

L2TP is a standard protocol that unlike PPTP, relies on the User Datagram Protocol (UDP) portion of TCP/IP. This means that it can work over more network platforms than PPTP. However, L2TP does not provide all of the features of PPTP. For example, PPTP can stand on its own because it can provide negotiation between the two systems, encryption of the communications and authentication for the user. L2TP only provides authentication on its own. This is why organizations marry L2TP with IPSec; IPSec will then provide the negotiation and encryption services while L2TP will authenticate the user. In addition, IPSec provides for mutual machine authentication, making sure you are linking to the right machine when you set up the connection.

Since L2TP is more modern, many organizations prefer to rely on this protocol along with IPSec for traditional VPNs. However, with the release of Windows Server 2008, Microsoft is introducing the Secure Socket Tunneling Protocol. SSTP relies on the Secure Sockets Layer (SSL) to create a simpler but as efficient Internet tunnel. This protocol uses the same strategy you would use when interacting with a commercial Web site such as a bank to encrypt all communications. The advantage of SSTP is that it relies on standard HyperText Transfer Protocol (HTTP) sessions to provide the VPN link. Working with HTTP is much simpler than working with IPSec or L2TP. In addition, SSTP is secure because user credentials are not sent until an encryption tunnel has been created, keeping them secure.

Each of the three VPN protocols relies on mutual identification and the creation of a tunnel before secure communications can begin. Several different authentication mechanisms can be used for the creation of this secure tunnel, but the simplest relies on the use of a trusted PKI certificate. In this case, client computers will automatically trust the certificate and connections will be implemented without the need to interact with the client system. If you use any other authentication mechanism, you will need to perform an activity on the client computer. For example, if you use a shared password, then you must enter the password on the server and also enter it on the client PC. This might work well on one or two PCs, but when you need to create VPNs for hundreds of systems, this becomes very impractical very quickly.

In addition, because SSTP relies on HTTP to operate, it uses port 443 for communications between the client and the VPN server. Port 443 is part of the standard ports that are usually open on firewalls. This means that when you rely on an SSTP VPN, you will most likely not need to do anything at the firewall level to have the connection work because port 443 is one of the standard ports organizations allow on their firewall configurations. Using either of the other two VPN protocols would require you to open additional ports, something that organizations are loathe to do with reason. The fewer ports you open on the firewall, the fewer chances you have of letting someone you don't want into your network.

NOTE For information on how to configure a server running Windows Server 2003 to support VPN connections, go to http://technet2.microsoft.com/windowsserver/en/library/00c498a8-95e7-4780-942e-c4594b01f6151033.mspx?mfr=true. For information on setting up IPSec VPN connections on Windows Server 2008, go to http://technet.microsoft.com/en-us/network/bb531150.aspx. For information on setting up SSTP VPNs on Windows Server 2008, go to http://technet.microsoft.com/en-us/magazine/cc162322(TechNet.10).aspx.

Working with Network Access Protection

Vista includes a client for Network Access Protection (NAP) that works with both Microsoft's NAP implementation in Windows Server 2008 and/or Cisco's Network Access Control. Basically, NAP allows you to protect your network from connections to systems that do not meet a specific health status when they request the connection. Connections can be through VPNs, DHCP, routers or switches, Terminal Services, or Web pages. Each time a connection request is forwarded to your centralized services, the client must provide its health status. If the health status does not conform to your policies, then the client is placed into a quarantine network where it will be updated so that it can meet the health requirements. After the client has been updated and it can prove so, the client is allowed to connect to the network.

NAP implementations not only allow you to create secure networks, but can also allow you to configure who has access to both your wired and wireless connections, making your network even more secure than ever. And, when you support VPN connections, you can ensure that your clients can only connect when they conform to a specific set of rules. For computers you control, you can rely on Group Policy and tools such as Windows Server Update Services to correct any unhealthy status. For computers you do not control, you can redirect the user to a Web page that outlines what the user must do to manually update their system to meet your health requirements.

NOTE Any computer that does not include the NAP client, either through the application of a service pack or through its integration into the platform, will simply not be able to connect to a NAP-enabled network. This behavior occurs whether the client is trying to make an internal or an external network connection.

You can configure the behavior of the NAP client through Group Policy (Computer Configuration ➪ Policies ➪ Windows Settings ➪ Security Settings ➪ Network Access Protection), as shown in Figure 11.19. Work with your server team to coordinate the settings you must apply to this section and then deploy these settings to each of your PCs. Doing this will help you create a secure network.

You'll find that you can control a series of different behaviors with NAP.

NAP relies on the Network Access Policy Service (NAPS) in Windows Server 2008. NAPS also provides the controls for remote access and VPN connections. This centralized control center will work with your firewall configurations, rely on PKI certificates and control connections to the network that originate internally through routers, DHCP or Terminal Services or connections that originate externally through the VPN mechanisms you put in place. NAP brings together all of the elements of Layer 5 in the Castle Defense System to help you implement a secure and protected network at all time.

FIGURE 11.19

Working with Network Access Protection client settings

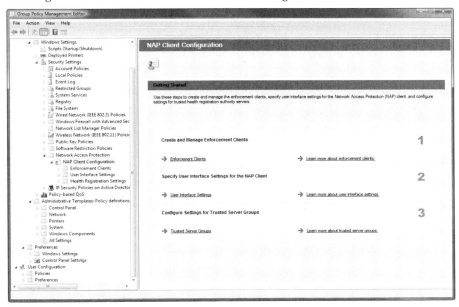

From the client side, you find that you can control the following behaviors through NAP client management:

- Enable or disable NAP enforcement
- Configure how you want the NAP client interface to appear on client computers, controlling items such as the branding text and graphics that appear
- Control to which Health Registration Authority (HRA) server or servers your clients will connect to
- Control which cryptographic mechanism clients will use when connecting to HRA servers

Most of these activities are performed by the server administrators that implement and administer the NAP service on your Windows Server 2008 systems. However, you should familiarize yourself with the various features and components of NAP in order to provide assistance during this process.

> **NOTE** NAP is a very comprehensive technology that has a lot of moving parts. To learn more about NAP in general, go to `http://technet.microsoft.com/en-us/network/bb545879.aspx`.

Summary

Security is not something you set up and then forget. As mentioned earlier, security is a cycle which must be continuously monitored and continually updated. In fact, this is one of the administrative tasks you must perform on an ongoing basis: task VA-18: Security Policy Review and Update. This basically means you need to review your existing security policy, determine if it continues to be adequate, and if not, update it and communicate the changes to all interested parties.

Along with information protection, the defense mechanisms you put in place will ensure your organization will have a proper business continuity strategy, one that will protect your assets and ensure you can carry on your operations as well as being prepared for the worst.

Chapter 12

Protecting User Data

The reason organizations rely on computers is to create, modify, and otherwise manipulate business data. Because of this, the job of protecting business data generated by information workers is probably the most important aspect of any PC administrator's responsibilities. Users complain when their computers don't work as they expect, but should they lose their data, they will do much more than complain. This is why it is important for any organization running personal computers to put in place and manage a proper data protection strategy.

Too many organizations are happy to provide a home directory to users, grant them a minimal amount of space on a central server, and then leave it at that. This is not a data protection strategy, or if it is, this is its barest form. Proper data protection strategies must rely on more than simple centralized folders. When you want to protect data, you need a full information lifecycle management strategy. In Windows Vista, this means:

- Identifying which data to protect
- Putting in place a modern data protection mechanism
- Protecting travelling data
- Protecting critical mobile systems

Keeping users happy by providing full protection for their data is the focus of this chapter.

Protecting User Profiles

In Windows, user data is stored within the user profile along with any configuration information and data related to the user's preferences. Data includes user-generated documents, desktop preferences, Internet favorites, and so on. Application settings are also contained within the profile and include items such as custom dictionaries, custom toolbars, and anything else that pertains to the application itself and how it has been customized by the user. Other application-related data — data that pertains to every user of the system — is stored within special profiles that apply to all users.

Profile information is not only stored within the file system, but also is included in special sections of the Windows Registry under the HKey_Users hierarchy. When users are logged on, their profile information is copied from the HKey_Users hierarchy into the HKey_Current_User section of the Registry. It remains there until the user logs off at which point updates are copied back to HKey_Users. Some information is stored in memory only while the user is logged on. This information is contained within the NTUSER.DAT file, a core profile file, which requires special handling because it is always locked while in use.

The first thing you notice when you begin looking at profiles in Windows Vista is that they are completely different from previous versions. Information is stored in a different file structure than with any of the legacy versions of Windows. Because of this, Microsoft has introduced the concept of *junction points,* redirection points that appear as normal folders to applications and users. Junction points provide backwards compatibility for older applications that need to address the legacy folder structure used for profile storage. Finally, the profile folder structure itself has been completely modified to provide better support for features such as *roaming profiles* — profiles that are stored on network shares to make them accessible to users on any computer in your network.

> **NOTE**   If you view junction points in Windows Explorer and you double-click on them, you will get an access denied error which is not pretty, but this is the implementation in Vista. For more information, see `/www.realtime-vista.com/general/2007/04/access_denied_to_documents_and.htm`.

Microsoft modified the profile structure in Vista to facilitate profile management, as shown in Figure 12.1. Because of this, several items have changed within the profile file structure:

- Profiles are stored under the C:\Users folder.

- Data assigned to every user is stored within the C:\Users\Public folder.

- Data used to generate a new profile is stored within the C:\Users\Default folder.

- Application data that is required for all users is stored within the C:\ProgramData folder.

- A new folder, C:\Users*username*\AppData contains user-specific application data. Note that *username* is the user's account name in Windows.

- The AppData folder includes three subfolders:

    - Local includes data that does not move with the user when they change from computer to computer. Most often, data in this folder is too large to transfer from the local PC to a network share. For example, Outlook personal storage files (.PST) are located in this folder.

- LocalLow includes data that is local but considered low priority.

- Roaming includes data that can be copied to a network share for availability to roaming users. As shown in Figure 12.2, the Start Menu is located under this folder.

- Data folders include Contacts, Desktop, Documents, Downloads, Favorites, Links, Music, Pictures, Saved Games, Searches, and Videos. Some apply to business use while others are more focused on personal use.

When you plan to protect user data, you must carefully consider which of the folders in the user profile you will protect.

FIGURE 12.1

The Vista user profile structure

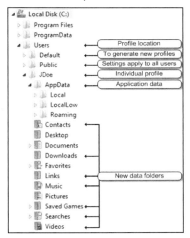

FIGURE 12.2

The contents of the Roaming folder in the Vista user profile

Providing User Data Protection

The way you protect user data in Vista has changed from previous versions. In past versions of Windows, administrators protected user data through two key features:

- **Home Directory:** This feature was a network share that would be provided to end users to store information on the network. Information in this share was protected through server backups

- **Roaming Profile:** This feature captures an entire user's profile and stores it on the network. When users log onto a PC, the entire profile is downloaded from the network. When users log off, the updated profile is copied back to the network share. Roaming profiles are monolithic; that is, the entire profile is copied back and forth. If a user has a 10MB document on the desktop, the document will be moved back and forth. Because of this, users with large profiles can experience unexpected delays at log on and log off.

Although both technologies are still available with Windows Vista, they are considered legacy technologies because of their monolithic nature. With the introduction of Windows XP and Windows Server 2003, Microsoft introduced a new concept for profile protection: folder redirection.

Folder redirection is controlled through Group Policy and serves to automatically redirect key user folders to network shares. The process is completely transparent to users. When folders are redirected, they automatically benefit from offline caching and are therefore available to users even when the network connection is no longer available. When the network connection returns, the contents of the local cache is automatically re-synchronized with the contents from the network share. In addition, folders can be discretely selected within Group Policy.

This makes folder redirection not only ideal for networked users, but also for mobile users because they have the ability to take data with them. When they reconnect to the network, their work is protected through synchronization, and, because the data resides on the network, it is backed up on a regular basis.

In Windows XP, folder redirection provided protection for four key folders. In Vista, this has been expanded to ten folders, which makes folder redirection more granular. By enabling folder redirection in Group Policy, you enable the system to create a centralized folder based on the user's name — much like the old home directory process. This folder is secured so that only the user will have access to it by default. Subfolders are created within the main folder for each of the folders you've elected to redirect. In addition, the folder on the user's desktop is automatically redirected to the newly created networked folders.

Synchronization of the data between the local PC and the network share begins as soon as the process is activated. If the user folder already exists, the user's data is moved from the PC to the network share. The data is cached back onto the PC. That is when the synchronization process begins. When a folder is redirected, its location changes to the network share, as shown in Figure 12.3. From then on, the local cache is managed through the Vista Sync Center. Users can choose the properties of a folder to ensure that it is synchronized and up to date, as shown in Figure 12.4.

FIGURE 12.3

Local folders are redirected to network shares

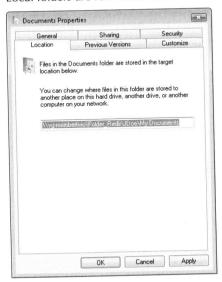

FIGURE 12.4

The Vista Sync Center is used to manage offline files

Completing a data protection strategy

Folder redirection provides extensive protection for ten key user folders, but unfortunately, this does not provide complete profile protection because it leaves key profile content unprotected. For example, folder redirection cannot protect the NTUser.DAT file that holds in-memory profile content because it is always locked when in use and therefore cannot be synchronized. In addition, the data located in the Local and LocalLow folders is not protected by folder redirection. Therefore, you must supplement folder redirection with additional profile protection.

The additional profile protection is done by combining folder redirection with roaming profiles. This can give you the best of both worlds:

- You rely on folder redirection to protect and synchronize data folders, and you rely on the roaming profile to protect the rest of the user content.

- Roaming profiles are smaller because you exclude the content that is protected by folder redirection from the roaming profile.

- Data is available in real time because of folder redirection.

- Logon and logoff times are faster because the content protected by roaming profiles is significantly less than through traditional roaming profiles.

- You protect only the content you need to protect.

But, this means a change in the way you provide user data protection. When organizations relied on home directories, they provided a minimal amount of space on central servers for users to store information. Now, with the combination of folder redirection and roaming profiles, you will need to allocate more storage space to each user. Ideally, 2GB of space per user would be adequate. If you are using Windows Server 2003 R2 or Windows Server 2008, then you can manage this space allocation through their quota management features and therefore make sure users do not exceed it.

You should implement this protection mechanism whether or not your users roam from PC to PC. Storage space is less expensive today than it has ever been before, so allocating appropriate space on a per-user level is easy. Storing profile information in a central location allows you to back it up as well as make it available to users from any computer. In addition, should anything untoward happen to the user's PC, you don't have to worry about trying to protect key data because it is not stored locally. When problems arise on PCs, you know you can flash their OS installation at any time because you no longer have to worry about user data.

> **NOTE** This is a powerful data protection strategy and falls in line with the first level of defense in the Castle Defense System, as described in Chapter 11.

> **NOTE** You can also rely on the combination of folder redirection with roaming profiles to migrate user data from Windows XP to Windows Vista. That's because both technologies work in each version of the Windows client OS. When users move from an XP computer to a Vista computer, the data is automatically transferred from one format to the other. Vista profiles are considered version 2 profiles and because of this, new profile folders with a .V2 extension will be created on the server. For detailed information on how to use this strategy to

migrate user data during a deployment, look up Chapter 8: Working with Personality Captures from the free eBook: *The Definitive Guide to Vista Migration* by Ruest and Ruest available at www.realtime-nexus.com/dgvm.htm.

Putting data protection in place

To put the data protection strategy in place, you need to perform several tasks:

1. Prepare the central server share(s) and the groups that will support folder redirection.
2. Enable the Distributed File System to make the share available in all locations (optional).
3. Enable roaming profiles and exclude specific folders from the profile.
4. Enable the folder redirection Group Policy Object (GPO).
5. Test the strategy before applying it to users.

Each operation requires care and structure in its application. The following sections outline how each step is performed.

Preparing for data protection

Because both folder redirection and roaming user profiles rely on networked storage, you need to make sure your storage locations will be ready before you begin the redirection process. Although roaming profiles are a function of the user account in Active Directory, folder redirection is a function of Group Policy. In addition, Group Policy can control how the roaming profile will be managed as well as how profiles are managed in general.

If you only have a single, central site, then it will be easy to configure both folder redirection and roaming profiles. Just direct each to the same network share to store the contents under folders created for each user in the organization. If, however, there are multiple sites or locations in your organization, then you'll have to consider creating redirection folders in each location. After all, you don't want users to synchronize folders or profiles over the wide area network (WAN), do you?

Both systems allow for either central or regional redirection. Roaming user profiles are the easiest to set up because they are set as a property of the user account. But with folder redirection, you need to prepare two elements before you can support regional users:

- You must prepare special AD groups that will regroup users in each location. In many cases, you may already have these groups in place. Using groups allows you to create a single GPO for folder redirection. If you want to create multiple GPOs, you can create one GPO for each region and assign them to Organizational Units (OU) that represent the regions and contain the accounts for the users located in that region.

- You need to prepare shared folders in each location.

You might also want to use this strategy if you want to direct user folders from different departments to different file servers even if all your users are in a single location.

Use the following steps to create the groups in AD and then create the file shares. You will need Account Operator rights in AD to perform this task.

1. **Use Active Directory Users and Computers to create the appropriate groups.** Because these groups will contain users, they should be Global Security groups. For regional folder redirection support, create regional groups that contain the accounts of all of the users in a given regional site. For departmental redirection, create departmental groups to contain the users. In most organizations, groups with this purpose will already have been created. If not, create them. Use a clear naming convention to make them easy to identify.

> **NOTE** When you work with groups in Active Directory, you should rely on the AGLP rule. AGLP stands for Accounts which go into Global Groups, which are then inserted into Local Groups. Finally, Permissions are assigned to the Local Groups. For more information on using the AGLP rule, look up Prerequisites for group management in Active Directory at http://searchwinit.techtarget.com/tip/0,289483,sid1_gci1273040,00.html.

2. **Create file shares.** Because users will not be accessing these file shares because they will access data through folders on their desktops, such as Documents, you do not need to make these shares visible to users. Therefore, you can create the shares using the $ character in the name of the share, effectively hiding it from normal network browsing. Two share structures are required; one for folder redirection and one for roaming profiles. Begin with the first.

3. **Create the first share structure.** On a file server will sufficient space for each user, create a top-level share named FolderRedir$. Set Everyone Full Control in the share permissions and assign Authenticated Users modify or change permissions at the NTFS level.

4. **Create the second share structure.** On the same file server, create a top-level share named RoamingProf$. Set Everyone Full Control in the share permissions and assign Authenticated Users modify or change permissions at the NTFS level.

5. **Repeat the process if either regional or departmental share structures are required.**

Both the required groups and the shares are ready. Proceed to the next step.

Enabling the Distributed File System

This step is optional and really only applies to organizations that use remote sites and expect to have to support users roaming from one office location to another. When users rely on folder redirection and roaming profiles and move from one office to another during the performance of their work, they can find themselves in situations where they need to load their profile from a remote location instead of from the local network. There is however an easy way to avoid this situation.

Windows Server 2003 R2 and Windows Server 2008 both include a very powerful technology called the Distributed File System (DFS). Although DFS is not new to these versions of Windows Server, its implementation in these versions has changed so much that it is basically a completely different product. DFS includes two different components:

■ **DFS Namespaces:** This component is designed to replace the traditional letter-based network share mapping. Instead of using a traditional universal naming convention (UNC) shares in the \\servername\sharename format, DFS Namespaces uses domain-based shares in the \\domainname\sharename format. The file share name is therefore based on the name of the Active Directory domain instead of on a single server's name. Domain-based DFS Namespaces are then assigned targets or specific servers that host a copy of the share. Organizations that have remote sites assign a target for the share in each site. Each target contains the same files. Users that move from site to site continue to address the share through the domain-based UNC but do so through Active Directory's site identification. They are automatically directed to a local target for the share, avoiding WAN communications to access data.

■ **DFS Replication:** This component is used to maintain consistency between the contents of one target with all others. DFS Replication uses delta-based compressed replication, replicating only changed data blocks from one location to the other instead of replicating entire files, to keep the target content up to date.

Together, these two technologies ensure that users can access the same content from any location without having to cross the WAN. For travelling users relying on roaming folders and folder redirection, DFS is a boon because it can be used to make their data available automatically in any of the offices in which they can find themselves.

If you decide to rely on DFS to provide data availability to your traveling users, then you need to perform several tasks:

1. **Identify which users roam from office to office.** Ideally, you can put these users into a special "roaming" Global Security group in AD.

2. **Create the DFS Namespace.** Use the same share names as with non-roaming users, but make them domain-based DFS shares.

3. **Assign targets to the DFS Namespace.** Assign one target per remote site along with one target in the central office.

4. **Configure DFS Replication for the Namespace.** Doing this ensures that each target has the same content.

5. **Use the new DFS Namespace to assign the Group Policies that will enable folder redirection and redirect users' roaming profiles to the DFS Namespace share.**

Proceed as follows to perform these activities. You need Server Operator permissions to perform this task.

1. **Begin by logging onto the File Server Management console.** Either this can be done on a server where the File Server role has been deployed including the DFS components or, preferably, on a desktop that has the Remote Server Administration Tools (RSAT) deployed.

NOTE To use the RSAT for Windows Server 2008 on Vista, you must have Vista Service Pack 1 deployed.

2. **Connect to a File Server and then move to the File Server Management ⇨ DFS Management ⇨ Namespaces node in the Tree pane of the console.**

3. **Right-click on Namespaces or use the Action pane to select New Namespace.** Doing this launches the New Namespace wizard.

4. **Assign a server to host the Namespace by typing in the name of the server or using the Browse button to select the server. Click Next. If the server's DFS service is not running, the wizard will offer to start it. Click Yes.** (Note that any server that will host a target will do to host the namespace.)

5. **Create the namespace.** You only need to type in the latter part of the share name since the domain name will automatically be assigned. Two Namespaces are required: RoamingProf and FolderRedir. Assign the first name, and then repeat the procedure to assign the second name.

> **NOTE** DFS Namespaces cannot be hidden, therefore you do not need to add the $ sign at the end of the Namespace names.

6. **Click Edit Settings to modify the share permissions. In the Edit Settings dialog box, click Browse to place the share on the appropriate disk and folder. Click OK and then click Next.** Shares should be on a data disk, usually D: and should be placed within a special DFSRoots folder to properly identify them. Also, assign permissions so that administrators have full control and users have read and write privileges (see Figure 12.5).

FIGURE 12.5

Setting DFS Namespace location and permissions

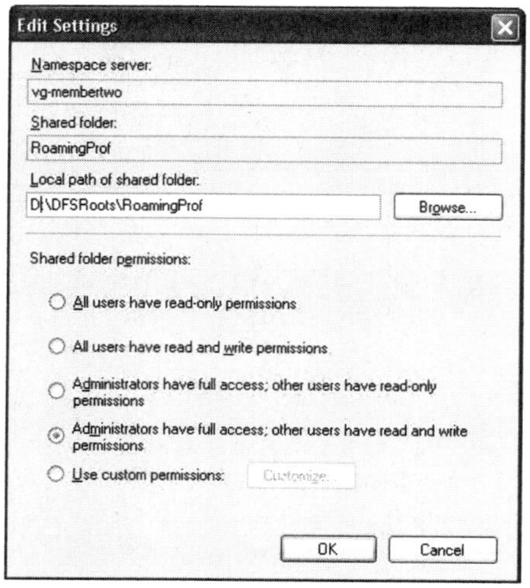

7. **Make sure that you select Domain-based namespace.** This ensures that the Namespace is stored within the directory and is made available to any location in your network. This dialog box lists the share name for your Namespace; make note of it. Click Next.

8. **Review the changes to perform and click Create. Click Previous if you need to modify the settings.**

9. **Review the tasks the wizard performed and click Close.**

10. **Repeat the procedure for the second namespace.**

Now you're ready to assign targets to the Namespace. Once again, this is done in the File Server Management console.

1. **Select the Namespace to which you want to add targets.**

2. **Click Add Namespace Server in the Action pane.**

3. **In the Add Namespace Server dialog box, click Browse to locate the servers you want to add as targets.**

4. **Again, click Edit Settings to assign the folder to the appropriate location and set proper permissions. Use the same settings as in the previous procedure. Click OK to assign the new target.** If the server's DFS service is not running, the wizard will offer to start it. Click Yes.

5. **Repeat the previous step to assign additional servers to this Namespace. Repeat the entire procedure to assign targets to the other Namespace.**

Now you're ready to set replication rules for the targets for each Namespace. Once again, this is done in the File Server Management console.

1. **Move to the File Server Management ⇨ DFS Management ⇨ Replication node in the tree pane of the console.**

2. **Right-click on Replication or use the action pane to select New Replication Group.** This launches the New Replication Group wizard.

3. **In the first page of the wizard, select Multipurpose replication group.** Selecting this enables you to set replication to keep content synchronized between locations.

4. **Click Next, name the Group, and click Next again.** For example, you can use Roaming Data Protection for the group name and assign a description.

5. **Use the Add button to select replication group member servers. Add all of the target servers in the Namespaces you created earlier. Click Next.**

6. **Select the Full mesh replication topology and click Next.** This step ensures that all members can initiate replication to all other members and will maintain identical content in each location.

7. **Select how much bandwidth replication will be allowed to use and identify the schedule.**

a. If your users spend entire days in remote offices when they travel, then you can use a daily replication schedule because they won't need to access their data in another location for 24 hours.

b. If your users are in several different offices in a single day, then you should use a more frequent replication schedule. In addition, you should throttle replication.

c. Use a value that is in keeping with the WAN links and available bandwidth on each link. Normally, 64 Mbps is sufficient.

d. Select Replicate during the specified days and times, and then click Edit Schedule.

8. **In the Schedule window, you can use the schedule which best fits your needs. Select the bandwidth to use, and then select the available times for this bandwidth. Click on Details to view the results of the schedule you set (see Figure 12.6). Click OK and then Next when done.**

FIGURE 12.6

Setting a Replication schedule

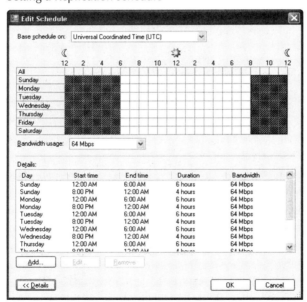

9. **Select the primary replication member and click Next.** This server will be the initial master during the first replication pass.

10. **Select the folders to replicate. Click Add to select the first folder, use the Browse button to locate the folder, use the same name as the target and make sure**

Permissions are set to Existing permissions. Click OK and repeat to add the second folder. Click Next when done.

11. **Select the local paths on target servers for each folder you replicate and then select the target server, click Edit, Enable replication, and click Browse to identify the local path.** This should be the same path as the Namespace path on each target server.

12. **Click OK and repeat for each target server. Click Next when Done.**

13. **Repeat the selection of local paths for the second folder to replicate.**

14. **Review your choices and click Create when ready. Click Previous to make modifications to your settings if needed.**

15. **Click Close when ready.** Windows displays a replication delay message indicating that replication will not begin until the target servers pick up the configuration from Active Directory. For example, in large organizations with extensive replication latency, this configuration would not be picked up by members until the latency period has passed. This is okay because you are still not ready to replicate data because your configuration is not yet complete.

16. **Click OK.** Your DFS strategy is complete.

Enabling roaming profiles

Now enable roaming profiles for your users. Locate your user accounts in AD DS and set them to use roaming profiles. Direct the profiles to local servers for users that do not travel and direct the travelling users' profiles to the new DFS Namespace for roaming profiles. You need Account Operator permissions to perform this task. Also, perform this task during off hours so that you have time to complete the entire operation before users access their profiles. To enable roaming profiles, use the following steps:

1. **Open Active Directory Users and Computers and locate the user accounts.**

2. **Right-click on the account name and select Properties.**

3. **Move to the Profile tab and type in the path of the shared folder to host the profile.**

   The path to the profile should be in the form of \\servername\RoamingProf\%username% for non-travelling users and for travelling users, it should be \\domainname\RoamingProf\%username% where the domain name is the full DNS name of your domain.

4. **Click Apply.** The profile path should change to the account name of the user.

5. **Verify that this is the case and click OK.**

Alternatively, you can perform this task with a script. Use the following script structures to perform this task. The first is for non-travelling users and the second is for travelling users.

```
dsmod user UserDN -profile \servername\RoamingProf\%username%
dsmod user UserDN -profile \domainname\RoamingProf\%username%
```

Use the user's distinguished name in the command line. For example, user Jane Doe in the People OU in the TandT.net domain would be "cn=Jane Doe,OU=People,dc=tandt,dc=net". Make sure that you do not use spaces between each section of the name and make sure that you enclose the entire name in double quotes.

Ideally, if you have many users to modify, you can export the user account name list from AD and then use a text editor to build the command structure around each user name, export it to text only, and save the file with a .CMD extension. Run the new .CMD file you created to modify the profile location for each user.

> **NOTE** Microsoft provides a guide for roaming user management in Vista at `http://technet2.microsoft.com/WindowsVista/en/library/fb3681b2-da39-4944-93ad-dd3b6e8ca4dc1033.mspx?mfr=true`. Use the online guide because it includes more information than the downloadable document.

Enabling folder redirection

Now, you're ready to enable folder redirection. In fact, you will need to perform three tasks:

1. Enable folder redirection.
2. Exclude folders from the roaming profile to keep it small and fast to load.
3. Set Group Policy settings for general profile management.

Each task is performed through the Group Policy Management Console. You need Group Policy Editing and Creation rights to perform these tasks. Also, make sure that you perform these tasks from a Vista PC or from a Windows Server 2008 machine otherwise you will not have access to the full redirection policy. Begin with Folder Redirection.

Ideally, your users will be regrouped in OUs, so you can target the GPO more easily. If not, you might consider regrouping users in appropriate OUs to make it easier to manage them. Use the following procedure to assign your Folder Redirection policy.

1. **Launch the Group Policy Management Console.** You can do this by typing `gpmc.msc` in the Start Search box in the Start Menu. Accept the elevation prompt.
2. **Expand the domain until you find the OU(s) containing user accounts.**
3. **Right-click on the target OU, select Create a GPO in this domain and link it here.**
4. **Name the policy appropriately. For example, you can name it Folder Redirection. Click OK.**
5. **Now, right-click on the new policy link and select Edit.**
6. **Expand User Configuration ⇨ Policies ⇨ Windows Settings ⇨ Folder Redirection.**
7. To set a folder redirection policy, you must right-click on each folder you want to redirect to set its properties. Begin with the first folder, AppData (Roaming), and then move on to each of the others. Use the following values to update the settings for each folder.

    a. If you have travelling users, then you must use the Advanced – Specify locations for various user groups setting.

b. If you want to redirect all folders to the same location, then use Basic –Redirect everyone's folder to the same location.

c. When using the Advanced option, click Add. Then use Browse to select the Security Group. Use the Create a folder for each user under the root path option and type in the Root Path (see Figure 12.7). Click OK when done and repeat for each user group. Figure 12.8 shows the redirection settings.

FIGURE 12.7

Specifying Groups and Locations

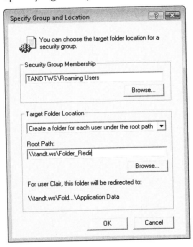

8. **Exclude the folders you redirected from the roaming profile. To do so, you must move to the User Configuration ➪ Policies ➪ Administrative Templates ➪ System ➪ User Profiles ➪ Exclude directories in roaming profile**.

9. **Open the setting's Properties, click Enable, and type in the profile paths to exclude.** Paths are relative to the root of the profile. For example, to exclude all of the folders you can redirect, you would exclude the following folders:

```
AppData\Roaming; Desktop; Documents; Pictures; Music; Videos;
Favorites; Contacts; Downloads; Links; Searches; Saved Games
```

You do not need to exclude the Start Menu because it is a subfolder of the AppData (Roaming) folder.

10. **Your policy is ready. Close the Group Policy Editor.**

11. **Review the policy settings and make sure it is enabled in the GPMC.**

FIGURE 12.8

Specifying Redirection Settings

Now you need to make sure your PCs manage user profiles properly. This means either creating a new GPO to apply to PCs or editing an existing GPO to include these settings. Use the following procedure to create a new GPO or to edit an existing GPO.

1. **Right-click on the target OU containing PCs and select Create a GPO in this domain, and link it here.**

2. **Name the policy appropriately and click OK.** For example, you can name it User Profile Management.

3. **Right-click the new policy link and select Edit.**

4. **Expand Computer Configuration ➪ Policies ➪ Administrative Templates ➪ System.**

5. **Locate the Verbose vs normal status messages setting and view its Properties. Set it to Enabled and click OK.** You change this setting because Vista does not display much user information during log on and log off. Because of this, users may complain that log on and log off times are too long. Changing this setting will display what Vista is doing during the log on and log off process and users will understand why it takes longer.

6. **Move to the Computer Configuration ➪ Policies ➪ Administrative Templates ➪ System ➪ User Profiles location. Modify the Delete user profiles older than a specified number of days on system restart and set it to 30 days.** Doing this cleans up unused profiles from your PCs.

7. **Close the Group Policy Editor and verify that the settings are appropriate in the new policy. Close the GPMC.**

Now test the policies by logging in and out of a PC with a user account. Verify that the proper folders have been created in your shared storage locations. Your basic user data protection strategy is complete.

NOTE Using this data protection mechanism fully addresses task VA-37: Transfer User Settings as identified in Chapter 10 because user settings are stored centrally and therefore never need to be transferred in the event of a change of PCs or even when the operating system on their PC is re-imaged.

Using the Encrypting File System

Protecting user data while it is within the internal network is mostly a matter of providing proper protected storage for user data, but when the information leaves the office, then protecting it requires a bit more than central storage. Fortunately, Windows Vista offers several features in relation to data protection while in transit on portable computers. One of these, the Encrypting File System (EFS), will protect all user data, even temporary files, by encrypting them. To view the data, users must have the decryption key. No decryption key, no data. It's as simple as that.

EFS is an extension of the NTFS file system build into Windows. NTFS is in fact a database system that adds and controls extended attributes to file objects. These attributes include security elements as well as the ability to either compress or encrypt data. Both compression and encryption are transparent attributes that are tied to the file object, but that are self-eliminating; a file object can either be compressed or encrypted, but not both at the same time.

Understanding EFS

The encrypting file system uses public key infrastructure (PKI) encryption to provide access control protection to files and folders stored on either NTFS or Web-based Distributed Authoring and Versioning (WebDAV). EFS operates on most newer versions of Windows including Windows 2000, Windows XP Professional, Windows Server 2003 and, of course, Windows Vista. EFS is not supported on Basic or Home Editions or any other older version of Windows.

EFS requires the use of both symmetric and asymmetric keys to encrypt data. The symmetric key or file encryption key (FEK) is randomly generated by EFS and is used to encrypt the file. Then, the user's public or asymmetric key is used to encrypt the symmetric key. Because it includes the capability to add more than one public key to the encrypted symmetric key, EFS can support the sharing of encrypted files between multiple users. This also provides a path for data recovery in the event of a mishap. If EFS was based on symmetric key pairs alone, it would not provide a very efficient protection mechanism because anyone with the decryption key could open the file. By relying on a public key infrastructure, EFS provides a very strong level of protection to encrypted data. EFS uses standard X.509 certificates for encryption.

EFS uses a standard process to encrypt files (see Figure 12.9). But before it encrypts a file, EFS begins with a number of verification checks — making sure that the file isn't already encrypted, identifying if there is enough disk space to encrypt the file, identifying whether the file is a system file or not, and so on. By default, system files cannot be encrypted. Next, it generates the FEK and protects it with the user's public key and any other public key that is designated as authorized.

After the FEK is protected, EFS generates the required metadata. This includes the data decryption field (DDF) that will contain the FEK and any public key used to protect it. A second key field that is stored within the metadata is the data recovery field (DRF). If one or several recovery agents have been assigned, then the DRF will contain their public keys. Other information stored in the metadata includes the version of EFS used and the encryption algorithm used to encrypt the data.

At this stage, EFS is now ready to encrypt the data. To do so, it begins by creating a temporary file in the same directory as the encrypted file. This temporary file serves as a backup of the original in case the encryption process goes awry. Next, it takes the original file and basically empties it of content and writes the metadata to it. It then proceeds to read data from the temporary file, encrypt it, and store it back into the original file. After the writing is complete, the temporary file is deleted. The original file is now considered encrypted because it contains both its original data and the EFS metadata.

If at any time during the process something goes awry, EFS uses the temporary file to restore the file to its original state. This is one reason why EFS and compression are self-eliminating — both need to have access to temporary space during the process of writing the file. When decrypting a file, EFS uses the same process in reverse.

Interacting with EFS and PKI

EFS requires an asymmetric key pair to operate. If a proper PKI is already implemented and the user has a key pair, EFS will use the user's public key to encrypt the FEK. But, if no PKI exists, Windows will automatically generate a key pair and assign it to the user. This key pair can be assigned as valid at the workstation or workgroup level and within an Active Directory (AD), at the site, domain, or organizational unit level. Within AD, it is best to keep PKI scopes at the domain level. This reduces the number of policies to maintain.

When key pair scopes are managed at the workstation or workgroup level, each and every machine involved must be addressed manually. This is because a core portion of any EFS strategy must involve a recovery policy — a special PKI policy that provides support for the designation of recovery agents in the event of the loss or damage of the encrypting user's private key. When working with individual workstations or small workgroups, this policy must be duplicated on every machine. Active Directory eliminates this by providing support for a corporate infrastructure for public key management. This is one reason why it is best to use the features integrated with Windows Server 2003 or 2008 and Active Directory to implement and manage a Windows-based public key infrastructure.

In addition, using a proper PKI will allow you to perform automatic key recovery. If you do not use a PKI, then you will be able to recover data from encrypted files, but you will never be able to recover lost keys. In short, if a user has a lot of encrypted data and you do not use a PKI in support of EFS, you, as the Data Recovery Agent (DRA) will have to either decrypt each of these files manually or re-encrypt them with a new EFS key. Although it is more work to implement a PKI at first, using a PKI will save you lots of administrative overhead in the end.

FIGURE 12.9

The EFS encryption process

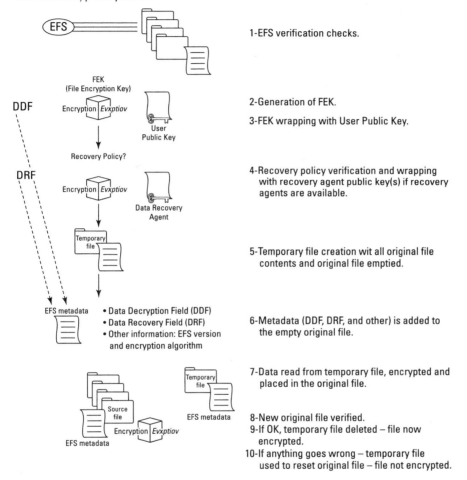

1-EFS verification checks.

2-Generation of FEK.

3-FEK wrapping with User Public Key.

4-Recovery policy verification and wrapping with recovery agent public key(s) if recovery agents are available.

5-Temporary file creation wit all original file contents and original file emptied.

6-Metadata (DDF, DRF, and other) is added to the empty original file.

7-Data read from temporary file, encrypted and placed in the original file.

8-New original file verified.

9-If OK, temporary file deleted – file now encrypted.

10-If anything goes wrong – temporary file used to reset original file – file not encrypted.

When you do use a PKI in support of EFS, the Certificate Authority in Windows Server will automatically create a backup copy of the encryption keys it assigns users. If a user loses this key, all you need to do — that is, you or the Certificate Authority administrator — is access the secure CA database to retrieve the user's lost key. After the user has access to the lost key again, they have access to all of their encrypted files, a much simpler process than relying on DRAs though you should have DRAs anyway. Finally, using PKI with EFS will make it easier for users to share encrypted files.

NOTE   **To get access to automatic key recovery, you must use an Enterprise Edition of Windows Server as your Certificate Authority.**

> **NOTE** Although Windows Server and AD give you the technology required to support the distribution and management of key pairs to your internal user base, they do not provide any means to truly identify you as who you are. This level of identification is at the core of any PKI implementation. Someone, somewhere — preferably a reputable someone, somewhere — can vouch that they have taken the time to identify and validate who you are. One of the best ways to do this in combination with an internal Windows-managed PKI is to obtain a corporate certificate from an external trusted certificate authority (CA) and use it as the root of your internal public key infrastructure. The fact that they are trusted simplifies the use of their certificate because it is automatically included in most Web browsers. The fact that they are external serves to validate who you are because the corroborator is a third-party organization. And the fact that you integrate this root certificate into your own lets you profit from the integrated services your operating system of choice offers while facilitating in-house certificate management.

EFS can be applied to either folders or individual files. Because folder inheritance is an intrinsic part of both NTFS and WebDAV, it is a good idea to focus on the encryption of entire folders rather than on individual objects. In fact, encrypting the folder is the default behavior of Windows (see Figure 12.10). This way, documents are automatically encrypted when placed into special folders. If this strategy is used, it is important to back it up with a strong training policy because of the potential for inadvertent decryption of files as they are removed from an encrypted folder and placed into folders that do not automatically encrypt data. By default, Windows displays encrypted data in green in the file system so that it is easier for users to identify.

FIGURE 12.10

By default, Windows wants to encrypt entire folders

In addition, Windows offers support for the encryption of offline files and folders. This lets you combine your data management strategy with a data protection policy by encrypting all files that can be at risk.

Working with EFS

Encrypting files is easy. All a user has to do is right-click on any file or folder, select Properties, click Advanced on the General tab, and check the Encrypt contents to secure data option. If the user selected a folder, then, when the user closes all of the dialog boxes, the system will ask if all content should be encrypted. That's it. From now on, the folder and the files contained within it will display in green in Windows Explorer.

To view the details of an encrypted file, the user needs to select it once again, view its Properties, click Advanced on the General tab and now, because the file is already encrypted, they will be able to click the Details button. Clicking Details displays the Encryption dialog box (see Figure 12.11). This displays who has access to the file as well as who can recover the file should an untoward event occur with the user's certificate. This interface also gives you access to the backup of the user's keys if you are using an internal CA to provide PKI keys.

FIGURE 12.11

Viewing the details of an encrypted file

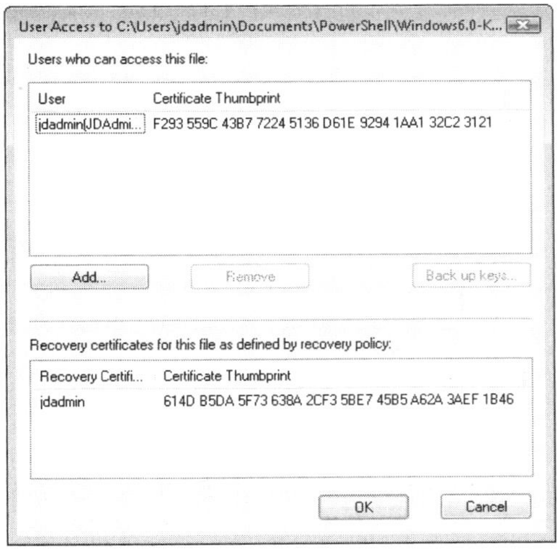

However, since putting in place an encrypting file system structure can be complex when you deal with it on a user per user basis, you should control encryption at the Group Policy level so that you have one single, structured EFS policy in place.

Implementing an EFS structure involves several activities:

- Identifying information that may be at risk
- Preparing a PKI for EFS use
- Implementing EFS for data that may be at risk

Perform each activity in turn. For the first activities, you may need to request help from your Certificate Authority administrator.

Identifying potential EFS uses

The first activity is relatively simple. In most organizations, the only data that is at risk is the data that is in transit inside portable or mobile computers. When the mobile system is lost and data is not protected, then your organization's information can be at risk. In some organizations, however, all data is considered at risk, and therefore all data is encrypted at all time.

If you choose to encrypt data that is located on mobile computers only, then you will need to regroup these computers into an OU within Active Directory to be able to more easily target them with an Encrypting File System Group Policy Object. If you want to encrypt data on all systems, then target your GPO to every PC in your network.

It is also a good idea to create a Windows Security group to contain the users you intend to assign EFS to. This helps identify them easily in the event of issues.

Preparing the PKI for EFS

The second activity is focused on using an existing PKI to prepare for EFS. Putting a new PKI in place is beyond the scope of this book because it focuses on server infrastructures more than on PC infrastructures. But keep the following in mind when you do put your PKI in place:

- Use an Enterprise Edition of Windows Server — either 2003 or 2008 — as your Certificate Authority.

- Obtain an official certificate from a third-party Certificate Authority to identify your organization and use this certificate as the root of your CA. Doing this will automatically identify your organization and the certificate it issues to others because most systems already trust third-party CAs.

- Use multiple levels of CAs to ensure redundancy for the infrastructure.

- Validate other uses for the CA. They support many more operations than just EFS. For example, if you are using Exchange in your organization, then you will need certificates for your Outlook Web Access Web site. This is another area where a PKI could help.

- Rely on user auto-enrolment to assign certificates.

- Make sure that your users are well informed on the uses of PKI and the importance of protecting their certificates.

Implementing a CA structure can be a complex operation. Don't take it lightly.

> **NOTE** For information on how to put a PKI in place with Windows Server 2008, look up *Windows Server 2008: The Complete Reference* by Ruest and Ruest from McGraw-Hill Osborne. For information on integrating a third-party root certificate into your CA structure, look up *The Case for Outsourcing PKI* under the Advanced PKI section at www.reso-net.com/articles.asp?m=8#c.

After it is implemented, you should begin issuing EFS certificates to end users. Windows includes a Basic EFS certificate template, but this template does not include certain useful options you might want in order to facilitate the management of these certificates. For this reason, it is a good idea to make a duplicate of this template, rename it to something such as Corporate EFS, and then customize it to your needs. Customizations include at least five settings that are not on the original template:

- On the General tab of the certificate template's Properties, choose Publish certificate in Active Directory.
- On the Request Handling tab of the template's Properties, choose Archive subject's encryption private key.
- On the Request Handling tab of the template's Properties, choose Enroll subject without requiring any user input.
- On the Security tab of the template's Properties, add the group you created earlier to grant access to this template. Grant the Read and Enroll or Autoenroll rights.
- On the Superseded Templates tab for the template's Properties, add the original Basic EFS template.

The first setting makes it easier for users to share encrypted files because they will be able to locate other user's certificates in AD. The second creates the user's backup certificate. The third lets users automatically generate the certificate. When users begin to use EFS, the EFS certificate will automatically be generated by the CA. Use Enroll rights to have the process issue the certificate on an as-needed basis. Use Autoenroll to distribute certificates to anyone who has access rights to them before they begin using EFS. The last option makes sure that your new template is used when user certificates are generated instead of the default template that is delivered with the CA.

Implementing EFS

Putting EFS in place requires a series of operations:

1. Find out if savvy users are already using EFS on their own.
2. Put the GPO settings required to enable EFS in place.
3. Prepare your data recovery agents (DRA).
4. Have your users use two-factor authentication to remove their certificate from the machine they work with.
5. Inform your users of the EFS policy you put in place and their responsibilities in relation to this policy.

Begin with the identification of who may be using EFS already. Savvy users can already have enabled standalone EFS on their own. If this happens, then you'll need to use a special approach for them. If you're working on this before anyone uses EFS, then you're lucky. All you need to do is disable standalone EFS through Group Policy. But if some of your users already use EFS, then you'll have to first disable EFS for those who are not using it, and then migrate the ones who are to the centrally controlled EFS policy. Do not disable EFS on the systems where it is already in use because your users will lose access to their data. To find out who is using EFS, use the following command line in a logon script:

```
Cipher /U /N >\\servername\sharename\%username%.txt
```

Basically, you use the cipher command to identify if users are running EFS and you are piping the result into a file named with the user name and placing the file on a central share somewhere in your network. Then, you can use the results to generate a Security group in AD, for example, a group named Standalone EFS Users, to contain the users who are already using EFS.

Now you're ready to prepare the GPO. If you do not have any users already using EFS, then you can make these GPO changes in the same GPO that you used for folder redirection earlier. If you do, then you have to create a new GPO. Use either of the two following procedures. You will need Group Policy Modification privileges to make these changes.

For organizations that are not yet using EFS:

1. **Launch the Group Policy Management Console.**
2. **Locate the User Profile Management GPO and right-click to select Edit.** You use this GPO because the settings you need to modify will apply to computer objects.
3. **Navigate to Computer Configuration ⇨ Policies ⇨ Windows Settings ⇨ Security Settings ⇨ Public Key Policies ⇨ Encrypting File System.**
4. **Right-click on Encrypting File System and select Properties.**
5. **On the General tab, set the policy to Don't allow. Click OK to enable the policy and close GPEdit.**

Remember to update your GPO description to reflect that it is also used for EFS.

For organizations that have users running EFS, use the following procedure:

1. **Create a new policy.** You must create a new policy because you will be preventing the users who are already using EFS from using this policy.
2. **Launch the GPMC.**
3. **Right-click the target OU containing PCs, select Create a GPO in this domain, and link it here.**
4. **Name the policy appropriately and click OK.** For example, you can name it Deny EFS Policy.
5. **Now, right-click the new policy link and select Edit.**
6. **Choose Computer Configuration ⇨ Policies ⇨ Windows Settings ⇨ Security Settings ⇨ Public Key Policies ⇨ Encrypting File System.**
7. **Right-click Encrypting File System and select Properties.**
8. **On the General tab, set the policy to Don't allow.**
9. **Click OK to enable the policy and close GPEdit.**
10. **Now filter this policy with the security group you created earlier.**
    a. Move to the Delegation tab for the policy in the GPMC, click Add to select the Standalone EFS Users group, and assign the Read property to them.

b. Next, click Advanced, deselect Allow Read, and select Deny Read for the Standalone EFS Users group. This blocks them from reading this policy.

Now that no users can use EFS except those that already have it. Because you elected to enroll users without any user input in the preparation of your EFS certificate template, and especially if you elected to automatically enroll users, everyone should have received a new certificate by now. This means you can assign a script to the Standalone EFS Users group to update their files with the new certificate. Run the following command in your script:

```
Cipher /U >\\servername\sharename\%username%.txt
```

This command automatically updates all of the standalone EFS certificates in pre-encrypted files to the new, centrally controlled certificate. It is a good idea to add a user count in the script, such as the generated text file to ensure that you know when all files have been updated for each user.

Now you're ready to define your central EFS policy.

1. **Begin by launching the Group Policy Management Console**. If you had standalone users, begin by deleting the Deny EFS Policy you created earlier, and then proceed to Step 5. If not, go to the next step.

2. **Locate the User Profile Management GPO and right-click on it to select Edit.**

3. **Move to Computer Configuration ⇨ Policies ⇨ Windows Settings ⇨ Security Settings ⇨ Public Key Policies ⇨ Encrypting File System.**

4. **Right-click on Encrypting File System and select Properties**. **On the General tab, select Not Defined and close GPEdit.** Doing this turns off the EFS blockage you put in place earlier.

5. **If you only want to apply EFS to mobile systems, then return to GPMC and right-click on the OU that contains mobile PCs to select Create a GPO in this Domain, and Link it here. Name the GPO EFS Policy, then right-click on the link to select Edit. If you want to assign EFS to all systems, then locate the User Profile Management GPO and right-click on it to select Edit.**

6. **Move to Computer Configuration ⇨ Policies ⇨ Windows Settings ⇨ Security Settings ⇨ Public Key Policies ⇨ Encrypting File System.**

7. **Right-click on Encrypting File System and select Properties.**

8. **On the General tab, apply the following settings (see Figure 12.12):**
   - Set the policy to Allow.
   - Select Encrypt the contents of the user's Documents folder.
   - Select Require smart card for EFS.
   - Leave Create caching-capable user key from smart card selected.
   - Select Enable pagefile encryption.
   - Select Display key backup notifications when user key is created or changed.

- Uncheck Allow EFS to generate self-signed certificates when a certification authority is not available.
- Use the Browse button to locate your Corporate EFS template.

FIGURE 12.12

Changing EFS Policy Properties

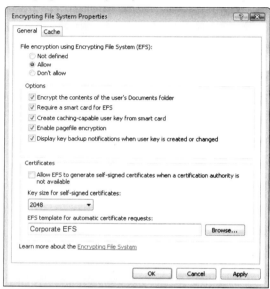

9. On the Cache tab, leave the Cache timeout option selected and select User locks workstation.
10. Click OK to enable the policy.
11. Now move to the Computer Configuration ➪ Policies ➪ Administrative Templates ➪ Network ➪ Offline Files section.
12. Double-click the Encrypt the Offline Files cache setting and Enable it. Click OK to close it. Close GPEdit for now.

This policy enables EFS on all of the computers in the target OU. It will automatically encrypt the Documents folder as well as the pagefile and all data in the offline cache. But, as you know, some data will not be covered by this policy. For example, data that is contained within the AppData\ Local and AppData\LocalLow folders will not be encrypted. If your users are running Microsoft Outlook, then it is possible that e-mail messages and personal stores are not protected. To ensure that all sensitive data is protected, you should supplement this policy with a logon script that targets all systems that should include encrypted data and includes the following command:

```
Cipher /e /s /a "%userprofile%\appData\Local
Cipher /e /s /a "%userprofile%\appData\LocalLow
```

This command ensures that all data is protected on the target systems. All other data folders are in the offline cache because of folder redirection.

Implementing an EFS recovery solution

Every organization planning to use EFS should devise a proper recovery policy. As seen earlier, recovery policies are used to assign the public keys of designated recovery agents to the data recovery field (DRF) of an encrypted file or folder. This allows the recovery agent to decrypt encrypted data in the event of a key loss or a user reassignment.

By default, a standalone machine will not have a recovery policy. That's because Windows Vista no longer requires the recovery policy to be in place before users can have access to the encryption capabilities it offers. In a domain, the recovery policy is enabled through the same policy which enables EFS.

Recovery agent private keys are very valuable because they are automatically included in each and every encrypted document and can therefore decrypt anything in your organization. Protect these keys as much as possible, removing them from machines and importing them only when a data recovery operation is required. Removing them is easily done. Keys can be stored on many types of removable storage, such as smart cards, floppy disks, CD-ROMs, DVDs, or even USB keys. Make sure that the removable storage is stored in a safe place that is immune to tampering or theft.

To begin, you need to deploy recovery agent certificates to the people you've designated to manage data recovery in the encrypting file system. This can be done by using the Certification Authority console, but there is a potential issue with using this console. As a best practice, you should make your data recovery agent certificates last much, much longer than the certificates you issue users. This ensures that your recovery certificates are always valid even if user certificates must be updated on a regular basis. By default, certificates you issue with the console will have the same duration as the Certificate Authority itself. Then, when they expire, you will need to maintain these older certificates to be able to recover files that were encrypted using the older DRA certificate. Using longer certificate duration avoids this issue.

By default, the cipher command can generate DRA certificates that have duration of 100 years. This should be long enough to recovery pretty well any file in your organization. To do so, use the following command to generate your certificates:

```
Cipher /r:Filename
```

Run this command within the security context of each user that will become a DRA. You'll need at least two DRAs in your organization. Each time the command is run, the new DRA will have to enter a password to protect the certificate files. Two files will be generated using the name you input as the file name. The .CER file only includes the certificate and is used to load the certificate into the EFS recovery policy. The .PFX file includes the certificate and the private key and is the file used to recover data.

After the recovery agent certificates have been issued, the recovery policy can be implemented. Use the following procedure. You need Group Policy Modification access rights.

1. Begin by launching the Group Policy Management Console.

2. Locate the GPO which contains your EFS policy. This can be the User Profile Management policy if you are assigning it to all PCs or the EFS Policy if you are only assigning it to mobile systems.

3. Right-click on the policy to select Edit.

4. Choose Computer Configuration ➪ Policies ➪ Windows Settings ➪ Security Settings ➪ Public Key Policies ➪ Encrypting File System.

5. Right-click on Encrypting File System and select Add Data Recovery Agent. This launches the Add Recovery Agent Wizard.

6. Click Next. Click Browse Folders because you generated certificates with the cipher command instead of the directory.

7. Locate the .CER files containing the DRA certificates. You will get a warning because Windows is unable to determine if the certificate is revoked once again because it was self-generated.

8. Click Yes to install the certificate.

9. Repeat for each DRA certificate to load.

10. Click Next.

11. Review your changes and click Finish or click Back to modify your settings.

Recovery certificates will now be displayed in your policy. You can right-click on each certificate and open them or view their properties. The Properties dialog box lets you add a friendly name and a description to the certificates. When you open the certificate, you will see that because it is self-generated, it is not trusted by your organization. You will also note that it has a duration of 100 years (see Figure 12.13).

Now you should add these certificates to the Trusted Root Certification Authorities store within the GPO to make them trustworthy.

1. Within the same GPO, move to Computer Configuration ➪ Policies ➪ Windows Settings ➪ Security Settings ➪ Public Key Policies ➪ Trusted Root Certification Authorities.

2. Right-click Trusted Root Certification Authorities and select Import. This launches the certificate import wizard.

3. Click Next, and then click Browse. Despite the information in this dialog box, you can use either the .PFX or the .CER files generated earlier with the cipher command. Only one file can be loaded at a time.

4. Locate the file and click Next. Select the .CER file because using the .PFX file will require a password to support the import of the private key.

5. Make sure that Place all certificates in the following store is selected and the Trusted Root store is indicated and click Next. Review your changes and click Finish. Click OK when Windows tells you the import was successful.

6. Repeat for each other DRA certificate.

Self-generated DRA Certificates have a duration of 100 years and are untrusted.

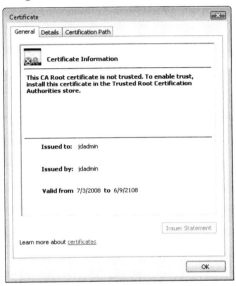

Now your certificates will be trusted by the users impacted by this GPO. From now on the DRA certificates will be added to all DRF fields of each encrypted file. Because the recovery policy is distributed by Group Policy, it automatically overrides any existing local policy. Should a member machine not be able to contact a domain controller to refresh its recovery policy, it will use a locally cached version of the policy to encrypt files.

In a workgroup, assigning a standard recovery agent is a bit more complex. That's because in a workgroup each machine has its own security accounts manager (SAM) database that is separate from all others. So to standardize the recovery agent, you first need to create one-on-one machine, export it to external storage and re-import it on the same machine. Make sure that you assign a strong password to the exported certificate. The export/re-import operation is necessary to have a separate copy of the certificate on removable storage. After this is done, you have to go to each machine and create the recovery agent, export it but then you re-import the agent that was created on the first machine. This automatically standardizes the agent on all members of the workgroup.

All is done through the Certificates console. Remember to keep the offline copy of the DRA well protected.

After the recovery policy is in place, it is relatively easy to recover files. If a single file is recovered, the recovery agent only needs to open it normally. Once opened, the file is in clear text and can be saved normally. If multiple files need to be decrypted, the recovery agent can do so through the file system, either by using the Windows Explorer and addressing the files' properties or through the cipher command.

 **Putting the DRA policy in place lets you address task VA-35: Encrypted Folder Recovery from the administrative tasks listed in Chapter 10.**

Preparing users for EFS

You're almost done. Now you need to help users load their certificates onto smart cards and teach them some EFS usage guidelines. There are several types of smart cards with and without readers. The simplest form of a smart card is a USB Key because it does not require an additional reader. But some organizations prefer to use smart cards that actually look like a card. In this case, you'll need to acquire readers for the cards as well as the cards themselves. Relying on smart cards is a good idea because it removes the certificate used for encryption from the PC and stores it on a separate device. This means that for anyone to either encrypt or decrypt files in your organization, they need two-factor authentication and provides a much more secure EFS policy.

In order to rely on this two-factor authentication, you must remove the user's certificate from the personal computer they use and place it on the smart card you distribute to them. This is one more reason why using a proper PKI makes sense. If users lose their smart card, then you always have a backup certificate for them.

The instructions for placing the certificate on a smart card will vary with the type of smart card you use, but in most cases, they require care and attention. This is one reason why it is a good idea to have users come in with their mobile system if you chose to only protect mobile data and assist them in this process. If you elected to protect all data, then you'll have to go around seeing each user at their desk.

This gives you the opportunity to perform the last two tasks at once. As you assist the users to move their certificates, you can also provide them with best practices for EFS use. Users should commit to the following guidelines:

- They should protect their smart card at all times.
- They should make a habit of removing their smart card whenever they lock their workstation.
- They should use long passwords or even better passphrases that include at least 11 characters. Brute force attack tools that try to obtain user passwords mostly fail when the password is 11 or more characters long. Correspondingly, you should make sure that the passwords for the default administrator and any other administrative account on the PC also use complex passphrases.

- Make sure that users know that all encrypted files are displayed in a different color within the Windows Explorer to facilitate their differentiation.

- When travelling, they should keep the smart card and the computer in separate containers. Lots of users put the smart card inside the computer bag along with the computer. This negates the two-factor concept because both are available if the bag should be lost.

- If users are granted local administrative rights — which they shouldn't — then they must make a habit of storing data in the default Documents folder. Placing data elsewhere may leave it unprotected.

You may have other recommendations for your users, but you should make sure they are at least familiar with these. Your EFS strategy is now in place and mobile data, at the very least, will be protected when it leaves your offices.

> **NOTE** In previous versions of Windows, you also had to change the Syskey mode to 3 to require a boot password for each machine that has encrypted files on it. This added one more layer of protection to these machines. Windows Vista does not require this change because EFS fully protects all user data files now and does not need additional protection mechanisms.

Running BitLocker Full Drive Encryption

Because EFS has been enhanced considerably with Windows Vista, and because you use EFS with smart cards, you may not need to run BitLocker Full Drive Encryption on your mobile systems. The basic difference between BitLocker and EFS is that EFS only encrypts the user's data on the mobile system. BitLocker encrypts the entire system drive including the operating system as well as all data for all users of the system.

> **NOTE** Only two Windows Vista editions support BitLocker: Enterprise and Ultimate. Keep this in mind if you decide to use BitLocker. All business editions of Vista support EFS.

The difference between BitLocker and EFS also extends to the way you put them in place. EFS is an extension of your data protection strategy and can be added once your systems are deployed. BitLocker, on the other hand, must be implemented during the installation of the operating system and cannot be added afterwards unless you have made specific preparations beforehand. This is because BitLocker requires two partitions: one small partition is used to begin the system boot process and the other is encrypted and will contain the entire OS (see Figure 12.14).

> **NOTE** BitLocker protects the entire contents of a system drive and therefore provides more protection than EFS does. This is because a malicious user that gains access to a system running EFS could eventually gain access to the files it contains through a brute force attack to obtain the user's password. Because EFS only protects data and not the entire system drive, the attacker gains access to system folders and can try to obtain the user's password from there. Two mechanisms can protect against this: using smart cards to remove the encryption certificate from the PC and using long and complex passwords. Most brute force tools today will have difficulty with passwords longer than 11 characters.

FIGURE 12.14

Creating partitions for BitLocker at system installation

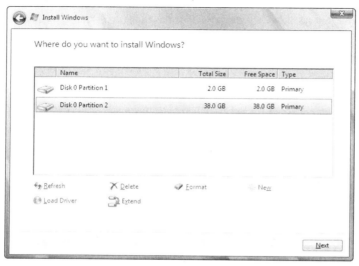

Most often, you will deploy BitLocker on systems that include a Trusted Protection Module (TMP) version 1.2. The TPM is a special microchip that is used to securely store decryption keys and user passwords. If you decide to deploy BitLocker on systems that do not include a TPM, then you will need to rely on external storage for the encryption keys, much like you would rely on a smart card for EFS encryption keys. This method is less secure than when using a TPM because even though the TPM is included in the PC, it cannot be tampered with. If, as with EFS, users leave a USB Key that includes the decryption keys within their computer bag, then their system will not be fully protected.

Because of this, you usually decide to deploy BitLocker when you build your systems. Both of the partitions you create must be primary partitions. Usually, 2GB is sufficient for the unencrypted boot partition while you assign the rest to the OS partition. The 2GB boot partition must be set as active so that it can launch the boot process.

> **NOTE** The Windows Recovery Environment (WinRE) also relies on two partitions: the first partition stores the recovery environment and the second stores the OS. Using two partitions for WinRE lets you recover broken system disks without having to resort to installation media. If you choose to combine BitLocker and WinRE, then you should store WinRE on the same partition as the OS. If not, the WinRE partition will not be encrypted and may become a security risk. Keep in mind however, that your technicians will need a different method of accessing WinRE in order to recover lost BitLocker partitions.

When you plan to deploy BitLocker, you'll have a couple of choices for installation:

- You can deploy BitLocker during the PC build process, using custom preconfigured BitLocker images. These images can be deployed with Windows Deployment Services or through unattended installations. Once the image is deployed, you rely on a Windows Management Instrumentation (WMI) script to enable BitLocker.

■ You deploy a standard PC build using two partitions. Then once the installation is complete, you either rely on a WMI script or the built-in manage-bde.wsf script to enable BitLocker.

Each process requires preparation beforehand so that your build process will support the creation of two partitions.

> **NOTE** Microsoft provides a complete BitLocker Design and Deployment Guide as well as sample BitLocker scripts at `http://go.microsoft.com/fwlink/?LinkId=96685`. Information on BitLocker can be found online at `http://go.microsoft.com/fwlink/?LinkId=77977`. In addition, Microsoft offers a planning and implementation guide for data encryption at `www.microsoft.com/technet/security/guidance/client security/dataencryption/default.mspx`.

Understanding BitLocker requirements

Deploying BitLocker in your environment is not a menial task. In fact, you must seriously consider the need for BitLocker before you put it in place. When in use, BitLocker requires a special encryption key mechanism. Then, this key protection mechanism is linked with the authentication method you've decided to implement to support system startup. Table 12.1 outlines the various protection mechanisms you can use with BitLocker. These mechanisms are used whenever the system boots from either a complete shutdown or from hibernation. Table 12.2 lists the authentication methods BitLocker supports.

TABLE 12.1

BitLocker Protection Mechanisms

Key Protection Mechanism	Comment
TPM 1.2 Microchip	The Trusted Protection Module is a special chip that securely stores the BitLocker encryption key.
Personal Identification Number (PIN)	This is a numeric value that is used in conjunction with the TPM to unlock the system.
Startup Key on Removable Media	The encryption key can also be stored on removable media. This includes USB keys, removable disk drives, and floppy disks. Obviously, the most practical media for this is the USB key. Startup Keys can be used with or without TPM chips.
Recovery Password	The Recovery Password is used to recover a BitLocker installation. This is a 48-digit number that is entered after the administrator presses the F1 and F10 keys during system startup.
Recovery Key	The Recovery Key is an encrypted file that can also be used to recover a BitLocker installation.

TABLE 12.2

BitLocker Authentication Mechanisms

Authentication Mechanism	Comment
TPM Alone	The TPM itself validates the boot process. No user interaction is required.
TPM and PIN	The TPM validates the boot process, but the user must enter a PIN before the process can complete.
TPM and Startup Key	The TPM validates the boot process, but the user must insert the Startup Key for the process to complete.
Startup Key Alone	No TPM is used. The user must insert the Startup Key before the boot process can complete.

As you can see, using BitLocker implies some changes to the processes you use to manage systems. Of all of the authentication mechanisms you can use with BitLocker, only the first listed in Table 12.2 does not require user interaction to boot. Of course, this level of authentication does not offer very much protection because the system opens by default. All of the other mechanisms require user input. Therefore, if you deploy updates to your systems and they require reboots, all systems using comprehensive BitLocker protection will fail during this boot process and will be in a locked state until the user returns. This leaves much to be desired as a remote management mechanism.

Integrating BitLocker with Active Directory

Another requirement you may have with BitLocker is Active Directory integration. When you integrate BitLocker with Active Directory, you are able to use the directory service to store BitLocker-related information including:

- BitLocker-enabled volume passwords
- TPM owner passwords
- Information which links these passwords with the appropriate computers

Storing this information in Active Directory makes it much simpler to recover BitLocker volumes should anything happen to them. However, in order to be able to store this information in AD, you must extend the AD DS schema or the AD DS database structure because the default installation of the directory does not contain the appropriate objects to store this information.

 In Windows Server 2008, Active Directory has been renamed to Active Directory Domain Services (ADDS).

Extending the AD schema is not done lightly and is definitely not done by PC technicians. If your organization decides to implement BitLocker, then you will need to work with your directory administrators to ensure that the AD is prepared properly and can accept BitLocker data.

NOTE The Active Directory extensions that are required to support BitLocker are available from the Microsoft downloads Web site. To obtain them, go to `http://go.microsoft.com/fwlink/?LinkId=78953`.

Relying on Group Policy to manage BitLocker

However, you do not need to modify your directory service to manage BitLocker and TPM settings through Group Policy though a modification gives you more control over these features. Several settings support the remote configuration of both components. You would typically apply these settings in order to ensure a consistent BitLocker behavior in your organization. Use the following instructions to do so. You need Group Policy Creation and Modification access rights to do so.

1. **Begin by determining if you can apply these settings in an existing Group Policy or if you need to create a new policy. You must create a new policy if no policy affecting target computers exists.** Because BitLocker is a function of the computer, not the user, this policy will be directed towards computer accounts. Ideally, you will already have regrouped the computer accounts that will be using BitLocker into a separate OU within the directory.

2. **Launch the GPMC. Right-click on the target OU containing the PCs that will use BitLocker and then select Create a GPO in this domain, and link it here.**

3. **Name the policy appropriately and click OK.** For example, you can name it **BitLocker Policy**.

4. **Now, right-click on the new policy link and select Edit.**

5. **Navigate to Computer Configuration ➪ Policies ➪ Administrative Templates ➪ Windows Components ➪ BitLocker Drive Encryption.**

6. **Change the following settings if you have made the schema update in Active Directory:**

   ■ Enable the Turn on BitLocker Backup to Active Directory Domain Services, check the Require BitLocker backup to ADDS option, and select to store Recover passwords and key packages. When you turn on this setting, BitLocker will require a connection to AD in order to be turned on. If no connection exists, then BitLocker will not be turned on.

7. **Change the following settings to enable BitLocker options:**

   ■ Enable Control Panel Setup: Configure recovery folder and assign the path through a variable, for example, `%SecureDriveEnvironmentVariable%\BitLockerBackup`. Although this does not force users to accept this location, it does display this location first as they go through the BitLocker wizard.

   ■ Do not enable Control Panel Setup: Configure recovery options if you have enabled backup of the recovery components in AD in Step 7. If not, then enable this setting and require both options. Note that a USB key will be required to store the 256-bit recovery key.

   ■ Enable Control Panel Setup: Enable advanced startup options and check Allow BitLocker without a compatible TPM only if your computers do not have a TPM 1.2 chip. If your computers include a TPM, then Disallow startup key with TPM and

Require startup PIN with TPM. Using a startup key means that a removable media device must always be present in the system for it to start. This is used only in the most secure environments. However, having users enter a 4- to 20-digit PIN adds additional protection without complicating the boot process.

■ Consider whether you need to enable Configure encryption method. By default, BitLocker users the Advanced Encryption Standard (AES) 128 bit with Diffuser encryption, but you can increase it to 256 bit. Only the most secure environments would enable this policy setting.

■ Do not set Prevent memory overwrite on restart. Windows overwrites memory at each reboot by default. This helps prevent the exposure of BitLocker secrets but it does however take longer to boot BitLocker volumes.

■ If your computers include TPM chips, then be very careful about using the last setting in this area. Configure TPM platform validation profile affects how the TPM chip determines whether or not it will release the BitLocker-encrypted volumes. The default configuration is sufficient in most environments. Changing this value will modify which values the TPM evaluates before releasing volumes and may affect your ability to recover information from BitLocker-enabled disks.

8. **Navigate Computer Configuration ⇨ Policies ⇨ Administrative Templates ⇨ System ⇨ Trusted Platform Module Services and change the following settings to control TPM options:**

■ If you have modified the AD schema, then enable Turn on TPM backup to Active Directory Domain Services and check Require TPM backup to ADDS. When you turn on this setting, BitLocker will require a connection to AD in order to be turned on. If no connection exists, then BitLocker will not be turned on.

■ The next setting, Configure the list of blocked TPM commands, must be treated very carefully. By default, Windows blocks a series of TPM commands. These commands are exposed through the TPM console (tpm.msc). Use this setting only if you are very comfortable with TPM commands.

■ Do not enable Ignore the default list of blocked TPM commands unless you are very familiar with TPMs and you want a very specific configuration for your environment.

■ Do not enable Ignore the local list of blocked TPM commands unless you are very familiar with TPMs and you want a very specific configuration for your environment.

9. **Navigate to Computer Configuration ⇨ Policies ⇨ Administrative Templates ⇨ System ⇨ Power Management ⇨ Sleep Settings to disable the following settings.** Disabling these settings will ensure that the only sleep state available to the PC will be Hibernation which requires an authentication to restore the computer to an operational state:

■ Disable Allow Standby States (S1-S3) When Sleeping (Plugged In)

■ Disable Allow Standby States (S1-S3) When Sleeping (On Battery)

10. **Close GPEdit.** Your BitLocker policy is now ready.

When BitLocker is set up, it might be a good idea for you to hide the BitLocker partition from the Windows Explorer to ensure that users don't inadvertently copy data to this partition. Do this during setup as your installers turn on BitLocker.

 Putting the BitLocker policy in place lets you address task VA-36: BitLocker Drive Encryption from the administrative tasks listed in Chapter 10.

Supporting BitLocker

Of course, if you use BitLocker, you'll run into situations where you need to support users that have issues with it. Therefore, you should create a BitLocker support policy. This policy should include:

- Documentation on all of your BitLocker configurations. Use standard configurations only. Keep them simple. Ideally, you will have only one or two configurations at most.
- Identification of who will be your BitLocker Recovery Agents (BRA). If you are already using EFS, these could be the same as the DRAs. You need at least two agents.
- Determination how you will recover systems:
  - Remote recovery lets you support users remotely when they have issues, for example, while they travel.
  - Local recovery lets you address the issue yourself directly on the problematic PC.
- Procedural documentation related to the acceptable recovery processes.

Of these, the remote recovery process is the most complex, and even then it doesn't need to be. Recovering a BitLocker volume can be done in one of three ways:

- Through the BitLocker Recovery Console, which is launched before Vista boots. This console supports unlocking a system volume.
- The BitLocker Control Panel's Recovery Wizard will unlock nonsystem volumes or volumes on other computers.
- The Windows Recovery Environment that can be launched either from the Windows Installation DVD or through a preinstalled partition includes a wizard that lets you recover a BitLocker volume.

When users find themselves in a situation where recovery is necessary, they or you will need to use the 48-character recovery password to unlock the BitLocker volume. Ideally, you will have stored these passwords into Active Directory so that they can be easily obtained. When the user is in a remote location, you give them the current 48-character password to unlock the drive after, of course, having validated that the user is who they say they are. They will need to use this password to unlock their system until they can come into one of your locations to have the system repaired.

When the computer is accessible, then you don't need to give out the password — just unlock the volume yourself. When you hand out the password to an end user in a remote location, you have to replace the used password with a new one.

There are two ways to obtain the recovery password. First, you can rely on the Get-BitLocker RecoveryInfo.vbs script which is part of the tools you downloaded to support your BitLocker deployment. But the easiest way to obtain the password is to use the interface which can be added to Active Directory Users and Computers: Find BitLocker Recovery Password. This provides you with a graphical interface for password location.

> **NOTE**   Obtain the add-on for Active Directory Users and Computers through Knowledge Base article number 928202 at http://support.microsoft.com/kb/928202.

After you have access to the system, use the BitLocker Control Panel to reset the recovery password for the system. If the system is damaged and needs significant repair, then you will need to use the BitLocker Repair tool. This tool can help you access data on systems that are damaged, and you are unable to repair them. You usually need access to another hard drive to be able to move data from the damaged system during the recovery procedure.

> **TIP**   Learn how to use the BitLocker Repair Tool through Knowledge Base article number 928201 at http://support.microsoft.com/kb/928201.

As you can see, BitLocker deployments are not to be taken lightly and must be properly planned. If you can at all, then rely on EFS instead of BitLocker because it is much simpler to deploy and repair when issues arise.

Summary

This chapter focuses on the P of the CASPR process. In this case, P stands for Protection of the data your users generate. It begins with a focus on how you should update user data protection strategies within your own network, moving from home directories to a more comprehensive data protection strategy.

In addition, you can protect user data that is cached locally on their system. Windows Vista provides a much more complete strategy for the Encrypting File System than ever before. For example, cached data is now protected on a per-user basis which lets multiple users work on the same system without issues related to cached data. Using EFS along with smart cards ensures your data is protected when it leaves the office on mobile computers. If you require even more protection than EFS offers, you can deploy BitLocker Full Drive Encryption, protecting the entire operating system and any other data partitions on computers that may leave your office.

Choose your data protection strategies carefully. Today, information theft is one of the most popular activities malicious users engage in. They perform these thefts through either spam techniques or through the pilfering of portable computers. Thousands of portable computers are lost or stolen every year. Make sure you don't fall victim to data theft even if you do become the victim of a lost portable computer.

Chapter 13

Recovering Damaged Systems and Lost Data

IN THIS CHAPTER

Using the Windows Recovery Environment

Using Windows Backup to protect and recover data

No matter how well you prepare your computer systems, someone somewhere will discover how to break them. This someone is usually one of your users, and the somewhere is usually in your organization. This is one of the rare truisms of computer system administration. You must be prepared and have a standard recovery procedure in place.

When you do so, you need to protect two different aspects of your systems:

- You must learn to recover computer systems. This topic was covered to a small extent in Chapter 12 as we discussed recovering BitLocker system volumes, but there are a lot of situations where systems are damaged and they do not include encrypted drives. Damage can range from one single component that no longer works to losing the entire system.

- You must learn how to recover data when the systems themselves are not damaged, but for some reason data has been lost. Once again, damage can range from the loss of a single file to the loss of an entire disk volume.

These are the two core topics of this chapter. Windows Vista includes a whole host of new features that are designed to help protect systems on an ongoing basis, and when things do go wrong, it includes quite a few new recovery tools that support recovering systems or data in any number of different situations.

Recovering Systems

In situations where things don't work as they should, you need to determine the level of the problem first, and then try to identify how you can fix the problem. The best way to do this is to identify potential problem levels. You usually have to work with three different problem levels:

- Level 1 relates to minor system issues. Most often, this will have something to do with a minor component not working properly in Windows.

- Level 2 becomes more serious and may have to do with systems not starting or with more comprehensive components being broken.

- Level 3 relates to very serious problems and the issues that correspond to nonworking systems.

Windows Vista includes a series of new tools that support the resolution of each of these types of issues. But first, you must determine just how you go about looking at the issues your users run into. Begin by using a basic troubleshooting strategy. A standard troubleshooting strategy was presented in Chapter 10. This strategy involves several steps that are linked in a flow-like process to help determine the root cause of a problem and identify potential solutions (see Figure 13.1). This is the type of strategy you must rely on to correct issues when they arise in your network.

As mentioned in Chapter 10, you need to answer the five questions when trying to troubleshoot a problem: Who, When, What, Why, and How. Answering these questions can go a long way toward resolving the issue you are dealing with. Of course, the length of time you spend on a problem will be determined by the severity of the problem. In addition, you need to maintain a problem tracking database, one where you document all problems and issues as well as their resolution.

> **NOTE**   If you do not have a problem tracking database, then look no further than Windows SharePoint Services (WSS). WSS is a collaboration environment that lets you bring together several sources of information in support of specific team efforts. In addition, Microsoft offers a custom WSS template for a site designed to manage help desk information. Obtain the Help Desk site template as well as others from `http://technet.microsoft.com/en-us/windowsserver/sharepoint/bb407286.aspx`.

Level 1: Dealing with system instability

Windows Vista includes several tools that provide information on system reliability and diagnostics, including the following:

- **Event Viewer:** This tool has been completely revamped to provide a solid infrastructure for event management. The Event Viewer was covered in detail in Chapter 9. This should often be one of the very first places you should look when issues arise.

- **Help and Support Center:** This tool has been updated since Windows XP. It includes information that stems from the local help store as well as online data if a Web connection is available. It profits from the new Vista search engine to help locate solutions more easily.

FIGURE 13.1

Using a troubleshooting flowchart

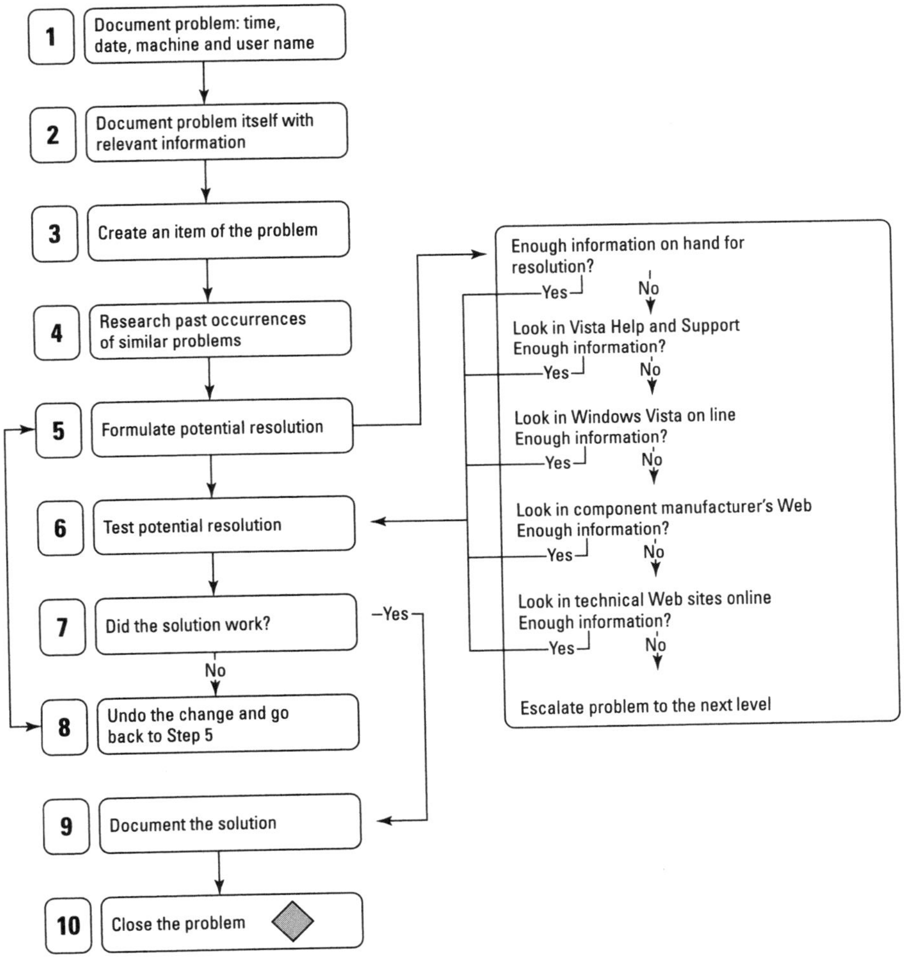

1	Document problem: time, date, machine and user name
2	Document problem itself with relevant information
3	Create an item of the problem
4	Research past occurrences of similar problems
5	Formulate potential resolution
6	Test potential resolution
7	Did the solution work?
8	Undo the change and go back to Step 5
9	Document the solution
10	Close the problem

Enough information on hand for resolution?
—Yes┘ No↓

Look in Vista Help and Support
Enough information?
—Yes┘ No↓

Look in Windows Vista on line
Enough information?
—Yes┘ No↓

Look in component manufacturer's Web
Enough information?
—Yes┘ No↓

Look in technical Web sites online
Enough information?
—Yes┘ No↓

Escalate problem to the next level

- **Performance Information and Tools:** This tool, located in the Control Panel, provides a single interface for the identification of potential issues related to system performance (see Figure 13.2). Reach the console through Control Panel ➪ System and Maintenance ➪ Performance Information and Tools. This console gives you access to the overall performance score on your PCs as well as quick access to tools such as:

  - **Manage Startup Programs** lets you improve performance by controlling which programs launch when Windows does.

  - **Adjust Visual Effects** enables you to control how a system uses Vista's graphical capabilities, notably the Aero interface, and possibly improve performance.

■ **Adjust Indexing Options** can let you reduce the amount of system resources that are used to index data. Vista uses up resources for indexing, especially in environments in which no corresponding Search technology exists on servers.

FIGURE 13.2

Using the Performannce Information and Tools Center

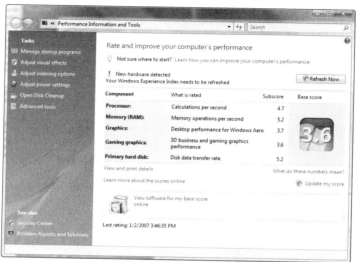

> **NOTE** To have server-based Search tools that correspond to those in Vista, you need one of two server-based technologies. Windows Server 2008 includes the same Search technology as Vista and works in conjunction with the client to offload search workloads. In addition, you can rely on Microsoft Search Server 2008 Express which also provides a corresponding server-based Search technology and runs on Windows Server 2003. Obtain Search Server 2008 Express free at www.microsoft.com/enterprisesearch/serverproducts/ searchserverexpress/default.aspx.

■ **Adjust Power Settings** can let you increase or decrease power usage in certain connected or disconnected scenarios and improve performance, possibly at the expense of battery life.

■ **Open Disk Cleanup** lets you remove temporary and other files located on your disks.

■ **Advanced Tools** leads you to a series of much more powerful troubleshooting tools (see Figure 13.3).

■ **Reliability and Performance Monitor:** This tool is an updated performance monitor that includes a reliability history for the PC.

- **Task Manager:** This tool provides information for ongoing performance as well as the list of running programs.

- **System Information:** This tool provides details about the different components of the PC.

- **Performance Options:** This tool lets you adjust visual effects, performance configurations, and Data Execution prevention.

- **ReadyBoost Devices:** This tool enables you to control how external flash memory can be used to increase system performance.

- **Disk Defragmenter:** This tool can help improve disk performance by defragmenting the data it contains. Disk Defragmenter works automatically in Vista and is enabled to run once a week by default.

- **System Health Reports:** These reports are produced through the Reliability and Performance Monitor. The reports give you a snapshot of the health status of a system when you activate it.

These tools let you resolve most of the problems that occur on systems that are still running.

FIGURE 13.3

Using Advanced Tools to troubleshoot performance issues

Using Vista's built-in diagnostics

In addition, Windows Vista includes several built-in diagnostics tools. These tools are based on Vista's new Windows Diagnostic Infrastructure (WDI), a framework that is designed to collect information about potential issues, provide automated resolution, and if these automated resolutions do not work, support your interactive troubleshooting efforts. WDI provides diagnostics at several different levels:

- **Disk Diagnostics:** This engine is designed to detect potential disk failures. It is also used to guide you through data backups, disk replacements, and data restoration procedures.

- **Memory Diagnostics:** This engine works with the online crash analysis database Microsoft maintains to help identify issues related to failing memory. It lets you test memory as the system restarts and mark bad memory sectors as unusable.

- **Network Diagnostics and Troubleshooting:** This engine helps identify network connectivity issues. Many of these issues can be corrected automatically with this engine.

- **Resource Exhaustion Prevention:** This engine will automatically warn users when system resources are too low and will do so before a system hang can occur. It identifies which processes are using the most memory and provides information on how you can reclaim these resources before the system crashes.

Diagnostic information from each one of these engines is stored within the appropriate Event Log including the automated repairs performed by the tool (see Figure 13.4). If the event indicates that the tool could not resolve the problem, then it provides information about how the problem might be resolved. In addition, if the system is connected to the Internet, then you can use the Event Log Online Help provided by Microsoft to find more information on a particular issue.

Using Problem Reports and Solutions

Windows Vista also includes an automated problem reports and solutions infrastructure. Find the Problem Reports and Solutions (PRS) interface by choosing Start Menu ➪ All Programs ➪ Accessories ➪ Maintenance. This tool logs all system issues as well as their solution. It gives you access to the problem history of any system. You can also use it to drill down into the problems that a specific PC has encountered. Problems are categorized based on origin and issue type. The details of each problem are documented, as shown in Figure 13.5, as well as potential resolution approaches.

However, this tool does not resolve all issues. For example, you might have a historical issue with a system that has not been resolved for some time, but you can use PRS to periodically check for updated solutions. Microsoft maintains a database of these issues and lists potential solutions including links to manufacturer Web sites when the issue relates to a specific component on your computer.

By default, PRS is configured to automatically verify for solutions online, but you can modify the settings. In fact, in Advanced Settings, you can even control a blocked list of problems to ensure that critical organizational information is not sent to Microsoft. Rely on this interface to map out if a "new" issue has ever occurred before on a system.

FIGURE 13.4

Using the Event Log to view diagnostics information

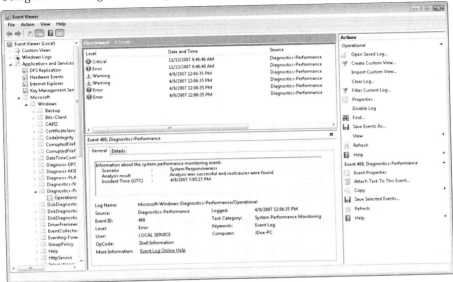

FIGURE 13.5

Using Problem Reports and Solutions to display information about a specific issue

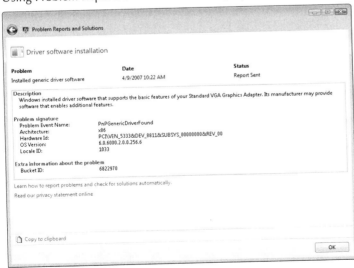

Using the Reliability Monitor

The Windows Reliability Monitor is a subset of the Windows Reliability and Performance Monitor (RPM) section of the Computer Management console. RPM is also available as a standalone snap-in for the Microsoft Management Console; however, the Computer Management console is still better to use because it includes so many other useful tools.

When you launch the Computer Management console (Go to Start Menu and then right-click on Computer to select Manage or Start Menu ⇨ Administrative Tools ⇨ Computer Management) and move to Reliability and Performance (Computer Management ⇨ System Tools ⇨ Reliability and Performance node), you see an instant summary of all of the core resources on the computer system, as shown in Figure 13.6. This overview includes CPU, disk, network, and memory resources. Below the Reliability and Performance node, you can see several different items:

- Monitoring tools includes both the traditional Performance Monitor and the Reliability Monitor.

- Data Collector Sets is where you store collection sets when you want to capture performance data over longer periods of time. It also includes Event Tracing captures.

- Reports include the performance reports you generate over time.

Both Reports and Data Collector Sets include User-Defined and System sections, segregating the items you generate from those the system itself generates.

FIGURE 13.6

The Reliability and Performance summary page

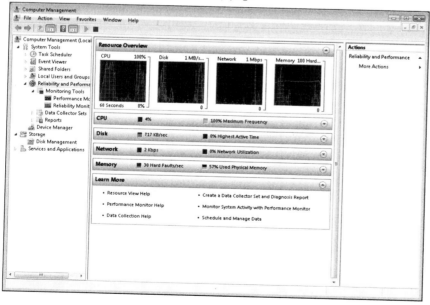

To view the Reliability Monitor, you need to move to Reliability Monitor under the Monitoring Tools node. Note that the Reliability Monitor tracks all system changes from the day it was installed to the day you are viewing it (see Figure 13.7). Each time a system change is performed, it marks it as a change point.

FIGURE 13.7

Viewing historical information within Reliability Monitor

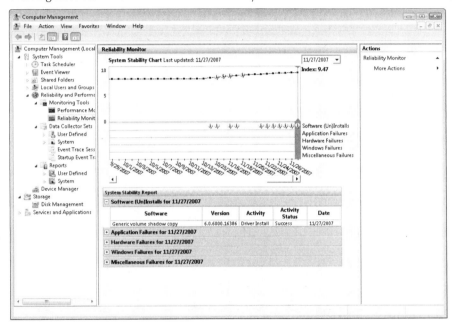

Reliability Monitor tracks the following different types of changes:

- General system changes such as system clock modifications
- Software installs or uninstalls
- Application failures
- Hardware failures
- General Windows failures
- Miscellaneous failures

Each failure is marked as a change point in the System Stability Chart histogram. You can click on any information bubble to view the actual change the system recorded. This makes it very easy to find out if a specific change occurred on a system before issues arose. Indeed, it helps you really discover the answer to the question: "Did you change anything on the system before this issue occurred?" As you know, users are often reluctant to answer "yes" to such a question because they fear it may be their fault. With Reliability Monitor, you avoid such guilt issues because the system itself tells you if a change occurred.

Reliability Monitor uses a scheduled task to pick up and record reliability information about each system. This task runs once a day and starts one day after the installation of the system. You can find this task by choosing Computer Management ⇨ System Tools ⇨ Task Scheduler ⇨ Task Scheduler Logs ⇨ Microsoft ⇨ Windows ⇨ RAC. This is a hidden task so you'll need to use View ⇨ à Show Hidden Tasks to see it. Do not disable this task if you want to rely on the Reliability Monitor when you need to troubleshoot system problems.

NOTE For more information on using Reliability Monitor to troubleshoot problematic situations, go to `http://technet2.microsoft.com/WindowsVista/en/library/d33c3cc1-a9dd-4b96-8062-edb21ee70f0e1033.mspx?mfr=true`.

Using the System Configuration tool

Another useful tool for system troubleshooting is the System Configuration tool. System Configuration (accessed by choosing Start Menu ⇨ Administrative Tools ⇨ System Configuration) lists the configuration settings for a system. This includes:

- General startup settings
- Boot configurations
- Service configurations
- Applications launched at startup
- Tool access

The last item, Tool access, gives you access to a wide selection of tools for system troubleshooting and may be the best part of the System Configuration dialog box itself (shown in Figure 13.8). This list of tools includes anything from general Windows version information to Remote Assistance and much more. Rely on this tool as an application launcher when you do not know which tool to go to when troubleshooting a particular problem.

Relying on System Restore points

Microsoft introduced the concept of a System Restore point with Windows XP. Basically, a system restore point is a point-in-time snapshot of the system's state before a modification is performed. By default, each time a significant configuration change is performed on a Vista PC, Windows captures the state of the computer before the change is implemented. Because of this, you can always return to this previous system state should the configuration change destabilize the PC for some reason.

FIGURE 13.8

Using System Configuration as a launch pad to access other troubleshooting tools

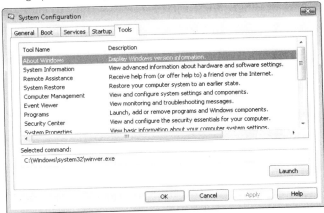

If you use application virtualization technologies to manage and deploy applications within your network, you will not need System Restore as much because a virtualized application does not modify the operating system in any way. Therefore, when virtualized applications are deployed, system restore points are not created. For more information on application virtualization, look up Application virtualization: Ending DLL Hell once and for all, a free Webcast on the topic at `http://searchwinit.bitpipe.com/detail/RES/1193672482_325.html?src=wc_swwit_editorial_11_29_07_c&li=68705`.

System restore points are created under different situations:

- Automatically whenever a new program or device driver is installed on the system
- Automatically every day
- Automatically when you use System Restore on a computer
- Manually through the use of the System Protection tool

This means that you can protect system configurations at any time. Restore points capture all sorts of data including system files, registry settings, and program files. It will also capture scripts or any other executable file on a system. System Restore can protect a PC even when you use it because it automatically creates a restore point before restoring the system to an earlier stable configuration, so if using System Restore does not solve the problem, then you can use it again to undo the changes it made.

NOTE System Restore does not modify user data files so you don't need to worry about them should you need to move to an older configuration. You should, however, always protect user data files.

Start System Restore by choosing Start Menu ⇨ All Programs ⇨ Accessories ⇨ System Tools ⇨ System Restore to return a system to a previous configuration (see Figure 13.9). This starts a wizard that leads you through the system restoration. By default, it selects a recommended restore that is the most recent restore point, but you can also select from a series of restore points. To do so, you need to select the Choose a different restore point option on the wizard's startup page. This leads you to a list of available restore points. Once again, by default only the restore points from the last five days are displayed. To list more restore points, select the Show restore points older than 5 days option, as shown in Figure 13.10. Then, after you've selected the restore point to return to, you click Finish. At this point, Windows will undo changes up to the selected restore point.

FIGURE 13.9

Starting System Restore

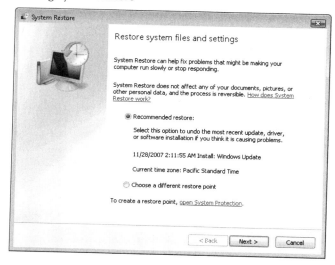

If you prefer to create a manual restore point, then click on open System Restore on the home page of the wizard. Doing this opens the System Properties dialog box and gives you access to the ability to create a specific restore point. System Protection is enabled by default for all hard drives in a PC. Each restore point takes up about 300MB or less. Restore points continue to be written to a disk so long as it contains sufficient disk space. If space is at a premium, the feature automatically over-writes older restore points. Learn to rely on this feature to protect stable system configurations.

NOTE There are several other tools within Vista to support system troubleshooting. Rely on Table 10.1 in Chapter 10 to identify other tools that can help in this situation.

FIGURE 13.10

Selecting a different restore point

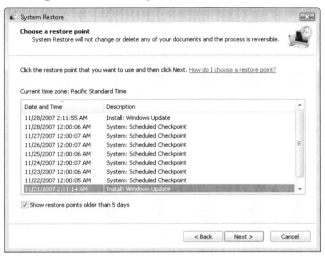

Level 2: Dealing with startup instability

Level 1 problems deal with system instability issues. In this case, the system starts up, but operates in an erratic manner. As you have seen, there are lots of tools that support the correction of these types of issues. Level 2 deals with startup instability or issues related to configuration or other changes that affect how a system starts up. Windows Vista includes several tools that support the repair of a system at system startup. They include two main tools:

- Last Known Good Configuration
- Safe Mode Startup

Both of these tools have been in Windows since its very earliest editions.

Using Last Known Good Configuration

Last Known Good Configuration (LKGC) is a startup option that relies on registry settings that were in use the last time the computer startup up successfully. LKGC has been around since the days of Windows NT. It was the only option you could rely on to correct startup instability issues.

Each time you make a significant configuration change, such as installing a new device driver or adding an application, this change modifies both the file system and the system registry. Each time you make significant changes to a system, Windows writes the existing configuration into a subset of the registry. Each time the system successfully starts, however, Windows replaces the content of the LKGC with the current boot settings. As you can see, the data in the LKGC is volatile and must be used as soon as you discover an issue otherwise it may no longer be valid.

If Windows detects that the system did not start properly, it will automatically display the LKGC at the next startup. If it doesn't and you want to access it, then you must press the F8 key repeatedly as the system is booting and before the Windows Vista logo appears. If the logo appears, then you are too late and must recycle the system once again. After Windows detects the F8 key, it will provide you with an advanced startup screen that displays the LKGC option (shown in Figure 13.11). To boot into the LKGC, simply select it and press Enter. The system starts with the data contained within this special registry store.

Most commonly, administrators relied on the LKGC to repair systems after installing video drivers that would not work with their installation of Windows. In this particular case, the LKGC would very rarely provide a solution and administrators needed to rely on other methods to repair the system. Although Microsoft did improve LKGC with time, you should still consider it a last resort and should only be used if nothing else works. Using LKGC can leave the system in an unstable state and should really only be used if for some reason there is unsaved data within the system and you cannot re-image it with a new OS installation until you recover this data.

FIGURE 13.11

Using F8 to access Advanced Startup options

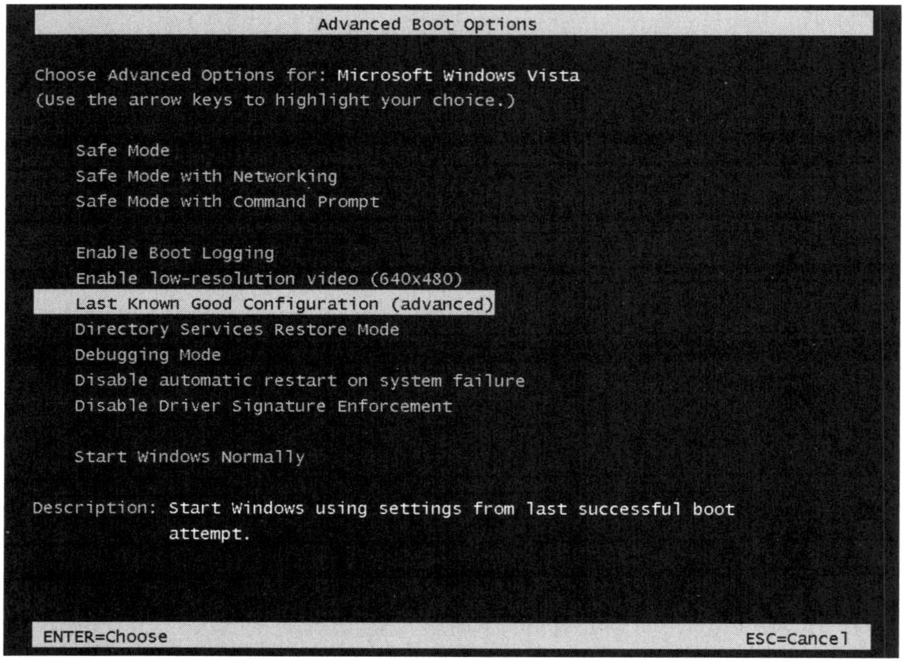

```
                    Advanced Boot Options

Choose Advanced Options for: Microsoft Windows Vista
(Use the arrow keys to highlight your choice.)

    Safe Mode
    Safe Mode with Networking
    Safe Mode with Command Prompt

    Enable Boot Logging
    Enable low-resolution video (640x480)
    Last Known Good Configuration (advanced)
    Directory Services Restore Mode
    Debugging Mode
    Disable automatic restart on system failure
    Disable Driver Signature Enforcement

    Start Windows Normally

Description: Start Windows using settings from last successful boot
             attempt.


    ENTER=Choose                               ESC=Cancel
```

Using Safe Mode startup

Another powerful startup option is Safe Mode. Windows includes three different safe mode startups:

- Safe Mode that starts Windows with only core drivers and services
- Safe Mode with Networking that uses only core drivers, but also includes networking
- Safe Mode with Command Prompt that uses only core drivers and automatically launches the command prompt

You usually rely on Safe Mode Startup when you face an issue with a newly installed driver that you cannot get to work. For example, if you installed a new video driver and your system does not respond correctly to this new driver, you can start Windows in Safe Mode to try to replace the video driver.

NOTE You can also use the Enable low-resolution video (640x480) to specifically repair video driver issues. This option starts Windows normally with all drivers and services, but runs it in low-resolution mode.

Safe Mode is useful for dealing with issues, such as needing to disable a device driver, return a driver to its previous version, or even launch a System Restore to return to a specific restore point. Safe Mode gives you access to the full Windows interface but without loading the more complex drivers your system may rely on.

Disabling a device is the easiest, but of course you wouldn't disable the video driver, so it has limited value. Disabling devices is done in the Device Manager. Use the following procedure:

1. **Use F8 to start the system in Safe Mode and log in after the system is started.**
2. **Once in Windows, launch Device Manager. Use Control Panel ⇨ System and Maintenance ⇨ Device Manager and accept the UAC prompt.**
3. **In Device Manager, locate the problematic device.** If the device is causing known problems in Vista, it will be displayed with a question mark beside it. If not, then expand the Tree pane until you see the device.
4. **Right-click on the device and select the appropriate action (see Figure 13.12).** You can Update Driver Software if you have a new driver on hand, uninstall the device, or simply disable it.
5. **Reboot the system in normal mode.**

You can also rely on Safe Mode and Device Manager to restore a device driver to its previous version. Use the same procedure mentioned previously, but this time, select the device's Properties. In Properties, move to the Driver tab and click on Roll Back Driver (see Figure 13.13). Windows displays a warning; click **Yes**. After the driver is rolled back, reboot the system into normal mode.

Finally, using System Restore in Safe Mode is the same as using it in normal mode. If System Restore can resolve the problem, then this might indeed be the best tool to use.

FIGURE 13.12

Using Device Manager in Safe Mode to disable a driver

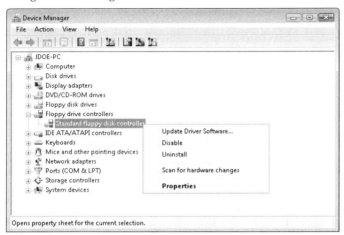

FIGURE 13.13

Rolling back a device driver

Level 3: Dealing with total system instability

Every now and then, you will run into major system issues — systems won't start, boot sectors on drives will be damaged, or Windows will be completely corrupted. When this happens, you need to rely on Vista's more advanced recovery tools. That's where the Windows Recovery Environment

(WinRE) comes in. WinRE is a self-contained operating environment based on Windows PE that can be used to give you access to non-working systems. As such, it includes a series of different tools that can be relied on to recover these systems. The tools in WinRE include:

■ Startup Repair that can automatically repair some problems that prevent Windows from booting up properly.

■ System Restore, which has been discussed at length.

■ Windows Complete PC Restore, which lets you restore a complete PC image. Complete PC Restore and Complete PC Backup are discussed later in this Chapter. Note that Complete PC Backup is only available in the Enterprise and Ultimate Editions of Vista.

■ Windows Memory Diagnostic Tool, which can verify RAM to identify potential problems.

■ Command Prompt, which then lets you run any commands against the PC and access common tools, such as Regedit.

In addition, WinRE gives you access to the shutdown and restart options for the system.

Working with the Windows Recovery Environment

WinRE is available in two flavors. The first is off the Windows Installation DVD. When you boot with this DVD, Windows Setup displays the initial setup screen where you choose the language and regional options for the installation. Then it moves you into the Install now screen. At this point in time, you can click on Repair your computer in the lower left-hand corner of the screen to access WinRE. After WinRE is launched, it looks for existing Windows installations on the system disk. At this point, you can load additional drivers if needed, or simply proceed to the System Recovery Options screen, shown in Figure 13.14, by clicking Next.

Alternatively, you can load WinRE onto a separate system partition and make it available in the Advanced Boot Options discussed earlier. Refer to Chapter 4 for instructions on loading WinRE onto each system. Loading WinRE requires two partitions on your system's disks, one for WinRE and one for the operating system itself. This is very much like loading BitLocker onto systems as was discussed in Chapter 9. Although it does make system recovery easier, in an organization where the operating system deployment process has been fully controlled as discussed in the first part of this book, there is little need to preload WinRE onto PCs. Preloading WinRE onto servers, however, is a completely different story and is well warranted in most cases.

NOTE Remember that you should spend only a certain amount of time on system recovery before you simply move on to system re-imaging. For example, if your imaging process only takes 30 minutes and you have implemented the folder redirection/roaming profile strategy outlined in Chapter 12, then it makes little sense to spend 30 minutes or more troubleshooting a serious system problem. Just re-image the PC and move on. However, if the problem is recurring, then you will need to spend time identifying its root cause. In that case, you might want to give the user a different PC so that they can continue with their work as you identify the cause of the issue.

FIGURE 13.14

Using WinRE to repair a broken system

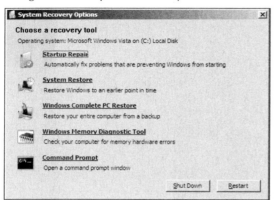

When it is installed on the system, WinRE can sometimes launch without assistance, although this is certainly a behavior to which you do not want to expose users. This happens when there is a boot failure. Windows detects the failure and then launches WinRE to perform automated repairs. But in some cases, the automated repair mode will not work. This includes:

- Partition Table damage or lost boot sectors on a system disk
- Missing or damaged Boot Manager (bootmgr.exe)
- Missing or damaged Boot Configuration Data

In this case, you must launch WinRE manually by using one of the approaches mentioned earlier in this chapter.

Running Memory Diagnostics

One of the most common problems users face with PC is corrupt memory modules. When you use a corrupt memory module, information stored within memory cannot be retrieved. This often causes Windows to fail because the missing information destabilizes the OS. For this reason, the WinRE environment includes a Windows Memory Diagnostics Tool (WMDT). Use WinRE to launch this tool. When you launch it (see Figure 13.15), WMDT will reboot the system and perform a memory scan, identifying potential bad memory blocks and mark them as such so that the system does not use them anymore (see Figure 13.16).

This is a stopgap measure at best and should be used mostly to identify bad memory blocks. Replace the bad memory modules as soon as possible.

FIGURE 13.15

Launching a Memory Diagnostics scan

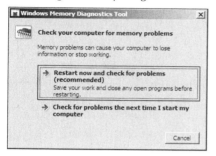

FIGURE 13.16

Scanning memory for bad blocks

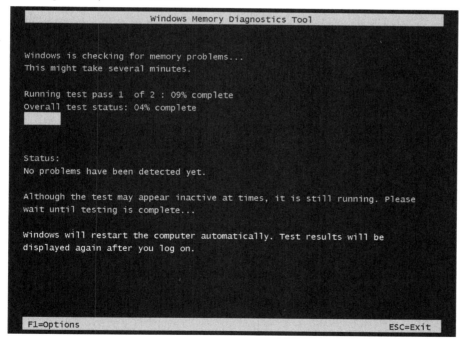

Using Startup Repair

Startup Repair is an automated tool that scans unbootable systems and automatically repairs them. It corrects issues, such as corrupt registry hives, missing system files and drivers, disk boot sector corruptions, and other startup issues.

To use it, launch WinRE and select Startup Repair. This launches a window that automatically scans the system for boot issues (shown in Figure 13.17) and then generates a report (shown in Figure 13.18). The report is generated whether or not Startup Repair finds issues. If you choose not to view the report after Startup Repair is run, you can always view it later. It is located in `%WINDIR%\System32\LogFiles\Srt`. Startup Repair files are named `SrtTrail.txt`.

FIGURE 13.17

Running Startup Repair

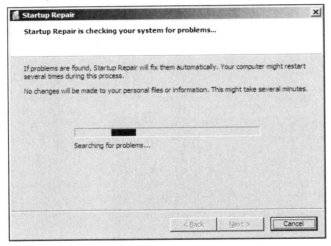

FIGURE 13.18

Viewing a Startup Repair report

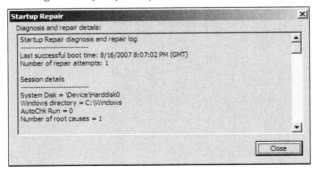

Working with Boot Configuration Data

When these tools do not resolve the issue, then you can try the more advanced recovery tools found in Windows Vista. One of these is the Boot Recovery tool (`bootrec.exe`). This tool can be used to repair damaged boot records on disks, missing or corrupt boot sectors, or even corrupt Boot Configuration Data (BCD) stores. With Windows Vista, Microsoft replaced the traditional `Boot.ini` file with a new BCD store. This store is now used to tell Vista where OS partitions can be found on a disk.

The Boot Recovery tool is accessed through WinRE. When in the System Recovery Options screen, select Command Prompt. Then, once the Command Prompt is launched, type:

```
bootrec /?
```

This will display the options for the command. Several options are available. Each is listed in Table 13.1.

TABLE 13.1

Boot Recovery Tool Options

Option	Description
/FixMBR	Using this option writes a new master boot record on the system disk. It does not overwrite the existing partition table, but sets the disk so that Vista can start.
/FixBoot	Using this option writes a new boot sector to the system disk. For example, if you install another OS onto a system where Vista is already installed, then the Boot Manager (`bootmgr.exe`) may have been replaced. This option repairs this issue.
/RebuildBCD	Using this option rebuilds the Boot Configuration Data store. During the rebuild operation, it lets you choose which compatible OS partition to add to the BCD.
/ScanOS	Using this option scans all disks to locate a Vista installation. Use this option after you have used the /RebuildBCD option to completely recreate the BCD store.

Microsoft also released a BCD store editor: `bcdedit.exe`. This tool includes a lot of different capabilities, all of which are very useful when you need to repair nonstarting systems. Table 13.2 outlines the options you can use with `bcdedit.exe`.

NOTE For more information on Boot Configuration Data in Windows Vista, go to www.microsoft.com/whdc/system/platform/firmware/bcd.mspx.

TABLE 13.2

Boot Data Configuration Editor Options

Command	Focus	Description
/createstore	BCD Store	Creates a new empty BCD store
/export	BCD Store	Exports the contents of the BCD store to a file
/import	BCD Store	Restores BCD store contents from previously exported data
/store	BCD Store	Indicates which BCD store to use
/copy	BCD Store Entries	Copies a specific entry in the BCD store
/create	BCD Store Entries	Creates a new BCD store entry
/delete	BCD Store Entries	Deletes a BCD store entry
/deletevalue	BCD Store Entry Settings	Deletes a specific element in an entry
/set	BCD Store Entry Settings	Sets a value for an entry
/enum	Output Control	Lists entries in a BCD store
/v	Output Control	Turns on verbose mode
bootsequence	Boot Manager Controls	Used to create a boot configuration order, but only for the next boot process
/default	Boot Manager Controls	Specifies the default entry to use when booting
displayorder	Boot Manager Controls	Specifies the order in which options are displayed to users
/timeout	Boot Manager Controls	Indicates the timeout value for a boot option
displayorder	Boot Manager Controls	Specifies the order in which options are displayed in boot management tools
/bootems	Emergency Management Services (EMS)	Enables or disables EMS booting for an entry

Command	Focus	Description
/ems	EMS	Enables or disables EMS booting for a boot entry
/emssettings	EMS	Sets global EMS values
/bootdebug	Debugging	Enables or disables debugging for an entry
/dbgsettings	Debugging	Enables or disables global debugging settings
/debug	Debugging	Enables or disables kernel debugging settings

As you can see, the BCD store and the commands you use to manage it are very different from previous versions of Windows. Remember that the best strategy is to use the user data protection mechanism outlined in Chapter 12 so that you minimize risk of data loss when systems fail. This way, you can re-image systems when the problems are too complex or too time consuming to repair.

Creating custom Windows PE recovery disks

Also, you see that it may be too time-consuming to use the Vista installation DVD to get to recovery options all the time since it requires moving through several screens. You can also use the procedures outlined in Chapter 4 to generate a custom Windows Pre-Execution Environment (WinPE) disk that includes WinRE. This way, your systems would boot directly into WinRE without having to pass through Windows Setup. This saves you a lot of time and speeds the recovery process for any unbootable system.

 For instructions on how to create a custom WinRE disk running on WinPE, go to http://blogs.msdn.com/winre/archive/2006/12/12/ creating-winre-using-waik.aspx or http://technet2.microsoft.com/ WindowsVista/en/library/61e08b15-82d8-46bd-a5f1-7947193e6ed81033. mspx?mfr=true.

Recovering Data

Although you should be protecting data according to the data protection strategy outlined in Chapter 12, it is still important to understand just how Vista supports information protection and recovery just as it supports system recovery. Once again, Vista offers support for data protection at three levels:

- Level 1 relates to minor data losses, for example, losing a single document or image on a PC.
- Level 2 relates to more comprehensive losses, but once again, losses focused on data and documents.
- Level 3 relates to major losses such as the loss of an entire system and its recovery.

The protection discussed in Level 1, Volume Shadow Copy, is available to three editions of Vista: Business, Enterprise, and Ultimate, and is an integral part of the operating system. The protection in Level 2 relies on the standard backup and restore tool contained within most editions of Windows Vista, Automatic Backup. Note that Automatic Backup is not included in the Starter Edition. The protection in Level 3 relies on Vista's Complete PC Backup tool which is also only available in the Business, Enterprise, or Ultimate editions of Vista.

Level 1: Dealing with minor data loss

The beauty of Level 1 protection within Vista is that it is focused on self-service and rarely involves the help desk after Vista users have learned how the feature works. With the release of Windows Server 2003, Microsoft introduced a new technology called the Volume Shadow Copy Service (VSS). Shadow copies or disk *snapshots,* as they are commonly referred to, are one of the major reasons why people implement shared storage. Shared storage systems — storage area networks (SAN) or network-attached storage (NAS) — include built-in technologies that support the capability of maintaining multiple concurrent copies of data. Among other things, these copies are used for backups (backing up a copy is much simpler than backing up live data because all files are closed) and restores (through special interfaces, users can even restore their own files). But the construction of these features is a complex task. Manufacturers have to basically design systems that will tell a running application to freeze all requests for data input and output for the time it takes to create the snapshot. This was a costly undertaking at best. Even worse, because most organizations implement heterogeneous solutions, they don't necessarily use the same drivers for backups as for undeletes. This is often a cause of instability.

By building snapshots into Windows, Microsoft has provided both VSS engines for its own applications (Exchange, Active Directory, and SQL Server) and a single standard set of APIs for application developers to write their own VSS engines, taking the onus away from the shared storage hardware manufacturer. In addition, VSS virtually eliminates the impact of data usage on backups and allows organizations to make data available in different formats for development and stress-testing purposes.

But, what's most impressive with VSS is what it can do for users. VSS automatically takes a snapshot of the files located in any shared folder where the service has been enabled. These snapshots include an image of the folder's contents at a given point in time. Depending on the space that you make available (each VSS snapshot is 100MB in size), you can have up to 64 different snapshots of a disk volume in Windows Server 2003 and much more in 2008. Because Microsoft has also made a client component of VSS — the Previous Versions client — available along with the VSS, users can have access to these snapshots. After it is implemented, users can recover almost any lost file by themselves, at the privacy of their own desk, without having to bother anyone and without the embarrassment of having to tell someone they've lost a file once again. The shadow copy service is designed to assist in the process of recovering previous versions of files without having to resort to backups. In this way, VSS is like an "undelete" utility.

In Windows Vista, VSS is on by default and takes snapshots of the entire contents of a disk on a regular basis. In addition, the snapshots have been reduced in size because only incremental changes are captured. Therefore, all data is protected while there is free space on a disk.

In Vista, the maximum size allocated to VSS is set to a value of 30 percent of free space or 15 percent of the overall size of the volume — whichever is less. This maximum size is static. It will not change when more or less free space is available, nor will it change after the size of the volume has been adjusted. However, you actually can manually adjust the size of this storage area by using the VSSAdmin tool from an elevated command prompt. For example, the command to increase the maximum storage size to 15GB on drive C: would be:

```
VSSAdmin Resize ShadowStorage /For=C: /On=C: /MaxSize=15GB
```

Use this command with care since in most cases, the default settings are appropriate.

To access VSS snapshots, you must use the Previous Versions tab on the Properties sheet of either a local disk, a local file folder, or a local file (see Figure 13.19). The Previous Versions client is installed by default in Vista and Windows Server 2008. However in XP and Windows Server 2003, you must deploy the Previous Versions client since it is not included in these operating systems. When you use the Previous Versions client, three options are available:

- **Open:** You can view the contents of the disk, folder, or file at the time of the snapshot.
- **Copy:** You can create a copy of the disk, folder, or file from the time of the snapshot.
- **Restore:** You can restore the copy of the disk, folder, or file to an alternate or the same location.

Users can access help information from directly within the Properties page by clicking on the How do I use previous versions? When users restore older versions of their documents, they must be careful to not overwrite the actual version unless of course, that is their goal.

> **NOTE** For information on the more arcane aspects of Previous Versions, look up www. realtime-vista.com/administration/2007/07/volume_shadow_copy.htm.

This feature is a boon to you as system administrator because it cuts down your workload. All you really need to do is ensure that users are familiar with the Previous Versions tab in the Properties sheet of the items they create. Then, you may never have to address a lost document ever again.

> **NOTE** Because Previous Versions is available on the desktop, users will come to expect it on all file shares as well. Even Windows SharePoint Services now boasts a VSS-like previous versions feature. However, VSS is not turned on by default on servers. You need to explicitly enable this feature to make it available. VSS is a function of the disk volume. Use the volume's Properties sheet and go to the Shadow Copies tab to turn it on. You should turn it on for any disk volume that hosts file shares that contain user data.

> **NOTE** Level 1 data protection practices address task VA-09: VSS Copy operation verification as outlined in Chapter 10.

FIGURE 13.19

Using Previous Versions to access backup copies of user data

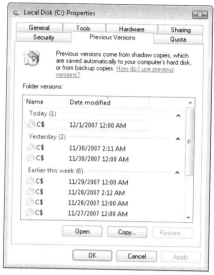

Level 2: Automating data protection

Make sure that you warn all users that Volume Shadow Copies do not replace backups. It is always a best practice to actually backup data as much as possible to enable multi-tiered protection mechanisms. Of course, if you are relying on roaming profiles and folder redirection, you will have enabled a networked backup mechanism to protect profile data. But there are still occasions when data may be at risk despite this strategy. For example, when users travel with their mobile PCs, they may be disconnected from the office for lengthy periods of time. When this occurs, their data is at risk until they can link back to the network and perform a synchronization. It is good practice to back up this data during this period to provide another layer of protection.

Vista includes two backup technologies: Automatic Backup and Complete PC Backup. Automatic Backup is available in almost all versions of Vista while Complete PC Backup is only available in the more advanced editions. To make things simpler, Microsoft has integrated both tools into one interface: the Backup and Restore Center (BRC). Access the BRC by choosing Control Panel ➪ System and Maintenance (see Figure 13.20). Note that you must have administrative access to create the backups through this interface.

Automatic Backup can also be accessed through the Backup Status and Configuration (BSC) interface, which is accessed by choosing Start Menu ➪ All Programs ➪ Accessories ➪ System Tools (shown in Figure 13.21). Once again, administrative access is required to create the initial backup schedule.

FIGURE 13.20

Using the Backup and Restore Center

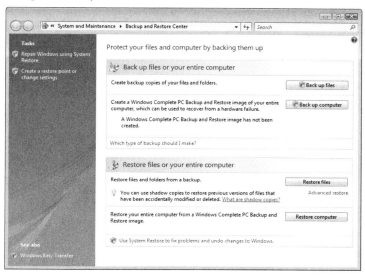

FIGURE 13.21

Creating a backup schedule

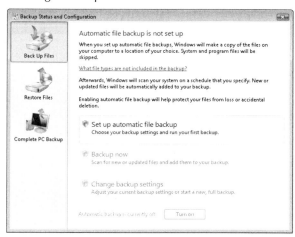

You can target another hard drive, a writable CD or DVD drive, or a network to store the backups. In an organization using a network, the best bet is to target networks as much as possible because then the backups are located on central storage. But, for users who travel a lot, the ideal strategy is to ensure that there are two hard disks in the notebook, or barring that, that there are two partitions on the same hard drive. This way they do not need to carry additional components to protect their data.

 **Tape is not a supported backup destination in either Vista or Windows Server 2008.**

There are also many other methods you can use to protect mobile data. For example, today it is fairly inexpensive to access large flash memory cards that can store 4 or more gigabytes of data. Placing one of these flash cards within the mobile PC and running backups against it is also painless for users. Barring this option, then you can use USB thumb drives or even external USB disks.

Setting up a backup schedule on a single PC

To set up Automatic Backup, use the following procedure:

1. **Launch the Backup Status and Configuration interface by choosing Start Menu ⇨ All Programs ⇨ Accessories ⇨ System Tools ⇨ Backup Status and Configuration.**

2. **Click Set up automatic file backup and accept the UAC prompt.**

3. **Select your target location and click Next.**

4. **Select the type of files you want to back up. (By default, all file types are selected, as shown in Figure 13.22.) Deselect those you do not want to protect and then click Next.** Note that moving the mouse over any category will display the types of files that will be protected in this category.

FIGURE 13.22

Using Automatic Backup to select files to protect

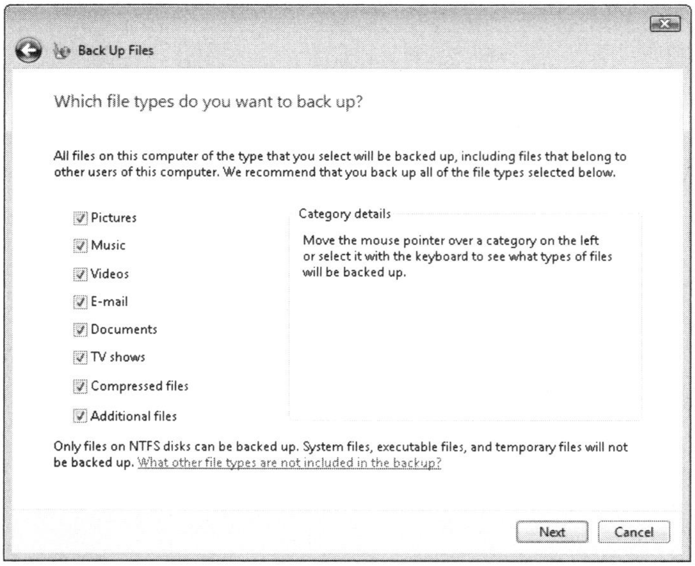

Back Up Files

Which file types do you want to back up?

All files on this computer of the type that you select will be backed up, including files that belong to other users of this computer. We recommend that you back up all of the file types selected below.

- ☑ Pictures
- ☑ Music
- ☑ Videos
- ☑ E-mail
- ☑ Documents
- ☑ TV shows
- ☑ Compressed files
- ☑ Additional files

Category details

Move the mouse pointer over a category on the left or select it with the keyboard to see what types of files will be backed up.

Only files on NTFS disks can be backed up. System files, executable files, and temporary files will not be backed up. What other file types are not included in the backup?

Next   Cancel

5. **Set the automated schedule.** Schedules can be Daily, Weekly, or Monthly and can be set for any time of day. Use whatever is appropriate to support your service level agreements.

6. **After you have set the schedule, click Save settings and start the backup.**

That's it. The backup process will start and begin by creating a shadow copy and then using this shadow copy to perform the backup. From that point on, you can rest easy because your user files are doubly protected. Users will be notified by balloon messages if they are logged on the system when backups are performed. The backup will be stored within a folder that indicates the computer's name. All user profiles will be backed up and stored within a compressed ZIP file.

NOTE   Vista's Automatic Backup does not back up files encrypted with the Encrypting File System. If you are using EFS along with roaming profiles and folder redirection, then use the Windows Server backup tool to back up these files on a regular basis from central storage. You can however use Complete PC Backup to back up encrypted files along with the entire operating system.

Restoring files on a single PC

If you need to restore a file, or even if a user needs to restore files, you can return to the BCS, but this time click the Restore Files button. Individual users can restore their own files by selecting Restore files (shown in Figure 13.23), but to access Advanced restore, you must have administrative access to the PC.

FIGURE 13.23

Using the Backup Status and Configuration interface to restore files

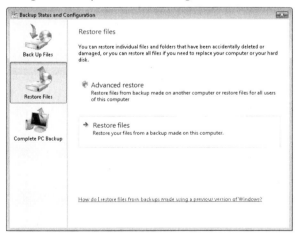

When you do access Advanced restore, you will have access to three choices:

- You can restore files from the latest backup made on this computer.
- You can restore files from an earlier backup made on this computer.
- You can restore files from a backup made on another computer.

The Advanced restore interface also gives you access to the Recycle Bin as well as System Restore. To restore files after a backup set is selected, you have three options:

- You can click Add files to select the files to restore.
- You can click Add folders to select the folders to restore.
- You can click Search to locate a specific file in the backup set.

Once the files or folders are selected, click Next to begin the restore process. Now you can either select to restore the files to their original location or select an alternate location. When ready, click Start restore to begin the restoration process. Click Finish when done.

It's as simple as that. Like all features in Vista, you can control backup behavior through Group Policy settings. The settings that apply to the entire PC are located under Computer Configuration ➪ Policies ➪ Administrative Templates ➪ Windows Components ➪ Backup. Similarly, the settings controlling backup behavior on a user-per-user basis are located under User Configuration ➪ Policies ➪ Administrative Templates ➪ Windows Components ➪ Backup.

Setting up backup schedules on multiple PCs

When you create a backup schedule on a single PC, you actually create three Scheduled Tasks (see Figure 13.24). Because you don't want to go from PC to PC to enable backup schedules, you should consider capturing these three tasks from one system, exporting them, and then importing them into each of the PCs you want to enable backup for. The three tasks are:

- **AutomaticBackup:** This task controls the schedule of the backup and will perform incremental backups automatically.
- **CheckFull:** This task is designed to verify if a full backup is required instead of an incremental backup.
- **Windows Backup Monitor:** This task monitors the backup operation and determines if notifications are required due to backup errors.

To automate the process of turning automated backups, use the following procedure:

1. **Prepare the backup schedule using BSC as outlined earlier. Wait until the first backup is created.**
2. **Launch the Task Scheduler by choosing Start Menu ➪ Administrative Tools ➪ Task Scheduler.**

FIGURE 13.24

Viewing the Automatic Backup Tasks within Task Scheduler

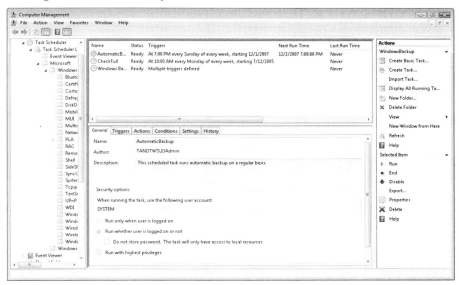

3. Choose Task Scheduler Library ➪ Microsoft ➪ Windows ➪ Windows Backup. Three tasks appear.

4. Right-click each task to select Export. Name each task and store them on a network-shared folder.

5. To enable the tasks on another Vista PC, move to the other PC, launch Task Scheduler, and click on Import Task in the Action pane. Locate each task and import it (shown in Figure 13.25).

Repeat on each PC on which you want to enable Automatic Backup. From now on these PCs will automatically back up user data.

If you want to perform this in a more automated fashion, you can use the schtasks command. Use the following commands to import each task:

```
schtasks /create /TN AutomaticBackup /S systemname /XML
    automaticbackup.xml
schtasks /create /TN CheckFull /S systemname /XML checkfull.xml
schtasks /create /TN "Windows Backup Monitor" /S systemname /XML
    windowsbackupmonitor.xml
```

where *systemname* is the name of the remote system to which you want to assign the task. Repeat for each system. Also, make sure you launch an elevated command prompt and you use an account with sufficient privileges on each remote PC.

FIGURE 13.25

Importing a task within Tasks Scheduler

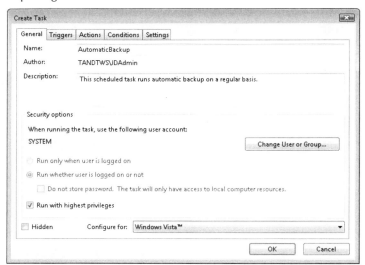

> **NOTE** The tasks you import in this fashion will work, but will not be stored within the Windows Backup category of Task Scheduler. For this reason, Automatic Backup will not display that automatic backups are turned on in the BSC. Don't worry, though. Backups will still run as expected.

Level 3: Protecting a complete PC

The last level of protection deals with the protection of a complete operating system configuration. For this, Microsoft has introduced the Complete PC Backup (CPC), which is available in the Business, Enterprise, and Ultimate editions. Complete PC captures the entire operating system configuration and stores it in a .VHD file, the format used for Microsoft's Virtual PC and Virtual Server virtual machine hard drives. Complete PC is an image-based backup tool that protects every aspect of a computer's configuration, including the OS, all installed applications, and user data files.

Complete PC can be launched in a number of ways. You've already seen that the Backup Status and Configuration interface has a Complete PC Backup button; so does the Backup and Restore Center under the Back up files or your entire computer option (refer to Figure 13.20). Complete PC is also one of the options available in WinRE, but here, you only have access to the Restore operation (refer to Figure 13.14).

To create a backup of your entire computer, proceed as follows:

1. **Log in with local administrator credentials.**

2. **Launch the Backup and Restore Center (Control Panel ⇨ System and Maintenance ⇨ Backup and Restore Center).**

3. **Accept the UAC prompt.**

4. **Click Back up computer.** Vista looks for appropriate backup devices and when it finds them, display a selection of choices to store the backup (shown in Figure 13.26).

FIGURE 13.26

Selecting the location of a Complete PC backup

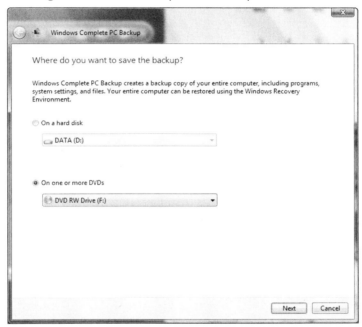

5. **Choose the appropriate location (DVD writer or external hard drive) and click Next.**

6. **Select the drive(s) to back up and click Next.** Normally, your PCs should have only one single drive unless you are using BitLocker. In this case, you need to back up both drives.

7. **Review your options and click Start backup.**

8. **Close the Backup window after the operation is complete. Close the Backup and Restore Center when done.**

Complete PC backups are incremental and always target the same backup file, so the backup file grows with time. Ideally, you would perform a defragmentation of the disk before performing the backup. Doing this creates a leaner and meaner backup and makes PC restoration more effective.

However, CPC will continue to back up into a storage destination until there is only 30 percent of space left on the destination. After it reaches the 30 percent limit, it begins discarding old data to make room for new data. There is no way to modify this 30 percent limit.

Keep a note of the following truisms when restoring Complete PC backups:

- When you restore the PC from a Complete PC backup, you recreate an image of the entire system. If you are restoring to a BitLocker partition, then you will need to run BitLocker again to re-encrypt the drive.

- Complete PC backups can only be restored to hardware that has a similar CPU and the same type of firmware (x86 and x64 systems use BIOS firmware whereas IA64 systems use EFI firmware). Ideally, the IDE controller uses the same driver as the source system as well.

- Complete PC backups must be restored to hard drives of the same or bigger size than the original hard drive. Restoring to smaller hard drives — even hard drives of the same size, but with less free space — does not work.

- If the machine is turned off or in sleep mode when a backup task is scheduled to run, Backup will not wake the machine. Machines must be already awake to run scheduled backup tasks.

- You cannot copy backups to multiple CD/DVDs to a hard drive and expect them to work. To be able to reuse a multi-CD/DVD backup for a restore operation, you must put it back on multiple CDs or DVDs.

- You can use the Microsoft VHDMount tool to locate individual files within a Complete PC backup, but this is not an officially supported method. VHDMount is a command line tool which makes the operation even more difficult. Obtain VHDMount with the free download of Microsoft Virtual Server at www.microsoft.com/technet/virtual server/software/default.mspx. Alternatively, you can mount a Complete PC VHD backup as a virtual machine in Virtual Server or Virtual PC and locate specific backup content in this manner.

Keep these caveats in mind when considering the use of Complete PC Backup.

As you can see, Complete PC Backup will protect your entire system's data, but you won't want to run complete system backups all the time. In fact, you might notice that Complete PC Backups are not scheduled, but are run interactively and with administrative credentials. Therefore, you run Complete PC Backups only at specific intervals.

Because of this, a complete PC protections strategy should include both regular Complete PC Backups and scheduled Automatic Backups. This strategy will provide the best protection for your systems.

> **NOTE** Levels 2 and 3 data protection practices address task VA-05: Backup Generation and Verification as outlined in Chapter 10.

NOTE You might find that the default backup features available in Vista leave a lot to be desired, especially in business situations. For this reason, you might consider looking at third-party backup solutions — solutions that offer centralized backup controls, full system backup through imaging, or backup to media that is unsupported in Vista — as a worthwhile endeavor. There is nothing more frustrating for a user than losing data despite your best efforts, and if this user is an executive, they will quickly approve any more comprehensive backup solution you suggest.

Summary

This chapter completes the CASPR process by focusing on system and data recovery. Each approach uses three levels of interaction. In system recovery, the levels address the following:

- Level 1 treats minor system instability issues.
- Level 2 treats system startup instabilities.
- Level 3 treats major system issues and unbootable systems.

Each level addresses increasingly complex issues, and while Vista offers many automated error-correction tools, you still need to be aware of the manual interactions you can take to resolve these system-related issues.

In data recovery, these levels address the following:

- Level 1 treats with user self-service data recovery.
- Level 2 treats with automated data protection strategies.
- Level 3 treats with complete system protection.

Once again, each level addresses increasingly complex data protection strategies. Chapter 12 outlined how to completely protect user data in a networked environment. If you can, then rely on this strategy to protect your user data. Then, perform centralized data backups. But, in some situations, you still need to provide additional data protection. In those cases, rely on the data protection strategies outlined here to provide complete system protection mechanisms.

Appendix

What's on the CD-ROM

This appendix provides you with information on the contents of the CD that accompanies this book. For the latest and greatest information, please refer to the ReadMe file located at the root of the CD. Here is what you will find:

- System requirements
- Using the CD with Windows
- What's on the CD-ROM
- Troubleshooting

System Requirements

Make sure that your computer meets the minimum system requirements listed in this section. If your computer doesn't match up to most of these requirements, you may have a problem using the contents of the CD:

- PC running Windows 98 or later
- An Internet connection
- A CD-ROM drive

The software provided on the CD has its own system requirements; please see the product's documentation for details.

Using the CD

To access the content from the CD, follow these steps.

1. **Insert the CD into your computer's CD-ROM drive.** The license agreement appears.

   Note to Windows users: The interface won't launch if you have autorun disabled. In that case, click Start ⇨ Run (For Windows Vista, Start ⇨ All Programs ⇨ Accessories ⇨ Run). In the dialog box that appears, type D:\Start.exe. (Replace D with the proper letter if your CD drive uses a different letter. If you don't know the letter, see how your CD drive is listed under My Computer.) Click OK.

2. **Read through the license agreement and then click the Accept button if you want to use the CD.**

   The CD interface appears. The interface allows you to install the programs and run the demos with just a click of a button (or two).

What's on the CD

The following sections provide a summary of the software and other materials you'll find on the CD.

Author-created materials

All author-created materials from the book, including code listings and samples, are on the CD in the folder named Author.

The Definitive Guide to Vista Migration

Rely on this free e-book to identify and prepare the administrative processes required to create and manage a Vista migration project.

Vista Migration Project Business Case Template

Rely on this Microsoft Word business case template to create your own justification for your Vista migration.

Vista Migration Project Plan

Rely on this Microsoft Project template to create and manage your own Vista migration project plan.

Vista Migration Presentation

Rely on this Microsoft PowerPoint presentation template to help promote your Vista migration project to peers and users.

Vista New Features Checklist

Rely on this checklist to identify which new features in Vista you plan to implement in your own deployment.

Applications

The following applications are on the CD:

Admin Script Editor 3.5

45-day trial for Windows. Admin Script Editor is a suite of scripting tools with support for the PowerShell, VBScript, KiXtart, AutoIt, and Batch scripting languages. It provides several code editing features as well as code generating tools for WMI, Database, XML, and Active Directory (AD). As discussed in Chapter 6, it also provides for the creation of graphical interfaces and custom dialogs. For more information, check out `www.adminscripteditor.com`.

Bart PE Builder v3.1.10a

Freeware for Windows. BartPE Builder allows for the creation of custom preinstallation environment images for targeted applications and in support of deployment scenarios. BartPE is discussed as a popular alternative to Windows PE in Chapter 6. For more information, check out `www.nu2.nu/pebuilder/`.

Expresso 3.0

Freeware for Windows. Expresso is a tool to assist in the writing of regular expressions. Regular expressions are often used in development and scripting. Specifically, this book mentions Expresso in Chapter 5 as a helpful tool in the authoring of custom XML files used for the inclusion and exclusion of items when using the User State Migration Tool (USMT). For more information, check out `www.ultrapico.com/Expresso.htm`.

GImageX v2.0.12

Freeware for Windows. GImageX is a graphical user interface for performing functions normally handled on the command line with the ImageX utility. This program is discussed in Chapter 6 as a popular GUI for ImageX. For more information, check out `www.autoitscript.com/gimagex`.

Lansweeper 3.1

Freeware for Windows. Lansweeper is a program for collecting and reporting software and hardware inventory over the network without need for client agent installation. For those that do not already have an inventory system in place, Lansweeper is recommended as a possible choice to obtain inventory data in Chapter 1. For more information, check out `www.lansweeper.com/`.

vLite v1.1.6

Freeware for Windows. vLite is a customization utility for Windows Vista WIM image files. It allows you to slipstream service packs, remove elements from an image, tweak certain settings directly as part of the installation, generate an Unattend.xml file, and burn the resulting image to CD/DVD. This tool is detailed in chapter 6 along with a walk-through on its use. For more information, check out `www.vlite.net`.

Shareware programs are fully functional trial versions of copyrighted programs. If you like particular programs, register with their authors for a nominal fee and receive licenses, enhanced versions, and technical support.

Freeware programs are copyrighted games, applications, and utilities that are free for personal use. Unlike shareware, these programs do not require a fee or provide technical support.

GNU software is governed by its own license, which is included inside the folder of the GNU product. See the GNU license for more details.

Trial, demo, or evaluation versions are usually limited by either time or functionality (such as being unable to save projects). Some trial versions are very sensitive to system date changes. If you alter your computer's date, the programs will "time out" and will no longer be functional.

eBook version of Windows Vista Deployment and Administration Bible

The complete text of this book is on the CD in Adobe's Portable Document Format (PDF). You can read and search through the file with the Adobe Acrobat Reader (also included on the CD); however, you will not be able to print the file.

Troubleshooting

If you have difficulty installing or using any of the materials on the companion CD, try the following solutions:

- **Run as administrator**. Often management tools like those discussed here require administrative privileges. Be sure to run such tools as administrator. In step-by-step documentation launching the tool as administrator is typically provided as an initial step in the procedure.

- **Turn off any antivirus software that you may have running.** Installers sometimes mimic virus activity and can make your computer incorrectly believe that it is being infected by a virus. (Be sure to turn the antivirus software back on later.)

- **Close all running programs.** The more programs you're running, the less memory is available to other programs. Installers also typically update files and programs; if you keep other programs running, installation may not work properly.

- **Reference the ReadMe:** Please refer to the ReadMe file located at the root of the CD-ROM for the latest product information at the time of publication.

- **Contact Customer Care:** If you have trouble with the CD-ROM, please call the Wiley Product Technical Support phone number at (800) 762-2974. Outside the United States, call 1(317) 572-3994. You can also contact Wiley Product Technical Support at **http://support.wiley.com**. John Wiley & Sons will provide technical support only for installation and other general quality control items. For technical support on the applications themselves, consult the program's vendor or author.

To place additional orders or to request information about other Wiley products, please call (877) 762-2974.

Index

A

AAS files, WIS use of, 120, 121
access denied errors, 446
Account Policy (Default Domain Policy), 303–304
Acronis True Image imaging solution, 14, 216
ACT. *See* Application Compatibility Toolkit
activating Vista. *See also* licensing Vista; volume licensing
    activated state, 82
    comparison of KMS and MAK, 92–93
    further information, 96
    grace period state, 82, 98
    Key Management Services (KMS) for, 85–89, 92–93, 95–97
    Multiple Activation Key (MAK) for, 84, 89–93, 97–98
    notification state and Reduced Functionality Mode (RFM), 82, 98–100
    with OEM licensing, 84
    re-imaging rights, 84
    with retail licensing, 83
    Software License Management Tool for, 93–94
    Volume Activation 1.0 versus 2.0, 84
    Volume Activation Key (VAK) for, 84
    Volume Activation Management Tool for, 94–95
Active Directory
    Active Directory Domain Services (ADDS), 269, 306
    AGLP rule for, 452
    basic components, 305–306
    BitLocker Full Drive Encryption integration with, 478–479
    collecting Vista events from machines using, 337–338
    containers for GPOs, 309
    creating groups and file shares in, 452
    domain, 306
    GPOs with, 301, 305–306
    preparing for data protection, 451–452
    required for Zero Touch Installation, 224
Active Directory Domain Services (ADDS), 269, 306. *See also* Active Directory

Active Directory Users and Computers tool, 343
Admin Script Editor suite (on the CD), 214–215, 521
administering workstations. *See* workstation administration
Administrative Tools, adding to Start Menu, 299
Administrator account, enabling in an answer file, 63
AdminPak.msi installation, 357–358
AdminStudio repackaging tool (Acresso Software), 23
ADMX/ADML templates for GPOs, 318–320, 415, 416–420
ADS (Automated Deployment Services), 264
Advanced Group Policy Management (AGPM), 322
Advanced Tools, 486
AGLP rule for Active Directory, 452
answer files. *See also* System Image Manager (SIM)
    changing the path to, 72
    component selections, 59–60
    component settings, 60–62
    configuration passes involved, 50–52
    embedding into customized image, 64
    enabling Administrator account, 63
    implementing, 64–66
    INI format no longer used for, 49
    restricting access to, 54
    steps for creating using SIM, 58–59
    System Image Manager tool for authoring, 52–63
    System Preparation Tool specification of, 71–72
    XML format for, 49–50
AppDeploy.com, 21
Append command (ImageX), 178, 179–180
application compatibility issues
    Application Compatibility Toolkit (ACT) for, 36–41
    Application Rights Auditor tool for, 31
    audit policies for resolving, 30–31
    broken applications, 28–29
    compatibility modes for resolving, 34–36
    Group Policy for resolving, 32
    identifying incompatibilities, 29–31
    modifying application security for, 32
    permission issues, 30
    Process Monitor tool for, 30

X

Z

Office heaven.

Get the first and last word on Microsoft® Office 2007 with our comprehensive Bibles and expert authors. These are the books you need to succeed!

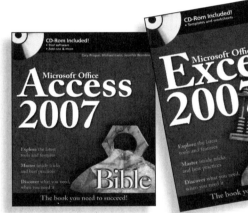

978-0-470-04673-9

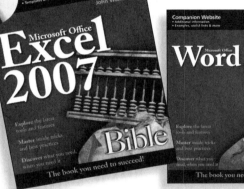

978-0-470-04403-2

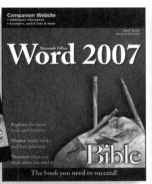

978-0-470-04689-0

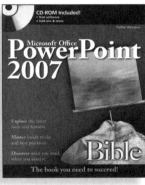

978-0-470-04368-4

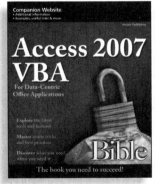

978-0-470-04702-6

978-0-470-04645-6

978-0-470-04691-3

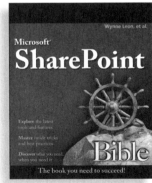

978-0-470-00861-4

WILEY

Now you know.

Wiley Publishing, Inc.
End-User License Agreement

READ THIS. You should carefully read these terms and conditions before opening the software packet(s) included with this book ("*Book*"). This is a license agreement ("Agreement") between you and Wiley Publishing, Inc. ("WPI"). By opening the accompanying software packet(s), you acknowledge that you have read and accept the followi ng terms and conditions. If you do not agree and do not want to be bound by such terms and conditions, promptly return the Book and the unopened software packet(s) to the place you obtained them for a full refund.

1. **License Grant.** WPI grants to you (either an individual or entity) a nonexclusive license to use one copy of the enclosed software program(s) (collectively, the "Software") solely for your own personal or business purposes on a single computer (whether a standard computer or a workstation component of a multi-user network). The Software is in use on a computer when it is loaded into temporary memory (RAM) or installed into permanent memory (hard disk, CD-ROM, or other storage device). WPI reserves all rights not expressly granted herein.

2. **Ownership.** WPI is the owner of all right, title, and interest, including copyright, in and to the compilation of the Software recorded on the disk(s) or CD-ROM "Software Media." Copyright to the individual programs recorded on the Software Media is owned by the author or other authorized copyright owner of each program. Ownership of the Software and all proprietary rights relating thereto remain with WPI and its licensers.

3. **Restrictions on Use and Transfer.**

   (a) You may only (i) make one copy of the Software for backup or archival purposes, or (ii) transfer the Software to a single hard disk, provided that you keep the original for backup or archival purposes. You may not (i) rent or lease the Software, (ii) copy or reproduce the Software through a LAN or other network system or through any computer subscriber system or bulletin-board system, or (iii) modify, adapt, or create derivative works based on the Software.

   (b) You may not reverse engineer, decompile, or disassemble the Software. You may transfer the Software and user documentation on a permanent basis, provided that the transferee agrees to accept the terms and conditions of this Agreement and you retain no copies. If the Software is an update or has been updated, any transfer must include the most recent update and all prior versions.

4. **Restrictions on Use of Individual Programs.** You must follow the individual requirements and restrictions detailed for each individual program in the "What's on the CD-ROM" appendix of this Book. These limitations are also contained in the individual license agreements recorded on the Software Media. These limitations may include a requirement that after using the program for a specified period of time, the user must pay a registration fee or discontinue use. By opening the Software packet(s), you will be agreeing to abide by the licenses and restrictions for these individual programs that are detailed in the "What's on the CD-ROM" appendix and on the Software Media. None of the material on this Software Media or listed in this Book may ever be redistributed, in original or modified form, for commercial purposes.

5. **Limited Warranty.**

   (a) WPI warrants that the Software and Software Media are free from defects in materials and workmanship under normal use for a period of sixty (60) days from the date of purchase of this Book. If WPI receives notification within the warranty period of defects in materials or workmanship, WPI will replace the defective Software Media.

   (b) WPI AND THE AUTHOR(S) OF THE BOOK DISCLAIM ALL OTHER WARRANTIES, EXPRESS OR IMPLIED, INCLUDING WITHOUT LIMITATION IMPLIED WARRANTIES OF MERCHANTABILITY AND FITNESS FOR A PARTICULAR PURPOSE, WITH RESPECT TO THE SOFTWARE, THE PROGRAMS, THE SOURCE CODE CONTAINED THEREIN, AND/OR THE TECHNIQUES DESCRIBED IN THIS BOOK. WPI DOES NOT WARRANT THAT THE FUNCTIONS CONTAINED IN THE SOFTWARE WILL MEET YOUR REQUIREMENTS OR THAT THE OPERATION OF THE SOFTWARE WILL BE ERROR FREE.

   (c) This limited warranty gives you specific legal rights, and you may have other rights that vary from jurisdiction to jurisdiction.

6. **Remedies.**

   (a) WPI's entire liability and your exclusive remedy for defects in materials and workmanship shall be limited to replacement of the Software Media, which may be returned to WPI with a copy of your receipt at the following address: Software Media Fulfillment Department, Attn.: *Deploying and Administering Windows Vista Bible*, Wiley Publishing, Inc., 10475 Crosspoint Blvd., Indianapolis, IN 46256, or call 1-800-762-2974. Please allow four to six weeks for delivery. This Limited Warranty is void if failure of the Software Media has resulted from accident, abuse, or misapplication. Any replacement Software Media will be warranted for the remainder of the original warranty period or thirty (30) days, whichever is longer.

   (b) In no event shall WPI or the author be liable for any damages whatsoever (including without limitation damages for loss of business profits, business interruption, loss of business information, or any other pecuniary loss) arising from the use of or inability to use the Book or the Software, even if WPI has been advised of the possibility of such damages.

   (c) Because some jurisdictions do not allow the exclusion or limitation of liability for consequential or incidental damages, the above limitation or exclusion may not apply to you.

7. **U.S. Government Restricted Rights.** Use, duplication, or disclosure of the Software for or on behalf of the United States of America, its agencies and/or instrumentalities "U.S. Government" is subject to restrictions as stated in paragraph (c)(1)(ii) of the Rights in Technical Data and Computer Software clause of DFARS 252.227-7013, or subparagraphs (c) (1) and (2) of the Commercial Computer Software - Restricted Rights clause at FAR 52.227-19, and in similar clauses in the NASA FAR supplement, as applicable.

8. **General.** This Agreement constitutes the entire understanding of the parties and revokes and supersedes all prior agreements, oral or written, between them and may not be modified or amended except in a writing signed by both parties hereto that specifically refers to this Agreement. This Agreement shall take precedence over any other documents that may be in conflict herewith. If any one or more provisions contained in this Agreement are held by any court or tribunal to be invalid, illegal, or otherwise unenforceable, each and every other provision shall remain in full force and effect.